M000191791

THE REVELATION
OF THE MONK OF EYNSHAM

EARLY ENGLISH TEXT SOCIETY

No. 318

2002

THE REVELATION
OF THE
MONK OF EYNSHAM

EDITED BY

ROBERT EASTING

Published for
THE EARLY ENGLISH TEXT SOCIETY
by the
OXFORD UNIVERSITY PRESS
2002

OXFORD

UNIVERSITY PRESS

Great Clarendon Street, Oxford OX2 6DP

Oxford University Press is a department of the University of Oxford.
It furthers the University's objective of excellence in research, scholarship,
and education by publishing worldwide in

Oxford New York

Auckland Bangkok Buenos Aires Cape Town Chennai
Dar es Salaam Delhi Hong Kong Istanbul Karachi Kolkata
Kuala Lumpur Madrid Melbourne Mexico City Mumbai Nairobi
São Paulo Shanghai Singapore Taipei Tokyo Toronto

Oxford is a registered trade mark of Oxford University Press
in the UK and in certain other countries

Published in the United States
by Oxford University Press Inc., New York

© Early English Text Society, 2002

The moral rights of the author have been asserted

Database right Oxford University Press (maker)

First published 2002

British Library Cataloguing in Publication Data

Data available

Library of Congress Cataloging in Publication Data

Data applied for

ISBN 0-19-722321-4

1 3 5 7 9 10 8 6 4 2

Typeset by Joshua Associates Ltd., Oxford
Printed in Great Britain
on acid-free paper by
Print Wright Ltd., Ipswich

For Caroline, Rachel, and Heather,
Margaret, David, and Helen,
and in memory of my father

PREFACE

At the beginning of the twentieth century, two scholars, Herbert Thurston and P. Michael Huber, unbeknown to each other, were each simultaneously preparing an edition of the *Visio monachi de Eynsham*.[1] Such unwitting collisions of scholarly endeavour are not uncommon. When I first started work on this edition in 1995, I learned via Professor Richard Sharpe that Professor Dr Paul Gerhard Schmidt and a team of researchers at Freiburg were also working on the *Visio*. Professor Schmidt and I were therefore able to consult to make sure that our work did not unduly overlap. He and his team, I learned, were not working on the Middle English translation or the Latin manuscript I was using as my base text, but were concerned more with the continental transmission of the *Visio*, including the German translations. The first fruits of their collaborative work, was published in 1998, a collection of essays, *Visio Edmundi monachi de Eynsham: Interdisziplinäre Studien zur mittelalterlichen Visionsliteratur,* edited by Thomas Ehlen, Johannes Mangei, and Elisabeth Stein (hereafter *VEME*). This volume is essential reading for any student of the Vision of the monk of Eynsham, or of the vast corpus of medieval vision literature. I have used it gratefully and thoroughly, and refer readers of my edition to it frequently; my work has been aided and shortened by their scholarship. The culmination of Professor Schmidt's and his team's work on this text will be their forthcoming edition from CCCM.

My labours have been solitary, but I am pleased to acknowledge various kinds of assistance. For permission to print the texts and reproduce the plates I thank The Bodleian Library, University of Oxford, and The British Library. I am also grateful to the following: Victoria University of Wellington for granting me Research Leave in 1995, when I started this project, and in the second half of 2000, when I completed it; Wolfson College, Oxford, where my wife and I were Visiting Scholars in 1995; Professor Richard Sharpe and Dr Janet Wilson, who each on different occasions provided me with friendly accommodation during my research trips to Oxford; Ingrid Horrocks and Michael Robertson, who typed out my manuscript of the Glossary;

---

[1] See Thurston, Huber1, and Huber2.

Dr Charity Scott Stokes for information on *Gaude* sequences; Mr Robert Penkett, for copies of his unpublished papers and for his comments on a draft of the Introduction and Commentary; Professor M. L. Samuels for his response to my query about the language of the *Revelation*; Dr Lotte Hellinga, for supplying information about L, and for her comments on a draft of my description of the printed copies and variants; and Dr Helen Spencer, Editorial Secretary of EETS, for overseeing publication. All errors of omission and commission remain my own. I particularly thank my friends and colleagues at Victoria University of Wellington, Dr Kathryn Walls and Mr Peter Whiteford, who generously stepped into the breach when I was on Research Leave. The book is dedicated in part to my sister and her family, who have also looked after me on my 'home' visits to England, and to my daughters in New Zealand, who have patiently borne my absences and long working hours. My greatest debt, as always, is to my wife, Dr Christine Franzen, for her unfailing support and constant love.

ADDENDUM

Notice of a non-surviving copy of the *Revelation* appears in a late fifteenth- or early sixteenth-century list of books loaned by the London charterhouse at Smithfield to the charterhouse at Hull: 'Item liber qui dicitur. a the Reuelacion to a monke of Enyshame', Public Record Office, London, Ecclesiastical Documents, E135/2/58, no. 7: see *Syon Abbey*, ed. Vincent Gillespie (Corpus of British Medieval Library Catalogues 9, London, 2001), p. 617. Whether this copy was in manuscript or print is unknown. On Carthusian interest in the Vision of Edmund, via the connection with Hugh of Lincoln, see below, p. xli, and Johannes Mangei, 'Die Bedeutung der Kartäuser' in *VEME*, pp. 135–61.

CONTENTS

LIST OF PLATES

The plates, after p. 216, give an example of one of the pages in quire [a] that were reset between L and O; see the discussion in Appendix 1.

ABBREVIATIONS AND SHORT TITLES

The abbreviations used for the titles of periodicals, series, manuscript sigla, and frequently-cited works are listed below. All other works referred to are cited in full at the first reference. If they are subsequently cited, the reference is given in abbreviated form (usually author and short title) and the full details may be found in the Select Bibliography.

AASS	*Acta Sanctorum Bollandiana*, ed. Jean Bollandus (Antwerp, 1643 *et seq.*)
AB	*Analecta Bollandiana*, 1– (Brussels, 1882–)
Arber	Arber, Edward, ed., *The Revelation to the Monk of Evesham. 1196. Carefully Edited from the Unique Copy, now in the British Museum, of the Edition Printed by William de Machlinia about 1482* (English Reprints 18, London, 1869; Westminster, 1895, 1901; English Reprints vol. 5, New York, 1966)
Bd	Oxford, Bodleian Library, MS Bodley 636 copy of the *Visio*
BEH	*Bede's Ecclesiastical History of the English People*, ed. Bertram Colgrave & R. A. B. Mynors (Oxford, 1969, repr. with corrections 1991)
BHL	A. Poncelet *et al.*, *Bibliotheca Hagiographica Latina* (Brussels, 1898–1901), and H. Fros, *Bibliotheca Hagiographica Latina: Nova Supplementum* (Brussels, 1986)
BL	British Library, London
BN	Bibliothèque nationale, Paris
Carozzi	Claude Carozzi, *Le Voyage de l'âme dans l'au-delà d'après la littérature latine (Ve–XIIIe siècle)* (Collection de l'École française de Rome 189, Rome, 1994)
CCCM	Corpus Christianorum, Continuatio Mediaevalis, 1– (Turnhout, 1954–)
DAI	*Dissertation Abstracts International*
Dialogi	*Grégoire le Grand, Dialogues*, ed. Adalbert de Vogüé & Paul Antin, 3 vols. (Sources chrétiennes 251, 260, 265, Paris, 1978–80)

DMLBS	*Dictionary of Medieval Latin from British Sources*, R. E. Latham *et al.* (London, 1975–)
DNB	*Dictionary of National Biography*, ed. L. Stephen & S. Lee, 63 vols. & suppl. (London, 1885–1901)
EETS	Early English Text Society, Original Series 1– (London, 1864–); Extra Series, 1–126 (London, 1867–1935); Supplementary Series 1– (London, 1970–)
HRHEW	Dom David Knowles, C. N. L. Brooke, and Vera C. M. London, *The Heads of Religious Houses: England and Wales 940–1216* (Cambridge, 1972)
Huber1	Huber, P. Michael, *Beitrag zur Visionsliteratur und Siebenschläferlegende des Mittelalters. Eine literargeschichtliche Untersuchung*, 1 Teil: Texte (Beilage zum Jahresbericht des humanistischen Gymnasiums Metten für das Schuljahr 1902/1903)
Huber2	Huber, P. Michael, 'Visio monachi de Eynsham', *Romanische Forschungen*, 16 (1904), 641–733
IPMEP	R. E. Lewis, N. F. Blake, & A. S. G. Edwards, *Index of Printed Middle English Prose* (Garland Reference Library of the Humanities 537, New York & London, 1985)
IISTC	*Illustrated Incunabula Short-Title Catalogue* on CD-ROM, 2nd edn., The British Library, 1998
L	London, British Library copy of the *Revelation*
LALME	Angus McIntosh, M. L. Samuels, and Michael Benskin, *A Linguistic Atlas of Late Mediaeval English*, 4 vols. (Aberdeen, 1986)
M	Metz, Bibliothèque municipale, MS lat. 651 copy of the *Visio*
Manual	*A Manual of the Writings in Middle English, 1050–1500*, ed. J. Burke Severs & Albert E. Hartung (New Haven, 1967–)
ME	Middle English
MED	*Middle English Dictionary*, ed. H. Kurath, S. M. Kuhn *et al.* (Ann Arbor, Michigan, 1954–2001)
MGH	Monumenta Germaniae Historica (Hanover & Berlin, 1826–)
ES	Epistolae Selectae
PLAC	Poëtae Latini Aevi Carolini
SRM	Scriptores Rerum Merovingicarum

Morgan	Alison Morgan, *Dante and the Medieval Other World* (Cambridge Studies in Medieval Literature 8, Cambridge, 1990)
MVSH	*Magna Vita Sancti Hugonis: The Life of St Hugh of Lincoln*, ed. Decima L. Douie and Dom Hugh Farmer O.S.B., 2 vols. (London, 1961–62). Repr. with corrections, Oxford Medieval Texts, 1985.
NS	New Series
O	Oxford, Bodleian Library copy of the *Revelation*
OED	*The Oxford English Dictionary*, ed. J. A. H. Murray *et al.*, second edition prepared by J. A. Simpson and E. S. C. Weiner, 20 vols. (Oxford, 1989)
PL	*Patrologiae Cursus Completus*, Series Latina, ed. J.-P. Migne, 221 vols. (Paris, 1844–64)
PRS	Publications of the Pipe Roll Society
Revelation	*The Revelation of the Monk of Eynsham* [The late ME translation of the *Visio*, edited here.]
RS	Rerum Britannicarum Medii Aevi Scriptores (Rolls Series, London, 1858–1911, 1964)
S	Oxford, Bodleian Library, MS Selden Supra 66 copy of the *Visio*
Salter	Salter, H. E., *The Cartulary of the Abbey of Eynsham*, 2 vols. (Oxford Historical Society 49 & 51, 1907–8) [Introduction to the Cartulary, 1.i–xxxvi; 'The Vision of the Monk of Eynsham', 2.255–371 (Introduction to the *Visio*, 2.257–83; text of the *Visio*, 2.285–371)]
SC	*A Summary Catalogue of Western Manuscripts in the Bodleian Library at Oxford*, 7 vols. (Oxford, 1895–1953, repr. 1980)
Sharpe Latin Writers	Richard Sharpe, *A Handlist of Latin Writers of Great Britain and Ireland before 1540* (Publications of the Journal of Medieval Latin 1, Turnhout, 1997)
SPP	*St Patrick's Purgatory: Two Versions of* Owayne Miles *and* The Vision of William of Stranton *together with the Long Text of the* Tractatus de Purgatorio Sancti Patricii, ed. Robert Easting, EETS 298 (Oxford, 1991)
STC	*A Short-title Catalogue of Books Printed in England, Scotland, & Ireland and of English Books Printed*

	Abroad, 1475–1640, first compiled by A. W. Pollard & G. R. Redgrave, 2nd edn. rev. and enlarged, begun by W. A. Jackson & F. S. Ferguson, completed by Katharine F. Pantzer, 3 vols. (London, 1976–91)
T	Cambridge, Trinity College, MS B.15.42 copy of the *Visio*
Thurston	Thurston, Herbert, 'Visio monachi de Eynsham', *AB*, 22 (1903), 225–319
VCH	The Victoria History of the Counties of England (London, 1900–)
VEME	*Visio Edmundi monachi de Eynsham: Interdisziplinäre Studien zur mittelalterlichen Visionsliteratur*, ed. Thomas Ehlen, Johannes Mangei, and Elisabeth Stein (ScriptOralia 105, Tübingen, 1998)
Visio	*Visio monachi de Eynsham*
VOWME	Robert Easting, *Visions of the Other World in Middle English* (Annotated Bibliography of Old and Middle English Literature 3, Cambridge, 1997)
Ward	Ward, H. L. D., *Catalogue of Romances in the Department of Manuscripts in the British Museum*, vol. 2 (London, 1893) [3 vols. 1883–1910, vol. 3 ed. J. A. Herbert]
×	times (e.g. 4× = four times)
Zaleski	Carol Zaleski, *Otherworld Journeys: Accounts of Near-Death Experience in Medieval and Modern Times* (New York, 1987)

INTRODUCTION

THE REVELATION OF THE MONK OF EYNSHAM AND THE VISIO MONACHI DE EYNSHAM

This volume contains the first modern edition of the fifteenth-century English prose *Revelation of the Monk of Eynsham* (hereafter, the *Revelation*), which is a translation of the late twelfth-century Latin prose *Visio monachi de Eynsham* (hereafter, the *Visio*). The *Revelation* survives in two copies of an early printed book, published in London *c.*1483 by William de Machlinia. I present the text of the *Revelation* in parallel with an edition of a manuscript of the so-called C text of the *Visio*, the version from which the Middle English translator worked; the C text has not previously been printed in its entirety.

At Easter 1196, in the Benedictine house of Eynsham, five and half miles WNW of Oxford, a young monk (or, perhaps more properly novice[1]) named Edmund, experienced a vision of purgatory and paradise during a two-day trance. The Latin account was apparently composed in 1196(–7?) by his brother Adam, then sub-prior of Eynsham, and from 1197 to 1200 chaplain to Hugh (of Avalon, bishop) of Lincoln, and later author of his biography, *Magna Vita Sancti Hugonis* (hereafter *MVSH*). Some thirty-three manuscripts of Adam's account, the *Visio*, survive in European libraries and one in the USA, and it was translated into French verse (not extant) and German prose as well as into the Middle English *Revelation*. Edmund's vision of the other world and its textual transmission are in the long line of such experiences and written accounts which

---

[1] The text of the *Visio* does not finally make it clear which is appropriate, though the *tituli* of the *Visio* in S and the *Revelation* at large respectively use the terms *monachus* and *monke*. Herbert Thurston, 'A Conjectural Chapter in the Life of St. Edmund of Canterbury', *The Dublin Review*, 135, 4th ser. 52 (1904), 229–57, p. 243, note, says that he calls Edmund 'novice' because though Edmund had been at Eynsham fifteen months, 'It is hardly credible that he could have been allowed to make his profession in the infirm state described to us'.

go back via earlier medieval visions such as those seen by Tnugdal, Barontus, and Dryhthelm, to the early Christian *Apocalypse of Paul*, earlier Judaeo-Christian apocalypses, and classical *katabasis* (descent to the underworld) literature. The *Visio* is one of the longest of such free-standing vision texts from the Middle Ages (cf. the lengthy *Visiones Georgii*), and the *Revelation* is much the longest as well as the latest of the Middle English texts in this genre.[2] The *Visio* is a fascinating document giving rich detail about the circumstances of Edmund's collapse into ecstasy, and describing at length numerous interviews that Edmund subsequently claimed to have had with souls in purgatory and the earthly paradise, where he was led by his beloved St Nicholas. The souls he talks to range from humble layfolk via fellow monastics to powerful prelates. The central concerns of his vision are ecclesiastical reform, the need for penance, and the

---

[2] For the most recent book devoted to such medieval visions, see Carozzi. For further access to accounts of this genre of visionary literature, and for a survey of the *Visio*, the *Revelation*, and writings on them to 1995, see *VOWME*, esp. pp. 89–99. I discuss the *Revelation* in the context of some other fifteenth-century English meditations and visions concerning the afterlife in ' "Send thine heart into purgatory": Visionaries of the Other World', in *The Long Fifteenth Century: Essays for Douglas Gray*, ed. Helen Cooper and Sally Mapstone (Oxford, 1997), pp. 185–203. For a selection of pertinent recent discussions (postdating my coverage in *VOWME*) of death, ghostly apparitions, visions, purgatory, judgement, and paradise, see Jean-Claude Schmitt, *Les revenants: les vivants et les morts dans la société médiévale* (Paris, 1994), trans. Teresa Lavender Fagan, *Ghosts in the Middle Ages: The Living and the Dead in Medieval Society* (Chicago & London, 1998); Jérôme Baschet, 'Jugement de l'âme, jugement dernier: Contradiction, complémentarité, chevauchement?', *Revue Mabillon*, NS, 6 (1995), 159–203; Caroline Walker Bynum, *The Resurrection of the Body in Western Christianity, 200–1336* (New York, 1995); John Lancaster Murphy, *The Idea of Purgatory in Middle English Literature*, Diss., University of California, 1995; Paul Binski, *Medieval Death: Ritual and Representation* (Ithaca, N.Y., 1996); Carl Watkins, 'Doctrine, Politics, and Purgation: The Vision of Tnúthgal and the Vision of Owein at St. Patrick's Purgatory', *Journal of Medieval History*, 22 (1996), 225–36; Peter Dinzelbacher, 'Das Fegefeuer in der schriftlichen und bildlichen Katechese des Mittelalters', *Studi Medievali*, 3rd series, 38 (1997), 1–66; Jeffrey Burton Russell, *A History of Heaven: The Singing Silence* (Princeton, 1997); Takami Matsuda, *Death and Purgatory in Middle English Didactic Poetry* (Cambridge, 1997); Jérôme Baschet, 'Vision béatifique et représentations du paradis (XIe–XVe siècle)', *Micrologus*, 7 (1999), 73–93; Jean Delumeau, *Que reste-t-il du paradis?* (Paris, 2000); *Imagining Heaven in the Middle Ages: A Book of Essays*, ed. Jan Swango Emerson & Hugh Feiss (New York & London, 2000); *Last Things: Death and the Apocalypse in the Middle Ages*, ed. Caroline Walker Bynum & Paul Freedman (Philadelphia, 2000); Isabel Moreira, *Dreams, Visions, and Spiritual Authority in Merovingian Gaul* (Ithaca & London, 2000); *The Place of the Dead: Death and Remembrance in Late Medieval and Early Modern Europe*, ed. Bruce Gordon and Peter Marshall (Cambridge, 2000); Ananya Jahanara Kabir, *Paradise, Death and Doomsday in Anglo-Saxon Literature* (Cambridge Studies in Anglo-Saxon England 32, Cambridge, 2001); and Robert Easting, 'Personal Apocalypse: Judgement in some Other-world Visions', forthcoming in *The Millennium, Social Disorder, and the Day of Doom: Proceedings of the 2000 Harlaxton Symposium* (2003).

requirements of social and spiritual justice. The vision itself is recounted in Edmund's reported speech in chapters 14–56. The opening thirteen chapters Adam devotes to telling of Edmund's condition before the vision, how he was found unconscious, how he was tended until his revival, and how he started to tell what he had seen. The final two chapters, 57–58, recount Edmund's return from his ecstasy and argue for the truthfulness of his vision. The *Visio* has a Preface, and the *Revelation* has instead a new Prologue and list of chapter headings.

The *Visio* was a Benedictine work, doubtless originally intended for monastic consumption. It was produced at the end of the twelfth century, which had seen the appearance of many such other-world visions, often revealed to laymen, notably Tnugdal (1148), and these were especially prolific in England, witness Ailsi (*c*.1110) written by Peter of Cornwall (1200), the boys Orm (1125) and William (1143–7), Owein at St Patrick's Purgatory (*c*.1146–7) written by H. of Sawtry (*c*.1181–4), Gunthelm (before 1161), and the Essex peasant Thurkill in 1206. As Le Goff has argued, during this period the concept of purgatory was becoming increasingly imaginatively organized.[3]

The *Revelation* was translated, and published by a London printer in the late fifteenth century, for a wider lay audience much concerned with penitential requirements and *post-mortem* purgatorial expectations. The publication of the *Revelation*, though rare in so far as it is the only ME vision of the other world to have been printed before 1500, sits alongside such late fifteenth- and early sixteenth-century printed texts as the *Speculum Christiani* (also published by Machlinia), the *Ars Moriendi*, *The Art and Craft to Lyve well and to Dye well*, the *Fifteen Tokens*, and *The Kalender of Shepherdes*. The fifteenth century saw the continued appearance of new vision texts, such as the *Vision of William of Stranton* (1406/9) and *A Revelation of Purgatory* (1422), both in ME, as well as the continued manuscript copying of the early Latin visions—for instance, twelve of the surviving copies of the *Visio* date from the fifteenth century—and the copying of vernacular translations. The three hundred years between the *Visio* and the *Revelation* increased rather than diminished people's interest in and the circulation of visions of the other world and the advice and teaching they provided about one's conduct in this life and the mutually beneficial relations that could and should

---

[3] Jacques Le Goff, *La Naissance du Purgatoire* (Paris, 1981), English translation, *The Birth of Purgatory*, by Arthur Goldhammer (Chicago & Aldershot, 1984).

exist between the living and the dead. The religious and historical contexts for the production and reception of a work such as the *Revelation* have recently and excellently been discussed by Eamon Duffy and Stephen Greenblatt.[4] The *Revelation* accommodates a lay readership's needs by interpreting monastic terminology and translating Latin biblical quotations, but the text was doubtless read by clergy and laity alike. One of the surviving printed copies, L, contains early readers' annotations in both English and Latin (see below, p. xlvi).

This introduction deals first with the Latin source, the *Visio*, and then with the Middle English translation, the *Revelation*.[5]

THE LATIN SOURCE:
VISIO MONACHI DE EYNSHAM

MANUSCRIPTS OF THE *VISIO*

Thirty-four surviving, two destroyed, and eight further attested Latin manuscript copies of the *Visio* have been identified.[6] The text was published four times within seven years, 1902–8, by Huber (twice), Thurston, and Salter.[7] Salter, working from the evidence of fifteen manuscripts, distinguished three authorial versions A, B, and C.[8] Huber and Thurston printed B texts. Salter printed text A as it

---

[4] See Eamon Duffy, *The Stripping of the Altars: Traditional Religion in England c.1400–c.1580* (New Haven & London, 1992), and Stephen Greenblatt, *Hamlet in Purgatory* (Princeton & Oxford, 2001).

[5] Line numbers for citations from the *Visio* are preceded by S, for MS Selden Supra 66, the base text for my edition of the Latin.

[6] I draw together, below, the listings by Mangei in *VEME*, pp. 136–8, 161, and Sharpe, *Latin Writers*, pp. 15–16. 'Thirty-four surviving' manuscripts of the *Visio* excludes BL, Cotton Caligula A.viii, the retranslation from French verse, but includes BL, Harley 3776, excerpts, omitted from Mangei's listing (of 37 manuscripts, which includes Caligula, no.15, and the three German versions, nos. 9, 12, and 21). The two destroyed manuscripts were at Chartres, bombed during the second World War (Mangei nos. 39, 40); the eight further attested copies are Mangei nos. 38, 41, and (from Sharpe's tally) nos. 42–47 (Mangei, p. 161, note 106).

[7] See Abbreviations: Huber1, Huber2, Salter, and Thurston.

[8] Salter argues that Text A ended at the conclusion of chapter 48, with an appendix from *hec ego* (chapter 57) to the end of chapter 58. Salter, 2.282, continues: 'Subsequently the author revised what he had written, and added ten chapters, but when he added chapter xlix he forgot to correct the last words of chapter xlviii, so that in Text B the author promises a continuation of his work at some distant date, and then immediately fulfils his promise in chapter xlix. Subsequently he corrected the whole work, and removed this and many other imperfections in Text C. This theory will account for the fact that

survives to chapter 28, and thereafter text C. Bihrer has identified a late redaction, and eight various further redactions.[9] In the following list, divided as far as possible into such groupings, I give as appropriate the number for each manuscript assigned by Salter (e.g. Salter 2) and the alphabetical *siglum* used by Huber in his two editions. Salter's 1–8 follow the numeration used by Thurston.

Paul Gerhard Schmidt and others are publishing a B and a C text together with a collection of the later continental redactions, forthcoming from CCCM. As this edition will contain full descriptions of the manuscripts, I limit myself here to a brief notice of them.

A TEXT

Oxford, Bodleian Library, MS Digby 34, pt. 2, ff. 100ʳ–126ᵛ (s. xiiiⁱⁿ)
  Salter 2. Ends *imputari*, cap. 28. Salter's base text to cap. 28.
  Contains four further other-world texts: *Tractatus de Purgatorio S. Patricii*, *Visio Karoli crassi*, *Qualiter vivo apparuit mortuus*,[10] and Bede's Vision of Dryhthelm (*Historia Ecclesiastica*, 5.12).

B TEXT

Cambridge, Corpus Christ College, MS 43, ff. 107ʳ–128ᵛ (s. xiv)
  Salter 6, Huber2 C. From Norwich?
Dublin, Trinity College, MS 370, pt. 1, ff. 50ᵛ–76ᵛ (s. xiii²)
  Ends cap. 35. From Crowland, Lincolnshire, St Guthlac, OSB.
Dublin, Trinity College, MS 494, pt. 2, ff. 77ʳ–112ʳ (s. xiiiⁱⁿ)
Heidelberg, University Library, MS Salem 9.31 (after 1224)
  Salem, Cistercian.
London, BL, MS Cotton Cleopatra C.xi, ff. 49ʳ–69ᵛ (s. xiiiⁱⁿ)
  Salter 1 (Salter mistakenly calls it Caligula), Huber2 A (Huber

whereas Texts B and C diverge considerably in chapters i–xlviii and the final appendix, they are almost identical in the remaining part. It is as if the author found that what he had hurriedly composed in 1197, though revised in Text B, yet needed further polishing in Text C, whereas that which had been composed at leisure for Text B satisfied him, and needed little alteration for Text C.' It is not clear why Salter thinks here that Adam wrote his initial account only one year after the vision; this must be a slip for '1196', as Adam makes plain: *que in quodam notissimo michi monasterio contigisse* anno presenti, *qui est uerbi incarnati annus millesimus centesimus nonagesimus sextus* (S61–63).

[9] In *VEME*, pp. 93–94 and 104–6, respectively.
[10] The *Visio Karoli crassi* and the ghost story, *Qualiter vivo apparuit mortuus* are both found in *William of Malmesbury, Gesta Regvm Anglorvm: The History of the English Kings*, ed. and trans. R. A. B. Mynors, completed by R. M. Thomson & M. Winterbottom (Oxford Medieval Texts, Oxford, 1998), ii.111, pp. 162–8, and iii.237, pp. 440–4, and see commentary in vol. 2 by R. M. Thomson in collaboration with M. Winterbottom (Oxford, 1999), pp. 85, and 228–9.

mistakenly calls it C.IX). Described by Ward, 2.493–502. Basis of Thurston's text.
Dore Abbey, Herefordshire, Cistercian.

London, Lambeth Palace Library, MS 51, ff. 32^v–54^v (1200)
Part of Peter of Cornwall's *Liber reuelationum*, Holy Trinity, London, OSA.

Oxford, Bodleian, MS Bodley 44 (*SC* 1868), ff. 170^r–189 (s. xiii^1 before 1260)
Salter 3. Ends *a carnibus*, cap. 51. From Reading, Holy Trinity Abbey, Berkshire, OSB.

Paris, Bibliothèque de l'Arsenal, MS 1030, ff. 96–124 (s. xv^2)
Salter 15. Paris, St Victor, OSA.

Paris, BN, MS lat. 2590, ff. 51–58 (s. xiii)
Salter 12, Huber2 P. Owner 1332–1339, Giovanni Visconti, bishop of Novara.

Paris, BN, MS lat. 6686A, f. 95ra–130ra (s. xiii)
Provenance unknown. Begins: *Incipit prologus dompni Petri abbatis Cluniaci in libello reuelationum de locis purgatorii et patrie celestis.*[11]
Divided into 32 caps.

Paris, BN, MS lat. 14,978, ff. 1–74 (s. xv)
Salter 14. Paris, St Victor, OSA.

Toledo, Biblioteca Capitular, MS 9–19, f. 106^v– (s. xiii)
Title: *Liber narrationum de penis purgatorii et sempiternis gaudiis.*

Lost manuscripts of the B text

Chartres, Bibliothèque municipale, MS lat. 84 (131), ff. 1–27 (s. xiii)
Salter 9, Huber2 F. Destroyed in 1944. Chartres, Saint-Père, OSB.

Chartres, Bibliothèque municipale, MS lat. 1036 (H.I.51), ff. 281–309 (s. xiv)
Salter 10, Huber2 Z. Destroyed in 1944. Chartres, Saint-Père, OSB.

Parc (near Le Mans), before 1620, Carthusian, St Mary.
Charles Le Coulteux refers to Clemens Bohicius, who entered the Carthusian house of Le Parc, Sarthe, France, in 1596 (d. 1622), and who reports a copy of the *Visio* at Parc: *Hactenus Acta, in*

---

[11] On the false attribution to Peter the Venerable, see Losert in *VEME*, pp. 8–9. Giles Constable, 'The Vision of Gunthelm and other Visiones attributed to Peter the Venerable', *Revue bénédictine*, 66 (1956), 92–114, at p. 96, wrongly thought the *Visio* was the first chapter of a *Libellus reuelationum*, followed by 31 other accounts.

quorum fidem noster Bohicius dicit asservari in Domo sua Parcensi codex continens quasdam visiones seu revelationes eidem monacho factas, maxime illam mirabilem plane ac terribilem quam habuit de rebus futuri animarum post hanc vitam status. Cujus etiam visionis præter cæteros meminit Dionysius Rikelius in Colloquio sive Dialogo de particulari judicio animarum, articulo 23. Eam vero contigisse anno 1196 narrat codex Parcensis, cujus autor præsens fuerat, qui suum ac monachi illius nomen tacuit.[12]

C TEXT

Brussels, Bibliothèque Royale, MS 8763–74 (1495)
Trier, St Alban, Carthusian.

Cambridge, Trinity College, MS B.15.42, ff. 62ra-86va (s. xv)
On the last leaf is a note dated 1468 giving the names William Caston and Caru (? Carew), which Doyle (2.75)[13] suggests are from the West Country.

Cologne, Stadtarchiv, MS GB oct. 94 (1469)
Kreuzherrenkloster.

Metz, Bibliothèque municipale, MS lat. 651, ff. 67^{r}–107^{v}, art. 6 (s. xiv)
Salter 11, Huber2 M. Base manuscript for Schmidt's C text edition.
Also contains *Magna Vita Sancti Hugonis*. Rettel, Marienfloss, Carthusian.

Oxford, Bodleian Library, MS Bodley 636 (*SC* 2002), ff. 25^{r}–50^{v} (s. xv)
Salter 5. Badly written, lacks mid cap. 13 to mid cap. 19. Preceded by *Visio Tnugdali*.
Owned by J. Penny in the fifteenth century.

Oxford, Bodleian Library, MS Selden Supra 66 (*SC* 3454), ff. 1^{r}–42^{r} (s. xiv^{ex} after 1377)
Salter 4. Basis of Salter's text from cap. 28, and basis of present edition.
Owned by John Parker, son of archbishop Matthew Parker, in the late sixteenth century.

---

[12] Dom Carolo Le Couteulx, *Annales Ordinis Cartusiensis ab anno 1084 ad annum 1429*, vol. 3 (Monstrolii, 1888), pp. 111–12. See also discussion by Thurston, *The Life of Saint Hugh of Lincoln* (1898), Appendix L, and Mangei in *VEME*, pp. 147–8.

[13] A. I. Doyle, 'Survey of the Origins and Circulation of Theological Writings in England in the 14th, 15th and early 16th Century', Cambridge Ph.D. Diss., 2301–2302 (1953).

Paris, BN, Réserve des Imprimés MS D. 1042 (s. xv²)

Salter 13. Cologne, St Pantaleon, OSB, Bursfeld. Bound with a printed book.

Xanten, Stiftsbibliothek, an cod. 204 A (1475)

Wesel, St John, Carthusian.

Further redactions (see Bihrer in *VEME*, pp. 104–7)

Barcelona, Arxiu de la Corona d'Aragó, MS Ripoll. 41,[14] ff. 3rb–34vb (s. xiii^{ex})

Ripoll. St Maria, OSB.

Incipit liber de penis infernalibus. Omni experientia quotidiana sentimus quod die post noctis tenebras redeunte . . . Dom Jean Leclercq, comparing this text with Toledo, says, 'Même texte, mais selon une rédaction légèrement différente.'[15]

Brussels, Bibliothèque Royale, MS 1960–62, ff. 37^r–47^r (s. xiii)

Louvain, Val-Saint-Martin, OSA.

Cambridge, Trinity College, MS B.15.36, ff. 42vb–51va (*c.*1200?)

Abbreviated from B or an earlier version? Omits Preface and ends *fuisse estimabam* cap. 57.

London, BL, MS Cotton Caligula A.viii, ff. 192^r–209^v (s. xiii)

Huber2 L. Described by Ward, 2.503–4; translated from an unknown French verse version, which Thurston, *The Life of Saint Hugh of Lincoln* (1898), p. 619, note 1, has conjectured may have been the work of Angier of St Frideswide, who translated Gregory's *Dialogi* into French verse in 1212. Salter, 2.278–9 prints its new preface. A new edition is in preparation by Elisabeth Stein, and see Stein in *VEME*, pp. 113–33.

London, BL, MS Harley 3776, ff. 89^v–92^r (s. xiv)

Short excerpts; described by Ward, 2.505–6.

Madrid, Biblioteca Nacional MS 9783 (Ee 103), ff. 108rb–109vb (s. xiii)

Cistercian.

Paris, BN, MS lat. 3338, ff. 178vb–192vb (s. xiii/xiv)

Blois, Bibliothèque des Comtes, Cistercian.

[14] Sharpe, *Latin Writers*, lists MS 44.

[15] 'Recherches dans les manuscrits cisterciens d'Espagne', *Analecta Sacri Ordinis Cisterciensis*, 5 (1949), 109–19, at p. 116. Zacharia García, *Bibliotheca Patrum Latinorum Hispaniensis*, vol. 2, Sitzungsberichte der Kais. Akademie der Wissenschaften in Wien, 169:2 (1915), p. 19, notes the ending of the text as follows: *Ec omnia . . . retulit Gilbertus, qui prius monachus ludensis, postea abbas de basinge . . . et nos de eius ore audita digessimus in tractatum. Explicit.* This suggests some confusion with the text of the *Tractatus de Purgatorio Sancti Patricii*.

Saint-Omer, Bibliothèque muncipale, MS 307, ff. 129rb–130vb (s. xiii^{1})
Fragment based on B. Saint-Omer, Saint-Bertin, OSB.

Late redaction (new edition in preparation by Andreas Bihrer, and see
Bihrer in *VEME*, pp. 93–94)

Basel, Universitätsbibliothek, MS A.VI.16, ff. 185^{r}–211^{r} (1487)
Huber1 B. Basel, Margaretental, Carthusian. The *Visio* is followed
by a copy of the *Tractatus de Purgatorio Sancti Patricii* (ff. 211^{v}–
224^{r}); also contains *Magna Vita Sancti Hugonis*.
Berlin, Staatsbibliothek, MS theol. lat. fol. 705, ff. 26^{r}–41^{v} (1560–1570)
Cologne, St Barbara, Carthusian.
Mainz, Stadtbibliothek, MS I 289, ff. 35^{r}–54^{r} (s. xiv)
Mainz, St Michaelsberg, Carthusian. The text is falsely attributed
to Peter the Venerable. Contains *Tractatus de Purgatorio Sancti
Patricii*.
St Gallen, Stiftsbibliothek, MS 142, pp. 324–44 (1477)
Huber1 G. Contains *Visio Tnugdali* and *Tractatus de Purgatorio
Sancti Patricii*.
Copied in 1477 by Matthias Bürer of Lindow, chaplain of the altar
of St Stephen in the church of the Virgin at Memmingen, from an
exemplar sent to him by the abbot of Maria Saal, Buxheim, a
Carthusian house near Memmingen. The text is falsely attributed
to Peter the Venerable on the authority of Vincent of Beauvais.[16]
Würzburg, Universitätsbibliothek, MS M. ch. q. 99, ff. 245^{r}–269^{r}
(1460–1464)
Würzburg, St Stephan, OSB, Bursfeld. Contains *Tractatus de
Purgatorio Sancti Patricii*.

Redaction unknown

Washington (DC), Library of Congress, MS 73 (Faye and Bond
129), ff. 72rb–81ra (s. xiv^{ex})
Middle Rhine? Shortened. Dijon, Sainte Trinité, Carthusian.

Lost manuscripts

Buxheim, Maria Saal, before 1477: exemplar for St Gallen MS,
above.
Medieval library catalogues in England list six further copies which
no longer survive: see Sharpe, *Latin Writers*, p. 16.

---

[16] See below, p. xxviii.

OTHER VERSIONS AND ACCOUNTS

There are three independent early New High German translations[17] from the late Latin redaction:

Dresden, Sächsische Landesbibliothek MS M 244, ff. 27^r–49^r (s. xv^1)

Gotha, Landes- und Forschungsbibliothek, MS chart. B 269, ff. 18^r–53^v (s. xiv)

Nürnberg, Stadtbibliothek, MS Cent. VI, 43b, ff. 140^r–166^r (s. xv^2)

The *Visio* was also excerpted and noted in other vision, chronicle, and theological texts, and in *exempla* collections:

The author of the *Visio Thurkilli*, probably Ralph of Coggeshall, in the preface to that work, refers to the *Visio* (see below, p. xxxv), and also, in *Radulphi de Coggeshall Chronicon Anglicanum*, ed. Joseph Stevenson, RS, 66 (London, 1875, repr. Wiesbaden, 1965), pp. 71–72, gives a brief notice and résumé of the *Visio*; reproduced by Schmidt, ed. *Visio Thvrkilli*, pp. 38–39.

Roger of Wendover, *Flores Historiarum*, ed. H. O. Coxe, 4 vols., Publications of the English Historical Society 12 (London, 1841–4), vol. 3 (1841), pp. 97–117.

Rogeri de Wendover Liber qui dicitur Flores Historiarum, ed. Henry G. Hewlett, 3 vols., RS, 84 (London, 1886–9, repr. Wiesbaden, 1965), vol. 1 (1886), pp. 246–66.[18]

English translation: *Roger of Wendover's Flowers of History*, trans. by J. A. Giles, Bohn's Antiquarian Library (London, 1849), 2.148–64, and Eileen Gardiner, who still calls Eynsham 'Evesham', *The Visions of Heaven and Hell Before Dante* (New York, 1989), pp. 197–218, and notes pp. 245–6.

---

[17] See Nigel F. Palmer, *'Visio Tnugdali': The German and Dutch Translations and their Circulation in the Later Middle Ages* (Munich, 1982), pp. 415–16; Bihrer in *VEME*, p. 106; new edition in preparation by Thomas Ehlen.

[18] Constance Davies, 'The Revelation to the Monk of Evesham', *Review of English Studies*, 11 (1935), 182–3, compared the *Revelation* to the chronicle version of Roger of Wendover and the mention of the vision by Ralph of Coggeshall in *Chronicon Anglicanum*, and hence deduced the existence of an earlier Latin text, but she did not know of the existence of the *Visio*. Davies, following Roger of Wendover, supposed 'Evesham' to be the correct reading. E. K. Chambers, in a brief reply in the same volume (p. 330), corrected this error and referred readers to Salter's edition of the *Visio*.

Matthæi Parisiensis, monachi Sancti Albani, Chronica Major, ed. Henry Richard Luard, 7 vols., RS 57 (London, 1872–83, repr. Wiesbaden, 1964), vol. 2 (1874), pp. 423–37.[19]

Matthæi Parisiensis, monachi Sancti Albani, Historia Anglorum, ed. Frederic Madden, 3 vols., RS 44 (London, 1866–9), vol. 2 (1866), p. 60. Matthew Paris gives a brief notice of the vision under the year 1196: *Circa illos dies facta est divinitus quædam mirabilis visio sive revelatio cuidam monacho Eveshamensi, de gaudiis paradisi, et de locis poenalibus et purgatorio. Quæ visio ideo plus credebatur, quia per aliquot dies jacuit idem monachus quasi in extasi, ut nec vivus nec mortuus judicaretur.* He does not include the *Visio* but refers interested readers to St Albans and *Euuesham* where it can be found written more fully.

Note that no distinction is made here between the terms *visio* and *revelatio*; that Eynsham is confused with Evesham; that Edmund's name is not given; and that his ecstasy is held to be a motive for believing the vision.

BL MS Additional 38,654, an incomplete copy (s. xiv[1]) of a treatise on virtues and vices, includes extracts from the *Visio*, naming Eynsham and Edmund: *cuidam fratri de Eynesham nomine Eadmundo* (f. 2[r]), and *quidam frater de Eynesham Eadmundus nomine* (ff. 10[r], 12[r], 14[r]).

Dionysius the Carthusian, *De Particulari Judicio in Obitu Singulorum Dialogus,* in *Doctoris Ecstatici D. Dionysii Cartusiansi Opera Omnia,* vol. 41 [*Opera Minora,* vol. 9] (Tournai, 1912), provides a brief résumé of the *Visio* in art. 23, pp. 450–60, and discusses it alongside other visions, including excerpts from the *Tractatus de Purgatorio Sancti Patricii, Visio Tnugdali,* and the Revelations of St Bridget. These visions, says Dionysius, *valde sunt inductivæ et inflammativæ ad Dei timorem, ad internam compunctionem, ad sanctam devotionem, ad pœnitentiam salutarem, ad mundi contemptum, ad cordis custodiam, atque ad emendationem in omnibus* (p. 465 col. 2). In *De Quatuor Hominis Novissimis,* in the same volume, he provides a similar résumé of the *Visio* (falsely attributed to Peter of Cluny), art. 47, pp. 558–61. In art. 54, p. 568 col. 2, he determines that Edmund's vision was in

---

[19] Umberto Cosmo, 'Una nuova fonte dantesca?', *Studi medievali,* 1 (1904–5), 77–93, inconclusively suggests the possibility that the *Visio* may have been known to Dante via Matthew Paris.

the imagination because his *anima* remained in his body during his trance and so that he could explain what he had seen by corporeal images: *evidenter probato quod tota ejus visio fuit imaginaria, et anima ejus in corpore remanente: quia in ejus corpore evidentia vitæ signa apparuerunt. His ergo et consimilibus monstrata sunt animarum in purgatorio aut inferno detentarum supplicia sub imaginibus et similitudinibus corporalium rerum, secundum quod utilius capere poterant, et reversæ ad corpus, id est ad pristinum usum sensuum, salubrius recitare viventibus, quibus spiritualia per corporalia declarari oportet.*

Four of the sinners seen by Edmund became the subject of short *exempla*: the drunken goldsmith (taken from chapters 19–23), the knight who broke his vow of going to the Holy Land (ch. 32), the knight who was too fond of hawking (ch. 33), and the simoniacal knight (ch. 46). All four were falsely attributed to Peter the Venerable (Peter of Cluny) by Vincent of Beauvais and included under 'De morte' in the *Speculum Morale*, Lib. II, Dist. xi, Pars I,[20] and also transmitted by Étienne de Bourbon's *Tractatus de diversis materiis praedicabilibus*. The drunken goldsmith was also transmitted again under 'De Gula' in the *Speculum Morale*, Lib. III, Dist. ii, Pars VIII,[21] and in other texts: Odo of Cheriton, *Parabolae* no. 20; a collection appended to a *Summa Poenitentia*; the *Liber Exemplorum ad usum praedicantium*; Humbert de Romans, *Liber de dono timoris*; the *Speculum Laicorum*; and *The Alphabet of Tales*.[22] The hawking knight and the simoniacal knight are also found in Humbert de Romans and the *Speculum Laicorum*.[23] The earliest extracts from the *Visio* to occur in an exemplum collection would appear to be those in Paris, BN, MS lat. 15,912, which McGuire dates 'at soon before or after the year 1200',[24] from the Cistercian daughter-house of Clairvaux at

---

[20] See *Speculum Morale* (Douai, 1624, repr. Graz, 1964), col. 739B-D. Gardiner, *Medieval Visions of Heaven and Hell: A Sourcebook* (New York, 1993), p. 98, perpetuates the misattribution, regarding Vincent's text as an independent vision.

[21] Ed. cit., col. 1359C.

[22] See references in Frederic Tubach, *Index Exemplorum: A Handbook of Medieval Religious Tales* (FF Communications 204, Helsinki, 1969), nos. 1806, 3784, 4005.

[23] See Tubach, no. 4005, and add H95#28, H401#495, 496. The error of Constable, 'The Vision of Gunthelm', (1956), pp. 95–96, of thinking that the *Visio*, source of these *exempla*, comes from Embsay in Yorkshire, instead of Eynsham, was corrected when the article was reprinted with addenda in Giles Constable, *Cluniac Studies* (London, 1980), Addenda, pp. 3–5.

[24] Brian Patrick McGuire, 'The Cistercians and the Rise of the Exemplum in Early Thirteenth Century France: A Reevaluation of *Paris BN lat. 15912*', *Classica et Mediaevalia*, 34 (1983), 211–67, p. 225.

Beaupré near Beauvais. McGuire lists several excerpts from an unidentified work: 'A third, much more difficult attribution in our MS is the title *De visione cuiusdam monachi*. These *exempla* are almost always short and vague, detached from an historical context and expressing moral truth about life after death.'[25] McGuire's description of these excerpts convinces me that we have here extracts from the *Visio*,[26] which we can thus add to the tally of other *exempla* that McGuire says reached the Beaupré compiler from England,[27] and in this case within a few years of Adam's composition of his account of Edmund's vision.

PREVIOUS EDITIONS OF THE *VISIO*

Hauréau, B., *Notices et extraits de quelques manuscrits latins de la Bibliothèque nationale*, 6 vols. (Paris, 1890–3, repr. Farnborough, 1967), I. 126–37, prints extracts from B text Paris, BN, MS lat. 2590, with brief discussion.

Huber1 (1902/3) prints the late redaction from St Gallen, Stiftsbibliothek, MS 142 with variants from Basel, Universitätsbibliothek, MS A.VI.16. Chapter divisions are taken from Arber. Although Huber1 is mentioned in Huber2 (p. 642), it appears not to have been seen by Thurston and Salter.

Thurston (1903) prints B text, based on Cotton Cleopatra C. xi, with lacunae and the chapter *tituli* supplied from Selden Supra 66 (C text), and other variants from Digby 34 (A text), Bodley 44 (B text) and Bodley 636 (hereafter Bd, a C text), and Cambridge, Corpus, MS 43 (B text). Huber divides the text according to the numbered chapter divisions in the *Revelation*, printing the *tituli* from S.

Huber2 (1904) prints B text from Chartres, Bibliothèque municipale, MS lat. 84 (131), collated with Chartres, Bibliothèque municipale,

---

[25] Ibid., p. 220.

[26] I quote McGuire's descriptions (p. 260, note 25) and interpolate in square brackets the numbers of the chapters in the *Visio* from whence the extracts must be taken: 'As f. 25ra: a woman in purgatory because of her biting wit and lack of patience [30]; f. 44ra: punishment of a prince for his adultery and for shedding blood [41]; f. 64ra: a knight is seen being punished in purgatory for his games with birds [33]; f. 74vb: terrifying punishments suffered by sodomites [24]; f. 81ra: an abbot is punished more harshly after death whenever his brothers disobey the Rule because of the lack of discipline that prevailed while he was alive [27]; f. 90vb: a bishop is seen being punished because of the sins of his youth, but his clothes give him partial protection because of his acts of mercy [29].'

[27] Ibid., p. 226 and p. 262, note 49.

MS lat. 1036 (H.I.51) and Paris, BN, MS lat. 2590, with variants from Metz, Bibliothèque municipale, MS lat. 651 (hereafter M, a C text). Salter points out (2.283) that the two Chartres manuscripts 'are copied from one another or from one archetype, and often have the same errors' and that Chartres 131 and BN, MS lat. 2590 'have some connexion', sharing many errors. Huber was correct in believing (pp. 642–3) that, of the manuscripts known to him, the *Revelation* was closest to the C text from Metz. Huber divides the text according to the numbered chapter divisions in the *Revelation*. He includes the rubrics from Chartres, MS lat. 1036, and M.

Salter (1908) prints A text from Digby 34, to where it ends in chapter 28, and thereafter prints C text from Selden Supra 66. Salter relies on Bd, and M as given by Huber2, to support readings for the C text. Salter gives variants from the B text, collated from Cotton Cleopatra C. xi and Bodley 44, and uses Corpus Christi College, Cambridge, MS 43 and the other B manuscripts cited by Thurston and Huber2. Salter divides the text according to the numbered chapter divisions in the *Revelation*, printing the *tituli* from Selden Supra 66.

There is no full modern translation of the *Visio*. Dinzelbacher provides a modern German translation of extracts, caps. 38–40, and 54.[28] Gardiner provides a modern English translation of the shortened version in Roger of Wendover (see above, p. xxvi).

EYNSHAM / EVESHAM

As the textual apparatus to the edition of the *Revelation* below, lines 3, 120, 122, shows, Machlinia's text erroneously speaks of 'a monke in the abbey of Euishamme', and 'a monasterye callyd Euyssham', hence the spine title of L, 'The Revelacion of the Monke of Evishamme', Arber's title, *The Revelation to the monk of Evesham*, and Sheppard's 'The Revelation of Saint Nicholas to a monk of Evesham'.[29] The English translator probably found the error in his Latin source; it stems originally from an easy misreading of the three minims of *in* as *ui*—*Euisham* instead of *Einsham*. Thus Corpus Christi College, Cambridge, MS 43 reads *Eveshamiae*; Roger of

---

[28] *Mittelalterliche Visionsliteratur: Eine Anthologie* (1989), pp. 122–7.

[29] See below, pp. xliv and xlvi. The misnomer is perpetuated in the discussions of the *Revelation* by Bynum, *The Resurrection of the Body*, see General Index, s.v. Visions of the otherworld, and Greenblatt, *Hamlet in Purgatory*, see Index, p. 316.

Wendover *Eveshamensis*; Matthew Paris *de Euesham*. A different misreading of the three minims of *-in-* as *-m-* yields Bodleian Library, MS Digby 34 *de Ameshamma*;[30] St Gallen, MS 142 *In Emesamensi*; St Omer, Bib. mun. MS 307 *uisio Edmundi monachi Eimeshamnensis* (f. 128vb) and *In Emeshamensi monasterio* (f. 129ra). The spelling of 'Eynsham' in the correct readings varies, as might be expected: e.g. Lambeth Palace Library, MS 51 *Enesham* (f. 32^{v} col. 1) and *Heinesham* (in the list of contents f. 9^{v} col. 2); BL, MS Cotton Caligula A.viii, f. 192^{r} and Bodleian Library, MS Selden Supra 66 *Eynesham*; Brussels, Bib. Royale, MS 1960–92 *in cenobio Egenesha-mensi*; Ralph of Coggeshall (RS 66, p. 71) *in Enigsamensi*.[31]

PRESENT EDITION OF THE *VISIO*
Oxford, Bodleian Library, MS Selden Supra 66 (SC 3454)

The *Revelation* is translated from a C text of the *Visio*,[32] and therefore, for the convenience of the reader, I present in parallel with the *Revelation* a copy of the C text, as this version has not previously been printed in full. For this I have used Bodleian Library, MS Selden Supra 66, ff. 1^{r}–42^{r} (hereafter S).

S is a late fourteenth-century, English, parchment manuscript of 45 leaves; the *Visio* is now the sole text, apart from notes at the end, and some additions preceding and following. According to the *SC* entry 3454, these are: ff. iii–iv, 'part of a Latin inventory of plate, cloth, &c., with their value, of the time of Henry viii: and fol. 43 is a list of testamentary bequests of money (of a London merchant?) of about 1500.' Collation [a–d]^{8}, [e]^{10}; pages measure 212 × 142 mm, written space 160 × 104 mm; 27 lines per page; writing below the top line; catchwords; some later signatures, cropped. The text, in black ink, in a regular book hand with some hair-line flourishes, is for the most part written continuously, with subsections of the narrative indicated by some 55 blue initials. It is usually next to these initials that marginal rubrics or *tituli* have been added in red, in a smaller script but similar hand to that of the text. There is one illuminated capital at the head of the text in *Usu*, and an eight-line initial at the head of the narrative, following the prologue, in *In*.

---

[30] MS appears to me to read *Ameshamma* (and is read thus by Thurston, p. 227), but the minims of *-m-* or *-in-* are difficult to interpret; Salter, 2.285, and Losert and Ehlen, in *VEME*, pp. 10 and 21, note 85, respectively, read as *Aineshamma*.

[31] See further Losert in *VEME*, p. 7, note 22.

[32] See below, pp. lviii–lx.

This manuscript has a close relationship with the *Revelation* for the chapter headings in the *Revelation* closely follow the *tituli* in S.[33] No other manuscript of the *Visio* listed above has these chapter *tituli*.[34] They are, as Salter says (2.277) not the work of the original author. Apart from the initial rubric, all the *tituli* were written in the margins after the text was copied. The outer edges of the leaves have been trimmed, mostly carefully preserving the *tituli*, some of which now therefore protrude slightly. The hand responsible for the inclusion of these *tituli* appears to be of the fourteenth century, thus ruling out any possibility that they could themselves be translated from the Middle English print, for the text of the Middle English translation appears not to antedate the print by very long—it is probably no earlier than 1470.

In the top margin of f. 1ʳ of S, in red crayon, is the name 'John Parker', i.e. archbishop Matthew Parker's son. On the facing folio the same hand reads *Vide in fine*, referring to f. 42ʳ where another, secretary, hand, believed to be archbishop Parker's, gives notice of further visions, on two parchment sheets stuck over another text in the same hand as, and following, the *Visio*.[35] A third seventeenth-century? hand adds further notes on another paste-down on f. 42ᵛ, referring to the visions of Elizabeth of Erkenrode, and the nun of Watton.[36] Hearne

---

[33] This was noted by Thurston, p. 234: 'His titulis qui fere concordant cum titulis in versione anglica impressa . . .'.

[34] Huber2 shows that Chartres, MS lat. 1036 had *tituli* for cap. 1, 8, 13A, 18, 19, 24, 28 (=S), 29, 30, 33, 36, 37, 38 (=S), 40, 41, 43 (=S), 46 (=S), 47, 48, 49, 50 (=S), 54, 56, M has *tituli* for cap. 1, 14, 19, 37, 41, 47 (=S), 48, 49, 50 (=S), 51, and Chartres, MS lat. 84 had them for cap. 41, 43 (=S), but these differ from each other and (apart from the instances noted, which are all short and simple) are not the same as for S and the *Revelation*. The re-translation from French verse, in BL, MS Cotton Caligula A.viii, contains 29 tituli, from *De filio aurifabri* (f. 196ᵛ) to *De gaudijs* (f. 208ʳ), but again these do not tally with those of S and the *Revelation*.

[35] *Hic videre Licet quam libenter passi sunt maiores nostri illudi vanis huiusmodi visionibus, quibus fere predicatores vsi sunt in comprobationem rerum et articulorum fidei quas tractabant. Preterita vt plurimum authoritate sacrarum scripturarum.*

Hec visio tanti habebatur apud maiores nostros vt eam in multis Libris scriptum propagari fecerint. Non incongrue asscribitur hec fabula revelacionis monacho de Eovesham, nam edificatio ipsius Cenobii initium habuit a visione ostensa Egiwino wiciorum episcopo primo fundatore, qui in charta Ewsham [margin] *sua (anno 714)* [margin] *protestatur Sanctam virginem mariam primum cuidam pastori gregum Eoves nuncupato et postea sibi cum duabus virginibus Librum in manibus tenentem apparuisse et Locum pro edificando monasterio ostendisse vnde illi nomen Eovesham dedit, vt Kenredus rex merciorum et Offa rex orientalium Anglorum testatur in charta sua Anno domini 709.*

[36] *Consimilis fabula narratur et asseveratur per fratrem Philippum de clara valla, de quadam puella, nomine Elizabeth, in monasterio vocat. Erkenrode in territorio Leodicensi, quod monasterium erat virginum Beati Barnardi. Vide in Alexandro Essebiensi. pag.ᵃ 185ᵃ.*

transcribed these notes 27 August 1711.[37] The hand in red crayon also underlines passages in the text and makes brief comments in the margin. Three further hands in black ink severally write *nota* in the margin, add brief notes, and one (a larger hand) identifies a few important features.

S presents an excellent copy of the C text with few errors. I have not undertaken to present a full collation of all the variants in all the C manuscripts, but I have checked the text against the printed editions of Huber2, Thurston, and Salter, and against the other original manuscript copies of the C text in England, Cambridge, Trinity College, MS B.15.42 (T) and Oxford, Bodleian Library, MS Bodley 636 (Bd), which are later than S and generally present less good texts, and also against a microfilm of Metz, Bibliothèque municipale, MS lat. 651 (M). I have used the readings of BdMT where they help when S is in error or questionable. For full collations of B and C texts, the reader is advised to consult the forthcoming edition by Schmidt in CCCM.

THE VISIONARY, AND THE AUTHOR OF THE *VISIO*

In 1998 Kerstin Losert scrupulously and cautiously examined the evidence for and against establishing the identities of the visionary and the author of the *Visio*. I shall not, therefore, rehearse all these arguments in detail. She concludes that one may with great probability ('mit grosser Wahrscheinlichkeit' (p. 30)) continue to

---

Item tale mirabile miraculum describitur ab Æthelredo abbate Rieuallensi de quadam sanctimoniali fœmina de Watton et de incestu eius. Vide Symion Dunelmensis, in fine libri.

On the nun of Watton, see Aelred of Rievaulx, *De Sanctimoniale de Wattun*, PL 195:789-95, and Giles Constable, 'Aelred of Rievaulx and the Nun of Watton: An Episode in the Early History of the Gilbertine Order', in *Medieval Women*, ed. Derek Baker (Oxford, 1978), pp. 205-226, who quotes, pp. 212-13, note 24, the same note (*Consimilis . . . 185ᵃ*) in a seventeenth-century hand from the end of Aelred's text in Cambridge, Corpus Christi College, MS 139, f. 151ᵛ. The beginning of the Corpus note reads: *Talis fabula narratur de quodam monacho de Euesham tempore Ric. primi Aᵒ 1196* [i.e. the *Visio*]. Constable refers to 'the parallel note' in S, and says he 'can find no closely parallel miracle either here [in the *Visio*] or in the *Vita* of Elizabeth of Erkenrode by Philip of Clairvaux, published in *Catalogus codicum hagiographicorum bibliothecae regiae Bruxellensis* (Brussels 1886-9) 1 pp 362-78'. According to Montague Rhodes James, *A Descriptive Catalogue of the Manuscripts in the Library of Corpus Christi College Cambridge*, 2 vols. (Cambridge, 1912), p. 320, the note found in Corpus MS 139 refers to Corpus MS 138, item 10, which is Philip of Clairvaux's account of Elizabeth of Herkenrode, starting on Parker's paginated p. 185; item 1 is *Alexandri Essebiensis epitome historiæ Britanniæ*.

[37] See *Hearne's Collections*, ed. C. E. Doble (Oxford Historical Society 13, Oxford, 1888), pp. 213-14.

entertain the long-held notion that the author, or what she prefers to term the 'first redactor', of the *Visio* was Adam of Eynsham. Sharpe had accepted Adam as the author in his *Latin Writers* (1997). And, while carefully canvassing all the counter-arguments, Losert leaves it an open question whether or not we can positively identify Edmund as the visionary of the *Visio* with the visionary clerk of the *Magna Vita Sancti Hugonis*, 5.3, also written by Adam of Eynsham, and whether or not Edmund was Adam's blood brother. Whilst perfectly conscious of the final uncertainty of these identifications, first posited by Salter, I accept them on the grounds of coherent probability, until such time as further evidence assists in confirming or refuting them.

The identity of the visionary and of the author of the *Visio* is not revealed within the text, but is given in rubrics added by copyists in some of the manuscripts, and the identity of the author is also noted by a contemporary writer. The principal evidence for the names of the visionary and the author is as follows. The *incipit* to MS Digby 34 (an early manuscript, *c.*1200), f. 100^r, reads:

Incipit prefatio domni Adam prioris de Ameshamma[38] *super uisionem*[39] *quam uidit Eadmundus monachus, bone indolis adolescens, frater ipsius, scilicet prioris, & in professione filius, anno ab incarnatione Domini M^o C^o xcv^{o}i.*

This names the visionary Edmund, notes that the author Adam, his brother (if we interpret *frater* here as blood brother)[40] was prior (which is probably an error for sub-prior) and also Edmund's spiritual father, that is, he served to instruct Edmund in the rule and customs of the abbey.[41] The rubric at the end of the preface in the same manuscript (f. 101^r) reads:

---

[38] See Eynsham / Evesham above.

[39] Thurston, p. 227, Salter, 2.285, Losert and Ehlen in *VEME*, pp. 10 and 271, note 85, respectively, all read *uisione*, but the MS clearly has a nasal abbreviation over the final *-e*, though in classical Latin this construction with *super* would have taken the ablative not the accusative.

[40] Losert points out that this is the only basis for the supposition that Edmund was Adam's brother, and that the term *frater* could equally mean fellow 'brother' of the monastery ('eine Ordensbruderschaft gemeint sein könnte', in *VEME*, p. 10). However, it may be that the larger expression *frater ipsius, scilicet prioris* suggests blood brotherhood: why else use *scilicet* when we have already been told that Adam was prior and Edmund a monk, and therefore *ipso facto* religious brothers–unless, perhaps, to indicate a brother monk of the *same* monastery; but this is spelled out in the ensuing *incipit* to the narrative. Moreover, the play of contrast on *frater* and *in professione filius* is the more pointed if the former denotes a blood relationship and the latter a spiritual one.

[41] See Salter, 2.285, note to line 3.

Explicit prefatio. Incipit uisio Eadmundi monachi de Amesham edita a uenerabili Adam priore de eodem loco.

The visionary is also named Edmund in: Peter of Cornwall's *Liber reuelationum*, Lambeth Palace Library, MS 51 (also early, and dated internally 1200), f. 32ᵛ col. 1: *De admirabili uisione Edmundi monachi de Enesham*;[42] BL, Cotton Cleopatra A.viii, a thirteenth-century copy of the text of the vision translated back into Latin prose, as the new prologue explains, from an unknown French verse translation, *de gallica edicione rithmice composita in Latinam transtuli*: the opening paragraph (f. 192ʳ) says: *Nomen uero serui dei memorati frater Edmundus uocabatur monachus de Aynesham*; St Omer, Bibl. mun. MS 307 *uisio Edmundi monachi Eimeshamnensis*; and the excerpts in BL, MS Additional 38,654 (see above, p. xxvii).

Adam is also named as author of the *Visio* by the author, probably Ralph of Coggeshall, of the *Visio Thurkilli*, which took place in 1206:

est et alia visio diligenti narratione luculenter exarata, que in monasterio de Einesham anno verbi incarnati MCXCVI contigit, quam domnus Adam supprior eiusdem cenobii, vir valde gravis ac religiosus, eleganti stilo conscripsit, sicut ab eius ore audivit, qui a corpore per duos dies et noctes eductus fuerat. non credo tantum virum, tam religiosum ac tam litteratum, nisi comperta et probabili auctoritate subnixa voluisse scripto mandare, maxime cum tunc temporis extiterit capellanus domni Hugonis Lincolniensis episcopi sanctissimi viri. interrogatus autem a nobis domnus Thomas prior de Binham, qui illis diebus extitit prior de Einesham, et qui diligenti scrutinio omnia examinaverat de monacho educto et que de eius visione perscrutanda erant, quidnam super his sentiret, respondit se non amplius de veritate huius visionis hesitare quam de domini nostri Iesu Christi crucifixione.[43]

Something is known, then, of the author of the *Visio*, but much remains conjectural.[44] Adam of Eynsham was, it seems, the older

---

[42] The reading *Uti uero de die mundi premisimus* (S19) has been optimistically miscorrected in Peter of Cornwall's copy to *Vti uero de edmundi premisimus* (f. 32ᵛ col. 2).

[43] *Visio Thvrkilli. Relatore vt videtvr Radvlpho de Coggeshall*, ed. Paul Gerhard Schmidt (Leipzig, 1978), p. 3, lines 12–25. Ralph of Coggeshall also writes of the vision of the monk of Eynsham (*in Enigsamensi coenobio*) in his *Chronicon Anglicanum*, s.a. 1196; this is reproduced by Schmidt in his Appendix I, pp. 38–39.

[44] The following brief account is indebted to Losert, and also to *Magna Vita S. Hugonis Episcopi Lincolniensis*, ed. James F. Dimock, RS 37 (London, 1864), pp. xxxiv–xlii; Salter, 1.vii–xxxiii and 2.257–83; Josiah Cox Russell, *Dictionary of Writers of Thirteenth Century England* (London, 1936), pp. 5–6; A. B. Emden, *A Biographical Register of the University of Oxford to A.D. 1500* (Oxford, 1957), 1.12; Dom David Knowles, *The Monastic Order in England*, 2nd edn. (Cambridge, 1963), pp. 381–91, and pp. 402, 631, and 652; *MVSH*; Hugh Farmer, *St. Hugh of Lincoln* (Kalamazoo, 1985); and Eric Gordon, *Eynsham Abbey 1005–1228: A Small Window into a Large Room* (Chichester, 1990).

brother of the visionary Edmund. They had another brother, William, who occurs in the Eynsham cartulary (Salter, 1.305, 159, 160, 162, 179, 245, 2.271). William held two small properties in the parish of St Peter in the East, and is described as *faber*. He had a son and heir also called Adam. The brothers were probably born at Oxford in the neighbourhood of Osney. Their father died on pilgrimage in the Holy Land not many years before 1194, probably during the time of the Third Crusade, 1189–92. The author Adam may have entered the Benedictine monastery of Eynsham when quite young and studied in the schools at Oxford before becoming a monk. At the time of Edmund's vision, Easter 1196, Adam was sub-prior. The prior was Thomas, who shortly after became prior of Binham, Norfolk.[45] Adam may have succeeded Thomas as prior of Eynsham, but this is uncertain; the incipit to MS Digby 34 calls Adam prior.[46] The abbacy was vacant for two and half years, from the death of Godfrey in about May 1195[47] to the blessing of his successor Robert of Dover at Lincoln, 11 November 1197. Adam started writing the *Visio* in 1196,[48] very likely with the support of bishop Hugh of Lincoln, and probably continued his revisions during the following year or two. On 12 November 1197 he left Eynsham to become chaplain to Hugh, and remained with him until Hugh's death, 16 November 1200.

At the time of Edmund's vision of the other world, Eynsham was involved in a dispute between Hugh of Lincoln and the crown over jurisdiction over the monastery, hence the delay in appointment of a successor to abbot Godfrey. Eynsham was an *Eigenkloster* of the bishops of Lincoln, and had been since its post-Conquest refounding by bishop Remigius before 1086, the community's removal to Stow near Lincoln in 1091, and its return to Eynsham at the behest of his successor Robert Bloet in 1094/5. Adam may have been the original compiler of the Eynsham cartulary, put together in 1196–7 to assist Hugh of Lincoln in his case against Richard I's claim to patronage of the abbey.[49] Adam's

---

[45] Salter, 1.xv–xvi. On p. xxxiii he erroneously substitutes the name Martin for Thomas.

[46] See Salter, 2.259, paragraph one, but Losert, pp. 16–18, questions this.

[47] Not 1196, *pace* Losert and Wieners, in *VEME*, pp. 13, 76, and 86, note 70. See below, Commentary 1511.

[48] See above, note 8.

[49] A writ of Henry II (at Rouen 1157–63) had reconfirmed the bishop of Lincoln's rights over Eynsham, and the bishop's power to appoint the abbot, with the king's advice and consent: see *The Registrum Antiquissimum of the Cathedral Church of Lincoln*, vol. 1, ed. C. W. Foster (The Lincoln Record Society 27, Lincoln, 1931), no. 135, p. 85, lines 5–11.

composition of the *Visio* and possibly of the cartulary would have been good reasons to support Hugh's choice of Adam as his chaplain. Mark Dengler has suggested that the selection of biblical citations in the *Visio* concerning good kingship and the responsibilities of the powerful is prompted by the conflict between the crown and the bishop over the right of election at Eynsham at this period.[50] Adam recounts Hugh's defence of his rights over Eynsham in *MVSH*, 4.8 (vol. 2, pp. 39–42). This legal contest was resolved in Hugh of Lincoln's favour in 1197. In Hugh's service Adam would have become familiar with a large number of distinguished men.[51]

When abbot Robert died in 1208, King John laid claim to the patronage of Eynsham. During the Interdict Adam fled abroad 1209 and did not return until 1213; the Interdict ended in June of that year; King John surrendered jurisdiction over the abbey of Eynsham to the bishop of Lincoln on 17 July.[52] During his exile Adam spent three months in Paris, befriended by Hugh's kinsman Reimund, whom he had met while accompanying Hugh on his last journey to Chartreuse in 1200. He also spent time at the Cistercian abbey of Clermaretz near Saint-Omer.[53] Adam was appointed abbot of Eynsham in the second half of 1213. Two former Benedictines who had become Carthusians of Witham had encouraged Adam to write his *Magna Vita Sancti Hugonis*, and he was probably engaged in its composition periodically until about 1212/13. Adam gave evidence to the commission of 1219 appointed by Honorius III to enquire into Hugh's life and miracles.[54] Hugh was canonized in 1220. Adam was deposed from his abbacy in 1228, *tanquam periurus et dilapidator manifestus*, probably 'as an incompetent business-manager'.[55] He had pursued various ambitious and expensive

[50] In *VEME*, pp. 59–71, esp. at pp. 69–70.

[51] On members of Hugh's staff see the Introduction to *English Episcopal Acta IV: Lincoln 1186–1206*, ed. David M. Smith (London, 1986), pp. xxiii–xxviii. For Hugh's extant charters dealing with Oxford houses see nos. 59–64 Eynsham, 67–68 Godstow, 142–8 Osney, and 149–50 St Frideswide.

[52] See *The Registrum Antiquissimum*, nos. 202–3, pp. 127–8.

[53] This could explain the presence of a MS of the *Visio* from Saint-Bertin at Saint-Omer.

[54] See Dom Hugh Farmer, 'The Canonization of St Hugh of Lincoln', *Lincolnshire Architectural and Archaeological Society Papers*, 6 (1956), 86–117.

[55] See Annals of Dunstable, *Annales Monastici*, ed. Henry Richard Luard, 5 vols., RS 36, vol. 3 (London, 1866), p. 109. Eric Gordon, 'Eynsham Charters. 2. Provision for Retired Abbots,' *The Eynsham Record*, 3 (1986), 6–11, at p. 6, note, corrects *HRHEW*, p. 49, which claims that after his deposition Adam became a monk at Crowland. Rather it was his successor, Nicolas, prior of Freiston, Lincolnshire, a dependency of Crowland

projects including expansion of the abbey lands and the establish-
ment of a new town at Eynsham. Salter (2.v) suggests that 'by
wasting the goods of the monastery he broke the oath he had made at
his consecration'. Adam was still alive in 1232, and assigned the
manor of Little Rollright on 20 May for his retirement, but probably
died soon after 1233.

As shown above, the name of the visionary is not given within the text
of the *Visio* either, but is identifiable as Edmund. Indeed, all the
persons who appear in the text are deliberately left anonymous, apart
from the guide, St Nicholas, as Adam explains in cap. 23 (S1130–44).
Losert has also examined with great care the lack of positive evidence
for Salter and subsequent writers identifying the Edmund of the *Visio*
with the anonymous young clerk whose auditions, and vision of the
Christ child in the Host, are recounted by Adam in *MVSH*, 5.3. But
again the conjunctions are both very suggestive and plausible.

While bishop Hugh of Lincoln, celebrating Mass in his manor at
Buckden, raised the Host for the consecration,

*cuiusdam clerici oculos superna clementia dignata est aperire; eique sub specie infantis
paruuli Christum suum demonstrauit mundissimis digitis sacri presulis reuerentissime
contrectari. Erat uero idem puer forma quidem permodicus set diuino quodam nitore
atque candore super estimationem hominis nimium decorus. Clericus qui hec uiderat
mira deuotione, nec mirum, successus plurimumque compunctus, tempus omne
continuabat in lacrimis quod intercessit ab illa eleuatione usquequo interim eam
leuari cerneret, frangendam iam et sumendam sub trina sui partitione. In qua rursum
eleuatione sub eadem qua prius ymagine natum intuetur de uirgine Filium Altissimi,
seipsum offerentem pro humana salute.*[56]

---

abbey, who was *monachus Croylandiae* (College of Arms, MS Arundel 10, f. 110ᵛ). See also
The Heads of Religious Houses: England and Wales, II. 1216–1377, ed. David M. Smith &
Vera C. M. London (Cambridge, 2001), p. 43.

[56] 'God in His mercy deigned to open the eyes of a certain clerk and showed him Christ
in the likeness of a small child in the chaste hands of the venerable and holy bishop.
Although very tiny, the child was very lovely and of a supernatural brilliance and
whiteness beyond man's imagination. The clerk who saw this not unnaturally felt great
devotion and compassion, and wept continuously from the time of the elevation until he
saw it elevated once more to be broken into three portions and partaken of. In the second
elevation he saw the Son of the Most High, born of a virgin, in the same form as before,
offer himself for the redemption of mankind.' *MVSH*, 5.3 (vol. 2, p. 86). Thurston (*The
Life of Saint Hugh*, p. 343, note 1), points out that there is here no elevation of the
consecrated Host 'in the modern understanding of the term'. Edmund sees the infant first
when the Host is elevated from the altar *before* the consecration, and a second time shortly
before the fraction.

This kind of vision of the body of the Christ child in the Host is found infrequently before the end of the twelfth century, but becomes much more frequent and elaborated among women visionaries in particular in the thirteenth and fourteenth centuries.[57] As Adam subsequently relates, the clerk (Edmund?) tells Hugh of a voice which he had heard earlier that week on the morrow of the feast of All Saints, while praying in a Lady Chapel in a church (in Oxford?) and saying the psalms for the souls of the dead. Having reached Psalm 101, he remembered and wept for his dead father, and then the voice had told him to go to bishop Hugh of Lincoln, 'and tell him from God to admonish earnestly the archbishop of Canterbury [= Hubert Walter] that with his assistance he should devote himself more zealously than hitherto to the reform of the Church and the clergy'. The voice lists a number of abuses, including the lechery of priests, churches given to those unfitted to rule them or being farmed out and leased 'to the highest bidder in the same way as taverns or shops', and neglect of the poor and needy. The voice ends with threats of divine vengeance now about to smite all the inhabitants of the land. Many of these concerns were taken up in the *Visio*, which, of course, antedates the *Vita*. The clerk is confused

---

[57] See Peter Browe, *Die eucharistischen Wunder des Mittelalters* (Breslauer Studien zur historischen Theologie, Neue Folge 4, Breslau, 1938), pp. 100–11; *Exordium magnum Cisterciense*, ed. Bruno Griesser (CCCM 138, Turnhout, 1994), 3.15.127–30, p. 184, and 4.4.108–9, p. 245; Peter the Venerable, *De miraculis*, 1.8, see *Petri Clvniacensi abbatis De miracvlis libri dvo*, ed. Dyonisia Bouthillier (CCCM 83, Turnhout, 1988), p. 28; Paul Gerhard Schmidt, 'Luzifer in Kaisheim. Die Sakramentsvision des Zisterziensers Rudolf (ca. 1207) und Abt Eberhard von Salem', in *Litterae Medii Aevi: Festschrift für Johanne Autenrieth*, ed. Michael Borgolte and Herrad Spilling (Sigmarinen, 1988), pp. 191–201, esp. p. 197: *. . . ubi calicem signavit, quando dicitur 'et sanguis', ilico infans positus super calicem apparebat . . . factaque benedictione et dicto 'Hoc est corpus meum' infans vivus in manibus eius apparuit . . .*; and Leah Sinanoglou, 'The Christ Child as Sacrifice: A Medieval Tradition and the Corpus Christi Plays', *Speculum*, 48 (1973), 491–509. The clerk's vision is recounted in *Nicholas Love's Mirror of the Blessed Life of Jesus Christ*, ed. Michael G. Sargent (New York & London, 1992), p. 232, lines 6–37. See also Peter Dinzelbacher, 'The Beginnings of Mysticism Experienced in Twelfth-Century England', in *The Medieval Mystical Tradition in England. Exeter Symposium IV: Papers read at Dartington Hall, July 1987*, ed. Marion Glasscoe (Cambridge, 1987), pp. 111–31, at p. 121. Thomas of Cantimpré reports people seeing Christ in varied forms in the Host at a house of regular canons in Douai: crowned with thorns, or youthful, or crucified, but most saw him as a child: see *Bonum universale*, 2.40.2, referred to by Robert Sweetman, 'Thomas of Cantimpré, *Mulieres Religiosae*, and Purgatorial Piety: Hagiographical *Vitae* and the Beguine "Voice"', in *A Distinct Voice: Medieval Studies in Honor of Leonard E. Boyle. O.P.*, ed. Jacqueline Brown & William P. Stoneman (Notre Dame, Indiana: 1997), pp. 606–28, at pp. 615–16. I have not seen Rosemarie Rode, 'Studien zu den Kind-Jesu-Visionen', Diss. Frankfurt, 1957.

and alarmed, not knowing who has spoken to him; he makes the sign of the cross and resumes his prayers more vehemently than before. The voice repeats its injunctions word for word. A certain pious virgin who regularly prays in the same church intuits that the clerk has received a 'heavenly message, as she called it'. He wishes that she, 'as one more worthy than myself to hear and understand divine revelations' might interpret it for him. She says that she knows that God has spoken to him twice. He asks her to pray for him, returns to his lodgings, and spends the rest of day in fasting and prayer. As he goes to bed, the voice returns, commanding him to go to Hugh as quickly as he can; Hugh will have faith in what the clerk tells him if he relates what he sees when he watches Hugh celebrating mass. He sets off before daybreak to seek the bishop.

As the clerk tells all this to Hugh, they both weep copiously. Hugh asks him to conceal his vision, and counsels him to become a monk, for 'it was not right for one who had heard and seen what he had to remain any longer in the world (*in seculi uanitate*)'. The clerk replied that he was ready to take the bishop's advice, and became a monk shortly afterwards (*cito postea*), 'and lived an exemplary religious life'. Adam concludes the chapter as follows:

Cui plurima quoque spiritualium uisionum misteria postmodum fuisse reuelata certissime experti sumus. Ex quibus non pauca, litteris dudum de mandato sancti presulis tradita, longe lateque uulgata noscuntur. A cuius ore hec ipsa que modo retulimus frequenter audiuimus. Cui inter alia id quoque reuelatum fuisse ab ipso accepimus, quia sanctam ciuitatem Hierusalem / que pridem nostris temporibus a Saracenis occupata est, nostris quoque diebus miraculose ab eorum instantia omnipotentissima Redemptoris nostri eripiet clementia. Quod eo magis, fauente eiusdem Domini nostri pietate, confidimus adimplendum, quo iam plurima uidemus impleta que implenda adhuc ei didicimus similiter preostensa. Set de hiis hoc interim dixisse sufficiat.[58]

Hugh of Lincoln was a Carthusian, and had been third prior of Witham, the first Carthusian house in England. When the Carthusian

---

[58] 'I know for certain that many other spiritual mysteries were subsequently revealed to him in visions. A few of these were written down by the order of our holy bishop, and were very widely known. What I have just related I have very often heard from his own mouth. One particular revelation among the rest which he imparted to me was that the holy city, which was captured recently in our own day by the Saracens, would be miraculously recovered from them also in our lifetime, through the mercy of our Saviour. I am completely convinced that this will take place in God's good time, for I have seen many things come to pass which he told me it had been revealed to him would happen. I have, however, said enough about these matters.' *MVSH*, vol. 2, pp. 91–92.

Bohicius recounts this story of the clerk's visit to Hugh at Buckden, he notes that the clerk subsequently had a revelation of the future state of souls,[59] and when Dionysius the Carthusian quotes from this it is from the *Visio*.[60] As Mangei points out, in discussing the Carthusian interest in and transmission of the *Visio* and the *Vita*, this shows that Dionysius, Bohicius, and Le Coulteulx, at least, all understood, rightly or wrongly, that the clerk in *MVSH*, 5.3 and Edmund of the *Visio* were the same person.[61]

If, with Salter, we accept this identification, then we learn from this chapter in *MVSH* that Edmund was about twenty five years old at the time of his vision of the Christ child in the Host, which took place in November 1194; he was therefore born about the end of 1169,[62] and probably in the neighbourhood of Osney. As a clerk he probably studied also in the schools at Oxford. On Hugh's recommendation he shortly afterwards entered a monastery, which must be Eynsham: Salter says this can be dated with certainty to the same month, November 1194.[63] The *Visio* tells us that at Christmas 1194 he was lying sick with quinsy somewhere near Eynsham (S849–51). This was fifteen months before his vision at Easter 1196.

The emotional intensity of the clerk's reactions to hearing the voice and seeing the vision in the Host, his copious weeping, the concerns expressed by the voice about the corruption in the church and the threatening vengeance of God, and his interest in the reconquest of the Holy Land, are all features which recur in the *Visio*, where their occurrence is arguably due both to the personality and behaviour of the same person, the clerk/Edmund, and also to the strong likelihood that his brother Adam wrote both texts.

Losert has sensibly questioned the wisdom of basing too large a supposition on too slender a collection of evidence, and has shown

[59] See the quotation from Le Couteulx above, under the manuscript listed from Parc, pp. xxii–xxiii.

[60] Dionysius the Carthusian, *De Particulari Judicio*, art. 23, and see *De Quatuor Hominis Novissimis*, art. 47. Dionysius also misattributes the *Visio* to Peter of Cluny (see above, pp. xxvii and xxii, note 11).

[61] Joseph Clayton, *St Hugh of Lincoln: A Biography* (London, 1931), pp. 125–8, mistakenly says that Adam was the clerk who saw the Christ child.

[62] At S78 the visionary is called *iuuenis* at the time he enters the monastery. As Ehlen in *VEME*, pp. 270–1 and note 84 has shown, this term means 15–20 in the Eynsham Customary; but it can mean between 28 and 49 in other divisions of the ages of man's life: Mary Dove, *The Perfect Age of Man's Life* (Cambridge, 1986), p. 58, says that Augustine reckoned 30 years was the upper limit for *iuuentus*; John Burrow, *The Ages of Man* (Oxford, 1986), p. 82, note 73, shows that for Isidore *iuuentus* reached to the fiftieth year.

[63] Emden, 2.626–7, says he was admitted a monk of Eynsham in January 1195.

how hypotheses readily harden into solid facts in the scholarly literature (pp. 20–23). She rightly says that there is nothing compelling or conclusive ('zwingend') to indicate the identity of the clerk and Edmund, but (pp. 23–24) points out the features that strongly suggest this interpretation: that the author of *MVSH* had close personal knowledge of the subsequent visions of the clerk; that a few were written down at Hugh of Lincoln's instigation;[64] that they were widely circulated; that this matches the *magni viri* that the author of the *Visio* claims required its composition; that the preface to the *Visio Thurkilli* also suggests Hugh's authorization of the composition of the account of Edmund's other-world vision; that there is no other surviving text which would fit the bill apart from the *Visio*; that Bohicius understood a relationship between *Visio* and *MVSH*. She also acknowledges (p. 28) that the lack of concrete evidence in favour of the idea that Adam wrote both is not in itself an argument against it: the *Visio* deliberately leaves names out, and there was no reason to incorporate the clerk's name in the *MVSH*. And there are other suggestive parallels between *Visio* and *MVSH*. Salter noted the closeness of the attack on corrupt priests in cap. 36 of the *Visio* and by the voice heard in *MVSH*, 5.3.[65] Losert (p. 29, note 112) mentions the use of the fairly rare word *defunctio* in the *Visio* cap. 33 (S1615) and in *MVSH*, 5.16 (vol. 2, p. 198),[66] and one could similarly adduce the occurrence in both texts of *parilitas* 'equality' (S599, 1874, *MVSH*, 5.18, vol. 2, p. 208),[67] and *dilectrix* applied to Mary Magdalene (see below, Commentary 381). Claude Carozzi has also noted the verbal parallel between Hugh's admonition to the clerk in *MVSH*, 5.3, to leave the vanity of the world (*in seculi uanitate*, quoted above) and the opening of the narrative of the *Visio*, Edmund's withdrawal to the monastery of Eynsham *a seculari uanitate*.[68] All in all, these considerations still seem to warrant acceptance, in terms of what I have called coherent probability, of Salter's hypotheses: that the clerk in *MVSH*, 5.3, was the Edmund of the *Visio*; that Adam wrote both texts; and that Adam and Edmund were blood brothers. But it is wise to remember that it has not yet been

[64] See Commentary 2932.

[65] Losert (p. 29, notes 110 and 111) says that Salter does not specify (2.274–5) the parallel passages that he adduces, but he does so for the attack on corrupt priests, 2.344, note 41 (see below, Commentary 1974–80), if not precisely for the account of tending lepers (Commentary 2343–52).

[66] Whence cited in *DMLBS*.

[67] This was first hinted at by Salter, 2.304, note to line 12, and 2.348, note to line 28.

[68] See below, Commentary 123.

possible to verify these hypotheses beyond all reasonable doubt. We can, however, take it as certain that the redactor and the visionary were indeed known to each other, which is not always the case in the transmission of vision texts; thus, the *Visio* may be aligned with others which claim a similar knowledge by the redactor, such as Barontus, Earnan, Boso, Alberic, Orm, and Gottschalk B,[69] but I imagine that Adam and Edmund's collaboration on the text was particularly close.[70]

THE MIDDLE ENGLISH TRANSLATION
THE REVELATION OF THE MONK OF EYNSHAM

THE PRINTED COPIES

There is no surviving manuscript copy, but two printed copies survive of the late Middle English prose *Revelation of the Monk of Eynsham* [erroneously *Evesham*][71] issued in London by the Flanders-born William de Machlinia[72] [Mechelen, Malines], *c.*1483:

L = London, British Library, shelfmark IA.55449, and

O = Oxford, Bodleian Library, shelfmark Auct.1Q.5.28.

For bibliography, see: *IISTC* No. ir00171550; *STC* 20917; HC 13885;[73] Proctor 9767;[74] Duff 357;[75] Sheppard 7518;[76] *IPMEP* 695;

---

[69] See Carozzi, p. 521.   [70] See further, p. xcvii.

[71] See Eynsham / Evesham, above, pp. xxx–xxxi.

[72] The *Revelation* is erroneously attributed to Caxton by Howard Rollins Patch, *The Other World* (Cambridge, Mass., 1950), p. 118, note 67.

[73] Ludovicus Hain, *Repertorium Bibliographicum*, 4 vols. (Milan, 1948), no. 13885 mistakenly says, 'Est forte Visio Tondali anglice.' W. A. Copinger, *Supplement to Hain's Repertorium Bibliographicum*, Part 1 (London, 1895, repr. Milan, 1950), gives the earlier shelfmark for L: C.21.c.

[74] Robert Proctor, *An Index to the Early Printed Books in the British Museum from the Invention of Printing to the Year MD, with Notes of those in the Bodleian Library*, 2 vols (London, 1898), 4 supplements 1899–1902, no. 9767, lists the *Revelation* under the works of Machlinia's first press.

[75] E. Gordon Duff, *Fifteenth Century English Books: A Bibliography of Books and Documents Printed in England and of Books for the English Market Printed Abroad* (The Bibliographical Society, Illustrated Monographs 18, Oxford, 1917), p. 99. The entry is titled: 'The Revelation of Saint Nicholas to a Monk of Evesham. 4° [William de Machlinia, 1485].' Duff prints the opening and closing passages, and notes, 'Owing to a mistake in imposition some pages were wrongly printed. The correct pages have been pasted over them. The name of the abbey should be Eynsham.' Facsimile XXV reproduces f. [a]4ᵛ. See pp. 122 and 130 for notice of the type faces.

[76] L. A. Sheppard, *A Catalogue of XVth Century Books in the Bodleian Library* [Unpublished MS, 1954–71].

Manual, vol. 2, V [326]; and *VOWME 6*. Both copies are available on microfilm: L, no. Mic C.12,359; O from University Microfilms Inc.[77]

My edition is based on L. O has reset pages in quire [a]; the variants are listed in Appendix 1, below. The only previously published edition of the *Revelation*, by Edward Arber, is from L. Arber did not know of the existence of O, and nor apparently did Johannes Mangei in *VEME*, p. 138, note 8. L is not, as Mangei says, still bound with Caxton's *Order of Chivalry* (see below).

L

For a full description of L see *Catalogue of Books Printed in the XVth Century now in the British Library*, Part XI (forthcoming).[78]

Quarto. [a–g^8, h^{10}.] 66 leaves, the first and f. 66^v blank, without title-page, pagination, or signatures.[79] f. [a]5^r: 30 lines, 150 × 93mm. Types 120 G., heading and first two words on f. [a]2^r, a few words elsewhere; 100B. Two- and three-line capital spaces left at the beginnings of chapters (four-line for the Prologue) with guide-letters; the second letter is usually a capital, which I print lower-case; no space left for the initial capital *I* for chapters 1 and 16; capitals supplied in black ink.[80] Undated (*c.*1483),[81] printed at Fleet Bridge. Paper, 200 × 138mm, stocks 16 (a remnant), 30, 33, 38, 40–42. Manuscript foliation, starting f. [a]1^r, 204–69. Folio [a]1^v notes the former shelfmark 'C21.c.3', and f. [a]2^r reads 'C21.c/2', cancelled. Text starts f. [a]2^r. Previously bound after IA. 55071 (*The Order of Chivalry*, Caxton, Westminster). Bound in late nineteenth-century gold-tooled blue sheepskin. From the Old Royal Library, once in the possession of Henry VII. Spine reads: 'The Revelacion of the Monke of Evishamme H.VII. R. Caxton.' Manuscript notes in Latin in two early hands, with underlinings (see Readers' notes in L, below).

[77] Eric Gordon, *Eynsham Abbey 1005–1228* (1990), p. 117, provides photographs of the openings of the prologue and of chapter 55 ['LV' is misread as '18'] from O (fols. 2^r and 62^r).

[78] I am indebted to Dr Lotte Hellinga for making information available to me according to the preparatory material for this volume.

[79] Manuscript signatures have been added for folios 1 and 3 in each quire and in [h] for f. 5 also.

[80] The printed guide-letter *y* (1st pers. sg. pron.) for chapters 28, 36, and 51 has been interpreted as *I* by the hand responsible for supplying the capitals. For chapter 21, the guide-letter *y* for *Ye* (2nd pers. pl. pron.) was interpreted *I*, and corrected to *3* by another hand. I have retained *Y* in each instance.

[81] Duff and Sheppard say 1485.

The print includes a good example of wrong imposition: the text of $[c]_1^v$ changed places with that of $[c]_7^v$, and that of $[c]_2^r$ with that of $[c]_8^r$; i.e. in quire [c] on the inner forme the type-pages for 1^v and 7^v (i.e. the verso of the volume's folios 17 and 23) have changed places, and likewise for 2^r and 8^r (i.e. folios 18 and 24).[82] The error was corrected by reprinting the forme, properly imposed, on single-sided sheets which were then pasted over the incorrect sheet-sides (see diagram, below). The inner forme was printed second, as the purpose of this shift was to avoid resetting and reprinting the outer forme. These pasted sheets have not subsequently been separated in L as they have in O.

The printer left the line of white at the end of chapter 18 one line early; this was filled by manuscript decoration.

Punctuation is by *punctus* (.), usually on the line but sometimes raised; colon (:); an occasional small cross (+); and *virgula suspensiva* (/).[83]

The printing is fairly coarse: letter spacing between and within words is often erratic, as is the provision of line-end hyphenation (see below, Notes on the presentation of the texts). There is a considerable number of compositorial slips, as the apparatus indicates, e.g. word-order inverted, *seyng sauyur* 1376; letters omitted, e.g. *prostate* (!) for *prostrate* 546; letters misplaced within a word, e.g. *brehetren* for *bretheren* 205, *Sorthely* for *Shortely* 1487; intrusive letters, e.g. *copynily* for *opynily* 389; possible distribution errors, that is, a character had been put back in the wrong box in the typecase, e.g. *tapte* for *rapte* 558; several confusions of *hem/him/hym*; a Spoonerism, *flyngers fayne* 1778–9 for *fyngers flayne*; and some compositorial oddities, e.g. *be caē* for *because* 1699.

---

[82] Ronald B. McKerrow, *An Introduction to Bibliography for Literary Students* (Oxford, 1927), p. 260–1 and note 1, cites Machlinia's error here from Gordon Duff, *Westminster and London Printers* (1906), p. 50, as an instance of a strange muddle 'due to a very simple cause, namely, to the sheets, after being printed on one side, having been turned the wrong way round when being perfected; or, alternatively, to the second forme printed having been placed the wrong way round on the bed of the press', but it is rather that of the adjacent pages of the inner forme, 3, 14, 15, and 2, numbers 3 (2^r) and 15 (8^r) have swapped places, as have 2 (1^v) and 14 (7^v). McKerrow rightly corrects Duff: 'the pages of the third gathering, as printed, run, 1, 14, 15, 4 . . . 13, 2, 3, 16 (not as Duff states 1, 14, 16, 4, an arrangement which could not possibly have come about in this manner, for 14 and 16 would belong to different formes).'

[83] Terms used by M. B. Parkes, *Pause and Effect: An Introduction to the History of Punctuation in the West* (Aldershot, 1992), see pp. 301–7.

Readers' notes in L

An early hand in Latin (black ink) has underlinings in the text, and added many notes in the margins from cap. xv to the end. I have not deemed it worthwhile collecting and printing them all, for they are mainly a brief running summary of key words and ideas. Some notes enumerate or list the different places of pain, or people, or sins appearing in a sequence (e.g. caps. xxxv, xxxvii, xliii, xlvii, l, lviii). This reader shows an interest in the punishments of ecclesiastics and judges, e.g. cap. xvi *Ve Prelatis Iudicibus* adding *Potentes potenter tormenta paciunt* (f. 220^r) and cap. xxvii with many summary notes and the exclamation *Ve ve prelatis malis* (f. 238^v), cf. *Heu heu* (cap. xliii, f. 252^r). Faced with the goldsmith's drunkenness, he exclaims, *Oh consuetudo detestabilis* (cap. xxi, f. 228^r). The longest note (f. 230^r) compares the goldsmith's claim that the words *Ihesus Nazarenus* are a remedy against death with the similar claim in the Life of St Edmund, archbishop of Canterbury (see Commentary 1174). Where the text misprints *Ibo* for *Job* (f. 223^r), this reader has 'corrected' it to *Philo*, and been properly corrected in turn by a later hand.

A second Latin hand is found on three occasions, indicating comparisons with a text of the Latin *Visio*. On f. 207^v this writer says (incorrectly) that the Latin dates the vision 1096 (for 1196); on f. 218^r an omission is signalled at the end of cap. xiii; and on the last folio (269^r) it is noted that the *Revelation* agrees with the Latin but not in everything: *concordat cum latino haec, non tamen plene in omnibus*.

A third reader makes three brief notes in English: 'the cause of the revelation' and 'no cause to dowte of the veritie of thys revelacion' (f. [a]2^r, 205^r), and 'never suche a revelation' (f. [a]2^v, 205^v).

O

Description is as for L, with the following differences.

Sheppard 7518 points out that f. [a]4^v has a 'different setting', and notes the vellum cover: the book is separately bound in white calf-skin and bears the gold stamp of the Bodleian Library on both covers. The spine reads in a seventeenth-century (?) hand, 'The Reuelation Purgatory [*sic*] by St Nicolas to ye Monk- of Eueshā. Sheppard entitles the work 'The Revelation of Saint Nicholas to a monk of Evesham' [*sic*].[84]

---

[84] *IISTC* adopts and corrects Sheppard's title: 'Revelation of St. Nicholas to a Monk of Eynsham'. The text is listed under 'Evesham' in the list of translations 1475–1560 in H. S.

The manuscript foliation, starting f. [a]1^r, is 1–66. Unlike L, O contains no manuscript signatures, and initial capitals for chapters have not been supplied following the guide-letters. On f. [a]1^v is the shelf-mark 'Linc. B.15.7'; figure '7' is inscribed on the book's outer edge.

O represents a variant state. Not only does f. [a]4^v have a different setting, as Sheppard noted, but so also do ff. [a]3^r, [a]5^r, and [a]6^v; i.e. the complete second outer forme in O has been reset; for the spelling and substantive variants here between L and O see Appendix 1. In a private communication (24 November 1995), Dr Lotte Hellinga suggests that this resetting was caused by another 'wrong imposition of pages in the forme': these four pages in the second outer forme must have changed places and had to be reset. Otherwise O and L are virtually identical,[85] except that in O the pasted correction sheets in quire [c] have later been separated, so that it is easy to see the wrongly imposed pages and how the problem was corrected.

Diagram of the wrongly-imposed and corrected quire [c]

This diagram shows the misimposed sheets (marked error) and the correction sheets, with folio numbers for ease of consultation with the prints. The arrows indicate where the single-sided correction sheets were pasted over the errors. As noted, in L these correction sheets remain pasted down, whereas in O they have been separated.

e = error, b = blank, c = correction, ← → = blank sides pasted over error

	/e ← b/c		c/b → e/		/	/	\	\	\e ← b\c		c\b → e\	
quire [c]	1^r	1^v	2^r	2^v	3	4	5	6	7^r	7^v	8^r	8^v
folio	17^r	17^v	18^r	18^v	19	20	21	22	23^r	23^v	24^r	24^v
O fol.	17^r	x17^v	x18^r	18^v	19	20	21	22	23^r	x23^v	24^r	—v
L fol.	220^r	220^v	221^r	221^v	222	223	224	225	226^r	226^v	227^r	227^v
L sig.	c1				c3							

WILLIAM DE MACHLINIA

William de Machlinia probably worked as a stationer in London before going into partnership with the printer John Lettou in about 1481.[86] Lettou had first set up a press in London the previous year. At a press near one of seven London churches dedicated to All

---

Bennett, *English Books & Readers 1475–1557*, 2nd edn. (Cambridge, 1969), p. 298. See further, Eynsham / Evesham, above, pp. xxx–xxxi.

[85] Note the three other corrections in O recorded at the end of Appendix 1, below.

[86] For full details of surviving Machlinia editions, see *IISTC*.

Hallows (*iuxta ecclesiam omnium sanctorum*), they printed the first undated edition of the *Tenores novelli* of Sir Thomas Littleton (d. 1481), and other law books including Yearbooks of law cases for the 33rd, 35th, and 36th years of Henry VI (i.e. 1454, 1456, and 1457). Their association was short-lived. By early 1483 Machlinia seems to have been working alone near Fleet Bridge. None of his productions is dated. He printed the *Promise of Matrimony*, containing a treaty of 1475 providing for the marriage of the Dauphin to Elizabeth, daughter of Edward IV, and an agreement of 1482 made by the Dauphin for his marriage to the daughter of Maximilian, Duke of Austria. In *c.*1483 Machlinia printed the *Revelation*, and a second edition of Littleton's *Tenores*, which bears the colophon: *Impressi per me Wilhelmi de Machlinia in opulentissima Ciuitate Londonia iuxta ponte qui vulgariter dicitur Flete brigge*. Thereafter he continued to print further Yearbooks, a school text *Vulgaria Terentii*, Wotton's *Speculum Christiani*, the closest in appeal to the *Revelation* of any of his productions, and *Chronicles of England*, amongst others. His later work is from a press in Holborn. He is not known to have printed anything after about 1487.[87]

Duff called Machlinia's print of the *Revelation* 'one of the most remarkable volumes of the fifteenth century', and pertinently noted that it is curious that no other early editions were issued as it seems 'exactly the kind of book which must have been popular'.[88] In fact, the *Revelation* is the only vision of the other world in Middle English to have been printed before 1500, whereas on the continent a number of vision texts were printed as incunables, especially German and Dutch versions of the *Visio Tnugdali*.[89]

ARBER'S REPRINT OF THE *REVELATION*

The only previous publication of the *Revelation* since the fifteenth century is that by Edward Arber (see 'Arber' under Abbreviations and Short Titles, above), text on pp. 15–112. Arber transcribed the text from L and did not know of the existence of O. Neither did

[87] George Smith, *William de Machlinia: The Primer on Vellum Printed by him in London about 1484* (London, 1929).

[88] E. Gordon Duff, *The Printers, Stationers and Bookbinders of Westminster and London from 1476 to 1535* (Cambridge, 1906), p. 50.

[89] See Palmer, '*Visio Tnugdali*', pp. 221ff, and his 'Illustrated Printed Editions of *The Visions of Tondal* from the Late Fifteenth and Early Sixteenth Centuries', in *Margaret of York, Simon Marmion, and* The Visions of Tondal, ed. Thomas Kren (Malibu, 1992), pp. 157–70.

Arber know of the *Visio*, but he did know the abridgement in Roger of Wendover (p. 7). His transcription though fair is not free from errors, but I have not thought it necessary to list them all. He provides a brief introduction considering the productions of John Lettou and William de Machlinia (pp. 3–7), and surveys the contents of the *Revelation*, with extracts in modernized spelling (pp. 8–14). He provides no commentary or linguistic comment.

MODERNIZED VERSIONS OF ARBER'S REPRINT

John Thomson, *The Revelation to the Monk of Evesham: A Remarkable Psychological Production of the Middle Ages, now for the first time sufficiently rendered into presentday English* (Glasgow, 1904). This is a privately reproduced, manuscript, prose modernization of Arber's 1869 reprint of Machlinia's text, by 'John Thomson, Printer, Translator, Editor' (p. 146). It contains a devout three-page 'Editor's Preface' approving the work's spiritual worth, and invoking an anonymous poem published by A. A. W. in *The Recipient*, 1 (1866), 64, and Swedenborg. The translation aims 'to elucidate and nothing more' (p. 4).

The Revelation to the Monk of Evesham Abbey in the Year of Our Lord Eleven Hundred and Ninety Six, concerning the Places of Purgatory and Paradise. Rendered into Modern English by Valerian Paget (London, 1909). Paget provides a 'free translation into current language and paraphrase' (p. 7) of Arber's text (pp. 31–319). The introduction (pp. 7–24), with extracts from the text and from Arber's introduction, lauds the vision as 'one of the most valuable and remarkable heirlooms of English literature' (p. 7) and likens the 'scathing denunciation of the corruption of the religious community' (p. 8) to Milton's *Lycidas* [cf. the *Revelation*, lines 2283–92]. Paget claims that, 'For combined grandeur and sweetness of spiritual conception it is hard to find anywhere an equal to the concluding pages of the "Revelation," devoted to the description of paradise. Dante himself is not so direct or vivid' (p. 16).

G. G. Coulton, *Life in the Middle Ages*, 1 (Cambridge, 1928), pp. 42–51, prints modernized extracts from Arber.

LANGUAGE OF THE *REVELATION*

There is no evidence for the identity of the English translator, and the language of the translation suggests that it probably does not predate its printing by many years. Smith[90] points out that 'Machlinia's practice of never giving dates of printing, and sometimes, as in the case of the Primer and other books, altogether omitting printed signatures, shows him to have been drawn to imitate the methods of the production of manuscripts of his time rather than those of contemporary printers'. This is pertinent to the language of the *Revelation*. Unusually for an early printed book in England, the language is dialectally distinct. M. L. Samuels assigns the language of the *Revelation* to NE Worcestershire, but perhaps one should rather say N Worcestershire,[91] verging on NW Worcestershire on the border with SE Shropshire, roughly within the area bounded by LPs 7600, 7610, 7550, 4239, and 7620 in *LALME*.[92]

[90] George Smith, *William de Machlinia* (1929), pp. 18–19.

[91] M. L. Samuels, 'Spelling and Dialect in the Late and Post-Middle English Periods', in *So meny people longages and tonges: Philological Essays in Scots and Mediæval English Presented to Angus McIntosh* (Edinburgh, 1981), pp. 43–54, at p. 43, writes: 'It is well known that there are dialect survivals in manuscripts of the early sixteenth century, and even in print, if the printer was foreign, a dialectal exemplar's spellings could be preserved intact. A startling example of this is *The Revelation of the Monk of Evesham*, printed in 1482 by William de Machlinia from an exemplar by a scribe whose dialect is sufficiently well preserved in the printed version for it to be localizable exactly in N. E. Worcestershire'. Samuels' article is reprinted in *The English of Chaucer and his Contemporaries*, ed. J. J. Smith (Aberdeen, 1988), pp. 86–95. Samuels' analysis is indebted to a questionnaire completed by J. S. Gómez Soliño; see the latter's discussion of the language of the *Revelation* in 'Variación y estandardización en el Ingés moderno temprano:1470–1540', Diss., University of Oviedo, 1984, pp. 481–3. Soliño points out that the *Revelation* is an interesting case of a non-English printer at the beginning of his career publishing a book in London without realizing that not all of its linguistic features coincided with the more prestigious language of the period. (He also notes that Evesham is in the county of Worcester, but this is irrelevant given that the supposed connection of the text with Evesham is an error.) Whether intentionally or not, Richard Beadle, while referring to Samuels' published statement, shifts the provenance in the direction I venture to suggest may be more accurate, saying, 'Early English printed texts that strongly preserve the dialectal characteristics of their original author or a prior manuscript copy are very rare. [But the *Revelation*] is exceptional in retaining the north-west Worcestershire dialect of its exemplar . . .'; see 'Middle English Texts and their Transmission, 1350–1500: Some Geographical Criteria', in *Speaking in our Tongues: Proceedings of a Colloquium on Medieval Dialectology and Related Disciplines*, ed. Margaret Laing and Keith Williamson (Cambridge, 1994), pp. 69–91, at 69–70. Beadle adds that the *Revelation* 'was one of a number of rather haphazard products of a short-lived London printing business occupied by William de Machlinia, a Belgian, who on this sort of evidence would appear not to have registered the linguistic factors that other printers of the time were taking into account'.
   An older view is expressed by T. L. Kington Oliphant, *The New English*, 2 vols. (London, 1886), 1.321, who comments on a selection of significant linguistic forms and spellings, using Arber's reprint, and says the *Revelation* 'seems to have been translated from the Latin about 1470; it was printed about 1482; I suspect that it was compiled not far from Tyndale's birthplace' [i.e. in Gloucestershire].

[92] See Key Map 2, vol. 4, p. 335.

Samuels locates the text north of Bromsgrove;[93] I suggest it may be
north and west of Bromsgrove in the Kidderminster area. The
closest LPs are 7610 and 7600, respectively north and east of
Kidderminster, but there are also close connections with LPs 7620
SW of Kidderminster, and 7550 and 4239 west of Kidderminster, in
SE Shropshire. The key features which combine to suggest this
localisation are those found on the following dotmaps in *LALME*
(vol. 1):

209 IF: forms with medial *e*: concentrated in Herefordshire, N
Worcestershire, and SE Shropshire

   ȝef 12 ×, *ȝefe* 1 ×, *yef* 1 ×, *yefe* 14 ×, ((*and*) *yf* 17 ×)

210 IF: spellings with *-ff-* occur in N Worcestershire and SE
Shropshire

   ȝeffe 4 ×, *yeffe* 5 ×

195 (AL)THOUGH: 'though' with *au* or *aw*: concentrated in
Herefordshire and Worcestershire

   thaugh 6 ×, *thaught* 1 ×, *thawgh* 2 ×, *thawghe* 4 ×, *thawght* 1 ×
(*though* 2 ×)

139 WAS: 'wes' type: Herefordshire, NW Worcestershire, and SE
Shropshire

   wes 2 × (*was* 459 ×)

526 STEAD: *stid(-)* and *styd(-)*: pockets occur in NW Worcestershire and SE Shropshire

   stydde 1 ×, *stidfastly* 1 × (*stedfaste* 1 ×, *stedfastly* 1 ×)

1032 HELD pt: 'hild' and 'hyld': NW Worcestershire and Herefordshire

   hild 1 ×, *hylde* 5 ×, *behilde* 5 ×, *behylde* 18 × (*behelde* 1 ×)

235 ERE conj.: spellings implying initial [j]: found almost exclusively
on the N Worcestershire and SE Shropshire border:

   ȝere 1 ×, *yere* 1 × (*ere* 1 ×)

---

[93] Soliño, 'Variación y estandardización', p. 482, cites a private communication from
Professor Samuels giving this location.

537 THOUSAND: 'thousond' type: a pocket in NW Worcestershire

thowsondis 1 ×

126 ARE: 'byn' type: occurrences in SE Shropshire and N Worcestershire

byn 16 × (*be* 30 ×, *ben* 10 ×)

The following features help corroborate the localisation:

1183 Development of initial *w-*: pocket in SE Shropshire
wolde 1 × 'old', *wothys* 1 × 'oaths' (there are no reverse spellings)

1169 Development of initial *y-* / *ȝ-*: N Worcestershire / SE Shropshire

ȝere 1 × 'ere', 'ever', *ȝese* 1 × 'ease', *ȝesely* 1 × 'easily', *ȝestewarde* 1 × 'eastward', *ȝesy* 1 × 'easy', *ȝesyur* 1 × 'easier', *ȝestur, ȝestir, ȝestyr* 1 × each 'Easter' (alongside *Estur* and *Estyr*), *ȝirne* 1 × 'iron' (there are no reverse spellings)

478 NEITHER spelling with *-ow-* (alongside *-e-* and *-o-* spellings), widespread in the Midlands and North, but a concentration in Worcestershire

265, 266, 269 STRENGTH, LENGTH sb/vb: forms in (respectively) *-ngh strengh* 1 ×, *-nght strenght* 3 ×, *-nth* text has *strenthe* 4 ×, *strenthyd* 1 ×, *lenthe* 3 × (*lengthe* 1 ×)

Other features worthy of note are as follows.[94]

Spellings and pronunciation

Initial *d-* for *th-* : *dat* 'that' 1429, *de* 'the' 2319, *dedyr* 'thither' 1264, 1815, 2855, *drede* 'thread' 2957.

Medial *-d-* for *-th-*; e.g. *todyr* 'the other' 3 ×, *wordly* 'worthily' 859.

Medial *-th-* for *-d-*: *vnther* 1299.

Final *-th* for *-d*?: *offendyth* 'offended' pa. t. 1528, 1775, *apperyth* 'appeared'? 46 (this occurs in the list of chapter headings, cf. *apperyd* 405). This usage may be an error, as the *apperyth/apperyd* readings suggest; I have emended the *offendyth* instances to *offendyd* for ease

---

[94] A selection of interesting items is also noted by Oliphant, *The New English* (1886), 1.321–3.

of comprehension, but retained *apperyth* 46 as it could stand for a legitimate pr. t.

th for *t*: *abboth* 103, *doutheles* 2825, *dowtheles* 569, *Thewysday* 2455.

t for *th*: *feytfully* 882, *neuertelesse* 1402, *tankyde* 2353.

t for *d*: *tytyngys* 'tidings' 1049.

Unvoicing of final *-d* following voiceless consonants, consequent on the syncope of unstressed inflexional syllables, e.g.: *clypte*, *ponyshte*, *worschipte*.

There are several instances of intrusive letters: initially before vowels: ʒ- or *y-* before *e*: *ʒere* 'ever' 728, *yere* 'ere' 1185 (and see Development of initial *y-* / ʒ-, above); *h-* in *harmys* 'arms' 2075, 2350, *hopynne* 'open' 512, *hordende* 'ordained' 1996; and *w-* in *wolde* 'old' 959, *wothys* 'oaths' 2478; and medially: *b* after *m* in *sembly* 'seemly' 2244; *-h-* in *thinghes* 1352, *thinghys** 1643, *thynghes* 2305, 2530, *thynghys* 2532, and *onspekehabule* 1573; and *-t-* in *iustys* 'juices' 229 (which I emend to *iuscys*). *vtwardly* 'utterly', not 'outwardly' (see Appendix 2 §7), includes both pre-vocalic *w* and intrusive *d* after *r*: the *Revelation* uses this idiosyncratic spelling 15 ×; it is not recorded in *OED* or *MED*; cf. *wydwardys* 'widower's' 1832.

Excrescent *-t*: *thaught* 2266, *thawght* 1810 'though'; *styftely* 'stiffly' 1880.[95]

Unhistorical *wh-* for *w-* by back spelling indicates loss of aspiration in words deriving from OE *hw-*:[96] e.g. *whe* 'we' 2529, *whent* 'went' 1814, *where* 'were' 682, *whyt* 'with' 1878, 2106, 2111, cf. *whytowte* 1083, *whyt-owte-forthe* 2112, *whytowtyn* 903, and cf. *betwhene* 2674, and *swhete* 2674; hence also *w-* for *wh-*: *wat-sum-euer* 2871; *were* 'where' 3 ×; *wiche* 'which' 2, *wyiche* 1927 (plus *which(e* / *whyche* 286 ×); *hois* 'whose' 2 ×, *hoys* 8 × (plus *whoys* 4 ×), *ho* 4 ×, *hoo* 1 × (plus *who* 7 ×), *home* 23 × (plus *whom* 4 ×, *whome* 24 ×). Also characteristic of the fifteenth century is *wh-* for *h-* in *wholde* 'holde' = held 1009, *whore* 'hoar' 553: *OED* cites this instance (**Wh** headnote), saying, 'Early in the fifteenth century appear spellings with *wh* of words with initial *h-* followed by an *o*-sound.' Cf. *white-safe* 'vouchsafe' 409, 417, *whytesaue* 2780, *OED* 6. δ². The inverse of

[95] E. J. Dobson, *English Pronunciation 1500–1700*, 2 vols., 2nd edn. (Oxford, 1968), 2. §437, discusses excrescent [t] after [f], and acknowledges that the 'phonetic reason for the development is obscure' (p. 1004).

[96] Ibid., 2. §414.

the *w-/wh-* and *-th/-t-* switches instanced above in the form *whyt* 'with' is found in *Wythssonday* 'Whit Sunday' 2450 and *wythnes* 'whiteness' 2703.

Loss of *w-* before *r*: *ronge* 'wrong' 1060.

Alongside final *-er, -ir, -yr* are instances of *-or* e.g.: *greuossor* 1681, *ʒesyor* 784, *opynnor* 616, *prayor* 369, *semlyor* 1705, *worthior* 964; and *-ur*: *besyur* 2637, *byttur(ly* 887, 1493, *chaptur* 32, *deuowtur* 2637, *Estur* 4×, *esyur* 660, *fyngur* 1172, *gladlyur* 933, *grettur* 279, *holsummur* 1393, *holyur* 1043, *monsturs* 2075, *oppressure* 1877, *prayur* 30 etc., *to-gedur* 985, *vppur* 2855, *vtturmaste* 2607, *whyttur* 2729; cf. noun pl. ending in *-us*: *vsus* 1029.

Lowering of short *i* to *e*, e.g. *dede*, *fegure* (alongside *figure/fygure*), *geue*, *kendler*, *leue*, *leuyd*, *seth*, *sex*, *pety/pete*, *wekyd(nes*, *wreten*, *wretyn*, and neutralization of unstressed syllables: *feleschippe/fele-shyppe/felishyppe*.

False word division: *my neris* 'mine ears' 514, *my nyes* 'mine eyes' 497, 502, 514, *myn nowne* 'mine own' 865.

ensonge 'evensong' 2438: *MED* sole citation for this spelling is from the West Country, (1453) *LRed Bk.Bristol.*

The text favours *on-* for *un-* (see Glossary).

A handful of spellings suggest pronunciation changes associated with the Great Vowel Shift. The spelling *defoyled* 'defiled' 1329 indicates a stage in the diphthongization of [ī];[97] cf. *feyghtyng* 'fighting' 2886, and *they* 'thy' 917, 994, 2900.[98] The spelling *my* for 'me' 1078, 1205, 1339, 2337 may also be explained as indicative of Great Vowel Shift raising.[99]

Spelling variants of any one word are usually mixed throughout the text, but in some instances some forms predominate earlier and others later, which may reflect either the settling in of the scribe of the compositor's exemplar, or of the compositor, or possibly the

---

[97] Cited in Henry Cecil Wyld, *A Short History of English*, 3rd edn. (London, 1927), p. 187.

[98] *MED* s.v. thin *pron.* labels *thei* 'N or NEM', citing *þey* 2.(a) as variant in *Siege Troy (1)* 31/371 a1400(?a1350), *þei* 2.(c) *Alex. & D.* 509 c1450(c1350), and *theyn* 3.(d) *Morte Arth.(1)* 3403 c1440(?a1400). These do not match the Worcestershire provenance of *Revelation.*

[99] *OED* s.v. me *pers. pron.* 2.a cites *mi* from *Cursor M.* 3611, but *MED* s.v. me *pron.* (2) recognizes *mi* only as an error.

work of two compositors. I list the clearest examples, giving the number of occurrences of the different spellings and the range of line numbers within which they occur; * = emended:

predominantly earlier in the text	predominantly later in the text
bretheren 30 ×, 41–2688	*brethirne* 6 × and *brethyrne* 4 × after 2648
forth 5 ×, 431–1319	*forthe* 15 ×, 1104–2976
I 'I' 30 ×, no examples after 2620	*Y* 696 ×, 70 × after 2620
strenght 3 ×, *strengh* 1 ×, 132–432	*strenthe* 4 ×, 1441–2919
ware pa. t. pl. 26 × [1 × *], 7–2254 (4 × after 990)	*were* 214 ×, 85–2963 (161 × after 1003)
whom(e 28 ×, 396–2719	*home* 23 ×, 1488–2987

Morphology

Verbs: Pr. 3 sg.: ends in non-Northern *-th*.

Pr. pl.: ends in Midlands *-n*, but occasionally in the Southern *-th*: *beholdyth* 2280, *conteynyth* 1173, *doth* 271, *remeynyth* 2220 alongside *remaynyn* 1244.

Pa. t. pl. of 'to be': *wes* 'were' 669, 2795, *was* 1348, *ware*, *where*.

Pa. t and pp. assimilated dental suffix in verbs with final dental in the stem: *amende* 1610 'amended', *correcte* 1610 'corrected', *defende* 1168 'defended', *enfecte*, *infecte* 'infected' 1633, 2344, *preuent* 'prevented' 2385, *profet* 'been useful' 1961, *profet* 'profited' 2001, *repente* 'repented' 2373, *torment* 'tormented' 661, 714. The weak pp. inflexion is also lost in words that do not have final dental in the stem: *blyster* 'blistered' 2347, *turne* 'turned' 1361, *scape* 'escaped' 2387.

Imper. pl.: ends in *-ith*: *sechith* 292, *settith* 366.

Syncope of inflexional pr. t., pa. t., and pp. endings after *r* and *w*, e.g.: *delyuerd* 3 × (plus *delyuered/delyueryd* 8 ×), *fauerd* 1 × (plus *faueryd* 1 ×), *fauerth* 1 ×; *dround/drownd(e* 3 ×, *folowd(e* 2 ×, *folowth* 1 × (plus *foloweth(e* 2 ×, *folowyth* 1 ×), *halowd* 1 × (plus *halowed* 1 ×), *swelowd(e* 2 ×.

Nouns: double plural: *pensys* 1128, 2401.

Pronouns: 3 sg. poss. separate 'his': *Cryste ys* 139, *abbot is* 187.

a certen neybur of herns 1662: *OED* s.v. hers *poss. pron.*[1] cites this, but emends it unnecessarily to *herys*. I take it rather as an interesting example of where, as Oliphant (1.321) puts it, 'South and North meet': *hers* is the northerly form, *hern* from the South and Midlands (see *OED* s.v. hern *poss. pron.*[1]).

3 sg. nom.: *hit* 98 ×, *hyt* 134 ×, *it* 6 ×, *yt* 12 ×.

3 pl. nom.: *they* 267 ×, *thay* 1 ×; poss. *her* 180 ×, *here* 1 ×, *ther* 17 ×; obj. *hem* 238 ×, *theym* 2 ×.

Adjectives: inflected pl.: *felows virgyns* 891, *lyberals facultees* 2495–6; cf. the anomalous *thingys whiche es*, corrected in O and printed below as 'thingys whiche' 283–4.

Comparative: *more* + comparative 24 ×; superlative: *mooste* + superlative 2 ×.

Syntax

There are instances of the growing complexity of compound verbs in the period, e.g.: *lest Y shulde haue ben reprouyd* 581, and *thys . . . sowle . . . was goyng to be broughte* 849, which is cited in *OED* (s.v. *Go* v. 47.b.) as the earliest occurrence of the 'going-to' future.[100]

The usage of prepositions and phrasal verbs frequently differs from modern practice, e.g. *after my power, aftyr the mesure* 'according to'; *what Y might hope after* 'for'; *by the space of* 'for'; especially the use of *of: done of yow* 'by'; *worshipte of the couent* 'by'; *seyde of* 'by'; *commaundyd of* 'by'; *reprouyd of presumpcion* 'for', *in comparyson of* 'with'; *of an euyl custome* 'because of', 'in'; *hit wellid out of blode* '—'; *sesid him of his telling* '—'

Post-posited adj.: *company innumerabulle* 637.

Obj. gen.: *ther knowlege* 'knowledge of them' 798.

Vocabulary

The *Revelation* was read for the *OED* in Arber's edition, but is not cited in *MED* (apart from the single word *colloke*). As a localizable translation, probably no earlier than 1470, it valuably includes a number of interesting words and forms, some newly recorded, some probably fairly late occurrences. Some fifteen words, usages, or spellings do not appear to be recorded elsewhere, including straight borrowings from the Latin, *abrasyng* 2070 and *aduocatour* 1109; anglicizations, *ongoyngable* 733, *wepyng* as n. pl. 271; and other uniquely occurring forms, *adigression* 616, *strompetly* 839, and

---

[100] James Finch Royster and John Marcellus Steadman, jun., 'The "*Going-to*" future', in *The Manly Anniversary Studies in Language and Literature* (Chicago, 1923), pp. 394–403 at p. 398, note 5, quote Oliphant, *The New English*, 1.322, 'A new phrase for the future . . . this reminds us of the Old English *hē gǽþ rīdan*.' For a possible, but obscure, earlier occurrence of this construction, see Tauno F. Mustanoja, *A Middle English Syntax*, Part 1 (Mémoires de la Société Néophilologique de Helsinki, 23, Helsinki, 1960), pp. 592–3.

spellings, *plutte* 1882, *wydwardys* 1832. (For details for all the words mentioned here, see Appendix 2, below.) In addition, the *Revelation* preserves a number of early occurrences. Over 35 words are first citations in *OED* and do not occur in *MED*. Of these, many are again adopted directly from the Latin; some have not survived in the language, such as *attente* 317, *discerpte* 1106, *gratulacyon* 2766, and *tradicion* 'betrayal' 140; others have continued in use, e.g. *intercessours* 2300 and *pompys* 848. Similarly, of those words or usages which are not adoptions from Latin, but which are first recorded here, some have since dropped out of use, e.g. *afterward that* 285, *glotyners* 2034, *pensys* 1128, *slowfulnes* 1901, *wordly* 'worthily' 859. Others are nowadays more common expressions which just happen to be first recorded in the *Revelation*, such as *ded and gonne* 1424, or *hedlong* 2120 with an *-o-* and not earlier *-i-*. Another group of words comprises those which are the first or sole citation in *OED* but which have since been antedated in *MED* (Appendix 2 §4). Many of these first appear in the record not long before the publication of the *Revelation*, and were probably fairly recent additions to the language at the time of the translation: *adolescente* 2682, *benyuolente* 1832, *dedifyed* 466, *despexion* 1433, *enarrabulle* 976, *incredibulle* 543. Other words or uses antedate *OED* and are not recorded in *MED*: *affixed* 468, *audybille* 256, *barenly* 1972, *byshoprye*, *bysshoppery* 1888, 1956, 2169, *carnaly* 2206, 2267, 2577. The expression *preuent of dethe* 944, glossed 'prematurely overtaken by death', is one not closely paralleled in *MED* or by other quotations in *OED*, and shows, as Oliphant (1.323) says, that 'here the idea of *forestalling* begins to come in', cf. *OED* prevent *v.* II.†5. and 6., first attested in the sixteenth century. As well as the words for which the *Revelation* provides the first or early recorded occurrences, there are also examples of what appear to be late survivals, including *euyn-heyre* 'co-heir' 2693, *euynworthy* 'suitable' 878, *here* 'their', *mawe* 'belly' 823, *medelyng* 'mixture' 2911, *none man* 14, *reboudye* 1783, *sey* pp. 'seen' 2013, *sickelew* 2650, *sykyng* 'sighing' 253, *sounned* 1783, *sparyd . . . oute* 'shut out' 2810–11, and *(ouer-)wrechidful* 643. Further details, including uncommon words and words used in senses not recorded by *OED* and *MED* are given in Appendix 2.

THE *REVELATION* AS TRANSLATION

The *Revelation* translated from a copy of the *Visio* text C close to MS Selden Supra 66 [S]

Ward, writing before Salter's division of the *Visio* manuscripts into versions A, B, and C, says that the *Revelation* follows BL, Cotton Cleopatra C.xi [a B text] 'as a general rule, very faithfully',[101] and gives parallel extracts showing its closeness to this version as against Roger of Wendover and the Latin translation (BL, MS Cotton Caligula A.viii) of a lost French verse version.[102]

The *Revelation* is indeed, as a general rule, a sufficiently faithful translation to show that without doubt the translator worked from a C text, or second authorial revision, of the *Visio*.[103] In brief, Salter posited that Adam initially wrote to the end of chapter 48 (A); later, he revised these chapters and added chapters 49–58 (B); and later still, revised the whole text (C).[104]

The following comparisons, from a large number of possible examples, are sufficient to demonstrate that the *Revelation* (*Rev.*) was translated from a C text of the *Visio*. (Quotations of text A are from Salter; of B from Thurston; of C from my text of S.)

A/B ubi inuentus fuerat
C   ubi **conuentus** fuerat (S159)
Rev. where **the couent** was (208)

A/B Mitte etiam ad bene tibi notum ancillarum dei/Domini
      monasterium
C   Mitte etiam ad bene tibi notum **uicinum** ancillarum Dei
      monasterium (S371–2)
Rev. Sende also to the monastery of nonnys **here-by**, that þow
      knowyst wele (440–1)
(This comparison was noted by Salter, 2.296.)

A/B Suscepi autem manu aperta
C   Suscepi **uero** manu aperta (S437)
Rev. **Trewly**, than Y toke in my hopynne hand (512)

A/B per totum fere sequens biduum, id est usque ad uesperam
      sab(b)ati

---

[101] Ward, 2.495.
[102] See Ward, 2.497–502, and Elisabeth Stein in *VEME*, pp. 113–33.
[103] See also the account of Huber2, above, p. xxx.
[104] See above, note 8.

C   usque ad **sequentis** sabbati uesperum (S584)

Rev.   tyl the euetyde of Saturday **foloyng** (627)

A/B   Ne autem offendamus potentes ad bibendum uinum fortesque
        ad concinnandam ebrietatem, qui negant uitio, cui deseruiunt,
        mortalis peccati thecam esse prefigendam, maxime cum con-
        tigerit illud non continuam febrem sed interpolatam imitari
        (cum tamen frequentior ac durior ac pene inexorabilis esse
        prenuntia mortis soleat quartana, quam febris continua), ne,
        inquam, eos qui huiusmodi sunt nimis exaggerando temulentie
        crimen scandalizemus, dicamus hoc quod uerum scimus,
        hunc, cuius modo et peccatum ut caueatur & periculum
        innotescimus ut timeatur, cum in pristina uita ad ebrietatem
        nimis fuisse pronum, tum illo triduo quod in seculo uidit
        ultimum, in huius admissi reatu deguisse continuum. Si ergo
        pridem michi constitisset eum, licet nobis carum, tali ueraciter
        ex causa in fata concessisse, nil facto dignius censerem pro illo
        quam non orare . . .

C   Hic ergo, cuius peccatum ut caueatur & periculum modo
        innotescimus ut timeatur, cum in pristina uita nimis ad
        ebrietatem fuisset pronus, illo triduo quod in seculo uidit
        ultimum in huius admissi reatu fuit fere continuus. Quod si
        michi pro certo pridem constitisset eum scilicet ex tali causa
        cessisse in fata, quid de eo dignius censerem quam pro illo non
        orare . . . (S862–7)

Rev.   Therfore, thys man, whoys sine and perelle we speke of now,
        þat hyt schulde be feryd and dredde, yn hys wolde days was
        ouer-prone and redy to dronkenes, for the last thre days þat
        euer he saw in thys worlde he continewyde, dayly almoste, yn
        the same synne. And yf Y had know for certen, a day before,
        þat he had dyed of seche a cause as hit ys afore seyde, what
        schulde Y thynke or fele of hym more worthior than not to
        pray for him . . . (958–64)

There are, moreover, a number of instances where S deviates from
other C manuscripts, and the *Revelation* follows the S reading. Thus,
an ymage of thy Redeemer (468) follows S397–8 *tui Redemptoris
ymaginem*, where other manuscripts read *cui*; *But he went not
onponyshte* (2451–2) follows S2165 *Sed non impune iuit*, where *iuit* in
S is an interlined correction, but is not found in other manuscripts; the
rather awkward expression *al only of tho thyngis that myghte be hadde*

(2639) can be explained by the reading in S2319–20 *sola tantum quod adhibere posset*, where other manuscripts read **solatium**, the S form *sola tm̄* doubtless being an error for *solatiū*; and *gladnes* (2792) follows S2455 **exultacione**, not *admiracione* of C texts BdMT.

These instances indicate that the English translator worked from a text very close to S. This is corroborated by the close correspondence between the ME chapter headings and the *tituli* in S, which survive only in this manuscript.[105] In the *Revelation* the chapter headings are also listed after the new prologue. These are not a verbatim copy of the headings as they occur chapter by chapter in the text; sometimes the headings in the list are closer to the Latin than those in the body of the text, and *vice versa*.

That the translator did not work from S directly, however, is probably sufficiently indicated by the incorporation of the headings for chapters 13 and 39 (557, 2079), which are *not* found in S, but is suggested also by other details, e.g. the goldsmith feels the devil who 'strangles' him go down his throat like an *owle* (1090), whereas S and all other manuscripts, as far as I know, read like a 'toad'. The translator's copy of the *Visio* must have read *bubonis* for *bufonis*, or the translator misread his copy.[106]

In short, the ME translator worked from a C text of the *Visio*, and of the surviving manuscripts of the C text, S is closest to the text that must have been used by the translator, and for this reason, as well as for its high quality, I have chosen S as the basis of my edition of the Latin.

The preface to the *Visio*

The *Visio* contains a preface for which the *Revelation* substitutes a new prologue. In the preface, Adam draws on Gregory the Great, *Dialogi*, 4.43.2,[107] explaining that the time of judgement and the end

---

[105] See above, p. xxxii.

[106] Some other details suggest that the translator worked from a manuscript other than S: *And there also mette with vs another senyor* (481), *Occurrit etiam nobis alius . . . senior* Salter A, *O. e. n. et alius . . . s.* text B, but *Occurrit etiam nobis . . . senior* S; *at the fyre* (683), *ad ignem* Thurston's B text and M, but S *ad ignes* and Salter A; *lustys of her body* (850), *carnis illecebras* Salter A, Thurston B, but S *carnis illecebram* and Huber2 B; *that this seyde to me* (1496), *et hec dixit michi* A/B, but S *qui hec dixit*; *he browghte me forthe* (2890), *eduxit me* Bd, but S *eduxit*; and see Commentary 481, 484, S473, 704–5, 2622.

[107] See Commentary S1–30. On the recent debate over the authorship of the *Dialogi*, see Marilyn Dunn, 'Gregory the Great, the Vision of Fursey and the Origins of Purgatory', *Peritia*, 14 (2000), 238–54, who argues that they may have been written in England in the 670s.

of the world is drawing near, and as it approaches, like day
succeeding night, the darkness of ignorance is dispelled by an
increase in the number of revelations of the future life. Such
revelations have been transmitted from the time of the fathers, and
more recent ones have also been committed to writing so that faith
might be strengthened, hope enlivened, love kindled, and the fear of
the Lord (which is the beginning of wisdom) acquired. They tell of
hell where the rich man (Dives) was buried; of those who insuffi-
ciently cleansed their sins (i.e. those in purgatory); and the joy of
those who wait with a blessed expectation in the pleasant place of rest
and light (equated in the *Revelation* with the Earthly Paradise).
Those in heaven above, where the just rejoice in the sight of God,
enjoy unspeakable bliss.

Adam says he has been urged to write down the vision by great
men who command him by the merit of their sanctity and the
privilege of their authority; Salter is probably correct to infer Hugh
of Lincoln, and Thomas, prior of Eynsham. Adam notes that he
knew of these things most certainly, for he himself was involved in
the events he is about to recount (*certissime agnoui, utpote quibus
interfui*). He disclaims all lies, for liars are doomed, so no-one should
doubt the truth of his account.

The prologue to the *Revelation*

Machlinia's print provides a new prologue and a list of the chapter
headings. In the prologue, the visionary, unnamed, is called *a certeyn
deuowt person, the wiche was a monke in the abbey of Einshamme*
[misnamed *Euishamme*]. The monk was *rapte in spirite* and led by the
hand of St Nicholas (not mentioned in the *Visio* preface) for two days
and nights *to see and knowe the peynys of purgatorye and the iowys of
paradyse*. Whereas in the *Visio* the identity of Edmund's guide is
concealed from the reader until cap. 20 and was unknown to
Edmund until told by his friend the drunken goldsmith in the
second field of purgatory, here in the *Revelation* St Nicholas's role is
foregrounded. The benefits of the protection of one's patron saint are
thus made more prominent in the vernacular translation. The
Revelation being a late fifteenth-century work, its positive identification and naming of purgatory is also not unexpected; purgatory is
named as the place Edmund visits no fewer than 27× in the
Revelation; in the *Visio, c.*1196–7, the only occurrences of related
terms are: *purgatoriis* 1×, *purgatorum* 1×, *purgari* 1×, and *purga-*

cionis 3 × . This does not, of course, mean that the *Revelation* has in any way distorted the eschatology of the *Visio*. It is simply that, as Le Goff has indicated, the noun *purgatorium* was not widely used before the thirteenth century, though this does not mean *pace* Le Goff, that the concept of a purgatorial place or places or state was not well established until then.[108]

Edmund's revelation is said to have been granted to him not only for his own sake, *butte also for the confort and profetyng of all Cristyn pepulle, that none man shuld dowte or mystruste of anothir life and world* (13–14), where all must go and receive appropriate reward. This is a common emphasis in other-world vision texts; revelations are for the benefit not merely of the visionary but for all those who hear or read of his experience; they are part of the continuing revelation of God's salvific purpose, and striking prompts to belief[109] and penance. They are therefore to be accepted as true, and the prologue invites readers and hearers to consider the opening sections of the text, detailing Edmund's condition and circumstances before and after the vision, and the ending which shows the vision to be *approuyd* or verified by *grete myraclis*—referring to the *meruelus curacion* or healing during Edmund's trance of an ulcer on his leg. A *ful feyre myracle* this is called at the end of the *Revelation*; the *Visio* does not use any such term.

The *Revelation* will therefore quench all *resons and mocions of infydelite* and cause people to dread God and love Him and praise Him in His works, for such another revelation *was neuer shewid in this lond ne in no nothir that we rede of*. This kind of publisher's blurb was what Adam and Edmund had carefully aimed to avoid, in monastic humility preserving their own anonymity.

---

[108] Le Goff, *La Naissance du Purgatoire* (1981). There have been many counters to Le Goff's claim that purgatory did not properly exist as a concept before the noun did: see, e.g. Adrian H. Bredero, 'Le Moyen Age et le Purgatoire', *Revue d'histoire ecclésiastique*, 78 (1983), 429–52; J. G. Bougerol, 'Autour de "La Naissance du Purgatoire"', *Archives d'histoire doctrinale et littéraire du Moyen Age*, 50 (1984 *for* 1983), 7–59; Graham Robert Edwards, 'Purgatory: "Birth" or Evolution?', *Journal of Ecclesiatical History*, 36 (1985), 634–46; Robert Easting, 'Purgatory and the Earthly Paradise in the *Tractatus de Purgatorio Sancti Patricii*', *Cîteaux*, 37 (1986), 23–48; P. Dinzelbacher, Review in *Ons geestelijk Erf*, 61 (1987), 278–82. Le Goff claimed that the noun *purgatorium* first appears in the 1170s, but Dinzelbacher points out an earlier instance in Bernard of Clairvaux's *De Diversis*, 42.5: see 'Das Fegefeuer', p. 3, note 13.

[109] A seminal statement about the efficacy of other-world visions for producing belief in those who had only heard but not seen is Gregory the Great, *Dialogi*, 4.37.2: *Superna enim pietas ex magna misericordiae suae largitate disponit, ut nonnulli etiam post exitum repente ad corpus redeant, et tormenta inferi, quae audita non crediderant, saltem uisa pertimescant.*

The narrative

Passages omitted by the Revelation

It is dangerous to speculate on omissions in a translation: we cannot know exactly what was in the translator's copy of the source text, nor precisely why the translator made certain choices, and some minor omissions might be inadvertent. But with this proviso it can be useful to identify certain kinds or patterns of omission made in the Middle English version. Thurston was of the opinion that the *Revelation* 'omits a number of significant details, especially the incidental comments of the writer'.[110]

Apart from the *Visio*'s preface, the largest omission made by the *Revelation* is *Visio* cap. 13A, in which Adam provides an analogue to Edmund's experience of the bleeding crucifix. Seven years earlier the same cross at Eynsham had given forth blood and a monk had been cured by drinking a potion containing the blood washed from the feet of the crucifix. Adam learned of this from the monk who prepared the potion and from him who drank it. Edmund's account of tasting the blood is corroborated, says Adam, by the monks finding blood on his hands and on the outside of his nose and face, though his nose did not appear to have been bleeding. And when they inspected the place in the chapel where the crucifix was, they found drops of dried blood on the floor, which they scraped up, dissolved, and preserved. And when the cross was raised for the adoration it was found to have blood on the side and feet of the crucifix, which one of the sacristans washed off before the monks were to kiss the cross. Without thinking, he threw out the blood-stained water, but the cloth remained discoloured. When he heard of Edmund's experience, the sacristan was terrified at what he had done, and prayed to God for forgiveness. Eventually, he had a dream in which a voice told him that the blood was to be venerated, as it had come from the side of the Lord on the cross. Adam concludes his digression by asserting that Edmund was fortified to withstand the terrors of his vision of the other world by his experience of the blood, and he assures the reader of the fidelity of his written composition, which follows the words and sense of Edmund's daily oral accounts of his experiences.

Also omitted are two sections from *Visio* cap. 21 ostensibly within the voice of the drunken goldsmith, a section (S939–49)

---

[110] Thurston, *The Life of Saint Hugh of Lincoln* (1898), p. 619.

lamenting our inability to fulfil the penitential requirements of the
seasons preceding Easter and Christmas, and a passage of self-
castigation citing 4 Kings 19:3 (S963–8). From cap. 23 are omitted
two further sections in Edmund's voice: three lines of transition
between two segments of the narrative concerning the goldsmith
(S1103–5), and thirty-six lines thereafter, the rest of the chapter,
which consists firstly (S1109–29) of a meditation on the necessity of
almsgiving with a pure heart, and secondly (S1130–44), still in
Edmund's voice, though speaking in the plural as if to cover both
himself and Adam, an explanation and apology for not naming
names in the text. They decided it was a better policy (*consilium*) to
omit all names to avoid creating sorrow and scandal, given that
many of the matters were so hard and so recent for friends to cope
with. They also omitted their own names and situation to avoid the
importunate curiosity of those who might wish to consult Edmund
about their deceased friends or relatives. (They did not have the
needs of future editors in mind.)

Similarly omitted is a substantial section at the end of cap. 41, a
section with its own rubric: *Quod monachus non omnia que uidit in
scripto redegerit* (S1894–1918). Edmund explains that just as nothing
is recorded about many things that he saw, so not everything has
been said about the few things that *are* here recorded. Rereading
what Adam has written, Edmund finds that it is as if nothing has
been said about the pains he witnessed. He appeals therefore to the
reader's prudence to compensate for the insufficiency of the written
account. The sheer scale of what he has seen is not matched by what
is written, but might appear incredible or tiring to the reader. He
has recorded the fate of a few of those whom he especially loved in
this life. He actually saw innumerable hosts of souls. He found
many there whom he thought still alive at the time of his vision. He
received certain knowledge there of the death of some of them (like
the goldsmith who recounted his own death); about others, he was
so stunned to see them in the other world that when he returned he
was not certain of their deaths. He has neglected to enquire about
infinite numbers of the souls, both from his guide and from others;
but he has become more certain of the deaths of some by the
undoubtable testimony he has heard since his vision. Later there are
further omissions of Edmund's thoughts on the process of recounting his vision. Not translated are a brief phrase, *que breuitatis causa
non exprimo* (S2300); a self-consciously paradoxical reflexion on not

omitting to say that the glory of many was inexpressible (S2395–7); and five lines expressing both reluctance to utter what many with only human reason will regard as incredible, and willingness to tell what he can for the benefit of those who listen with the right spirit of devotion (S2443–9). In the last chapter, the translation omits Adam's opening statement (S2579–85) of how, while studious of brevity, he has written what he learned from Edmund following now the sense and now the words of his brother, and how, like others who know him well, he is convinced of the truth of his account.

The *Revelation*'s omission of all these sections indicates the translator's interest in preserving only the essential narrative of Edmund's vision, unimpeded even by corroborative 'evidence' or hortatory or explanatory elaboration, avoiding minor as well as major narratorial intrusions, e.g. *ut iam dixi superius* (S496–7).

S1732–40 are also omitted, part of the diatribe against negligent and ambitious but fruitless ecclesiastics, voiced in chapter 36 concerning Baldwin, archbishop of Canterbury. It is less clear why these lines have been omitted by the Middle English translator; maybe they were considered dangerously hard-hitting. Conversely, it is obvious that the Middle English is brought up to date by the omission of S1766–8, which mention the recent (i.e. third) crusade (of 1189–92). S1313–20, on the bestial, indeed demonic, associations of sodomy, may conceivably have been omitted on grounds of sensitivity,[111] but this seems unlikely given the translator's willingness to expand a sentence on lesbianism (see below), so these lines are probably ditched as another intrusion into the progress of the narrative. Three short passages are omitted from the praise of the prior encountered in the field full of flowers or paradise in cap. 51 (S2316–19, 2321–2, 2326–7), the last a quotation from Solomon, but I cannot offer a sound explanation for these omissions.

The *Revelation* also omits some brief passages which personalize the narrative by pertaining directly to Edmund: e.g. *ea tempestate . . . descenderatis* (S849–51) addressed to Adam, recalling Edmund's illness at the time of the goldsmith's death; *Continuis . . . effectum* (S353–7), Edmund's calling on Christ, Mary, and all the saints that he might be granted a revelation of the other world; *Multos . . . cruciatos* (S640–1), which notes that many of the tormented souls

---

[111] Could that also explain the omission of those guilty of incest from the list of sinners at *Revelation* 2033?

seen by Edmund were personally known and dear to him; *Nimium . . . premebatur* (S1257), an expression of Edmund's extreme sorrow for the suffering of the sodomitical lawyer in cap. 26; a temporal detail (S2169); and *Eorum nempe . . . sciui* (S2561–5) on Edmund's confused sense on coming round from his vision. The intention seems to be to reduce some of those elements that focus on the visionary rather than the vision. Edmund as an individual was obviously of less interest to an audience three hundred years later than to his brother. Similarly omitted is a geographical detail deemed of no interest to a later audience: *ad capellam que uicina est domui in qua decumbebam* (S1272–3) is translated *came to his chirche* (1422).

For the most part, however, it must be said, the *Revelation* is a close translation. Adam's Latin is not always easy, and the translation is not always elegant. But apart from the more substantial omissions so far noted, occasional words, phrases, clauses, and sentences are omitted, though remarkably few given the texts' length. Some of these minor omissions (and I am not attempting to list them all) may be intended to make the *Revelation*, a vernacular printed work, more accessible to the laity, by excising details to do with the monastic life, e.g. *ubi ueniam petere fratres solent* (S137–8); *ad oratorium* (S408–9). The *Revelation* drops the concept *de mistica Babilone* (S1849); omits biblical citation used as commentary (S1930–2); excises the numbers of the three psalms sung over a dying prior (S2351), and reference to Edmund's sobbing and weeping (S2426–7); and ignores the notion of nuns panting with pious desire for the embrace of the celestial spouse (S2059–60). As if to make the vision seem as clear as possible, a qualifying moment is dropped: in the second place of purgatory, Edmund says, *fluuius dixerim an stagnum nescio* (S689); *Revelation* retains only *ponde* (747). And as if to avoid prompting doubt about the veracity of the vision, the translator omits passages in the final chapter where Adam suggests that some might think Edmund's protracted illness and trance were faked, only to dismiss such an accusation (S2592–5 *dicant . . . laborauerat*; S2597–8 *fuerit . . . fraudulencia*; and S2598–9 *effossa . . . lumina*).

But, as noted above, there are many instances of omission where it is hazardous to argue the reason. Consider, for instance, this passage on the drunkard's death (S852–4):

de quo id etiam vulgatum fuerat, ex nimio vino ingurgitatus,
uitam ebrietate uendiderit, letum leticia non bene cautus institor emercatus

The *Revelation* omits the rhetorical reiteration of the second line. Was this to avoid a redundant flourish, or was it simply caused by eye-skip from *ingurgitatus* to *emercatus*?

Additions in the Revelation

Significant additions in the Middle English are few. I have mentioned above the recurrent use of the term 'purgatory',[112] a familiar, indeed, vital concept for the laity in the late fifteenth century, and, as with the omissions, the translator's additions seem largely geared to serving the needs of a lay readership. Thus, for instance, translations are included of the Latin quotations from the Bible, and explanations of technical monastic terms are given, e.g. *locutorium*: 'the colloke, the which ys a place where they may speke to-geder' (387–8), or *infirmaria*: 'A fermorye among religious men is called a place or an howse ordende to kepe seke bretheren' (294–5). These were obviously new and hard words for a lay public (*OED* records 71 first occurrences of words in the *Revelation*).[113] In the following passage the words in bold are additions by the translator, trying to clarify a rather confusing passage dealing with the monastic practice of giving disciplines (flogging)—Edmund believes he has received the discipline but is told that he has not for it was against the monastic rule to do so at that particular hour. The translator introduces additional direct speech:

'Knowe not 3e that this ys trowth that Y haue to yow **here** seyde?'
Than seyde hys confessor ageyne, 'In no wise, ther was no seche thynges done **of vs**, nether myght be done, for the ordyr wil not **that we shuld haue gone that tyme of the night into the chaptur-howse to geue discyplynys.'**
Than he seyd **to hym,** 'Dowtheles Y had went hether-to, **that tho discyplynys and other thynges had be done of yow to me.** Ful wele Y knowe withowtyn dowte, **that Y resceyued thoes dyscyplynys aboue-rehersyd in the chaptur-howse** . . . (563–72)

This brief passage is unusual for the amount of new material introduced en route. It is prompted by the trickiness of the narrative at this point: Edmund has been hallucinating; he has imagined that

---

[112] See, e.g. the beginning of ch. 17, additions in bold: Of the secunde place of **purgatory**. 'Therefore, after that **we were paste the firste place of purgatorye**, we came to the seconde place of **purgatorye and** tormentys, in the whyche was an hye hylle, vppe al-mooste to the clowdys, and was deuyded fro the forseyde **fyrste** place of purgatorye . . . (738–42).

[113] See Appendix 2.

he has received the discipline and cannot understand why his interlocutors, who he thought had administered it, are denying it. The translator is clearly making some effort to clarify this for the reader. In fact, he adds an 'Adigression' on the subject at the end of the chapter (604–17), speculating that the figures Edmund believed to have given him the discipline *were douteles holy angellys*. This digression is the longest addition in the translation apart from the new prologue.

Devotion to the saints is also enhanced in the translation: *beatam . . . Margaretam* becomes *the blessyd virgynne and martir sent Margaret* (860–1, cf. 902); and St Nicholas, the patron of both the goldsmith and Edmund, is repeatedly invoked: the goldsmith asks Edmund to ensure his wife and son do their devotions *and seruys to hys patron and aduocatour Sent Nycholas* (1230–1, cf. 1235, 1252, 1260, 1471, 2246). In lieu of the long omission at the end of ch. 23, the *Revelation* adds a sentence advocating devotion to the saints: *Wherfore, ful expedyente hyt ys to alle men, whyle they leuyn in thys world, deuoutely to serue the holy seyntys of God, by the whyche they may haue in her grete nede the grace and mercye of Almyghty God, as hyt ys schewyd and prouyd often-tymes* (1237–41).

One sentence added at the end of chapter 36 spells out more clearly the state of the knowledge that the souls in purgatory have about their salvation, a matter of great importance to an audience at the end of the fifteenth century. The Latin ends the chapter with a sentence translated thus: *Sothly, in al this visyon Y saw no man that vtwardly* [utterly] *hadd loste hope of saluacion, nethir þat was in certente of eternal dampnacion* (2017–18). In other words, in purgatory the souls are not deprived of hope and are bound for salvation, a perfectly orthodox sentiment. The *Revelation* then adds: *Neuertheles, some þat were in greuys peynys had no knoulege when they shulde be sauyd, and þat was most peynful to hem. And some that were in peynys knew a certente of her delyuerans, and that was to hem a grete solace, as hit ys here seyde aboue* (2019–22). These two sentences supply further distinctions: some know *when* as well as *that* they will be saved, and some do not, and the lack of such knowledge is one of the principal pains of purgatory (as experienced by the sodomitical legist in chapter 26, 1407–10).[114] The translator refers back to the end of

---

[114] St Bridget also considered such uncertainty of salvation the worst pain of purgatory: see the discussion by Duffy, *The Stripping of the Altars* (1992), p. 345, and Easting, 'Purgatory and the Earthly Paradise', pp. 37–38.

chapter 35, where this issue is discussed: Edmund speaks of the purgatorial souls' faithful trust in deliverance, a trust *the wyiche they knewe and haue by oure Lordys mercye* (1927), the translator adds.

Edmund's surprise at learning about the existence of lesbianism is also slightly expanded by the translator, who adds the following sentence: *I neuyr herde before nether hadde any suspycyon hethirto that the kynde of wemen hadde be deprauyd and defoyled by suche a foule synne* (1327–9).

Commonplace pious sentiments and expressions frequently provide minor expansions: e.g. to the priest's care for his parishioners, telling them how they should leave their sins, is added *and fulfille owre Lordyis commandmentis* (2714–15); to the nomination *the meke Redemer of mankynde* is added *oure swete Lorde and Sauyur, Ihesus Criste* (2748–9); to the rewards awaiting Reginald Fitzjocelin is added *yn the euerlasting blysse of heuene* (2180). And the rubric for the final chapter is more enthusiastic: *Argumentum ad uisionem monachi confirmandum* becomes *A proffe that thys reuelacyon ys of God and most nedys be trew for the grete myraclys that our Lord shewyd on this same monke that same tyme* (2940–2). Adam does not call Edmund's healing a miracle (see above, p. lxii, and below, p. lxxxiii).

Other distinctive features of the Revelation *compared to the* Visio

Arber calls the style of the *Revelation* 'rapid, clear, unhesitating, unhalting'. This is generous. He adds: 'There is great craft and subtlety in producing *vraisemblance*—despite inconsistent narration—by innumerable graphic touches, circumstantial details, and natural dialogues' (p. 8). Arber did not know the *Visio* and how these virtues are derived from the Latin.

As is usual with translations from Latin, the English text is longer, even though it omits more than it adds: the *Visio* contains 22,195 words, the *Revelation*, 34,150, and even allowing for editorial choices of sentence division, the English sentences are comparably longer, on average 34 words to the *Visio*'s 18. It is easy to see why, when, not untypically, an expression like *si . . . temptarem exponere* is inflated to *ȝef Y schulde sey or be aboute to schew and declare* (2027–8), or when the short sentence *Monachicum ab infancia usque ad senectutem & habitum gesserat & animum* (S2308–9) is doubled in length in translation: *And he bare euermore whyle he leuyd in thys world the habet of a monke, bothe on his body and in hys herte, fro the tyme of hys chyldhode on-to hys oolde aage and to hys laste ende* (2626–9). We can

see from these two examples that when, in the first sentence of the
translation, *inualitudine* becomes *febulnes and wekenes* (126), the
translator is starting as he means to continue, with the duplets so
favoured in much later fifteenth-century English prose. For instance,
in a few lines we find the following pairings for single words in the
Latin: *suffragys and helpys* (780) from *solaciorum* (S715); *meritys and
deseruingys* (779) from *meritorum*; and *3esyor and softyr* (784) from
micior; the pattern is endemic: *enfourmed and taught by comyning
and spekyng* (678–9), *whome no truste or helpe releuyth or helpyth*
(837), *Of the vnclene and foule vyce and synne of sodemytys* (1305).

On occasions the translator, by amplifying, loses track of the
syntax, and ends up with an anacoluthon, e.g. the first of the two
sentences *Than the heuynly leche . . . in hys dethe* (1376–83); the prose
is not rescued by conjoining these two sentences into one. Sometimes
the syntax comes apart in long sentences with subordinate and
embedded clauses. For example, translating S1705–10, not a particularly complex sentence, but one where the verb of a relative clause
comes at the end of the sentence, 35 words after its subject (*qui . . .
profecerat*), the English writer shifts uneasily from the relative (*the
whiche*) to a repeated subject and passive construction *and at the last
he was promotyd* (see 1936–42). Such a sentence is neither rapid, nor
clear, nor unhalting; but it would be unfair to the translator to focus
only on the sticky places.

The translator is, indeed, capable of brief and pointed formula-
tions, e.g. Adam's taut observation on the coherent facility of
Edmund's effusions of devotion, *pocius legere scripta, quam propria
fundere uerba uideretur* is neatly rendered *hit semyd rathir he redde hem
thanne seyde hem* (323–4). Sometimes shortening is also a simplifying
of the rather high-flown Latin of the *Visio*,[115] especially where it is
dealing with monastic practices that are of less significance for the lay
audience for whom the translation is clearly intended; thus

*sicque usque ad noctis horam qua ad matutinarum laudes festiua Domino exultacione
persoluendas conuentus pulsantibus signis cepit preparari, peruigil in lacrimis &
graciarum accione permansit.* (S304–7)

---

[115] Salter, 2.274, calls Adam's Latin 'too ambitious' but 'idiomatic'. For fuller
consideration of the Latin style of the *Visio*, see Schmidt, ' "Visio diligenti narratione
luculenter exarata." Zu Sprache und Stil der "Visio Edmundi monachi de Eynsham"', in
VEME, pp. 31–38, where he addresses Adam's use of biblical citations (see also Dengler in
the same volume), and rhetorical use of *variatio*, and calls the text 'ein auf hohem
Reflexionsniveau konzipiertes Dokument elaborierter Schriftlichkeit' (p. 36).

Ande so he bode waking in prayor and terys til the howre of night that they range to matens. (368–70)

The concrete *prayor* for *graciarum accione* is typical here, as is a simple rendition elsewhere in the text of the Ovidian expression *thori socia* as *my wyfe* (1078). Adam's inventive Latin is often thus made more straightforward for the lay reader by a reduction of metaphor, as when an abbess's passage *ad interminabilem perpetue lucis diem* becomes *tawarde the euerlastyng lyfe and ioys of heuyn* (2315–16), or when at a young monk's death *stola immortalitatis feliciter commutauerat* becomes *and so blessydly he passyd out of this worlde* (2686–7).

The Middle English sometimes breaks up the (often lengthy) periods of the Latin, appropriately turning participial phrases or embedded clauses into separate sentences. This can have the effect of highlighting certain moments; e.g. when Edmund swallows, as he thinks, one drop of the blood dripping from the side wound of Christ on the crucifix, he says he does not know if that was a sin: *an in hoc peccauerim ignoro*. In the translation, this clause is made into a separate sentence following the deed: *And whether Y offendyd God in that poynt or no, Y wote nere* (516–17). The subject and main verb, which are sometimes left until the end of a long sentence in the Latin, can also be properly brought to the head of the English sentence (e.g. 211 *They herde . . .*).

An awkwardly Latinate syntax in the Middle English shows that the translator was not a complete master of his craft: *hit was perseyuyd in him* (196) remains too close to *ei . . . deprehensum est*; *ut plorantes solent* 'as weepers are wont to do' is translated *as wepyng doth* (271): the southern plural 'do' is a little weak for *solent*, and *wepyng* as an absolute or nominal use of the participial adjective is undertranslated, unless a following word like 'folk' has dropped out. Ablative absolutes are carried over, resulting in rather abrupt expressions that do not sound comfortable in English, e.g. *habita deliberacione* becomes *auysement takyn* (222–3), but we need to beware of judging the translator by modern preferences. These and similar moments are the concomitant vice of the virtue of trying to give a faithful rendering of the Latin. Too close an adherence to the Latin can yield forms which, though plausible, are uncommon, like the doubly inflected *felows virgyns* (891) from *sodales . . . uirgines*, or the attractive adverb *wepyngly* (225) from *flebiliter*. Spellings are taken over in Latin form: *remediis* (650) and *iniuriis* (712) are plurals from Latin ablative plurals.

The translator omits the rhetorical question *Quid multa?* (S171) and also in the mouth of the drunken goldmith *Quid multis immoror?* (S971), but is not immune to inserting his own rhetorical appeals. He turns first-person narrative into direct address to the reader in order to draw attention to the importance of alms-giving for assisting one's suffering in purgatory: *Vidi enim* becomes *See nowe and consydre* (1452–3). And out of a good final cadence, *subito insipiens & uecors inuentus est* (which has partly achieved its effect by offsetting *insipiens* against *sapiens* near the beginning of the sentence), he creates a new sentence, with exclamation and increased patterning: *Loo, so sone and sodenly he ys founde onwyse and madde* (1458–9).

The most pervasive verbal tic is the recurrence of assurances of the veracity of the vision and its insights. The word *Soth(e)ly* introduces no fewer than 90 sentences, and *sothe* and *sothly* occur a further 8×. As a variation on this, forms of the word 'truly' introduce another 78 sentences, and 'true' and 'truly' occur a further 19×. Thus, 15% of the text's 1,100 sentences open with a rhetorical bid for credence. True it is that *uero* occurs 115× in the *Visio*, but this still means a more than 70% increase in the number of the translation's truth claims.

A brief dialogue is continued by turning indirect into direct speech, in a well-chosen moment when Adam explains, by implication, to Edmund that part of the latter's experiences before the main vision were hallucinatory (565–8). Similarly, at 1204 the translation suddenly shifts momentarily into reported direct speech. This helps to clarify the relationships when Edmund recounts Adam's recounting of the goldsmith's son's recounting of his mother's recounting of what his dead father's spirit had told her. This complicated string had caused variants in the Latin versions:

Salter's A text: *& retulit* [mother] *michi* [son] *(inquid* [son]*) illius* [father's] *verba*
Thurston's B text: *& retulit* [son] *ipsa illius* [mother] *verba*
C text S1084–5: *& retulit* [son] *michi* [Edmund] *ipsa illius* [mother] *verba*

Revelation 1204–6 has the son speak: '*and thenne afterward sche told vnto my* [me] *hys wordys, the whyche he hadde tolde and seyde vnto her*'. Indirect speech also becomes direct in the *Revelation* when abbot Godfrey explains how the continued wickedness of those formerly in his charge increases his pains in purgatory (1596–9). Elsewhere

Edmund thinks to himself, why are so few unchaste priests in purgatory, and *responsum est michi quod . . .*, the question is answered anonymously (perhaps, by implication, by his guide St Nicholas); in the *Revelation*, we find *to thys hit was so answard*, and the answer is in direct speech: because such priests were not penitent '. . . *the grete multytude of hem byn vtwardly dampde'* (2010–16); i.e. they are not in purgatory but in hell. The abbess, explaining how she has benefited from the masses said for her, is also allowed direct speech in the translation (2331–6), and the simoniac knight's direct speech about God's mercy starts earlier at 2385. All such moments of direct speech heighten the immediacy of the narrative and help to fix important ideas in the reader's or hearer's awareness. But the direction of change is not all one way. Elsewhere the translator removes the last sentence of Henry II's direct-speech lament (S1886–8) and absorbs it into the following narrative sentence, and at 2396–9 one sentence from the middle of the simoniac spirit's speech is turned into two sentences of narrative.

The *Revelation* makes St Nicholas appear more prominent by naming him no less than 40 ×; in the *Visio* he is named 13 ×. This suggests the English translator is more interested in the saint's powers of intercession and spiritual guardianship, functions that could appeal to a lay readership concerned with personal salvation and the assistance to be derived from devotion to the saints (noted above, p. lxviii). These functions are prominent also in the appearance of St Margaret and her virgins to intercede on behalf of the prostitute, one of her devoted followers. It is this attitude which prompted the changes to the heading for chapter 1 (which is derived from S1–3, the *incipit* to the *Visio* preface): *Here begynnyth a* **meruelous** *reuelacion* **that** *was schewyd of Almyghty God by Sent* **Nycholas to a monke** . . . (118–19, additions in bold).

There is a modification indicative of a shift in emphasis in confessional practice between the late twelfth and late fifteenth centuries:

Sacerdotum plures qui incontinencie sue reatus penitendo & confitendo reliquerant, sed penitenciam non peregerant, innumeris & immensis suppliciis & ardoribus ibi confectos misera per omnia sorte uidi. (S1769–72)

Also many prystys, that by the grace of God lefte her vycyus leuing of onchastyte, in very contricion of herte with confession of mouth when they leuyd, and be-cause they had not do penans sufficiently, Y saw hem in torment in innumerable peynys. (2004–7)

The most significant additions here are *by the grace of God* and *in very contricion of herte*, stressing for the late fifteenth-century audience a fourfold pattern of requirements for absolution: grace, contrition, confession, and penance. As Robert Penkett has noted, the *Visio* here omits the first two.[116] The translation's **sufficiently** also spells out the need for the completion of penance, indicated by the Latin *peregerant*.

The *Revelation* does indeed successfully transmit the 'innumberable graphic touches, circumstantial details, and natural dialogues'[117] of the *Visio*, and for the most part copes remarkably fluently with the sometimes elaborate Latin. The translator has made minimal cuts, and provided occasional interpretative glosses; both modifications help to focus the attention of the potential lay reader on the progress of the narrative, and on its spiritual import.

EDMUND'S VISION OF THE OTHER WORLD

Although it is not always possible to maintain a precise distinction, for convenience I divide the following discussion of the *Visio* and *Revelation* into sections on the texts' treatment of the preliminary 'historical' matter—chronology and events surrounding the vision—and the vision itself of purgatory and paradise.

Before recounting what Edmund told of his vision, Adam goes to some lengths to establish Edmund's physical and spiritual condition and the details of his movements immediately before and after his ecstasy, just as at the end of the text (chapter 58) he speaks of the healing of an ulcer on Edmund's leg during the time of his trance.

The time scheme is complicated as Adam recounts what he and his fellow monks saw of Edmund's condition and movements before and after his vision (chapters 1–8), and what Edmund recalls (chapters 9–13), confusedly, of events before the death-like collapse during which his *meruelous reuelacion* (118) takes place from after midnight Maundy Thursday / early Good Friday morning till before compline on Easter Saturday, 20 April 1196, a duration of maybe forty-two hours or more. For the reader's benefit, I attempt here to

---

[116] Penkett, Robert, 'Sinners and the Community of Saints: Aspects of Repentance in a Late Twelfth-Century Visio', Lambeth MA thesis (1996), p. 60.

[117] Arber, p. 8.

present in a single chronological sequence an outline of these events. Edmund's hallucinatory/visionary experiences are set between square brackets; line numbers for citations from the *Visio* and *Revelation* are in parentheses; chapter numbers are in bold.

CHRONOLOGY

Christmas 1194 Edmund is sick of a quinsy, somewhere near Eynsham (?Osney) **20** (S849–50). January/February? 1195 Edmund enters the monastery of Eynsham, where for fifteen months he is ill for most of the time **1**. February–April 1196 his condition is worse **1**. Before Lent he prays for a vision of the other world and at the beginning of Lent, about Ash Wednesday, six weeks before Maundy Thursday **9**, [a figure in a dream tells him that if he continues to pray and seeks the prayers of others, including the community of nuns at Godstow (unnamed), his wish will be granted **9**].

Towards Easter 1196 Edmund begins to strengthen **1**. On the evening of Wednesday 17 April he walks with a staff about the infirmary and goes to the church where the community offers the night offices between midnight and daybreak, and experiences *grete conpunccion and swetenes* (144–5) following the service of Our Lord's betrayal and Passion **1**.

He attends Matins early Maundy Thursday morning 18 April (*as he did the daye before* (179) **1**. [Edmund believes he is disciplined by his two confessors (after Matins?) during the night of Wednesday/ Thursday **9**, but it is an hallucination **13**. He thought that he would have preferred to stay in the chapter-house all night at his devotions but he was disturbed by the brethren leaving the church after Matins **13**]. He weeps and praises God from midnight till *sex of the belle* (147) in the morning **1**. On leaving the chapter-house, as he thinks, he meets brother Marten **13**. He returns to bed lest he be *reprouyd of presumpcion* (581–2) **13** [for wishing to stay in the chapter house all night.] He remains at his devotions, weeping, until *hora sexta* (about 11.00 a.m.–12 noon) on Thursday, when he confesses to two of his brethren, probably Adam, his brother, the sub-prior, and Thomas, prior **1**. They fear he is near death; he says he does not feel that he is. Edmund asks if the priors had disciplined the brothers the previous night. They think he says this because of *grete febulnesse of his hedde, or by alyenacion of hys mynde, the whiche perauenture he hadde falle in by his infirmyte and inmoderate weping or fastyng, howe-be-hit that he* *with hym had meruailous wisdam and discrecion al the tyme of hys sekenesse* (170–3) 1. Edmund spends the rest of Maundy Thursday in devotions 1.

On Thursday night he falls asleep 1 [at the hour to rise for Matins on Good Friday morning 9. A voice tells him to rise and go to the chapel dedicated to St Lawrence and all the martyrs, and he will find a cross behind the altar 10]. He wakes, rises, and goes to Matins early Good Friday morning, 19 April 1 [10]. [About the beginning of the third nocturn of Matins he is called from the altar where he is praying by a noise *lyke as a man hadde smytte the stony pament wyth his fote, and so went in-to the chaptur-howse* (588–9) 13. It was the same hour as the previous night. When the brethren have begun Matins he meets a senior in the church porch, one of those who (he thinks) disciplined him the previous night, i.e. early Thursday morning 10. They go to the chapter-house and return, and they meet another senior in the church porch, to whom he beckons to have the discipline. The second senior bids him wait awhile.] He goes alone to St Lawrence's altar and removes his shoes. He finds and worships the cross 10. [It bleeds from the wounds in the right side and right foot of the crucifix, and he tastes the blood. This takes place behind the altar (north side) about midnight on Thursday 11. He sees two lights pass to the south side of the altar: he follows hoping to see there *sum spiritualle thyng* (531) 12. He hears the voice of the second senior.] Not knowing how, he comes into the chapter house 13. [Edmund confesses; the second senior disciplines him six times. The senior goes in his albs and sits *in the abbotis sete, that was there in the chaptur-hows* (545–6).] *And thanne I came and lay prostrate* [*before hym*. He confesses again. A certain worshipful senior *that had a face and a chere as an angelle* (551–2) takes him by the hand and says *'Folowe þow me'* 12. This turns out to be his guide, St Nicholas (13 Adigression, and 20).] *Here Y felte my-selfe fyrst rapte in spyryte* (558) 13.

At prime (about 6.00–7.00 a.m.) on Good Friday, Edmund is found without his staff, prostrate, bare foot, and unconscious, in the chapter-house before the abbot's seat. His eyes and nose are bloody 2. He is washed and taken to his bed in the infirmary 2. The monks discover the crucifix bleeding in the church. It had been set on the floor between the altar and the east wall during Lent. Edmund's staff and shoes are found by the crucifix 3. The monks take discipline, i.e. are flogged with rods, and lie prostrate in the church saying, *wepingly* (225), the seven penitential psalms 3.

Edmund lies unconscious all Good Friday and until almost sunset on Easter Saturday 20th April 3, despite the brothers trying to rouse him with needles, scraping the soles of his feet, and blowing a great horn 3.

Gradually he recovers consciousness just before the monks gather for collation and compline on Easter Saturday 4. His eyes run with a yellow humour of water. He begins to mouth a few words, calling on Mary, and comes to, *lyke as a man had awaked fro a grete slepe* (269–70) 4, thinking that he is still in the church early on Good Friday morning 5. The brethren bring him a silver crucifix, which he worships 5. The bells ring for collation; the monks leave for supper and compline. One (Adam?) remains and Edmund tells him much 6. He tells some of his visions also to *a few persons of wytnesse, on whois deuocyons he had taken a specyalle trust* (356–7) 6. He says he is healed and expects to live *long ynow* 6. He takes a little bread and honey, and prays until the bell rings for Matins on Easter Sunday morning 7, when he rises and enters the choir in the church, without any support, for the first time in eleven months. He attends Matins and the performance of the Easter Resurrection enactment, the *Visitatio Sepulchri*, and Mass 7. Afterwards he goes with the brethren to the *colloke*, and they ask him to tell *hem of seche thinges as befylle hym and as he had seyn, for ther goostly edifiyng and comfort* (389–91) 8. He *dissymylyd alle thing a lytyl while* (395), but tells what had befallen him to the two to whom he had confessed on Maundy Thursday (8, as in 1). On Easter Sunday, he also tells Adam about the bleeding cross that he saw about midnight Thursday 11. Adam (?) explains to Edmund that he and the prior did not go to the chapter-house late on Wednesday and Thursday nights and did not give him disciplines 12.

The *Revelation* includes an 'adigression' at the end of chapter 13 to clarify that the imagined brethren, who Edmund thought had administered disciplines to him, *were douteles holy angellys, that so apperyd* (609–10), and to establish here, rather than waiting another seven chapters (as in the *Visio*), that Edmund's guide was St Nicholas, *as hit shalle be aftirward more opynnor declarid* (615–16).

The fact that this whole introductory section of the text is not *more opynnor* than it is, is mainly because Adam has not seen fit to pre-empt knowledge that was subsequently revealed, but has presented it in the order it came to him. It is confusing for the reader to untangle because at the time of these occurrences Adam and Edmund both found it difficult to understand what was going on, and Adam has accurately reproduced that uncertainty by adhering to the chronology of understanding rather than of occurrence. Speaking in the third person, he explains in chapter **6** how, through discussion with Edmund, he, *bi leyser and gret dylygens, lernyd and knewe an ordir of euery-thing synglerly, more opynner and fullyor than he knewe afore* (346–8).

EVENTS SURROUNDING THE VISION

If, as I have suggested above (pp. xxxiii–xliii), we accept the unproven likelihood that Edmund is the same person as the clerk in *MVSH*, 5.3, then we know that he was already given to visionary experience before his other-world vision on Good Friday and Easter Saturday 1196. Indeed, even without such an identification, Edmund appears as one susceptible to visions, a condition doubtless enhanced by the delibitating effects of his protracted illness. We are told that before his vision of the other world he been ill for fifteen months, from about the time of his entering the monastery, during which period sometimes for stretches of nine days or more Edmund's stomach could hold down nothing but a little warm water (124–9). In the last three months before Easter *he was more sorer dyseasyd and feblyd than euer he was before* (134–5). Some six or more weeks before Easter, feeling himself near death, Edmund prays God,

> to reuele and shewe to me, in some maner of wise, the state of the worlde that is to come and the condicion of the soulys that byn past her bodyes after this lyfe; and thanne, this opynly knowen, Y might the bettyr vndirstonde what within shorte space (as Y supposyd) were to be dred, and what Y might hope after, whanne Y shuld passe fro thys worlde to that worlde, and so by this to stabylle myselfe in the drede and loue of God. (418–24)

There can be little doubt that he and the Eynsham monks knew of other-world visions seen by other people. They were many and widely reported, and had been a staple of monastic reading for centuries. In England, the most influential such vision was that of the Northumbrian layman, Dryhthelm, reported by Bede (in the *Historia Ecclesiastica*, 5.12), and other English examples include the visions of the monk of Wenlock, of Orm, of the boy William, and of Gunthelm. The most famous recent account, written only a dozen years before and ten miles north of the clerk's vision of the Christ child at the bishop of Lincoln's manor at Buckden, was H[enry] of Sawtry's account of Owein's experiences in the *Tractatus de Purgatorio Sancti*

Patricii.[118] Given that this was written in a Cistercian monastery that was on Hugh of Lincoln's route from Lincoln to Buckden and London, and given Hugh's patronage of Eynsham, it seems likely that the monks of Eynsham would at least have heard of the *Tractatus* within a decade of its composition *c.*1181–84. In monastic circles texts recounting visions of the other world may even have been used (a little like the Book of the Dead, in Tibet), for reading to those who appeared terminally ill or on the point of death. In the ninth-century vision of the monk Wettin, Wettin specifically asks for the Fourth Book of Gregory the Great's *Dialogi*, containing influential accounts of other-world visions, to be read to him after he has had one brief vision himself; two of his fellow monks read to the end of the ninth or tenth folio before he relapses into sleep and his major vision. He dies the following day. Edmund, sensing the approach of his own death, prays to God for a revelation of the world to come, and is told by a figure who appears to him in his sleep to pray further and seek the prayers of others, including the nuns at Godstow (unnamed), and *þou shalte opteyne and gete thy peticion* (434–5). So Edmund is prepared to receive the vision which indeed follows. His physical and spiritual states are receptive. As we have noted in the chronology above, Edmund also experiences visionary hallucinations—seeing moving lights, tasting the blood from the crucifix, imagining flagellation—and other quasi-mystical feelings of *grete conpunccion and swetenes* (144–5) *afore þat he was rapte* in the ecstasy wherein he sees things *spiritually in anothir world* (341–2). Peter Dinzelbacher[119] has examined in detail the language and imagery used to describe Edmund's experience of infused sweetness and loving emotion in front of Jesus on the crucifix as evidence of 'what perhaps could be called premystical experience' (p. 113), of a kind characteristically associated with the charismatics of the later Middle Ages. In so far as Edmund has multiple visionary experiences, some of a charismatic kind, he is different from most of the other male recipients of other-world visions, for whom such an experience is a one-off occurrence. There is no indication that Dryhthelm, or Barontus, or Tnugdal, or Owein, or Thurkill, for instance, ever

---

[118] See *SPP*.

[119] Peter Dinzelbacher, 'The Beginnings of Mysticism', and also, 'Das Christusbild der heiligen Lutgard von Tongeren im Rahmen der Passionsmystik und Bildkunst des 12. und 13. Jahrhunderts', *Ons geestelijk Erf* 56 (1982), 217–77, at pp. 228–9, and *Christliche Mystik im Abendland* (Paderborn, 1994), pp. 154–5.

had any other vision, but Edmund, a religious at the end of the
twelfth century is at a turning point which leads to the later often
multiple visionary experiences of (more usually) women mystics.[120]

Edmund's illness must have been a major contributory factor to
his vision. He had survived fifteen months in which he *labouryd with
gret febulness and wekeness of body* (126). The majority of medieval
visions of the other world were experienced by people who had been
ill, indeed so ill that they appeared either dead or close to death
during the time of their vision, e.g. Dryhthelm, Fursey, Barontus,
Wettin, Heinrich von Ahorn, Gottschalk, and Thurkill. Owein and
Tnugdal are different: but Owein undergoes fifteen days of harsh
fasting and preparatory exercises and enters St Patrick's Purgatory
expecting this to take him to the other world, and though,
conversely, Tnugdal is healthy but suddenly collapses while eating
a hearty meal, his bodily symptoms during his ecstasy are similar to
Edmund's. As with the collapsed Edmund, light breathing is
detected in Bernold, the first monk of Saint-Vaast, Boso, Orm,
and Gunthelm; a certain warmth or redness of face is also discerned
in Tnugdal and Bernold; Edmund is insensible, like Boso, Alberic,
and Thurkill; his feet are cold, like Fursey's; he makes no movement,
like Barontus, Heinrich von Ahorn, Alberic, Gottschalk, and Thurkill; and similar language is used, e.g. Edmund is called *exanimis*, as
are Baldarius, Bernold, Orm, and Tnugdal; or in *excessu mentis*, like
Bonellus.[121]

Adam's account of Edmund's physical, mental, and spiritual states
prior to the vision is unprecedentedly long and detailed amongst other-
world vision texts, and is valuable for what it reveals, amongst other
things, of contemporary monastic attitudes to sickness and spiritual
experience. The reported details of Edmund's illness suggest that his
brother may have had some medical training. Adam shows that
Edmund is mentally alert during his illness and during the out-
pourings of prayer and exhortation which follow his revival.
Although, as Adam acknowledges, Edmund's profuse weeping and
sobbing and worshipping of the cross at this point was thought
tedious by *some stondyng by* (312), yet Edmund's *meruailus prayers*

[120] Peter Dinzelbacher broadly distinguishes these two kinds of visionary modes as
Type I and Type II in *Vision und Visionsliteratur im Mittelalter* (Monographien zur
Geschichte des Mittelalters 23, Stuttgart, 1981).
[121] See the discussion of terminology by Dinzelbacher, *Vision und Visionsliteratur*,
pp. 45–53.

and obsecracyons were not merely rhapsodic effusion: *Thoes wordys the whiche he made in his supplicacions ware so redy and prompte and also repletyd with grete reson and hyenesse of witte, that hit semyd rathir he redde hem thanne seyde hem* (321–4). Adam's later work, the *Magna Vita Sancti Hugonis*, shows him to be a writer more accurate in depicting events and more subtly alert to the niceties of mood and temperament of his subject than is commonly found among hagiographers.[122] Similarly, in the *Visio*, Adam encourages acquiescence in his narrative by the care with which he handles tricky material. His detailed reports of the events surrounding the vision are clearly intended to reinforce the reader's belief in the truthfulness of his account and hence also in the reliability of Edmund's vision. Adam must have been aware immediately that there were members of the monastery who had no faith in Edmund's vision at all. We learn this also from Ralph of Coggeshall, author of the *Visio Thurkilli* (1206), who in his preface refers to Edmund's vision alongside Gregory's *Dialogi* Book 4, the *Tractatus de Purgatorio Sancti Patricii*, the *Visio Tnugdali*, and the visions of the monks of Strata Florida in Wales and of Vaucelles in France. The extract concerning Edmund's vision taken from Ralph's preface, quoted above (p. xxxv), continues discussing his conversation with Thomas, prior of Eynsham at the time of the vision:

multaque alia nobis retulit probamenta ad commendationum predicte visionis. hec iccirco dixerim, quia multi contubernalium suorum huic visioni contradicunt, sicut fere de omni revelatione quibusdam dubitatur.

Apart from any scepticism about visions in general, many of the Eynsham monks probably decried Edmund's vision because he reported harsh words about some of his brethren uttered by the soul of their deceased abbot Godfrey, including attacks on the rifeness of homosexuality within the monastery (ch. 27). We know that even as devoted a collector of vision texts as Peter of Cornwall initially had doubts about Edmund's vision, though he does not specify what those doubts were. Peter, prior of the Augustinian canons' house of Holy Trinity, Aldgate, London, started compiling his huge collection, the *Liber reuelationum* in 1200, only four years after Edmund's vision. After he had had a B text of the *Visio* copied

---

[122] Douie and Farmer, *MVSH*, vol. 1, p. VIII, report the acknowledged specialists in saints' lives saying of *MVSH* that 'Its reliability and fullness of detail [are] almost unsurpassed in medieval hagiography'.

near the beginning of his collection, Lambeth Palace Library, MS 51, he had it crossed out: 'every page has a neatly ruled saltire of two black lines and one red'.[123] But a note by him explains why he subsequently attempted to have the crossings-out erased: *Hanc uisionem ego Petrus in hoc libro cancellaui putans non posse esse ueram, sed postea per ueridicos testes et qui rem cognouerunt probaui eam esse uerissimam.* ('I, Peter, cancelled this vision in this book thinking it could not be true, but afterwards, via veracious witnesses who knew the matter, I have proved it to be most true').[124] Peter's copy of the *Visio* is the earliest dated copy to survive.[125]

So far I have discussed Adam's depiction of Edmund leading up to the point where he starts to relate his vision, and I have suggested that Adam's account shows particular care to give circumstantial detail establishing Edmund's frame of mind (and that of the other monks), both out of a desire to be truthful and accurate and also to counter or forestall disbelief. At the end of the vision the question of credence crops up again. In a passage not translated in the *Revelation*, at the beginning of cap. 58, Adam tells how he has studiously expressed the vision, now following the sense and now the words of him who saw it, and that he, Adam, and many others who know the visionary well (*familiarius*) are sufficiently persuaded that they ought to have sure faith (*fidem indubitatam*) in his words. The English resumes: *Mony instruccyons and opyn examples byn here at the begynnyng of thys narracyon, that euydentely prouyn thys vysyon not to be of mannys conceyte but vtwardely* [utterly] *of the wylle of God, the whiche wolde haue hyt schewed to Crystyn pepul* (2943–6). Adam rehearses the failure to wake Edmund with needles and noise, how his eyes were sunk into his head, and how his breathing was

---

[123] M. R. James and C. Jenkins, *A Descriptive Catalogue of the Manuscripts in the Library of Lambeth Palace* (Cambridge, 1930), p. 77.

[124] The text of the *Visio* starts at the top of f. 32vb, with *De Edmundo monacho* in the top margin. The note is added in the blank foot of the preceding column, and is itself preceded by a new rubric written in the same hand: *De admirabili uisione Edmundi monachi de Enesham qua uidit infinitas penas malorum & gloriam bonorum.*

[125] On Peter of Cornwall's work and personal interest in visions, see Robert Easting and Richard Sharpe, 'The Visions of Ailsi and his Sons', *Mediaevistik*, 1 (1988), 207–62. Zaleski aptly suggests that 'there seems to have been a real campaign to win support for Adam's account of Edmund's vision' (p. 82), and that Adam and other authors' harping on evidence 'may be because the mundane settings in which medieval visions occur [unlike early apocalypses] highlight their extraordinary character in a way that strains credulity' (p. 83).

undetectable for two days. But Edmund's sudden cure is the most remarkable testimony of God's truth in him, and of this cure the most notable sign is the apparent healing, *yn the space of hys raueshyng* (2970), of an open ulcer on his leg, which no medicine had been able to cure for nearly a year, and which had tormented him like *an hoote plate of yrne bownde faste to hys legge* (2965–6). The only difference from his other leg is that where the ulcer had been there was now no hair. Cures of illnesses during trances and visions are reported elsewhere (for example, Heinrich von Ahorn was similarly cured of his ailment during the time of his vision),[126] though not as frequently as miracle cures in saints' lives; they may have some psychosomatic basis, as in passing through the hallucinations of the crisis stage of a fever. It is interesting to see, however, that Adam's principal proof of the truth of the revelation is not Edmund's return with knowledge of the dead which is subsequently confirmed by living witnesses, or his sight of the crucified Christ in Paradise, or the blood on his face and on the crucifix, but a stretch of hairless skin on Edmund's leg. Adam soberly counters doubt about the ecstatic life of the spirit with tangible evidence of the flesh. It is the *Revelation*, not Adam, that calls this healing *a ful feyre myracle* (2960) and translates *diuine . . . medicine* as *the meruelus curacion of God* (2973).[127]

THE VISION

What of the vision proper, which is related in chapters 14 to 57? Contrary to the opinion of some commentators,[128] Edmund's vision

---

[126] See Commentary 2969–70.

[127] Edmund's healing is the opposite of the burn wound visible on Fursey after his return from the other world: *Atque superfusus aqua, incendium inter scapulas illius, quod de iniquo sumpsit uiro, et in facie eius apparuit. Mirumque in modum quod anima sola sustinuit in carne demonstrabatur* (Carozzi, p. 692, lines 16–18). On Adam's cautious attitude to miracles, a stance probably reinforced by his association with Hugh of Lincoln from before the time he became his chaplain, see Dimock's comments in *Magna Vita S. Hugonis Epscopi Lincolniensis*, RS, 37 (1864), pp. xlvi–xlvii, and see, e.g. *MVSH*, 5.20, vol. 2, p. 230, on the need to verify miracles following Hugh of Lincoln's death: *ueritatem super hoc et super aliis que procul dubio audiri contingeret signis, diligentissime semper inquirendam primitus et non nisi certissime probata quolibet modo propalanda et publice predicanda nouimus.* Bynum, *The Resurrection of the Dead*, p. 296, likens the healing of Edmund's leg to the discovery sixteen years after her death of a healed tumour on the neck of St Etheldreda. See also Zaleski, p. 79, on other visionaries' physical manifestations of their experiences.

[128] E.g. Morgan, p. 223, says that Edmund 'visits the three areas of torment in Hell', and Russell, *A History of Heaven*, p. 106, says Edmund was guided through 'hell and purgatory'.

does not deal with hell and heaven, but with purgatory and the Earthly Paradise. In this it is like the *Tractatus de Purgatorio Sancti Patricii*.[129] This is not the place to add to the controversy which was prompted by Le Goff about whether or not purgatory could be said to exist before the noun *purgatorium* was used.[130] Suffice it to say that a purgatorial place or places or state or torments had existed in Christian conceptions of the other world long before the word *purgatorium* was first used in the second half of the twelfth century. It is very clear, for instance, in Bede's 'Vision of Dryhthelm', the place that Dryhthelm thought was hell but was not, and before then in Gregory the Great, to whom Adam refers, saying that whoever does not believe that miracles can be performed by those *in purgatoriis*, should read of Paschasius the deacon in Gregory's *Dialogi* [4.42]. Although the *Visio* may not use the noun *purgatorium*, Edmund's and Adam's concept of purgatory is beyond doubt; it is quite clear that the vision is about *the peynys of purgatorye and the iowys of paradyse*, as the new preface to the *Revelation* puts it. As noted above, the *Revelation* employs the term 'purgatory' 27 × without distorting the eschatology of the Latin; for instance, when Adam writes *in hoc purgacionis loco*, the ME translator gives *in this place of purgatorye for my purgacion* (1112–13). Purgatory takes up 35 chapters (14–48), paradise 9 chapters (49–57); such proportions are common in such visions.

What is *un*common about Edmund's vision is that the purgatorial torments, in other visions frequently described at length and with fascinated horror, are here, though present, given far less promin-ence. They are outstripped by the attention given to the speeches made by the souls that Edmund encounters as he is led by his guide St Nicholas. (According to Salter, Edmund and Adam probably grew up in the island of Osney, under the spiritual protection of St Nicholas; there was a chapel of the saint at Osney abbey.)[131] Edmund is less interested in the topography of the other world and the physical depiction of purgatorial pains than in the spiritual process of the souls' purification, the progress of their salvation, and the efficacy of alms and other suffrages performed by the living for the benefit of souls in purgatory. Morgan (p. 155) correctly observes that amongst

---

[129] See Easting, 'Purgatory and the Earthly Paradise', and *SPP*.

[130] See above, note 108.

[131] St Nicholas's chapel at Osney Abbey was on Osney Lane: see *A History of the County of Oxford*, vol. 4, ed. Alan Crossley,VCH (1979), p. 365.

medieval other-world visions the *Visio* 'concentrates most fully on the individual', a topic that has been explored by Kim Dian Gainer in relation to developing practices of confession. Gainer explores the confessional scenes of the prostitute, the goldsmith, and the priest, whom Edmund interviews, and argues that the *Visio* demonstrates a new interest in the interior life of individuals, prompted by the act of confession, for consideration of the inner spiritual life was encouraged by confessional manuals before the Fourth Lateran Council's decree *Omnis utriusque sexus* of 1215.[132] As Gainer says, 'the descriptions of the torments sometimes serve only to remind the reader of the importance of the individual's state of spiritual development'.[133] Penkett aptly observes that the *Visio* is unique among other-world visions 'in its frequent and comprehensive remarks on contrition, compunction, confession and satisfaction',[134] and he explores the *Visio*'s treatment of each of these aspects of penance, especially in the context of the changing patterns of penitential practice in the twelfth century, shifting from the older methods of fixed penalties[135] to the newer confessional stress on the individual's circumstances.[136] The emphasis of Edmund's vision, then, is quite different from that of earlier such texts, which tend to group sinners according their sin. The late twelfth- and early-thirteenth-century visions of Gottschalk (1189), Edmund (1196), and Thurkill (1206), all favour 'the presentation of individuals with case histories, often in such detail that the vision reads more like a document of social history than an account of the other world'.[137] Carozzi (p. 623) suggests that with the *Visio* other-world

---

[132] See also Alexander Murray, 'Confession before 1215', *Transactions of the Royal Historical Society*, 6th series, 3 (1993), 51–81.

[133] See Gainer, 'Prolegomenon to Piers Plowman: Latin Visions of the Otherworld from the Beginnings to the Thirteenth Century,' Diss., Ohio State University (1987), p. 180, and discussion pp. 178–93. Gainer is prompted by Mary F. Braswell, *The Medieval Sinner: Characterization and Confession in the Literature of the Middle Ages* (Rutherford, New Jersey, 1983). See also Caroline Walker Bynum, *Jesus as Mother* (Berkeley & Los Angeles, 1982), ch. 3, pp. 82–109, who canvasses the recent growing discussion of the notion of the twelfth century's (re-)discovery of the individual or the self, balancing this with an examination of group alliances.

[134] Penkett, 'Sinners and the Community of Saints' (1996), p. 23.

[135] See John T. McNeill and Helena M. Gamer, *Medieval Hand-books of Penance: A Translation of the Principal* Libri poenitentiales *and Selections from Related Documents* (New York, 1938, repr. 1990).

[136] See further P. Anciaux, *La Théologie du Sacrement de Pénitence au XIIe Siècle* (Louvain, 1949).

[137] Morgan, p. 54.

visions reach a limit, the continuation of the genre threatened on the one hand by concentration on mystical phenomena (which, as mentioned, tend to become more prominent in thirteenth-century visions) and on the other by dispersion into individual cases. Indeed, following the *Visio Thurkilli*, the genre of other-world visions tends to give way to other more charismatic forms of visionary experience.[138]

PURGATORY

By the late twelfth century, passage through purgatory was long understood to be a necessary preliminary to attaining heaven for the vast majority of the faithful, excluding those who die unrepentant in a state of mortal sin, who go straight to hell, and saints, martyrs, and the rare souls of the just and faithful who by their penitence and penance might be sufficiently purged to be admitted to the company of the blessed immediately after death. Similarly, visions of the afterlife usually started with the places of punishment first and then proceeded to paradise. This is the pattern in the *Visio* as in the visions of Dryhthelm, the monk of Wenlock, Alberic, the boy William, Tnugdal, Owein, and Thurkill—what Zaleski (calls the 'Drythelm [sic] line')[139]—as also in the visions of Wettin and Gottschalk, as Caesarius of Heisterbach pointed out: *Lege Visiones Witini, Godescalci, et aliorum, quibus concessum est videre poenas malorum et gloriam electorum, pene ubique visio poenalis praecedit.*[140] In some cases, the order was reversed, e.g. the Irish *Fis Adamnáin* and the Visions of Barontus, Boso, and Gunthelm, but the order experienced by Edmund was well established, and conformed also to a long pattern of preaching which sought to convert by stressing fear before love, e.g. as advocated by Isidore, *Ante necesse est timore converti ad Deum, ut metu futurarum poenarum carnales illecebrae*

---

[138] Morgan, p. 3 (and cf. p. 112) says, 'No new visions [of the other world] are recorded after that of Thurkill in 1206', but the genre does not die out completely, of course, witness such later examples as a Yorkshire vision of the fourteenth century (Robert Easting, 'Peter of Bramham's Account of a Chaplain's Vision of Purgatory (*c.* 1343?)', *Medium Ævum*, 65 (1996), 211–29); the *Visiones Georgii* (1353) and other visions seen at St Patrick's Purgatory, by Ramon de Perellós 1397, William of Stranton 1406/9, Laurence Rathold de Pászthó and Antonio Mannini 1411 (see the survey and references in Michael Haren and Yolande de Pontfarcy, eds., *The Medieval Pilgrimage to St Patrick's Purgatory: Lough Derg and the European Tradition* (Enniskillen, 1988)); and the *Vision of Edmund Leversedge* (1465), ed. Nijenhuis (Nijmegen, 1991).

[139] See Zaleski, p. 75, and note 2.

[140] *Dialogus Miraculorum*, 5.44.

devincantur. Deinde oportet, abjecto timore, ad amorem vitae eternae transire.[141]

Purgatory as seen by Edmund is divided into three places. Adam deals with each in turn in chapters 15–26, and then in chapters 27–48 he goes back to recount further meetings that Edmund had with the souls of those whom he knew.

The first place of torment (chapters 15–16, 27–33) is *fowle and myry of thicke cley* (634). All kinds of sinners suffer all kinds of pains. They are *bounden to-gedyr flockemel, in ther equalyte of synnys and in likenesse of profession equaly to soffyr* (643–4). Edmund is given knowledge of each of their sins and *the mesure and qualite of ther satisfaccion* (648). The souls have *hope of euerlasting blisse* (652). Some of the pains are briefly listed (682–92). As in all these visions, they are horrendous, but they are basically *inenarrabulle* (637) 'unutterable', and, in comparison with the accounts of Tnugdal, Owein, and Thurkill, Edmund tends to pass over them without graphic elaboration. Especially punished are bishops and abbots, judges and prelates; those of less *worldely dygnyte and prosperyte* (699) suffer lesser pains. I would, says Edmund, suffer temporal death for the release of my worst enemy from such torments—a striking sentiment that was noted by later writers (see Commentary 711–18).

The second place of purgatory (chapters 17–23, 34–48) has a high hill, almost up to the clouds. Beyond it is a valley, dark and deep, with a stinking pond. One side of the hill is burning, the other freezing. The hill and the valley are *so full of sowlys, as hyues swarmyn ful of bees* (757–8). The souls are circulated between the heat, the cold, and the pond, punished more or less according to *the qualite of her merytys and deseruingys afore-done, and also for the quantite of suffragys and helpys done of her frendys for hem after her dethe* (778–81). The second place is worse than the first. Edmund recognises many acquaintances. Here St Margaret releases a prostitute who had revered her (though in this case it is not stated whether or not Edmund knew the prostitute). Devils are tossing the woman about like a ball (a tennis-ball in the *Revelation*) with fiery instruments. With her sleeve St Margaret whisks away the wicked spirits *as hyt had be flyes yn a whyrlewynde* (911–12). Here also Edmund meets an alcoholic goldsmith from Osney whom he knew well, and who

---

[141] *Sententiarum*, 2.8, in *PL* 83:609.

similarly reveres St Nicholas. Five chapters are devoted to the goldsmith's account of his fight against drink and the suffering it has caused both before and after death.

The third place of purgatory (chapters 24–26) is full of worms and demons tearing, liquefying, and reconstituting the souls of homosexuals, who are compelled by horrible monsters to meddle with them. Not surprisingly, homosexuals are the object of attack in earlier visions of the punishments of the after-life, including the *Apocalypse of Peter*. Edmund has a shock, for he discovers what he had never even suspected before, namely *that the kynde of wemen hadde be deprauyd and defoyled by suche a foule synne* (1328–9). He meets a doctor of lawe that he knew sometime in his childhood and youth, but did not know was dead. The lawyer did not confess during his fatal illness for he hoped to recover, and also for shame. Edmund asks St Nicholas if there is no way this soul can be helped, but is told that it lies in Christ's will at Doomsday to decide. This is the closest the vision comes to suggesting that a soul seen by Edmund might not ultimately be saved,[142] but the implication is rather that the lawyer's purgation will last till the Last Judgement. The *Revelation* leaves out Edmund's statement that he pitied the lawyer for the weight of the calamity which weighed him down.

The identity of the people whom Edmund encounters is not readily ascertainable for they are all anonymous, as noted above, p. lxiv. My initial guide to identifications is Salter, one of the first editors of the *Visio*, whose scholarship transformed our historical knowledge of Oxford and Oxfordshire. In this introduction I shall not attempt to discuss all the twenty-seven contemporary characters whom Edmund meets in purgatory and paradise; for some I offer a brief notes in the Commentary. As is to be expected, Edmund encounters many figures in the other world whom he knew or knew of via their associations with Eynsham or Oxford or bishop Hugh of Lincoln.

Many of the important ecclesiastical figures who seem to appear in the vision are persons with whom Hugh of Lincoln had an active

---

[142] There is no warrant for understanding that this or other figures met by Edmund are believed to be in hell, as does Kreutzer in *VEME*, p. 46, notes 41 and 42. Matsuda, *Death and Purgatory*, p. 51, rightly observes of this passage that, as 'in the *Visio Tnugdali*, the apparent denial of any assurance of salvation to those souls who died with a grave sin is a didactic device intended to warn against excessive hope in post-mortem purgation and, as here, to bring home the importance of alms and works of charity performed before death. The lack of assurance does not indicate that the place is hell.'

engagement. This, one might say, is not surprising, given his role as bishop of the largest diocese in England. However, Edmund's vision of the other world appears to be closely connected with Hugh's interests and activities. This is the case irrespective of whether Edmund is to be identified with the visionary clerk in *MVSH*; if he were, the case would naturally be the stronger. But Hugh of Lincoln's interest in Eynsham and *vice versa* would still be a significant factor in the vision even if this identification were false, for, as we have seen above (p. xxxvi), Eynsham was an *Eigenkloster* of the bishop of Lincoln. Moreover, at the time of the vision the abbacy of Eynsham was vacant, for two and a half years, 1195–7, and Hugh was therefore, as it were, *in loco abbatis* during this period. Hugh therefore had good opportunity to know Adam the sub-prior, and the visionary Edmund at the time of his vision, nineteen months before he chose Adam as his personal chaplain.

In chapter 27 Salter identifies the rector of a religious house that Edmund knows well as abbot Godfrey of Eynsham, who served as abbot for 44 years. Godfrey is found in the first field of purgatory, suffering for his nepotism and negligent care of his flock. He is pained on account of the wickedness of those at Eynsham whom he did not reprove, and names for Edmund four members of the house in particular whom he advises to repent lest they be damned. (In accordance with Edmund and Adam's strict policy, the names are not given.) Among the sins of the brothers is sodomy. We can see why it preys upon Edmund when what he considers the sin that cannot be named is rife in his own community. In their discussion, we learn that there were members of Eynsham abbey who were *accendyd by zele of rightwysnes and feruor of relygyon, and dyd also grete labur and dylygens that, alle inordinate fauors putte a-syde, the puryte and honeste of her ordre myght be kepte* (1601–4), but Godfrey had not supported them and whatever reforms these few had achieved had not been thanks to the abbot's encouragement. Salter supposes that Edmund has in mind Thomas the prior and his brother Adam, the sub-prior. Apart from the anonymity, this is certainly plain speaking. It shows Edmund's zeal for the reform of ecclesiastical corruption, a zeal that is recurrently displayed in the vision. This was the burden of the voice that the clerk/Edmund(?) had heard in 1194, and which directed him to Hugh of Lincoln, where he saw the vision of the Christ child. Edmund repeatedly stresses the need to improve church discipline. The evils of prelates also crop up in earlier other-world visions seen by monks, such as the monk of Rheims, recounted by Ansellus Scholasticus. The lechery of ecclesiastics, the appointment of unfit clerics, the farming of benefices—these are concerns found in both Edmund's vision and in the audition of the voice which prompts the clerk to visit Hugh, and these were issues that Hugh did take action on. 'He was deeply concerned for the reform of clerical morals and for the edification and instruction of his clergy, both in his cathedral and throughout his diocese.'[143] At the monastic level, chapter 31 is devoted to the very severe pains assigned to venial sins committed by religious, such as immoderate laughter, speaking idle words, and wandering out of the cloister. Doubtless, Edmund's fifteen-month illness, which prevented his full participation in his chosen monastic life, made his perfectionist's anxieties the greater.

In the first place of purgatory Edmund finds also a woman recluse (ch. 28), but gives no reason for her presence there, as she passes lightly and swiftly on her journey to paradise; an Englishman (ch. 29) who was a bishop abroad (not conclusively identified), punished for his vicious living in his youth; a poor man's wife who was rancorous to those who offended her (ch. 30); and a young knight who broke his vow to go the Holy Land (ch. 32), a vow he took for vainglory to please his lord: every night he has to travel a little further on his pilgrimage, and at every dawn wicked spirits drag him back to purgatory. If we identify Edmund as Adam's brother and the visionary clerk, it would strengthen his involvement with this anonymous knight, for then we know from *MVSH*, 5.3, that their father had died on pilgrimage to the Holy Land. The clerk had been

---

[143] H. E. J. Cowdray, 'Hugh of Avalon, Carthusian and Bishop', in *De Cella in Seculum*, ed. Michael G. Sargent (Cambridge, 1989), pp. 41–57, at p. 52. Antonia Gransden, *Historical Writing in England c.550 to c.1307* (London, 1974), pp. 314–15, points out that Adam's account in *MVSH* describes Hugh's assiduity 'in reforming the morals of his clergy, and in the choice of clergy for the benefices in his gift', and that Hugh 'refused to promote unsuitable candidates to prebends or livings, even if backed by the king'; see *MVSH* vol. 1, pp. 113–15, 119–20 and vol. 2, pp. 95–97, 131. Hugh also undertook diocesan visitations: 'Following the provincial lead of Archbishop Richard of Canterbury (1174–84) and his immediate successors Baldwin (1185–90) and Hubert Walter (1193–1205), Hugh seems to have been among the first to conduct a systematic visitation of monastic houses': David M. Smith, 'Hugh's Administration of the Diocese of Lincoln', in *St Hugh of Lincoln*, ed. Henry Mayr-Harting (Oxford, 1987), p. 33. Of contemporary bishops, Bartholomew of Exeter is also reputed to have undertaken diocesan visitations, a practice not well established in England until later in the thirteenth century: see C. R. Cheney, *From Becket to Langton: English Church Government 1170–1213* (Manchester, 1956), p. 141.

bewailing the memory of his father when the voice spoke which sent him to Hugh. It is hard to believe that such a personal loss would not have played a part in Edmund's strictures on broken vows of pilgrimage to Jerusalem. The clerk also prophesied the recovery of the Holy City. Edmund also meets here another knight (ch. 33) who delighted in his hawks slaying little birds—he did not know it was a sin. His hand is torn by the beak and claws of a bird like a sparrowhawk.

In the second place of purgatory Edmund meets a number of ecclesiastics, firstly, three bishops (ch. 35). Of these, one seems to be Hugh Pudsey (du Puiset), bishop of Durham, earl-palatine of Durham and earl of Northumberland, who is accused of sitting among secular judges and being a violent oppressor against right-eousness, and another, Joscelin, bishop of Salisbury, punished for unchastity, though he later became a monk, which helped him towards salvation. He was the father of Reginald of Bath, of whom more later. The third bishop is as yet unidentified (see Commentary 1897). All three are suffering in purgatory for *negligens of her office, delectacion of worldly worschippe* (1910–1), and failing to correct those in their charge. This is a recurrent attack, found also in chapter 36, which certainly deals with Baldwin, archbishop of Canterbury. His early career, as a Cistercian monk and abbot of Ford, seems to have saved him from a worse fate, which his dealings as archbishop justified. The vision constantly reinforces the benefits of the monastic life. Baldwin's famous quarrel with the monks of Canter-bury, over his plan to found a new college of secular priests either at Hackington, near Canterbury, or at Lambeth, is probably hinted at by Edmund saying that Baldwin studied *to troble hem the whiche he knew were agenste his promoting of the byshoprye and dignite that he had* (1955–6). However, he was helped in purgatory by Thomas Becket, *home he had gotyn to him there a special patron and helper, be-cause when he went to the Holy Londe a pilgrymage in his lyfe-tyme, he hordende there an hospitalle for pilgrimmys and intytylde hit in the name of Sente Thomas, to the gret sokyr and conforte of Crystyn pylgryms* (1993–8). His pilgrimage there also helped him greatly. Baldwin died at Acre in 1190, doubtless another reminder of Edmund's father's death on such a pilgrimage. The language of the attack here on unchaste priests handling the mass is also very close to the words of the voice that the clerk reported to Hugh two and half years before Edmund's vision of the other world, as recorded by Adam some dozen years later in *MVSH* 5.3.[144] Hugh of Lincoln had taken an active part in trying to sort out Baldwin's problems and he was doubtless gratified to learn from Edmund's vision that the former archbishop was progressing well, if painfully, in purgatory.

Edmund finds it impossible to describe all the pains of all the sinners whom he saw and knew, and all the torments suffered by all the different kinds of sinners. Who can tell all this, he says, when *they þat were good relygyus men sofred ful sore and greuys peynys only by-cause they delyted and toke a plesure of the feyernes of her handys and longe fingers?* (2037–9). So, with Edmund, I skip over the poisoners, and women who forsook their babies or aborted them; usurers; and apostates returning to the world like a dog to its vomit. Throughout the vision Edmund evinces a ready sympathy for some of those he meets as they suffer their passage through purgatory, both those he knows and those he does not. However harshly he condemns the sins, he is quick to show concern for many of the sinners. Thus, when he encounters Godfrey, who greets him with gentle voice, Edmund responds, despite all Godfrey's reputed failings, *with compassyon of herte* (1521), *conpacienti affectu*. Edmund has a good Christian's concern for the underdog. The harshest torments and criticisms are for mighty prelates who abuse their power and neglect the cure of souls in their charge, but the drunken goldsmith and the prostitute are saved by their devotion to their favourite saints, and by their humility. Edmund is clearly no supporter of the death sentence for common theft, and thieves who are repentant are (rather charmingly) *with a special certen worschipfulnes put to ful softe and esy peynys* (2048–9).

In chapter 41, Edmund sees Henry II sitting on a horse which breathes black flames. The king is fully clad in white-hot armour; spikes on his saddle pierce his bowels, for murders and adultery; he is tormented for killing and maiming those who slew his deer, *whiche by the law of kinde ought to be slayne to euery man* (2130–1); and, alas for all kings and governors, Henry is suffering for oppressing the people with undue taxes. He is relieved and eased only by the prayers of religious men, to whom in his life *he was full benyuolent oftyn-tymes* (2147–8). Henry's founding of the first Carthusian house in England at Witham, Somerset, and his love of Hugh of Lincoln, whom he originally invited from the Grande Charteuse to take

---

[144] See Commentary 1974–80.

charge at Witham, inevitably come to mind here. It was at Eynsham that Henry II presided over the meeting at which Hugh was elected bishop of Lincoln (see Commentary, Chapter 41).

In chapter 42 we meet Reginald, bishop of Bath and Wells, who is credited with performing miracles after his death even though his soul is in purgatory. He had offended by negligence of his office, but had always punished his faults by wearing a hair shirt and by *dyuers chastmentys and ofte wepyngs* (2168). Reginald was one of the delegation sent by Henry II to the Grande Chartreuse to secure the appointment of Hugh to Witham, which was in Reginald's diocese—so this is another way in which the vision connects to Hugh's life. Edmund meets also an abbess in the second place of purgatory, who is most likely Agnes of Godstow, recently deceased (chapter 44). She has messages for Edmund to convey to her natural sisters, who were nuns under her care. She confirms that she has been greatly assisted by the masses and prayers that her nuns have had said for her by certain religious persons.[145] She had tended two leprous nuns with great care. Others in the nunnery, she says, *lothyd alle-moste to see or vysyte hem or to toche hem, but to me, me thoughte and semyd full swete to haue and opteyne hem yn my lappe or holde hem in my harmys, and forthermore alsoo to wesse hem in bathys, and also to wype her sores wyth my sleuys* (2348–52). Readers of Adam's later *MVSH*, 4.3, will recall how he recounts that Hugh used to wash and dry the feet of lepers and kiss them affectionately, while Adam confesses that it made him shudder not only to touch but even to see their swollen, livid, and deformed faces. Abbess Agnes's ministrations are tender and loving, but do not demonstrate that extreme of pious enthusiasm more frequently found in the thirteenth century (see Commentary 2343–52). Edmund learns that the Godstow lepers' sufferings crowned them with a martyrdom which admitted them straight into the company of the Lamb.

PARADISE

The manuscript evidence indicates that Adam concluded the first version of the *Visio* with chapter 48, the end of the discussion of purgatory,[146] and that the ten chapters on those already saved were

---

[145] As Bynum puts it, the Revelation 'is, among other things, propaganda for prayers for the dead. It leaves the impression that everyone the monk meets in the afterlife is able to work his or her way toward reward'; see *The Resurrection of the Body*, p. 290, note 38.

[146] For the B text reading of the end of cap. 48, complete with concluding doxology, see Thurston, p. 307, or Salter, 2.281.

added subsequently in the revised B version. Thereafter he once more revised the whole text as the C version, the one translated as the *Revelation*.

Edmund passes beyond the places of purgatorial pains into the field of paradise, the Earthly Paradise (chapters 49–54). The *Revelation* uses the word 'paradise' 22 ×; the *Visio* 4 × (S adds the word 4 × more in the *tituli*, including *paradisum terrestrem* once (S1339–40) in a heading omitted from the *Revelation*). Edmund meets four religious in the field of paradise: another abbess (presumably Edith II of Godstow), whom Edmund knew when he was a child, and who has just completed fourteen years in purgatory; a prior dead three years whom Edmund knew from his early years, and a young monk of his, of whom Edmund had heard, though he had never previously seen him in life. The fourth is a priest who saved many by his preaching and good example.

More remarkably, in chapter 54 Edmund shows how further on *owre Lordys Passion was representyd and shewyd to the sowlys that were in paradise* (2738–9): *crucis Christi misterium adorabatur, uelut presencialiter in carne dominica passio celebrabatur* ('the mystery of Christ's cross was adored, the Lord's Passion celebrated as if present in the flesh'), or as the *Revelation* puts it, *the holy crosse of Crystys Passyon was presented and schewed to hem . . . as oure Lorde had be present in Hys body* (2744–6). Christ's body is shown in all its bloody pain, but Mary was *not now in heuynes and mornyng, but right gladsum and ioyng* (2756–7) at this *spectaculum* (translated as *vysyon*). I know of no other other-world vision in which the souls in paradise see the Passion *representyd and schewde in a vysyon* (2781–2) (*ymaginaliter representare*). It is a fitting part of the climax for Edmund, whose first vision that we know of was probably of the Christ child in the Host, and who had a preliminary vision/hallucination of drinking a few drops of Christ's blood just before his major vision on Good Friday and Easter Saturday. When Thomas, the prior of Eynsham at the time of Edmund's vision, later says he has no more doubt about the truth of the vision than of the Crucifixion of our Lord (see above, p. xxxv), he must also have remembered Edmund's account of this spectacle of the Crucifixion beheld by the souls in paradise.

After this, in chapter 55, St Nicholas leads Edmund to a gate in a crystal wall. A cross rises and falls within the gate, now admitting, now debarring the many souls who seek entry. As St Nicholas leads Edmund in by the hand, the cross descends and separates them. St Nicholas enters, Edmund is left outside. Nicholas bids Edmund have certain faith in Christ; his hope and trust return, the cross lifts, and Edmund enters too. Beyond the wall is a brilliant light, which sharpens and fits one's power of sight to see it, much as the light in Dante's *Paradiso* strengthens his sight. On the far side of the wall, souls ascend stairs, without labour or difficulty, to meet and offer thanks to Christ *yn lykenes of man*, seated aloft on a throne. Edmund realizes that this is not the *hye heuyn of heuyns* where angels and the souls of the righteous *ioyin yn the seyghte of God, seyng Hym yn Hys mageste as He ys* (2858–9). Souls ascend with ease from the top of the wall to *the hey heuin* (2857, 2862), but no living creature may. Edmund is nonetheless filled with unspeakable joy.

In chapter 56 St Nicholas rehearses what Edmund has seen, in fulfilment of his prayer six weeks before for a vision of the other world. He has seen what is possible for him to see: *the perels of hem that offendyn and erryn; the peynys of synners; the reste also of hem þat haue done her purgacion; the desyrys of hem that be goyng to heuynward and the ioys of hem that now byn cumme to the courte of heuyn; and also the ioy of Crystis reynynge* (2881–5). Here the *Revelation* omits (presumably accidentally) from this list the mystery of our Lord's Passion, duly noted in the Latin in chronological order before the joy of Christ's reigning. The perils and pains clearly signify purgatory, though it is not named here; the rest and quiet of those who have been purged refers to the Earthly Paradise, the fair field full of flowers wherein he meets the abbess, prior, monk, and priest. It is here that the Passion is represented. The desires of them that are going heavenward must refer to the crowds assembling to enter the gate in the wall, and within the wall is the court of heaven (*celi curia*) where Christ reigns. As is appropriate, the final vision of God in majesty is withheld until after Edmund's real death. For now St Nicholas tells him, *thow muste go ageyne to they-selfe, and to thyne, and to the worldys feyghtyng* (2885–6). If Edmund continues in the dread of God, he will return to perceive the joys he has seen, *and mekyl more*.

In chapter 57 a great pealing of bells breaks out; Edmund's mind is *suspendyd to here hyt* (*animo suspensus*). And then he finds himself coming round, in his bed, thinking it is still just after Matins early on Good Friday morning, but he is told that it is Saturday evening, Easter Eve.[147] His other-world journey has been virtually coterminous with

---

[147] Russell, *A History of Heaven*, p. 106, erroneously states that Edmund's 'vision lasted from Maundy Thursday to Easter Monday'.

Christ's Harrowing of Hell, like Dante's later traverse of hell and purgatory. The *Visio Anselli* and Vision of Orm had also been connected with Easter,[148] and in the BL, MS Additional 34,193 text of the *Vision of William of Stranton* William descends into St Patrick's Purgatory on Easter Day;[149] it was a liturgically obvious choice of season for such a journey. Edmund had imagined himself being disciplined (at about the time of Christ's flagellation) and tasting the blood from Christ's wounds on the Cross; his descent into unconsciousness and the visionary tour of purgatory parallel Christ's death and Harrowing of Hell; he witnesses the Crucifixion represented in paradise; and he sees Christ enthroned as man.[150] The bell which rings to compline in Eynsham marks the beginning of Easter, the first time the bell, as opposed to a slab of wood (*tabula*), has been struck since the beginning of Lent. It subsequently melds in Edmund's mind with the bells he heard ringing in paradise which *betokynde the same solennyte of Jestir* (2984–5). Edmund comes round, healed, at the beginning of the season of the Resurrection, and rises without help from his bed to go to Matins on Easter Sunday: *whan the bretheren rose to matens, he went with them, and as he had rose with our Lorde, the which sum-tyme that same howre rose fro deth vnto lyfe* (370–2). At the service he witnesses the performance of the *Visitatio Sepulchri*. Thereafter, the ringing of bells always reminds Edmund of *the ful swete pele and melody the whyche he herde when he was amonge the blessyd sowlys yn paradyse* (2978–80). In other words, the whole of Edmund's visionary experience and of its recounting in the *Visio* is thus framed by and consciously modelled on the liturgical pattern and spiritual significance of Easter.

A note of interpretative caution is perhaps in order here. Whereas some earlier critical accounts (say, pre-1960) of the transmission of vision texts may have underestimated the contribution of the writer, and overestimated the degree of direct reportage of the visionary's oral account, there is now perhaps a tendency to go too far the other way and to attribute too much to the efforts of the writer and to

---

[148] The descent *ad inferorum regionem*, led by Christ, in the other-world vision of the monk of Saint-Rémi of Rheims, told by Ansellus Scholasticus, took place before the night office on Palm Sunday: *Namque completa tristicia dominice passionis, cum gaudia tractaremus resurrectionis, ante officium nocturnale . . .* (Jean Leclercq, 'Une redaction en prose de la "Visio Anselli" dans un manuscrit de Subiaco', *Benedictina*, 16 (1969), 188–95, p. 192, lines 11–12).

[149] See *SPP*, pp. lxxiv–lxxv.

[150] For further discussion of the liturgical significance of the timing of Edmund's vision, see Carozzi, pp. 622–3, Ehlen in *VEME*, pp. 287–9, and Penkett, 'Sinners and the Community of Saints', pp. 49–59.

diminish too drastically the responsibility of the real-life visionary. For instance, when discussing the shaping of the *Visio* in terms of the correlation between the liturgical season of Easter and the pattern of Edmund's collapse, vision, and recovery, just noted, or when observing the moments in which the *Visio* includes comment on the nature of visionary experience, whether spiritual, intellectual, or experiential, Ehlen[151] attributes such liturgical and theoretical aware-ness to the redactor only rather than to the visionary also, and regards the *persona* of the visionary as a construct. Granted, the *way* the visionary is presented is the result of the shaping activity of Adam as writer, but this does *not* mean that the person Edmund, however emotionally extravagant he may have been, was not himself also intellectually aware of these same issues. It seems to me inconceivable that, as a devout member of a Benedictine community at the end of the twelfth century, he should be ignorant of them, irrespective of the fact that Edmund and Adam's production of the text was a collaborative venture, and allowing that the actual committal to writing and shaping of the presentation was Adam's responsibility. It is clear that where the visionary is an illiterate peasant, like Gottschalk or Thurkill, or a layman, like Owein or Tundale, then the ecclesiastical redactor is almost bound to have the principal impact on the representation of the vision. But in this case, Edmund is a regular religious, known intimately to the author of his vision, indeed living in the same monastery, so we might expect Edmund's contribution to and understanding of the full import of the written account to be the greater.

The Vision of the monk of Eynsham is one of the most extensive accounts we have among medieval visions of the other world; Morgan (p. 123) says, 'in its complexity and level of detail it is unsurpassed'; in length it is rivalled only by the *Visiones Georgii* (1353). Brian Patrick McGuire has said that the content of the *Visio* 'is perhaps less exciting in literary terms'[152] than the *Visio Tnugdali* or the *Tractatus de Purgatorio Sancti Patricii*. To be sure, it spends less energy on describing and organizing the topography of the other world and plotting Edmund's journey through it, and unlike these

---

[151] In *VEME*, pp. 286–98. My comments are not meant to detract from the excellence of Ehlen's essay, which is indispensable for an understanding of the *Visio*.

[152] Brian Patrick McGuire, 'Purgatory, the Communion of the Saints, and Medieval Change', *Viator*, 20 (1989), 61–84, at p. 80.

visions it is not imbued with the excitement of knightly adventure and the frissons of their secular (anti-?)heroes' embroilment in the purgatorial punishments. Edmund does not suffer himself in the pains of purgatory as do Owein, Tnugdal, Gottschalk, and Thurkill. But, as McGuire notes, the *Visio* is full of rich detail reflecting the average content of monastic life; it is used to praise one faction of the monks for fighting laxity, to remind the members of the monastic community of their belonging to an unseen world, and to reinforce the conviction that 'there was a constant traffic of souls in both directions'.[153] In Edmund's day, the abbey at Eynsham saw the traffic of many of the leading figures of church and state passing through as well, and though such personalities may have had less appeal for Machlinia's readership, the printing of the Middle English translation nearly three hundred years after Adam wrote indicates that the *Visio*'s spiritual intentions were still immediately pertinent, and therefore translator and publisher thought it should be made accessible for a lay audience. Another five hundred years on and Eynsham abbey has long been reduced to undulations in a sheep field, but the *Visio* and the *Revelation* will now reward readers who want to learn more of the range of religious experiences and life in the late twelfth century, from those of a goldsmith with drink problems in Osney to an archbishop with ecclesiastical problems in Canterbury. Apart from the impaling of Henry II, there is nothing much here about secular politics, as there had been in earlier visions of the other world, especially Carolingian texts, but there is also much about church and monastic politics. Principally, we find here a fascinating range of historical figures imagined speaking in confessional mode about their inner lives. Edmund's vision of the other world reveals for us, after all, other visions of this world.

NOTES ON THE PRESENTATION OF THE TEXTS

The Middle English translation, *The Revelation of the Monk of Eynsham*, is presented in parallel with an edition of the manuscript copy of the *Visio monachi de Eynsham* which is closest to that used by the translator.

[153] Ibid., p. 81.

In both texts, abbreviations have been silently expanded; punctuation, sentence division, and paragraphing are editorial; missing letters are enclosed in diamond brackets; emendations are enclosed in square brackets, though a dagger at the end of a word indicates an emendation which drops one or more letters. Original readings for all emended forms are given in the apparatus. Where one text is not running, the page is left blank.

The *Visio* is edited from S, Bodleian Library, MS Selden Supra 66. Tironian *et* has been printed as *&*, and I have preserved the *u/v* distinction but not the use of long *i/j* as the second or last *i* in a sequence. Marginal *tituli* or rubrics are printed as chapter or section headings in bold. Chapter numbers have been supplied to match those in the *Revelation*; to maintain the parallel numeration, the chapter omitted from the translation has been numbered [XIII A], following Salter. In the apparatus, the reading following the lemma is S, unless otherwise stated; selected readings from other C text manuscripts BdMT are supplied when S is in error or questionable (see above, p. xxxiii).

The *Revelation* is edited from L, the copy in the British Library. Readings which differ in the Bodleian Library copy, O, are listed in Appendix 1, and incorporated in the text as appropriate. For clarity's sake, I have regularized the use of points before and after roman numerals, which is inconsistent in LO. Capitalization, letter-spacing, which is not always regular in the incunable, and word-division are also editorial: e.g. *a s, ho pyng, afaste,* and *assone* are printed *as, hopyng, a faste,* and *as sone*; single lexical units originally presented as separate words are hyphenated, e.g. *a nothir* and *alto toryn* are printed *a-nothir* and *al to-toryn*, but are not hyphenated when found split at the end of a line, whether or not the text supplies hyphenation: Machlinia sometimes uses a double slanting hyphen, sometimes not. 7-shaped ampersand is printed *and*; *y* used for thorn is printed *þ*; *yᵗ* is printed *þat*, *wᵗ* is printed *with*. *ȝ* used for final [s] or initial [z] is printed *z*; *ȝ* used for yogh is retained as such. Nasal suspensions have been silently expanded, where possible in accordance with the same or similar words written out in full, e.g. *īmoderate* has been printed as *inmoderate* 1772 on the model of the same spelling in full at 172. I have endeavoured to note occasions where the compositor has inadvertently substituted *u* for *n* and *vice versa*; these do not appear to be turned letters, for *u* has a forward stroke on the second ascender which is not usually confusable with turned *n*, though the type is not so regular that discrimination is always readily possible. I have printed Latin quotations in the *Revelation* in italics only when the text signals them as quotations. In the apparatus, the reading following the lemma is L, unless otherwise stated.

VISIO MONACHI DE EYNSHAM
AND
THE REVELATION OF
THE MONK OF EYNSHAM

Incipit prefacio de susequenti uisione que contigit apud Eynesham tempore regis Ricardi primi. Anno Domini M.ˡᵒ C.ᵐᵒ iiij.ˣˣᵒ xvi.ᵗᵒ.

Usu notissimum habetur quod, diem sole post tenebras noccium reportante, paulatim vmbrarum densitas lumine succedente atteritur, 5 donec pleno fulgore facies terre et rerum forme illustrentur, & sic uideri incipiant que uisum penitus latuerant; uisa eciam certa agnicione comprehendantur, que in luce dubia uideri utcunque, sed discerni cercius nequibant. Totus autem mundus inuoluitur tenebris, in aliis tanquam in profunda nocte funditus caligans, in 10 aliis uelut in crepusculo dubie uidens. Aderit post hec ueri manifestacio diei, cum scilicet in regno Patris eorum gaudebunt omnes electi, beata immortalitate felices, solem iusticie perpetuo cernentes. Aurora huius diei est resurreccionis vniuersorum & iudicii tempus, quo uere diuiditur lux a tenebris, iusti videlicet ab impiis. Tunc nox 15 in diem commutabitur, ut, qui modo fidei merito et deuocionis cognoscimur a Deo, dum in eum credimus & eum non uidentes, iam cognoscamus eum sicuti cogniti sumus ab eo, ipsum facie ad faciem contemplantes. Uti uero de die mundi premisimus, quod oculis iugiter cernimus, quia ipso iam iam terris imminente noctis umbra 20 tenuatur & uicine lucis candor magis ac magis aperitur, sic nimirum eterne uicinitas diei, mundi scilicet fine quasi obscurissime noctis termino instante, lucis sue graciam euidencius aperire ubique pene terrarum cepit, & fiunt passim mire uite future reuelaciones; ut ea que patres per fidem cernebant in speculo & in enigmate, nunc 25 manifesta reuelacione, ab aliis quidem uideantur, & audita per illos

qui uiderunt ab aliis cercius agnoscantur; | pleraque etiam huic seculo inaudita & quasi ab oculis in hac mortalitate degencium penitus occulta ipsis reuelacionibus producuntur in lucem, et fiunt certa que dubia erant, & que prorsus latuerant claris uisibus exponuntur. 30 Legimus sane multas temporibus patrum de statu seculi uenturi factas reuelaciones, & ab ipsis patribus successure posteritatis noticie stili beneficio transmissas. Legimus quoque nonnullas huiusmodi manifestaciones, que nostris diebus et reuelate sunt diuersis, & per fideles excepte scriptoque commandate personas, quibus & fides non 35 incertis roboretur argumentis, animetur spes, & caritas inflammetur; maxime autem inicium sapientie, scilicet timor Domini, adquiratur:

cautela quoque augeatur, que in uite presentis lubrico gressum dirigit & a lapsu protegit tendencium ad patriam superne hereditatis. Videtur Dominus secundum quod peciit ab Abraham diues in inferno sepultus, ut in omnibus & suis prospiciat amicis ad salutem et inimicis omnem auferat excusacionem, non eo solum contentum esse quod Moysen & prophetas, apostolos eciam et uiros apostolica sanctitate illustres ad preparanda mortalium & excitanda torpencium corda seculo concessit, nisi eciam ea que apud inferos sunt viuentibus in hoc mundo innotescat, queque eciam in locis penalibus perferant, qui hic maculas peccaminum minus diluerunt, et quanta felicitate perfruantur, qui labe uiciorum discussa, superni aditum regni in regione amenitatis & lucis, in loco quietis & suauitatis, beata expectacione prestolantur. De hiis enim que super celos sunt, ubi exultant iusti in conspectu Dei, sicut multa & ineffabilia bona credere omnibus fidelibus & plerisque contemplari permissum est; sic de ipsis aliquid pre excellencia rerum digne referre omni creature que in terris consistit impossibile est. Igitur ut magnis | uiris, quibus & sanctitatis merito & auctoritatis eorum priuiligio paruitas mea et condicionis ordine & deuocionis affectu usquequaque addicta habetur, pro uiribus satisfaciam, qui id oneris michi imperito ineuitabili prescriptu obedientie imponunt, quedam ualde preclara, &, ut nonnullorum habet estimacio, ad tocius catholice matris ecclesie consolacionem & edificacionem atque instruccionem multorum, si fideliter audiantur, efficacissima, que in quodam notissimo michi monasterio contigisse anno presenti, qui est uerbi incarnati annus millesimus centesimus nonagesimus sextus, certissime agnoui, utpote quibus interfui & que fratri cuidam in uisione ostensa sunt, ex parte scribere disposui, et hinc quidem summis votis fidelium edificacionem quos presenti relacione letificandos spero exoptans, hinc eciam serui inertis & pigri notam & penam euitare satagens; hanc namque imminere michi pertimescerem, si conseruos tante edificacionis stipe ingrato silencio fraudarem. De ueritate autem dicendorum fidelium nemo dubitare maluerit, quia, sciens perdendos a Domino omnes qui loquuntur mendacium, magis silerem funditus, quam quicquam obnoxium mendaciis scriptitando, tot ipse primo menciens redderem falsiloquos, quot fore contingeret scripti nostri narratores.

Explicit prologus. Incipit narracio.

¶**The prologe of this reuelacion.**   [a]2^r
L.205^r
O2^r

The reuelacion that foloweth here in this boke tretyth how a certeyn
deuowt person, the wiche was a monke in the abbey of E[in]shamme,
was rapte in spirite by the wille of God and ladde by the hand of
5 Seint Nycholas the space of .ii. days and .ii. nyghtes to see and
knowe the peynys of purgatorye and the iowys of paradyse, and in
what state the sowlis ware that ware in purgatorye and also in
paradyse. Sothly, in bothe this placis he sawe and knewe many
persons, bothe men and women, the whiche he knewe welle before
10 when they lyuyd in thys world, and spake with hem there mowthe to
mowth in bothe the placys as he founde hem, as hit folowth wele
aftir in this boke. This reuelacion was not shewed to hym only for
hym, butte also for the confort and profetyng of all Cristyn pepulle,
that none man shuld dowte or mystruste of anothir life and world,
15 the whiche euery man and woman moste go to, and, lyke as they
deserue here in this world by here lyuyng, so there to be rewardyd.
And as for the trowthe of this reuelacyon, no man nother woman
ought to dowte in any wise, for and a man wele rede and vndirstonde
the begynnyng with the ending, he shalle so largely see hit approuyd
20 in grete myraclis by Almyghty God shewyd vnto the same person
that same tyme, that alle resons and mocions of infydelite, the
whiche risith often-tymes of mannis | sensualite, shalle vtwardly be   [a]2^v
excludyd and quenchid, and gretely shalle cause alle Crysten pepulle   L.205^v
that herith hit to drede God and loue Hym and also to preyse Hym   O2^v
25 in Hys werkys, for seche anothir reuelacion and so opyn, Y trowe,
was neuer shewid in this lond ne in no nothir that we rede of.

¶ **Here endyth this prologge.**

¶ **Here begynne the chapitres of this reuelacyon.**

¶ Howe this monke fyl in-to a sore and greuys sekenes
30 and gaue hym to confession and prayur and compunccion
of teeris   Chapitur I
¶ Howe he laye also prostrate in the chaptur-howse as thaugh
he had ben dedde   ij

---

3 Einshamme] Euishamme   21 mocions] mocyons O

51 the] O, *om.* L   53–6 How] *Capital* O, how L   71 .iii.] +iii. L, iii O

[a]3ᵛ L206ᵛ O3ᵛ

[a]4ʳ L207ʳ O4ʳ

74 xxvi] O, xxv L   93 bisshoppe] bsshoppe   104 deuoutely] deuontely

[I] Qualiter monachus in egritudinem inciderit et qualiter   75
uacauerit confessioni, orationi, & lacrimarum
compunccioni.

In quodam igitur cenobio erat iuuenis quidam nuper ad monasticam
uitam fideli deuocione a seculari uanitate conuersus, qui circa
primordia conuersionis sue uehementer egrotare incipiens, per 80
annum integrum & menses tres graui corporis inualitudine laborans,
cibi et potus abhominaciones ita incurrerat, ut per nouem aliquando
dies, uel eo amplius, nichil preter modicum aque calide perciperet.
Medicorum ei nulla potuit quicquam remedii conferre industria, sed
in contrarium uertebatur quicquid leuaminis causa ei a quolibet 85
homine uidebatur exhibitum. Languebat igitur grabato decumbens,
f. 2ᵛ uiribus corporis plurimum destitutus, nec loco | mouere preualens,
nisi ministrancium labore deuect[us]. Ita tribus mensibus solito
acerbius macerabatur, tamen ex insperato, imminente iam resurreccionis dominice annua sollemnitate, cepit aliquantulum leuius se 90
habere, & uiribus parumper restitutis, baculo innisus per cellam
infirmorum solus deambulare. Interea cum iam adesset nox qua
officium de tradicione Domini sollemni more consueuit celebrari, cui
cene etiam dominice succedit dies, magne deuocionis instinctu ad
maiorem ecclesiam vna cum fratribus qui secum debilitatis gratia in 95
infirmaria pausabant, baculo subuehente, perrexit; ubi conuentus
nocturnales Domino laudes persoluebat; ubi tantum compunccionis,
gratie celestis respectu afflatus, percepit, ut modum excederet sancta
deuocio: vnde nec a fletibus & Dei laudibus a medio noctis usque ad
sextam diei sequentis horam se potuit continere, hinc miseracionum 100
Domini quas humano contulit generi cum gaudio & ueneracione
memor, inde preteritarum negligenciarum & presentis sue imperfec-

88 deuectus] BdT, deuecto SM

¶ Howe this monke came agayne throwe the gate of paradyse   lvi
¶ Of the swete melodye of bellys that he herd in paradyse
and how he came to him-selfe ageyne   lvii
¶ Approfe how this reuelacyon is of God and moste nedys be
115 trewe for the grete myraclys that God shewyd on hym that
same tyme   lviii

¶ **Expliciunt capitula.**

¶ **Here begynnyth a meruelous reuelacion that was schewyd**   [a]4ᵛ
of Almyghty God by Sent Nycholas to a monke of   L207ᵛ
O4ᵛ
120 **E[yn]shamme yn the days of kynge Richard the fyrst and**
the yere of owre Lord .MC. Lxxxxvi.   ¶ **Ca primum**

In a monasterye callyd E[yn]ssham there was a certen yong man
turnyd wyth feythfull deuocyon fro thys worldys vanyte to the lyfe of
a monke, the whiche abowte the begynnyng of hys conuersion fylle
125 yn-to a grete and a greuys sekenes and by the space of .xv. monthys
was sore labouryd with gret febulnes and wekenes of body. Also hys
stomake abhortyd so gretly mete and drynke, that sum-tyme by the
space of .ix. days or more he myght resceyue noo thyng but a lytyl
warme watyr. And what-sum-euer thyng of leche-crafte or fesyke
130 any manne dedde to hym for hys conforte or hys amendement, noo
thyng hym helpyd but al turnyd contrarye. Therfore he lay seke yn
his bedde, gretly destitute of bodely strenght, so that he myght not
moue hymselfe fro one place to anothyr butte by helpe of seruauntes.
Alsoo yn thre the laste monethys of hys sekenesse he was more sorer
135 dyseasyd and feblyd than euer he was before. Neuerthelesse, than
commyng on the feste of Estur, sodenly he beganne sumwhat to
amende yn hys bodely myghtys, and with hys staffe walkyd aboute
the fermorye. Sothly, on thes euyn of Schere Thursdaye, in the
whiche nyght the office and seruice of owre Lord Ihesu Cryste ys
140 tradicion and | Passion was solenly songe wyth grete deuocion, he   [a]5ʳ
wente wyth hys staffe to the chyrche wyth his bretheren, the whiche   L208ʳ
by-cause of sekenesse rested hem also with hym in the fermorie, were   O5ʳ
the couent nyghtly seruice and laudes offerd vppe to owre Lord. And
there, by the respecte of heuynly grace, so grete conpunccion and
145 swetenes he rescyued that hys holy deuocion excedyd mesure.
Wherfore he myght not conteyne hym fro wepyng and laudyng

120 Eynshamme] Euyshamme   122 Eynssham] Euyssham

cionis cum dolore et luctu detrimenta deplorans. Circa sextam vero
ipsius diei horam accersiri ad se fecit duos e fratribus, vnum post
alium, quibus suscipiendi confessiones & penitentibus absolucionem 105
dandi ministerium creditum fuerat, & utrique in quantum possibile
erat omnium culparum & minimarum quarumlibet transgressionum
ordinis siue preceptorum Dei confessionem pure & integre in summa
contricione cordis & lacrimarum effusione fecit, & absolucionem
uehementi desiderio quesitam percepit. Requisitus uero ab vno 110
eorum, quid sibi tam immoderati fletus & luctus occasionem
dedisset, suspicati enim sunt vniuersi, quod se de seculo celerius
migraturum sentiret aliquo modo, respondit se nil tale sentire; immo
curiosius sciscitanti fratri hoc tandem confessus est:

'Sciatis,' inquiens, 'domine, quod nocte transacta tantam in 115
capitulo, ubi simul fuimus, cordis suauitatem & exultacionem
f. 3ʳ percepi spiritus, quod uix meipsum capere pre gaudii | magnitudine
aut ferre ualeo.'

Requisiuit etiam utrum consuetudinis esset, quod ipsa nocte
priores, sacris induti uestibus & albis, disciplinas fratribus darent. 120
Hec ab ipso audiens predictus frater credebat illum ex nimia
inanicione capitis, quam forte inedia simul & langore immoderato
contraxisset, in mentis alienacione talia proferre, licet mirabili
prudencia atque discrecione toto egritudinis sue tempore preditus
fuisset. Quamobrem commendans eum Domino, nil ab eo ulterius 125
inquirendum censuit moxque discessit. Eger autem in Dei laudibus
totum exegit diem. Sequenti nocte, modico prelibato sompno, strato
se excuciens, cum ex more illius temporis pro conuocandis ad
matutinas fratribus tabula percuteretur, iter ad ecclesiam, sicut
pridie fecerat, aggressus est. Qualiter uero in ecclesia tunc se 130
habuerit, uel quando inde discesserit, uerbis illius in sequentibus
pandetur.

God fro mydnyght tyl sex of the belle yn the mornyng, what for
remembryng wyth worshippe and ioye the merceis of owre Lord, the
whiche [He] ha[th] doon for mankynde, and also remembryng wyth
150 sore wepyng hys offencys and synnys doon by-fore-tyme, and the
hurte and the state of hys present imperfeccion. And abowte sex [of]
the belle yn the mornyng he made to be called to hym .ij. of his
bretheren, one aftyr a-nothyr, whiche hadd powr to here confessyons
and gyue to penitentes absolucion, and to them bothe made purely
155 and holy, as mekylle as he cowde, hys confession of al hys synnys and
of the lest offence of hys religion or of the commawndementys of
God, and wyth grete contricion of herte and effusion of terys desired
hys absolucion and had hyt. Than on of hem askyd hym why he
sorowde and wepte so inmoderately, for al they had went þat he
160 schulde fele hym-selfe sone to passe owte of this worlde. Than he
seyde he felte hym-selfe no-thyng so. Sothly, than he tolde to his
brother, þat diligently enquiryde this of hym, and seyde,
    'Sir, ȝe schal vndyrstonde and know that | thys laste night, whenne   [a]5ᵛ
we were to-gedyr in chaptur-howse, Y resceyuyd so grete swetenesse   L208ᵛ
165 of herte and gladnesse of sowle, that onnethis Y myghte hoolde or   O5ᵛ
bere my-selfe.'
    He askyd also and hyt were by the relygion that the priowrs shuld
geue that nyght to the bretheren dyscyplynys in hooly vesture and
aubys. And whenne he herd hym enquyre this, he hadde wente that
170 he had seyd hyt of grete febulnesse of his hedde, or by alyenacion of
hys mynde, the whiche perauenture he hadde falle in by his infirmyte
and inmoderate weping or fastyng, howe-be-hit that he with hym
had meruailous wisdam and discrecion al the tyme of hys sekenesse.
Wherfore he commendyd hym to our Lord, no-thing els enquyring
175 of hym, and so went his weye. The seke brother spendyd al that daye
in laudyng and presyng God, and the next night folowing, after he
hadde slepte a lityll while, rose vp of his bed. And when the chaptur
was ronge, as the tyme requyred, to calle the couent to matens, he
went than to chirche, as he did the daye before. Sothely, how he
180 behauyd hym thenne in the chirche, and whan he went thens, hit
shalle be schewyd in his wordys foloyng.

149 He] O, *om.* L   hath] O, had L   151 of] O, *om.* L

[II] **Qualiter monachus iacuerit in capitulo quasi exanimis tot⟨o⟩ extento corpore.**

Facto autem mane sequentis diei, id est Parasceues, cum fratres ad 135
prime hore solemnia peragenda consurgerent, et ecclesiam adituri
ante capitulum transirent, conspiciunt eum coram sede abbatis, ubi
ueniam petere fratres solent, nudis pedibus iacere, recta tocius
corporis strage, vultu solotenus defixo, quasi ueniam a quolibet
presidente ex more postularet. Quo uiso stupefacti accurrunt; et 140
uolentes eum ammouere, uelut exanimem et sine motu alicuius
menbrorum reperiunt, oculis in profundiora dimersis, & ipsis
luminum sedibus ac naso multo sanguine illitis. Igitur expirasse
iam illum vniuersi proclamant. Pedes quidem habebat frigidissimos,
sed reliquo corpori aliquantulum uidebatur inesse caloris. Motus in 145
eo arteriarum nullus, multo intercurrente more spacio, poterat
dinosci: anelitum tandem, licet perexilem, & precordialem motum
uix ei superesse deprehensum est. Itaque uerticem ipsius, pectus,
f. 3ᵛ manusque ac pedes | frigida diluentes aqua, primo eum corpore toto
uiderunt trementem modice, sed mox quieuit & insensibilis perman- 150
sit. Diuciusque hesitabant quid in re tali faciendum sibi esset, dum
nec penitus exanimari nec meliorari aliquatenus cerneretur. Ad
lectulum uero suum, inito consilio, tandem deferunt eum, adhibitis
custodibus a quibus diligencia peruigili seruaretur.

[III] ⟨D⟩e **figura crucifixi ⟨c⟩ruentata.** 155

Interea fratribus super tali euentu stupentibus, nempe mirantur
talem tamque insolitam egroti consistenciam, & multo plus qualiter
id ei accidisset, uel quemadmodum sine alicuius adminiculo susten-
taminis eo loco, ubi conuentus fuerat, peruenisset, nunciantur alia
que incomparabiliter plus admiranda, sed pauenda, sed ueneranda 160
subtexam. Corporis enim dominici figuram ligno in crucis modum
affixam, que a conuentu annis singulis adorari ipsa die deuotissime &
in ueneracione passionis Christi deosculari consueuerat, sanguine
recenti circa vulneris locum in latere & pede dextro cruentatam non
sine ingenti metu & admiracione audierunt. Secretarii equidem 165
ecclesie ante quadragesimale tempus ipsam crucem a desuper altari
ad terram deposuerant, interque maceriam & altare locatam, sic
usque tunc di[m]iserant. Baculus autem et calciamenta predicti

168 dimiserant] BdT, diuiserant S; dimiserunt *H2, Thurston, & Salter*; omiserant M

¶ Howe he laye prostrate al his body in the chaptur-hows
as he had be dedde.   ¶ Ca ii

On the morow nexte foloyng, that ys Good Fredaye, whenne the
185 couent rose to cum to chirche to seye Prime, as they ede afore the |
chaptur-hous they sawe the same seke brother lye prostrate and bare-   [a]6ʳ
foote before the abbot is sete, hois face was flate to the ground, as   L209ʳ
thaugh he shuld by the ordyr aske mercy of euery presydent. Than the   O6ʳ
bretheren, seyng this, meruelyd and rane thedir, and willing to take
190 hym vp, they founde hym as a man lyfeles without any mocyon of any
membre of his body. Trewly, his yes ware falle doun depe into his
heed, and tho yes and nose of him ware blody or as a manne had ouyr-
leyde hem with mekyl bloode. Wherfore they seyde alle that he was
dede. His feete ware ful coolde but in the rem[n]ande of his body was
195 found a lytyl warmenes. No mouing of his pypys might be knowen
long tyme, and at the last onnethis [h]it was perseyuyd in him a litill
thynne breth and a mouyng of his herte. Thenne they weshid his
heedde, breste, handys, and feete with colde watyr. And than first they
sawe al hys body a lityl to tremyl and quake, but anoon he sesyd and
200 was insensybulle. So, long tyme they musyd and dowtyd what they
might do to hym, whyle they sawe hym not verily dedde, nothyr any-
thing amendyng. At the last, by conselle, they had him to his bedde,
and there to be kepte with grete attendans of kepers.

¶ Of the blody figure of the crosse.   ¶ Ca iii

205 The mene-whyle, the bre[the]ren merueled and wondred on suche a
soden happe and beyng of the seke brother, and more they wondrid
howe hyt | happyd, and yn what wyse, wythowte any helpe, he myhht   [a]6ᵛ
comme thedyr to that place, where the couent was. Sothely, othyr   L209ᵛ
thyngys that now foloyn, the whyche Y schal telle of, wythowte any   O6ᵛ
210 comparsone ben more to be dred, feryd, and worshipte than any-
thyng aboue-seyd. They herde anone aftyr, and that not wythowte
grete meruelle, that the fygure of owre Lordys body affyxed on a
crosse, whyche fygure and crosse ȝerly ys wonte ful deuowtely to be
kyssyd and worshipte of the couent yn remembrance of owre Lordys
215 Passion, was founde fresch bledyng and newe abowte the place of the
grete wounde yn the ryhht syde and also at the ryght foote. Trewly,
afore Lente the sextense of the chyrche had let done the same crosse to

194 remnande] remuande   196 hit] bit   205 bretheren] brehetren

fratris infirmi prope locum ipsum in cumulum admiracionis reperta
sunt.   170

Quid multa? Conueniunt vniuersi fratres in capitulum super hiis
omnibus que acciderant nimis attoniti, & habita deliberacione omnes
& singuli disciplinas cum immensa contricione animi susceperunt,
prosternentesque se in ecclesia septem penitenciales psalmos pro
impetranda diuine propiciacionis clemencia flebiliter decantauerunt. 175
Frater uero sepe nominatus tota die illa cum sequenti nocte & in
crastino fere usque ad solis occasum in eodem quo ceperat permansit
statu. Succos diuersarum specierum uel herbarum ori eius uiolentius
adaperto remedii gracia iniecerunt fratres, sed confestim quasi
f. 4ʳ preclusi essent faucium meatus, quicquid immittebatur | effluebat. 180
Emplastra etiam pectori eius et brachiis frustra alligarunt; acubus
plantas eius scalpentes & pungentes, nichil quod animati hominis
esse uideretur perspicere in eo potuerunt, preter ruborem, qui genas,
& modicum teporem pocius quam calorem, qui reliquum optinebat
corpus. Genarum eciam & faciei color frequenter in liuorem ciner- 185
eum & pallorem conuerti & denuo mirum in modum reuiuiscere &
nitere uidebatur. Cornu quoque pregrandi sed nequ[ic]quam in
aurem eius uehementer bucinari fecerunt.

[IV] **Qualiter monachus ab extasi reuersus est.**

In crastino autem, videlicet die magno sabbati, instante iam hora qua 190
fratres ad collaciones & completorium erant conuenturi, ceperunt
primum cilia oculorum eius paululum agitari & ita marcescere ac si
bullienti aqua essent decocta, & demum croceus quidam humor more
lacrimarum in genas leniter defluebat. Hec uidentes qui aderant,
fratres conuocant, mox eum putantes migraturum. Paulo ante uero 195
labia quoque eius moueri uidimus, compressis tamen faucibus, ac si
predulce quidlibet ori suo illapsum gluciendo insumeret. Post
defluxum autem lacrimarum ut prelibauimus, quemadmodum si
dormiens quis ploret, crebra & minuta imo pectore uisus est
ingeminare suspiria, & post modicum sono uix audibili sed minime 200
intelligibili profundo in gutture uerba quedam uoluere, sed que
proferre nequibat, uidebatur. Redeunte autem sensim spiritu, uox

187 nequicquam] S *correction in smaller hand in margin for* nequaquam

the grownd, and so tyl Good Fredaye they hadd lefte hyt betwyxe the
auter and the walle. And for a more wondyr the staffe and schewys of
220 the same seke brothyr ware fondyn by the same place.

Sothely, than all the brethirne came to-gedyr in-to the chaptur-
hows, gretly astonyd apon these thyngys that befylle, and, auysement
takyn, alle that were there, wyth grete contricion of herte, toke
discyplynys of roddys, and, lyyng prostrate yn the chirche, seyden
225 wepyngly the .vij. salmys of penanse, for-to gete owre Lordys
mercye. Trewly, thys seke brother, all þat daye whiche was Gode
Freday with the nyght folo[w]yng and the nexte day aftyr, all-mooste
tyl the sonne sette, contynewde yn one state. Also the bretheren
wyth strengh of handys opynde hys mowth and caste yn hyt ius[c]ys
230 of dyuers spycys and herbis | for hys releuyng, but anone after h[it]   [a]7^r
wente owte ageyne, what-somme-euer was putte in-to hys mowthe,   L210^r
as thaugh hys throte hadde ben stopped. Emplasters alsoo to his   O7^r
breste and armys they bonde, but alle was vayne. They prickyd with
neldys and scrapyd the solys of hys fete, but no-thyng myght be
235 perceyuyd in hym of a lyuys manne, saue a lityll rednes of chekys
and a litil warmenes of body. The colowre of hys face oftyn-tymes
was chaunged to ashis and ageyne meruaylously the colowre of hys
face was reuyuyd and welle shewyd. Alsoo they made a grete horne
to be blowyn there, but no-thyng hit botyd.

240 ¶ Howe he came ageyn to hym-self on Ȝestur euyn abowte
complen tyme.   Ca iiii

Thenne on the morowe, that ys Estur euyn, and the same owre that
the couent came togedyr to the collacion and to complenne, the briys
of hys ye-lyddys beganne firste a lytil to moue, and so they semyd as
245 they hadde ben sode in boylyng watyr. And atte last there came don
fro hys yes on hys chekys a yelowe humour of watyr in manere of
terys. Thanne they that were wyth hym, seyng thys, called anone for
the bretheren, supposyng that he shuld haue sone passed fro thys
world. They sawe also, a lytyl afore thys tyme, hys lyppys a lytyl to
250 moue, with his chekys compressyd as he had resceyued or swelowde
sum swete | thing fallyn in-to hys mowth, and after that a flowyng   [a]7^v
owte of terys, as hyt is seyd here before. Alsoo he was seyn often and   L210^v
many diuers tymys sykyng alow in his breste as a manne slepyng had   O7^v

219 schewys] e *changed by hand to* o   227 folowyng] fologyng   229 iuscys]
iustys   230 hit] he

hec prima ab ore eius insonuit, quam intelligerent audientes,
'O sancta Maria, O sancta Maria'; et denuo, 'O domina mea,
sancta Maria, O domina mea, sancta Maria.'   205

Qualiter monachus planxit pro amissione gaudii quod in excessu mentis uid⟨erat.⟩

(Verba ipsa dicturus sum sicut ab illo audiuimus nichil adiciendo.)
'O,' inquit, 'domina mea, sancta Maria,' nam hoc frequentissime
repetebat, 'pro quo peccato perdo tam magnum gaudium?' Et 210
iterum, 'Domina mea, sancta Maria, quando recuperabo tam
grande, quod nunc perdo, gaudium?' Hec autem sepius & alia in
hunc modum, quibus immensi nescio cuius gaudii deflebat priua-
f. 4ᵛ cionem, adhuc tamquam in sompnis | & clausis semper oculis
iterabat.   215

Deinde repente, quasi de alto euigilans sompno, excussit caput, &
nimis amare flere, et grauiter decurrentibus lacrimis singultire, ut
plorantes solent, cepit: palmisque complosis & digitis constrictis
subito erexit se & resedit; caputque in manus & super genua
deponens lamentabilem nimis planctum, sicut ceperat, continuare 220
diucius non cessabat. Tunc a quodam assidencium ei fratrum leniter
inquisitus est, quid sibi uellent tam ingentes fletus, uel quomodo se
habere sentiret. Tunc ille paululum quieuit & sic leni demum uoce
respondit: 'Bene, bene,' inquit, '& uere bene hactenus me habui, sed
nunc male & uere male me habeo.' Et iterum uehemencius quam   225
ceperat plangere & plorare adiecit.

Sed quia nimis longum, immo & impossibile omnino est, omnia
que tunc uelut in excessu mentis dixit commemorare & quantum
fleuit exprimere, hiis ad presens omissis, summatim que ab illo
postmodum, iam plene sibi reddito, in summa mentis contricione 230
referri audiuimus, perstringere uel ex parte curabimus.

[V] Qualiter cepit baculum & calciamenta querere & quam deuote crucem adorauerit.

Inter lamentaciones itaque & suspiria, oculos cum ingenti annisu,
compressis & reductis ter uel quater ciliis, demum aperuit & 235

---

206 *Rubric in right-hand margin om. by Thurston and Salter*

wepte. And anone after, as hit semyd, he reuoluyd certeyn wordys
255 benethe in hys throte, butte he myght not speke them owte, saue
onely in a voyce onethys audybille and noo-thyng intelligibille.
Sothely, thanne hys spyrite beganne a lytyll and a lytill to comme
ageyne, and these wordys and voyce he first sownyd that might be
vndyrstond, 'O sancta Maria! O sancta Maria!' And agayne, 'O my
260 Lady, sancta Maria! O my Lady, sancta Maria!' (I shalle seye tho
wordys as I herde theym, noo-thyng addyng therto.) 'O,' he seyde,
'my Lady, sancta Maria!' These wordes often-tymys he rehersed.
'For what synne,' he seyde, 'lese Y soo grete ioye?' And agayne he
seyde, 'My Lady, sancta Maria, when shalle I recouere so grete ioye
265 that Y lese nowe?' These thynges and many other often-tymes he
rehersed, yet as a man ware a-slepe and hys yest† euer closyd, the
whiche I wote not of what grete ioye he sorowde and wepte hym-
selfe departyd fro.

Sothely, aftyrward sodenly, lyke as a man had awaked fro a grete
270 slepe, he lyfte vppe hys hed and ful bitterly beganne to wepe and
with rennyng terys sorofully sobbyd, as wepyng doth, and, ioynyng
his handys and fyngers to-gedur, reysid him-self and sate vp. Then
he put downe his hed in his handys on his kneys, and as he beganne
afore ful lamen|tably to wayle and sorowe, so sesyd not lo[n]g tyme [a]8ʳ
275 aftyr. Thanne one of his bretheren that was with hym askyd what L211ʳ
causyd hym so sore to wepe and howe he felte hym-selfe. Than he O8ʳ
restid a litil while and at the laste softely seyde to hym, 'Wele, wele,
and verely wele Y was hedir-to, but now euyl and verely euyl Y am
and fele my-selfe.' And ageyne more grettur he wepte and sorowd
280 than he dyd before.

And by-cause that hit ys ouer-longe and also as inpossible to
remembre al thyng that he seyde than and how mekil he wepte, we
leue nowe and purpose to drawe shortly to-gedir tho thingys
whiche† we herde hym telle of in gret contricion of herte and of
285 mynde, aftyrward that he was fully comme to hymselfe ageyne.

¶ Howe he sought after his showis and how reuerently he
worshipt the crosse.   [Ca v]

Sothly, amonge his lamentacions and sykynges that he† had, he
asayde with gret strenght onys or twies or thries to opene his yes,

266 yes] O, thyes L   274 long] loug   283 tho] thoes O   284 whiche]
whiche es L, whiche O   288 he (1)] the

utraque manu circumcirca querere baculum in ecclesia relictum
cepit: et non inueniens, 'Requirite,' inquit, 'hic baculum nostrum;
sed & calciamenta nostra prope columpnam sumite & redeamus in
infirmariam.'

Cui cum diceretur a fratribus, 'Iam respice, frater, & uide te in 240
infirmaria & in stratu tuo locatum; baculus tuus & calciamenta en
presto sunt,' ille deinceps, 'O,' inquit, 'quando huc uel quomodo
aduenimus? Nonne modo in ecclesia simul ad matutinas fuimus?'

Audiens uero se iam biduo ibidem quieuisse, & paschalis solemni-
tatis in crastino dominicum diem fore, uehemencius cepit plorare. 245
Et, 'O,' inquit, 'nonne, fratres, crucem dominicam in die Parasceues
adorare debueramus, & adhuc in commune non adorauimus?'

Cumque audiret hoc pridie a fratribus impletum, illum autem
detinente egritudinis impedimento minime interfuisse, 'O,' inquit,
f. 5ʳ 'ego postquam | in ecclesia fui, nulla egritudine laboraui. Sed uadam, 250
queso, crucem Domini nostri adorare.'

Tunc allatam sibi crucem argenteam nimia cum ueneracione
amplexatur, pedes lacrimis & osculis rigat & lambit, et usque ad
tedium quorundam circumastancium gratiarum acciones pro beneficiis innumeris, quorum nonnulla singillatim commemorauit, 255
Redemptori cum Patre & Spiritu Sancto persoluit, & denuo pro se
& vniuersitate sancte & catholice matris ecclesie, immo et pro omni
gradu et condicione fidelium, & attencius pro inimicis, si qui essent,
suis uel amicorum suorum diuisim, oraciones & miras obsecraciones
fecit, tricies uel pluries, ut estimo, super pedes crucifixi capite 260
demisso incumbens, oscula cum fletu imprimens, singultu plerum-
que orantis & gracias referentis uocem interrumpente. Verba que in
illa supplicacione protulit, tanta ratione & sensuum profunditate, sed
& sermonum prompta facilitate referta erant, ut pocius legere scripta,
quam propria fundere uerba uideretur. Quorum tenore predulci & 265
tunc multos excitauit audiencium fletus et semper dum illa recorda-
mur, non minimum compunccionis, deuocionis & dileccionis in
Dominum & fratres nostros, omnes scilicet homines, nobis prestant
incentiuum. De clemencia & longanimitate Redemptoris magnifica
quedam ad singulas oraciunculas interserebat.   270

290 that were closid, and atte last they opened. Thanne he beganne with
bothe his handys al aboute to seche aftyr his staffe, that he lefte in
the chirce. And whanne hyt kowd not be fownde, he seyd, 'Sechith
here owre staffe and take owr showys by the piller and goe we ageyne
in-to the fermorye.' (A fermorye among religious men is called a
295 place or an howse ordende to kepe seke bretheren.)

Thanne, | whanne hit was seyde of some of his bretheren,   [a]8ᵛ
'Behoolde, brother, nowe and see yow in the fermorye and set in   L211ᵛ
your bedde, and loe, yowre staffe and showys byn here redy,' thanne   O8ᵛ
he seyd, 'O, howe came we hedyr and whanne? Were not we ryght
300 nowe in the chirche to-gedyr at matens?'

Thanne his bretheren told hym that he had be there now .ii.
dayes, 'And to-morowe wil be Estur daye.' And whanne he herd this,
more grettyr he beganne to wepe, and seyd, 'O, should we not,
bretheren, haue worshypte on Good Freday owre Lordys crosse?
305 And yet we haue not in comonne worshipte hit.'

Thenne whenne he herd of his bretheren, that owre Lordys crosse
was worshipte the day before, and he might not be-cause of sekenes,
he seyde to hem, 'Aftyr that I came into the chirche Y felte no disese.
But Y praye yow that Y may go to worshipe the crosse.'

310 Thanne ther was brought to hym a crosse of seluyr, the whiche
reuerently he clyppyd to hym, and with cossis and terys watryd the
fete of the crosse. And vnto the tedusnes of some stondyng by, he
thankyd owr Lord and Redemer, and the Fadyr and the Holy
Gooste, for innumerabulle benefetis, of the whyche he rehersyd
315 mony, synglerly for hym-selfe, and vnyuersally for al Holy Chirche,
and also for al degreys and condycyons of alle Crystyn pepulle, and
more attente for hys enmyes, yef any there ware, or for the enmyes of
hys frendys, he made meruailus prayers and obsecracyons. And, as Y
suppose, .xxx. tymes or more, he inclynde hys hede doone to the
320 fete | of the crosse with terys and sobbyng, that often-tymes his   [b]1ʳ
voyce sesid of prayng. Thoes wordys the whiche he made in his   L212ʳ
supplicacions ware so redy and prompte and also repletyd with grete   O9ʳ
reson and hyenesse of witte, that hit semyd rathir he redde hem
thanne seyde hem. Ho-is swete seyng steryd mony than that herd
325 hym to weping and deuocyon, and euer while we remembre them,
causyn vs to haue a grete inwarde cumpunctyon, and also loue and
deuocyon to our Lord, to our bretheren, and to alle men. And of the
grete humylyte and goodnes of oure Redemer, he put betwene certen
grete thingis at euery synguler shorte prayer.

[VI] Qualiter cuidam sibi familiari in parte na⟨r⟩rauit que in extasi uiderat.

Interea signum ad collacionem pulsari cepit, & asportantibus crucem fratribus, que illi allata fuerat, & discedentibus, 'Iam,' inquit, 'uere scio quia Pascha Domini est.' Hoc qua de causa dixerit, postmodum 275 exponetur.

Remorante autem secum quodam fratre sibi in sancto proposito familiariter dilecto, eius callida pie quodammodo circumuentus instancia, cum adhuc in quodam propter illa que uiderat detineretur animi stupore, multa ex hiis que acciderant ei ante ipsam qua raptus 280 fuerat extasim & ex hiis, que spiritu abductus seculo uiderat, passim et, ut ita dixerim, frustatim commemorauit; que omnia frater ille in corde suo conseruabat, & hiis que palam ei accidisse nouerat |
f. 5ᵛ conferens, postmodum occasione ex hiis omnibus sumpta, expressius & plenius ordinem singulorum cum ingenti addidicit diligencia: non 285 tamen vniuersa que uidit in tam prolixo, scilicet duorum dierum & totidem noccium, spacio cuiquam narrare uoluit. Quarundam enim uisionum mencionem inter narrandum fecit, sed mox ceptam subticuit historiam, nec ullis adhuc precibus ad earum explanacionem potuit induci.   290

Sed nec cuncta nos ad presens referre sufficimus, que ipsius relacione perpaucis quidem arbitris, & super quorum deuocione specialem exceperat fiduciam, credita nouimus; neque scripto ullatenus seu lingua, uisionum tam expresse, sicut ipse solet, possumus intimare proprietatem. Inter alia uero sciscitantibus utrum de 295 infirmitate se speraret euadere, uel in corpore diucius uiuere, respondit, 'Satis,' inquiens, 'uiuam, nam & de infirmitate iam satis conualui.'

[VII] Quomodo rogatus est a fratribus ut propter longum ieiunium aliquid manducaret.   300

Post hec cum iam sero esset, multum rogatus ut aliquid sumeret post tam prolixam inediam & ieiunium, 'Apponatur nobis,' inquit, 'parum

330 **¶ Howe he told to one of his bretheren, that he louyd**
famylyarly, suche thingys as he had seyn.   **¶ vi**

The mene-while, as the tyme requyryd, hit range to the collacyon,
and the bretheren the whiche had brought to him the crosse went
thense. And thenne he seyde, 'Nowe Y knowe veryly that this is the
335 holy tyme of Estur.' And for what cause he seyde so, hit shal be
declaryd aftyrward.

Trewely, than bode with hym a certeyn brother that louyd him
famyliarly in holy purpose of relygyon, and mouyd hym sum-what
by a wyse and a meke instans, ȝet beyng holde in a certeyn stupour
340 and wondyr of mynde of suche thinges that he had seyne, bothe of
tho thinges the whiche befyll him afore þat he was rapte, and of tho
thinges that he had seyn | spiritually in anothir world, in al placis. [b]1ᵛ
And as Y haue seyde or may sey, synglerly and particularly he tolde L212ᵛ
and remembrid mony thynges, the whiche the forseid brother that O9ᵛ
345 herde him bare hem al in his herte, telling him also of tho thinges
that he knewe opynly betyd him. And so aftirward bi leyser and gret
dylygens, lernyd and knewe an ordir of euery-thing synglerly, more
opynner and fullyor than he knewe afore. Neuertheles, as for al thing
that he sawe in soo longe space, that is to seye .ii. dayes and .ii.
350 nightys, he wolde not telle to no man. And amonge in hys tellyng he
made mencyon of some visyons, but anon as he had begonne, sesid
the proces of them, and nothir ȝet for any prayur might be inducyd
to telle any more ther-of.

But nethir we at this tyme be sufficient to telle al thinges, the
355 whiche sothely we knewe by his owne seyng, that he had tolde before
to a few persons of wytnesse, on whois deuocyons he had taken a
specyalle trust; nethir in any wise we may or can reuele and shewe so
opynly the proprite of his visions, nether by writing, nether by
telling, as he coude and didde. Also, amonge other thinges he was
360 askid and he hoped to scape his seknes or shulde leue any lenger in
this bodely lyfe. And then he seide, 'I shal leue long ynow and of my
seknes Y am fully recoueryd.'

¶ How he was desired of his bretheren to take sum mete
after so longe a faste.   **¶ Ca vii**

365 Than after this at euyn he was gretly desired to take some mete after
so longe a faste. And | than he seyde, 'Settith before vs the bred and a [b]2ʳ

quod alia uice superfuit mellis & mica panis.' Quo facto, talis cibi
satis perexigua refeccione soluit ieiunium, sicque usque ad noctis
horam qua ad matutinarum laudes festiua Domino exultacione 305
persoluendas conuentus pulsantibus signis cepit preparari, peruigil
in lacrimis & graciarum accione permansit. Surgentibus uero fratribus & ipse cum eis, immo uelut cum Domino ipsa quondam hora
ab inferis resurgente, surrexit, & non sine gratulabunda admiracione
intuencium, ecclesiam nullo usus sustentamine adiit, chorum ingres- 310
sus est, quod fere vndecim elapso mensium spacio ante non fecerat,
ibique in fletus continuacione perstitit, usque dum matutinis percantatis &, sicut in eadem ecclesia illa die annua consuetudine fieri
solet, uisibiliter exhibita representacione dominice resurreccionis et
angelice manifestacionis, mulieres ad sepulcrum alloquentis, ac regis 315
sui peractos iam triumphos ipsis & per ipsas discipulis denunciantis,
ac demum apparicionis ipsius Christi dilectricem suam Mariam in
f. 6ʳ ortolani effigie | appellantis, missis etiam celebratis, sacre commu-
nionis meruit participacione saginari.

[VIII] Qualiter duobus confessor⟨ibus⟩ suis que in uisione   320
uidera⟨t⟩ ex parte narrauit.

Post hec iam plenius, Deo hospite, gratulabundus & alacer in
locutorium a fratribus deducitur, ac religiosa eorundem sollicitudine
impensius conuenitur, obnixius postulatur, ut seriatim que sibi
acciderant, queque uiderat, edificacionis gracia eis intimaret. Multa 325
enim ostensa sibi fuisse multis ex signis vniuersi intellexerunt, qui
uerba eius expergiscentis pridie audierant & lacrimas eius indesinentes uiderant. Quo aliquamdiu cuncta dissimulante, cum illi
uehemencius petendo instarent, tandem illis duobus, quibus confessus fuit in die cene Domini, ut premissum est, singulis eorum 330
separatim, que inferius digesta sunt, interfluentibus iugiter lacrimis
et gemitu crebrius uocem absorbente, narrauit; et quedam quidem
utrique, alia tantum isti, alia tantum illi, non sine pie cuiusdam &
multum circumspecte dispensacionis respectu, insinuauit. Hoc
autem dicendi exordio usus est.   335

litil hony that was lefte the tothir tyme.' And whanne hit was so done,   L213^r
with a ful litil refeccion ther-of, he brake his faste. Ande so he bode   O10^r
waking in prayor and terys til the howre of night that they range to
370 matens. Sothely, whan the bretheren rose to matens, he went with
hem, and as he had rose with our Lorde, the whiche sum-tyme that
same howre rose fro deth vnto lyfe. And so came to chirche, not
withowte ioyful merueling of them that sawe him, and, without
sustentacion or helpe of any-thing, entrid into the quire, and so he
375 did not a .xi. monthis before. And there, in gret deuocyon and terys,
bode and contynewid til matens was doon, and tyl the resurreccion of
our Lorde, the whiche yerely in the same chirche is wont to be shewid
vysybly, and howe the angel apperid and spake to the wemen at the
sepulture of the victoriose resurreccion of ther Kinge, and also that
380 they shulde tel to His disciplys His glorious resurreccion, and at the
laste til our Lord apperyd to his wel-belouyd Mary Mawdelen and
named her Maria in the figure of a gardner, and til the messys ware
doone and had resceyuid the holy comyning of Cristen men.

¶ How he tolde to .ii. of his confessorys a parte of suche
385 thinges as he had seyne.   ¶ Ca viii

After this, nowe that he had resceyued oure Lordys precyous body,
ioyful and light he was, and brought of his bretheren into the colloke,
the which | ys a place where they may speke to-geder, and there   [b]2^v
opynily† they came abowte hym, desiring him to tel hem of seche   L213^v
390 thinges as befylle hym and as he had seyn, for ther goostly edifiyng   O10^v
and comfort. For al they vndyrstode, that herde his wordys the day
before, when he was fully cumme to him-selfe, and sawe his
contynuall weping, that by mony thinges, grete thingis and meruelus
had be shewde him. And whan they with grete instans askid him, he
395 dissymylyd alle thing a lytyl while. At the laste, vnto his .ii.
confessorys, to whom he was confest on Sh[e]re Thursday, as hit
is seyd afore, to hem bothe separatly he told thees thynges, the
whiche here-after be digestyd and wreten, with grete weping and
syking, the whiche sumtyme sesid him of his telling. And sum
400 thinges he told to hem bothe, and sum thinges onely vnto the thoon,
and sum othir only to the tothir, and that not without a consydera-
cion of a certen meke and a good auisement. And this he gon to telle,
as hit nowe folowethe.

    389 opynily] copynily   396 Shere Thursday] shrethursday

[IX] Que fuit peticio mon⟨a⟩chi specialis & de cuiusdam
apparicione sibi facta & cetera.

'Cum,' inquit, 'graui & prolixa, sicut uidistis, tabescerem ualitudine corporis, et ore semper atque animo Dominum benedicerem, &
gracias illi referrem, quod me indignum paterno uerbere castigare   340
dignaretur, postposita omni spe recuperande sanitatis, cepi, quamquam nimis segniter, tamen utcunque sicut sciui & potui, meipsum
preparare, quo cicius & facilius futuri seculi calamitates euaderem, &
perpetue salutis quietem, cum de corpore euocandus essem, inuenire
potuissem. Dumque hec pro posse meo sedule mecum agerem,   345
aliquanto tempore elapso, incidi in talem cogitatum, ut Dominum
petere deberem, quatinus reuelare michi qualicumque modo dignaretur, qualis esset futuri seculi status, que animarum corpore
exemptarum post hanc uitam foret condicio, quatinus hiis ad
liquidum cognitis, plenius dinoscerem quid michi in breui, ut   350
putabatur, ex hac ad illam uitam migraturo sperandum, quidue
metuendum existeret, & per id in timore pariter et amore diuino
f. 6ᵛ proficerem quamdiu in hac ancipiti uita superfuissem. | Continuis
igitur uotis huic nostro desiderio satisfieri cupiebam, & nunc
Dominum, nunc dominam nostram, nunc sanctos quos familiarius   355
diligebam, nunc omnes similiter Dei electos interpellando, affectus
michi inseparabiliter inserti requirebam effectum; cum, ecce, quadam
nocte, imminente iam quadragesime inicio, quam proxime transegi-
mus, michi, quod rarissime ualebam, paululum dormienti assistere
uisa est quedam uenerabilis omnino persona, & ita effari: 360
'"O," inquit, "fili, multa tibi est precandi deuocio, magna
intencionis tue perseuerancia, nec poterit apud clemenciam Redemptoris inefficax esse tam pius tamque continuus oracionis tue conatus.
Uerumtamen amodo animequior esto & oracioni deuotus insiste; tibi
etiam oracionum suffragia a religiosis quibusque personis attencius   365
exquire. Noueris proculdubio quod hec agens celerem pie peticionis
consequeris effectum."

'Nominatim etiam expressit quarundam uocabula et officia personarum,
'"Multum," inquiens, "tibi scias profuturum, si talium interces-   370
sione adiuueris, quos diuina pietas libencius exaudire consueuit. Mitte
etiam ad bene tibi notum uicinum ancillarum Dei monasterium,"
et nominauit illud, "ab eis tibi oracionum adminicula implorans;

345 sedule] sedulo BdMT

¶ **What was his peticion specially and how a certen person**
₅ **apperyd to him in his slepe.**   ¶ **Ca ix**

'Sothely,' he seyde, 'whan Y was laborid, as ye sawe me, with
greuys and longe wekenes of body, and euermore with herte and
sowle Y blessyd our Lorde and thankid Him, that He wolde
whitesafe to chaste me onworthy in a fadyrly chastment; and than,
₁₀ al hope put aside as for any recoueryng | of bodely helth, Y began— [b]3ʳ
thaugh hit were slowly—neuertheles, Y disposed me, as Y cowde   L214ʳ
and mighte, to make me redy, how Y might the sandyr and lyghter   O11ʳ
scape the peynys and sorows of the world that is to cumme, and how
Y might fynde the reste of euerlastyng life, when Y shuld be callid
₁₅ oute of my body. And when as Y remembrid these thinges, after my
power, besely, than, after a litil while past, a thoughte fyl to my
mynde that Y shulde praye our Lord God that he wolde white-safe
to reuele and shewe to me, in some maner of wise, the state of the
worlde that is to come and the condicion of the soulys that byn past
₂₀ her bodyes after this lyfe; and thanne, this opynly knowen, Y might
the bettyr vndirstonde what within shorte space (as Y supposyd)
were to be dred, and what Y might hope after, whanne Y shuld passe
fro thys worlde to that worlde, and so by this to stabylle myselfe in
the drede and loue of God, as long as I shuld leue in this dowtefulle
₂₅ lyfe. And so, on a certeyn night in the begynnyng of Lente that ys
laste past, apperyd to me in my slepe a certen worshipful person
stondyng by me and seyng to me,
'"O, sone," he seyde, "gret ys thy deuocyon in praying, and mekyl
is thy perseuer[en]s, wherfor thy contynual prayer and meke
₃₀ demening may not be onspedeful before the presens and goodnes
of God. Neuertheles, fro hens-forth be of goode conforte and
contynew deuoutly in prayur, and for more strenght seche the
helpe of prayers of some religious persons, and ȝef þow so do,
doutles þou shalte knowe þat sone þou shalte opteyne and gete thy
₃₅ peticion."
'Sothely, | than he named to me some persons, and the namys of [b]3ᵛ
ther offices, seyng this,   L214ᵛ
'"Knowe wele, that mekil yt wille the profete, ȝef þow maye haue   O11ᵛ
the prayers of suche persons, the whiche the goodnes of God ys
₄₀ wonte right gladly to here. Sende also to the monastery of nonnys
here-by, that þow knowyst wele," and namyd hit, "besechyng hem to

429 perseuerens] *see Commentary*

plurimum siquidem delectatur Deus in sancto proposito & laudabili
deuocione illarum; quamobrem & uotis earum superna fauet benigni- 37
tas."

'Hiis dictis, alloquentis ymago cum ipso ablata est sopore. Ego
experrectus uisionem fixo seruaui animo, & licet non propalata
intencione mea, quantum potui, eam sanctorum supplicacionibus
adiuuari instancius sategi. Iamque decurso sex ebdomadarum spacio, 38
cum in nocte illa, que cene Domini die illucescente finitur, in
capitulo, sicut meministis, a uobis et a socio uestro disciplinas
percepissem, ab utroque scilicet singillatim sex, pro ipsa uidelicet
die vnam & quinque pro transactis sextis feriis quadragesime, quibus
morbo impediente a suscepcione disciplinarum compulsus sum 38
abstinere, tantam inter hec dulcedinem mentis & affluenciam lacrimarum michi infusam sensi, quantam nullis possem uerbis effari.
Vnde & die sequenti iugiter flere dulcissimum habui. Proxima deinde
f. 7ʳ nocte post larga suspiria, instante iam hora | qua ad matutinas
surgendum erat, placidum sum resolutus in sompnum.'
                                                              39

[X] **Qualiter monitus est in somnis crucem Domini
ado⟨rare⟩.**

'Tunc uero hanc, nescio cuius ministerio delatam, auditu percipio
uocem, hec monita preferentem,

'"Surge," inquit, "& ingressus oratorium accede ad altare, quod in 39
ueneracione sancti Laurencii & omnium martirum habetur consecratum, & retro ipsam aram inuenies crucem, tui Redemptoris
ymaginem, sua morte uitam mundi comparantis, affixam uidebis;
ipsamque in memoriam Saluatoris supplex & deuotus adiens &
deosculans, cordis contriti & humiliati sacrificium offer, sciturus 40
Domino acceptum fore tibique salubre deuocionis holocaustum,
cuius ibidem pinguedine affluenter donaberis."

'Hic discusso sopore euigilo, et cum fratribus ad ecclesiam
matutinas auditurus peruenio; quibus a conuentu iniciatis seniorem
quem nostis in uestibulo ecclesie obuium habui, qui vnus est eorum, 40
a quibus nocte precedenti disciplinas sumpsimus. Quem nutu solito
ad dandam simili ordine tunc quoque nobis disciplinam inuitantes,
alacriter capitulum ingredimur pariter, et uoti compotes effecti, ad
oratorium leti redimus. Occurrit etiam nobis in eodem loco, quo

praye for the. Mekyl God is pleasid in her holy purpose and laudable conuersacion, wherfore His goodnes gretly fauerth their willes and desires."

45   'And whan this was seyd to me, bothe the slepe that Y was in and the person that spake to me went away. Than sodenly Y wakyd, and stedfastly kepte in mynde this vysyon, and as sone as Y might, Y desired the same persons to pray for me, not vttering to them the cause wherfore they shulde pray for me. Than, .vi. wekis paste, in 50 the night that was nexte afore Shere Thursday, as ᵹe can remembre, whan Y had taken of yow and of youre felowe discyplynys in the chaptur-hows—that ys to seye, .vi. of yow and .vi. of him for that day, and .v. other for the sexte feriis of Lente paste, fro the whiche Y was compellyd that tyme to absteyne bycause of sekenes—so grete 55 abundans of grace of terys and swetenesse of herte Y felte me repletyd there in the resceyuyng of tho discyplynys, that Y can-not shewe it in telling by no wordys. Wherfore, the nexte day after, hit was to me ful swete often-tymes to wepe. And than the next nyght, after grete sykynges, beyng than the houre to ryse to matens, Y fylle 60 in-to a pleasaunt slepe.'

¶ **Howe he was warned in his slepe to worshipe the crosse of oure Lord.**   ¶ Ca x

[b]4ʳ
L215ʳ
O12ʳ

'Sothely, than, as Y was a-slepe, Y perceyued a voyce (but Y wist not fro whens hyt came), seyng to me in this wyse,
65   '"Arise vppe and goe into the chapell, and to the awter that is dedifyed and halowd in the worschipe of Seynte Laurence and of alle martyres. And there behynd that awter þowe shalte fynde a crosse, and an ymage of thy Redemer affixed to the same crosse, redemyng the world by Hys deth. And that same crosse, mekely and deuowtly 70 go to, and kys in remembraunce of thy Sauyur, and offir to Hym with meke herte a sacrifice of prayers, knowyng wele hit to be accept of God, and to the an holsum deuocion, in the whiche þow shalte ful abundantly delyte."
'Than after this Y wakyd, and with the bretheren Y came to the 75 chirche to here matens. And when the bretheren had begunne matens, Y mette with a senyor, that ᵹe knowe wele, in the chirche porch, and was on of hem that Y toke disciplinis in the night before. Than whan Y saw hym, Y made a signe to hym to discyplyne me in lyke wyse ageyne as he dyd afore. And so lightely we went bothe to-

istum inueneramus, senior, a quo simile munus signo indice 41
postulantes, parum expectare, manu innuente, iussi sumus. Tunc
ego relictis sociis, qui in parte utpote uiribus debilitati consederant,
solus ad altare michi in sompnis notatum progredior: quo appropians
calciamenta depono, genibusque pauimento impressis, baculum
manu tenens, & caput solotenus frequenter inclinans, ad locum 41
tendo quo Saluatoris uexillum inueniendum audieram. Nesciebam
sane, nullo videlicet indicio antea instructus, quod ibi crux deposita
fuisset. Inuenio tamen sicut michi predictum fuerat, moxque totus in
lacrimas resolutus, totoque corpore pauimento coequatus, ipsam
deuotissime adoro & multimodarum precum libamina suppliciter 42
fundo: denuo genibus innitens ad eam usque accedo, & post diucius
repetita supplicacionum & gratiarum accionum uota, crebra pedibus
f. 7ᵛ crucifixi oscula imprimo, | & fletibus quibus medullitus michi
liquescere uidebar sedulus rigo.'

[XI] ⟨D⟩e sanguine effluente de ⟨l⟩atere crucifixi & de pede   42
⟨d⟩extro, & de duobus luminibus.

'Interea dum ad vultum ymaginis lumina grauida lacrimis attollo,
mirum dictu, sed nimis iocundum uisu & suaue auditu, in frontem
michi sencio guttas quasdam leuiter instillasse; digitosque admouens
sanguinem ex rubore deprehendo. Contemplor denique latus domin- 43
ici corporis ita cruorem emanare, ut solet uiui hominis caro, cute
flebotomo recisa. Erat quidem locus ipse, quo ista uisebam, sui
scilicet posicione obscurior, sed uisa sunt michi circa utrumque
latus crucifixi flammea duo rutilare lumina, qualia possent bene
ardentes cerei ministrare; nichil uero licet curiosius inspiciens 43
uidere potui, quod materiam tanto uel alimentum daret splendori.
Suscepi uero manu aperta nescio quot defluentes guttulas, & exinde
oculos, aures, & nares michi diligenter liniui. Postremo, an in hoc
peccauerim ignoro, vnam eiusdem sanguinis stillam labiis ingessi &
ex nimio cordis desiderio etiam glutiui. Quod reliquum pugillo 44
exceperam, seruandum decreui. Pedem quoque dextrum ymaginis
sanguinare conspexi. Hesterna uero die quando michi redditus sum,

80 gedyr into the chaptur-howse and with one assent gladly we came
ageyne. And there also mette with vs another senyor in the same
place where Y mette the first, to whome Y made alsoo a signe for-to
haue a disciplyne. And he beckid with his hand that Y shulde tarye a
lityl while. Thanne | lefte Y my bretheren, that Y came with to
85 chirche, the whiche were sekelew sittyng a–parte, and alone Y wente
forth to the awter that was notyd to me in my slepe. And whenne Y
was nygh the awter, Y put of my showys and knelyd on my kneys
apon the pament, and ofte-tymys inclyned my heed doon to the
grownd. And so went behynde the awter to seche the crosse that Y
90 herd of before. Trewly, Y knew not afore in any wise by any mannys
telling that any crosse was let doon there. Neuertheles, Y found hit,
as hit was tolde me before. And anon Y was resoluyd al into terys of
deuocyon, and lyyng prostrate al my body, ful deuowtly Y worshipte
that holy crosse, seyng many deuout prayers. And than after, Y cam
95 knelyng on my kneys to the same crosse, and aftyr seyd lengur
deuoute supplicacions and thankynges to God, kyssing oft-tymes the
fete of the crucyfyxe, and besily with the terys of my nyes watrid
hem.'

¶ **Howe he sawe the right side of the crucifixe bledyng don**
300 **to him and the right fote also and of the .ii. lightys that**
apperid there.   ¶ **xi**

'The mene-while, as Y lift vppe my nyes, that were sore of
weping, to the face of the crucifyxe, Y felte some dropys fallyng don
to me. I putte ther-to my fyngerys and Y wele perceyued and knewe
305 by the rednes that hit was blode. Also Y behylde the right syde of the
ymage of oure Lordis body, and hit wellid oute of blode, as a
mannys | flesh is wont to blede whenne hit is cuppid. Trewly, the
place that Y sawe this in was derke, for hyt was behynde the auter
aboute mydnighte. But I sawe there .ii. lyghtis shynyng at bothe the
310 sydes of the crosse, as hit had be .ij. tapers wele brenning. I lokyd fro
whens that light shulde cumme and Y cowde see no place fro whens
hit came. Trewly, than Y toke in my hopynne hand Y wote nere how
mony dropis of that precious blode, and there-with diligently Y
anoyntid my nyes, my neris, and my nose-thrillys. And at the laste Y
315 put one drope of þat blessyd blode in-to my lippys, and of the grete
desyre and deuocyon of myne herte, Y swelowd hyt doone. And
whether Y offendyd God in that poynt or no, Y wote nere. The

[b]4ᵛ
L215ᵛ
O12ᵛ

[b]5ʳ
L216ʳ
O13ʳ

cum nichil sanguinis meis in manibus inuenissem, nimis indolui, semperque dolebo super tanti precii amisso thesauro.'

[XII] ⟨Q⟩ualiter in capitulum uenerit, ⟨&⟩ disciplinas   44₅
susceperit, & qualiter in extasi mentis raptus sit.

'Uerum, ut cetera studiis uestris uel in parte satisfacturus euoluam, lumina illa que altrinsecus circa crucem radiabant, elongari repente uidi, & in meridianam altaris plagam pariter transferri. Quod cernens ego, qui in parte procumbebam aquilonari, scilicet ad latus 45₀
crucifixi dextrum, festinanter eo transire cupiebam, quo lumina emigrabant, sperans me aliquid spirituale ibidem uisurum. Quo perueniens, audiui mox sonitum longiuscule retro me factum, a fratre scilicet illo a quo disciplinas expectabam suscipere. Relictis itaque hiis que ibidem uideram, nescio quali modo in capitulum 45₅
confestim deueni, & post disciplinas, ut prius, feceram sex uicibus, iterata confessione mea & oracione eius pro me, ut moris est, cum
f. 8ʳ absolucione ipsius ac benediccione *In nomine* | *Patris & Filii & Spiritus Sancti. Amen.* Optabam sepius confessionem repetere & pluries disciplinari. Incredibilis enim quedam michi ad singulas 46₀
percussiones uice doloris infundebatur dulcedo & inestimabilis suauitas. Sed illo abnuente surrexi. Ipse uero in sede abbatis, ut erat, albis indutus resedit. Tunc ego prosternens me coram eo & ueniam petens, ac repetens *Confiteor Deo & beate Marie & omnibus sanctis* & que sequuntur, denuo absolucionem, premisso *Misereatur* 46₅
tui omnipotens Deus & cetera, ac subiuncta benediccione, ab illo percepi. Cumque ad benediccionem eius respondissem "*Amen*," continuo accedens ad me quidam senior angelicum habens uultum, ueste indutus bissina, que nitore sui niuis candorem superaret, capillo canus, statura mediocris, erexit me, hoc tantum dicens, 47₀
"Sequere me." Tenebat autem manum meam dextram, tam firmiter quam leniter sua eam manu complexus.'

remnand ther-of Y hild in my hand, purposyng to haue kept hit.
Also Y behilde and sawe the right fote of the same crucifi[x]e bl[e]de.
520 Sothely, ȝisterday, whan Y was restoryd to my-selfe ageyne, and
founde no-thing of that precious blode in my handys, sore and gretly
Y sorowde, and euer shal, for the losse of so grete and precious
tresowre.'

¶ Howe he came in-to the chaptur-howse and toke
525 discyplynys and how he was there rauesht.   Ca xii

'Forthermore, to satisfye yow, Y shalle nowe telle of other
thynges. The .ii. lyghtes, that Y sawe shynyng abowte the crucyfyxe
afore-seyde, sodenly paste thens to the sowthe parte of the awter.
Thanne Y, that was knelyng in the | north side of the auter, at the   [b]5ᵛ
530 right side of the crucyfyxe, seyng hit paste and gon to the tother side,   L216ᵛ
folowd after, hopyng that Y shulde see there sum spiritualle thyng.   O13ᵛ
And whan Y came thedir, Y herde the sowne of a voyce behynde me,
of the same old fadyr that Y mette with last before in the chirch
porch, of whom Y desyred to be discyplyned, and he bade me tary a
535 litil while. Than lefte Y alle that Y sawe there, and Y not howe,
nether in what wise, anoon Y came in-to the chaptur-howse. And
whan Y had seyd my *Confiteor*, as the vse ys, and he had prayde for
me and assoyled me with this beneson, *In nomine Patris et Filii et
Spiritus Sancti. Amen*, he gaue me disciplynys .vi. tymes, as he didde
540 afore. Often-tymes Y desired him that Y might reherse my confessyon and to take dyscyplynys of hym, for at euery stroke that he
gaue me, in the stydde of sorowe and peyne, they were turnid to me
an inestymable and incredibulle swetenes of ioyfull conforte. But he
wold geue me no more and so Y rose vpe. Sothely thanne he went in
545 his albys and sate done in the abbotis sete, that was there in the
chaptur-hows. And thanne Y came and lay prost[r]ate before hym,
askyng my *Veny* and rehersyd ageyne my *Confiteor* etc., and he seyde
ouer me *Misereatur tui omnipotens Deus* etc., and so assoyled me
ageyne wyth thys blessyng, *In nomine Patris et Filii et Spiritus Sancti.*
550 And whenne [Y] had answarde, *Amen*, anoon ther came to me a
certeyne worshipful fadyr, a senyor, that had a face and a chere as an
angelle, clothid in white, brightyr and | whittir thanne the snowe.   [b]6ʳ
The heere of his hedd was whore and his stature of medy heyth. He   L217ʳ
toke me vppe and seyde allonly to me these wordys, "Folowe þow   O14ʳ

519 crucifixe] crucifiye; blede] blode   546 prostrate] prostate   550 Y] he

[XIII]

'Hic primum sensi me in excessu mentis raptum.'

Ad hec frater ille, cui omnia retulit que supra digesta sunt, 475 inquisiuit dicens: 'Et putas,' inquit, 'frater, adhuc, quod ego uel ille alius senior, ut dicis, reuera de nocte tibi disciplinas exhibuimus, uel capitulum albis induti ingressi sumus?'

Qua ille percunctacione stupefactus, 'Nonne,' ait, 'utique uerum esse scitis quod assero?' 480

Cumque audiret ab inquirente hoc omnino nec se fecisse, nec ordine contradicente facere ullatenus potuisse, ille uehementer admirans ait,

'Hoc nempe indubitanter uerum fuisse actenus credidi. Nullatenus autem dubium gero, id me uigili & integro sensu corporaliter 485 pertulisse, a uiris speciem uestri satis expresse preferentibus: nam & ictus audiui & sensi, et uocem exorantis & absoluentis bene quasi uestram utriusque noui & intellexi. Prima uero nocte cum, de ipso capitulo vobis recedentibus, in magna, quam ibi conceperam, cordis leticia ipso in loco usque ad lucem remorari cogitarem, strepitu 490 egredientis de ecclesia conuentus post finitas matutinas parumper f. 8ᵛ inquietatus sum, et | retractans mecum ne forte presumpcionis arguerer, si ibi pernoctarem, cum fratribus ad lectulum nostrum iui, obuiumque habui fratrem Martinum cum exirem a capitulo. Peruigil autem tota nocte illa permansi, & in ingenti alacritate animi 495 ita ferie sexte matutinas expectaui. Quibus cum interessem, ut iam dixi superius, circa principium tercie nocturne, de altari ubi oraueram accercitus, sonitu ut premisi facto quasi hominis pede lapideum cederetur pauimentum, capitulum adiui. Ipsa etiam hora fuit qua, nocte anteacta, postrema uice simili de causa illo perrex- 500 imus. Cetera, ut retuli, omnia euenerunt nobis. Hoc tamen nullatenus recordari ualeo, quomodo de oratorio hac ultima uice illuc deueni. Neque enim sine baculo eatenus incedere ualebam, & ipsum circa altaris sacrarium me scio reliquisse. Qualiter uero interiacentem uiam longiorem, subobscuram & gradibus aliisque 505 offendiculis quatuor aut quinque in locis impeditam confecerim, nequeo meminisse. Nam & cum ad meipsum sero redissem adeo impressa erant menti mee, que circa altare & crucem corporaliter

555 me." Trewly, than he hylde me by the right hand so sewerly as
softly, and so clippid my hand in hys.'

¶ **How he felte hym-selfe here first rapte.**   ¶ Ca xiii

'Here Y felte my-selfe fyrst [r]apte in spyryte.'
Than hys brother, that was hys confessor, to whome he tolde alle
560 these thynges aforeseyde, askyd hym and seyde, 'And trowiste ȝet,
brother, that Y or the tother senyor gaue discyplynis þat night, as
thou seyste, or went in-to the chaptur-howse in albys?'
Than he wondrede at his asking and seyde, 'Knowe not ȝe that
this ys trowth that Y haue to yow here seyde?'
565 Than seyde hys confessor ageyne, 'In no wise, ther was no seche
thynges done of vs, nether myght be done, for the ordyr wil not that
we shuld haue gone that tyme of the night into the chaptur-howse to
geue discyplynys.'
Than he seyd to hym, 'Dowtheles Y had went hether-to, that tho
570 discyplynys and other thynges had be done of yow to me. Ful wele Y
knowe withowtyn dowte, that Y resceyued thoes dyscyplynys aboue-
rehersyd in the chaptur-howse, of men that shewed your persons and
liknes, wakyngly and bodely and wyth hole mynde, for Y felte and
herde the strokys of hem, and also Y wele vndyrstode and dyscernyd
575 the voyce of them that prayde for | me and assoyled me, as Y shulde   [b]6ᵛ
haue knowe of you bothe. Trewly, the first night, when Y went owte   L217ᵛ
of the chaptur-hows, Y thought to haue byddyn ther in the same   O14ᵛ
place tyl the mornyng, in the grete gladnes of herte and deuocyon
that Y had resceyued there, but Y was sum-what troubulde and
580 disesyd by the noyse of the couent, when they went oute of the
chirche after matens. And lest Y shulde haue ben reprouyd of
presumpcion, ȝef Y had taride there al night, Y wente with oure
bretheren home to oure bedde. And whenne Y went out of the
chaptur-hows Y mette with brother Marten. And that night bode Y
585 waking in grete lightnesse of sowle tyl matens of the next nyghte.
Thanne the next night after, when Y was at matens, aboute the
begynnyng of the thirde nocturne, Y was callid fro the awter, whereas Y was praying, with a sowne made lyke as a man hadde smytte the
stony pament wyth his fote, and so went in-to the chaptur-howse.
590 Alsoo hyt was the same owre in the whiche the laste nyghte, at the
laste tyme, we went thedyr for the same cause. And alle other

558 rapte] tapte   572 your] yor (r *superscript*)

expertus fueram, ut magis ibi quam in capitulo me crederem
constitutum.'

Hec de hiis frater ipse narrauit.

510

[XIII A] **De duobus egrotantibus curatis per sanguinem
crucifixi & quid fratres inde egerint, et de uisione super hoc
monacho fact[a].**

De cruce autem, quam prenominatus frater in sompno premonitus 515
adorauerat, nos antiquorum fratrum attestacione olim cognouimus,
quod & alia dudum uice sanguinem distillauerit. Quidam uero e
fratribus ante hoc septennium grauibus & repentinis febribus
molestissime urgeri cepit. Tunc, de consilio cuiusdam senioris,
eiusdem crucifixi pedes diluit sacrista, & bibendam febricitanti 520
eiusdem ablucionis obtulit aquam; qua gustata, plene conualuit
infirmus. Supersunt enim utrique, qui et pocionem confecit & qui
conualuit, quorum relacione hoc cognoui; qui actenus eiusdem ligni
uirtutem magnis attollunt preconiis. Quorum uero frater ille, de quo
iam plura retulimus, nimis dolere se dicebat, sanguinis amissionem, 525
f. 9ʳ quem manu collegerat, constat | nimirum quia, inuentus in capitulo,
cum uelut exanimis aqua perfundebatur, de manibus sicut & de
oculis, fronte, ore, ac naso uel reliquis membris eius ipsum
sanguinem fratres diluerunt & penitus exterserunt. Nasus uero
circa medium exterius quidem sanguine concretus erat indurato, 530
sed liquido patebat ipsum de naribus nequaquam profluxisse. Ipse
uero asserebat quia, recedente lumine quod circa crucem uiderat,
cum illi obuiam festinanter transire niteretur ut superius dictum est,
aliquid sibi de manu in pauimentum decidisset; cuius rei fidem
experiri cupientes, lustrauimus curiose designatum locum, & ipsum 535
altare purpureo sanguine aspersum nescio quot locis, ubi crux
steterat, inuenimus & guttulas aliquot pauimento dilapsas utroque
ex altaris latere euidenter conspeximus; quas reuerenter abrasimus, et
puluerem de ipsis conspersum reponentes cum diligencia reseruamus.
Dum autem in die Parasceues ipsa crux de retro altari a sacrista 540
tolleretur ad adorandum de more a conuentu, ex inprouiso digitos
misit super latus, quod sanguine adhuc madebat intinctum. Qui
pauefactus circumstantibus quidem manum ostentabat, sed inscius
vnde id cruci accidisset manum detersit. Latus uero crucifixi
eiusdem adhuc uestigia cruoris manifesta conseruat. Pedem uero 545

376 facta] facto

thynges, lyke as Y haue told yow, befylle me. Thys onely Y canne
not remembre in any wise, howe Y came at the laste tyme fro the
chapel that Y was inne, to the chaptur-hows. For withowte a staffe Y
595 myght not goe thedyr, and abowte the sacrarye of the same auter Y
knowe wele Y left [hit] my-selfe. And howe Y paste ouer the waye
that lyth betwene the chaptur-hows and the place that Y was in, and
also the lettynges of gricis and other obstaclis .iiii. or .v., Y can-not
remembre. | For when Y was cumme to my-selfe ageyne, thoes   [b]7ʳ
600 thinges the whiche Y had experiens of bodely about the awter and   L218ʳ
the crosse ware so fressh in my mynde that I wende Y had be founde   O15ʳ
rather there than in the chaptur-howse.'
And this he tolde of tho thingis aboue rehersid.

¶ Adigression.

605 ¶ Now, as touching tho persons of whom he was brought in-to the
chaptur-hous and to whome he seyd [h]is *Confiteor*, the whiche
prayde for him, assoylyd him, and gaue him also disciplynys, in the
liknes of his own bretheren, and he knew no nothir wise that time
but they had be his bretheren, they were douteles holy angellys, that
610 so apperyd and dyd to him by the wille of God. And as towching that
worshipfull olde fadyr, whois face was like an angel and hys clothing
whittir than the snowe, that toke hym by the hand when he lay
prostrate in the chaptur-hous, and seyde to him, 'Folow thow me,'
was the holy and blessid bishoppe Sente Nicholas, whome specially
615 he louid, and worshipte dayly, as hit shalle be aftirward more
opynnor declarid. And nowe after this adigression go we ageyne to
the narracion.

596 hit] *om.*   606 his] is

similiter cruentatum alius quidam e sacristis incauta uelocitate, non
bene preuentus, quia mox a uenerantibus crucem deosculandus erat,
diluit & extersit. Aquam nichilominus eadem ablucione rubricatam
inprouide eiecit, lintheolum conseruans illius detersione purpura-
tum. Postmodum autem, cum conuentus seriem fratris iam crebro   550
memorati insinuacione percepisset, expauit uehementer quod fecerat,
& (ut est bene) timoratus Dominumque sedulo exorabat, quatinus
huius reatus ueniam ei indulgeret. Ambigebat tamen non modice,
quid de sanguine huiuscemodi sentire debuisset. Et ecce non post
f. 9ᵛ   multum temporis cum in stratu suo multa | inde cogitando obdor-   555
misset, uisus est sibi uocem audire in sompnis hec protestantem:
   'Sanguinem, super cuius estimacionem fide titubas, ita noueris
debere uenerari, sicut ipsum qui pacientis in cruce de latere Domini
noscitur emanasse.'
   Quo circa, nos nichil temere discutere presumimus; magis autem   560
diuina miracula humiliter ueneramur, tanta deitatis magnalia Spiritui
sancto, cuius patrantur maiestate, discernenda committentes. Dulce
tamen est vniuersis intueri, quanta superne pietatis dispensacione
actum sit, ut frater, qui, graui percussionis uerbere diu examinatus,
iam consolacionis munere diuinitus erat refouendus, tali ac tanto   565
summi regis munimine etiam corporaliter vndique septus tueretur,
ut nec spiritualium tormentorum uel hostium contuitu, quos erat
uisurus, terreretur, nec corporei strepitus uel inquietudinis uehe-
mencia, qua sicut retulimus multipliciter fuerat exagitandus, ab
intime speculacionis serenitate vllatenus intempestiue auocaretur.   570
Hiis quadam necessaria digressione intersertis, ad rem gestam
redeamus, illius qui hec experiendo & uidendo cognouit, uerba uel
sensa exprimentes. Ipsum ergo non modo uelut loquentem immo
etiam tanquam ista scribentem inducimus, cuius cotidiana relacione
de hiis edocti, que scribimus in nullo ab eius uerbis deuiamus.   575

[XIV] Qualiter in extasi positus sit monachus & secutus fuerit ductorem suum.

   'Senem itaque uenerabilem,' ait frater predictus, 'qui me & uocis
imperio et ductu manus vie sue comitem asciuerat, alacriter comi-
tatus sum; pariterque incedentes, manus simul consertas habebamus   580
omni tempore quo corporeis sensibus orbatus mente absens per-
mansi. Hoc autem fuit a medio noctis que sexte ferie aurora
terminatur, quo scilicet tempore in capitulo mentis excessum incurri,

¶ Howe this monke was rapte and foloude his leder Sent Nicholas. ¶   Ca xiiij

620 'Gladly than,' seide this monke, 'wente Y with that worshipfull
olde fader, the whiche by commandement of moth and leding of
hande had take me vp to be a felow with him of his wey, and al the |
while that Y lay destitute of my bodily wittis, we went bothe to-   [b]7ᵛ
geder hande in hande. Sothly, this was fro mydnight of Shere   L218ᵛ
625 Thursday, the whiche endith in the mornyng of Good Fredaye, in   O15ᵛ

usque ad sequentis sabbati uesperum quo ad mundane conuersacionis publicum sum uobis cernentibus a quietis qua fruebar secreto 585
expulsus.'

[XV] **Qualiter ueniunt in primum locum tormentorum.**

'Ibamus igitur per uiam planam recto orientis tramite quousque
f. 10ʳ peruenimus | in regionem quandam spaciosam, nimis uisu horren-
dam, palustri situ & luto in duriciem inspissato deformem. Ibi erat 590
uidere hominum multitudinem infinitam, quam estimare nemo
sufficeret, uariis & inenarrabilibus expositam suppliciorum immani-
tatibus. Ibi utriusque sexus, vniuerse condicionis, professionis, &
ordinis turba innumerabilis; ibi quoque omnium peccatorum admissores, diuersis quique addicti pro culparum uarietate et personarum 595
qualitate generibus tormentorum. Videbam & audiebam per late
patencia illius campi spacia, cuius metas nulla circumspiceret acies
oculorum, miserorum choros nimium miserabiles, turmatim collec-
tos & gregatim, criminum parilitate & professionum similitudine
constrictos, pariliter estuare & similiter eiulare sub penarum 600
cumulis. Quoscunque uidi pro quibuscunque affligi peccatis, liquido
aduertebam & peccati eorum genus & modum & satisfaccionis
qualitatem, qua solummodo uel de reatu suo penitendo & confitendo, uel aliorum remediis beneficiorum adiunctis, meruissent in
illo penali exilio ad patrie celestis ingressum preparari. Uniuersos 605
enim ibi positos in spem salutis quandoque capescende aliquatenus
respirare dinoscebam. Quosdam grauiora cernebam equanimius
ferre supplicia, & quasi de consciencia reposite sibi mercedis
bonorum, que egissent, operum & fiducia beatitudinis consecuture
animo semper leuiter reputare horrenda, que perferebant, supplicia. 610
Gemebant quidem, & flebant & eiulabant urgentibus penis, & inter
hec ad anteriora paulatim, semper scilicet minora uel miciora
pertendebant, ut sic dixerim, palestre illius certamina. Nonnullos
conspiciebam de loco quo torquebantur repente exilire, & uiam ad
ulteriora tendentem ocius festinando carpere; quos subito emergens 615
ab imis flamma, quasi dirupto malefidi soli gremio, inuoluebat,
dureque conflagratos, cum flagris ac tridentibus & uario tormen-
f. 10ᵛ torum apparatu accurrentibus tortoribus, omnem in eos | seuiciam
exacturis, denuo restituebant. Nichilominus, sic exusti, sic cesi, &
cedendo precordialiter discerpti, denuo euadentes simili semper 620

whiche time Y was rauyshte in spirite as Y laye in the chaptur-hows,
tyl the euetyde of Saturday foloyng, in the whiche euetyde, as ȝe
sawe, Y was put oute fro that secrete reste and spiritualle sightis, that
Y had before, to thys opyn and worldly conuersacion.'

630 ¶ **How Sent Nicholas brought this monke to the first place**
of peynes.   ¶ Ca xv

'Thenne went we ȝestewarde by a pleyn weye in a right path til we
came to a certen regyon, that was ful wyde and brode and ouer-
horabulle and gastfull in sight, fowle and myry of thicke cley.
635 Trewly, there we sawe an infenyte nombre of men and wemen,
that no man might nombre, put forth to the gretnes of dyuers and
inenarrabulle peynes. There was a company innumerabulle of men
and women of euery condicion, of euery profession, and of euery
ordyr. There were the doers of al synnys ordente to dyuers kyndes of
640 peynes, after the diuersite of synnes and qualite of persons. I herde
and sawe bi the opyn and brode space of that filde, whois endys no ye
might see, the wrechid companyes of men and wemen ouer-
wrechidful, bounden to-gedyr flockemel, in ther equalyte of synnys
and in likenesse of profession equaly to soffyr, and like-wise to | crye   [b]8ʳ
645 in here grete and greuys peynes. And who-sum-euer Y sawe there to   L219ʳ
be made redy in that peynefull place to heuyn-warde, opynly Y   O16ʳ
knewe and vndyrstode for what synnes they were ponysht and the
kynde of the synne, and the mesure and qualite of ther satisfaccion,
the whiche they deseruyd owther by contricion and co[n]fession of
650 her offensis, or by the remediis and helpinges of othir benefetis done
for hem. Trewly, al tho that Y sawe put there, sum-what Y knewe
hem confortyd for the hope of euerlasting blisse the which they
hopid sum-tyme to cum to. And some Y sawe paciently sofyrre right
grete peynes, and for the gode werkys the whiche they had done of
655 ther consciens, that was reseruyd and putte vppe in mede for them,
and also, for the grete trust that they had to haue euerlasting blisse,
euermore countid lygh[t]ly in her sowle the horrabulle peynes that
they bare. Treuly, they wepte and sorowde and cryed oute for grefe
of peinys, and amonge this, as they went forth farthir, euermore her
660 peynys were lessid and to hem more esyur. Also Y behilde mony of
them that sodenly scapyd out of the place that they were torment in
and sander hastid hem-selfe thanne other to go the weye that was

649 confession] cofession   657 lyghtly] lyghly

condicione ulterius tendebant, de grauissimis iugiter ad tolerabiliora succedentes.

'In hac profeccione alii multum, alii parum, alii pene nichil proficiebant. Quibusdam uero de atrocissimis ad crudeliora non profectus sed miserabiliter restabat defectus; & singuli quidem, 625 secundum quod suis pristinis iuuabantur uel impediebantur meritis, & presentibus carorum suorum adminiculabantur pro se exhibitis beneficiis. Uerum de hiis euidencius quod uel mente intellexi, uel alloquiis quorundam instructus percepi, ut inferius declarabitur, paulo post enodabo.' 630

[XVI] De diuersitate penarum.

'Infinite erant species quas ibi uidi penarum. Hii ad ignes torrebantur. Hii in sartagine frigebantur. Hos vngues ignei usque ad ossa & solucionem compagum radendo sulcabant. Illos balnea pice & sulphure cum fetore horrifico aliisque liquaminibus, plumbo & ere, 635 & aliis generibus metallorum calore solutis, excoquebant. Istos uermes monstruosi ueneniferis rodebant dentibus. Illos denso ordine substrati sudes flammatis aculeis, dum furcis regirantur, vnguibus distrahuntur, flagellis innumeris ceduntur, diro laniabantur exemplo. Multos pridem agnitos michique in seculo familiares atque 640 karissimos ibi uario exitu conspexi cruciatos. Quorum nonnulli episcopi uel abbates extiterant; alii aliis dignitatibus, quidam in clero, quidam in seculari foro, quidam in claustro floruerant, quos duplici super immunes personas uidebam cruciari dolore. Nam clericos & monachos, laicos & feminas, tam laicas quam sanctimo- 645 niales, eo minoribus uidi addictos cruciatibus, quo in uita priori minoribus fuerant honorum fulti priuilegiis. In ueritate, speciali quadam pre ceteris acerbitate supplicii vniuersos angi perspiciebam, quos iudices aliorum uel prelatos nostra etate noueram extitisse. Quoniam autem longum est de singulis, pauca saltim de ce[rt]is 650

650 certis] T, ceteris S

before hem. But anone fro benethe, lyke as the grownde hadde be broken, ther brake vppe a flame of fier that inuoluyd hem, and the
665 deuyls þat mette with hem sore bete hem with scorgis and forkis and other dyuers kyndes of tormentyng, and soo ageyne retourned apon hem alle her wodenesse. Neuertheles, they beyng so betyn and brokyn and inwardly | brent, ȝet they scapyd ageyne, and in lyke condicion as hit is seyd afore, the ferther they went, the lessur wes
670 ther peynys and the ȝesyur.

'Sothely, in this passage some did gretely profet, some but lytyl, and some al-moste neuer a dele. To some ther goyng was no profetyng but a myserabulle fayling, for they went fro ful cruel peynes to wers. And eche of them, aftyr ther olde merytys and
675 deseruynges, owthir were holpe in her weye or lettyd or els releuyd, and that was by the present benefetys done and shewyd for hem of their frendys in this world. Sothely, thoes thynges the whiche Y conseyued in mynde, or was enfourmed and taught by comyning and spekyng with some of them there, anone aftyr Y wille opynly shewe
680 hem, as hit is benethe in this present wrytyng declared.'

¶ **Of the grete diuersitees of peynes.**   ¶ Ca xvi

'Infynyte kyndes and diuersytees of peynys where there that Y sawe. Some of hem were rostyd at the fyre. Some were fryed in a panne. Some were al to-rasyd with fyry naylys vnto the bonys and to
685 the lowsing of her ioyntys. Some were soden in bathis of pyche and brymstonne with an horabul stenche and other thingis melted by heete, as ledde, brasse, and other dyuers metellys. And some were gnawyn with the venummys teth of wondyrfull wormys. Some also were caste done thicke on a rowe and smyt throw with sharpe stakys
690 and palys who-ys endys | were alle fyrye. And whyle some were hangyn on galows, odyr were al to-drawyn wyth hokys, and some were betyn sore wyth scurgys, and so in hard example they were al to-toryn. Trewly, of tho persons mony were bisshoppis and abbotys and other were of other dignitees. Sothely, some flowryd in prosperite in the
695 spyrytualte, some in the temporalte, and some in relygyon, the whiche were seyn ponisht in dowbulle sorowe aboue other perso[n]s. For Y sawe them that were clerkys, monkys, noonys, lay-men and lay-wemen, so mekyl lesse ordende and put to peynys, howe mekyl the lesse they had before of worldely dygnyte and prosperyte. In trowthe,

[b]8ᵛ
L219ᵛ
O16ᵛ

[c]1ʳ
L220ʳ
O17ʳ

f. 11^r quibusdam personis, quid & qua ex causa | perferebant uel antea post
obitum suum pertulerant, perstringam; nam & hoc in singulis michi
conspicuum fuit. Nulla tamen hominis lingua sufficienter uel
leuissima illius regionis supplicia ualet exprimere nec estimacio
concipere. Uarietatum etiam multiplicitatem qua uicissim alternanti- 655
bus subduntur penis, nemo uere fateor dinumerare preualeret. Testis
michi Deus est, quia si uiderem quempiam hominum, qui me &
omnes caros meos omnibus dampnis & iniuriis que homini in hac
uita constituto possunt irrogari, et etiam extrema leti sorte affecisset-
si, inquam, tam immanissimum hostem meum illis suppliciis que ibi 660
uidi deputatum conspicerem prolixius cruciandum, milies si fieri
posset pro eius erepcione temporalem mortem appeterem; adeo
quecunque ibi penalia sunt doloris & angustie, amaritudinis &
miserie, mensuram excedunt & modum. Viderimus nos quantis
nisibus, quam castigatis moribus, quam laboriosis mandatorum Dei 665
& omnium denique bonorum operum exercitacionibus, deberemus
conari, ut nos ipsi tot tantisque preripi mereremur erumpnis & ut
karissimi parentes & quondam dilectores nostri & amici d[u]lcissimi,
hiis pro suis excessibus deputati, pietatis & misericordie exhibicio-
nibus pro redempcione sua deuote a nobis impensis inde cicius 670
eruerentur.

'Prius quam speciales aliquorum describam agones, quos ibi
repertos ab ipsis recognitus ipse agnoui, uolo breuiter summatim
percurrendo commemorare, que suppliciorum stadia, postquam hoc
penale transiuimus ergastulum, alias mesto compassionis affectu 675
lustrando conspexi. Erat sane huius prout uidebatur palestre imper-
meabilis longitudo; sed nos, scilicet dux meus & ego, ex transuerso
illam pretermeauimus, sicut & alios quos inferius memorabo tor-
mentales fines. Confinia nempe cruciatuum transiebamus; sed inter
ipsos non incessimus, licet hoc, ut uidebatur michi, inpauidi, et 680
indempnes & prorsus illesi potuissemus.'

668 dulcissimi] dilcissimi

700 Y sawe hem greuyd in a more specyal bittirnesse of peynys aboue
other, the whyche Y knewe in my tyme were iugys and prelatys of
other. And by-cause hyt ys ouer-longe to telle singlerly of euery
persone, what they soffryd and wherfore they soffryd, some thynges Y
wylle gedur to-gedur of some certeyn persons, what they sofryd afore
705 ther dethe and after ther dethe, for that was opyn to me of euery
person. Neuerthelesse, there ys no mannys tonge that may suffycy-
ently telle the lyghtys[t] peynys of that place, nethyr by estymacyon
conceue h[e]m in mynde. Also the dyuersyte and multyplycyte of
peynys, to the whiche they be caste vndyr euer amonge, fro one to a-
710 nother, veryly, Y knowlege no man may noumbre. I take God to
wytnesse, that and there were any man the whiche had done to me, or
to my frendys, alle the hurtys and iniuriis that may be done of any man
in | thys lyfe, or ellys he had flayne vs—Y sey, and Y had so grete an   [c]1^v
enmy put into peynys that Y sawe there to be torment long tyme, a   L220^v
715 thousand tymes, and hit were possybylle, Y wolde sofyr temporal   Ox17^v
dethe for hys delyuerans, for alle thing ther ben so peynfull of sorowe
and anguysshe, byttyrnes and wrechydnes, that they excede mesure
and mode. Let vs nowe that be† in this worlde alyue, see and
considere by this how gretely we ought to geue vs in chaystyng
720 oure wekyd condycyons, and to amende oure leuyng, and also how
mekyl we schulde labur to exercyse vs to kepe the commawndementys
of God and to do good werkys, by the whyche and the mercy of God,
we may deserue to be delyuerd afore of so grete euyllys. And also that
owre dere frendys, as fadyr and moder, systyr and broder, and othyr
725 that were sum-tyme owre louers, ther sore ponysht for her offencys,
myght be delyuerd the soner fro thens by good dedys and werkys of
mercy and pety deuowtly done of vs for ther redempcion and helpyng.
    'And afore ӡere Y make any special mencion by wrytyng of the
[s]ore peynys and tormentys of sum persons that Y fownde and knew
730 ther, and they also knew me, Y wyl schortly wryte yn here the placys
of peynys that Y behelde as Y went abowte with heuy compassion
aftyr we were paste the fyrst peynful place and region. Sothly, to
owre semyng the lengthe of thys fyrste place afore-seyde was ongoyngable, but we, that ys to seye, my leder and Y, went on to the
735 syde ageynste hyt, as we dyd othyr peynful coostys of tormentys, but |
amonge them we came not, how-be-hyt, as hyt semyd to me, we   [c]2^r
myghte haue done wythowt any fere or hurte or harme.'   L221^r
    Ox18^r

707 lyghtys] *final round* s *changed by hand to long* s t *ligature.*   708 hem] hym
718 be] be it   729 sore] fore   734 to the] *reversed*

f. 11ᵛ [XVII] | **De secundo loco tormentorum.**

'Post hunc igitur ad alium tormentorum deuenimus locum. Mons uero, ipsis nubibus celsitudine sui pene contiguus, locum disterminabat utrumque. Huius nos iuga tam facili quam ueloci gressu 685 subegimus. Erat itaque sub remoto ipsius montis latere uallis profundissima & tenebrosa, altrinsecus iugis rupium eminentissimis cincta, cuius longitudinem nullius perstringeret aspectus. Ima illius uallis fluuius dixerim an stagnum nescio, tenebat, amplitudine latissimum, teterrimo latice horrendum, quod nebulam fetoris 690 indicibilis iugiter exalabat. Imminens uero hac ex parte stagni† montis latus rogum, ad ipsam usque celi cameram, succensum emittebat. Ex opposito autem promontorio collis eiusdem, tanta frigoris immanitas certatim niuis & grandinis seuientibus procellis rigebat, ut illo eatinus algore nichil penalius me conspexisse 695 putauerim.

'Tractus prescripte uallis & utriusque montis latera, que frigoris & ignis facies horrenda inuaserat, ita multitudine feruebant animarum, ut solent aluearia crebro apum examine scatere. Quibus hoc generale fuit supplicium, quod nunc in amne mergebantur fetido, nunc inde 700 erumpentes hinc obuiis uoluminibus ignium uorabantur, & demum fluctuantibus flammarum globis tanquam fornacis scintille in altum delate, & in alterius ripe profunda demisse, turbinibus uentorum, frigoribus niuium, & grandinum asperitatibus excipiebantur; & inde precipitate ac quasi refugientes uiolenciam tempestatum, iterum 705 fetoribus fluuii, & iterum concremacionibus debacchantis incendii reddebantur. Quosdam flamme, quosdam frigora, diucius cruciabant, & quidam in amnis fetore moram ducebant largiorem. Alios quasi oleas in prelo ita in mediis flammis comprimi, quod dictu quidem mirum est, & iugiter artari uidebam. Omnium qui illic cruciabantur 710
f. 12ʳ ista | fuit condicio, quod ad perficiendam purgacionis sue plenitudinem, omnia illius laci a principio usque ad finem permeare cogebantur spacia. Maxima tamen & multiformis erat ibi afflictorum distinccio, quia istis leuior et ocior indulgebatur, pro meritorum qualitate & collatorum sibi post funera solaciorum quantitate, 715 transitus. Maioribus obnoxii reatibus & restriccioribus adiuti remediis, graui & diutino detinebantur supplicio. Omnibus uero, quanto plus ad finem illius loci proximabant, eo micior restabat cruciacio. Crudelissimam uero in principio constituti perferebant, quamquam,

691 stagni] stangni   718 loci] a written above o

¶ Of the secunde place of purgatory.   ¶ Ca xvij

'Therefore, after that we were paste the firste place of purgatorye,
740 we came to the seconde place of purgatorye and tormentys, in the
whyche was an hye hylle, vppe al-mooste to the clowdys, and was
deuyded fro the forseyde fyrste place of purgatorye. And thenne
lyghtely and swyftely we wente on thys same hye hylle. And there
was vndyr the farthyr syde of thys hylle a full depe valeye and a
745 derke, set with bocis and brackys on euery syde hangyng owte, whoys lenthe no man myght see. And in the lower parte of the seyde
valeye was a full brode ponde of horrabull blake watyr. And owte of
that same fowle ponde bysyly brake a myste of an indycybylle
stenche. Trewely, the toon syde of that same hye hylle, whyche
750 hangyd toward the ponde, caste oute fro hym an horrabulle
brennyng fyre vppe on-to the heuyn. And alsoo on tothyr syde of
the forseyde hye hylle was so grete and inestymable coolde, that ys to
seye, of snowe and hayle, wyth many other cruell stormys, that me
thowghte and semyd, that Y sawe no-thyng so peynefull and cruel as
755 þat colde was.

'The lenthe of that valey afore-|seyde and bothe the sydys of the   [c]2ᵛ
hylle, the whiche had in hem that horabulle fyre and coold, was so   L221ᵛ
full of sowlys, as hyues swarmyn ful of bees. To the whyche sowlys   O18ᵛ
thys was a comynne and a generalle tormente, that nowe they were
760 drownd in the forseyde ponde and fro thens takyn vppe and caste into fiere, and so at the laste they ware bore vppe an hy by the grete
vyolente flamys of fier, as sparclys byn of a brennyng fornece, and so
lette down on the to[t]her syde of the hylle to the horrabulle coolde
of snowe, hayle, and sharpenesse of stormys, and afterward caste
765 downe hedlonge in-to the greuys stenche of the ponde aboue-seyde,
and ageyne takyn vp and caste in-to the brennyng fier. And some of
hem were lengur ponysht in fier thenne other, and some in coolde.
And some ware taryde lengur in the greuys stenche of the ponde
than other. And some Y saw ware bounde and compressid in the
770 myddys of flamys of fier, that meruelous hit is to speke, and as
grapys be compressyd in a pressure. Trewely, the condicion of al that
ware there torment and peynde in that secunde place was this: alle
the space of the ponde aboue-seyde they were compellyd to goe
throwe, fro the begynnyng to the endyng, for-to fulfylle her
775 purgacion. Neuerthelesse, ful grete and monyfold was the distinc-

763 tother] torher

ut premisi, non omnes equaliter penam. Grauissima istius loci 720
tormenta immaniora fuerunt, quam loci superius a nobis inspecti
immanissima; similiter & minima illius loci leuiora erant quam istius.
Vnde fiebat quod multi ibi grauius quam hic uidebantur torqueri.

'Hic uero multo plures notorum meorum quam superius, repperi
& agnoui. Quibusdam utrobique collocutus sum. Stature eorum non 725
satis patebat mensura, quam pridem noueram: quorundam enim
uelut attenuata suppliciis & imminuta forma uisebatur; alii de
quantitate solita nil deposuerant. Ceterum cognicioni intuentis in
nullo preiudicabat ista diuersitas. Ita michi prompta fuit & manifesta
omnium cognicio, sicut eo tempore quo nobiscum degebant in 730
seculo.'

[XVIII] **Qualiter beata Margareta quandam meretricem liberauit a demonibus.**

'Hic iam referre libet perpulcrum quoddam magne pietatis opus,
quod tunc quidem meroris pariter & congratulacionis michi prestitit 735
insigne spectaculum, et quod toti mundo egregium esse ualeat pie in
Deum & sanctos ac sanctas eius ueneracionis documentum.

'Dum enim ea que supra retuli aliaque quamplura stupens
conspicio, & longiores cum notis meis confabulaciones protraho,
audiebatur eminus strepitus commocionis magne, ingensque tumul- 740
tus quasi latrunculorum uociferancium super preda quam cepissent,
et hosti quem uicissent inconditis cachinnacionibus insultancium. Et
ecce post commocionem sequebatur nefanda immo & ualida |
f. 12ᵛ malignorum spirituum cohors, animam olim a se illaqueatam in

cyon and dyuersyte of her peynys and tormentys. For some had
lighter ponyshment than some, and some was grauntyd a more
swyfter passage thens then to some other, and that was for the
qualite of her merytys and deseruingys | afore-done, and also for the   [c]3ʳ
780 quantite of suffragys and helpys done of her frendys for hem after   L222ʳ
her dethe. And they that were of grettur offensys and synnis, and   O19ʳ
seldyn or slowly holpyn, longe tyme and sore were holdyn in peynys.
And sothely, the more nere they al came to the ende of the place, the
more ӡesyor and softyr waxed their peynys. The moste cruell peynys
785 were in the begynnyng, howe-be-hit, as Y seyde afore, not al equaly.
Sothely, the peynys and tormentys of thys seconde place were mekyl
more harder and scharper than the peynys and tormentys that we
sawe in the fyrste place, wherfore hyt was so, that mony that ware yn
the secunde place ware sorer ponysht than they that ware yn in the
790 fyrst place.

'Here trewly fownde Y and knew mony mo, some-tyme of myne
aquentans, than Y dyd yn the fyrst place. Notwythstondyng, yn
bothe the placys Y spake with some. The mesure of ther statur
apperyd not sufficiently as Y knew hem before yn thys worlde. For
795 the stature and forme of some of them was as hyt had be lessyd or
thynnyde by tormentys. And some had lefte no-thyng of ther
quantite. Neuertheles, thys dyuersiteys of her shappys yn no-thyng
lettyd my knowlege. For ther knowlege was to me so prompte, so
redy, and so opyn, as hyt was that tyme when they leuyd wyth vs yn
800 thys worlde.'

¶ How Sent Margaret delyuered a sowle of a synful woman fro the deuyls.   ¶ Ca xviij

|'Here nowe hit lykyth me to telle a certen fayre dede and werke of   [c]3ᵛ
grete pete and mercye, the whiche that tyme was to me a beholdyng   L222ᵛ
805 of heuynes and also of consolacion, the whyche may be to alle the   O19ᵛ
worlde a nobylle document and techyng why the peple schulde haue
God and hys holy seyntys, bothe of men and wemen, in worschuppe
and in reuerence.

'Truly, whyle Y behylde meruelyng thoo thyngys aboue-seyde and
810 mony other, and hylde long talkyng there wyth hem that Y knewe
before, Y harde a-ferre a grete noyse and a crye, as hit had be theuys
that had takyn a pray or else as they had ouercum their ennemy with
fowle mockys and scornys. And loe, after that noyse and creye

seculo & modo inde abstractam ducencium, infernalibus mox ut 745
sperabant claustris ingerendam. Deus bone, quas cruces, que
supplicia infligebant captiue sue noui illi hospites, eo in exsulem
immaniores, quo eam nouerant magis auxilio destitutam.

'Quis vnquam referenti crederet audiens nefandos diaboli satellites
uicissim miserabilem illam ab isto ad illum quasi pilam iactari; hunc 750
igneis tridentibus, illum furcis flammeis excipere uel excipienti
auferre. Quis credenti ullo sermone exponeret, quomodo iecur,
qualiter cordis intima, quomodo abditos uiscerum recessus, flammi-
gera terebrabant spicula furencium lanistarum, et tamen, ut Deus
ipse testis est, hec tanta taliaque tormenta tam uere quam seue 755
irrogabant illi, pertulit illa, ego conspexi. Neque enim, ut carnalium
oculorum natura consueuit, tantummodo superficiem eorum que
uidebantur, perstringebat obtutus, sed que in occultis bona uel
mala senciebant, qui afficiebantur letis aut tristibus, omnia intuenti
peruia fuerunt atque conspicua. Ita ergo infelix anima presencium 760
dolore & eternorum angebatur metu malorum, nec spes ulla euadendi
miseram refouebat, meritorum suffragiis desolatam. O amaritudo
omnium amaritudinum amarissima, quam nec fiducia mitigabat
leuaminis, & exaggerat desperacio finis. Pridem libenter honestatis
clamidem reiecerat, & meretricio operi in seculo uacans, nunc 765
confusionis operta diploide, interius reprobe accionis consciencia &
exterius demonum sibi insultancium molestia urgebatur. Senciebat-
que in se completum illud beati Iob, *Ducunt in bonis dies suos, & in
puncto ad inferna descendunt*. Et item illud, *Merces carnis, ignis &
uermis*. 770

'Dum igitur quasi triumphalibus pompis hostium infelix ob carnis
illecebram sic agitur in gehennam, ecce repente de sublimi celorum
f. 13ʳ cardine | lux copiosa descendit, cuius radiis predicti tenebrarum
ministri ebetati, ad terram pariter cum illa dilabuntur. Descendit
autem cum luce premissa multitudo uirginum niueis uestibus, auro 775

folowde a cursyd companye of wyckyd spyrytys and a myghty,
815 ledyng with hem anone, as they hopyde to helle, a soule of a
woman late departyd fro her body. O good God, what peynys and
tormentys tho cruell enmyes leyde apon her. And the more they
knewe her withoute helpe, the more wodder were they on her.

'What man heryng euer wolde beleue to any creature tellyng how
820 tho wekyd spyrytys and tyrandys of the Deuylle castyd that soule
amonge hem as a tenyse-balle wyth fyrye instrumentys, now fro on to
another. But hoo may in any wyse telle or schewe to any man beleuyng
howe her mawe and inwarde bowellys were smytte thorowe wyth the
fyrye dartys of tho cruell tormentours. And as God ys my wytnes, Y
825 behylde and sawe her sofyrre so grete and horrabulle peynys and
tormentys verely as they leyde | hem on her cruelly. Nowther these
thyngys ware vnto my syghte as naturaly a man seyth with bodely yes,
that ys to saye, the vtwarde peynys that a man sofryth yn bodye, but
also what they felte ynwardly, good or euylle, and with what
830 heuynesse or wyth what gladnes they were smytte wythinforthe in
her sowllys, alle was to me that tyme playne and opyn. So therfore
thys vnhappy sowle, what for the presente sorowe or dolour that sche
sofryd and hadde and the fere of euerlastyng damp[n]acyon, was in
grete anguys and sorowe of peynys and tormentys. For there was no
835 hope that confortyd her to scape, desolate and destytute of alle helpe
and socoure. O byttyrnesse, of alle bytternesse mooste byttyrste,
whome no truste or helpe releuyth or helpyth, and desperacyon of
the ende encresythe. The daye before, she lefte her mortalle body, in
the whyche sche leuyd strompetly and vycyusly, and nowe sche ys
840 keuerd wyth the vesture of schame and vellonye. And wyth-yn sche ys
byttyn wyth the conscyens of schameful dedys done wyckydlye, and
wythoutforth sche ys mouyd wyth mockyng and scornyng of deuelys
heuely. Sothely, sche felte thanne in her fulfylled the wordys of the
holy man I[ob], seyng thys wyse of suche persons: *Ducunt in bonis dies*
845 *suos, et in puncto ad inferna descendunt.* That ys to seye, "They lede her
days in goodys after their plesure, and in the twynkeling of an ye they
falle done to helle".

'Therfore, while thys onhappy sowle, by the vyctory[o]se pompys
of her enmyes, was goyng to be broughte into helle for | the synne
850 and onleful lustys of her body, loe, sodenly† anon came done an hye

[c]4^r
L223^r
O20^r

[c]4^v
L223^v
O20^v

833 dampnacyon] dampuacyon   844 Iob] Ibo   848 vyctoryose] vyctoryse
850 sodenly] sondenly

& margaritis intermicantibus, refulgencium. Graciam & gloriam vultus uel aspectus earum non describo, que tanta fuit quantam nec animo recolere ipse qui uidi digne sufficio. Inter istas vnam speciosissimam, beatam scilicet Margaretam, agnoui, quam mox ut uidit anima prefata, criminum periculosius quam demonum captiua, 780 miserabilibus uocibus exclamare cepit.

'"O," inquit, "sponsa Christi preciosa, miserere mei, subueni desperate, & ob scelera propria iuste meritis suppliciis addicte. Confiteor, & uere confiteor, quia in omni uita mea mandata Dei contempsi, corpusque meum omni pollucionum labe fedaui: num- 785 quam Deum nec aliquem sanctorum siue sanctarum preter te uel affectu dilexi uel facto uenerata sum. Te solam de supernorum ciuium numero ex corde semper amaui, omni die sabbati coram tuo altari luminaria de meo exhibui; corrupte uite mee consuetudi-nem dudum bene sospes & mei compos, ob honorem & dileccionem 790 tui prorsus deserui; confessionis remedio tocius uite mee flagicia diluisse me credidi, sed hanc, heu pro[h] dolor, nec precedens contricionis feruor, nec condigne satisfaccionis fructus congruam reddiderunt ad tot & tantas tamque inueteratas sordes diluendas. Adherent igitur, heu michi, non remisse iniquitates mee, quas dignis 795 accionibus tegere neglexi. Siccine ergo domina mea, dulcedo mea, peribunt michi deuocionis mee munia tibi fideliter impensa? Immo egone sic peribo, non modo michi sed & tibi, cui soli non perire impense studui, cum michi & omnibus perii?"

'Hec & alia in hunc modum uociferando & miserabiliter eiulando, 800 ac dure & amare supra quam credi possit lacrimando (nam Deum testor, quod in modum grandinis lacrimas ab eius oculis erumpentes conspicere michi uisus sum), | talia, inquam, dum ista congeminat, beata uirgo & martir Margareta ad sodales, que simul aderant, uirgines conuersa, 805

f. 13ᵛ

792 proh] pro

fro heuyn a gret lyght, by the whyche bryghtnes and bemys the
forseyde wykyd spiritys and minystrys of the Deuyl ware dullyd and
made onmyghty and fyl done to the gronde wyth the sowle that they
had. Sothly, than yn the same lyght came done a multitude of
855 virgenys schynyng yn clothys whyte as the snow and sette abowte
wyth golde and precius stonys. The grace and ioy that was yn the
beholdyng of her facys and chere Y make no mension of, for hyt was
so gret and ynestymable, that Y can-not remembre my-selfe that saw
hyt, how Y myght wordly speke of hyt. Amonge the whyche, on that
860 was mooste feyryste, wele Y knew, and seche was the blessyd
virgynne and martir Sent Margaret. And anon as the forseid sowle
saw her, the whiche was more thrall for her synnys than of the
deuyllys, beganne myserably to crye and seyde,
   ' "O blessyd and precius spowse of Cryste, haue mercy on me and
865 helpe me, that for myn nowne propyr synnys am yn desperacyon and
ryghtfully put to peynys and tormente. I knowlege, and verely
knowlege, that yn al my lyfe Y dyspysyd the commawndementys of
God and gaue my body to al onclene leuyng, and nothyr God, ne any
of hys sentys of men or wemen, that Y louyd affectualy or dyd any
870 worshippe to hem yn dede. The only of the nowmbre of the holy
sentis yn heuin euermore hertely Y haue louyd, and euery Saturday of
myn own goodys afore thine auter Y offerde vppe candelys. | And the   [c]5^r
custome of my fowle leuyng, now late beyng hoolle of my mynde and   L224^r
body, for thy loue and worshippe vtwardly Y lefte; I beleuyd also, that   O21^r
875 by the remedy of confession, al my synnys hade be weshte awey. But
alas, for sorowe, my confession was not sufficient to weshe† and do
awey so gret and so mony fowle synnys and olde, by-cause Y lackyd
before the feruor of contricion and dyd not for my synnys euy[n]-
worthy penans. Therfor my synnys cleuyn fast to me, not ƺet
880 forgeuyn, the whiche Y slowthyd too wype awey by goo[d] werkys.
Loe, ther-fore, my lady, and my swetnes and conforte, schalle my
ƺystys of deuocyons peryshe, the whyche Y haue done feytfully to the?
And schalle Y thys peryshe nowe also, not only to my-selfe, but also to
the, to whome only Y haue studyd besely and thowght not for-to
885 peryshe, and now Y peryshe to myselfe and to al thyngys?"
   'These thyngys and many othyr yn thys wyse sche seyde wyth sore
and byttur wepyng, and crying more tha[n] a man may beleue. For Y
take God to recorde and to my wytnes, that Y saw the terys breke

'"O," inquit, "dulcissime sorores, uidetis periculum huius qua-
liscumque olim ueneratricis mee, et scitis peruicaciam demonum qui
sibi ius in illam usurpare multis racionum fulti presidiis non
differunt. Agite ergo, quod solum remedii superest, eterno Iudici
& pio Redemptori preces fundamus, quatinus ipse qui omnia potest, 810
ob sui clemenciam & graciam nostri huic ouicule suo sacro sanguine
olim redempte, iam uero uirulentis luporum dentibus prefocate, sicut
nouit, aliquatenus dignetur subuenire."

'Hec cum perorasset uirgo gloriosa, incunctanter vniuerse, ad
solum genibus demisse, palmis in sublime porrectis, grata gratifico 815
& immortali sponso suo pro peccatrice thura litant oracionum. Nec
tardius quod petunt diuinitus impetrato, ab oracione surgunt. Hinc
uirgo prefata, non minori vultus quam animi constancia, sinistris
spiritibus terribilis & minax, propius accedens, quasi flabello de
manica sua facto, ictus in nequam spiritus moliebatur. Qui mox ut 820
solent musce turbinibus acte hac illacque diffugiunt, captiuam suam,
male malo eatenus stipatam comite, iam bene solam relinquentes.
Extimplo apparuit in loco remociori fossa bullientem habens aquam
ad summum plena. In hanc illam ream pariter & absolutam
demersam uidi.   825

'"Hic," ait miseratrix piissima & potentissima liberatrix eius, beata
Margareta, "hic penitenciam, quam peragere dissimulasti in seculo,
consummare necesse habes, interuencione mea plurimum habitura
leuaminis, & maculis deinde tuis expiatis per me gaudiis admittenda
sempiternis."   830

'Dici uero non potest quam hillaris & gaudens peccatrix illam
dictatam exceperit sentenciam, in qua sic debitam agnouit iram, ut
indebitam sentiret clemenciam. Ita uirginalis acies specioso potita
triumpho celo recipitur.'

owte of her yes as they hade be hayle stonys. And thys whyle sche
890 sorowde, the glorius virgyn and martyr Sent Ma[r]garet turnyd her
to her felows virgyns, that were there wyth her, and seyde,

'"O," sche seyde, "ye moste swete systers, ye see now the perelle
of thys woman, sum-tyme my seruant, and ye knew a[l]so the
ynportune malice of the deuyls, the whyche pretendyn by mony
895 weys of reson to haue her to hem. And therfore let vs now do that
thyng, the whiche only ys | lefte of remedy and helpe for her. Pray   [c]5ᵛ
we now to the euerlastyng Iuge and meke Redemer, that He, the   L224ᵛ
whyche al thing may doo, wille wythsaue as He knowyth beste, of   O21ᵛ
Hys goodnes, and at owre desyre, sumwhat to helpe thys wrechyd
900 sowle, sum-tyme redemyd by Hys precius blode fro the cruelle
power and venummys tethe of these wekyd spiritys."

'And whan thys blessyd virgyn and martyr Sent Margaret had
seide these wordys, anone whytowtyn any taryng, al thoo virgyns
bowde downe to the grownd on her kneys and lyftyd vppe her
905 handys, prayng for that synful woman to her ynmortalle spowse,
owre blessyd Lorde and Sauyur Ihesu Cryst. And anon as they had
of God ther peticion grantyd, they rose vppe togedyr fro preyer.
Than anone thys blessyd virgyn, Seynt Margaret, wyth stabylle
contynawnse of face and sowle, gastfulle and thretyng the wekyd
910 spiritys, came nere and made of her sleue a maner of a schorge, and
lyfte hyt vppe, as sche wolde haue smitte hem. Then they anon, as
hyt had be flyes yn a whyrlewynde, fleyd away hethur and thedur,
leuyng alone her bownde sowle. And sodenly þa[n] yn the farthir
syde apperyd a dyke ful of boylyng watyr vppe to the brymmys.
915 Therfore yn thys dyke Y sawe her put yn.

'And then seyde to her that blessyd and mercyfulle helper, Sent
Margaret, "Here now thow muste fulfylle they penanse, the whiche
thow schuldyst haue done before yn they lyfe. And by my prayur
thow schalt haue mekylle helpe and releuyng of thy peynys. And
920 aftyrwarde, when thy synnys be fully purgyd and clensyd, by me
thow | schalt be admytted to rese[y]ue euerlastyng ioye and blisse."   [c]6ʳ

'Treuly, hit can-not be seyde howe ioifully this synful woman toke   L225ʳ
tho wordys seyde to her, in the whiche sche knewe an ende of her   O22ʳ
due penanse, and afterward myght fele the goodnes and mercy of
925 God. So than, thys vyctoryose dede done, þat glorius sight of
vyrgynys ascendyt vppe to heuyn.'

890 Margaret] Magaret   893 also] aso   904 her kneys] her-kneys
913 þan] þat   921 reseyue] reserue

f. 14^r [XIX] | De quodam aurifabro per beatum Nicholaum a   835
dampnacione liberat[o].

'Exigit similitudo miraculi, ut hic quoque non imparis misericordie, nec inferioris potencie, sanctissimi presulis Nicholai retexam
opus eximium, in quodam famulo suo, michi dudum familiariter ob
quedam bona que illi uidebantur inesse cognito & dilecto, nuperrime 840
patratum; quod ideo hic libencius replico, quia ductoris mei cum
nomine meritum quoque iste de quo nunc agitur primo michi
declarauit, licet forte preuaricari uidear prescriptam narracionis
seriem, qua superius dixi me prius loca penalia michi ostensa
summatim percursurum, quam speciales aliquorum retexerem cru- 845
ciatus: sed hoc aliorum respectu dictum accipiatur, de quibus
innumeras quas inferius seriatim dilucidem narraciones referendas
suscepi ad cautelam legencium siue audiencium.

'Igitur meminisse uos credo ea tempestate qua me sinancia
percussum in uillam ubi semineci similis decumbebam uisitaturus 850
descenderatis, aurificem quendam eiusdem loci ciuem subita morte
expirasse; de quo id etiam vulgatum fuerat, ex nimio vino ingurgitatus, uitam ebrietate uendiderit, letum leticia non bene cautus
institor emercatus. Hunc ergo ubi sortem uocacionis sue accepisse
diceres nisi inter illos de quibus specialiter Iohannes in epistola sua 855
scribit dicens, *Est peccatum ad mortem; non pro hoc dico ut quis oret?*
Quis uero tam absolute peccatum ad mortem dicetur admittere,
quam qui uitam exuit & mortem excipit manens in crimine? Hic
autem non modo usque ad mortem in crimine mansit, sed mortem
incurrit admittendo illud crimen, quod omnium malorum est 860
seminarium. Ebrietas enim, ut ait quidam, nullum uicium excusat.

'Hic ergo, cuius peccatum ut caueatur & periculum modo
innotescimus ut timeatur, cum in pristina uita nimis ad ebrietatem
fuisset pronus, illo triduo quod in seculo uidit ultimum in huius
admissi reatu fuit fere continuus. Quod si michi pro certo pridem 865
f. 14^v constitisset eum scilicet ex | tali causa cessisse in fata, quid de eo
dignius censerem quam pro illo non orare, ne penes iustum iudicem
nil preter repulsam cassa oratio repperisset? Orare tamen pro illo,
licet egre, consueueram, non usquequaque certificatus de fama
tam luctuosi euentus. Contigit ergo celesti prouisione, quod in hoc 870
loco tormentorum, quem postremo depinxi, hunc michi e uicino

836 liberato] liberatus

¶ How a goldsmyth was sauyd by Sent Nycholas.   ¶ Ca xix

'Here [n]ow folowyth also another like myracle of ful grete mercy
and pety, of the excellent might and poure of the blessyd byshope
930 Sent Nycholas. Therfore now Y wille telle a nobyl dede and werke
late done in a certen seruant of his, the whiche not longe a-go welle
Y knewe, and famylyarly louyd for some gode thingys þat was seyne
of him; the whiche therfore the more gladlyur Y wil telle, for this
man þat Y now speke of, the whiche by his occupacion was a
935 goldsmith, told and declaryd to me first the merite and the name of
my leder, with whome Y went hande in hande. And thaugh Y be
seyn here now sum-what to breke out f[ro] the order of the
narracion, be-cause Y seyde before, that ere Y made any mencyon
of the tormentis and peynys of any persons specially, first Y wulde
940 shortly telle of the peynful placys that were schewyd to me—but let
that be takyn of tho persons the whiche afterward Y wille opinly
declare, to the profet of hem þat lyste to here or rede this reuelacion.

'Therfor as Y suppose, ȝe remembre how a certen person, a
goldsmith and a cytson of this place, was | hastly preuent of dethe   [c]6ᵛ
945 and sodenly dyed. Of whom also hyt was opynly noysyd that hyt so   L225ᵛ
be-fylle hym for ouer-mekylle drynkyng wyne. And therfore how   O22ᵛ
myght a man sey to whome thys man schulde be sortyd, but amonge
them that Sent Iohan the apostylle specially spekyth yn hys pystylle,
"*Est peccatum ad mortem; non pro illo dico vt oret quis*"? That ys to sey,
950 "Ther ys synne contynewde vn-to dethe. Y sey no man pray for hym
that contynewyth hys synne to hys dethe." Who so absolute may be
seyde that contynewyth hys synne to hys dethe, as he that contynewyth yn dedly synne and so lesyth lyfe and takyth dethe? Sothly,
thys man bode not only yn the synne of dronkynnes to hys dethe, but
955 also he fylle yn-to dethe doyng that same synne, the whiche ys the
seede and cause of al euylle. And as a certen wyse man seith,
"Dronkinnes excusith no vise."

'Therfore, thys man, whoys sine and perelle we speke of now, þat
hyt schulde be feryd and dredde, yn hys wolde days was ouer-prone
960 and redy to dronkenes, for the last thre days þat euer he saw in thys
worlde he continewyde, dayly almoste, yn the same synne. And yf Y
had know for certen, a day before, þat he had dyed of seche a cause
as hit ys afore seyde, what schulde Y thynke or fele of hym more
worthior than not for to pray for him, le[s]te my prayur before the

928 now] uow   937 for] fro   964 leste] lefte

conspexi. Quem confestim agnoscens, & pre multis aliis a me uisis
spe bona tormenta tollerare, leuiusque afflictum, cernens, opido
miratus sum. Ductor uero meus, intuens me illum attensius
respectantem, sciscitatus est an illum agnoscerem, & audiens illum 875
michi notissimum fuisse,
'"Ergo si," inquit, "nosti eum, loquere illi."

'Ipse uero intuens in nos & recognoscens, ineffabili gestu leticie
applaudebat ductori meo & expansis manibus crebra tocius corporis
inclinacione illum ueneratus atque salutans, pro impensis beneficiis 880
innumerabiles graciarum referebat acciones. Ego interim eum salutaui & ille me gratulabundus resalutauit. Tunc a me inquisitus
quomodo immania tam cito pertransisset supplicia, que illum
pertulisse ipso eius aspectu cognoui, ita infit.'

[XX] **Monachus hic primo sciuit quod beatus Nicholaus fuit** 885
ductor suus.

'"Uos," inquiens, "dilecte mi, in seculo vnanimiter me vniuersi
quasi pro perdito & dampnato habetis, nescientes clemenciam &
misericordiam presentis domini mei sancti Nicholai, qui me infelicem & seruum suum inutilem, meritam non est passus dampnacio- 890
nem perpetuo subire."

'Ad quem ego, "Reuera," inquam, "ut asseris, omnes amici tui
repentina clade, qua te preuentum doluimus, animo consternati
sumus, existimantes profecto te iudicium subisse dampnacionis, cui
uidimus ante mortis periculum omnia Christianitatis abnegata 895
remedia. Verum quia secus quam putabamus successisse tibi iam
letus comperi, magnopere a te ipso audirem omnem euentus tui
seriem, quo scilicet ordine & temporaliter obisti, & mortis eterne
discrimen effugisti."

'Et ille, "Libens," ait, "quod cupis tibi enarrabo."' 900

873 cernens] valde *interlined*

65 ryghtwes Iuge schulde be voide and no-thing helpyng hym?
Neuertheles, Y vsyd to pray for hym, thawghe yt ware slowly, not
verely certifide of so soroful a fame and happe. Sothely, hyt was so,
by the prouision of God, that thys goldesmyth was | in the secunde   [c]7ʳ
place of peynys, and also Y sawe and behylde hym by me, whome   L226ʳ
70 anone Y knewe and gretely meruelde, seyng hym, afore mony other   O23ʳ
that Y behylde, in goode hope and lyghtly sofryng hys peynys.
Trewly, thanne my leder lokyd on me, howe stidfastly Y behylde
hym, and askyd me and Y knew hym. And Y seyde, "Ful wele."

'Than he seyde, "And þow knowe hym, speke to hym."

75 'Sothly then this goldsmyth lokid on vs bothe, and knowing vs,
wyth an enarrabulle gestur and behauing of gladnes, ioyde to my
leder, and, with bothe his handys spred opyn, ofte bowde done al hys
body, worshippyng and greting hym with innumerable thankys for
hys benefetys and goodnes shewyd to hym. And the mene whyle Y
80 salute hym, and he ioyfully salute me ageyne. Than Y enqueryd of
hym how hit was, that so sone he was paste the horable peynys, the
whiche Y knewe by his sighte he had sofryd. Then he answarde this.'

¶ Here thys monke knewe first that Sente Nicholas was hys leder.   ¶ Ca xx

85 '"My dere frynde," he seyde, "al ȝe to-gedur in the worlde haue
me as loste and dampde, not knowyng the goodnes and mercy here of
my present lorde, Sente Nicholas, the whiche had not sofrid me, an
onhappy and an onprofetable seruaunt of his, to be dampde and loste
euerlastyngly."

90 'Than seyde Y to hym, "Trewly, as thou seyste, alle we that ware
thy frendys sorowde that thou didest so sodenly, and | gretly   [c]7ᵛ
abashyd ynwardly, supposyng verely that thow hadyste be   L226ᵛ
dampde, and by-cause also thow hadyste no helpe ne remedy by-   Ox23ᵛ
fore they dethe of the holy sacramentys of the chyrche. Sothly, by-
95 cause Y fynde the othyr-wyse than we wende, Y am glade, and fayne
Y wolde here how and yn what wyse thow deydyst so, and
scapydyste eternal dam[p]nacion."

'Thanne he seyde, "Gladly, what-sum-euer thow desyre, Y wylle
the telle."'

997 dampnacion] damnapcion

[XXI] Narracio aurifabri de subita eius morte.

'"Nosti enim quibus studiis uitam meam in seculo dicaueram,
f. 15ʳ quantum | ad ea que in prospectu intuentibus patent. Crimini
maximo ebrietatis mala deuictus consuetudine finetenus deseruiui,
non tamen uolens quantum ad interioris hominis uotum: multum 90
enim michi displicebat multumque dolebam quod uicium hoc
pestiferum deserere non potui. Frequenter etiam erexi me contra
me, quasi firmiter proponens quod iugum seruitutis huius turpissime
qua detinebar abicerem; sed mox bibendi uoluptate & conbibencium
importunitate, quibus ex equo inique compotare urgebar deuictus, 91
trahebar denuo captiuus in regnum peccati, quod erat in gula &
faucibus meis. Inter hec uero per misericordiam Domini nostri, qui
neminem uult perire, in dominum meum, quem felici comitatu
presentem sequeris, sanctissimum Nicholaum, cuius eram parochia-
nus, talem habui deuocionem, ut nulla vnquam occasione pretermi- 91
serim, quin eius ueneracioni quicquid potuissem deuotissime
exhiberem. Quantumlibet sero ebrietati indulsissem, matutinas
deuote nullatenus pretermittere consueui, sed mox pulsante signo,
ipso frequenter ocior capellano accurrebam. Lampadem in oratorio
domini mei sancti Nicholai de meo proprio iugiter exhibebam. Que 92
uero ad tocius ecclesie cultum, siue in luminaribus, siue in rebus
diuersis, forent necessaria, sedulo quasi familiare ipsius mancipium
procurabam, et ubi proprie facultatis minus suppetebant uires,
comparochianos mouebam ad conferendum que defore uidebantur.
Dona uero conferencium suscipiebam oportunis usibus fidelissime 92
expendenda. Bis in anno scilicet ante Natale Domini & ante Pascha,
purissimam, prout sciebam, peccatorum meorum sacerdoti faciebam
confessionem, penitentiam suscipiens & in parte studiose illam
adimplens; non enim sufficienter que precipiebar obseruabam; hinc
nonnunquam omittens facienda, hinc & cauenda admittens. Dies 93
dominico aduentui sollemniter in ecclesia dicatos ex mandato
f. 15ᵛ sacerdotis mei in abstinencia quadragesimali transigebam, | quibus
sponte mea tot de prioribus adiciebam dies quot numerum explerent
quadragenarium. Ita in die natalis Domini corporis & sanguinis
ipsius uiuifica percipiebam misteria, sed proh dolor, cum illis 93
sacrosanctis diebus dominice Natiuitatis caucius & sacracius uiuere
oporteret, ego in contrarium ex mundana consuetudine deuoluebar
institutum.

901 *Titulus on f. 15r.*

'"Ye knew wele how Y dysposyd me yn my leuynge whan Y was
yn the worlde, as thoo thingys that were opyn to mannys syghte.
Also Y contynwyde yn the fowle synne of dronkynnes vn-to my last
ende, of an euyl custome. Neuertheles, hyt was not my wylle, for
gretly hyt dysplesyd me, and mekyl Y sorowyde that Y kowde not
leue that vyse. Sothly, oftyn-tymes Y rose ageynst my-selfe, sewurly
purposyng to leue and caste awey the fowle vyse of dronkynnes that
Y was wholde yn. But anon, what for the luste of drynkyng and the
inportunyte of feleshyppe that Y dranke with, Y was constraynde to
drynke aftyr the mesure of myne olde custome, wherby Y was
ouercumme, and drawyn ageyne, bonde yn-to luste and custome of
the same sinne, that was yn mine owne onmeserabulle taking and
appetite. Treuly, amonge this, | by the mercy of God, the whiche   [c]8^r
wylle that no man perysh, yn my moste blessyd lorde, Sent   L227^r
Nycholas, whome now ye folowe graciusly and presently, and   O24^r
whoys pareshon also Y was, seche deuocion Y had to hym, that
for any occasion Y neuer lefte, but what-sum-euer Y myght do to his
worschippe Y dyd hyt ful deuowtly. And how mekyl euer Y gaue me
towarde euyn to dronkynnes, Y vsyd euer-more to be at matens, for
anon as they range Y wulde be ther, and oftyn-tymes afore the
parysh pryste. Also Y fownde contynwaly a lampe of myne owne
coste yn Sent Nycholas chapelle. And thoo thyngys that were
necessarye to the ornamentys of alle the chyrche, as yn lyghtys or
any othyr thyngys, Y wolde dylygently orden therfore, as Y had be
hys famylyar seruante and mawncypylle. And wher Y had not
sufficyent of myn owne goodys to do hyt, Y wolde moue othyr of
the parysh to helpe, as hyt semyd nedefulle. Sothly, the 3y[f]tys that
men or wemen gaue, Y toke hem, and to be-ho[u]able vsus ful treuly
Y spende hem. Also, twyes yn the yere, that ys at Cristynmas and at
Estyr, [Y] wolde clene confesse me of al my synnys, as wele as Y
[k]owde, to owre parysh pryste, takyng penanse for hem, and yn
parte Y dyd fulfille hem diligently. Treuly, Y dyd not obserue and
kepe tho thingys that Y was commaundyd of my gostely fathyr, for
oftyntymes Y lefte sum thyngys that Y schulde haue doo, and thoo
thingys that Y schulde haue be ware of. And of the commawndement

1028 3yftys] 3ystys   1029 be-houable] be honable   1031 Y] *om.*
1032 kowde] bowde

'"O miserabilem & omnino preposteram insensibilitatis humane uecordiam. Cum enim in preparacionem sancti Pasche uel Natalis Domini diutina carnis maceracione soliti simus emundari, ut diuinis conspectibus fiducialiter in solemni sacrorum dierum reuolucione, quibus nos celitus uisitatos & liberatos agnouimus, tanquam uasa honoris representari mereremur, supernorum munerum benediccionibus refouendi, nos e contrario mox ut affuisset uotiue expectacionis tempus, ita noxiis & ludicris, uanis & uoluptuosis studiis occupandos tradebamus, quasi premissam hoc tantum fine subiissemus continenciam, ut tunc auidi & inexplebiles peruersitatum omnimodarum redderemur executores.

'"Quo ex usu contigit, ut michi quoque in extremis insultaret incentor malorum, angelus Sathane, qui etiam de perdicione mea gratum patri suo diabolo detulisset obsequium, nisi domini mei Nicholai pietas obstitisset. Grates illi semper referat pro erepcione mea fidelium suorum pia deuocio, quia tam iuste dampnandum, tam seuere cruciandum absoluit, tam pie, tam benigne refouit.

'"De more siquidem, ut predixi, die Natalis Domini, que vicinior discrimen exitus mei de corpore antecesserat, cum essem viuifica celestis mense participacione refectus, quod meminisse sine ingenti horrore non ualeo, nimia potacione in ebrietatem traductus sum, non sine iniuria tanti hospitis, quem mentis habitaculo susceperam.

'"In crastino ad ecclesiam, ut moris michi fuit, ante lucem processi, quod pridie commiseram lugens ac dampnans & de cetero dampnare proponens. At id frustra. Merito enim tanti excessus | quem in tam sacra die post tanti percepcionem sacramenti negligenter admiseram, impletur in me illud quod in populo quodam hostibus suis resistere non ualenti, rex ipsorum deflet euenisse: 'Uenerunt,' inquiens, 'filii usque ad partum, & uires non habet parturiens.' Sic, sic nimirum, uirile sobrietatis propositum, quod mente conceperam, occasione potandi ingesta, instigante aduersario & uirtutis instancia destitutus, in facto non edidi, sed turpiter sicut heri, sic & hodie uicio blandiente succubui. Quid multis immoror? Die postera non ante a sobrietatis hostili insectacione destiti, quam funditus ipsam a sensuum meorum inhabitacione bibendo profugaui.

f. 16ʳ

of my gostely fadyr, Y fastyd the dayes of Aduent as Y dyd the Lent
sesyne. To | the why[c]he dayes of Aduent, Y addyd, of myne owne [c]8ᵛ
fre wylle, as mony days afore Aduente as wold make vppe the L227ᵛ
noumbre of the dayes of Lente. And so on Crystenmas daye Y wold Ox24ᵛ
be hosylde and resceyue the holy sacrament of owre Lordys
precio[u]s body and blode. But alasse, for sorowe, when that Y
shuld haue be that holy dayes of owre Lordys byrthe more holyur
and deuowtur in my lyuyng then other tymes, Y turnyd me contrary
vnto other werkys and besynesses of a worldly custome.

    ' "Wherfore hyt happyd vnto me also in myne laste ende, that the
wekyd angelle of that deuyl Sathanas, the whyche ys causer and
kendler of alle e[u]yl, scornyd me. And also he hadde browghte
plesaunte worde and tytyngys of my dampnacyon to hys father the
Deuyl, ȝeffe the mercye and goodnes of my lorde, Sente Nycholas,
had not wythstonde hym. Therfore euermore to hym be thankyngys
of al his trew seruawntys for my dely[u]eraunce, for he had lowsyd
and delyueryd me. And as ryghtwesly as Y was to be dampde and
cruelly to be ponyshte, as mekely and as mercyfully he hath noryshte
and kept me.

    ' "Sothely, on Crystynmas daye, after that Y had resceyuyd the
good Lorde, that Y can-not remembre withowte grete horror and
heuynes, Y was drawyn of an euyl custome, as Y seyd afore, by ouer-
moche drynkyng the same daye in-to dronkynnesse ageyne, to the
grete iniurye and ronge of seche a Lorde, whome Y had resceyuyd a
lytyll before in-to my sowle.

    ' "And on the morow Y wente to chyrche, as Y | vsid to do, sore [d]1ʳ
waylyng the fowle vice, the whiche Y dyde the daye before, L228ʳ
purposyng to be ware of hyt and to do no more. But hit was as O25ʳ
voyde and vayne, for by the occasion that Y had of drinkyng, and the
Deuylys steryng me therto, Y was destitute, and loste the stabulnes
of vertu and the mighty purpos of soburnes that Y had conceuyd.
And so Y fulfilde [n]ot my purpose in dede, but fowle as Y dyd
ȝysterdaye, so Y dyd to-daye, and by delectacion of ouer-mekyl
drynkyng fyl downe agayne to dronkinnes. Sothely, the next daye
after folowyng, the whiche ys the thirde daye after Crystynmas daye,
I lefte not myne olde custome of drinkyng, wherby Y had loste the
vertu of soburnes and all my wyttys also.

1038 whyche] whythe   1042 precious] precions   1048 euyl] enyl
1052 delyueraunce] delyneraunce   1068 not] uot

'"Iamque nocte profunda de loco potacionis lares proprios, 975
propriumque cubile repetens, sic ut eram uestitus, calceis etiam
non solutis, modice dormiui. Nec mora; expergefactus surgere
uolebam, dicens, quod uerum credebam, quia iam pulsatum fuisset
ad conuocandum eos qui matutinas essent audituri. Sed prohibente
thori socia non longe post tempus affore surgendi abstruente, lectulo 980
iterum non resurrecturus me restituo. In momento enim post hec,
dormicio prius quidem sompni & confestim etiam mortis me inuasit.
Qualiter uero michi senserim mortem obrepsisse non tacebo. Demon
quidam, quem ad ebrietatis malignum desiderium incentorem
habueram, reputans secum quod me omni remota contradiccione 985
ad tartarum pertraheret, si in tali articulo defungerer, presumens
etiam quia tunc ad quecumque uellet in me potestatem haberet, quod
eatenus illum sequendo sibi paruissem, uerens autem quam maxime
ne aliquando meritis domini & patroni mei contra ipsum per uitam
emendaciorem preualuissem, si viuendi spacia largiora non defuis- 990
sent, sic me ex improuiso, presumpta potestate abusus, crudeliter
prefocauit. Sensi enim instar bufonis eum, os meum quod tociens
male patulum bibendo laxaueram ingressum, mox per gule fistulam
f. 16ᵛ ad cordis abdita perserpere. Extimplo inimici agnoui pre-|senciam,
nec immemor tamen miseracionum Domini uel miseriarum mearum, 995
fixo iam proposito, Domino in mente uoui, quod puram, fidelem, &
integram de omnibus peccatis meis facerem confessionem & ebrietatis uicium omnimodis in eternum abdicarem. Ad hec fideiussorem
michi fore sanctum poscebam Nicholaum, ipsum ut potui medullitus
inuocando. Uerum ad huiusmodi deliberacionem momentaneum uix 100
michi spacium indulgebatur. Malignus enim super cor meum
confestim decumbens, ipsumque brachiis nefandis vndique complexus, horrificum etiam ueneni ore hiante uomitum egerens, lateque
diffundens, in ictu oculi sedibus suis euulsum de corpore spiritum
eiecit. 100
'"Agebar statim per loca tenebrosa incredibili spirituum malignorum; qui me trahebant, furore, atrocissime multipliciterque uer-
beratus, discerptus, confossus, dilaniatus & perustus, nescio quo loci
pro libitu eorum ad cruciatus & mortem immortalem deputandus. Et
ecce piissimus, quem corde inuocaueram in extremis & semper in 101
uita licet peccator colueram, dominus & aduocatus meus sanctus
Nicholaus adueniens, me potenter de manibus eorum eripuit, & in
hoc purgacionis loco constituit; ubi etsi dira perpessus sim tormenta,
nichili ea duco, timore malignorum spirituum sublato, & tirannica et

' "Thenne, whenne hit was derke nyghte, Y went oute of the place
075 where Y dranke, and came home and wente to bed as Y was, clothyd
and schod, and a lytyl Y slepte. And anone Y woke and wold haue
resyn, and seyd, as Y had wente, that then yt had ronge to matens.
But my wyfe told me, 'Nay', and so Y layde my downe ageyne.
Trewly, thanne fyrst Y toke a slepe, and anone after, Y toke my
080 dethe. And howe Y felte deth sodenly cumme apone me, Y wille telle
yow. A certen deuyl, that tempted and steryd me to the vyce of
dronkynnes, thowghte to hym-selfe that, and Y deyed in seche a
perylle, whytowte any contradiccion he wolde me drawe to helle,
presumyng also to haue thenne power on me to doo what-somme-
085 euer he wolde, for myne obedyens and consentyng in that vyce to
hym. But ageyne, full | mekyl he drede, leste by the merytys of my   [d]1ᵛ
patron Sent Nicholas, Y schulde any tyme preuayle agenst him by   L228ᵛ
amendement of my lyuyng, yf Y lyued any lengur, and so by hys   O25ᵛ
presumptuous power cruelly me strangulde. Trewly, Y felte him like
090 an owle goo in-to my mowthe, the whiche oftyn-tymes ful euylle Y
opynd to drynke, and so thorowe my throte [s]lyly came downe to
my harte. And anone Y knewe that hit was the deuil. Notwith-
stondyng, Y was ȝet myndfull of the mercijs of God, and also of
myne owne wrechydnes, and with stabulle purpose vowyd in my
095 mynde to God that Y wold purely and holy confesse me of alle my
synnys, and vtwardly for euer forsake the wyse of dronkennes. And
to this Y called as inwardly as Y kowde on Sent Nicholas to be my
borowe. Sothely, to this auysement onnethe was graunted me the
space of a moment. Trewely, thanne the wekyd spiryte sate downe
100 anone apon my herte, and clypte hyt wyth his cursyd armys on euery
syde. Also he drew out of his mowthe an horrable voment of venyne
and caste hit al abrode, and so, in the space of a twyn[k]elyng of an
ye, he expellyd and caste me oute of my bodye.
' "And anone after that, Y was hade forthe thorowe darke placys
105 by the cruelle and incredible wodnes of wykyd spirytys, the whiche
al to-bete me, discerpte me, stekyd me, drewe me, and al to-brend
me, and caryed me with them, Y wote not wheder, but as they
wolde, to euerlasting tormentys. Than anone my moste meke and
dere aduocatour, Seynt | Nicholas, to whome Y called with all myne   [d]2ʳ
110 herte at my laste ende, and whome euer in my lyfe Y haue   L229ʳ
worschipte, thawghe Y were a synner, came thanne and mightily   O26ʳ
toke and deliueryd me oute of her handys, and here hath sette me in

1091 slyly] flyly   1102 twynkelyng] twynbelyng

importabili eorum seuicia frustrata, qua in me debacati sunt. Ad hec 101
autem etiam quietem & gaudium sempiternum per ipsum dominum
meum quandoque me percepturum certissime confido. Quin etiam
modo & semper, ex quo hiis penis subactus fui, cum nimis angebar &
estuabam grauiori supplicio, clementissima ipsius uisitacione releua-
tus sum.   102

'"In artificio sane quo uitam meam meorumque transigebam in
mundo, fraudes nonnunquam, in rudi adhuc etate constitutus &
metu egestatis seductus, inferre presumpi; hoc itaque acerbissime
nunc luo & pridem multo acerbius lui. Frequenter enim in cumulo
nummorum ardencium precipitatus intollerabiliter nimis exurebar; 102
ipsos quoque igneos denarios ore hians uorare compulsus, omnia
f. 17ʳ uiscera | mea michi ardere sensi. Actenus etiam crebro illos numerare
compellor, & ex contrectacione ipsa manus & digitos pessundatos
habeo. Sitis incendio nimium acri uiscerum michi itidem interiora
cum gutture, corde & faucibus iugiter tabefiunt."   103

'Hec & alia multa ab isto ita manifeste audiui, sicut ab ullo in
corpore uiuencium possent enarrari.'

[XXII] Documentum aurifab⟨ri⟩ contra mortem subitane[a]m.

'Quiddam uero inter cetera michi dixit quod lectorem celare non 103
debeo. Subita enim morte extinctos ibi innumerabiles conspexi, &
fere omnes atrocitate immoderata uexabantur. De nonnullis autem id
agnoui, quia positi in deliberacione peccandi, cum uentum esset ad
perpetracionem, cuiuscumque id esset, reatus, & diceret quilibet
eorum in corde suo, "En expleo quod multum optaui," tradebatur 104
diuino nutu in exterminium mortis, ac si diuinitus audiret, "Stulte,
en repetitur anima tua ex te; ad quid cogitasti aduersus Deum immo
contra teipsum nequissima?"

1034 subitaneam] subitaneem

this place of purgatorye for my purgacion. And how-be-yt that Y
sofre here sore and harde peynys, Y cownte hit lightly whyle Y haue
115 no drede of the wekyd spyrytys, and also that her tyranny† and
inportable cruelnes ys sesyd and gone fro me. And sothely after this
for certeyn Y am and truste to haue reste and euerlastyng ioye be my
lorde Sent Nicholas. And nowe also and euermore sen the tyme that
Y was put here to this peynys, by the whiche whenne Y ame ouer-
120 sore greuyd and disesyd, ȝet by hys meke and moste meke and
blessyd visitacyon Y am wel confortid and releuyd ageyne.

'"In my [c]ra[f]te also, by the whiche Y gate to me and to myn
ow[n]e leuyng in the world, often-tymes in my beginnyng Y begylde
and dysceyued the pepulle for the fere of pouerte. And now, for that,
125 Y am ful bitturly ponyshte, and the todyr daye before mekyl more
harder therffore Y sofryd peynes. Trewly, often-tyme Y haue ben
caste downe hedlonge into a grete hepe of brennyng† money,
amonge the whiche Y brente ful intolerably. And tho fyrye pensys
Y was compellyd to deuoure with an opyn mowthe, that Y felte alle
130 my bowellys to brenne in me. And hethir-to, often-times Y am
compellyd to telle hem, and of the towchyng of hem myne handys
and fyngers ben sore peynde. Also by ouer-grete | brennyng and hete   [d]2ᵛ
of thirst my inward bowels, with herte, throwte, and chekys, waxen   L229ᵛ
wan and besyly begynne to fayle."   O26ᵛ
135 'These and many other thinges Y herde of hym, as opynly as hit
might be told of any man leuyng yn hys bodye.'

¶ Howe the goldsmyth also tolde to the monke a remedye
agenst soden deth.   ¶ Ca xxii

'Svm-thynge ther is, the whiche he tolde me amonge other, that Y
140 wyl not hyde fro the reder here-of. I sawe there innumerable pepulle
that dyde sodenly in this world, the whiche were ponyscht al-moste
owt of mesure. And of many thys Y knew, that they the whiche were
putte in delyberacyon and auysement for-to synne, and whenne they
came to the dede-doyng of what-somme-euer synne hyt was and
145 eche one of theym seyde in hys mynde, "Lo, now Y wylle doo and
fulfille that the wyche Y haue gretly desyred," he was takyn by the
wille of God to the vtmest peynys and ponissement of dethe, as
thawgh he hadde herde of this texte in the gospelle, "Stulte, en anima

1115 tyranny] tyrannny   1122 crafte] graste (g crossed out by hand, c inserted above)
1123 owne] owre   1127 brennyng] brennyning

'Qui tamen, sicut de isto, eo ipso exponente, cognouimus, in ipsa
mortis amaritudine positi, culpas suas corrigere & deserere cupientes   104
& proponentes, si daretur eis locus penitencie, Dei et sanctorum eius
auxilium & misericordiam in celeritate exitus sui anxius requisierunt;
quamobrem mors ipsa acerbissima ex miseracione omnipotentis Dei
reputata est eis in expiacionem non modicam commissorum, quam
plenissime in penalibus postmodum locis consequebantur. Inquisiui   105
igitur ab isto, de quo iam plura diximus, si possibile esset, ut
homines quouis remedio muniti tale uitarent tamque horrendum
cunctis exicium. Et ille ad hec,

'"O," inquit, "profecto, si scissem cum eram in seculo quod modo
scio, totum mundum contra hoc incommodum munissem & instrux-   105
issem, qualiter tutus & saluus foret ab ingruencia eius. Si enim
cotidie superscriberentur in frontibus & circa loca cordis digito uel
quolibet modo hec duo uocabula, misterium humane salutis con-
tinencia, scilicet 'Ihesus nazarenus', fideles proculdubio a periculo
f. 17ᵛ isto conseruarent immunes: post mortem quoque ipsarum | effigies   106
litterarum loca, in quibus solebant depingi in uiuentibus, decore
clarissimo in eis ipsis insignirent.

'"Scio preterea quia biduo post exanimacionem corporis mei me
insepultum obseruauerunt familiares mei, sperantes recuperacionem
meam propter ruborem & calorem, quem in facie & in toto   106
preferebam corpore, quod nimirum vini effecerat feruens replecio;
nam meus de corpore egressus tam uelox fuit ut, antequam uel ipsa
coniux mea aduerteret uel ad sacerdotem euocandum mitteret, carnis
exuuias penitus reliquerim."

'Hec ita ab isto uerissime cognoui.'   107

tua repetitur a te; ad quid cogitasti aduersus Deum immo contra ipsum te
150 *nequissima?*" That ys to saye, "Fole, lo, they sowle ys takyn fro the;
wherto haste thow thowghte agenst God and alsoo agaynest thy-selfe
full wekyd thynges?"

'Neuerthelesse, as we haue knowyn by hym-selfe the whiche told
thys, that whenne they were putte yn that byttyr scharpenesse of
155 dethe, coueytyng and purposyng to | correcte and amende her fautes, [d]3ʳ
ȝef they hadde any space of penaunce graunted vnto hem, and in her L230ʳ
swyfte and hasty departyng sekyd after the mercye of God and alsoo O27ʳ
after the helpe of his holy seyntys; therfore, of the grete mercy of
God her byttyr dethe was to hem a grete clensyng of her synnys, the
160 whiche they schuld haue sofryd afterward fully in placys of peynys
and tormentys. Forthermore, Y enquyred and askyd of thys goldsmyth, of whome Y haue nowe told and seyde many thingys, ȝeffe
hyt were possyble by any-thyng that the folke myght schonne and
eschewe soden dethe. Thenne he answarde and seyde in thys wyse
165 vnto me,

'"O," he seyde, "sothely, and yf Y hadde knowyn, whenne that Y
was in the world leuyng, suche thyngys as Y knowe nowe, Y wulde
haue taughte and defende all the world fro that grete hurte and
dammage, howe the pepulle and folke myght be sewre and safe fro
170 the fallyng of soden dethe. Trewly and verily, and the Crystyn
pepulle wolde wryte dayly on her forhedys and aboute the placys of
her herte wyth her fyngur, o[r] in any other wyse, these .ii. wordys,
that conteynyth the mysterye of the helthe and saluacyon of
mankynde, that ys to wytte and to saye, ¶ **Ihesus Nazarenus**,
175 wythowtyn dowte the trewe pepulle of oure Sauyur Ihesu Cryste
schuld be harmeles and preserued f[ro] suche a grete peryll and
hurte. And alsoo they schalle haue after her dethe the same letters
and wordys wretyn full opynly and clerely at her hertys and also in
her forhedys, in tokyn and in sig-|ne of grete worschyppe. [d]3ᵛ
180 '"I knowe also that my meyny kepte me .ii. dayes onberyde after L230ᵛ
my dethe, hopyng that Y schulde haue reuyuyd for the rednesse and O27ᵛ
hete the whyche was in my face and in my bodye, the whyche
douteles was of the feruent replecyon of wyne dronkyn before. For
my departyng of this world was so hastye and zwifte, that myne soule
185 was gonne and paste out of my bodye yere my wyfe vnderstode or
knewe hit or sende to calle for the pryste."

'These thyngys Y knewe ful trewly there of this goldsmyth.'

1172 or] of   1176 fro] for

[XXIII] Qualiter narrauerit filius aurifabri de apparicione
trina patris matri sue facta.

'Post .xv. uero dies ex quo ista uidi & audiui, uenit ad me iuuenis
quidam predicti aurificis filius, & multis perfusus lacrimis asserebat
sepedictum patrem suum matri sue, in stratu suo psalmos, uel   107
orationes quas noscet, ruminanti & Dominum deprecanti, dum
adhuc uigilaret, tribus continue noctibus apparuisse, & precepisse
ut ipsum filium suum ad nos mitteret, scitura a nobis plenissime
statum suum; quo cognito fiducialius & obnixius ad sibi subuenien-
dum animaretur; ipsa etiam cum suis ad caucius uiuendum eadem   108
ipsa relacione nostra excitari utiliter ualuisset. Testabatur cum
uehementi iuracione idem adolescens, se nocte tercia eiusdem
apparicionis patris sui diucius audisse sermocinantem matrem,
nunc inquirentem nunc respondentem, & retulit michi ipsa illius
uerba. Ipse uero colloquentis cum ea sermones non audiuit, sed   108
pacienter sustinebat colloquia eorum. Dixerat enim ei mater quid bis
a uiro suo antea audiuisset. Ira enim plenus, ut ipsa fatebatur,
improperabat ei se neglectum ab ea que post obitum eius per seipsum
admonita tantillum pro ipso facere noluisset. Qua excusante se
propter uisionum incertas uarietates & incertitudines uarias distu-   109
lisse, ne forte ipsam delirare crederemus,
    '"Mitte," ait ille, "incunctanter quo iubeo, & expone illi quociens
f. 18ʳ pro hoc ipso apparui tibi, dicetis-|que pro intersignis, quia in
affliccione magna fui cum postremo me uidit, et inter alia que
audiuit, exposui ei quantum michi auxiliatus est sanctus Nicholaus."   109
    'Rogauerat autem me multis precibus quatinus ipsis, scilicet relicte
sue & filio instanter, persuaderem & ex parte illius studiosius
preciperem, ne famulatus obsequium, quod ipse in uita sua & ipsi
exemplo eius sancto consueuerant deferre Nicholao, ulla occasione
negligerent, sed magis ac magis cum uite sue correccionem tamen   110
permaxime aduocati sui instantissime ueneracioni de die in diem
propensiorem operam adhiberent.
    'Nunc alium quoque quem postremo uidi locum miserorum
miseriis nimium miserabilem breuiter attingamus, ac deinde que ab
aliis audiui & circa ipsos uidi, ex parte communicabo.   110

¶ Howe the sone of the same goldsmyth tolde vnto the
monke, aftyr that he was cum to hym-selfe ageyne, that
190 hys fadyr had aperyd thries to hys mother aftyr hys
dethe.   ¶ Ca xxiii

'Sothely, aftyr .xv. dayes seth Y saw and herde thys, the sone of
the forseyd goldesmyth, a certen yonge man, came to me with grete
wepyng and tolde me that hys father had apperyd .iij. nyghtis to-
195 gedyr to hys moeder wakyngly, as sche was yn her prayers at home
yn her chambyr, and bade her that sche schulde sende to me to
knowe how hyt was fully with hym and of hys state, that, thys
knowyn, sche myght be the more confortyd and feythfullir and
deuowter to helpe hym, and also that she, by the same tellyng, may
200 the bettyr be ware gyde to her-selfe and | her meyny to God-ward.   [d]4ʳ
And the same yonge man wytnesyd wyth grete sweryng that the   L231ʳ
thyrde nyghte of hys father[i]s apperyng he herde hys mother   O28ʳ
talkyng and spekyng longe tyme with hym, and somme-tyme
enquyryng and also somme-tyme answeryng hym, "and thenne
205 afterward sche told vnto my hys wordys, the whyche he hadde
tolde and seyde vnto her." Trewely, he seyde that he herde no maner
wordys of hym talkyng or spekyng vnto her but pacyently taryde tyl
they hadde done. Sothely, hys mother told hym that sche hadde
harde of her husbond twyes before. And as sche knowleged and
210 seyde, sche seyde that he was full of ire and wrathe, and moche
blamed her because that he was forgoten and putte owte of mynde
fro her, whyche was warnyd by hym-selfe after hys dethe to doo a
lytyll thyng for hym, and that sche wulde not do so moche for hym,
but excused her that for the oncertente of vysyons sche dyfferde hyt,
215 leste that hyt sculd haue bene supposyd that sche hadde be
desceyued and begylde.
'And thenne he answerde and seyde, "Sende wythoutyn taryyng
thedyr as Y commaunde, and telle and saye to hym howe often-
tymes for the same thyng Y haue apperyd to the, and alsoo seye
220 apone these tokynys, that the last tyme the whiche he sawe me Y was
in grete peyne. And amonge othyr thyngys that he herde of me, Y
told hym how mekyl the holy confessour Seynt Nycholas hadde
holpe me."
'Trewly, he prayde me with grete instaunce that I schulde stere
225 and alsoo moue bothe hys | wyfe and hys sone, and on hys behalfe   [d]4ᵛ

1202 fatheris] fatherrs

'Uir ille de quo prolixior iam superior est facta relacio, ante .xv. menses quam ipsi sum locutus de seculo migrauit, qui reuera meritis aduocati sui in breui expleuit tormenta multa, ita ut uix quemquam uiderim, qui tantum in tantillo tempore profecerit. Vnde profecto liquet ueracem esse illam sentenciam, qua dicitur, *Non est ei bene, qui* ₁₁₁c *assiduus est in malis, & elemosinam non danti.* Danti enim elemosinam dicetur a pio retributore, *Quod vni ex minimis meis fecisti, michi fecisti*; nec poterit de mercede non esse securus, qui talem sibi obligauit. Hic autem uir predictus vni non quidem de minimis, sed de precipuis amicis Dei, quod potuit fecit, in se expertus sentencie illius ₁₁₁₅ ueritatem, *Sicut aqua extinguit ignem, ita elemosina extinguit peccatum.* Erit itaque aliquando bene danti elemosinas, & tanto cicius & melius erit ei, quanto libencius & deuocius dederit, & per aliquem [e]arum, ut ita dicam, portitorem & in magni regis curia magis Deo familiarem, illas Domino commendare sategerit. Quod totum quam ₁₁₂c prudenter iste procurauerit ex premissis satis elucet. Vnde licet uerum sit quod dicitur, *Non redimuntur elemosinis peccata nisi que* f. 18ᵛ *deseruntur*; iste tamen, qui ita assiduus | erat in malis, iccirco forsitan meruit redimi a peccatis, quia peccata sua oderat, & ut potuit confitendo & alia que enumerauimus bona exequendo illa impugna- ₁₁₂₅ bat. Quod & ipsum ut mereretur hinc forte concessum est ei, quia elemosinam, ut dictum est, tam deuote iugiter exercebat. Quam uerum sit autem quia in malis assiduo nec danti elemosinam non sit bene, ex hiis que sequuntur perpendi ualet.

'De cetero autem non ignoramus quia perspicacior hec nostra foret ₁₁₃₀ oracio, si nomina personarum & loca in quibus famosi deguerant hii, quorum fata reteximus, huic inserentur pagine. Uerumtamen ne tristiciam uel scandalum paterentur infirmi, de quorum fortasse amicis hic plura tam dura quam recencia scriberentur, neminem designari ex nomine consilium fuit. Preter hec importunitatem ₁₁₃₅ eorum a nobis excludimus, qui curiositatis instinctu magnam nobis gignerent molestiam, dum de suis caris nos consulturi confluerent, si a nobis hos uisos agnouissent. Lateant ergo nomina non modo eorum de quibus hic sermo texitur, sub Dei testimonio uerissimus, sed & nomen lateat relatoris & locus in quo degit; res ipse ubique ₁₁₄₀ diuulgentur ut hinc discatur feruencius, impleatur perfeccius ab vniuersis lex Domini immaculata, scientibus cunctis & per hec exempla plenius certificatis, quia factores uel neglectores illius retribucio manet siue hos in bono, siue illos in malo, multa nimis.'

1118 earum] carum

commande hem, that the seruyce and worschyppe the whyche he was
wonte to do in hys lyfe and they also by example to Sent Nycholas,
for no cause nethyr for any occasyon schulde be lefte, but dayly more
and more wyth amendement of her lyuyng dylygently schewe and do
1230 her deuocyons and seruys to hys patron and aduocatour Sent
Nycholas.

'Also this foreseyde man and goldsmyth, of whome Y haue nowe
told and spokyn, as hyt ys seyde afore, dyde aboute a .xv. monthys
agone, the whyche trewely, by the merytys of the holy confessour
1235 Sent Nycholas, hys patrone, yn a shorte tyme was spede oute of
mekyl sorowe, that onethe Y myght see any that profette so mekyl
there as he dede in so lytyl tyme. Wherfore, ful expedyente hyt ys to
alle men, whyle they leuyn in thys world, deuoutely to serue the holy
seyntys of God, by the whyche they may haue in her grete nede the
1240 grace and mercye of Almyghty God, as hyt ys schewyd and prouyd
often-tymes.'

[XXIV] **De tercio loco tormentorum.** 1145

'Sed iam que restant de tercio quem inspeximus loco, qui super omnia que mente concipi possunt exicialis est, ut possumus, exprimamus. Nam prout magnitudo mali quod ibi est postularet, uere fateor nemo uel extrema illius supplicia exprimere sufficeret. Huius inexplicabilem loci horrorem eo securior uidere potui, quo 1150 eum quem semper amando & specialiter colendo desideraueram, iam noui mecum esse ductorem. Quanto enim in uenerando michi extiterat familiarior, tanto illius consorcio efficiebar securior, & ad immania supplicia intuenda, que nunc quoque absens sine immensi f. 19ʳ horroris concussione re-|cordari nequeo, geminata ex agnicione illius 1155 fiducia, factus sum usquequaque constancior.

'Relinquentes igitur predictam uere lacrimarum uallem quam secundo adiuimus loco, peruenimus ad campum maximum, in demerso, ut uidebatur, terre gremio situm & ab vniuersorum, preter eorum qui ibi uel torquebant uel torquebantur, accessu 1160 sequestratum. Tegebat autem superiora campi illius chaos quoddam horrificum, quo permixtim rotabantur fumus sulphureus, fetoris immensi nebula, & flamma picee nigredinis, que instar moncium hinc inde emergens confuse per inane spargebatur. Planicies uero loci ita multitudine uermium constrata scatebat, uti domorum aree iuncis 1165 solent operiri. Et hii super omnem estimacionem horridi, monstruosi, & deformes, terribili oris rictu & naribus ignem spirantes execrabilem, turmas miserorum uoracitate inexplebili lacerabant; quos, iamiam absumptos, demones ubique discursantes insaniencium more in miseros seuientes, nunc eosdem frustatim per membra 1170 singula igniferis truncabant ferramentis, nunc omnem carnem funditus ad ossa abradebant, nunc igni iniectos, ut solent metalla, liquefaciebant eos & in modum ignis ardentes reddebant.

¶ Of the thyrd place of the peynys and tormentys that ben
in the purgatorye.   ¶ Ca xxiiij

'But nowe let vs schewe, as we maye, thoes thynges that remaynyn
1245 of the thyrde place, the whyche we sawe and behylde. For aboue alle
thyng that may be conceyued of any mannys myn-|de, hyt excedeth   [d]5ʳ
of cruelnes and dedly tormenting. For veryly Y knouleche, as for the   L232ʳ
quantyte of euyl þat ys there, no man may suffyse to expresse or telle   O29ʳ
the lest peynys of that place. The grete horrabulnes of þat place, so
1250 mekylle the seurer Y myght see and beholde, that Y knewe hym to
be wyth me, and was also my gyde and leder at that same tyme, the
holy bysschop and confessour Sente Nycholas, whome Y haue euer
specyally worschipped and loued. Trewely, the more famylyare that
Y hadde hym in worshyp, the more surer was Y made of hys
1255 felysschippe and companye, to see and beholde the horrabulle peynys
and tormentys, the whiche nowe beyng absent [Y] cannot remembur
withoute grete horrour and gastfulnesse of mynde, but Y was made
of euery syde ful stabulle and sure, for the felysshyppe and
knowleche the whyche Y hadde of my gyde and leder, the holy
1260 confessour Sent Nycholas.

'Therfore, leuyng the forseide secunde place that we were at, as
hit ys aboue rehersyd, we came to a ful gret fylde, and, as hyt
semyd, hyt was sette yn a lowe grownde, sequestrate and departyd
from al othir, that no maner persone myght dedyr come, excepte tho
1265 that were there ponyschte or schuld be ponyschte. Trewly, the ouer-
part of that fylde was keueryde wyth a ful horrable clowde, yn the
whyche was myxte and medylde to-gedir a fume of brymstone wyth
a myste; a gret stenche and a flame black as pycche was medylde
wyth hem, the whyche brake owte on euery syde lyke hyllys and so
1270 spredyd all abrode. And the playnnes of that | place was so repletyd   [d]5ᵛ
and fulfylde withe wormys, as flowrys be wonte to be strawyn with   L232ᵛ
russhys. And they were aboue alle estymacyon horrabulle, wundyr-   O29ᵛ
full, and vnshappely, the whyche wyth a gastfull opyn mouth
brethyd oute cursyd fyre at her nosys. And with an onspekable
1275 deuowryng al to-tore the wrechyd companyse of folke that ther were,
the whyche, ryght nowe so wastyd and consumydde, deuylys ranne
ouer-all lyke as madde men, and were also full cruell and wodde
apone tho wrechys. Trewely, thanne the deuylys ponyshte hem wyth
fyry instrumentys synglerly by euery membre of her bodye, and

1256 Y] *om.*

'Parum est, Deum testor, immo tanquam nichil, quicquid dicere
nitimur de penis illius loci. In breuissimo enim temporis spacio 1175
centum uel eo amplius penarum diuersitatibus omnimodis adnullatos
& mox restauratos, iterum in nichilum fere redactos & denuo
redintegratos eos intuebar, quos illo loco uita perdita cruciari
cogebat: & harum uicissitudinum nullus erat finis, nulla meta,
nullus terminus. Ignis illius tam edax fuit incendium, ut quasi 1180
tepere crederes quicquid feruere uel exurere solet. Uermes autem
dirupti & mortui ac per frusta comminuti sub infelicibus in
congeriem glomerabantur. Hii fetore tam execrande putredinis
adeo vniuersa replebant, ut feculencia illa omnem predictarum
penarum excederet cruciatum.   1185

'Restat adhuc quod, hiis omnibus magis exosum & graue pariter ac
f. 19ᵛ uerecundum, | illius loci tollerare cogebantur dampnaticii.'

[XXV] **De uicio sodomitico.**

'Omnes enim qui ibi puniebantur, sceleris illius, quod nec
nominari decet non modo a Christiano sed nec a quolibet ethnico, 1190
in seculo fuerant patratores. Hos itaque monstra quedam ingencia,
igneam qualitatem preferencia, uisu horribilia, iugiter impetebant, &
quamlibet renitentes ac refugientes sibi abusionis genere dampnabili
permisceri cogebant. Horreo referens, & sceleris obscenitate dum
inde loquor in meipso confundor. Ita uero inter nefandos complexus 1195
pre dolore nimio palpitabant, rugiebant, ululabant, & deinde uelut
exanimati & in mortem deficientes collabebantur innouandis mox
cruciatibus excipiendi. Inauditum sane & insuspicabile michi eatenus
fuerat femineum sexum talibus immundiciis fuisse deprauatum.
Neque enim que apostolus de talibus commemorat satis aduerteram, 1200

1280 thanne afterward they rasyd and al to-teryd their fleshe vtwardly
vnto the bonys, and thenne after thys, whenne they hadde so done,
they caste them into the fyre, and there they were made lyquyd, as
hyt were metalle, and also toke hem oute ageyne as brennyng fyre.

'Lytyl yt ys, Y take God to recorde, and as no-thyng what-somme-
1285 euer Y be aboute to telle of the peynys and tormentys of that place.
For in a ful schorte space of tyme, by alle maner dyuersytees of an
hondyrdfolde peynys and tormentys or more, Y behylde and sawe
howe they were consumed and wasted to noughte and thenne anone
restoryd ageyne. And ageyne almoste they were with peynys
1290 broughte to nought and anone made hole ageyne, the whiche in
that same place the loste lyfe of hem was compellyd to sofre. And of
these alteracyons of tymes, in the whyche by grete peynys and
tormentys they were | brought to nought, anone restoryd ageyne,   [d]6ʳ
ther was non ende, no marke, ne terme. Also the hete and brennyng   L233ʳ
1295 of that fyre was so feruent and deuouring that what-sum-euer hyt   O30ʳ
brent hyt wulde be lyke as a thyng that ware al-moste consumyd or
wastyd. And thenne the wormys that were there war[e] ded and
brokyn and made smalle vnto pecys, and then they were gedyrd on
grete hepys to-gedyr and leyde vnther the vnhappy synfyl wrechys
1300 that were there, wherfore they so fulfylled alle thyng with so grete
stenche that hyt excedyd alle the tormentys and peynis before-seyd.

'And ȝet remayneth one thyng, the wyche they that were in that
place were compellyd to sofre, the whiche ys more hatfull, peynful,
and schameful than any-thyng aboue-seyde.'

1305 ¶ Of the vnclene and foule vyce and synne of sodemytys.
¶ Ca xxv

'Sothely, alle thoo that were there ponyssht and peynde were in
thys worlde whyle they leuyd doers of that foule synne, the whiche
oughte not be namyd not only of a Crystyn man but also of none
1310 hethyn man. Certen grete monstrus, that ys to seye grete bestys
onnaturally schapyne, schewyd hem-selfe in a fyrye lykenesse,
horrabulle and gastfulle to sight, and oftyn-tymes vyolently came
apone hem and also in a fowle damnable abusion compellyd | hem to   [d]6ᵛ
medylle with hem, howe-be-hyt that they refusyd and wulde hyt not.   L233ᵛ
1315 I abhorre and ame asschamed to speke of the fowlnesse and vnclenes   O30ᵛ
of that same synne. Thanne betwene her peynfull and cursyd

1297 ware ded] warded

ubi utriusque sexus innaturalem prostitucionem condempnat, et si
causam perpendissem, tantam tamen impudenciam temporibus
Christianis a sexu naturaliter pudibundo potuisse presumi nullatenus
credidissem.

'At, pro[h] dolor, talium caterua tam innumerabilis, quam mis- 1205
erabilis, ibidem reperiebatur. Personas eo loco multorum nec agnoui
nec diligencius inspexi, quia obscenitatis enormitas & tormentorum
ac fetoris immanitas nimium michi ingerebant tedium & horrorem.
Molestum michi fuit supra quam credi possit uel ad breue momen-
tum ibi consistere, uel que ibi erant intueri. Fetorem tamen, sicut 1210
nec aliarum lesionem penarum, per experienciam [non] sensi, non
enim si sensissem, ulterius, ut michi uidebatur, uiuere potuissem:
immo intellectualiter in mente horum omnium intollerabilem mag-
nitudinem satis perpendi. Miseri uero illi hec vniuersa & alia infinita
que nullus enarrare sufficeret sensibiliter experiebantur. Denique 1215
inter lamentabiles querimoniarum fletus dum clamaret vnusquisque
eorum, "Ue! Ue! quare peccaui? Quare penitendo peccata non
correxi?" etiam suppliciorum dolores memorabant, & resultabat
f. 20ʳ clamor flencium & plangencium nimia uociferacione, ut puta-|res
hunc in toto mundo audiri.'   1220

[XXVI] **De quodam legista sodomidico.**

'Itaque licet, quantum potui, que ibi fiebant intueri refugerem,
vnius tamen clerici, quem olim uideram, non potui mutuam
agnicionem effugere. Hic autem suo tempore inter legistas uel

1205 proh] pro   1211 non] M, *om.* SBdT

clepynges, they roryd and ȝellyd and cryed owte, and afterward they
fylle done to-gedyr lyke as yf they hadde ben gonne and ded and
anone takyn vppe ageyne, and so forth putte vnto newe peynys.
1320 Trewely, Y remembryd not wele at that same tyme the seyyng of the
holy postre Sent Powelle in hys pystylle of seche persons, where he
condempnyth the foule vyce and synne agaynest nature bothe of men
and wemen. And ȝeffe Y hadde sene and consyderyd the cause
namely nowe in tyme of Crystendame, cowde not in any wyse haue
1325 be-leuyd that suche a foule synne and vyse myght haue be presumed
and done, specyally of wemen, the whyche naturelly schuld be more
schamfull thenne other. I neuyr herde before nether hadde any
suspycyon hethirto that the kynde of wemen hadde be deprauyd and
defoyled by suche a foule synne.

1330   'And alas, for sorowe, for ther was founde a company of suche, so
innumerabulle as they were myserable. Many of tho personys that
were there in that place Y knewe not nethyr wele behylde hem, by-
cause that the qualyte of her foule synne, and the grete stenche and
tormentys that was there, smytte me wyth full grete horrour and
1335 tedusnes. Full greuys hyt was vnto me, and more thanne a man may
beleue, to be there in that place a moment whyle, or to beholde
suche | thynges as ware there. Neuerthelesse, Y felte no stenche by   [d]7^r
experyence whylys Y was there as Y dyd no nothir hirte of peynys,   L234^r
for my thoughte and yf I hadde felte hit Y myghte noo lengur haue   O31^r
1340 leuyd. Nothwithstondyng, Y consyderyd and perceyued sufficyently
in mynde the intollerable gretnes of alle thyng. Trewely, thoo
wrechys that were there sencybly hadde experyence and felte alle
these peynys and other mo infynyte, that no man maye tel of. And
amonge her sorowfulle lamentacyons of complaynyng, whyle euer-
1345 ychon of hem cryed, "Alas, alas, why dyd Y so synne? Alas, why dyd
not Y penans for my synnys and amende my lyuyng?" they felte and
remembryd her greuys peynys. Sothely, their voycys of wepyng and
sorowyng was exaltyd and lyfte vppe with so gret a cry that a man
wolde haue wend hyt schulde haue be herd thorow all the world.'

1350 ¶ **Of a doctour a lawe that was a sodemyte.**   ¶ Ca xxvi

'Trewly, thawgh Y refusyd as mekyll as Y myghte to see and
beholde tho thinghes that were done yn that place, Y cowde not
auoide the knoweleg of on clerk, the wyche Y sawe and knew sum-
tyme. Thys clerk in hys days was a doctur of lawe and also amonge

decretistas peritissimus habebatur. Earum etiam facultatum auditores 1225
in scolis quam plurimos instituerat, & subinde magnatum familiar-
itatem sibi conciliarat. Hinc redditibus ecclesiarum ampliatus, cum
affluentibus in diem opibus magis magisque inhiaret, nutu Dei, qui
omnes vult ad penitenciam conuerti, incidit in langorem, quo per
nouem circiter menses uexatus est. Hoc uero pia Saluatoris dis- 1230
pensacione agebatur, ut uel percussione doloris commonefactus
corrigere satageret, que blandiente corporis incolumitate exicialiter
deliquerat. Ille e contra de sospitate corporis temporali, quam
nimium diligebat, solicitus erat, quam & consecuturum se inaniter
presumebat. Vnde nec miserendo anime sue, quod primum & 1235
precipuum est genus elemosine, confiteri peccata studuit, nec
pauperibus compaciendo, uel sanctis Dei obsequia munerum humiliter offerendo, pro eorum redempcione elemosinas de rebus saltim
exterioribus & caducis erogare, quoad uixit, curauit. Uidens itaque
celestis medicus quia nichil proficeret in eo cura pietatis adhibita, 1240
dum non egrederetur de uasculo corrupte carnis nimia rubigo, neque
per affliccionem, misericorditer mala, que in uiuente nequibant
emendari, finire uel in moriente disposuit. Quid enim clemencius
cum hiis ualet actitari, qui secundum duriciam & cor impenitens de
die in diem thesaurizant sibi iram in die ire & reuelacionis iusti 1245
iudicii Dei, quam ut cicius auferatur dies mundi in quo mali huius
thesauri cumulus in perniciem accressit possessoris, & in mortis
noctem recipiantur, qua nemo poterit thesaurizare, quia nec operari?
Quid salubrius fiet hiis, qui stricto per insaniam mucrone ictum sibi
inferre propriis vulneribus cupiunt, quam ut ligentur, sublatis 1250
f. 20ᵛ quibus | abutebantur armis, & sic parcere uel ligati compellantur,
qui male soluti sibi parcere nescierunt?

1355 other that were docturs of lawe he was had in that sciens ful
excellent. Full many lerners of that faculte he ordende yn scolez,
wherby he gatte to hym gret famyliarite of worshippeful men. | This [d]7ᵛ
clerke was largely posseste with beneficys and rentys of the chirche, L234ᵛ
and ȝet, that not-withstonding, dayly he coueytyd to haue more and O31ᵛ
1360 more, wherfore by the wille of God, the whiche wolde haue alle men
to be turne to penans, he felle yn-to grete sekenes, by the wh[ic]he he
was sore vexid and desesid abowt a .ix. monthys. Sothely, hyt was
done of a meke dispensacion of oure Sa[u]yur, that he shulde by the
schorge of sekenes and sorowe dispose to corect and amende hys
1365 synful leuyng, the whyche, whene he was yn gode helthe of body,
fowle and dedly trespast oftyn-tymes to God. Bu[t] he contrary-wyse
was ouer-carkefulle of hys bodely hel[þ]e, the whyche he louyd ouer-
mekyl, and so vaynely presumyd and thowght to haue hyt ageyne,
wherfore he neuyr wolde dyspose hym to be confest of hys synys and
1370 specialy of hys fowle and onclene leuyng, for the helthe of his sowle,
the whyche ys the fyrst and chefe dede of almys that a man schuld
doo, nethyr had any compassion on powre pepul to geue hem any
almys, nethir any-thyng dyd to the sentys of God, as yn offeryng to
Hym mekely hys seruys for the redempcion of hys synys, nethir
1375 studyd or karyd to do any almys of his erthely and transitory godys
as long as he leuyd. Than the he[u]ynly leche, oure Sauyur, seyng
that he was neuer in his dayes the bettyr for the sekenesse the whiche
he hadde for his warnyng, the whyche he schoyd and gaue vnto hym
for a gostely medeson, nethir wente owte of hys onclene leuing, in
1380 the whiche vnclene leuing he was in by the affliccyon | of hys grete [d]8ʳ
sekenesse. Therfore the euyll and wekid faites and dedys that cowde L235ʳ
not be clensyd and purged in hys yonge aage, oure Lord Ihesu Crist O32ʳ
mercefully putte an† ende of hem in hys dethe. What more mercye
myghte be done vnto hem the whyche after their hardnesse and
1385 inpenytente herte, tresur to hem fro daye to daye the wrathe of owre
Sauyur Ihesu Cryste, in the daye of Hys wrathe and also of schewyng
Hys ryghtfull iuggement, and alsoo to be resceyued in-to the nyght
of dethe, in the whiche nyghte of dethe no man may helpe hym-selfe,
for thanne no man may labure any-thyng for-to deserue thanne that
1390 sone her lyfe of thys world be schortyd and alsoo fro hem takyn
aweye, in the whyche her synnys and mysdedys encresyn and

1361 whiche] whcihe   1363 Sauyur] sayur   1366 But] Bur, *corr. by hand* L
1367 helþe] helpe   1376 heuynly] henynly   Sauyur, seyng] *reversed*   1383 an]
and

'Clericum hunc olim michi in puericia notum, post autem a prouincia qua degebam remocius separatum, obisse nesciebam. Quamobrem in talibus eum penis reperiens, duplici admiracione 1255 tenebar, quia & viuum adhuc & semper honestum eum putaueram virum. Nimium miserans calamitatis pondus quo premebatur, inquirebam utrum misericordiam se aliquando consecuturum speraret.

'Qui respondens, "Ve," inquit, "ve! ve! scio, scio quia citra diem 1260 iudicii ueniam omnimodis non merebor: an autem uel tunc incertum habeo. Semper enim ex quo in hec mala demersus sum, deterioratur pena mea de pessimis ad peiora me trahens."

'Cui ego, "Et quare uel in extremis non es confessus peccata tua, nec egisti penitenciam?"   1265

'Et ille, "Quia spem," inquit, "habebam recuperandi sanitatem, & fallente diabolo erubui tam turpe facinus confiteri, ne despeccior inter eos haberer, in quibus male splendidus apparebam & gloriosus. Leuia quidem peccata confessus sum uenerabili presbitero quem & tu nosti, & interroganti an aliorum michi conscius essem peccatorum, 1270 precepi ut tunc quidem abiret, & iterum si quid occurrisset memorie sibi intimarem. Quo recedente & uix usque ad capellam que uicina est domui in qua decumbebam progresso, mori incipiebam. Ille a ministris reaccersitus, iam me inuenit hominem exuisse. Nichil autem de mille penarum generibus, quas omni die perfero, sic me 1275 excruciat quomodo infausta representacio erroris mei quo tenebar in seculo, qua cogor actualiter turpitudini antique passionis deseruire: preter supplicii enim indicibilem uehemenciam, confusione intollerabilius premor, dum in conspectu omnium de tali & tanto flagicio execrabilis fio. Ve! ue! quis vnquam crederet gloriam & fauorem, 1280 quibus conspicui inter homines habebamur, tanta contemptibilitate & ignominia permutandos? Unde permaxime confundor, quia fedus f. 21ʳ cunctis intuentibus | ostendor, qui omnibus apparebam gloriosus."

growyn to her perdycyon and destruccyon? And what thing myght
be more holsummur to them, the whyche by her folusnesse and
madenesse with a scharpe swerde koueyten and desyren to adde
395 strokys to her owne propre wowndys, thanne that they be bounde,
and also her wepynys takyn aweye, the whiche they mysusyd to her
owne propre hurte and dammage?

'Thys forseyde clarke, the whyche Y knew sum-tyme in my
chyldhode and yong aage, Y vndyrstode nor Y knewe not that he
400 was dysceste and ded. For that same tyme in the whyche Y knewe
hym he remouyd fro that prouynce or place ther-as he was wonte to
dwelle in before vnto a-nothir prouynce or place. Neuertelesse, yn
alle suche peynys and tormentys, as hit ys aboue seyd, Y sawe and
fownde | hym, and Y merueyled of hit, for Y had wente he had be yet   [d]8ᵛ
405 a-lyue and also an honest person. Than Y spake to hym and askyd   L235ᵛ
whethyr he hopyd any tyme to haue the mercye of God.   O32ᵛ

'And than he seyde, "Alas, alas, Y knowe, and knowe that a-this-
halfe domys-daye Y schall haue algate no mercye. And whethir Y
schalle haue any thanne, Y am not certeyn. Sothely, euermore sethe
410 Y was putte here to these peynys, they encresyn more and more."

'Then Y seyde to hym, "And why were þow not confeste of thy
synnys at thy laste ende and dydyst no penaunce for hem?"

'Than he seyde, "By-cause Y hopyd to haue recouered, and also
by the disceyte of the Deuyl, my gostely ennemy, Y was aschamed to
415 confesse so fowle a synne, leste Y shulde haue be of les reputacyon
and dyspysed amonge them the whiche Y semyd gloryous and fayre.
Y confeste me of lytyl and smale synys to seche an honest person and
a worschipfull pryste that þow knowyst wele. And whanne he askyd
me 3ef Y had any other thynges to be confeste of, Y bade him go his
420 waye and tolde him that 3ef any other thyng cumme afterward to my
mynde Y wulde sende for hym ageyne and tell him. And whanne he
was gonne and onethis came to his chirche, Y begunne to deye.
Thenne anone he was cald for ageyne and whenne he was cumme he
fownde me ded and gonne. Trewly, ther ys no-thyng of a thowsand
425 peynys that Y sofyr dayly so greuys to me as ys the vnhappy
presentacion of my fowle and vnclene leuyng that Y vsyd in the
world, and now beyng here am | compellyd to doo actually the same   [e]1ʳ
foule passyon. And besyde the horrabulle gretnesse of peynys that Y   L236ʳ
am in, Y am more confounded of schame whyle dat Y am by the   O33ʳ
430 same synne made cursyd and abhomynable in the syght of al men.
Alas, alas, whoeuer wolde haue wende that the worschyppe and

'Hec ille cum nimia eiulatione profatus est. In momento autem
dum miseriam tanti quondam uiri in magno animi stupore admiror,   128
innumeris eum modis uidi excruciari, & ipsis cruciatibus uelut in
nichilum redigi & instar plumbi in liquidum quid per vim caloris
dissolui. Sanctum autem qui astabat sciscitatus sum an possent
aliquo modo remediari tanta hominis tormenta.

'Ille ad hoc, "Cum uenerit," inquit, "extremi dies iudicii, tunc   129
Christi uoluntas fiet. Ipse solus nouit corda omnium, & tunc iuste
omnibus retribuet."

'Nichil itaque certum de liberacione istius agnoscere potui. Ex hiis
igitur quod prefati sumus superius satis, licet perpendi, *Quia non sit
ei bene, qui assiduus est in malis, & elemosinam non danti*. Vidi enim   129
quam maxime per elemosinarum largicionem idest per opera misericordie, que Dominus in euangelio commemorat, omnes adiuuari &
refrigerari in aliis penarum locis, qui ea in uita sua exercuerant. Iste
uero aliquando sapiens in oculis suis & in se confidens alteriusque
patrocinium bonis operibus implorare detrectans contra peccata   130
quibus in perdicionem agebatur, subito insipiens & uecors inuentus
est. Ecce quod & nunc de isto & paulo ante de illo aurifice expositum
est, liquido illam sentenciam libri Sapientie confirmat dicens,
"*Exiguo*," inquit, "*conceditur misericordia, potentes uero potenter
tormenta pacientur.*" Ille enim, &si peccator, tamen exiguus fuit in   130
oculis suis, neque de sapiencia sua uel uirtute presumebat, sed
infirmum se & imprudentem propter peccata sua, & propter
impotenciam suam reputabat: vnde magni, fortis, & sapientis,
aduocati suffragium, quibus potuit, elemosinarum donis ambiebat.
Sicque cupitam percepit misericordiam. E diuerso quasi ex adipe   131
honoris, opum & sciencie istius egressa est iniquitas, & quia se
exceptum putabat a labore hominum, en quam seuo exemplo cum
hominibus non flagellatur? Quod enim de iniquitate Sodome legitur
f. 21ᵛ in propheta, adhuc in filiis suis uiget, qui per superbiam | &
abundanciam in reprobum sensum traditi, faciunt que non conue-   131
niunt, contumeliis afficientes corpora sua in semetipsis. Quos non
homines probabili satis ratione dixerim: quia & scelus quod oper-

1293 de liberacione] BdMT, deliberacione S

fauour the whiche Y hadde amonge men sculde be turned to seche
confusyon and despexion as it is nowe? Wherfore ful gretely Y am
confowndyd and asshamed, for nowe to euery creature Y appere
foule and abhomynable, the whiche before apperyd to euery man
gloryous and honorabulle."

'And thys he seyd with full sore and grete cryyng and wepyng.
And whyle Y meruelde the wrechidnes and peynys of so grete a man
sum-tyme, Y sawe howe he was ponysshte in innumerabulle wysys,
and by thoo tormentys he was brought as to nought and dyssoluyd
by strenthe and hete of fyre and so made lyquyd, as led ys whenne
hyt ys multe. Sothely, thanne Y askyd Sent Nycholas my leder yf
this mannys peynys myght be remedyde or helpe by any mene.

'And thanne he seyde, "Whanne the daye of dome ys cumme,
thenne schall† Crystys wille be fulfyllede. He onely knowyth the
hertys of alle men, and then he wole doo to euery man ryghtfully."

'Therfore I coude knowe no-thyng for certen of this mannys
delyberacyon. Therfore thoo thyngys the whiche we haue spokyn of
here before may wele be consyderyd as the scripture seyth in thys
wyse, "*Non est ei bene qui assiduus est in malis, et elemosinam non
danti.*" | That ys to saye, "Hyt ys not wele with hym that ys besye in
euyll, nethir with hym that dothe non almys." See nowe and
consydre howe gretely they be holpe in placys of peynys by the
doyng of almys-dedys, as oure Lorde spekyth in the gospelle, the
whiche dyd hem in her lyfe. Thys clerke in hys lyfe was wise and
wyttye in hys owne conceyte and, trusting to him-selfe, set ful lytyl
to seche helpe of other by almis-dede and good werkys for his
synnys. That hathe wrought nowe to hym damnacyon. Loo, so sone
and sodenly he ys founde onwyse and madde. Concey[u]e nowe what
ys here nowe seyde of thys clarke and a lytyl before what was seyde
of a goldsmyth, and opynly hyt confermethe the sentence of the
scrypture seyng in thys wyse, "*Potenter potentes tormenta sustinebunt
et exiguo conceditur misericordia.*" þat ys to seye, "Myghty men
myghtyly schalle sofyr tormentys, and to a meke man ys graunted
mercye." That goldsmyth, and though he were a syner, ȝet was in
hys owne syghte meke and lytyl, the whiche nethir by hys connyng
ne[t]hyr of any othir vertue presumyd, but countyd hym-selfe
euermore onwyse and onstable by-cause of hys synnys. Therfore,
by the mene of almys-dedys, and serues as he myght doo, gate to
hym the helpe and soffragys of hys grete and myghty aduocatour and

[e]1ᵛ
L236ᵛ
O33ᵛ

antur a natura eos humana in bestialem, immo in demoniacam, degenerare ostendit insaniam, & semel admissi erroris pertinacia mentem rationalem eos funditus conuincit exuisse.   132

'Linguam preterea istius assidua uidi conflagracione in modum facule ardentis de ore ipsius prominentem exuri. Constat uero hoc illum propterea sustinere, quia iusticiam sepius, ueluti homo potens in sermone, munerum uel personarum accepcione peruerterit. Non enim ociosa tantum loqui consueuerat, sed quod deterius est in   132 uerbis nociuis, iusticie & ueritati contrariis, nimium excesserat. Nec mirum si pro huiuscemodi lingue excessibus, huiusmodi perferebat lingue cruciatus, cum de diuite illo in euangelio legatur quod propter ociosa, que inter epulandum garriebat, eius lingua cruciabatur in flamma.   133

'Venit autem cito post hec ad nos sacerdos ille uenerabilis, cui clericus iste leuia tantummodo delicta sua se confessum esse dixerat, & inter cetera, cum audisset a nobis qualiter abire eum iusserit, & mox illo abeunte expirauerit, ut iam dictum est, in fletum amarissimum prorupit, Deum testans quia hec uerissima esse certissime   133 sciret; ac remota omni ambiguitate constare sibi, quia hec ab illo perceperim, eo quod solus ille preter se ista cognouerit. Hunc igitur clericum solum in illa multitudine infelicium agnoui, qui hec dixit.'

Hinc diuert[un]t monachus et ductor suus ad paradisum terrestrem.   134

'Cicius uero inde discedentes peruenimus ad regionem feliciter quiescencium, in qua multos a nobis cognitos in multa felicitate inuenimus. Uerum de loci illius amenitate & ibidem consistencium iocunditate, uel etiam de meritis eorum ea que nobis comperta sunt, ut Dominus dederit, postmodum disseremus. Nunc ad ea que   134 omisimus de penis & meritis quorumdam, quos in seculo uideram & in locis memoratis cruciatibus addictos inueneram, stili cursum reflectamus.'

1339 diuertunt] diuertit

patron Seynt Nycholas, and so in tyme of nede he had [h]elpe and
mercy as he desyred. And also euyn contrarye-wyse thys clarke of the
excellente connyng, ryches, and worschippe that he hadde, procedyd
forthe | hys wekednesse. And by-cause he thoughte hymselfe excepte   [e]2ʳ
475 in this worlde fro the comon labur of men, lo, in so cruell and byttur   L237ʳ
example he is not nowe ponysshte with othyr men.   O34ʳ

'Also Y sawe there hys tonge ha[ng]yng forthe oute of his hede
and besyly brennyng as hyt were a bronde of fyre, and þat veryly he
sofryd by-cause that often-tymes he peruerted ryghtwesnes, as a man
480 myghty in wordys takyng ȝeftys and mennys persons. For he vsyd
not only to iangyl idyle wordys, but also frowardly in wordys
contrarye to [t]rothe ouer-mekyl he had excedyd. Therfore no
meruelle though he were ponyshte this wyse for suche excessys
and fawtys, whenne oure Lorde spekyth in the gospelle of the ryche
485 man, the whiche for hys light speking and iangelyng at mete was sore
ponyshte in hys tonge in a flame of fyre.

'S[h]ortely after this, came to me that worschyppefull pryste to
home this clerke was confeste of hys smale synnys, as hit ys rehersed
before. And amonge other thyngys the whyche this worschipful
490 pryste herde of me, Y tolde howe this clarke afore-seyde, whenne he
was confeste, bade hym goo hys waye as for that tyme, and so anone
dyde as hyt ys seyde before. And when Y had told him this, he wepte
ful bytturly and toke God to recorde that hit was very trouthe, as Y
seyde and knewe wele, that the forseyde clerke seyde so to hym.
495 Therfore, only of that multytude of wrechys Y knewe this clerke,
that this seyde to me.

'Sothely, thanne sone after that we were paste thys third place we   [e]2ᵛ
came to a regyon where the soulys, the whiche hadd done her   L237ᵛ
purgacyon in purgatorye, ioyfully restyd, in the whyche place many   O34ᵛ
500 Y knewe wele and founde hem there in grete felycyte and conforte.
Trewely, as touchyng the ioys of that place and the iocundnes and
gladnes of them that were there, as oure Lorde wylle ȝeue vs grace,
we schall afterward schewe and declare. But fyrst let vs turne ageyne
thys narracyon to thoes thynges the whyche we haue lefte oute, of
505 the peynys and merytys of some personys in especyalle, the whyche
Y sawe and founde in tho placys of purgatorye, as hyt ys seyde
before.'

1471 helpe] pelpe, *corr. by hand* L   1477 hangyng] hauyng   1482 trothe]
wrothe   1487 Shortely] Sorthely

[XXVII] **De hiis quos in primo loco tormentorum monachus**
f. 22ʳ **uiderat cruciari. | De quodam rectore cenob⟨ii⟩.**   135⟨

'Rector igitur religiose cuiusdam congregacionis, quem bene
noueram, anno presenti regimen animarum, quod aliqua diu in sui
ipsius & gregis sibi commissi dispendium tenuerat, mortis beneficio
absolutus deposuit: de cuius moribus, in utramlibet partem se
habentibus, multa que noui, tedio lectoris consulens, pretereo.   135!
Hunc igitur in penis ad quos primo loco uenimus, inter primos
quos uidimus agnoui. Erat autem in tormentis maximis & nunc in
igne nunc in balneis fedis sulphure & pice mixtim feruentibus
grauissima perferebat supplicia: vultu exsanguis nimiumque defor-
matus aspectu erat. Qui statim ut me uidit satis supplici affatu   136⟨
compellari me cepit ac salutare: quem & ego conpacienti affectu
resalutaui & multa ei locutus sum. Querebam enim an propter delicta
iuuentutis sue talia ac tanta pateretur, quando forsan negligencius
ordinis sacri, quem in infancia susceperat, obseruasset instituta.

'Ille econtra, "Dura," inquit, "& amara ualde perpecior, nec tam   136!
pro excessibus quos in propria persona admisi torqueor, licet in
multis offenderim, quam pro peccatis & nequiciis michi pridem
subditorum. Nam mea utcumque ferrem peccata & hiis debitas
equanimiter sustinerem penas; hec enim crebra confessione, disciplinarum percepcione, oracionibus assiduis, & aliis pluribus modis 137⟨
redimere & castigare consueueram. Ex hiis tamen grauius me
premunt amor parentum et carnaliter propinquorum, quorum aliis
cum minus digni essent ecclesiastica adquisiui beneficia, aliis multa
de bonis ecclesie quam regebam indiscrete contuli; qui mei curam in
hac modo necessitate omnino postponunt. Amor uero excellencie & 137!
honoris ac fauoris humani michi principaliter nocuit. Heu dolori
meo, sicut modum sic & terminum, nisi Deus misereatur, funditus
ademit. Ambitus enim honoris retinendi auidus & amittendi timidus
ita excecauerat oculos cordis mei, ut discipline habenas subiectorum
uoluntati omnino laxarem, permittens eos uelut clausis oculis | 138⟨
f. 22ᵛ uoluptatibus & desideriis suis, ne forte illos adquirerem prelacionis
mee insidiatores, si suis leuitatibus meum opposuissem rigorem.
Preterea bonos & ordinem feruenti amore zelantes nec opitulando
nec saltim fauendo in religionis conseruacione iuui, sed quod nimis
preposterum fuit hiis cum emulis eorum clam derogare & professio- 138!
nis sacre transgressores fouere solebam. Quod totum partim proprie
leuitatis instinctu, partim obtentu tuendi primatus mei faciebam.

¶ Of .ii. personys that this monke sawe and spake with in
the first place of purgatorye, and first with a prior.

510   ¶ Ca xxvii

'Therfore, a prior, that was father of a relygyous place, the whiche
Y knewe full wele sumtyme, dysceste and deyde this same yere. And
of hys maners and condycyons Y knewe many thyngys the whiche Y
leue oute at this tyme by-cause of schortenes. Thys man and prior Y
515 sawe and knew amonge the firste that were in peynys of the fyrste
place of purgatorye that we came to. Trewly, he was in ful grete and
sore tormentys and sofyrd ful greuys peynys, sum-tyme in fyre and
sum-tyme in stinkyng bathys of brimston and pyche medild | to-
gedyr, hoys face and chere was ouer-wrechyd and dedful. And as   [e]3ʳ
520 sone as he sawe me he began mekely to calle me and grete me,   L238ʳ
whome with compassyon of herte Y grete also and spake to hym   O35ʳ
many thyngys. And Y enquyryd of hym whethir he sofreyd so grete
peynys for the fawtys the whiche he dyd in youthe, by-cause
perauenture he neglygently kepte hys ordre that he toke to hym in
525 hys chyldhode.

'And he seyde, "Naye. But neuertheles, ful sore and byttyr peynys
Y sofre here not onely for myne owne synnys and excessys, the
whiche Y dyd in myne own person, howe-be-yt that Y offendy[d] in
many thingys, but also for the wekydnes and mysgouernaunce of tho
530 personys the whiche a lytyl before Y had charge and cure of. For as
touchyng myne own synnys, Y wulde sofyr, as Y myght bere, thoes
peynys the whyche be dewe for hem. For Y vsyd to redeme and
schast myne owne synnys by ofte confessyon and takyng discyplynys
and besy prayers, and also by dyuers other weyes. Sothely, of these
535 thingis ful sore greuyth me nowe the carnal affeccyon and loue that Y
hadde to my frendys, as fadyr and mother and other of my kynne, of
the whyche to sum of hem Y gate benefycys of chyrchys, whenne
they were ful onworthy to haue hem, and to othir Y gaue right
ondyscretely many ʒeftys of the godys of the monasterye that Y was
540 prior of, and they nowe ful lytyl remembre me or doo any-thynge for
me in my nede. Trewlye, the fauyr of pepulle and the loue of
worschippe that Y had, me prinspaly noythe. And | alas, alas, for   [e]3ᵛ
sorowe, for, and God take not mercy on me, as Y am nowe in peynys   L238ᵛ
oute of mesure, so schalle Y be withoute ende. The couetyse   O35ᵛ
545 ambycyon that Y hadde to kepe my worschippe, and the fere that

1528 offendyd] offendyth

Nam ludicra & inania queque facere seu proferre, ac inter seculares
ociose peruagari, satis eis licebat, sicut & michi. Qua crudeli leuitate
mea abutentes quidam eorum nefanda plurima presumpserunt   139(
attemptare. Hinc autem desperabiliter torqueor, quia licet non ex
animo approbante, tamen sciente & quadam inani, formidine dissimulante, in abusionibus suis nonnulli ex ipsis de prauis in peiora
uergentes permanserunt. Alii in malis suis persistentes usque ad
mortem, me adhuc superstite in mundo, eternaliter perierunt. Alii   139.
nunc usque in mortuis operibus deterius viuentes, continuis enormi-
tatibus suis & sibi inextinguibiles & michi pariter, ut uereor,
succendunt ardores. Denique ab hora exitus mei de corpore indicibilibus sum addictus suppliciis, & tamen leuissima michi uisa sunt
que tunc pertuli, comparacione malorum in quibus modo sum.   140(
Eratque michi dies prima omnibus deinceps diebus remissior, dum
ex omnibus que illi post excessum meum ex praua consuetudine
committunt, quam per meam uidentur contraxisse incuriam, augen-
tur pene cruciatus mei. Et quia aliquos, preter cetera mala ipsorum in
crimen singulariter Deo odibile & hominibus detestabile, quod nec   140;
nominare licet, siue iam defunctos siue dampnabilius in carne
uiuentes, prolapsos sciui & correpcionis manum non adhibui,
nichil ita timeo quam meorum eatenus deterioracionem accrescere
michi tormentorum, quousque fetorem etiam, quo talium admissores
flagiciorum cruciantur, sustinere compellar. Hinc enim scio cunctis   141(
f. 23ʳ penis intol-|lerabiliorem, quas vndecumque rei alii perferunt pecca-
tores. Quociens enim dampnabile aliquid perpetrant quos superstites
post me reliqui, accurrunt demones michi cum nimia exprobracione
insultantes, penas priores nouis & attrocioribus semper accumu-
lantes."
                                                                      141;

Y hadde to leue hit, so blyndyd the syghte of my soule that Y lowsyd
the brydyl of correccyon to the willys of my sogettys and sofryd hem
to doo and folowe her desyrys and lustys, as my yes had be closyd,
leste, haply, ȝef Y had correcte hem and refraynde hem from her
50 lyghtnes, they wulle haue be to me as enemyes, to labure and to haue
me out of my worshippe and prelacyon that Y was in. Forthermore,
they that were gode relygyous men and had zele and loue to kepe the
ordyr, Y no-thing helpyd or faueryd in conseruacyon of the
relygyon, but full inordenatly and contrary to vertue Y wolde
55 wyth other that loued hem not speke euyl of hem and detracte
hem and cherysshe other that were ful euyl-disposyd and brekerys of
her holy professyon and order. And alle this Y dyd, a part of myne
owne lightnes and a parte be-cause Y wolde defende my prelacyon.
And for hem to pleye lewde gamys and to speke and clathyr tryfullys,
60 iapys, and other lewdnesse, and also to goo and wandyr amonge
secler folkys in ydelnes, hyt was leful to hem, as hyt was to me.
Therfore, some of hem, by thys cruel lyghtnes of me and that they
sawe in me, presumyd and sayde to do many full cursyd thyngys,
wherfore here Y am ponysshte withoute hope, howe-be-yt that Y
65 approuyd not her wykyd dedys. Notwithstonding, | Y knewe hem, [e]4ʳ
and of a vayne drede made lyke as yf Y had not knowe hyt, wherfore L239ʳ
many of hem bode stylle in her fowle abusyons, going fro euyll to O36ʳ
wars. And some of hem contynued in euyll vnto her dethe whyle Y
leuyd in the worlde, and now they be euerlasting dampde. Also some
70 other of hem ȝet hethir-to leuyn contynualy wars and wars in grete
synnys and dedly dedys, wherfore to hem and to me, as Y am agaste,
succedyth inextynguyble fyre. Also fro the howre that Y paste fro my
body, Y ame putte to onspekehabule tormentys, the whiche were, as
me semyth nowe, ful lyght in comparyson of the peynys that Y nowe
75 sofyr. Sothely, the firste daye after my dethe was to me more esuer
thanne alle the dayes that Y hadde setthe. And of the alle the synnys
and fautes that nowe they done after my dethe, of an euyl custome
that they hadde before, the whiche they be seyne to haue take by my
neglygens, my peynys therfore ben euermore encresyd. And by-
80 cause that Y knewe sum of hem that be ded and sum other the
whiche ȝette leuyn, that haue flyd and falle, besyde other synnys, to
that fowle and abhomynable synne that ought not to be named, and
therfore putte to hem no correccyon, no-thyng Y drede so mekyll as
the encresyng of my peynys so largely tyl Y be compellyd to sofyr
85 the foule and abhomynable stenche, the whiche they sofre and haue

'Dicebat enim michi quo die & quo loco & quo tempore, postquam migrauit a seculo, que persona quoque quale commisisset piaculum. Et referebat pleraque de factis plurimorum, asserens mox, ut a suis olim discipulis eadem mala impleta fuissent, hec sibi per angelos ministros Sathane improperari & suos continue cruciatus augmen-   14 tari.

'Constat uero quosdam e fratribus eiusdem cui iste prefuerat congregacionis, zelo iusticie & feruore religionis succensos, multam impendisse operam, etiam ante mortem ipsius, quatinus exordina- cionibus indisciplinatorum amotis, ordinis puritas seruaretur. Hoc   14 etiam michi conpertum fuit; quamobrem dixi ei, "Quomodo ergo longe lateque disseminatum est quod plurimum emendacionis prouenerit ante finem vestrum in domo illa cui prefuistis, cum tanta & tam enormia de incolis eiusdem loci uobis nuncientur?"

'Ille uero ad hec, "Vera esse scio que commemoras, nonnulla ibi   14 solito probabilius & correccius constare. Sed de eorum melioracione nullus michi fructus, nulla merces ascribitur, immo & augetur cruciatus; nimis enim infestus correccionibus eorum obstiti, & ne corrigerentur que uel correcta sunt, uel corrigerentur nisi obuiassem, quam maxime impediui. Confusione enim illa, que ut dicit scriptura   14 adducit peccatum, insipienter preuentus, peccatis meis exigentibus, erubui manifestam eorum correccionem, que minus erubui passim in vulgo, cum fierent, ignominiose diffamari. Tanta uero in quibusdam obstinacione conualuerunt germinis detestandi plantaria, ut & eos estimem prorsus incorrigibiles, & per eorum facciones, nisi mira   14 deitatis potencia auxilietur illis, qui nequiciis obstinatorum obsistunt, quicquid ibi ad emendacionem ceptum creditur in infectum dedu- cetur. Ue! ue! cur me vnquam talium consiliis credidi? Ve! cur tales f. 23ᵛ in sublime extuli, per quos adeo | diuine maiestatis incurri offensam, dum campum eis laxaui, quecunque uellent per se suosque complices   14 inique operandi? Illis uero quatuor" (& nominatim expressit uoca- bula eorum) "dicere poteris uerbis meis, quod eterna eos & ineffabilia manent in baratro gehenne supplicia, nisi celerius digna[m] Deo de

1448 dignam] MT, digna SBd

nowe, the whiche dyd the same fowle and abhomynable synne, for
Y know wele that the greuys peyne of that same stenche ys more
intollerable and peynfull than any other peynys | that synners   [e]4ᵛ
sofryn. And as ofte as they, the whyche Y lefte alyue, dampnably   L239ᵛ
90 offendyd, anone the deuyls ranne to me with grete scornes and   O36ᵛ
vpbraydys, and euermore and more with newe peynys encresyng
my tormentys."

'Also he tolde me what daye, what place, and what tyme after that
he was paste oute of thys world, and what person of hym hyt was,
95 and what synne he hadde done. And he told my many thyngys that
they dyde, and seyde, "Anone as they done any euyl, the whiche Y
had sum-tyme cure of, the mynystrys and wykyd angellys of the
Deuylle vpbraydyn me with the same, and anon they encresyn my
peynys."

00 'Sothely, ther was sum of the bretheren of that place, the whiche
this man aforeseyde was prior and father to, that were accendyd by
zele of rightwysnes and feruor of relygyon, and dyd also grete labur
and dylygens that, alle inordinate fauors putte a-syde, the puryte and
honeste of her ordre myght be kepte. And this Y knewe was trouthe,
05 wherfore Y seyde to hym, "Howe than was hit noysyd fer and brode
that many thyngys were wel reformyd and amendyd before your
ende in the place where ye were prior, yf hit be nowe schewyd yow
so mekyl euyl of hem that dwelle there ȝette."

'And thanne he seyde, "Trew hit ys, as ye saye, that mekyll thyng
10 was correcte and amende more than yt was wonte to be before.
Neuertheles, of her amendement haue Y no frute ne mede, but also
my pey[n]ys encresyng, because Y was ouer-mekyl agenst her
correccions, and leste Y schulde be correcte, or tho thingys
amendyd | that be amendyd, ful mekyl Y lettyd. Sothely, Y was   [e]5ʳ
15 asschamyd of her opyn correccyon, but lesse Y bashyd to here hem   L240ʳ
ouer-all schamfully dyffamyd. Trewly, her condycyons were so   O37ʳ
froward and obstynate that vtwardly Y hadde wende they had be
incorrygyble, and what-sum-euer ys beleuyd to be done ther fore
amendment, but yf the meruaylous power and myght of God helpe,
20 hyt wyl be broughte done ageyne to noughte. Alas, alas, why dyd Y
beleue euer to seche consels? Alas, that euer Y fauyrde and
magnyfyde seche persons, by the whiche Y dyd so offende the
mageste of God, so to let hem haue her wylle to doo what they
wolde. Sothely, foure persons there byn" (and tolde me her namys,
25 that Y schulde seye to hem), "but yf they sone do to God

1612 peynys] peyuys

maleficiis suis uel consiliis, quibus tam se quam sibi adquiescentes perdiderunt, satisfaccionem obtulerint. Et reuera si usque ad sup- 14 premum iudicii diem in satisfaciendo quantumuis laborarent, modicum omnino eis uideri debuisset in conpensacione & expiacione tam magne & tam diuturne prauitatis sue, qua meipsum extreme calamitati fecerunt obnoxium & domum pene cunctam multiplicibus malis infecerunt. Hos enim uix vnquam uel leuiter contristare 14 uolebam, sed ad nutum eorum, quocunque eis libuisset, inclinabar. Preterea debita michi in psalmis & missis suffragia intercessionum uix pauci ex omni congregacione plenarie soluerunt. Multi autem ex ipsis pro quibus ad penas precipue teneor, nichil omnino earum rerum adimplent. Pro hiis ergo omnibus & dolore presencium et 14 instancium formidine malorum vndique coangustor."

'Talia circa istum uidi qui michi sic locutus est.'

[XXVIII] De quadam inclusa.

'Inclusam uero quandam bone prorsus conuersacionis agnoueram, quam & impensius dilexeram. Hanc ibi quasi de seculo uenientem de 14 nouo uidi. Erat autem vultu admodum constanti & aspectu uenusto, quam uia quidem laboriosa fatigabat immodice; penis etiam ignium, quibus alii hinc inde inuoluebantur, illa frequencius attacta urebatur solummodo. Ipsa uero hec quasi pro exiguo ducens, iter ad paradisum ocius festinando multumque proficiens indesinenter agebat. 14 Hoc cum uiderem, teste Deo, fantasma & quasi sompnium id reputabam, quia illam nullatenus mortuam esse credebam. Dicebam uero in memetipso, "Puto quia meritum ancille Christi in ymaginacione ista sic michi insinuatur: nam in ueritate ea ipsa, que adhuc uiuit in corpore, hic esse non potest." 14

'Hodie autem tercius dies est quo locutus est mecum quidam olim f. 24ʳ conuicaneus predicte ancille Dei, quem | rogaui ut eam uerbis meis salutaret, deuote supplicans, quatinus pro me attencius orare dignaretur. Is autem respondit, "Imo tu magis pro illa uenerabili & communi amica nostra intercede obnixius. Mortis enim debitum 14 iam eam soluisse cognoscas."

euynworthy penaunce for her cursyd dedys and consels, by the
whiche they haue loste hem-selfe and other also, the whiche haue
done after hem, they schalle haue the indycyble and euerlastyng
tormentys of helle. And trewly, yf they dyd penauns and satisfaccion
630 tyl domys-daye they schulde thynke hit but lytyl in-to the recompensacyon and expyacyon of the grete and longe schrewdenes and
cursydnes, by the whiche they haue broughte me to this peynys that
Y am in nowe, and with her wyckydnes they haue al-moste enfecte
and cumbrid alle the howse. Sothely, onethys or litil, any-tyme tho
635 foure persons Y wulde displese, but Y was inclynyd and bowyd to let
hem do what they wolde. Also fewe ther ben of al the couent that for
me and for myn helping, fully haue done and seyde the messys and
psalmys wyth other | soffragys and prayers, the whiche of dewty they [e]5^v
schulde seye and do for me according to oure relygyon. And many of   L240^v
                                                                      O37^v
640 hem for whome Y am now in sore peynys, haue done none of these
thingys ȝet for me, therfore what for sorowe and drede that Y haue
of these present tormentys, Y am peynde on euery syde."

'Seche thin[g]hys sawe Y aboute this prior, and this wyse he spake
to me, as hit ys aboue rehersyd.'

645 ¶ Of an ancres that he sawe and knewe in the same place.
                                                    ¶ Ca xxviij

'Y knewe also a certen ancresse, the whiche was of a gode and
honeste conuersacyon, whome gretely Y louyd, and Y sawe her ther,
as sche had comme late fro the world. Trewly, sche was stable and
650 stedfaste in contynauns and feyre of beholdyng, home the laborus
weye that sche had gon a lytyl had weryde, and with the peynys of
fyre that other were inuoluyd, here and there sche was ofte-tymes
tochyd and sum-what brente. But she ful lytyl counted hyt, and
hastyd her spedly, gretly profeting on the iorney that goyth to
655 paradyse. And this whan Y sawe, Y take God to record, Y had wende
hyt had be sum fantesy and as hit had be a dreme, for Y beleuyd in
no wise that sche was ded. Than seyd Y vnto myselfe, "Y trowe that
the merytorye leuyng of this ancres and seruaunte of Cryste so ys
schewde to me by ymagynacyon, for trewly, sche that ys ȝette aly[u]e
660 in her bodye may not be here."

'Sothely, the thirde | daye after that Y was cum to my-selfe [e]6^r
                                                              L241^r
                                                              O38^r

1643 thinghys] thinhys   1659 alyue] alyne

'Obstupui, fateor, uehemencius, & uerum fuisse, quod de illa conceperam, tunc primo uel ipse credere cepi. De cetero hanc generalem fore omnium moriencium condicionem euidentissime agnoui. Vniuersos qui ad percipiendam ante extremum resurreccio- 148 nis & iudicii tempus quietem destinati sunt, ab hora mortis sue semper duriora relinquentes, leuiora subibant tormenta, nisi forte occasione sui aliqua a uiuentibus committerentur, que sibi iuste imputari potuissent, dum ante mortem satisfaccionis munere non obtinuissent, ut eis ignosceretur, transmissa ad posteros materia 149 delinquendi. Illos uero quos grauior astrinxit causa, qua puniri eternaliter demeruissent, incipiebant quidem a penis grauissimis, que successu grauiorum indies iugiter augmentabantur, & fiebat eis omnis dies sequens precedente amarior.'

[XXIX] **De quodam episcopo.**   149

'In predictis etiam penis episcopum quemdam longe lateque famosum strenuitatis immense prerogatiua qua preminebat, natum quidem de terra hac, sed presulatus honore functum in partibus transmarinis, quem semel tantum uideram, recognoui. Obiit uero anno presenti circa festum sancti Michaelis, nam & diem transitus 150 ipsius tunc liquido noui, sed iam memorie excidit; mente scilicet mea circa multa que uidebam occupata, innumera eorum nec diligenter notare, nec omnia potui que notaueram arcius retinere. Ille uero quem superius memoraui de transitu incluse michi certitudinem attulisse, & hunc rebus humanis exceptum cercius denunciauit, sed 150 quo tempore obisset ignorabat. Repatriarat enim quidam adolescens eiusdem presulis consanguineus, qui illius dum uiueret adheserat famulatui, eique certum detulerat nuncium de obitu ipsius. Flammis autem pene continuis adurebatur & maxime propter lubricos ado- lescencie sue excessus. Aliis etiam modis innumeris torquebatur: 151 f. 24ᵛ cuius mencionem iccirco | non pretermittendam putaui, quia mirum

ageyne, a certen neybur of herns was here that Y spake with and
prayde hym to grete her wele on my worde, and also that sche wylle
whytsafe to pray for me. Than he seyde, "Praye ye also for her, our
665 good frende, for ye scalle vndyrstande that sche ys disceste and paste
to God."

'Ueryly, Y merueylyd gretly at hys seying. And than first Y
beleuyd that hyt was trewe that Y sawe of her in the first place of
purgatorye. Forthermore, this generall condicyon of alle folk that
670 deyon, Y knowe there opynly: that alle pepule the whiche be ordende
to perceue reste and blysse before the daye of dome, hadde euermore
fro the first howre of her dethe her peynys lesse and lesse. But yf hyt
were so, that any of hem had lefte to other that leuyd after, by euyl
exampulle, occasyon of synne, the whiche ryghtwysly they myght
675 wyte hit hem that dyd so before, and whyle they dede no satisfaccion
to God for hit before her deth, wherby seche occasyon of synning
lefte to other schulde haue be forgeuyn hem also, they þat greuysly
offendyd, by the whiche they deseruyd euerlasting dampnacion,
begunne to goo fro ful bittyr peynys to wars, and so by succeding
680 of her peynys, dayly her tormentys besyly encresyn, þat euery day
foloing is more greuossor to hem then was the daye before.'

¶ Of a certen bisshop that was there also.   ¶ xxix

'A certen bisshop Y knew there in peynys, the whiche onys Y
sawe, and he was bore in thys ground | of Inglonde and had hys   [e]6ᵛ
685 byshopriche be-yonde see. Trewely, he deyed thys same yere abowte L241ᵛ
the feste of Seynt Myghel the archangel. For than Y knewe opynly   O38ᵛ
the daye of his passyng, but nowe hit is fallyn out of my mynde, the
whiche that tyme was occupyed aboute many thingys that Y sawe.
Sothely, innumerabulle thyngys there were the whiche Y dyd not
690 wele note, nether cowde wele kepe in my mynde all thyngys that Y
had notyd. Trewely, the same man, the whiche tolde me of the
passyng of the ancres, as hyt ys seyde in the next chaptur before, told
me also of the passing of this bysshoppe, but he knew not what tyme.
Trewely, anothyr yong man, the whiche was cosyn and alye to the
695 same bysshoppe, and also in seruyce with hym whenne he leuyd, cam
home ageyn to his countrey of Inglonde and brought certen worde to
the todyr man, that tolde me that the forseyde bysshoppe was dede.
Trewly, Y sawe this bysshoppe al-moste contynualy brennyng in

quiddam circa ipsum specialiter uidi. Cum enim iugi arderet
incendio ignis, uestis semper honestissima, qua erat indutus, non
modo illesa sed seipsa formosior per flammas reddebatur.

'Cuius miraculi racionem michi dux meus exposuit dicens, "Hoc 151
ei priuilegium prisce consuetudinis sue beneficio comparatum:
enimuero," ait, "nudis semper specialius compati & eorum indigenciam liberalissime solebat releuare. Quare uestis eius decore non
carebit, donec penitencie spacio excurso stola diuinitus iocunditatis
& leticie donetur sempiterno."' 152

[XXX] De cuiusdam uxore.

'Uiri cuiusdam plebei vxor, bonis admodum vna cum marito
predita moribus & studiis, anno preterito huic instabili luci ultimum
ualefecit. Hanc familiariter olim michi caram ibi sub leui affliccione,
respectu aliorum, ad immensum glorie fastigium celestis alacriter 152
properantem gratulabundus aspexi. Inde uero grauiorem reatum
contraxerat & supplicium quia emulis suis & quibuscumque sibi
iniuste inimicantibus impacienti dicacitate conuiciari & obloqui et in
animo dolorem rancoris tenere consueuerat. Hoc tamen uicium,
inuincibile sibi propter imperfeccionem suam, & semper oderat in 153
se & frequencius deflebat. Quare & uicinior restabat ei & facilior
illius ueniam commissi. Fuerat enim in deuocione & oracionis studio
feruentissima, elemosine, hospitalitati, uel reliquis misericordie
operibus super possibilitatem facultatule sue dedita & intenta. Ad
ultimum uero diuturno langore ut fornacis aurum examinata, omnem 153
pene uiciorum scoriam deposuerat.

flamys of fyre, and moste be-ca[us]e of his vycyus leuing that he
700 leuyd in his youthe. Also he was torment in other innumerable
wysys, and be-cause Y sawe sum specyal thinge aboute him, Y
thought to remembre and specially to speke of him. Sothely, as he
brende besyly in fyre he had euermore a ful honest clothe apon him
there, the whiche not only was [not] hurte by the fyre but also yt was
705 yldyn and made by the fyre more feyrer and semlyor than hit was
afore.

'Thanne Sent Nycholas declared to me the reason of thys
meruaylous thyng, and seyde, "Thys preuylege he gate to hym
whenne he leuyd, | by a good dede the whiche he vsyd to doo. And [e]7ʳ
710 this hit was. Euermore he hadde compassion on powre pepulle that L242ʳ
were nakyd, and ful lyberally he vsyd to releue hem of that nede, O39ʳ
wherfore his clothyng schalle neuer lacke feyernes, tyl that he haue
fulfylled his penauns and take of God the stole of euerlastyng ioye
and blysse."'

715 ¶ **Of a certen woman the whyche was a pore mannys wyfe.**
¶ **Ca xxx**

'A woman also that was a poure mannys wyf dyde this laste yere
with her husbond, the whiche was wele condicionde and in mony
thyngys ful wele dysposyd. Sche was sum-tyme ryght famylyarly
720 belouyd of me, home ful gladly Y behylde there in lyghte peynys, in
comparyson of other, swiftely goyng forthe to the grete mede and
worschippe of heuynly ioyes. Trewely, in thys, that sche vsyd
inpacyently to s[c]olde and vpbrayde hem that dyd her wronge
and enmyte, and in her herte hylde ra[n]cour and sowernes agenste
725 hem, sche gretely offendyd and therfore sche hadde sofryd peynys.
Neuertheles, thys vyse was to her inuyncyble by-cause of her
inperfeccyon and euer sche hatyd hyt and often-tymes wepte that
sche coude not ouercome hyt, wherfore sche hadde the soner
forgeuenes of that synne. Sothely, sche was in her prayers ful
730 deuoute and wele disposyd to almys-dedys and hospytalte more
then sche might wele do of her owne godys. And before | her dethe, [e]7ᵛ
by long sekenes that sche had, sche was prouid and clensyd as gold ys L242ᵛ
in a fornes, by the whyche al-moste sche hadde caste fro her the O39ᵛ
scur[f]e and the hardenes of her synnys.

1699 be-cause] be caē   1704 not] *om.*   1723 scolde] stolde   1724 rancour]
raucour   1734 scurfe] scurse

'Ceterum omnino perrarum est, ut hiis diebus, quibus a mera illius nascentis pridem ecclesie simplicitate & innocencia omnium pene mores degenerant, quisquam in hac mortalitate degens, euangelicam ad plenum conseruet aut recuperet iusticiam & pur-   154 itatem, quas donec quisque promeruerit, nec in tabernaculo celestium habitare mansionum, nec in monte paradisiace amenitatis requiescere ualebit. Quamobrem quicquid animabus migrancium de hoc seculo immundicie equitatique contrarium inheserit in illo
f. 25ʳ seculo purgari habet, ut per supplicia purificatis aditus | pateat beate   154 quietis, & in quietis loco perfeccius ex desiderio diuine uisionis dignificatis animabus introitus reseretur celestis glorie. Hoc autem tantum de illis credi oportet iniquitatibus & maculis, quas inter uenialia concedunt annumerari uel sui qualitas in mali pondere leuis uel penitencie satisfaccio & confessionis. Nam de criminalibus que &   155 sui natura mortifera sunt & penitencie remedio leuigata non fuerunt, restat proculdubio ut talis quisque in futuro presentetur iudicio, qualis recessit de hoc seculo.'

[XXXI] De uiris religiosis quas penas, pro quibus delictis, pertulerint.
155

'Omnes uero tam pro magnis quam pro leuioribus peccatis certas & quasi singulorum peccatorum proprias uidi perferre penas. Grauia ualde michi uidebantur eciam que minima ibi & pro leuioribus inferebantur excessibus, ut pro risu immoderato & uerbis ociosis, pro cogitacionibus uagis cum nimis mentem per incuriam occu-   156 passent, uel certe que a uiris obseruanciam regularem professis [committitur] ordinis sui & institucionis transgressio facilis, scilicet in gestu indisciplinato & signis nimiis, in euagacione de claustro uel cellis inutili et indiscreta & in aliis, que in hunc modum sunt. Nam & aliquos uidi pro eo quod extra locum et horam legittime refeccionis   156 herbas uel arborum fructus non medicine sed uoluptatis impulsu comedere presumpsissent, prunas ardentes in ore uoluere, miserabiliter deflentes se non cibum sed supplicium, cum illa sumerent,

1562 committitur] BdT, *om.* SM

735 'Forthirmore, fulfeldyn hyt is in this dayes, in the whyche al-
moste the condicions of alle men gone oute of kynde, f[ro] the pure
and clere symplycyte and innocentnes of the very chirce of God, that
any man leuyng in thys lyfe kepyth or rekeuerythe fully the equyte
and puryte of the holy gospelle, the whyche, tyle a man fulfylle, he
740 may not dwelle in heuynly placys nethyr schalle reste in the
mow[n]te and hille of paradyse of ioye and blysse. Wherfore what-
sum-euer thynge of synne and vnclenesse contrarye to equite and
ryghtwysnes cleuyth and restyth on the sowlys that passyn hens out
of this world, hit shal be purged in a-nothir world, and so by her
745 penauns the weye and pathe of a ioyful restyng shal be schewyd to
hem that be purged and clensyd, and so thenne in placys of reste, the
entring of heuyn and euerlasting blisse ful largely shal be opynd to
tho soulys, for the perfette desyre that they shal haue ther to se God.
Sothly, this only must be takyn of tho synnys whiche, by her light
750 qualite or els by confessyon and satisfaccion don for hem, be granted
of God to be changyd and contyd among venyal synnys. For as
touching tho synnys þat be dedly, and were not in this worlde by the
remedy of confession and penans made light and venial, hyt ys
withoutyn doute þat he shal so be presentyd to his iugement in the
755 world þat is to cum as he is fonde in hys leuyng when he passyth
oute of this worlde.'

¶ **What peynys relygyous men sofryd for certen fawtes.**   [e]8^r
                                            ¶ **Ca xxxi**   L243^r
                                                             O40^r

'Sothely, Y sawe alle relygyous folke, bothe of men and wemen,
760 howe they sofryd certeyne peynys as wele for lytyl offenses as for
grete synnys, and as hit were propyr peynes for synguler synnys.
And full sore, as hit semyd to me, were the leste peynys that they
sofryd for ryght lytyl offenses, as for inmoderate lawghyng and ydyl
wordys spekyng, and that they sofryd her mynde neglygently ouyr-
765 mekyl to wandyr aboute in vayne thoughtys, or els for lyght brekyng
the rulys and fourme of her relygyon, as in lyghte and nyce behauing
of gestur, and in multyplyyng sygnys to mekyl and so for goyng and
wandryng out of her cloyster and cellys onprofetabully, and also for
many other thyngys in lyke wyse. For some Y sawe ful myserabully
770 wepyng, and rowlling hoote brennyng colys in theire mouthys for
eting frutys and herbys out of dewe placys and tyme, not for any

1736 fro] for   1741 mownte] mowute

comedisse. Pro risu uero immoderato, uerbera, pro uerbis ociosis in
facie, cesiones, pro cogitacionibus inutilibus & nimium ex more 15
uagis, aeris uariam inclemenciam perferebant. Qui in gestu dissolu-
ciori peccassent, uinculis asperrimis & nonnulli igneis artabantur.
Pro signorum numerositate superflua, quibus ludicra & ociosa
queque contulissent adinuicem, digiti negligencium uel excoriaban-
f. 25ᵛ tur uel tunsionibus quassabantur. Uagacio | instabilium dura de loco 15
in locum iactacione, distraccione & collisione inter se membrorum
molestius plectebantur. Sermones uero impuritate aliqua & irreligio-
sitate, qualibetue turpitudine sordentes, in uiris presertim ordinis
sacri, sicut capitalia crimina pene puniebantur. Uotorum quorum-
cunque fracciones & precipue cum aliquid impendentis periculi metu 15
quique domino uel sanctis eius pro erepcione uouissent, & securitate
recepta eiusdem uoti preuaricacionem non uitassent, inestimabilibus
penis luebantur.'

[XXXII] De quodam milite, qui uotum fregit.

'Inter eiusmodi preuaricatores iuuenem quendam de ordine mili- 158
tari, michi dudum familiarem, uidi medio in rogo ardere. Quem
sciscitatus cur tantis subderetur malis, hec ab eo audiui.
'"Vita," inquit, "mea omnino sterilis & uana, sed multorum
fertilis uiciorum, immo uiciis plena. Feda enim libidine, elacione
insolens erat. Uerum inde crucior precipue, quia crucem reieci, 159
quam sumpseram in uoto Ierusolimam adeundi, quamquam non
instinctu deuocionis sed inanis glorie obtentu, quam a domino cui
militabam captare sategi, illam susceperim. Omni uero nocte iter
illud quanta ualeo profeccione consummare laboro. Verum debilis
uiribus, destitutus sumptibus, aeris contrarietate, & asperitatibus 159
insuper uie non leuiter prepedior. Vnde uix breuissimam explere
ualeo dietam. Erumpente autem mane aduolant terrores mei, angeli
tenebrarum, omnique crudelitate debachantes ad locum me reuehunt
tormentorum, ubi totis semper diebus, cum quadam tamen melior-
acione hesterni doloris, licet permodica, incendor et multipliciter 160
affligor. Denuo nocte reddita, illo restituor in loco ubi pridie finiui
iter. Unde uiam omisse peregrinacionis demum aggredior, mane
iugiter suppliciis de more subdendus. Omnes quoque qui crucem
f. 26ʳ reicientes Ierusolimitanam postposuerint | quam uouerint peregrina-

medsyn or nede, but for luste and appetyte. And for inmoderate
lawghing they had betingys; for ydyl speche, strokys in her face; and
for vayne thoughtys they sofryd greuys and varyante trowb[u]lnes of
775 the eyre. And they that offendy[d] in dissolucyon of gestur and
behauyng were bonde with scharpe bondys, and many with fyry
boundys, and for superfluyte of signys, by the whiche they hadde
togedyr lewde pleys and ydyl gamys, sum of hem had her fyngerst†
f[l]ayne and some had hem by | knockyng sore broysyd. They also [e]8ᵛ
780 that were onstabule, wandryng here and there, were greuysly caste L243ᵛ
and throwe fro one place to anothir, by the whiche her lymmys were O40ᵛ
sore hurte amonge hem-selfe. Also they that spake wordis of
reboudye, the whiche sounned onclenesse or other-wise agenst the
honeste of relygyon, were ponysshte there almoste as sore as for
785 dedly synnys. Alsoo who-sum-euer brake any vowys made to God or
to hys seyntys, specyally in tyme of drede and perylle, for her helpe
and delyuerans, and afterward suerte takyn of the same vowe, sofryd
inestymable tormentys.'

¶ Of a certen knyght that brake a vowe.   ¶ xxxii

790   'Amonge hem that brake her vowys Y sawe a yong knyght
brennyng in the myddys of fyre, whome Y knewe sumtyme ful
wele. And as Y enquyred of him why he was putte in so grete
peynes, thys he tolde me.
      ' "My lyfe," he seyde, "that Y leuyd, was but baren and vayne and
795 also vycyous. For Y was insolent and nyse in pryde and elacyon, and
foule and vnclene by the vyce of lecherye. Notwithstonding, for thys
Y am nowe specyally ponysht by-cause Y caste aweye fro me the
sygne of the holy crosse, the whyche Y hadde takyn apone me in a
vowe that Y made to goo to the Holy Lond, howe-be-yt that Y toke
800 the crosse not for deuocyon but for vayne-glorye, the whiche Y loued
to haue hadde of the lorde þat Y seruyd. Trewely, euery nyght Y
labur in going | as mekyl as Y maye to make an ende of that [f]1ʳ
pilgremage. But what for febulnes of strenthe and contraryusnes of L244ʳ
the wedyr, and also scharpnes of the waye, Y am lettyd gretly, that O41ʳ
805 onethe Y may goo at on tyme a full lytyl dayes iourney. Sothely,
whenne the mornyng begynnyth, fleyn to me wykyd spirytys, beyng
wodde yn al cruelnes, and drawyn me ageyne to the place of my

1774 trowbulnes] trowbnlnes   1775 offendyd] offendyth   1778-9 fyngers
flayne] flyngers fayne

cionem, simili fatigacione hanc tenentur explere, si tamen, sicut & 160
michi celitus concessum est, uel in uite suppremo ex hoc digne
penituerint & per confessionis salutare refugium hoc crimen sibi
ueniale reddiderint. Alias peccatum istud suos admissores dampna-
cioni eterne astringit."'

[XXXIII] De alio milite. 161

'Alium quoque militem, qui ante hoc decennium miliciam uite,
que super terram est, defunccione salutari omiserat, ibidem recognoui. Hic autem tunc temporis omnes quidem penas euicerat
grauiores, sed prius in eis multipliciter estuauerat. Cuius ideo
defunccionem salutarem dico, quia & per tanti spacii cruciatus ad 161
gaudia tamen migrabat omnium seculorum. Auiculam quandam niso
similem pugno ferebat. Hic uero in uita pristina pre omnibus
prouincie sue hominibus benificenciam hospitalitatis, ut monet
apostolus, liberalius & studiosius quibusque aduentantibus exhibere
gaudebat. Annis ferme triginta continenciam uidualem, coniuge sua 162
quam maritali castitate dilexerat ad Dominum premissa, sectari
uidebatur. Dapsilis, omnibus affabilis & beneficus uixerat. Mirabar
itaque uehementer cur tanto tempore uir honeste morigeratus
quietem plenissimam minime percepisset. Uerum dixit michi hoc
mirandum non esse, cum in mundo diucius uiuens non potuerit 162
plurima non commisisse, presertim in puericia & iuuentute cum
delicacius nutriretur, et tum a sodalibus, tum feruore indiscrete
etatis, ad noxia multipliciter traheretur, que uidelicet in conuersa-
cione seculari, ubi conuiuencium moribus conformari oportet, ad
plenum nequiuerit expiare. Auem uero quam pugno gestabat, 163
penaliter sibi manum rostro & vngulis lacerare querebatur. Cuius-
modi tedium ea ex re molestius & infestius sibi imminere fatebatur,
quia in lusu auium, quarum uolatu alias raperet, omni uite sue
f. 26ᵛ tempore inani quadam uoluptate impensius delectari con-|sueuisset.

peynys, where euer-more al the days tyme Y am gretly peynde yn
fyre. Neuertheles, wyth a certen amendement of lessur dyssese,
810 thawght hyt be lytyl. And ageyne when nyghte comythe Y am
restoryd to the place where Y lefte laste my iourney, and so Y go
forthe on my pylgrimage, and when the mornyng ys cumme Y am
drawyn ageyne and caste to peynys. And al that haue vowyd to go to
the Holy Londe, and aftyr dyd caste fro hem her crosse, and whent
815 not dedyr, yn lyke wyse as Y go, they be compellyd to do her
pylgrymage, so yf they may haue the grace of God yn her laste ende
to repente hem, as Y had to repente me for brekyng of my vowe, and
than by the holsum remedy of confession thys synne þat was dedly
synne may be changyd to a venyal synne. Othyr-wyse al that breke
820 that same vowe be put to eternalle dampnacion." '

¶ **Also of another knyhht.**   ¶ **Ca xxxiii**

'Another knyght also, the whiche welle dyde and paste to God a
.x. ȝere a-gon, Y sawe and knew | there. This knyght, that tyme the [f]1ᵛ
whyche Y sawe hym, had ouercome alle his grete peynys that he had L244ᵛ
O41ᵛ
825 sofryd before, and therfore Y sey he dyd wele, for by that space of
penans he wente wele toward the ioys of paradyse. Sothely, he bare
there on hys fyste a lytyll byrdde lyke a sparhauke. Also in hys lyfe,
aboue alle men that were of that countreye the whiche he dwellyd in,
[he] gaue gladly and lyberally to all pore pepul that came to hym
830 hospytalyte. Trewely, his wyfe dide afore him almoste a .xxx.
wyntyr, after hoys dethe he leuyd continent and chaste, in a
wydwardys lyfe, redy and benyuolente to alle men whilys he
leuyd. And gretely [Y] merueylde why he, þat was so honeste of
leuyng and wele condycyonde in hys demening, had not ȝette
835 perceiuyd fully reste and ioye. Than he seyde to me that hit was
not too be merueylyde. For why, whenne he leuyd, he mighte ofte
offende in many wysys, specialy by-cause that in hys youthe and
childhode he was norishte and broughte vppe delycately, and, what
for felishyppe and hys yowthe, was drawyn to many noy[e]ful
840 thyngys of the whiche he kowde not fully be purgyd and made
clene in worldly conuersacyon, where he muste conforme hym to the
maners and behauyng of hem þat he dwellyd amonge. Sothely, he
complaynde that the hauke the whiche he bare on hys fyste paynfully
tare his hande with her bylle and scharpe cleys. This tedeusnes of

1829 he] *om.*   1833 Y] *om.*   1839 noyeful] noysful

Quod genus delinquendi nec in senio reliquerit uel defleuerit, quia   163
hoc in peccatum deputari nescisset.

'Multa etiam et alia uidi in loco quem primo inspexi tam circa
notos meos quam circa promiscuas omnium graduum & professionum multitudines, quorum singuli, ut longe superius breuiter sub
quadam generalitate complexus sum, innumeris afficiebantur   164•
penarum asperitatibus & amaritudinibus. Verum hec interim pauca
de multis dixisse sufficiat.'

[XXXIV] De hiis quos in secundo loco tormentorum monachus uiderit.

'Iam ex hiis, que loco secundo notauimus nobis insinuata, aliqua   164:
compendiose memoremus. Hoc in loco, ut prefati sumus, multo
plures quam in aliis nobis dudum familiares & notos, ea in quibus a
Dei cognicione & familiaritate abalienati sunt deuiando, scilicet a
mandatis eius, inter supplicia deflere conspexi.'

[XXXV] De tribus episcopis.   165(

'Tres ibi episcopos olim sepius a nobis uisos cathenis igneis arcius
constrictos inter globos ignium & procellas grandinum ac niuium &
turbines uentorum & interfluentis stagni fetores miserabili ordine
uolutari cernebam. Non multum ab inuicem dissimiliter cruciabantur.   165:
'Unus tamen pre ceteris immanissime ea potissimum ex causa
torquebatur, quia placitatoris loco inter seculares iudices consedere
plurimumque in hoc delectari soleret, multis etiam bona consciencia
nitentibus in litigando uiolentus contra iusticiam oppressor extiterit.
Hiante iugiter ore linguam sibi flammis ultricibus ardere querebatur;   166(
et cum uicissim nunc ignibus totus cremaretur, nunc niue madidus
geluque constrictus obrigesceret, nunc stagni fetoribus cenoque†
oblimatus sorderet, lingue semper sue continuabantur incendia.

1662 cenoque] BdT, scenoque SM

1845 peyne he sofryd, as he seyde, by-cawse that in haukyng, the whiche
he vsyd alle the tyme of hys lyfe, [he] gretely delytyd to see the
haukys whenne | they flowe, howe they toke other byrddys. The [f]2ʳ
whiche haukyng he lefte not in hys aage, nethyr thereof had any L245ʳ
compunccyon, for he knewe not that seche a thing were any synne. O42ʳ
1850 'Many other thingis also Y sawe and behylde in this firste place of
purgatorye, [i].e. as wele aboute hem that Y knewe, as aboute other,
bothe of men and women, of alle degreys and professyons, of the
whiche eueryche-on of hem were ponyshte in peynys innumerable,
ful scharpe and bytterly, as Y haue schortely aboue seyde, vnder a
1855 certen generalyte, wherfore these fewe thingys seyde now of many
thingys be suffycyaunt here at this tyme.'

¶ **Of tho persons that he sawe in the secund place of
purgatorye.** ¶ Ca xxxiiij

'Nowe of tho thingys the whiche Y sawe and notyd in the second
1860 place of purgatorye, sumwhat Y wylle schewe and declare to yow.
Sothely, in this secund place Y sawe and knewe many mo that were
sum-tyme of myne acquentanse than Y dyd in any other place, sore
wepyng and sorowyng in her peynys her synnys, by the whiche they
had brokyn owre Lordys commaundmentys, wherfore they were
1865 alyenate and made ferre fro his famylyare knowlege.'

¶ **Of .iii. bysshoppys þat Y fonde there.** ¶ Ca xxxv

'Thre bysshoppys that Y knewe wele sum-tyme I sawe there
straytely bownde wyth fyrye | chaynys, oftyn-tymes turnyng and [f]2ᵛ
walowyng ful myserabully, now yn gret fyre, and now yn scharpe L245ᵛ
1870 stormys of hayle and snow and whyrlewyndys, and aftyrward yn a O42ᵛ
fowle stynkyng ponde of blacke watyr. Trewly, they were ponysht
dyuersly, not fer from othyr.
'And on of hem was more bytterly torment than tothyr were, and
that was by-cause he vsyd yn hys lyfe to sytte amonge secler iugys yn
1875 place and tyme of pledyng, and ther-yn he toke a grete plesure and
delyte, and oftyn-tymes he was, to many that pledyd her causis of
god consciens, a vyolent oppressure agenst ryghtewesenes, and
therfore he compleynyd whyt an opyn mowthe that hys tonge
contynually brende yn flamys of fyre. And as he was now brennyng
1846 he] *om.* 1851 i.e.] .e.

'Alius continencie cingulo aliquando negligencius usus est. Quod nefas, in episcopo nimis immensum, crebra putentis demersione stagni illius, quod estus & frigora interiacere supradiximus, puniebatur. Profuit ei multum inter alia satisfaccionis bona quod calcato prelacionis ambitu humilem monachorum ante finem suum corde contrito susceperat habitum. Hoc | enim quibusque facientibus plurimum confert, quia & meritis & interuentu sanctorum, qui hoc habitu usi sunt, specialius iuuantur, & in ordine eorum resuscitandi noscuntur, qui mundum pro Domino funditus reliquerunt, si uel in extremis plena deuocione mundo renunciauerunt.

'Tercii peculiare fuerat uicium, inanis gloria. In cuius compensacione delicti frequencius altissimis flammarum spiris in sublime agebatur. Et quia per hoc uicium precipue a diuino amore in frigus itur mundani torporis, cadentem illum excipiebant partis opposite algores. Commune illorum trium exicium fuit animarum incuria, diuiciarum cura, despeccio erga pauperes, in principes adulacio, sollicitudo illicita & immoderata propinquorum, & ut vno sermone breuiter multa concludam, quilibet que sua erant quesisse, que Ihesu Christi neglexisse conuincebatur. Generale autem huius & complurium quos uidi prelatorum malum fuit neglectus officii suscepti, honoris delectacio, oneris dissimulacio. In hiis omnibus potestate qua prediti fuerant in sui perniciem & subditorum perdicionem se abusos inenarrabili luctu plangebant. Horum fere omnium tormenta ita sicut superius de quodam rettuli cotidianis fere cumulis augmentabantur, ut quicquid diutina uexacione & amicorum viuencium suffragiis in missis, elemosinis & ceteris huiusmodi mitigari de penis eorum debuisset, nouis & recentibus suorum criminibus, quos in uiciis suis perniciose fouerant, aut minime pro gradus sui debito corripuerant, amplius indies aggrauabantur. Quare vniuersi, qui tali condicione supplicia perferebant, de salute sua omnino dubii & ancipites pene desperabiliter fluctuabant. Nichil uero in tormentis ita exiciale ducebant, sicut indulgencie quandoque percipiende incertitudinem. Nichil e diuerso aliorum dolorem sic

1880 yn fyre and now wete, and styftely froryn yn snow and froste, and
now yn a stynkyng ponde, and now fowle ouerkeuryde yn fenne and
plutte, hys tonge euermore conteynuyd yn brennyng fyre.

'The tothyr of hem othyr-whyles neglygently brake hys chastyte,
the whyche dede, specialy yn a byshoppe, was ouerfowle and
1885 abhomynable, and therfore was he drownde oftyn-tymes yn the
fowle and stynking ponde that lythe betwene the gret hete and
colde, as hyt ys seyde be-fore. Sothly, a-fore hys dethe he lefte the
honowre and dignyte of hys byshoprye, and toke apon hym the meke
habette of a monke, the whyche gretly helpyd hym, amonge othyr
1890 dedys of satysfaccion. And al that so done, grete good and profette
ther-of cummyth to hem. For al they specialy | be holpyn by the   [f]3^r
meritys and prayers of the holy seyntys, the whiche vsid afore the   L246^r
same habette, and also ben knowyn and markid to rise vppe ageyne   O43^r
in the ordyr of hem the whiche, when they leuyd here, vtwardly lefte
1895 this worlde or els at her laste ende in ful deuocyon forsoke this
world.

'The thirde of these byshopys gretly delyted in worldly worshippe
and vayne glorye. For the whiche synne he was ofte-tymys bore vp
an hye in ful hye spyryst† of flamys of fyre. And bycause he fille fro
1900 the loue of God by seche synne vnto the coolde of worldly
slowfulnes, he was lette done brenning to the greuys coolde that
was on the todyr syde of the fyre, and be-cause of the comyn euyl
and peynys that thes thre ware in, was for the neglygens of soulys the
whiche they had cure of, and for the gret carke that they had of her
1905 riches and despexion of pore pepul, for flatering of princys and
inmoderate carke of her kynnefolke, and, as Y may shortly conclude
many thingys in fewe wordys, euerych-on of hem sought after tho
thingys that was to him-selfe and not tho thingys that longyth to our
Lorde Ihesu Criste. And the general euyll of these and many other
1910 prelatys that Y sawe was the negligens of her office, delectacion of
worldly worschippe, and dyssymulacyon of her charge, and in alle
these thingys ful heuely they sorowyd by-cause they mysusyd her
powre, that they had vndyr God, to the grete hurte of hem-selfe and
to the perdicion of her sogettys. And therfore the peynys of al seche
1915 prelatys were dayly encresyd more and more, as Y haue tolde before
of a certen prior, that what-sum-euer her frendys that leuyd in | the   [f]3^v
worlde dyd for hem, as in messys, almysdede, and seche other   L246^v
thingis by the whiche her peynys shold be lessyd, dayly her greuys   O43^v

1899 spyrys] spyrytys

mitigabat, quemadmodum fida consequende remissionis presumpcio.

f. 27ᵛ Incertis quoque de fine malorum suorum uel hoc ipsum | magnum quodammodo uidebatur esse solacium, quod dampnacionis sue certitudine non tenebantur. Nam hoc malum peremptorium, scilicet 1700 desperacio, quantum perpendere mecum secundum ea que uidebam ibi sufficio, omnibus cruciatibus plus cruciat, omnibus angustiis plus angustat, & penis omnibus magis grauat.'

[XXXVI] De quodam archiepiscopo.

'Uidi preter istos quendam meriti quondam & nominis magni 1705 uirum, qui post humile cenobitarum contubernium, ubi reuera deuote uixerat, in religione feruens, in corporis maceracione rigidus, in sacris meditacionibus strenuus, in multarum carismatibus uirtutum prestantissimus, ad pontificatus & demum ad primatus apicem in regione latissima profecerat. Uerum proth dolor quantum per hoc 1710 in oculis hominum creuerat, tantum in iudicio interni inspectoris decreuisset, si non diuina miseracione & precedentis uite meritis adiutus, in qua in humili habitu bene placuerat Domino, in bono proposito & labore Deo acceptabili uite terminum conclusisset. In pontificali enim regimine minori iusto solercia, maxime cum sciencia 1715 magna premineret, saluti inuigilauit populorum. Indignissimorum etiam promocionibus ad honores ecclesiasticos ignauiter consensit. Regiis nutibus propter iuris execucionem displicere, quia specialiter regio fauore tantum honorem uidebatur adeptus, aut formidauit aut erubuit. Denique & simultatum equo tenacior, multa quibusque 1720 studuit irrogare aduersa, quos promocioni sue in primis nouerat renitentes. Hiis & huiusmodi excessibus enormiter offenderat. Hoc etiam sibi ad maiorem reputabatur culpam, quod religionis & sapiencie auctoritatem, quibus opinatissimus celebrabatur, & quibus multis prodesse ualuisset, sub cuiusdam ignauie modio 1725

peynys were encresyd for the synful leuyng of hem the whiche they
1920 dedly fauerd and brought vp in her vicys, or els be-cause they dyd
not correcte hem in dewe forme, as yt longeth to her offyce.
Wherfore, al thay þat for seche causys sofrid peynys, gretly douted
of her saluacion and were almoste in desperacion. Sothly, ther is no-
thing so greuys to hem that be in peynys as the oncertente of her
1925 delyuerans, and also ther ys no-thing that so mekyl swagyth the
peynys and sorowys of other as dothe a very hope and feythefull
truste, the wyiche they knewe and haue by oure Lordys mercye, to
be delyueryd. And they that were certeyn to haue an ende of her
peynys and were not bonde to the certente of dampnacion, þat same
1930 certente was to hem a ful grete solace and conforte. For as touching
the euyl and hurte of desperacion, as mekyl as Y can consider and
remembre me after tho thingys that Y sawe there, hyt greuyth,
disesyth, and tormentyth tho soulys that haue hit, more than al other
peynys done.'

1935 ¶ Of an archebysshoppe of Canturbery.   ¶ Ca xxxvi

'Y sawe also besyde these aboue-seyde a certen person that
sumtyme was of grete name and fame, the whiche after the meke
conuersacion of monkys relygyon that he leuyd in before, in the
whiche he had leuid ful deuoutely, as in bodely penauns, in holy
1940 medytacions, and many other vertues right excellently, and at the last
he was promotyd and made archebishope of Canturbery and primate
of Inglonde. But alas, for sorow, for | trewly, the more therby he   [f]4ʳ
grewe in the sight of the pepul, so mekyl he had fal and decresyd in   L247ʳ
the sight of God, the whiche behilde him inwardly, and the sander   O44ʳ
1945 had endid his life ȝef he had not be holpe by the mercy of God and
the merytys of his good leuyng afore, by the whiche, when he was in
relygyon a monke ful wele in good purpose and labore acceptable to
God, he had plesyd oure Lorde. Sothely, when he was bisshope of
Canturbery and also specyaly ful excellent in conning, ful lityl hede
1950 he toke to his cure and to the gostely helthe of the peple. For he
onwysyly promoted ful onworthy persons to beneficys of the chirche,
and also he dredde and was aschamyd to execute the lawe for
displeasing the King, by hoys fauor, hit semyd, he cam to that
dignite. Also he studyd and thought by a colur of symulacyon,
1955 odyrwise then he schulde, to troble hem the whiche he knew were
agenste his promoting of the byshoprye and dignite that he had. In

inutiliter deprimendo occultauit. Qui enim hoc faciunt suppliciis enormibus deputantur; quia & scandalum magis parant ecclesie Dei quique sanctitatis & sapiencie titulis illustres, | dum nec uicia & abusionum male sata & peius radicata plantaria euellunt, nec uirtutum & honestatis insignia edificare & plantare pro iure officii sui in plebe sibi subdita satagunt, quam alii qui utriusque boni prerogatiua destituti, cum sint eque inutiles, noscuntur. Enim uero ab istis exigi non potest, quod eis creditum non est. Quamobrem & leuiter ferendum esse creditur si inutilitate natiua terram occupant nitore mundane ambicionis quasi foliis quibusdam vmbrosis pulcri, sed fructus dulcedine uacui: illorum uero torpor & remissio etiam istis securitatem perniciosam transmittit, ut credant se strenuos ministerii sui executores in quo tam famosis rectoribus uel predecessoribus uel collegis suis aut pares inueniuntur aut parum inferiores.

'Deus tamen & ab insciis, quod habere debuerunt ut fierent capita in populis, expetit; & sciolis, quod steriliter habuerunt, in ipsorum perniciem & penam immaniorem conuertit.

'De publica autem presbiterorum & clericorum incontinencia maxime periclitantur moderni pontifices, quia tam enorme scelus in iniuriam celestium sacramentorum, in quibus omnis fidelium salus & uita consistit, que isti, quantum in ipsis est, temerare, cum sint polluti et fedi, non uerentur, corrigere dissimulant.

'De negligencia decanorum, officialium, & archidiaconorum pleraque que uidi referre supersedeo, & qualiter, illis uel consencientibus uel propter numerum aut personarum accepcionem dissimulantibus, Christianitatis status omnis euertitur. Id enim in viuencium operibus uel moribus euidencius ostenditur. Horum itaque dissolucio & langor erga zelum domus Dei tum maxime clero & populo tum precipue & sibi & suis auctoribus dampnacionem adquirit eternam.

'De hiis uero omnibus & aliis in hunc modum innumeris, prefatus in regione sua presulum maximus graui sub | questione laborabat. Iuuit autem precipue hunc preciosissimus martir et Anglorum archiepiscopus sanctus Thomas, quem suffragatorem hinc potissimum optinuerat, quia in terra promissionis ad quam peregre deuenerat xenodochium instituerat nomine sancti Thome intitulatum ad magnum scilicet refugium peregrinorum. Quod factum ibi primo cognoui, sed pridie quidam monachus id michi sciscitanti, an uerum esset, retulit per ordinem qualiter illud institutum est. Auxit preterea non modice remedia ipsius peregrinacionis labor, quem in expedi-

f. 28ʳ (margin)

1730
1735
1740
1745
1750
1755
f. 28ᵛ (margin)
1760
1765

these thingys and seche other he had gretly offendyd. Also in this he
was more to be blamid and more offendyd, þat he hyd and kepte
close ful onprofetably the auctorite of relygyon and wysdom that he
had fro hem of home he was ful excellently named and to home he
might ful gretly haue profet; and ho-sum-euer so do, they be
ordende to ful grete peynis, for they be a sclaunder to the chirche
of God while they plucke not vppe and distrey the wekyd leuing and
rotyd wysys, the whiche be sowyn in the hertys and conuersacion of
the peple of God þat they haue cure and charge of, nethir be aboute
by her office to edifie and plante in her sogettys the nobulnes and
condicions of vertu and honeste, | no more than other that lacke
bothe holynes and gode vnderstanding.

'Neuertheles, our Lorde sechyth as wel of hem that had no
conning in seche thingis as they shuld haue had for-to be hedys of
the peple, as of other the whiche had connyng and vnderstonding,
how-be-it þat they had hit but barenly, and turnith hit to the more
tormentys and peynys of hem bothe.

'Also, for the opyn and foule onchaste leuing of pristys and
clarkys, bishoppis nowe-a-dayis ful gretly perishe be-cause they
correcte not so grete a synne, the whiche is a ful grete iniurye and
wrong to the heuynly sacramentys of Holy Chirche. For in thoo
blessyd sacramentys al the lyfe and helpe of Crystyn peple is
conteynyd, the whiche, as mekyl as is in hem, be not aschamyd to
defoule when they be right foule and pollutyd.

'Sothly, of the negligens of denys, of archedekons, and of other
officers, mony thingis Y saw, the whiche Y leue out to tel, and how
by her consenting and simulacyon and for taking ʒeftys and mennys
persons, al the state of Cryndome almost ys ouercomme and
subuertyd. For this ys opynly shewyd in the werkys and condicions
of hem that now leuyn. Also the dissolucyon and sloufulnes of seche
persons, þat shulde haue a zele and a loue to the peple of God,
requyryth and askyth eternal dampnacion, as wel to the clergy as to
the laye-folke, and most to hem-selfe and to her auctors.

'Trewly, for these thingis and many other inumerable in this wise
the forseyde archebishoppe laborde in gret peynys vnder greuys
complayning. Sothly, he was wel holpen there by the gloryus martir
and archebishoppe of Englonde, Sent Thomas of Canturbery, home
he had gotyn to him there a special patron and helper, be-|cause
when he went to the Holy Londe a pilgrymage in his lyfe-tyme, he
hordende there an hospitalle for pilgrimmys and intytylde hit in the

[f]4ᵛ
L247ᵛ
O44ᵛ

[f]5ʳ
L248ʳ
O45ʳ

cione Ierusolimitana sustinuit, que nuper de omnibus pene mundi partibus contra inimicos crucis Christi, qui ipsam urbem peccatis incolarum exigentibus peruaserunt, profecta est.

'Sacerdotum plures qui incontinencie sue reatus penitendo & confitendo reliquerant, sed penitenciam non peregerant, innumeris 1770 & immensis suppliciis & ardoribus ibi confectos misera per omnia sorte uidi. Verum cogitanti intra me quod nimis pauci ibi reperi[r]-entur ad multitudinem nimiam eorum quam ubique terrarum castimoniam polluendo penas demeruisse post mortem suspicabar, responsum est michi quod ideo paucissimi de multitudine talium ibi 1775 torquerentur quia uix & rarus quisquam ex eis uere penitens super iniquitate & fornicacionibus suis inueniatur: vnde multitudinem ipsorum maximam ad illos, quos in carne morientes mors eterna excipit, pertinere et illorum penis indicibilibus coniungi non esset ambiguum. 1780

'Ego autem in tota uisione ista neminem conspexi, qui spem funditus amisisset indulgencie & sub certitudine estuaret perdicionis eterne.'

[XXXVII] Quedam descripcio monachi de quibusdam hominum generibus & de eorum penis. 1785

'Longum supra modum foret si uiritim omnium condicionum uel graduum uel ordinum personas quos ibi noui recenserem: fastidio-sum etiam nimis lectori, si singillatim supplicia criminum singu-lorum, prout nobis ostensa sunt, temptarem exponere. Nullum in scripturis sanctis peccati genus describitur, cuius in hiis locis certa 1790 non sint auctoribus suis preparata tormenta. Pretereo igitur f. 29ʳ homicidas, | adulteros, fornicatores, incestuosos, mendaces, periuros, commessatores, proditores, auaros, superbos, inuidos, detractores, odientes proximos, & cenodoxie seruientes, & alias in hunc modum

1772 reperirentur] repperirentur M, reperientur ST

name of Sente Thomas, to the gret sokyr and conforte of Crystyn
pylgryms. Trewely, this dede Y knew first in purgatory when Y saw
the forseyd bisshop in sore peynys, but ʒesterday Y enquered therof
yf hit were trew, and a certen person, a religius man, told me how yt
was ordende and begunne. Forthyrmore, gretly hit profet him the
labur þat he had when he went on pilgremage to Ierusalem where he
made þat place.

'Also many prystys, that by the grace of God lefte her vycyus
leuing of onchastyte, in very contricion of herte with confession of
mouth when they leuyd, and be-cause they had not do penans
sufficiently, Y saw hem torment in innumerable peynys. Trewly,
then Y thoughte to myselfe þat ful few prystys were ther fonde of the
gret nombre þat is of hem in al the world, that had deseruyd peynis
after her dethe for breking her chastyte, and to thys hit was so
answard:

'"Therfor ful few ben here torment of the nombre of seche
persons, for onethe it is seldynne sey þat any man of hem were
very penitent and contrite while they leuyd for her synnys, wherfore
hit ys no doute but þat the grete multytude of hem byn vtwardly
dampde."

'Sothly, in al this visyon Y saw no man that vtwardly hadd loste
hope of saluacion, nethir þat was in certente of eternal dampnacion.
Neuertheles, some þat were in greuys peynys had no knoulege when
they shulde be sauyd, and þat was most peynful to hem. And some
that were in peynys knew a certente of her delyuerans, and that was
to hem a grete solace, as hit ys here seyde aboue.'

¶ A certen descripcion of diuers kynd of synfull peple and
of her peynys.   ¶ Ca xxxvij

[f]5ᵛ
L248ᵛ
O45ᵛ

'Hyt were to longe and oute of mesure yeffe Y schulde reherse by
name al tho persons the whiche Y sawe and knew there, of all
condicions, of all degreys, and of all orders. Also ʒef Y schulde sey or
be aboute to schew and declare synglerly the peynys and tormentys
of euery syngler cryme, like as hit was schewde to me at that tyme,
hit wulde be ouer-teduse and weriful to the redder therof. For ther
ys no synne wretyn in holy scripture but ther ys ordende in tho
placys certen peynis to al that be doers of hem. T[he]refore, Y leue
oute and pas by men-[s]leers, auowtres, fornicators, lyers and

2032 Therefore] Trefore   2033 men-sleers] menfleers

mille pestes, quarum ibi merces copiosa nimis diuisim suis prepar-   179
atur operariis. Quis enim hec omnia referre ualeat cum bene
religios[o]s uiderim pro eo tantum, quod manuum decore &
digitorum producciori nitore gloriari solerent, amara nimis perferre
supplicia? Uiatores repentinis latronum insidiis trucidatos modestius
cruciari pro suis quibusque reatibus uidi. Fures uero, quod omni-   180
modis pretereundum non est, qui suspendio adiudicati sacerdoti
tantum, uel quod maxime iuuat, puplice crimina & opera sua mala in
uera cordis contricione confessi sunt, ipsumque mox patibulum
paciencter in remissionem peccatorum omnium subierunt, remittentes
ex animo persecutoribus & inimicis suis iniurias & afflicciones, ipsam   180
etiam mortem suam, cum speciali quadam uenerabilitate in penis
micioribus uidi contrectari. Alios pro simili punit[os] scelere, qui
confiteri iam leto imminente obiecta facinora palam noluerunt,
sperantes (scilicet diabolica fraude decepti) quod, negantes vnde
criminabantur, dimitterentur illesi, propositum autem firmum   181
habentes relinquendi peccata sua ac digne penitendi, si speratas
percepissent inducias, tunc etiam presbitero, si adesset, parati
confiteri, sed hiis omnibus frustrati, Dei solius & sanctorum eius
misericordiam in uite supremo enixius interpellantes, nimia uidi
attrocitate uexari. Venie tamen consequende spem nec isti amiserant.   181
Igneis autem patibulis lorisque flammeis compediti & suspensi,
mediis in rogis palpitabant, quos flagris & tridentibus cedentes et
discerpentes tortores immanissimi facinora sua cum insultacionibus
nimiis improperabant.'

[XXXVIII] De ueneficis.   182

'Ueneficos & mulierculas, que fetus suos aut editos exposuerant
f. 29ᵛ abdicatos aut interfecerant uel conceptos abor-|tire maleficiis suis
coegerant, dilacerari multimoda cede & vngularum abrasione uidi.
Metalla etiam diuersa, ut es & plumbum, igne soluta, admixtis
quibusdam fetidissimis sordibus, potare cogebantur. Quod genus   182

1797 religiosos] M, religiosis SBdT   1807 punitos] puniti SMT

forswerers, glotyners, trayturs, couetyse folke, proude pepul, enuyus
035 pepul, sclaunderers, hateful peple, and a thousand mo of this wyse,
to home all ys ordende ther synglerly ful grete peynes and greuys.
And ho may tel of al these thingys when they þat were good relygyus
men sofred ful sore and greuys peynys only by-cause they delyted
and toke a plesure of the feyernes of her handys and longe fingers?
040 Also weyfaring men þat were slayne of theuys in her iornay, Y saw
hem ponyshte for her synnys in an ȝesy wise. Theuys also, of home
hit is not to be lefte oute in no wise, that were for her synnys iugit to
han[g]ing in this world, and were only confeste to a priste, or els
opynly, þat moste helpith, of her wykydnes and euyl dedys, in very
045 trew contricion of herte, and so anon toke her dethe, paciently
forgeuing with herte al her enemyes and | al maner wrongys and   [f]6ʳ
trespassys done to hem and alsoo her dethe, in remyssyon of al her   L249ʳ
synnys, Y saw al seche with a special certen worschipfulnes put to ful O46ʳ
softe and esy peynys. Also other that were ponyshte and hangyd
050 lyke-wyse for thefte and other mysdedys, and wulde not opynly
confesse her synnys in tyme of her dethe, but hoping by fraude and
disceyte of her gostely enmy the Deuyl to scape harmles at that tyme
for the denying and excusing her synnys, how-be-hit that they
purposyd in her herte to be confeste to a priste of hem afterward,
055 and to do for hem condigne penans, and also vtwardly to leue hem,
ȝef they coude haue, and opteyne space therto as they hopid, and ȝet
coude not haue hit, but schulde deye, and than in the laste ende of
her lyfe mekely besought God and his holy seyntys of mercy and
helpe, al seche were ful greuysly torment in peynys for her synnys.
060 Not-withstonding, nethir these had loste hope of mercy and forgeuenes. Neuertheles, they were gy[u]yd in fyry feturs and hangyd
vp in the myddys of fyre on gybbettis, home the cruel tormentours
and fyndys al to-bete and brake with scorgys and forkys, and
vpbrayde hem of crymys and synnys with grete scornys and mockys.'

065 ¶ **Of posynners that he sawe there.**   ¶ **Ca xxxviij**

'They that were posynners and poy[syn]yd folke, and also wemen
that hadde caste awey and forsake her babys the whiche they had
bore, or had slayne hem, or ellys by her cursyd crafte had causyd
hem to be bore afore her tyme, I sawe suche persons by full ofte
070 betyngys and abrasyng of naylys al to-toryn. | And also they were   [f]6ᵛ

2043 hanging] hanuing   2061 gyuyd] gynyd   2066 poysynyd] poynsyd

poculi execrandum, interiora eorum exurens, omnia miserabili clade
penetrabat & emissum per secreciora iterum miseris bibendum
ingerebatur. Immania uero quedam repencium monstra portentuosis
lacertis ipsas complectencia, vnguibus alcius immersis in ceruices &
costas, uberibus huiusmodi feminarum dependebant, ore uipereo &   183
dentibus sugentes & corrodentes mammas earum.'

[XXXIX]

'Feneratores, nummorum cumulis instar moncium igneorum
coaceruatis immersi, auaricie flammam malo suo se iniquis aluisse
compendiis, dum in seculo uixerant, indefessis eiulatibus testaban-   183
tur.'

[XL] **De fugitiuis.**

'Fugitiui de sacris professionibus, quibus diuino se famulatui
deuouerant, & post uotum mundanarum sordium uomitum ritu
canino repetentes, tantis ibi afficiebantur malis, ut eorum exponere   184
supplicia, que uidi, nullo sciam eloquio. Amarissima uix penitudo &
resipiscencia in extremis, adiuncta confessione, tales quidem interdum a gehennali suspendit interitu, sed ipsa eorum apostasia nimiis
& diutissimis cruciatibus punitur.'

[XLI] **De quodam principe.**   184

'Quid uero de principe quodam, quem inter tocius mundi principes uidimus potentissimum, dicam, quem hinc tantis cernere erat
calamitatibus pressum & vndique coangustatum ut in eo specialius
impletum uiderim quod de mistica Babilone in Iohannis Apocalipsi
precipitur? "Quantum," inquit, "dilatauit se & in deliciis fuit,   185
tantum date ei tormentum & luctum."

compellyd to drinke dyuers metals, as bras and ledde multyn by fyre, L249ᵛ
and medylde with full stinkinge thingys, the whiche brente her O46ᵛ
inward bowels and so went greuysly thorow hem, and when it was
out hit was brought to hem to drinke ageyne. Trewly, certen grete
2075 monsturs of creping bestis with horrabul and gastful harmys cleppyd
seche wemen, and stykyd her naylys ful depe in her neckys and
sydys, and ha[ng]yng at her brestys, sokyd her pappys with her
venummys mouthe and al to-gnew hem with her cursyd tethe.'

¶ **Of vsurers also.**   ¶ **Ca xxxix**

2080   'Usurers also Y sawe, howe they were dround in gret hepys lyke
hyllys of brenning money, complayning with grete sorowe and
wayling, by-cawse they quenchyd not in hem, when they leuyd in
thys worlde, the euyl flame and synne of couetyse.'

¶ **Of fygytyuys oute of religion.**   ¶ **Ca xl**

2085   'Religyous persons that were fugytyuys, that is to sey, that ranne
oute of her order by the whiche they had bonde hem-self to the
seruice of God, and after turnid ageyne to the worlde and gaue hem
to wordely leuing, as a dogge þat turnith ageyn to his vomet, so
gretely they were there smyt with peynys þat Y can in no wise tell
2090 nethir declare her tormentis, and onethe ful bitter repentans and
confession at her laste ende sauyd seche persons otherwhile fro
euerlasting dampnacion. Neuertheles, her apostasye was ful long
tyme and greuysly ponyshte.'

¶ **Of a certen kyng of Inglond.**   ¶ **Ca xli** [f]7ʳ
                                                              L250ʳ
2095   'But what schal Y sey of a certen prynce and sumtyme king of O47ʳ
Englond þat Y sawe, the whyche in his lyfe was ful myghty amonge
al the princys of thys world? Sothely, he was on euery syde pressyd
and peynyd, that a man myght sey of h[y]m as Seint Iohan the
euangelyste seythe yn hys Apocalyps, thys wyse: *Quantum se dilatauit*
2100 *et in delicijs fuit, tantum datur ei tormentum et luctum.* That ys to sey,
"How mekyl he dydde extende and magnifyde h[y]mselfe and was in
onleful lustys and delytys, so mekyl geue ȝe to hym torment and
he[u]ynes."

2077 hangyng] hauyng   2098 hym] hem   2101 hymselfe] hemselfe
2103 heuynes] henynes

'Quis enim uel mente concipiat quantis cruciatibus corpore toto & membris omnibus torquebatur, qui equo insidens, piceam ore & naribus flammam cum fumo & fetore tartareo iugiter in supplicium f. 30ʳ sessoris efflanti, armis omnibus tanquam ad | bellum erat indutus, 1855 que ei supplicium inenarrabile extiterunt? Ipsa enim arma quibus tegebatur uelut candens ferrum cum malleis contunditur igneum scintillabant imbrem, quo totus medullitus exurebatur. Exterius uero flammea, nimio pondere sui onerabant, nimioque ardore incendebant utentem eis. Itaque de galea, scuto, lorica, & ocreis taceo, quorum 1860 omnium concremacione & onere, quantum cruciaretur, nullus estimare sufficeret. Optabat sane, si fieri posset, tocius orbis dacione tormentum redimere, quod per vnius calcaris usum, quo uectorem suum in uaria urgebat precipicia, tollerabat. Sella, que sub ipso erat, clauis & uerubus igneis hinc inde prefixa, eminus intuenti horrorem 1865 permaximum incuciebat. Sedentis uero in ea iecur & precordia uniuersa aculeis illis transfigebantur. Nocebant eum tam crudeliter sanguinis humani iniusta effusio & legittimi thori adulterina transgressio. In hiis duobus frequencius mortaliter deliquerat. Seuientes enim carnifices hec ei improperabant, insultantes preterea uehemen- 1870 tissime quia in ulcionem ferarum irracionabilium, que de iure naturali communiter omnibus cedere deberent, homines racione utentes & eodem sanguine Christi redemptos & nature indifferentis parilitate consortes aut multasset leto aut membris diuersis crudeliter mut[i]lasset. Super hec omnia egram penitus & parum deuotam 1875 penitenciam in uite termino habuerat.

'Subsidia uero paucissima superstites filii & amici, quibus bona temporalia immensa contulerat, ut miserabiliter querebatur, defuncto exhibuerant.

'"Nichil," inquit, "remedii omnes pridem fautores & alumpni mei 1880 in hiis erumpnis michi prestiterunt. Heus! siccine omnem laborem meum & sollicitudinem perdidi quibus pro heredibus meis ditandis frustra desudaui? Heu obsequencium fallax adulacio, quid contulit michi infortunato, quorum gracia tot gazas pessundedi, quibus tot f. 30ᵛ inaniter redditus conferre sategi, pro quibus | in tantis deliqui viuens 1885 & iam defunctus per illos in nullo remedia percepi? Uiri tamen sacre religionis aliquantulum meam suis oracionibus lenierunt calamitatem."

'How ys that may conce[u]e yn mynde what gret peynys al hys body
2105 and lymmys were smytte wythe? He sate apon an horse, that blewe
owte of her mowthe and nose a flame blacke as pycche, medylde whyt
a smoke and stenche of helle, yn-to the greuys torment of hym that
sate aboue, the whyche was armyd at al pecys as he schulde haue gone
to batelle. Trewly, the armyr that he were, was to hym intollerabul
2110 peyne, for they were as bryght brennyng ȝirne ys, when hyt ys betyn
whyt hamers and smytyth owte fyry sparclys, by the whyche he was
wyth-ynforthe al to-brende, and whyt-owte-forthe the same armyr
brende yn ful gret hete, and ladyd hym that ware hym wyth ful sore
bor[th]yn. Also as tochyng hys helme, hys shylde, and hys haburgyn,
2115 and hys legge harnes, Y leue owte, for by the brennyng hete and peyse
of hem al, howe mekyl he was peynyd no man | can telle. Sothely, he   [f]7ᵛ
wulde haue geuyn alle the world, yf hit might haue be, so that he   L250ᵛ
might haue be delyueryd fro on spurre with the whiche he was   O47ᵛ
compellid to stere his wrechid hors to renne, wherby oftyn-times he
2120 fylle down hedlong. Also the sadyle þat he sate in was stekyd thorow
on bothe the sydys with fyrye brochys and naylis, the which was a
gasteful sight for any man to beholde, and the maw and inwarde
bowels of him þat sate in the sadelle were sore smyt thorow by the
scharpnes of tho brochys and naylys, and this cruelly was he ponyshte
2125 for the onrightful scheding of mennys blode and for the foule synne of
auowtrye þat he vsyd. In thys too thingys he dedly offendyd ofte-
tymys. And tho cruel tormentours, wykyd fyndis, ful gretly with
derisions and scornys vpbraydyd him, because he wuld be auengid on
men þat [s]lew his venery, as harte and hynde, boocke and do, and
2130 seche other, the whiche by the law of kinde ought to be slayne to euery
man, and therfore sum of hem he putte to dethe or els cruelly wulde
mayme h[e]m, and for al thys he dyd neuer but lytyl penance as long
as he leuyd.

'Also ful myserably he complaynde þat nethir his sonnys nethir his
2135 frendys, the whiche he lefte alyue and to home he had gotyn mekyl
temporal godys, dyd or schewyd for him any-thing after his deth for
his helpe and releuyng.

'"No-thing," he seyde, "my sonnys and frendys haue done for me
in these peynys. Alas, lo, Y haue loste alle my labur and besynes that
2140 Y haue done ydylly to make myne heiers riche and mighty. Alas, for
the false and deceuabul flatring of pepul. And now what haue they

2104 conceue] concede   2114 borthyn] borhtyn   2129 slew] flew
2132 hem] him

'Intellexi preterea quod inde precipue spem gereret adipiscende misericordie, quia religiosis uiris pro Domino sepius beneficus & 189₄ affabilis extitisset. Tercium uero, vnde preter premissa grauius ingemiscebat afflictus, uaria extitit depressio populorum, quos uehemencius aliquociens indebitis onerauit exaccionibus.

Quod monachus non omnia que uidit in scripto redegerit.

'Hucusque compendiose multa percurro &, sicut de pluribus 189 nichil, ita & de paucis a nobis cognitis non omnia que ueraciter & utiliter dicere possem retexo. Vniuersa enim complecti nec multa uolumina possent. Nemo autem exaggerando aliquid me suspicetur uel de penis uel de querelis referre dolencium. Secretorum testis & conscius Deus ipse nouit, quod relegens que iam scripta sunt de 190₄ quorundam suppliciis & recolens que circa ipsos conspexi, tanquam nichil expressum sit de miseriis eorum, ita inania pocius quam leuia reputo in comparacione uisorum ea que digesta sunt. Colligat igitur ex hiis lectoris prudencia aliquod edificacionis sue emolumentum, discatque ex minimis & paucissimis que scripta relegit, ingencia 190 metiri, que uel referri ob sui magnitudinem & numerum innumerabilem nequiunt uel, si utcumque possent, magis forte tediosa & minus credibilia infirmis quibusque & tediosis uiderentur. Paucorum adhuc mencionem subinfero, quos in hac pridem mortali uita specialius dilexi. Numerus autem eorum quos recordacioni nostre 191₄ & aspectui representauit illa hora, innumerabilis est. Quosdam notorum, quos uiuere credebam adhuc, ibi mortuis admixtos obstupui. De dormicione quorundam eorum certitudinem plenam ibidem concepi. De quibusdam uero pre admiracione nimia, scilicet non credens eos obisse, certus non sum redditus. Nam & sciscitari 191 propter alia infinita, que contemplabar, dissimulaui, uel a ductore meo uel ab ipsis; sed iam indubitata quorundam relacione super f. 31ʳ eorum | decessu certioratus sum.'

brought or done for me vnhappy, to home Y gate and ge-|dirde so [f]8ʳ
mekyl tresur and riches, and to whome Y gaue so many rentys and L251ʳ
possessions, and for home so gretly Y offendyd God while Y leuyd, O48ʳ
and now Y am dedde non of hem doyth any-thing for me?"

'Trewly, Y saw him sumwhat esyd and releuyd of his peynys only
by the prayers of religious men, to home in his life for God he was
full benyuolent oftyn-tymes, and therby Y vndirstode specyally that
he hopyd to be sauyd. Forthermore, be-syde al these thingys aboue-
seyde, ful greuysly he sorowyd and was peynde, for by-cause he
oppressyd diuers tymes the pepul with ondue taxys.'

[XLII] **De quodam episcopo, qui licet in penis esset, tamen miraculis corusc⟨a⟩uit.**

'Iam quartus, ut arbitror, elapsus est annus, quo pontifex quidam in archipresulem electus cita morte preuentus episcopatus onus ante deposuit quam honorem consequeretur, ad quem petebatur, gradus eminencioris. Extiterat autem in abscondito interioris hominis bene religiosus pureque deuotus, asperrimo cilicii usu multisque aliis cruciatibus carnem macerans corpusque proprium domans. In facie uero non multum a secularibus distare uidebatur, nonnunquam pro uitanda inanis glorie aura, que uirtutum semper floribus probatur inimica, leticiam vultu pretendens & uerbis, cum interius esset corde contritus & affectu compunctus. Illud autem sapientis memoriter tenebat, "Frons tua populo conueniat, cum intus sint omnia dissimilia."

'Episcopus autem, de quo nunc agimus, excessus tam quotidianos, qui in magnis sollicitudinibus & negociis sepe difficilibus constituto subripuerant, quam minoris quoque etatis, quando seculi lasciuiam minus declinauerat, lacrimis frequentibus & uaria ut predixi castigacione corporis punire solebat. Uerum in episcopali officio multa per negligenciam grauiter offenderat, sicut & alii de quibus superius mencionem feci.

'De isto plurimorum iam vulgatum assercione audiui quod per ipsum miracula curacionum in quibusdam debilibus & infirmis post eius transitum fuerint perpetrata. Quod fortassis uerum esse non negamus, Domino huiusmodi beneficiis famulum suum honorante, ut daret intuentibus ostensionem, quod sibi grata fuerint merita ipsius, que in uite austeritate occulta & mentis puritate interna suis conspectibus, qui corda intuetur, placuissent. Uerumtamen in penis adhuc & ipsum, restante sibi proculdubio multa premiorum recompensacione, inueni. Qui uero non credit fieri aliquociens miraculum meritis eorum qui in purgatoriis uexantur, quartum librum *Dialogi* beati Gregorii relegat & ibi plenius huius rei exemplum, scilicet de Paschasio diacono, reperiet.'

1947 premiorum] SM, meritorum BdT *and marginal correction* S

¶ Of a bysshoppe þat was there in peynys and ȝet God
shewid miraclys for him after his dethe.   ¶ Ca xlii

'Nowe as Y remembre, a .iiii. ȝere agon a certen bisshoppe was
chose to be an archebysshope but he was than hastely preuente of
dethe and so disceste and lefte bothe. Trewly, this bysshoppe was
inwardly in his leuing ful wele disposyd and religyusly, for he was
pure and deuoute in herte and clene of body, that by the vse and
weryng of a scharpe herre and other dyuers penauns, tamyd wele his
owne flesche. He conformyd hys face and chere as hit semyd mekyl
after the behauing of secler pepul, and, to eschue and refuse the
fauer of vayne-glorye, the whiche is euer prouyd an enmy to vertu,
he shewid alwey in wordys and contenans gladnes and iocundnes,
when he was withinforth contrite in herte and in his affeccions.

'Also this bisshop vsyd, as it is seyd before, to ponyssh as wel his
dayly fautys, by the whiche in grete curys and harde thingys he | had   [f]8ᵛ
offendyd, as he dyd other synnys, the whyche he had done in hys   L251ᵛ
yong age, by dyuers chastmentys and ofte wepyngs. Also in hys office   O48ᵛ
of bysshoppery, he had offendyd greuysly in mony thingys by hys
neglygens, as other bysshoppys dyd, of home Y haue made mencyon
aboue.

'Of this bysshoppe Y harde nowe opynly by the seyng of many
folke, that by hym myraclys were schewed and done after hys dethe
on seke pepull and febull. And I suppose hyt ys trouthe that oure
Lord dyd worschype hys seruaunte with seche benefettys, te geue
other example and vndyrstondyng that [t]he herde and clene leuyng,
the whyche he leuyd ynwardly, plesyd owre Lord ful wele, the
whyche beholdyth only mennys hertys. Sothely, ȝet fownde Y h[y]m
yn peynys, remanyng to hym wythowtyn dowte ful gret mede and
rewardys yn the euerlasting blysse of heuene. And he that beleuythe
not them, the whyche byn yn the peynys of purgatory, sum-tyme to
doo myraclys yn thys world, let h[y]m rede the .iiii. boke of the
Dyaloge of Seynt Gregory, and ther he schal see fullyur an example
of thys thyng, schewyd and done at Rome of an holy man þat was
callyd Pascasius a decon.'

[XLIII] **De quodam abbate.**

'Abbas quidam sane religiosus magneque frugalitatis ante hoc
f. 31ᵛ decennium, | transiturus e seculo, fidelissimo cuidam monacho
delegauit solidos non paucos, quos in scriniis habebat, in pauperum
refrigeria pro salute anime sue dispensanda. Qui sagaciter uotum
testatoris adimplens deuote largiebatur egenis subsidia. Si quem
fame uel langore afflictum grauius, si quos a claris natalibus &
honestis moribus ad indigencie necessitatem redactos didicisset, qui
& mendicare confunderentur, & uictualia comparare vndecunque
non ualebant, aperiebat benediccionibus manum suam & replebat pro
uiribus animas eorum, etiam calciamentis uel uestibus tegens eos.
Anachoritis & uiduis necnon & senibus deuotis uel clericis multa
tribuebat, omnibus indicens quatinus pro anima illius qui hec sibi
per manus suas largienda destinasset orare sedulo meminissent.
Quod etiam ab illis haut segniter implebatur. Hic ergo fidelis
dispensator, cum omnia dispergendo que acceperat pauperibus
erogasset, in langorem & ipse decidit; quo tempore non modico
excoctus ante hos quatuor annos hominem sancto fine beatus exuit.
Hos utrosque ibidem repperi. Uerum abbas suppliciis adhuc detine-
batur acrioribus ea potissimum ex causa, quod propinquis &
carnaliter se contingentibus nimie teneritudinis affectu fuisset obnox-
ius, nimiumque erga illos munificus, de bonis monasterii sui plus in
eis, quam deceret, expendisset.

'Plane hoc uicium, amor scilicet propinquorum intensior equo,
omnes fere, etiam qui in aliis probabiliter se gesserant, sacri ordinis
professores et quoslibet ecclesiasticos dispensatores in illis penis
plurimum grauabat. Vt enim de illis taceam qui ecclesiastica,
quibus locupletati sunt, beneficia in luxu uestium & uentris con-
cupiscencia, in equis & uariis uanitatibus & mundi pompis absu-
munt, illi etiam qui ita frugaliter hiis utuntur ad necessitatem, ut
nichil horum admittant ad superfluitatem, racionem nichilominus
f. 32ʳ exactissime de | illis tenentur exsoluere, que suo fuerint necessario
usui residua. Debent enim ea primitus & abundancius indigentibus
sue cure subditis ministrare, deinde mediante discrecione parentum
indigenciam, remota superfluitate, & quorumlibet inopum sine culpa,
immo cum fructu misericordie, poterunt releuare. Hanc enim
regulam ecclesiarum uicariis & personis, abbatibus & episcopis
statutam ibi primo didici, quam sine graui uindicta non licet
preuaricari. Prius enim quam ista uidi longe aliter de hiis sensi,

¶ Of a certen abbotte†.   ¶ Ca xliij

'A certen abbot that was wele and religyous[ly] dysposyd and a
man of gret sobirnes deyde a .x. ȝere a-goo, the whyche be-quethyd at
hys laste ende to one of hys bretheren mekyl mony for-to dele to | the   [g]1ʳ
powre folke for the helpe of his sowle. Thenne this monke wysyly   L252ʳ
and deuoutely fulfylled the abbottys wille and gaue alle that money   O49ʳ
to t[h]e pore pepul and nedy. And where he knewe any þat were
colde and hungery or smytte with sekenes, and were bore of honeste
folke and wele condicyonde and were fallyn to pouerte, wherby they
had not to bye her leuyng, and to begge they wer aschamyd to seche,
he wulde opyn hys hand [a]fter his powre and releue hem with mete
and drynke, schoys and clothys. Also to ancrys and to wedowys, to
wolde folke and to powre scolers, he gaue mekyl, commaunding hem
al to praye deuoutely for the soule of him for whome that money was
geuyn. And also they dyd ful spedly. And whenne this trewe and
feythfull monke had geuyn to pore peple alle that was be-takyn hym,
he fylle in-to sekenes, by the whyche longe tyme he was wele prouyd
and purgyd, and dysceste a foure ȝere a-goe and made a blessyd
ende. And bothe the forseyde abbotte and the monke Y fonde there
in purgatorye. Trewely, the abbot was holdyn ȝette in scharpe
peynys, and moste by-cause that ful carnaly and ouer-mekyl he
louyd hys kynnys-folke, and also was to hem ouer-large in ȝeftys of
the goodys of hys monasterye, and spende on hem mekyl more than
was conuenyent to do.

'Playnly that same vyse, that ys to seye, carnalle loue to kynred
more thanne ryght requyryth, full sore gre[u]yth al-moste alle maner
of peple that were profeste to holy relygyon in her lyfe, and also al
them that | were dyspensours of Holy Chirche goodys, as bysshopys   [g]1ᵛ
byn and suche other the whyche spende hem probably in other vysys   L252ᵛ
than they schulde. And as Y cese of hem then whiche wastyn the   O49ᵛ
godys of the Holy Chyrche, wherby they were made ryche, in
dyssolucyon of clothyng, in voluptuous metys and pompys of the
world, so schalle they that vsyn scarsly to her nede the godys that
they haue, though no-thing of hyt be spende in vanyte, ful straytely
geue acomtys of suche godys as they haue and kepe and remeynyth
aboue her [n]ede. Sothely, they sch[u]ld first geue of here goodys
more largely to the pore pepulle of her parishonse, and afterward by

2186 abbotte] ababotte   2187 religyously] religyous   2192 the] tpe
2196 after] hfter   2211 greuyth] grenyth   2221 nede] yede   schuld] schnld

quia longe aliter morem ipsorum se habere sciui. Qui uero ista bene
ut iustum est obseruant, tanquam serui boni, ita pro hiis remuner-
antur, ac si de suis patrimoniis hec pro Domino prestitissent.

'Predictus igitur abbas, inter duros agones penarum ad requiem
anhelans paradisi, monachum prefatum qui respectu sui satis leuiter 10
uexabatur in parte quadam a tormentis difficilioribus remota intuens,
frequenti inclinacione sui, manibus etiam protensis grates ei piissimo
affectu exsoluebat pro pietate sibi in premissa solidorum distribu-
cione impensa. Monachus autem uenusto admodum aspectu, ueste
nitida rarissimis tamen maculis respersa, iocunda etiam quodam- 20
modo alacritate sui graciosum de se prebebat intuenti spectaculum
abbati. Quod dum mecum stupens admiror, hanc ab ore ductoris mei
de eo audiui testificacionem.

'"Noueris," inquit, "hunc quem cernis multa cordis sinceritate &
corporis castimonia Domino placuisse, plurimaque per eum in loco 20
quo degebat mala ne fierent fuisse impedita. Fuit enim iusticie zelo
feruidus, odio habens malum ex animo. Multas etiam sepe contra-
rietates & probra pacienter sustinuit pro defensione honestatis &
religionis, machinantibus hiis qui religionis habitum ad hoc portant,
ut religionem destruant, in castris spiritualis milicie non spiritui sed 20
carni officiosissime obsequentes. Per tales, prothdolor, hodie speciale
quondam sancte ecclesie decus & gloria paulominus ad nichilum
f. 32ᵛ redigitur, dum crescit super numerum multitudo | carnalium, cui
cedit paucitas spiritualium, magis eligens aliena mala dissimulando in
sese quiescere, quam increpando furencium in se bella concitare. Qui 20
& si sileant & quiescant, a talium insidiis quieti esse non ualent. Sicut
enim quondam Ysmael, qui secundum carnem natus est, perseque-
batur Ysaac qui secundum spiritum, ita et nunc carnales spiritualibus
inexorabiles conflictus ingerunt, frementes & tabescentes quia eos
suis peruersitatibus nequiunt conformare. 20

discrecyon helpe her faders and moders as they nede, alle superfluyte
putte asyde, and also releue other pore folke, and so deserue mede of
₂₅ God withoute any offense. For ther in purgatorye Y knewe first this
rewle ordende to bysshoppys and abbottys, persons and vicars of the
chirche, the whyche can-not be brokyn withoute grete veng[a]ns.
And ȝere Y sawe these thyngys so ordend, full fer Y thought† odyr-
wyse of hem, for Y knewe afore that the maners and condycyons of
₃₀ seche prelatys were ferre fro hyt and odyr-wyse demenyd. And alle
that kepe and fulfille this lawe and ordenans, as ryght and reason
requyryth, schalle so be rewardyd of God for hem, as they hadde
geuyn alle suche godys of her owne propre patrymonye.

'Therfore, thys abbot afore-seyde, amonge sore and greuys peynys
₃₅ and tormentys, hastyd hym toward the reste of paradyse. And as he
sawe and behylde | the forseyde monke hys brother, the whiche was   [g]2ʳ
there in a certen parte besyde remouyd fro the greuys peynys and   L253ʳ
tormentys that were there, and ful lyghtly peynde in comparyson of   O50ʳ
hym, bowde hym-selfe oftyn-tymes to the same monke, and thankyd
₄₀ hym with bothe hys handys for the grete charyte that he schewyd for
hym in the dystrybucyon and delyng of the forseyde money that he
delyueryd to hym. And the monke schewyd hym-selfe to the abbot
that behylde hym ful gracyous of syghte and gladsum of chere. For
he was right feyre and sembly in whyte clothyng, thawghe they were
₄₅ resperste and had on hem a few spottys. And whenne Y sawe thys, Y
merueyled in myselfe. Thenne Sente Nycholas, þat hylde me by the
hand, tolde me this of hym:

'"Knowyst this monke that thou seyst? He seruyd and pleasyd
God ful wele in hys lyfe wyth grete clennes of herte and chastyte of
₅₀ bodye, and mekyl euyl, the whiche schulde haue be done in the place
were he was, he lettyd and was agenste hyt. For he was feruent in
zele of ryghtwys[n]es and hatyng euyl of herte. Wherfore many
reproues oftyn-tymes pacyentely he sofryd for the defense and
honeste of his religion, and specyaly of hem the whiche ware the
₅₅ habet of religyon apon hem for that entent that they myght dystroye
the vertuus leuing and conuersacion of relygyon, ful besyly seruyng
not her spiryte but the wrechidnes of her flesh and the worlde, in the
monasteriis of spyritual and gostely leuing. And alas, for sorow, for
now by seche persons the specyal worschyppe and honoure that
₆₀ Holy | Chirche was of before is almost brought to nought, whyle the   [g]2ᵛ
                                                                         L253ᵛ
                                                                         O50ᵛ

2227 vengans] vengns   2228 thought] thoughtr   2252 ryghtwysnes]
ryghtwysues

' "Plures quoque, quod nimis lugendum est, spiritu incipientes, tempore procedente uel pusillanimitate uicti uel simplicitate seducti, in hoc certamine succumbunt in corrupcionem & miserabilem uite torporem, exemplis & persuasionibus infelicium abstracti & illecti. Verum hec tanta cenobice uite dispendia, que instar celestis rei puplice temporibus patrum insignissime floruit, modernos prelatos maxime respiciunt, qui hec sciunt & negligunt, immo ita hec contempnunt, ut nec ea sic se habere aduertant. Sciunt enim ad quid uenerunt, sed ignorant ad quid uenisse debuerunt. Venerunt enim ad luxum & ad gloriam mundi, uenisse autem debuerant ad imitacionem paupertatis Christi, ad sollicitudinem Pauli, ad custodiam circumspectam gregis sibi commissi. Hoc ergo sequuntur, hoc curant, hoc querunt, ad quod uenerunt: gregem uero Domini non pascunt, immo depascunt, & a rectitudine quam forte habent deicientes spiritualiter mactant, & sibi eos conformantes perdunt, non se pastores sed lupos exhibentes & fures. Talium promociones reges & pontifices & alii iam procurant potentes: ipsi quoque subiecti tales propensius exquirunt non rectores sed peruersores animarum suarum; sub quibus omne, quod eis libuerit, liceat. Quare iusto Dei iudicio & regna turbantur & ecclesie confunduntur & status terrigenarum prorsus euertitur. Fiunt enim hoc ordine Deo execrabiles, qui pro uiuis & defunctis pii ad Deum & exaudibiles fore deberent intercessores, quorum specialius meritis & interuentu omnium conseruari & augeri debuerat incolumitas | Christianorum, omnisque clades a plebe Dei propelli & amoueri."

f. 33ʳ

multytude of carnal and worldly men encresyn aboue noumbre,
home the fewnes of spyrytuall men sofryn, chesyng rather to
dyssymylle and not to knowe her euyll, and so to reste hem-selfe,
than by her blamyng and resysting stere and moue agenste hem the
55 wrathe and trowbullus hastynes of suche euyl-dysposyd persons.
And thaught they soo do, ȝette they can-not be sewer fro the spyes
and fraudys of hem. And as sum-tyme Ysmael, that was bore carnaly,
pursewyd Ysaac, that was bore spyrytualy, that ys to seye, by a
spyrytual promyse of Almighty God, lyke-wyse hyt is nowe. For
70 carnal folke ben ful greuys to spyrytuall pepul, be-cause they cannot
peruerte hem to her frawardnes.

'"Also many ther byn, that gretely hyt ys to sorowe, the whyche in
her leuyng begunne spyrytualy, but by processe of tyme owther they
be ouercumme by onstabulnes or els ben dysceyuyd by sympylnes,
75 and also they falle done fro her purpose and begynnyng vnto the
myserabul and wrechyd corr[u]pcyon and slowfulnes of this world,
entysyd and drawyn by the examplys and councelys of euyll-
dysposyd persons. Trewly, these grete hirtys of relygyous leuyng,
the whyche before in the tyme of faders ful nobly flowryd and schone
80 as an heuynly lyght, ful gretely beholdyth the prelatys of Holy
Chyrche in thys dayes, that knowen thys and despysen hyt, in so
mekyl that they vndyrstonde not hem-selfe, that hyt ys so wyth hem.
They kn[o]we veryly what thynge they be cum to, but they | [knowe
not] what thinge they schulde haue cum to, be-cause þat they be cum
85 to the luste and plesure of thys world, but they schulde haue cum to
the folowing of Crystes pouerte, and to the karke and dilygente
kepyng of her cure, that ys, the pepul of God commytted to hem.
And therfore, that they seche and that they care for, that they be cum
to and that they haue. The pepul of God they fede not but distroye,
90 and hem perauenture that they haue turnyd fro ryhhtwysnes, they
fleyn spirytually and lesyn for her conformyng to hem, not shewyng
hem-selfe faders and pastors, but woluys and theuys. Trewely, the
promotyng of suche persons, kyngys and bysshoppys and other grete
men procuron and gete, and her sogettys ful mekyl loke ther-aftur,
95 not beyng rectors and faders, but peruersours and destroyers of her
sowlys, the whiche thynkyn that alle thynge, that ys vnder hem, that
lykyth, ys leuefulle. Why by the rightwes iugemente of God byn
remys trowbuld and chyrchys confowndyd and the state of erthely
folke vtwardly subuertyd? And for seche demenyng they be acursyd

[g]3ʳ
L254ʳ
O51ʳ

2276 corrupcyon] corrnpcyon   2283 knowe] knewe   2283-4 knowe not] *om.*

'Hec & in hunc modum plurima de lapsu & defectu sacre religionis sancto Dei Nicholao conquerente & de preconiis eorum, qui in hiis periculis uiriliter stare & alios corroborare non segniter curant, sublimia quedam commemorante, alios atque alios, quos ante noueram, uariis dextra leuaque uidebam detineri cruciatibus. Pre ceteris uero quos pridem cariores habueram hiis curiosius intendebam.'

[XLIIII] **De quadam abbatissa.**

'E quibus uenerabilis quedam abbatissa fuit, que anno presenti spe felici presentis uite erumpnas euadens, ad interminabile[m] perpetue lucis diem peruentura a corpore migrauit. Hec michi quam plurima de statu suo tam presenti quam preterito insinuauit. Germanis etiam sororibus suis sub uirginitatis titulo inter sacras uirgines in monasterio, cui prefuerat, ad amplexus celestis sponsi piis desideriis anhelantibus, quibusdam certorum intersignorum indiciis nonnulla per me illis intimanda mandauit. Ex quibus quedam hic referam, aliis quibusdam suppressis, que auditu forent graciosa, ni uetuisset ea aliis diuulgari quam ipsis pro quibus ea specialiter mandasse videbatur. Aiebat itaque se non modicum leuamen psalmis, oracionibus, & lacrimis ancillarum Dei quibus mater spiritualis extiterat percepisse. Gracias illis referendas mandauit quod & per seipsas multa ei contulissent beneficia, & quod sedulo a quibuscunque ualebant religiosis missarum & oracionum ei sategissent impetrare suffragia; insuper annuas hostias pro se diatim sine intermissione Domino fecissent immolari. Scirent procul dubio hinc premia ipsis deberi ingencia, se uero acerbissima per hec supplicia euasisse & de residuis adhuc penis, si perseruerarent in inceptis, cito euasuram. Referebat quoque multum sibi profuisse quod ante susceptum gradum regiminis compacientissimam se quibusque afflictis sororibusque multa benignitate prestitisset & quod quibuslibet sese extremis uilibusque officiis deuocius persepe mancipasset.'

2055 interminabilem] BdMT, interminabile S

00 of God, the whyche schulde be deuowt and meke intercessours to
God, bothe for h[e]m that byn a-lyue, and for h[e]m that byn dede,
by hoys meritys and prayers specialy the welfare of al Crystyndome
myght be preseruyd and encresyd, and al euyl fer put awey fro the
pepul of God."

05 'And whyle Sent Nycholas conplaynyd of seche thynghes and of
many othyr yn thys wyse, and remembryd also some thyngys that
were of grete commendacyon and | laude of certen persons, the
whyche yn her tyme stode ful manly yn seche perels, and strenthyd
othyr so to doo, Y saw ful many on euery syde me, the whyche Y
10 knew be-fore, sore holdyn yn ful greuys peynys and tormentys.
Trewly, Y lokyd most apon hem that Y knew a lytyl be-fore and
louyd ryght specialy.'

[g]3ᵛ
L254ᵛ
O51ᵛ

¶ **Of an abasse also.**   ¶ **Ca xliiij**

'Of the whiche, a certen worschipful abbas was ther, that blessedly
15 paste thys same ȝere owte fro thys world tawarde the euerlastyng lyfe
and ioys of heuyn. Sothely, sche tolde me many thyngys bothe of her
state that sche was paste and of her state that sche was yn. Also sche
seyde many thingys to me the whyche Y schulde telle to her owne
naturale sisters, that were vnder de tytyl of virgynyte amonge othyr
20 holy virgenis yn the same monasterye that sche was abbas of, by
some certen tokyns, of the whyche some Y wolde telle that schulde
be to the herers of hem ful gracius and good, but that sche bade me
telle hyt to no nothyr, saue to hem that sche commawndyd me. Sche
seyde also that sche hathe resceuyd mekyl releuyng and helpe of her
25 peynys by the deuowte prayers and psalmys of her systers, the
seruantis of God to† home be-fore sche was a spiritual modere. And
sche commawndyd me to thanke hem for mony good dedys the
whyche they haue done for her, and for the sofragys of messys and
othyr holy prayers that they haue gotyn for her, as they myghte, of
30 certen re-|ligious persons.

[g]4ʳ
L255ʳ
O52ʳ

'"And more-ouer they haue made and ordende to be offerd to
oure Lord dayly withoute any cesyng for me messys and other
deuoute prayers. And therfore lete h[e]m knowe withouten doute
that they schalle haue therfor ful grete mede and Y also haue scapyd
35 ful scarpe peynys. And yf they perseuere as they haue begunne, sone
Y hope to scape the remnande of my peynys."

2301 hem] hym *2x*   2326 to] tho   2333 hem] him

[XLV] De duabus monialibus lepro⟨sis⟩.

'"Fuerunt nempe," ait, "quodam tempore in monasterio nostro
f. 33ᵛ due | tenere quidem etatis uirgungule, lepre contagio miserabiliter
supra modum infecte, in tantum ut uirulenta pernicies carnes earum   20
plerisque in locis usque ad ossa excederet, cutis superficie immaniter
pustulis frequentissimis turgescente. Has vniuersis pene sororibus
tangere uel aspicere horrori erat. Michi autem ipsas sinibus meis
confouere & ulnis, lauare in balneis, manicis etiam meis ulcera earum
detergere dulcissimum uidebatur. Ipse uero in summa equanimitate   20
& graciarum accione plagam sibi diuinitus illatam perferentes, ita tali
delectabantur incommodo ac si percepissent a suo quem tenerrime
dilexerant sponso uarii ornatus pignora graciosa. Hinc longo pridem
coronate martirio iam sine macula felices sequuntur agnum quo-
cumque ierit. Huius quoque pietatis obtentu celerrimum in omni   20
angustia mea persensi refrigerium."

'Alia autem multa predicta michi abbatissa nunciauit, conquerens
inter alia sibi non exiliter obfuisse in penis, quod clericum quendam,
amicorum omnium solacio destitutum, etate paruulum, cuiusdam
episcopi commendacione ei ad educandum traditum, mox penitus   20
neglexisset; qui ob hoc uitam diucius protraxit erumpnosam. De sui
quoque monasterii cetu aliquot sanctimoniales feminas leuioribus in
penis ibidem recognoui.'

'Sche tolde my also that gretely hyt helped her that before she was made abbas sche schewyd and behauyd her-selfe with grete compassyon ful mekely to some of her systers that were sore vexed wyth grete sekenesse or temptacyon, and ful ofte dyd alle maner of seruyce deuowtely that were right foule and abiecte in the monasterye.'

¶ **Of .ii. yonge nonnys that were lepurs.**   ¶ **xlv**

'"There were," sche seyde, "on a tyme in owre place, .ii. yonge vyrgyns, the whiche were ful sore infecte with the grete plage of lepur, and for as moche that in many placys of her bodyes the flesche was falle downe to the bonys, and the skynne aboue oftyn-tymes horrably blyster owte of bleynys. And alle my systers of owre monasterye lothyd alle-moste to see or vysyte hem or to toche hem, but to me, me thoughte and semyd full swete to haue and opteyne hem yn my lappe or holde hem in my harmys, and forthermore alsoo to wesse hem in bathys, and also to wype her sores wyth my sleuys. And they ful wele and gladly sofryd that plage of | lepur and tankyde God of that chastement and dyssese, and so delytyd hem yn hyt as they had resceyuyd of hym gracius ȝy[f]tys of diuers ornamentys. And where a lytyl whyle agon they were peynyd yn the worlde by a longe martyrdome, now ful blessydly they folowyn the heuenly lambe, her spowse Ihesu Cryste, wyhtowtyn any spotte, wher-sum-euer He goo. And for the pety and charyte that Y had and schewyd to hem yn her nede, Y haue euermore had yn al my peynys a swyfte refreschyng and releuyng of helpe."

'Also many othyr thyngys the same abbas tolde me, amonge the whyche sche complaynyd that for on thyng that she dyd she had sofryd sore peynys, and that was by-cause, neglygently, sche lefte a certen chylde, a yonge scoler, that was destitute of al hys frendys, and was comyttyd to her of a certen byshoppe for to be browght vppe, and therfore the chylde leuyd longe tyme yn grete dyscomforte and heuynes. Also Y saw and knew sum of her systers, that were noonys of her monastery, ther yn that place of purgatory yn lyght peynys.'

[g]4ᵛ
L255ᵛ
O52ᵛ

2354 ȝyftys] ȝystys

[XLVI] De quodam milite symoniaco.

'Miles quidam cuiusdam ecclesie patronus uiginti septem marcis   21〈
cuidam clerico uendiderat personatum. Qui postea facti penitens in
recompensacionem tanti piaculi crucem susceperat, sepulcrum
Domini, si daretur facultas, aditurus, suisque erratibus ueniam
petiturus. Ea tempestate terram promissionis barbaries gentilium,
expugnatis Christianis, peruasione nefaria occupauerat. Ad quorum   21〈
perfidiam propulsandam Christicolis de cunctis mundi partibus
adunatis, hic miles sese coniunxit; vbi tactus incommodo, pro
Domino exul spontaneus uitam in castris terminauit. Hunc igitur
f. 34ʳ mediocribus in suppliciis positum repperi. | Fatebatur autem quod
pro crimine symonie superius memorato grauissimos pertulisset   21
cruciatus, adiciens quod nisi diuina preuentus miseracione ante
mortis horam adeo super hoc penituisset, eternum nullatenus
effugisset interitum.

'"Pene uero," ait, "tante iniquitati debite, multum pro labore
peregrinacionis, quam pro Domino suscepi, michi sunt alleuiate.   21
Indultum preterea diuina bonitate fuit michi, ut dudum per
quendam fidelem clericum in sompni uisione admonitum uxori
quondam mee mandarem, quatinus pro salute mea quinque missarum tricennalia cum officiis psalmorum, leccionum, & oracionum,
que pro defunctis recitari mos ecclesiasticus instituit, per honeste &   21
continentis uite presbiteros, quos etiam nominatim expressi, sollicite
procuraret celebrari. Quod ipsa fideliter impleri satagens, ipsosque
sacerdotes postea ut digni erant remunerans, maximam michi
penarum mearum mitigacionem impetrauit. Nam circa primordia
post decessum meum cotidie frequencius denarios, quos pro uendi-   21〉
cione ecclesie perceperam, ardentes uorare compellebar. A cuius
immanitate supplicii iam superna pietate & illius potissimum remedii
subuencione immunis sum redditus. Asperitate frigoris adhuc immo-
deracius coartor, quia nudis & algentibus inclemencior uixi &
incompaciens. Quamuis enim sepius alimoniam famelicis largirer,   21〉
tenacitatis tamen uicio denarios in refrigeria eorum cauebam expen-
dere."

70 ¶ **Of a knyghte that sinnyd yn simony.** ¶ Ca xlvi

'A certen knyght that was patron of a chyrche solde on a tyme a personage to a certen clerke for .xxvij. marke. Sothely, aftyrwarde he repente hym of that dede, and for the satysfaccion of so grete a synne he toke the crosse to go [to] the Holy Londe, and to vyset owre

75 Lordys scepulcur, ȝef he myghte, and for | hys offensys, there to aske God forgeuenes and mercy. Trewly, that tyme, the hethyn folke had put thens Crystin pepul and so occupied the Holy Londe. Then were Cristen pepul gedyrde of al coostys of the worlde to fyghte agenste hem and to dryue hem away, and so thys knyghte yoynde hym-selfe

80 to goo amonge hem. And aftyrwarde he was smytte wyth sekenes, and endyd hys lyfe yn that yourney. Sothly, Y fownde thys knyghte there ȝet yn mene peynys. And he tolde me that for the synne of symony that he dyd, as hyt ys a-fore seyde, he had sofryd ful greuys peynys and gret.

85 ' "And more-ouer," he seyde, "yf Y had not be preuent by the mercy of God to repente me ful sore afore my dethe for that synne of symony, yn no wyse schulde [Y] haue scape eternal dampnacyon. And the labur of the pylgrymmage that Y toke for God tawarde the Holy Londe gretly esyd me of thoo peynys, that were due for the same synne. Also

90 hit was grawntyd me by the goodnes of God that Y schulde sende to her that was my wyfe, by a feythful clerke warnyd yn hys slepe of me, that sche schulde orden to be seyde for me .v. tricennarijs of messys, wyth the offycys of *Placebo* and *Dirige*, as the chirche had ordende for hem that byn dede, and of seche prystys that were of honeste and chaste

95 lyuyng, of the whyche, some Y tolde by name."

'Than sche made these messis, wyth othyr thyngys a-fore-seyde, to be trewly done for hym. And aftyrwarde sche rewardyd hem, as they were worthy, by the whyche, he seyde, hys peynys were ful gretly abatyd.

100 ' "For a-|bowte the begynnyng, after my dethe, oftyn-tymes Y was compellyd dayly to deuoure tho pensys hoote and brennyng that Y had takyn of the pryste and person afore-seyd. And nowe by the mercy of God Y am delyueryd fro that grete tormente, and that was moste for the suffragiis the whiche was done for me. And ȝette Y am

105 constrayned ful sore to sofyr the scarpnes of colde, by-cause whenne Y leuyd Y had not compassyon on powre and nedeful people that were clothles and coolde. And oftyntymes whenne Y gaue hem mete

[g]5ʳ
L256ʳ
O53ʳ

[g]5ᵛ
L256ᵛ
O53ᵛ

2374 to] *om.*   2387 Y] *om.*

'Ad quem ego, "Si adhuc," inquam, "pro uobis fieret missarum celebracio, nonne perfectam reciperetis quietem?"

'Et ille, "Eciam," inquit, "si modo septem pro me tricennalia cum officiis coherentibus, scilicet *Dirige* & *Placebo*, exsoluerentur, spero quod hiis completis mox de penis transferrer ad quietis eterne mansionem."

'Hec ille. Animaduertendum uero est quod idem defunctus, sicut michi certissime iam compertum est, quinque castissimos sacerdotes, ex nomine electos, in uisione ad hec pro se peragenda missarum f. 34ᵛ officia designauerit; | quorum persone & nomina & mansionum loca, que singula diligenter expressit, tam sibi dum in corpore uixerat, quam clerico quo mediante hec uxori sue nunciata sunt, quam eidem etiam mulieri fuerunt incognita.'

[XLVII] De monacho sacrista.

'Iuuenem quendam sub monachili habitu religiose in multis se habentem aliquando uideram; qui sacriste etiam officio in ecclesia sua fungebatur. Ymagines autem tres uel quatuor in ueneracione sancte Dei genitricis Marie, auro & coloribus decenter ornate, Saluatoris in forma puerili yconas in gremio gestantes, in ecclesia illa per singula altaria disponuntur, magnum intuentibus pie deuocionis prebentes incentiuum. Ex consuetudine uero ecclesie singulis precipuis festiuitatibus per annum, totis a uespera usque ad uesperam diebus & noctibus, singule lampades ante singulas ymagines ardere consueuerant, totam suo fulgore ecclesiam reddentes choruscam.

'Contigit autem quodam tempore in diebus sacriste illius olei magnam in regione illa fieri penuriam, quia & vnde fieret nulli indigenarum suppetebat materies & aduenarum rarus quisquam eisdem in horis id genus mercimonii in uenalibus proponebat. Vnde habita desperacione adquirendi liquoris prefati in usus quosque necessarios, predictus sacrista, ubi licenciosius fore putauit, lampadum interim resecauit usum, ita quod in Pentecoste, uel in ascensione Domini, lampadibus que in istis solemnitatibus ardere consueuerant, ignem non admouit. Sed non impune iuit: tercia

2165 iuit] *interlined* S, *om.* BdMT

and drynke Y wuld be ryght wele warre by the vyce of hardnes to
spende no money apon hem."

2410 'Thanne seyde Y to hym, "What and there were done ȝet ageyne
messys for you, schuld ye not trowe ye resceyue perfetly reste?"

'Thanne he seyde, "ȝys. And there were done for me .vii.
tricennariis with the officys longyng to hem, this ys *Placebo* and
Dirige, Y hope that anone as they were done for me, Y schuld be
2415 delyueryd fro peynys to euerlastyng reste."

'Here nowe hyt ys to be vndyrstonde that thys same knyght after
his deth, as Y knowe hyt nowe withoute any doute, apperyd in a
vysyon to the same clarke afore-seyd, and assygned hym .v. ful
chaste prystys and chosyn by name, that schuld seye these messys
2420 and other thingys, lyke as hyt ys seyde aboue. Hoys persons and
namys and the placys of her dwellynges, the whyche dylygentely he
expressyd, were to hym-selfe, while he leuyd in hys bodye, and to
þ[e] clarke that he apperyd to, and also to hys wyfe that dydde for |
hym, vtwardly onknowen.'

[g]6^r
L257^r
O54^r

2425 ¶ **Of a certen yonge monke that somme-tyme in hys dayes**
was sexten of the chirche.   ¶ Ca xlvij

'A certen yonge man, a monke, that somme-tyme Y had seyne, the
whiche in many thyngys behauyd hym relygyously, and he was also
sexten of the chyrche where he dwellyd. Sothely, there were in thys
2430 same chyrche .iii. or .iiii. ymagys of our blessyd Lady, Seynt Marye,
hauyng in her lappys the ymage of oure Sauyur Ihesu Cryste yn
fourme of a lytyl babe, and they were sette at euery auter on right
wele peynted and feyre arayed wyth golde and diuers other colours,
the whyc[h]e schewyd to the people that behylde Hym grete
2435 deuocyon. And before euery ymage hynge a lampe, the whyche,
after the custome of that same chyrche, were wonte to be lyghted at
euery pryncypale feste thorowe alle the yere, bothe by nyghte and by
daye, enduryng fro the first ensonge vnto the second ensonge, afore
the forseyde ymages of owre blessyd Lady, Seynte Marye. And alsoo
2440 thylke lampys lyghtnyd alle the chyrche abowte.

'Trewely, hyt happonde apon a tyme in the forseyde sextenys
dayes, that grete scarsnesse of oyle was in that countreye that same
tyme, and also there was no man that there had any oyle thanne to
selle. And seldyn hyt was that any stranger at that sesyn putte forthe

2423 þe] þ   2434 whyche] whycde

namque feria Pentecostes, cum sanissimus uideretur, & per omnia
incolumis, repente acutis febribus usque ad mentis alienacionem
uexatus, secunda feria sequentis ebdomade defungitur. Mane uero
die sabbati, que festum sancte Trinitatis antecedit, cum adhuc in
extremis ageret, intuetur in uisione angelorum reginam, Deique 2170
matrem piissimam, in limine cuiusdam coclee, que vni de supradictis
ymaginibus uicina imminet, consistere. Qua uisa, sui non immemor
langoris atque periculi exclamare uidebatur, "O sancta Maria,
miserere."

f. 35ʳ   'Illa | uero ad hec, uoce & aspectu seuerior, ita infit: "Tu," inquit, 2175
"luminis decus michi preripuistis in terris: ego tibi preripiam uite
presentis lumen."

'Hac ille (nec mirum) comminacione perterritus prosternere se
uidebatur ad pedes domine cum nimio eiulatu, ueniamque postulare
commissi, emendacionem de cetero polliceri. Ad hec illa cuius etiam 2180
mine de misericordia manare consueuerunt, clemencius in eum
respiciens & manu innuens, limen cui suprastabat ei ostendit,
dicens, "Sede hic."

'Tunc ille ad uestigia eius residere tremebundus cepit, cum illa
subito disparuit. Ille uero ad se reuersus, fratres conuocauit, 2185
uisionem seriatim exposuit, & ut sequenti nocte, cum die succedente,
luminaria de more inextincta lucerent cum magnis adiuracionibus
precepit, & summa cum instancia flagitauit; uouitque quod, si
redderetur cupite sospitati, ad gloriam perpetue uirginis & matris
ueri luminis et solita conseruaret & ecclesie luminaria perpetim 2190
conseruanda augeret. Sed nequiuit reuocari sentencia quam mater
ueritatis ueraci ore dictauerat. Obiit enim post hec die tercia, quasi
premissa in illa, que intercessit, sancte Trinitatis sollemnitate ex
luminarium restitucione aliqua sui reatus satisfaccione. In penis uero
hactenus ipsum uidi detentum, quia sepe & multum in ordinis uel 2195
diuini officii execucione negligens extitisset, & in cibis & potibus, in
risu & iocis remissius quam deceret sese habuisset.'

2445 any suche chafer for-to | selle. Where-fore, the forseyde sexten, by- [g]6ᵛ
cause he wyste not where he myght gete oyle for necessary vsys, the L257ᵛ
mene whyle he withdrew the lyghte fro the forseyde lampys, as hym O54ᵛ
thowghte he myghte lefully doo, how-be-hyt that he had some yn
store. But he drede leste hyt wolde not suffyce tyl he hade more, so
2450 that on Ascensyon Day and Wythssonday he put no lyght to h[e]m,
the whiche yn these festis specialy were wonte to brenne. But he
went not onponyshte. Sothely, the thyrde day yn Whytsson weke,
when he was seyen yn al thyngys ryght hole and sownde, sodenly he
was smyte wyth a ful scharpe axces, and so a-vexid ther-of that he
2455 was madde and owte of hys mynde, and on The-wysday the nexte
weke aftir he dyde. And on Saterday by-fore hys dethe, when he was
almoste at hys laste ende, he saw yn a vysyon the quene of heuyn,
owre blessyd Lady, Sent Mary, stondyng on a grice of a certen
wyndyng steyer yn the chyrche, that was by on of the same ymagys
2460 of owre blessyd Lady aforeseyde. And when he saw her he cryde to
her, remembryng hys sekenes and perelle, and seyde, "O holy and
blessyd Mary, haue mercy on me."

'Than sche andswerde hym scharply, bothe yn worde and yn
chere, seying thys wyse: "Thow haste take fro me the worshyppe of
2465 my lyghte yn erthe, and Y schal ageyn take fro the lyghte of thys
present lyfe."

'Sothely, whenne he herde and vnderstode this thretyng, he was
sore aferd and abasshid, and no meruelle, and caste hym-selfe done
at her fete with grete wepyng and sorowyng and askyng for[g]euenes |
2470 of hys trespas, and promysed amendement. Thenne oure blessyd [g]7ʳ
Lady, hoys thretyng ys wonte to be of mercye, mekely behylde hym L258ʳ
and made a signe with her hand schewyng hym the grice that sche O55ʳ
stode apon, and seyde, "Sytte done here."

'Thanne he begunne, as hym thoughte, to sytte done ful sore aferd
2475 at her fete, whenne sche sodenly vanyshte awey. And whenne he was
cumme to hym-selfe ageyne, callyd for hys bretheren and tolde h[e]m
thys vysyon that he had seyne, and prayde hem and also bade hem
with grete instaunce and wothys, that the nexte nyghte with the daye
folowyng, the lampys afore-seyd schuld by lyghtynde and brenne, as
2480 the custome was before. Also he made a vowe that, and he myght haue
hys helthe ageyne, he wold contynally kepe forthe and encrese the
forseyde lampys to worschyppe and lawde of the gloryous vyrgyn and
moder of God, oure blessyd Lady, Seynt Marye. But he cowde not

2450 hem] hym   2469 forgeuenes] foreuenes   2476 hem] hym

[XLVIII] **De quodam clerico scolastico qui sancte uixerat.**

'Clericum quendam preterea in ipso iuuentutis flore ex hac luce
sublatum quem spiritu scientie illustrante omnes pene coetaneos tam   2200
in diuinis quam in liberalium arcium disciplinis uidimus transcen-
disse, faciliori purgacione mediocriter afflictum, ad paradisi gaudia ex
bone consciencie testimonio hillariter pertendentem, eodem in loco
uidi. Uixerat enim moribus probis & studiis preditus, pudicicia
fulgidus, caritate beniuolus, aliisque uirtutum carismatibus Deo &   2205
bonis omnibus acceptus. Precipue uero egregium culmen optime
structure bonarum accionum impositum preferebat, dileccionem
scilicet sancte uirginis Dei matris Marie, in cuius ueneracione |
f. 35ᵛ extiterat deuotissimus, crebras persepe & prolixas coram altaribus
eius spiritu contrito & humiliato exercens in oracionibus & fletibus   2210
excubias, multisque stipem necessariam pro illius amore impendens.
Vnde proculdubio restabat ei in celis ab eadem piissima angelorum
celique regina preparata merces immarcessibilis gloriaque perhennis.
Illius quoque beneficiis ab hora exitus sui multiplicia receperat
refrigeria, continuo illius solacio inter penarum gemitus misericor-   2215
diter refocillatus. Aeris solummodo intemperancia affligi uidebatur,
per frigus scilicet & estum, cum michi ostendebatur. Dictum uero
michi est sciscitanti, utrum & alias vndelibet sustineret penas, quod
preterea sitis quoque interdum cruciaretur ardore, quia iusto parcius
desideria egenorum, cum multis abundaret facultatibus, exsaciasset.   2220
Et quidem bene compaciens uidebatur & egenis multa erogare dum
uixit: sed tamen pauperes multociens fastidiuit, ex quo diues
apparuit, in tantum ut, quibus ipse pauperior affabilis uixerat &
subuentor deuotus, iam locupletatus, austerior aliquociens cerneretur: vnde cum ingenti metu animaduertendum est, quam districte   2225
ab hiis qui ecclesiastica perceperint beneficia, exigetur racio dis-

calle ageyne the worde and sentence that sche seyde to hym. And so he
2485 dyde the Tewsday after Trynyte Sonday. And as for the restoryng of
the forseyde lampys, some satysfaccyon he dydde for his offense and
trespas. Trewly, ȝette hethir-to was he holdyn in peynys and
tormentys by-cause often-tymes he had offendyd in kepyng of hys
relygyon and in seying of dyuyne seruyce. And also he was lyght of
2490 behauyng and ondyscrete as in etyng and drynkyng, lawghyng,
spekyng, iapyng, and in many other mo.'

¶ **Of a certen clerk that leuyd holyly.**   ¶ Ca xlviij

'Forthermore a certen clerke that paste oute of thys world in hys
yowthe Y sawe there in the same place, the whyche by the inspyracyon
2495 of the Holy Goste, bothe in connyng of dyuynyte as in other lyberals
facultees, passyd al-moste alle other that were hys felawys. Sothely, he
was there peynde in a light and a mene wyse, gladly goyng forthe, by
the testymony and witnes of a goode consciens that he had, toward the
ioys and reste of paradyse. Trewely, he was ful wele dis[p]osyd of
2500 maners and condicions and studeyng in scolys, pure of chastyte and
benyuolente in charyte, with other ȝeftys of grace by the whyche he
plesyd oure Lord ful wele. Also he had gotyn to hym specyaly the loue
of the moste gloryus vyrgyne, the modyr of God, oure blessyd Lady,
Sent Marye, home he seruyd ful deuoutely in hys lyfe, and ful oftyn-
2505 tymes wachyd longe in prayers before her auter with a ful meke
spyryte and a contryte herte, and for her loue gaue to pore pepul
mekyl almys, wherfore withoutyn doute thys remaynyd to hym of the
same blessyd Lady in heuyn, euerlastyng ioye and grete mede. And
f[ro] the houre of hys passyng oute of thys world he had resceyued
2510 mekyl refresshyng, and by her contynual solace and helpe was
mercyfully also in hys peynys sokyrde and conforted. Sothely,
whenne he was schewyd to me he was sumwhat dyssesyd and
peynyd only by the intemperans of the eyre, as in coolde and in
hete. Then Y enquyred | and he had sofrid any other peynys afore.
2515 And hyt was tolde me that he had sofryd other-whyles amonge the
peynfull hete of thirste, and that was be-cause whenne he abowndyd
in temporal goodys he was more harder to the pore pep[ul] than he
schulde haue be, or ryghte wolde. And trewely, he had gret
compassyon of hem, and mekyl he dyd in hys lyfe to helpe and
2520 releue hem. But neuertheles, oftyn-tymes he was wery of hem, and

2499 disposyd] dishosyd   2509 fro] for   2517 pepul] peplu

pensacionis sue, dicente in euangelio Saluatore, "*Cui plus committitur, plus exigetur ab eo.*"

'Iam uero quia multa ex hiis que in locis tormentorum comperimus, ut potuimus, festinanter fideli pocius quam falerato sermone 2230 digessimus, hic de penis uel in eis positis animabus narracionem interim terminamus. Post hec de gaudio & exultacione bonorum in sede amena & iocunda feliciter quiescencium aliqua que uidimus exprimere prout Dominus dederit, temptabimus.'

[XLIX] De paradiso & hominum multitudine quam 2235 monachus in illo uidit.

Nunc de solaciis quiescencium et eterna gloria bonorum aliqua utcunque dicamus. Nam sufficienter nemo posset. Ait itaque frater predictus:

'Postquam diucius per diuersorum suppliciorum genera ince- 2240 dentes, per tria ut iam supra memorauimus loca uarios miserorum
f. 36ʳ labores inspeximus & dolores, ad ulteri-|ora tendentibus lumen nobis gratissimum paulatim cepit apparere. Hinc odoris fragrancia suauissimi, & non multo post campi multimoda florum iocunditate uernantis amenitas incredibilem nobis prestitit uoluptatem. Hoc in 2245 campo hominum seu pocius animarum milia infinita repperimus, felic[i] quiete post excursa supplicia iocundancium. Quos autem in prima illius campi margine inuenimus albis quidem sed non satis nitentibus utebantur uestibus: nigredinis uero aut cuiuslibet macule nichil eis uidebatur inesse, minori tamen gracia candoris pollebant. 2250 Inter quos plerosque dudum bene michi cognitos recognoui; ex quibus multorum interim suppressa mencione, de paucis aliquid uobis breuiter referam.'

2246 felici] BdM, felice S

specyaly after that he was waxin rycher, in so mekyl that before, when
he was powrer and had not so mekyl, he was more lyberale to powre
folke than he was after, whenne hys goodys were encresyd. And
therfore full sore hyt ys to drede howe streytely they shulde ʒeue
2525 acomtys of her dispensacyon that haue resceyued benefytys and
ryches of the chyrche, owre Lord Yhesus seyng thys wyse yn the
gospel, *Cui plus commit[t]itur, ab eo plus exigetur.* That ys to sey, "To
home more ys commytid or be-takyn, of hym more shal be askyd."

'Now sothly, by-cause whe haue here trewly wretyn yn wordes
2530 mony thynghes that we fownde and saw yn placys of peynys, let vs
here ende owre narracion of hem. And aftirward, as God wyl geue vs
grace, we wyl asaye to telle and declare some thynghys that we saw of
the conforte and gladnes of the blessyd sowlys, the whyche restyd
hem yoyfully yn the ful mery and yocunde place of paradyse.'

2535 ¶ **Also of paradyse and of the multitude of pepul that he**   [g]8ᵛ
     sawe and founde there.   ¶ **Ca xlix** L259ᵛ
                                                                            O56ᵛ

'Nowe of the solace and conforte of the blessyd sowlys that byn
scapyd her peynys and be at reste and of her euerlastyng ioys, sum-
what Y wille tel yow as Y can and may. For no man may sufficiently.
2540 And whenne we were paste and gonne these thre placys of peynys, as
hyt ys aboue seyde, and had beholde the grete peynys and dyuers
tormentys of synnarys, we wente forthe farthir. And as we wente
farther, there begunne to appere a lytyl and a lytyl more and more a
full feire lyghte vnto vs, and with-al brake oute a ful plesaunte swete
2545 sauyr. And anone after, we cam to a fylde, the which was full of alle
maner of feyre and plesaunte flowrys, that gaue to vs an oncredyble
and inestymable conforte of ioye and plesure. Sothely, in thys fylde
we sawe and founde infynyte thousandys of sowlys ful iocunde and
merye in a ful swete reste after her penauns and after her purgacyon.
2550 And hem that we founde firste in the begynnyng of that filde had
apon hem white clothyng, but hyt was not very bryght nethyr wele
schynyng. Nothwithstondyng, they had no spotte of blacknes or of
any other onclennes on hem, as hyt semyd, saue thys, as Y seyd
before, they were not very bryght schynyng whyte. Trewely, amonge
2555 these, many Y knewe, the whyche sum-tyme Y sawe and knewe ful
wele whenne they leuyd in thys world. Of the whyche schortely sum-
|what Y wylle telle yow and of other Y purpose to cesse.'   [h]1ʳ
                                                                    L260ʳ
      2527 committitur] commititur   O57ʳ

[L] De quadam abbatissa.

'Quedam uite admodum uenerabilis abbatissa, quam adhuc puer 2255
noueram, ante hos quatuordecim annos migrauit ad Dominum. Fuit
autem tam pudicicie, quam tocius honestatis zelo feruida, misericordie uisceribus affluentissima, in custodia gregis sibi commissi
solers & deuota. Hanc, inter eos quos exteriores iam dicte amenitatis
[oras] habitare uidi, [primam] recognoui. Nuper uero de locis 2260
tormentorum euaserat, & uestibus immaculatis, parum tamen can-
dentibus, induebatur. Marcida specie et tali habitudine uidebatur,
quasi longa egritudine confecta & ex balneis nuper fuisset egressa.

'Transeo cetera leuiora propter que meruerat penas, iras etiam
iusto acerbiores, inanis glorie motum inter uirtutum merita & 2265
laudancium blandimenta non plene edomitum, & alia pretereo
innumera, in quibus etiam bonorum ignorancia sepe delinquit
infirmitas. Hoc sibi precipue penas dicebat peperisse, quod carnales
propinquos carnali teneritudine dilexerat & eis de bonis monasterii
quod regebat multa contulerat, plerisque ancillis Christi, quarum 2270
mater spiritualis fuerat, tam uictus quam uestitus inedia laboranti-
bus. Stupebam ad ista uehementer quippe qui certissime noueram
f. 36ᵛ uix quempiam hodie prelatum inueniri, qui in tantis | diuiciis tanta
circa propinquos parcitate utatur, quanta utebatur illa. Vix enim
necessaria, ut de superfluis taceam, alicui suorum vnquam impen- 2275
derat. Nepotes & neptes seu alias cognatas sibi personas non
matrimonio iungebat carnali, sed monasteriis Christo famulaturas
tradebat. Tanta quoque vultus & uerborum austeritate uigebat in
consanguineos, ut cum extraneis omnibus amicabilis esset & cum
multa benignitate affabilis, suis tantum affinibus terribilis uideretur & 2280
immitis. Erratus suorum & solertissime inquirere solebat &, quando
fortuitu deprehendere potuisset, seuerissime puniebat. Honestatem
morum exigebat & castitatis decorem ab omnibus quos in monasterii
tocius seruientes officiis habebat, sed maxime ab hiis qui aliquo
affinitatis titulo seipsam contingebant. Non denique frater, non soror 2285
ea penes illam confidencia utebatur, qua ceteri a sua parentela remoti.

'Ista retexens & etiam quod bonam educacionem in multis fecisset,
quos religionis propositum cum habitu laudabiliter suscepto seruare
deuote noueram, hec ab eadem audiui abbatissa:

'"Uera quidem," ait, "sunt que commemoras, sed tamen pro 2290
carnali affectu quo medullitus non carui, cum essem spiritualis

2260 oras] Bd, horas T, *om.* SM   primam] BdMT, *om.* S

¶ Of a certen abbas the whyche he sawe and knewe there
also.   ¶ Ca. l.

2560 'Here in thys place was a certen abbas that was of worschipful
conuersacyon, the whyche Y knewe whenne Y was a chylde, and sche
dyed a .xiiii. yere agone. Sothely, sche had grete feruour and zele to
chastyte, and to alle other honeste. Also sche was wyse and warre and
deuowte in kepyng her sisters, to whome sche was commytted. Thys
2565 abbas Y sawe amonge them that were in the begynnyng of that ioyful
place. For sche was but as newe cum thedur fro her peynys, and sche
had apon her clene clothyng but not verey whyte schynyng. And
sche semyd by her chere and dysposycyon as sche had be longe tyme
sicke or dissesyd and had cumme late fro bathys.

2570 'I passe by here to tel of summe lyghte thyngys for the whyche
sche had sofryd ryghte scarpe peynys. Sothely, sche had not
ouercumme in her leuyng the vyce and mocyon of vayne-glorye,
amonge the merytys of vertu, and commendacyon of flatryng and of
other thyngis innumerabulle Y passe by, in the whyche the febull
2575 ignoraunce of good pepul often-tymes offendythe. Trewely, sche told
me that sche had sofryd peynys specyaly by-cause sche louyd her
kynnys-folke ouermekyl carnaly, and to hem gaue mekyl goodys of |
the place that sche had rule of, whenne some of her systers to home   [h]1ᵛ
sche was a spyrytuall moder lackyd sum-tymes suche thyngys as   L260ᵛ
2580 longed to her leuyng and clothyng. And whenne Y harde thys of her, O57ᵛ
gretely Y meruelyde. For Y knowe not onethe any prelate in thys
dayes that vsyd so grete scarsnes to her kynnys-folke as sche, me
semyd, dydde to her cosynis. And as tochyng superfluyte, as fer as Y
knew, onethe sche gaue any-tyme to hem that were of her kynne ther
2585 necessarijs. Also her neueys and necys, and othyr that were of her
kynne, she cowpulde hem not to carnal matrymony, but be-toke hem
to religyon for-to serue God. And so sterne sche behauyd her yn
wordys and yn chere, to hem specialy, that when sche was seyne to
othyr strangers frendely and ʒesely, sche was only to her cosynis
2590 ryghte gastful and on-mylde. Also sche vsyd to enquyre ther fawtys
ful warly, and when perauenture sche myghte fynde hem fawtye, ful
bytturly therfor sche wol[d]e hem ponyshe. Also sche wolde haue the
honeste of maners and the clennes of chastyte obseruyd and kepte, of
al seruantys and persons that sche hade longyng to the monasterye,
2595 but mooste of hem þat were of her kynne. And ther was no brothyr

2592 wolde] wolbe

propositi debito tam professionis quam regiminis racione obnoxia,
apud districtum iudicem per rigorem, superficietenus exhibitum,
excusacionis locum minime inueni; ea quam maxima ex causa, quod
murmuracionis causa† et exemplum sollicitudinis superflue ancillis   2295
Christi pro cura suorum ex meo facto nascebatur. Oportuerat enim
me lesionem pocius michi commissarum precauere animarum, quam
parentum, quos semel cum seculo pro Christo reliqueram, tempor-
ales utilitates procurare."

'Hiis et aliis multis que breuitatis causa non exprimo a predicta   2300
uenerabili femina auditis, ad interiora illius campi properauimus.'

[LI] De quodam priore qualiter sancte obierat.

'Hic quendam pie recordacionis uirum, qui prioratus officio in
quodam monasterio functus ante hoc triennium sarcinam carnis
f. 37ʳ exuit, uidi & agnoui. Uidebam | e[um] beata cum spiritibus iustorum   2305
quiete felicem, penis omnibus exemptum, iocunditate qua donatus
fuerat hilarem, certa expectacione uisionis diuine, qua erat muner-
andus, incomparabiliter leciorem. Monachicum ab infancia usque ad
senectutem & habitum gesserat & animum. Uirginitatem mentis &
corporis humilitatis sinu tutauerat. Humilitati pacienciam indissolu-   2310
bili federe copulauerat. Abstinenciam rigidiorem uigiliarum prolix-
itate reddebat, deuocione utrasque superare nitebatur. Psalmodie &
laudis diuine officia tunc solum non mutus omiserat, cum magis pro
tempore necessaria caritatis obsequia compulissent. Nemo temptatis
misericordius illo compaciebatur: egrotantibus nullus eo deuocius uel   2315
sollicicius obsequebatur. Ita se iuxta apostolum omnibus omnia

2295 causa] causas SBdT, M causas *final* s *over erasure*   2305 eum] MT, enim S

ne syster that sche vsyd to fauer, as dydde othyr that were not of her
kynne.

'And when Y had seyde thys to her, and also that sche had
browghte forthe many that Y knewe to kepe deuowtly her purpose
2600 and habet of relygyon that they had takyn apon hem, thys wyse the
same abbas seide to me ageyne:

'"Sothe | hyt ys," sche seyde, "as yet† sey. But neuertheles, for the   [h]2ʳ
carnal affeccyon and loue that Y had ynwardely to my frendys when   L261ʳ
Y was bownde to the due gostely leuyng of religion, as wele by the   O58ʳ
2605 reson of my professyon as by the office that Y bare, Y kowde fynde
non excuse be-fore the streyte iugement of God, yn the whyche Y
was examynde to the vtturmaste poynte of my leuyng. And moste
by-cause that occasyon of gruggyng and example of ouermekyl
besynes grewe to my systers, by my fawte and negligens for the
2610 carke and besynes that they had to her frendys. Trewly, Y schulde
rathyr haue be warre and takyn hede of the hurte of her sowlys of
home Y had cure and charge, than the superfluyteis and prouysyon
of wordly goodys to my frendys, the whyche Y lefte onys wyth the
worlde for God."

2615 'And when thys worschippful abbas had tolde me thys and many
othyr thyngys also, we wente forthe farther yn-to the same ioyful
fylde.'

¶ Of a certen prior that leuyd deuowtly and dyed holyly.   ¶ Ca li

2620 'Y saw and knew also yn thys ioyful place a certen worshipful
person þat was a prior of a monasterye the whyche dyed a .iij. ȝere
agonne. Trewly, Y saw hym ful blessydly amonge þe holy spiritys
and blessyd seyntys yn a ioyful reste, exempte and delyueryd frome
al peynys, gladsum and mery of þat place þat he was yn, but mekyl
2625 more gladder and that yncomparable | for the certen bydyng that he   [h]2ᵛ
boode, to haue the sight of God. And he bare euermore whyle he   L261ᵛ
leuyd in thys world the habet of a monke, bothe on his body and in   O58ᵛ
hys herte, fro the tyme of hys chyldhode on-to hys oolde aage and to
hys laste ende. Also he kepe[d] and hydde the floure of hys vyrgynite
2630 in the bosum of mekenes and he cowpuld to hem ful suerly the vertu
of pacyens. Trewely, he vsyd gret abstynence and longe wacchyng,
and bothe too he ouercome by holy deuocyon. And whenne necessyte

2602 ye] tye   2629 keped] kepeth

exhibuerat, ut cum suus in necessariis raro, in refrigeriis rarissime, in
uoluptuosis nunquam esse crederetur, in utilibus semper pro posse
aliorum erat. Nunquam peticionibus afflictorum sola tantum quod
adhibere posset denegauit. Sola penes eum insinuacione, ut mer- 2320
entibus subueniret, opus fuit. Indigencium enim non dico preces, sed
uota quoque anticipare satagebat remediorum impensis. Cum talibus
uite sanctissime studiis corporis etiam multiplici ualitudine multis
ante obitum suum annis continue laborauerat, adeo ut vi langoris
vnius oculi biennio ante mortem funditus priuaretur aspectu, cum 2325
reliqua corporis membra uaria clade pene deficerent. Verum, ut ait
Salomon, spiritus hominis sustentat imbecillitatem eius; nunquam
propter hec a conuentu, nunquam a choro potuit auelli: communem
refectorii mensam cum fratribus adiens, fratrum pocius quam sua
saginabatur refeccione. A carnibus post adolescencie annos funditus 2330
abstinuerat; fratribus tamen, debilitate aut morbo confectis, eas
sedula deuocione pro eorum reparacione uolebat offerri. Tandem
dissenteriam incurrens, cum ad uite iam extrema perductus fuisset,
f. 37ᵛ dominici | corporis uiatico premunitus, sacrique olei delibutus
vnccione, decem ferme diebus absque cibo permansit, diuinis 2335
tantum beneficiis & fratrum exhortacioni intentus. Nocte uero, que
transitus sui precessit diem, instante iam nocturnalis officii hora,
uidit Dominum nostrum Ihesum Christum cum matre sua uirgine
illibata comitatum ad se accedere & nutu benignissimo ad se
sequendum inuitare. Statimque accitis ad se fratribus uisionem 2340
exposuit & se in crastino migraturum a seculo corde letissimo
predixit. Quod & factum est.

'Longum foret si vniuersa percurrerem que ante exitum suum
dixit, cum omnia uerba eius & oraciones, quibus & se & filios suos
Domino commendabat & ad perseueranciam boni operis informabat, 2345
non tam uerba fuerunt hominis quam Spiritus Sancti qui loquebatur
in eo. Circa terciam itaque diei sequentis horam in cinere & cilicio
recubans, horis diurnis, horis etiam de sancta Trinitate & de beata
Dei genitrice, quas ab infancia deuote frequentauerat, cum fratribus
percantatis, passione quoque dominica secundum quatuor euangelis- 2350
tas cum psalmis centesimo primo et centesimo .iiᵒ. & centesimo .iiiᵒ.
ante eum recitatis & ab eo intentissime cum gemitu & spiritus
contricione perauditis, inter crucis dominice oscula, inter saluta-
ciones beate uirginis, fratribus benedicens, diem clausit extremum.
Hunc igitur tantum & talem uirum, michique a primeua etate 2355

2353 perauditis] corr. from peraudidis

compellyd hym to be aboute werkys of charyte, as hys office
requyred for the tyme, he wulde euer amonge be seying some
2635 salmys or other deuowte prayers to God. No man had more
compassyon to hem that were in temptacyon than he, ne no man
was more deuowtur and besyur in seruyce to seke men than he. Also
he neuer denyed hem her petycyons and askynges that were
dyssesyd, al only of tho thyngis that myghte be hadde. And for-to
2640 helpe hem that were in heuynes, a becke of warnyng was suffycyent.
And whenne he was of seche holy leuyng and conuersacyon, and also
laborde cont[y]nualy mony ȝerys before hys dethe in grete wekenes
of bodye, so that by hys febulnes and dissese he had vtwardly loste
the sight of on of his yes a too ȝere before his obite, when other
2645 lymmys of his body faylde him for dyuers other dyssesis, and
notwithstonding alle thys, ȝette wolde he neuer be fro the couent
ne fro the quere ne fro the comyn table of the frayter, where he was
more fedde of the refeccyon of his brethyrne | than of hys owne. [h]3ʳ
Sothely, aftyr hys yonge age, he vtwardly absteynide hym fro flesche L262ʳ
2650 metys; neuertheles, he wolde to his brethirne þat wer sickelew and O59ʳ
febul besyly and deuowtly profer hem flessche metys for her
recoueryng. And at the laste he fyl yn-to a sekenes þat ys called
dissenteria. And when he was al-moste browghte to hys ende, he toke
hys gostely conforte and socur, the holy and blessyd sakyrment of
2655 owre Lordys precius body and blode, with hys laste anoyntyng, and
so bode al-moste .x. days withowte any mete, intendyng only the
benefitys of God and the exhortacion of hys brethyrne. Trewly, the
nyghte before the day þat he paste to God, abowte the owre of
diuyne seruyce, he saw owre Lord Ihesu and owre blessyd Lady,
2660 Seynt Mary, cummyng to hym, and with a ful meke sygne they made
a tokyn to hym that he schulde folow hem. And anon aftyr, callyd for
hys brethirne, and declaryd to hem the visyon that he had seyne, and
tolde hem before, and þat with a ful glade herte, þat he schulde passe
hens on the morow nexte, and so he dydde.
2665   'Longe hyt were ȝef Y schulde telle and remembre al thyng that he
seyde before hys ende, how he commendyd hym-selfe and hys
brethirne to God, and exhortyd hem to contynew yn good leuyng,
hoys wordys and exhortacion was not of man, but of the Holy Gooste
that spake yn hym. Sothly, then on the morow aftyr, abowt the howr
2670 of tyrse, lying yn ashys and yn herre, when he had seyde the seruice
of the day, and of the Holy Trinite, and of owre blessyd Lady, the

2642 contynualy] contnualy

amicissimum deuote mox uisum salutaui & multa ab eo benignissime
resalutatus audiui.'

[LII] De quodam sancto adolescente monacho.

'Ostendit autem michi adolescentulum quendam monachum, qui
sacre religionis habitum adhuc puer ardentissima deuocione ques- 2360
itum & puro ac mundo corde & corpore in monasterio predicti
prioris aliquamdiu gestatum, morte preuentus immatura, stola
immortalitatis feliciter commutauerat. Non quidem eum in corpore
positum uideram, sed de innocencie & deuocionis illius puritate &
sancto eius transitu multa crebro a fratribus eiusdem loci referri 2365
audieram.

f. 38ʳ   'Dixit | itaque michi senior prefatus: "Hic," ait ille, "meus est
filius de quo frequenter audisti. Hic meus fuit in deuocione &
spirituali proposito socius, hic comes est michi tendenti ad celum.
Hic in beatitudine eterna coheres michi futurus est sempiternus." 2370

'Idem uero adolescens horam transitus sui fratribus euidenter
predixerat. In eius quoque decessu audita celestis cantilena fuit, ut
multi perhibent, qui in monasterio eodem consistunt. Prior quoque
pro uariis negligenciis suis & suorum, quos regebat, diuersis
erratibus aliquantas pertulerat penas. Nunc uero predicto adoles- 2375
centi, qui sicut in minutis deliquerat ita in minimis senserat penas, in
candore & gaudio equalis fuit. Eminencioris uero glorie fiduciam pro
maioribus uirtutum meritis prior habere uidebatur.'

whyche he vsyd euermore of a childe, and when he had herde
deuowtly the Passion of owre | Lorde after the .iiii. euangelystys, and
other salmys with grete compunccyon of herte, betwhene the swhete
2675 kyssyngys of oure Lordys crosse and the salutacions of oure blessyd
Lady, blessyng hys brethyrne, deuoutely expyryd. Therfore thys
worschyfful fader, wyth home fro my ryghte yonge aage Y was ful
wele acquentyd, anon as Y sawe hym, deuoutely Y grete hym, and he
grete me ageyne ful mekely and tolde me many thyngys.'

[h]3ᵛ
L262ᵛ
O59ᵛ

2680 ¶ **Of a certen yonge monke there of his.**   ¶ Ca lii

'Sothely, thys worschipful fader and prior schewyd to me ther also
a certen adolescente, a yonge man the whyche in hys chyldhode with
gret feruent deuocyon entryd in-to relygyon and was a monke in the
same place and monasterye þat thys worschypful fader aforeseyde
2685 was prior of, and there he leuyd a good whyle, but no longe tyme, for
he was preuent hastely and sone of dethe, and so blessydly he passyd
out of this worlde. Trewly, Y neuer saw hym in body. Neuertheles,
often Y haue harde the bretheren of the same place tel of his pure
and innocent leuing, and also of hys holy passing, mony thingys.
2690   'Then seyd the forseyde prior to me of hym, "This ys my sonne,"
he seyde, "of home often-tymes thou haste herde. He was my felowe
when Y leuyd in the worlde in holy leuing and deuocyon. He ys now
also my felowe going to heuyn, and schalle be an euyn-heyre with me
eternaly in euerlasting ioye and blysse."
2695   'And the same yong | monke also tolde opinly to hys brethirne
before his dethe the howre of hys passyng. And also heuynly melody
was harde at hys passyng, as many can telle that were ther in the
monasterie the same tyme. Treuly, the forseyde prior, what for
diuers negligencys of hys owne doyng and for othyr diuers fawtys of
2700 hys brethirne, he had sofryd some lytyl peynys. And the same yonge
monke also, as he had offendyd yn ful smale and lytyl thyngys, so he
had felte afore sum-what of lytyl peynys; not-wythstondyng, they
were bothe equale yn wythnes and yn ioy. Sothly, the forseide prior,
as hyt semyd, had a truste of a more greter rewarde for the more
2705 goode dedys and meritys of vertu, the whyche he had by lengur
leuyng deseruyd.'

[h]4ʳ
L263ʳ
O60ʳ

[LIII] De quodam uenerabilis uite sacerdote.

'Uidi quoque in eisdem locis uenerabilem quendam sacerdotem, 2380
quem predicacionis uerbo & animarum saluti precipuam suis temporibus uidimus exhibuisse diligenciam. Zelo siquidem rectitudinis
cum uite exemplis ita predicacionis graciam habebat coniunctam, ut
non modo in parochiis quas regebat, sed per diuersarum longe
lateque ecclesiarum populos innumeras multitudines nunc a morti- 2385
feris criminibus reuocaret, nunc in uirtutum meritis feliciter profi-
cientes & usque ad finem debite consummacionis in iusticia et
sanctitate perseuerantes exhiberet. Quosdam ita diabolicis laqueis
irretitos, ut diabolo, quod dictu quoque nefas est, seruitute premissa
uisibiliter eius se dominio mancipassent, orando & predicando ex 2390
baratro perdicionis reuocauit, et per confessionis & penitencie
satisfaccionem mult[o]s, qui nunquam in grauioribus deliquerant,
reddidit miserante Deo in fide & bonis operibus perfecciores. Quibus
tamen ex causis modico tempore uarias pertulerit penas, quia iam
multa de similibus dixi, interim sileo. Hoc uero silendum non est, 2395
quod sibi & per eum cooperante Deo innumeris aliis gloria restabat
inenarrabilis.

f. 38ᵛ | 'Hinc ad interiora predicte amenitatis accedentibus nobis maior
semper & lucis claritas et odoris suauitas & ibidem degencium candor
et iocunditas arridebat. Cur autem diucius immorer personas eorum 2400
& merita recensendo, quos ibi uel ignotos prius in seculo uel notos
uidi? Omnes enim, quos locus iste tenet, superne Ierusalem ciues
sunt ascripti; omnes de seculi istius certamine demonum triumpha-
tores migrauerunt; penas omnes tam facile transierunt, quam uiciis
mundanis minus fuerunt irretiti.'   2405

[LIV] De representacione dominice passionis inter agmina
bonorum facta.

'Iam uero, que ad interiora progressi uidimus, nec lingua retexere
nec mens humana digne ualet perpendere. Quis enim digne uerbis
exponat, qualiter in medio beatorum spirituum, quorum infinita 2410
2392 multos] BdT, multis SM

¶ **Also of a worschipful pryste.**   ¶ **Ca liij**

'Y saw also yn thys same place a certen worschipful priste, the
whyche yn hys lyfe dydde mekyl good to the pepul by hys holy
10 preching. Treuly, he had grace of prechyng so ioynyd wi[t]h the zele
of ryghtwesnes and with good example of leuyng, þat he callid not
only the pepul of hys owne paryshons fro wekyd leuyng and dedly
dedis, but also he enformid and tawghte innumerable pepul of other
parishons ferre and brode, how they schulde leue her synnys and
15 fulfille owre Lordis commandmentis, and how they schulde dayly
encrese and perfet in goode and vertuus leuyng and so to continew to
a dew and a conuenient ende. And sothly, summe were so | ferre   [h]4ᵛ
fallyn yn-to the Deuyls bondys by her euyl and wekyd leuyng,   L263ᵛ
whome he callyd ageyne by prayur and holy prechyng, that visibly O60ᵛ
20 they myghte aftyrwarde vnderstonde and know how they had be-
takyn hem-selfe to the Deuyl and hys seruice, the whiche he made,
of oure Lordys infinite mercy, by confession and satisfaccion and
penanse-doyng, ryght wele and parfet yn the feithe and yn good
leuyng. Neuertheles, for what causys he had also sofryd before a lytyl
25 while diuers peynis, Y leue oute here by-cause Y haue seyde a-fore
many seche-lyke thyngys.

   'And as we wente more ynward and farthir yn-to þat ioyful place
of paradyse, we had euer more a clere lyghte and felte a swetur sauer,
and hem that we founde and saw ther were more whyttur and
30 gladder than were othyr that we saw before. And wher-to schulde Y
tarye here now to nowmbre tho persons and her merytys the whiche
Y saw ther, that Y knew summe-tyme before yn the worlde, and hem
also that Y knew not before? For al that were ther yn that place were
ordende to be the cytsonnys of the hye and euerlastyng Ierusalem,
35 and al had paste the stryfe and batel of this worlde and were victurs
of deuyls, and so lyghtly they went thorowe al peynys as they were
before les comyrd and holde by wrechyd leuyng a[n]d wordely vicys.'

¶ **How owre Lordys Passion was representyd and shewyd to
the sowlys that were in paradise.**   ¶ **Ca liiii**

40 | 'Nowe sothely, tho thyngys the whiche we sawe as we wente   [h]5ʳ
forthe farthir in-to the same place, nethyr tonge may telle, ne L264ʳ
mannys mynde maye worthely consyder. Who ys he that may   O61ʳ

   2710 with] wich   2737 and] aud

milia ibi circumstabant, crucis Christi misterium adorabatur, uelut
presencialiter in carne dominica passio celebrabatur? Uidebatur pius
generis humani Redemptor tanquam in crucis stipite appensus,
flagellis toto corpore cruentus & liuidus, sputis dehonestatus, cor-
onatus spinis, confossus clauis, & lancea perforatus; per manus &   24
pedes riui profluere purpurii cruoris: ex sacro autem latere sanguis
largiter stillabat & aqua. Huic mater non iam lugubris & anxia sed
gaudens & hilaris vultu serenissimo tanto tamque inenarrabili astabat
spectaculo. Inde discipulus ille, quem diligebat Ihesus, inter quosdam alios visus est astitisse. Iam uero quis vnquam uel tacita mente   24
coniciat, quanta cum alacritate ad hoc tam uitale spectaculum
vndique concurrebatur, que intuencium erat deuocio, quis adoran-
cium concursus, quante pro tantis beneficiis graciarum acciones &
Christo gloriam concinencium quam mira fuit exultacio? Hec michi
alcius recolenti dolor nescio an deuocio, compassio an congratulacio   24
animum distrahunt infelicem; fauces, lumina, singultus, & lacrime
indesinenter fatigant. Stupor uero & admiracio meipsum funditus
f. 39ʳ alienum & quodammodo michimet absentem | reddunt. Quis enim
non immanissime doleat tam uenusti decoris pulcritudinem tam fedis
subactam fuisse iniuriis & penis? Quis non compaciatur nimio affectu 24
tante pietati tam impiis exagitate suppliciis & obprobriis? Quid uero
deuocionis quantumque congratulacionis habet quod hiis suppliciis
diabolus uincitur, tartarus debellatur, alligatur fortis, arma eius
diripiuntur & spolia, perditus homo reparatur, et preda demonum,
a penali erepta ergastulo inferni, choris inseritur angelorum? Quis   24
uero non admiretur et stupeat tantam in Saluatore nostro clemenciam, tanteque uiscera pietatis, ut, quod semel in carne passibili
sustinuit pro nobis in mundo, hoc immortalitatis iam gloria uestitus
ob nimium humanarum animarum amorem ad earum gaudium et
deuocionem ampliandam ymaginaliter representare dignetur in para-   24
diso?

2432 suppliciis] BdMT *add* & contumeliis

worthily tel in worde how, in the myddys of tho blessyd and holy
sowlys, the holy crosse of Crystys Passyon was presented and
45 schewed to hem, of the whiche infy[ni]te thousandys were there
stondyng aboute hyt, and as oure Lorde had be present in Hys body,
so they worschypte and halowed Hys blessyd Passyon. Trewly, there
was seyne the meke Redemer of mankynde, oure swete Lorde and
Sauyur, Ihesus Criste, as he had be done fresche on the crosse. For
50 alle Hys body was blake and blody of scurgys and betyng, and cruelly
disfigurde by fowle spyttyng, crownyd with scarpe thornys, and
smytte throw with grete naylys. Hys syde was sore persyd with a
spere, and fro His handys and fete ranne out blode redde as purpul,
and fro His holy syde cam downe blode and water ful largely. And at
55 this grete and wondyrful spectacul stode His holy moder, oure
blessyd Lady, Sent Marye, not now in heuynes and mornyng,
b[u]t right gladsum and ioyng, and þat was in a ful feyre demenyng.
And ther also stode with herre the swete dyscipil of Criste, Seynt
Iohnne, the blessyd euangeliste. And ho may now conceue in mynde
60 how thoo holy soulys ranne thedir on euery syde gladly and lightly to
see and beholde þat blessyd sight? O what deuocyon was there of
hem that behilde that glorius vysyon. O what concurs was ther of
worschipping and thanking our Lorde Ihesu Criste, and how
meruelus was her ioyful gladnes. Trew-|ly, remembryng these† [h]5ᵛ
65 thingys in my-selfe, Y wote not whedir sorow or deuocyon or   L264ᵛ
compassion or gratulacyon drawyn nowe myne onhappy soule   O61ᵛ
dyuers weyes. For wondyr and meruel of tho thingis makyn me
alyenate fro my-selfe and sum-what absent to my-selfe. Who ys he
that wolde not ful gretly sorow to see so feire and so solemly a body
70 to be caste vnder so grete iniuriis and sore peynys? And who wolde
not with al his harte haue compassion apon His mekenes, so mouid
and vexyd with tormentys and vpbraydys of seche wekyd folke? And
what ioye and conforte may nowe here be thoughte, that by His
Passion and meke dethe helle ys foughtyn agenst, the Deuyl ys
75 ouercome and bounde, his power and strenthe is destroyed, and man
that was loste ys restoryd ageyne to grace, and takyn oute of the
peynful prison of helle, and ioynyd blessydly to the holy angelys of
heuyn? And ho wolde not meruel on the grete mercy and goodnes of
our Sauyur, Cryste Ihesu, the whiche now beyng inmortalle wyl
80 whytesaue þat Hys Passyon and dethe, the whyche He sofryd onys in
this worlde bodely for the redempcion of mankynde, be representyd

2745 infynite] infyinte   2757 but] bat   2764 these] thesese

'Multa que hic uidi & audiui interim pocius silencio quam stilo credenda existimo. Hoc ipsum autem, quod iam uictus deuocione uestra retuli, tam inuitus profero, quam insolitum & pene illis incredibile scio, qui presencia tantum & ea humana dumtaxat racione 24 estimare didicerunt. Uobis tamen, quos scio illius participes esse spiritus, qui omnia scrutatur, etiam profunda Dei, ex omnibus que passim uidi aliqua uel summatim ideo fidentur insinuo, quia quam tutis auribus quam deuotis mentibus loquor, non ignoro.

'Denique post moram non modicam in tam beata uisone expletam, 24 uisio ipsa repente disparuit. Frequencia autem eorum qui conuenerant, adorato loco ubi steterat gloria tanti sacramenti, sensim cepit rarescere, & singuli ad proprias sedes cum gaudio & leticia rediere. Ego precedentem ducem nostrum inter mansiones lucidissimas gaudio & exultacione plenus ad ulteriora subsequebar. Hic iam 24: consistencium candor, hic odoris fragrancia, hic armonia Deo f. 39ᵛ laudes canencium inestimabilis, & omnia sensibus | uix credenda mortalium.'

[LV] De ingressu porte paradisi et de gloria Domini que intro apparuit.
24(

'Multo inter hec iam emenso uie spacio, et crescente semper ante nos locorum iocunditate, uidi eminus quasi murum cristallinum, cuius altitudo peruideri non potuit, longitudinis quoque metam nequiui comprehendere. Quo iam appropinquantibus nobis, portam uidi lucidissima introrsus claritate micantem, apertumque eius 24(aditum, sed crucis tantum vnius obice signatum. Accedebat illuc cateruatim multitudo eorum, qui uiciniores erant, ingredi exoptans. Crux uero in medio porte sita, mirabile dictu, nunc se attollens ad superiora, latum aduentantibus pandebat ingressum, nunc ima petens intrare cupientibus aditum negabat. Quam uero gaudenter 247 introibant admissi, quam reuerenter subsistebant exclusi iterum crucis eleuacionem prestolantes, exprimere non sufficio. Substitit hic mecum dux meus aliquamdiu & has uicissim crucis eleuaciones & demissiones, accedencium nunc introitum nunc exclusionem, diucius stupens intuebar. Demum accessimus & nos. Incedebamus autem, ut 247 predixi, manibus inuicem consertis. Igitur accedentibus nobis crux

and schewde in a vysyon to the holy sowlys that byn in paradyse, that
her deuocyon and loue schuld be the more accendyd and incresyd to
Hym?

2785   'Many other thingis Y saw and herde there, the whyche Y trowe at
this tyme is bettur to leue hem out than to wryte hem.

'And than aftyrward sodenly this blessyd syghte and holy vysyon
was takyn fro thens. Than al that grete multytude of soulys that
came thedir to worschippe the holy crosse of Crystys Passion, wente |
2790 ageyne euerichon to her owne places with ioy and gladnes. Treuly, Y   [h]6ʳ
folowyde euermore my duke and lodisman, Sent Nicholas, that went   L265ʳ
forthe farthir and farther, repletyd now with grete ioye and gladnes   O62ʳ
amonge the ful brighte and light mansyons of blessid sowlys. And
the whitnes of hem þat were here in this place, and the swetnes of
2795 sauer, and also the melodye of synging laudys to God, wes
inestymable and onethe to mannys vnderstondyng credyble.'

¶ Of the entryng of the gate of paradyse and of the ioy that
apperyd withinforth.   ¶ Ca lv

'Forthermore nowe, whenne we were paste all these placys and
2800 sightys aforeseyde, and had gonne a good space more inward, and
euer grew to vs more and more ioye and feyernes of placys also, at
the laste we sawe aferre a ful glorious walle of crystal, hoys heythe no
man might see, and lenthe no man might consider. And when we
came thedyr Y sawe within-forthe a ful feyre, brighte, schynyng gate
2805 and stode opyn, saue hit was signed and leide ouer with a crosse.
Treuly, theder came flockemele the multytude of tho blessyd sowlys
that were next to hyt, and wolde cum in at that feyre gate. The
crosse was sette in the myddys of that gate, and nowe sche was lyfte
vppe an hye and so gaue to hem that came thedyr an opyn and a fre
2810 entryng, and afterward sche was lettyn done ageyne, and so sparyd
other oute that wuld haue commyn in. But howe ioyful they were
that wente | in, and how reuerently they taryde that stode withoute   [h]6ᵛ
abydyng the lyftyng vppe of the crosse ageyne, Y cannot telle by no   L265ᵛ
wordys. Sothely, here Sent Nycholas and Y stode stille to-geder, and   O62ᵛ

erigitur, iter patet ingressuris. Socius meus libere ingreditur, seque-
bar et ego; uerum crux ex improuiso super manus nostras descendit,
meque a ducis mei consectatu arcebat. Quod senciens ego, nimiumque pertimescens, ista piissimi comitis monita audiui: 2480
' "Ne paueas," inquit. "Fidem tantum certissimam habeto in
Dominum Ihesum Christum & securus ingredere."

'Post hec redeunte fiducia crux cessit & intraui. Quantus uero
inestimabilis fulgor claritatis, quanta luminis gracia interius vniuersa
possederit, a me nemo requirat. Hoc enim non uerbis promere, sed   2485
nec mente sufficio recordari. Splendor ille choruscus & blandus,
serenus & lenis, sic intuentem rapiebat in se, sic nitoris immensitate
ferebat super se, ut nichil in eius comparacione crederem esse,
f. 40ʳ quicquid | eatenus me contigit uidisse. Splendor iste quamlibet
ineffabilis, quamlibet inestimabilis, tamen non reuerberabat sed   2490
pocius acuebat obtutum. Micabat quidem ineffabiliter sed multo
inestimabilius inspicientem demulcens, uisioni sue mirabiliter coaptabat.

'Inferius nichil aliud occurrebat intuenti nisi lux & murus candore
perspicuus, per quem ingressi sumus. Erant quoque ab imo usque ad   2495
summitatem eius gradus mira pulcritudine disposti, per quos
ascendebant agmina letancium, mox ut fuissent per ianuam intro-
gressi. Nullus fuit ascendencium labor, difficultas nulla, non quelibet
in ascendendo mora; superior semper alacrius quam inferior scande-
batur gradus. In plano itaque deorsum consistens, deducebam longo   2500
oculorum intuitu per hos gradus ascendentes in sublime, quos modo
per ianuam uideram intrantes. Ad alciora uero ocul[o]s defigens
conspexi in trono glorie residentem Dominum & Saluatorem nostrum in specie humana, & in circuitu accedentes et cum graciarum
accione adorantes eum, ut michi uidebatur, quingentorum uel   2505
septingentorum spiritus bonorum, qui nuper itinere predicto ad
locum troni conscenderant. Plerique etiam remocius per summos
muri sepedicti fines huc illucque uelut spaciando deambulare
uidebantur. Michi autem certissime constat quod celum celorum
ubi exultant iusti in conspectu Dei uidentes eum in maiestate sua,   2510
sicuti est, ubi etiam milia milium ministrant ei & decies milies
centena milia assistunt ei, non erat locus ille sedentis in trono, quem
ego uidebam: sed inde iam remota difficultate & omni dilacione,
ascenditur ad celum illud, eterne deitatis uisione beatum, solis
angelis & iustorum spiritibus angelica iam perfeccione consummatis   2515

2491 acuebat] BdT *add* intuentis   2502 oculos] MT, oculis S

815 the lyftyngys vppe of the crosse and the lettyngys done ageyne,
wherby somme wente in and some taryde withoute, Y behilde long
tyme with grete wonder. And at the laste Sent Nycholas and Y came
thedyr to the same gate hande in hande. And when we came thedyr
the crosse was lyfte vp. And so they that were there wente in.
820 Sothely, than my felowe, Sent Nycholas, frely wente in and Y
foloude, but sodenly and onauysyd the crosse of the gate came
done apon owre handys and departyd me fro my felawe, Sente
Nycholas, and when Y sawe thys, ful sore aferde Y was.

'Then seyde Sent Nycholas to me, "Be not aferde, but haue only
825 ful certen feythe in our Lorde Ihesu Criste, and doutheles thou
schalt come yn."

'And aftyr thys, my hope and truste came ageyne, and the crosse
was lyfte vppe, and so Y cam in. But what brightnes and clerenes of
light was there within-forthe al aboutys, no man aske ne seche of me,
830 for Y can-not only telle hit by worde, but also Y can-not remembre
hit in mynde. That gloryous schyning light was brighte and smothe,
and so raueshte a man that behylde hit, that hit bare a man aboue
hym-selfe by the grete brightnes of lyghte, yn so mekyl that what-
sum-euer Y sawe before, hit was as no-thing, me thought, in
835 comparyson of hit. That bryghtnesse, thawghe hyt were inestymable,
neuerthelesse, hyt dullyd not a mannys syghte, but rathyr scharpyd
hyt. | Sothly, hyt schynyd ful meruelusly, but more ynestymably, hyt   [h]7ʳ
delytyd a man that behylde hyt, and wondirfully cowpulde a mannys   L266ʳ
syghte to se hit.   O63ʳ

840 'And wyth-ynforthe, no-thyng Y myght see but lighte and the
walle of crystalle throw the whyche we came yn. And also, fro the
gronde vppe to toppe of that walle were grycis, ordende and
dysposyd feyre and meruelusly, by the whyche the ioyful company
that was cum yn at the forseyde gate gladly ascendyd vppe. Ther was
845 no labur, ther was no difficulte, ther was no taryng yn her ascendyng,
and the hier they wente, the gladder they were. Sothely, Y stode
benethe on the grunde, and longe tyme Y saw and behylde how they
that came yn at the gate ascendyd vppe by the same grycis. And at
the laste, as Y lokyd vppe hier, Y saw yn a trone of ioy sittyng owre
850 blessyd Lord and Sauyur, Ihesus Criste, yn lykenes of man, and
abowte Hym, as hyt semyd to me, were a fyue hondred sowlys, the
whyche late had styed vppe to that glorius trone, and so they came to
owre Lorde and worsch[i]pte Hym and thankyde Hym for Hys grete

2853 worschipte] worschpte

peruium, ubi facie ad faciem uidebitur immortalis et inuisibilis Rex
f. 40ᵛ seculorum, qui | solus habet immortalitatem & lucem habitat
inaccessibilem, quem nullus mortalium uidit, sed nec uidere
potest. Uidetur autem a mundis corde, quos nec cordis nec corporis
corrupcio deprimens grauat. In hac tamen uisione tantum leticie &   252
gaudii, tantum iocunditatis et exultacionis concepi animo, ut,
quicquid humanis dici potest uerbis, minus sit ad exprimendum
cordis mei gaudium quo ibi fructus sum.'

[LVI] Qualiter monachus egressus est ianuam paradisi.

'Hiis igitur et aliis innumeris uisis & auditis sanctus Dei Nicholaus   252
hec michi breuiter est locutus:

'"En," inquit, "uel ex parte iam, fili, ut petisti & nimio desiderio
concupisti, seculi futuri statum, pericula errancium, supplicia peccatorum, purgatorum quietem, tendencium desideria, gaudia eorum
qui iam ad celi curiam perueniunt, passionis dominice misteria, &   253
Christi iam regnantis gloriam, ut tibi possibile fuit, conspexisti. Iam
tibi ad tuos & ad seculi pugnas est redeundum. Percipies autem si
perseueraueris in timore Domini bona que oculis conspexisti &
multo hiis maiora, que solus uidere merebitur, qui sine fine illa
possidere dignus erit."
253

mercy and grace schewyd and done to hem. And some were seyne on
2855 the vppur partys of the walle as they had walkyd hethyr and dedyr.
Trewly, Y knew for certen that thys place, were Y saw oure Lorde
syttyng yn a trone, was not the hye heuyn of heuyns, where the
blessid spiritis of angels and the holy sowlys of ryghtwys men ioyin
yn the seyghte of God, seyng Hym yn Hys mageste as He ys, where
2860 also innumerable thowsondis of holy spiritys and angels serue Hym
and assiste | Hym. But than fro thens, wythowten any hardnes or
taryng, they ascende vppe to the hey heuin, the whyche ys blessyd of
the syghte of the euerlastyng Godhed, where al only the holy angels
and the sowlys of ryghtwes men, that byn of angels perfeccion, seyn
2865 the ynuisibl[e] and inmortalle Kynge of al worldys face to face, the
whyche hathe only inmortalite, and dwellyth yn lyghte that ys
inaccessyble; for no man may cumme to hyt, the whyche no mortalle
man seithe, nethyr may see. Sothely, He ys seyne only of holy
spiritys that byn pure and clene, the whyche be not greuyd by no
2870 corrupcion of body, nethir of sowle. And yn thys vision that Y saw,
so mekylle Y conceuyd yn my sowle of ioy and gladnes, that wat-
sum-euer may be seyde of hyt by mannys mowthe, ful lytyl hyt ys,
and onsufficient to expresse the ioy of myne herte, that y had there.'

[h]7ᵛ
L266ᵛ
O63ᵛ

¶ **How the monke came owte ageyne throw the same gate**
2875 **of paradyse.**   **¶ Ca lvi**

'Therfore, when Y had seyn al these syghtys aboue-seyde and
many othyr innumerable, my lorde, Sent Nycholas, that hylde me by
the hande, seyde schortly thys to me:
'"Loo, sonne," he seyde, "now a party aftyr they peticion and
2880 grete desir thow haste seyne and beholde: the state of the worlde þat
ys to cumme, as hyt myghte be to [the] possible; also the perels of
hem that offendyn and erryn; the peynys of synners; the reste also of
hem þat haue done her purgacion; the desyrys | of hem that be goyng
to heuynward and the ioys of hem that now byn cumme to the courte
2885 of heuyn; and also the ioy of Crystis reynynge. And now thow muste
go ageyne to they-selfe, and to thyne, and to the worldys feyghtyng.
Treuly, thow schalt haue and perceue the ioys that thow haste seyne
and mekyl more, ȝeffe thow contynew and perseuer yn the drede of
God."

[h]8ʳ
L267ʳ
O64ʳ

2865 ynuisible] ynuisibly   2881 the] *om.*

'Hec dicens satis mestum & supra quam dici potest merentem, quia de tanta beatitudine ad mundi erumpnas me redire debere cognoui, per ianuam qua ingressi sumus eduxit, multum instruens & exhortans quatinus immaculato corpore et innocenti corde cum pie religionis studio diem uocacionis mee prestolari satagerem: 2540

'"Diligenter," inquiens, "mandata Dei obserua & uitam tuam ad exempla iustorum institue. Sic enim fiet ut in eorum collegio post exactum uite mortalis terminum perpetuo beatus merearis admitti."'

[LVII] **De classico quod monachus audiuit & qualiter ad se reuersus fuerit.** 2545

'Dum adhuc mecum talia loqueretur subito classicum mire suauitatis cepit audiri, quasi tocius mundi campane uel quicquid sonorum est vna simul pulsacione concuteretur. In hoc classico mirabilis suauitas & uaria melodie permixtio magnitudine nescio | 2550
f. 41ʳ an dulcedine soni plus stupenda fuit. Ad tam insolitum auditum sollicite attentus & nimium animo suspensus, mox ut sonitus ille desiit audiri, a ducis mei dulcis comitatu me ex insperato destitutum uidi. Ad meipsum uero reuersus, uoces mox audiui fratrum nostrorum qui lectulo nostro astabant; uiribus etiam corporis paulatim 2555 redeuntibus, oculis quoque in usum uidendi sensim patefactis, sicut ipsi uidistis, pristine egritudinis molestia funditus deleta, non modo incolumis, uerum debilitate qua diu fueram oppressus exclusa, tam ualidus & fortis quam mestus et lugubris coram uobis resedi. Putabam autem me in ecclesia coram altari esse, ubi crucem 2560 dominicam primitus adoraueram. Eorum nempe memoria que ibi corporaliter egeram et perspexeram multo magis herebat animo meo quam eorum que in capitulo, licet ea posterius perpessus fueram. Eorum uero que circa me corporaliter acciderunt postquam in capitulo prostratus fui, nichil omnino sensi aut sciui. Moram 2565 quoque in uisione illa, que michi ostensa est, me aliquam fecisse non credidi, sed tantummodo sexte ferie matutinas tunc primum percantatas fuisse estimabam.

'Hec ego uobis, que michi in corpore uel in spiritu reuelata sunt,

890 'And when he had seyde thys to me, he browghte me forthe
throwe the same gate that we came yn. Wherfor ful heuy and sory
was Y and more than a man may suppose, for wele Y knew that
Y must turne ageyne fro that heuynly blysse to thys worldys
wrechidnes. And gretely he exhortyd me how Y schulde dyspose
895 me, to abyde the day of my callyng oute of my body yn clennes of
herte and of body, and mekenes of spirite wyth dylygent kepyng of
my religyon.

'"Dylygently," he seyde to me, "kepe the commaundementys of
God, and dyspose they leuyng aftyr the example of ryghtwes men.
900 And truely, so hyt schal be, that aftyr the terme of they bodely
leuyng thow schal be admyttyd blessydly to her feleschippe euerlastyngly."'

¶ Of the swete pele and melodye of bellys that he herde in
paradyse and also how he came to hym-self ageyne.
¶ Ca. lvii

905
'And whyle the holy confessour, Sent Nycholas, thys wyse spake
ʒet with me, sodenly Y harde | ther a solenne pele and a rynggyng [h]8ᵛ
of a meruelus swetenes, and as al the bellys yn the worlde, or L267ᵛ
whatsumeuer ys of sownyng, had be rongyn to-gedyr at onys. O64ᵛ
910 Trewly, yn thys pele and rynging brake owte also a meruelus
swetenes, and a variant medelyng of melody sownyd wyth-alle. And
Y wote not whether the gretnes of melody, or the swetnes of
sownnyng of bellys, was more to be wondirde. And to so grete a
noyse Y toke good hede and ful gretly my mynde was suspendyd to
915 here hyt. Sothly, anone as that gret and merueles sownnyng and
noyse was cessyd, sodenly Y saw my-selfe departyd fro the swete
feleschippe of my duke and leder, Sent Nicholas. Than was Y
returnyd to my-selfe ageyne, and anone Y hard the voycis of my
brethyrne, that stode abowte our bedde. Also my bodely strenthe
920 cam ageyn to me a lytyl and a litil, and myn yes opinde to the vse
of seying, as ʒe sawe ryghte wele. Also my sekenes and febulnes, by
the whiche Y was longe tyme ful sore dissesid, was vtwardly
excludyd and gonne fro me, and sate vppe before yow so stronge
and myghty as Y was afore by hyt soroful and heuy. And Y wende
925 that Y had be then yn the chirche afore the auter, where Y
worshipte fyrste the crosse. And as tochyng the taryng that Y
made yn thys vysyon, Y had wende hyt had be noone, but al only

caritate illectus & coactus uestre sanctitatis imperio, quam potui 25ͽ
compendiose narraui. Vos autem queso et cum immenso lacrimarum
fonte supplex postulo, quatinus pro me infelice & misero instancius
apud Dominum intercedere dignemini, ut supplicia, que uidi,
reorum euadere & gaudia que agnoui iustorum innocenter & pie
viuendo, soluto mortis debito, merear introire, dulcemque Dei & 25ͽ
Domini mei Ihesu Christi faciem, dominam quoque meam sanctam
Mariam in eternum merear intueri.'

[LVIII] **Argumentum ad uisionem monachi confirmandum.**

Quibusdam igitur tum breuitatis studio tum aliis certis de causis
pretermissis, ego qui hec utcunque magnorum uirorum compulsus 258
imperio literis tradidi, omnia hec, ipso qui hec uidit referente, didici,
& quam potui studiose narracionis eius nunc sensum nunc etiam
f. 41ᵛ   uerba expressi. Ceterum michi sicut & plerisque aliis, qui | illum
familiarius nouerunt, satis persuasum est ex multis rebus fidem
indubitatam uerbis illius habere debere. Ut enim secreciora preter- 258
eam, multa sunt documenta manifesta, ex quibus circa principium
huius narracionis nonnulla memoraui, que euidenter probare uidentur non humano commento sed nutu diuino hec innotuisse fidelibus.
Uerum sit tanta infidelitas, uel, ut temperancius loquar, sit infirmitas
ista quorundam, ut premissis non credant, licet talem ac tantam 259
tamque inauditam hominis infirmitatem tam cito, tam insperato in
testimonium ostense uisionis uiderint curatam: dicant, si uelint,
fictam egritudinem cuius racionem nullus medicorum sciuit: men-
ciantur tantam hominis fuisse peruicaciam ut simulata eius dormicio,
qui iugi prius insompnietate per longum tempus laborauerat, & 259
uocibus repentinis clangencium, non punccionibus adhibitis stimu-
lorum aliquatenus exagitari potuerit: fuerit tanta uersute simulacionis
fraudulencia, ut, oculis in ima demersis, effossa uisus sit habere
lumina, omnimodis spirare biduo non sit uisus, arteriarum motum
post longissima horarum spacia uix tandem ad modum tenuissimi fili 260
permiserit sentiri: lacrimas etiam postmodum per multos dies fere
indesinentes irrideant: uidimus in eo preter hec omnia quiddam satis
pulcrum nec minus certum superne curacionis indicium. Habebat

the space of on matens while, and now as Y vnderstonde, Y was
teryde .ij. days and more.

2930 'And now as compendeusly as Y kowde, Y haue here tolde yow of
al tho thingys the whiche Y sawe and were schewyd to me yn body
or yn spirite, | at the instauns and commandement of youre holynes [h]9ʳ
and deuoute charyte. And nowe Y beseche yo[u] mekely, and that L268ʳ
with sore weping, that ye will withsaue to praye to God for me, an O65ʳ
2935 vnhappy wrecche, þat Y may scape the grete and greuys peynys of
synners the whyche Y sawe, and cum to the ioys of the holy sowlys
that Y knewe, and alsoo to see euerlastyngly the gloryous face of oure
blessyd Lorde and Sauyur, Ihesu Criste, and oure blessyd Lady,
Sent Marye.'

2940 ¶ A proffe that thys reuelacyon ys of God and most nedys
be trew for the grete myraclys that our Lord shewyd on
this same monke that same tyme.   ¶ Ca lviij

Mony instruccyons and opyn examples byn here at the begynnyng of
thys narracyon, that euydentely prouyn thys vysyon not to be of
2945 mannys conceyte but vtwardely of the wylle of God, the whiche
wolde haue hyt schewed to Crystyn pepul. Neuerthelesse, ȝefe there
be so grete infydelyte or infyrmyte of a[n]y persons that can-not
beleue to these thyngys aforeseyde, lete hem consyder the grete
sekenesse and febulnes of hym that sawe hyt, so sodenly and so sone
2950 helyd in-to a very wytnes and trowthe of this vysyon that he sawe.
Also let hem meruelle the grete noyse that was abowte hym, and also
howe that he was prycked in hys fete with nyldys, by the whyche he
kowde not in any wyse be mouyd. Forthermore, let hem take hede to
hys yes, that were so ferre fallyn done in-to hys hede, and was not
2955 seyne onethe | to brethe space of .ij. days. And also aftyr a ful longe [h]9ᵛ
space of howris onethe laste myghte be perseuyd yn hym a ful smalle L268ᵛ
meuyng as a thynne drede yn hys vytalle veynys. Also let hem O65ᵛ
consyder hys contynualle wepyng and terys, the whyche he had
aftyrward many days. And besyde all thes thyngys, we knowe also a-
2960 nothyr certen thynge, that was a ful feyre myracle and a very tokyn
of Godys curacyon schewyd on hym the same tyme, and as mekyl to
be merueld. Sothely, he had al-moste the space of an hole ȝere yn hys
lyfte legge a grete sore and a ful byttur, as hyt were a canker large
and brode, wherby he was peynyd intollerably. And he was wonte to

2933 you] yon   2947 any] auy

enim toto fere vnius anni spacio in sinistra tibia ulceris genus acerbissimum, et non modice latum, quo intollerabiliter cruciabatur. 2605 Dicere solebat talem sibi ex hoc adesse dolorem quasi ferri candentis laminam tibie iugiter alligatam gestaret. Nullum emplastrum, non aliquod vnguentum uel medicina alia, quamuis plurima adhiberentur a medicis, uel cruciatum eius lenire uel locum vulneris coartare f. 42ʳ ualebat. Sub illa uero dormicione ita plenissime | sanatus apparuit, ut 2610 ipse quoque nobiscum stupens miraretur dolorem cum vulnere ita deletum, ut nec cicatricis uestigium nec ruboris aut alboris indicium diuine superfuerit medicine. Hoc autem solo a reliqua tibia locus distabat sanati doloris, quod pilis omnino nudus fuit.

Delectabile sibi admodum perhibet esse quociens pulsari classicum 2615 uel sonare aliquod signum audierit, quia ex hoc sibi ad mentem redit classicum illud suauissimum, quod in regione beatorum audiuit. Sibi uero post excessum redditus, cum ei diceretur a fratribus iam Paschalem adesse festiuitatem, tunc primum asserentibus credidit, cum signum completorii pulsari audiuit. Iamque certus animaduertit 2620 classicum illud hoc innuisse quod apud celi ciues non sine ineffabili iocunditate exultacionis, nec absque festiua celebritate recolitur humane salutis effectus, quam in sollemnitate Paschali operatus est in medio terre, qui vno eodemque momento olim creauit ex nichilo celum & terram Ihesus Christus Dominus noster, cui est cum Patre 2625 & Spiritu Sancto honor et gloria in secula seculorum. Amen. **Explicit uisio monachi de Eynesham.**

2965 sey, that he had seche a sorow and peyne ther-of, as he had bore an
hoote plate of yrne bownde faste to hys legge. And ther was no
emplastur, no oyntmente, nethyr any othyr medicyn, how-be-hit that
he had mekyl of lechis, leyde to hyt, þat myghte ȝese hym of hys
peyne or drawe the wownde to-gedyr. Trewly, yn the space of hys
2970 raueshyng, he was so fully helyd that he hym-selfe meruelyd wyth vs
to fele and see the peyne and ache wyth the wownde so clene agonne,
that no tokyn of hyt, ne signe of rednes or of whythnes, remaynyd
aboue the meruelus curacion of God. Al only thys differens had hys
legge that was sore fro todyr legge, that where the forseyde sore was,
2975 that place was bare and had non heere.

Ful delectable hyt was to hym, as he seyde fro that tyme forthe, as
ofte as he harde any so-|lenne pele of ryngyng of bellys, by-cause hyt   [h]10ʳ
wolde then cum to hys mynde ageyne, the ful swete pele and melody   L269ʳ
the whyche he herde when he was amonge the blessyd sowlys yn   O66ʳ
2980 paradyse. Sothely, aftyr that he was cum to hym-selfe, and hys
brethirne had tolde hym that now ys the holy tyme of ȝestyr, than
fyrste he beleuyd, when he harde hem rynge solenly to complen, for
then he knew certenly that the pele and melodye, that he herde yn
paradyse wyth so grete ioy and gladnes, betokynde the same
2985 solennyte of ȝestir, yn the whyche owre blessyd Lorde and
Sauyur, Ihesus Criste, ros[e] vppe visibly and bodely fro dethe on-
to lyfe, to home wyth the Fadyr and the Holy Gooste be now and
euermore euerlastyng ioy and blysse. Amen.

2986 rose] roso

COMMENTARY

Line references for the *Visio* are preceded by S (for MS Selden Supra 66).

PREFACE TO THE *VISIO*

S1–2 *apud Eynesham*: On the history of Eynsham abbey, see the brief remarks in
the Introduction above, p. xxxvi, and consult Salter, and *A History of
Oxfordshire*, ed. W. Page, VCH, 2 (London, 1907), 65–67; *A History of the
County of Oxford*, ed. Alan Crossley, VCH, 12 (London, 1990), 98 ff; Eric
Gordon, *Eynsham Abbey 1005–1228* (1990), and Christopher A. Jones, *Ælfric's
Letter to the Monks of Eynsham* (Cambridge, 1998), pp. 5–17. For recent
excavations, see Gordon's contribution to Margaret Gray and Nicholas Clayton,
'Excavations on the Site of Eynsham Abbey', *Oxoniensia*, 43 (1978), 100–122 at
105–8, and D. R. M. Gainster, S. Margeson, M. Hurley, and B. S. Nenk,
reports in *Medieval Archaeology*, 34 (1990), 207; 35 (1991), 180–3; 36 (1992),
257–8; and 38 (1994), 240–1. The only surviving picture of the abbey is that of
the ruins drawn by Anthony Wood in 1657, Bodleian Library, MS Wood E.1, f.
45^r, reproduced in Gordon, *Eynsham Abbey 1005–1228* (1990), ill. 26, p. 97.

   Some Eynsham manuscripts (92 titles) are noted in the early-fourteenth-
century *Registrum Anglie de libris doctorum et auctorum veterum*, ed. Richard
H. Rouse and Mary A. Rouse (Corpus of British Library Catalogues, London,
1991), pp. 266–7. There is a striking twelfth-century image of the Virgin and
child in one of these manuscripts, Bodleian Library, MS Bodley 269 (*SC*
1935), f. iii^r, reproduced in colour as frontispiece in Gordon, *Eynsham Abbey
1005–1228*, and see C. M. Kauffmann, *Romanesque Manuscripts 1066–1190*
(London, 1975), p. 86, no. 52. The manuscript, shelfmark B III, written
c.1130–40, contains Augustine's commentary on Psalms 101–150. Penkett,
'Sinners and the Community of Saints', pp. 46–47, notes the presence at
Eynsham (shelfmark B IX) of Bodleian Library, MS Laud lat. 3 (see Gordon,
Eynsham Abbey 1005–1228, ill. 13, p. 27), containing Pseudo-Augustine, *De vera
et falsa poenitentia*, which stresses the need for contrition before absolution can
be given (*PL* 40:1113–30), an emphasis repeated in the *Visio*.

S1–30 Ehlen, in *VEME*, pp. 291–3, suggests as likely sources for the opening
section of Adam's Preface—the extended image of the night of ignorance giving
way to the day of revelation—Augustine, *Confessiones*, 12 and *Epistula* 187 (*PL*
33:832–48), and Bernard, *Sermones super Canticum canticorum*, 72 and 75, but
though they are plausible I do not find them compelling; probably the most
immediate prompt was Gregory the Great, *Dialogi* 4.43.2:

Nam quantum praesens saeculum propinquat ad finem, tantum futurum saeculum ipsa iam quasi propinquitate tangitur et signis manifestionibus aperitur. Quia enim in hoc cogitationes nostras uicissim minime uidemus, in illo autem nostra in alterutrum corda conspicimus, quid hoc saeculum nisi noctem, et quid uenturum nisi diem dixerim? Sed quemadmodum cum nox finiri et dies incipit oriri, ante solis ortum simul aliquo modo tenebrae cum luce conmixtae sunt, quousque discedentis noctis reliquiae in luce diei subsequentis perfecta uertantur, ita huius mundi finis iam cum futuri saeculi exordio permiscetur, atque ipsae reliquiarum eius tenebrae quadam iam rerum spiritalium permixtione translucent. Et quae illius mundi sunt multa iam cernimus, sed necdum perfecte cognoscimus, quia quasi in quodam mentis crepusculo haec uelut ante solem uidimus.

Cf. Rom. 13:12. Zaleski, pp. 81–82, briefly compares Adam's Preface with the other extended prefatory defences and explanations of visionary experience given by H[enry] of Sawtry (see *SPP*) and Ralph of Coggeshall (see *Visio Thurkilli*). I am preparing an edition and translation of Peter of Cornwall's contemporary preface (1200) to his *Liber reuelationum*, which speaks in similar terms, also quoting the *Dialogi*.

S15 *diuiditur . . . tenebris*: Gen. 1:4.

S18–36 Prompted by 1 Cor. 13:12–13.

S18 *cogniti sumus ab eo*: cf. 1 Cor. 8:3.

S33–35 As Carozzi notes (p. 527–8), many vision texts refer to earlier ones to authenticate their accounts; see, for example, references to the visions of Dryhthelm, the monk of Wenlock, Wetti, and visions told by Gregory the Great, used to defend the orthodoxy of the *Visio Bernoldi* (Maaike Van Der Lugt, 'The Textual Tradition of Hincmar of Rheims *Visio Bernoldi* with a New Critical Edition', *Bulletin du Cange*, 52 (1994), 109–49, section [A]7, p. 147). Other visions refer to their predecessors, as here, without naming particular visions or authors: e.g. Bede in his account of the Vision of Dryhthelm: *miraculorum memorabile et antiquorum simile* (*BEH*, p. 488), and Guido in his preface to the *Visio Alberici*: *Deus . . . alios vero quibusdam visionibus ac revelationibus informat et erudit, ut, qui scripturarum predicationibus et minis quadam mentis obstinatione sumus increduli, his saltem visionibus instructi nostrarum animarum ruinas timeamus, quibus in hac vita positis futuri seculi pena vel gloria manifestis indiciis ostenditur* (ed. Schmidt, p. 166).

S35–36 *fides . . . spes . . . caritas*: 1 Cor. 13:13.

S37 *timor Domini*: Ps. 110:10, Eccli. 1:16.

S40 *diues*: cf. Luke 16:19 ff.

S40–41 *diues in inferno sepultus*: Luke 16:22.

S43 *Moysen & prophetas*: Luke 16:29, 31.

S51 *exultant . . . Dei*: Response 1st Vespers Feast of All Saints.

S59–60 *ad . . . ecclesie consolacionem & edificacionem atque instruccionem multorum*: cf. S33–36. The instructional usefulness and edificatory values of visions are repeatedly invoked by the authors of vision texts: e.g. Gregory the Great, *Dialogi*, 4.40 *ad aedificationem audientium*; Vision of Heinrich von Ahorn: *Hec ueraci illius qui visionem uiderat relatione cum audissemus, ad edificationem fidelium memorie commendare studuimus* (ed. Steinmeyer & Sievers, p. 493); *ad utilitatem legentium* (*Visio Tnugdali*, ed. Wagner, p. 56); H[enry] of Sawtry: *utilitatem multorum per me prouenire desiderem . . . me numquam legisse quicquam uel audisse, unde in timore et amore Dei tantum proficerem* (*SPP*, p. 121, lines 9–13); *quia plerique audientium ex relatione predicte visionis non minimum profecerunt emendatiorem vitam eligentes* (*Visio Thvrkilli*, ed. Schmidt, p. 4, lines 14–16).

S67 Cf. Matt. 25:26.

S70–71 *perdendos . . . qui loquuntur mendacium*: Prov. 19:9.

PROLOGUE TO THE *REVELATION*

5 *Seint Nycholas*: St Nicholas is Edmund's guide during his soul journey in the other world. In the *Visio* he is not identified by name until (in cap. 20) he is recognized by the goldsmith, who was his parishioner (1017), i.e. according to Salter, 2.264–8, the goldsmith attended the chapel of St Nicholas in Osney Abbey. In ch. 21 we learn how the goldsmith believed that the intervention of St Nicholas had saved him from the clutches of the devil in recompense for his paying for a lamp in St Nicholas's chapel and for his devotion and prayers to the saint. In ch. 24, Edmund says that he has *'euer specyally worschipped and loued'* (1252–3) St Nicholas, and Salter, 2.273, suggests that, like the goldsmith, Edmund may have been a resident of the island of Osney.

In the *Visio Thurkilli* St Nicholas (*qui huic purgatorio prefuit*, ed. Schmidt, p. 16, line 1) determines how deeply purgatorial souls are immersed in an icy pool. Charles W. Jones, *Saint Nicholas of Myra, Bari, and Manhattan* (1978), pp. 238–9, briefly deals with the saint's appearance in the *Visio*, and compares Nicholas's role as Edmund's overseer in purgatory with that of Cato in Dante's *Divina Commedia*.

For valuable comments on the function of the guide in other-world visions, including the *Revelation*, see Zaleski, pp. 52–55.

11 *mowth*: *t* is faint and the cross-bar is not visible; it could be an *i* without a dot, as frequently, e.g. in *vndirstonde* 18; *h* has a horizontal bar: hence Arber, *mowith*.

16 *here* (2): 'their', last citation for this form in *OED*.

CHAPTER HEADINGS OF THE *REVELATION*

These have been added here by Machlinia and his translator (see Introduction, p. lx).

29–31 The heading for ch. 1 here is derived from the *titulus* to cap. 1 in the *Visio* (S75–77); cf. below, Commentary 118–21.

34–35 Cf. 204 which is closer to S155.

37–38 The heading here is closer to S232–3 than 286–7. (I have not given notice of all such variations.)

CHAPTER I

118–21 The chapter heading is based on the *Visio*'s *incipit* (S1–3).

122 Note that the name of the monastery, included here, is not given in the *Visio*, apart from, in S, in the *incipit*, S2. *Revelation* omits *nuper* (S78); for the translator and his audience the events are no longer recent.

123 *fro thys worldys vanyte*: Carozzi (p. 511) points out that the *Visio*, though written first, is in effect the continuation of the story of the clerk (Edmund?) in *MVSH*, 5.3, whom Hugh of Lincoln recommended to take the monastic habit, for *non esse conueniens ut qui talia uidisset et audisset in seculi uanitate ulterius spatiari uellet* (*MVSH*, vol. 2, p. 90); the *Visio* narrative here starts with Edmund *a seculari uanitate conuersus*.

127–9 Thurston, *The Physical Phenomena of Mysticism* (London, 1952), p. 344, mentions Edmund's going without food and drink, alongside alleged examples of longer abstentions, in a chapter 'The Mystic as hunger-striker': e.g. Marie of Oignies going without food for 35 days, or indeed St Lydwina (d. 1433) eschewing food for 28 years! But Edmund's abstention is seemingly involuntary and caused by sickness.

138 *thes euyn of Schere Thursdaye*: i.e. the night of Wednesday 17 April 1196, preceding Maundy Thursday, the latter known in Latin as *cena dominica* (S94) or *cena Domini* (S330, 381).

139–40 *Cryste ys tradicion*: Christ's betrayal, by Judas. Note that this is the first occurrence of *tradicion* in this sense in *OED*, and is taken directly from the *Visio*: *de tradicione Domini* (S93). The reader is directed to Appendix 2 for all subsequent early occurrences of words in the *Revelation*.

144/155 *compunccion / confession*: The *Regularis Concordia* 37, ed. and trans. Dom T. Symons (London, 1953), pp. 36–37, speaks of the arousal of compunction of the soul by the outward representation of that which is spiritual in certain practices of performing the night office on Maundy Thursday, and on p. 38, says that the monks should go to confession on that day. On Edmund's experience of sweet compunction and the extravagance of his weeping devotions, see Dinzelbacher, 'The Beginnings of Mysticism' (1987). The translator adds *swetenes* at 145, but the terminology is justified by the occurrence of *suauitatem* later at S116. For a recent account of compunction in texts from England, see Sandra McEntire, 'The Doctrine of Compunction from Bede to Margery Kempe', in *The Medieval Mystical Tradition in England. Exeter Symposium IV: Papers read at Dartington Hall, July 1987*, ed. Marion Glasscoe (Cambridge, 1987), pp. 77–90.

147 *sex of the belle yn the mornyng*: i.e. about noon on Maundy Thursday.

148–9 *the merceis of owre Lord, the whiche [He] ha[th] doon for mankynde*: He omitted after *whiche* is an understandable error in L and was corrected in O in the second setting of quire [a]. The subject pronoun is omitted elsewhere, and I have chosen to emend by adding *he* at 1829, 1846 and *Y* at 1031, 1256, 1833, 2387. I also adopt O's *hath* for L's *had* as another substantive correction matching S *contulit*; although the sequence of tenses in the translation could justify *had*, the perfect rather than pluperfect tense is theologically more sound, for the Lord has not ceased to be merciful. Cf. the interchange of *-d* and *-th* noted above, p. lii.

157 *contricion of herte*: The *Revelation* mentions *contricion* 6x more: 223, 284, 649, 878, 2005, 2045. Contrition equals attrition, or sorrow for one's sins, plus confession, plus the will not to commit the sin again; it requires oral confession and satisfaction; the sorrow must be heartfelt; exterior tears alone are no true sign of contrition; and the contrite heart is accompanied by grace. For details of this complex and rapidly developing concept in the twelfth century, see Anciaux, *La Théologie du Sacrement de Pénitence*, pp. 463–80.

161–2 *his brother*: The term is, of course, ambiguous, and could just mean 'fellow monk', as it does when referring to *.ij. of his bretheren* (152–3). Those two brethren, authorized to hear confession and give absolution, look like the priors of 167. The prior at the time was one Thomas; the sub-prior was Adam, the author, in all probability Edmund's blood brother (162), the *predictus frater* also of S121; Salter, 2.289, notes here that *predictus* is added in the B and C versions: 'Possibly in A *frater* meant "his brother", and to make the story more impersonal *predictus* was inserted, so that the meaning would be "the said monk".' See Introduction, pp. xxxiii–xliii. Thomas's knowledge of the matter, as reported by Ralph of Coggeshall, would be explained by the fact that it was to him and to Adam that Edmund in confession gave the most detailed accounts of his vision: see also 395–8, and the quotation from *Visio Thurkilli*, above, Introduction, p. xxxv.

167 *and hyt were by the relygion*: *utrum consuetudinis esset* (S119): i.e. if it were according to the rules of the monastery. As a novice, Edmund is not necessarily fully *au fait* with all the monastic customs, but he is also surprised, as it were, by the hallucination, which, we subsequently discover, makes him believe that he has been disciplined (i.e. flogged) in the chapter house during the night, after Matins.

170–1 *grete febulnesse of his hedde, or by alyenacion of hys mynde*: Not surprisingly, visionaries were not infrequently thought to be crazy, e.g. Heinrich von Ahorn's wife tries to shut him up for this reason when he tells of his vision: *alii de morte eum resurrexisse, alii eum insanire existimabant. Ipse autem se sane fore mentis asseruit, seniorem secum fuisse, secum plura locutum esse constanter affirmauit. Mulier his auditis propius accedebat et amplexans uirum, ut eum ab aliena locutione auerteret, alia aliaque illi uerba ingerebat et sic a narratione uisionis que precepta illi fuerat eum abstrahebat* (ed. Steinmeyer & Sievers, 4.493); and Thurkill; for further discussion, see Peter Dinzelbacher, 'Körperliche und seelische Vorbedingungen religiöser Träume und Visionen', in *I sogni nel medioevo*, ed. Tullio Gregory (Lessico Intellettuale Europeo 35, Rome, 1985), 57–86, pp. 74 ff.

177–8 *when the chaptur was ronge*: does not accurately translate *tabula percuteretur*. Salter notes (2.289), 'the rule was that bells should not be rung during Lent, but that a *tabula*, a slab of wood, should be struck to summon the brethren.' The odd construction may suggest the intended reading 'chapter-bell' for *chaptur*, but that again misses the point of *tabula* that Salter explains. (*OED* cites this passage (s.v. chapter *sb.* 3.) to illustrate, erroneously, the sense 'A short "lesson" or passage of scripture read in services of the Latin church' or b. 'An anthem in the Ambrosian rite said at Lauds after the psalms and before the antiphon, and varying with the day'.) One might understand the expression 'when the body of monks was rung for /summoned by ringing', cf. *OED* ring *v.*[2] B.10.b. first citation 1562; *chaptur* and *couent* would then be in apposition. The monks are here being summoned to Matins early Good Friday morning.

CHAPTER 2

S134 *toto*: Thurston and Salter, who do not indicate where letters are missing in the *tituli*, read *fuisset*, but only the first three letters survive where the rubric has been cropped (not, I believe, since their examinations of the manuscript), and the first two are definitely not *fu*. The wording of the rubric is probably here influenced by *totus corporis strage* (S138–9). Cf. the *Revelation*'s *laye prostrate al his body* (182).

185 *Prime*: about 7.00 a.m.

187 *abbot is*: possessive with separate pronoun. In L a second *t* has been inserted by hand in the gap before *is*.

The abbot's seat was in fact doubly vacant, not only because no-one was sitting in it at the time, but also in the sense that the abbacy itself was vacant at this time; see Introduction, p. lxxxix, and Wieners and Ehlen in *VEME*, pp. 75 and 256.

190–1 *without any mocyon of any membre of his body*: Such immobility is a not uncommon feature of the entranced state of visionaries; e.g. *Visio Baronti*: *nullum membrum agitare* (Ciccarese, p. 238); Elisabeth of Schönau I.1; Alpais of Cudot II.3; Orm *sine motu et sensu iacuit* (*AB*, 75 (1957), 77); *Visio Tnugdali*: *mortuus jacet nullo in eo remanente vite signo* (ed. Wagner, p. 8, lines 16–17);

Exordium Magnum 2.26; Heinrich von Ahorn: *iacet per triduum sine voce, sine tocius motu corporis* (ed. Steinmeyer & Sievers, p. 491); Godescalc: a slight movement of his mouth is the only vital sign which prevents him from being buried when he lies *sensibus pariter deficientibus* (ed. Assman, (A) p. 50, line 20): *Alterum vero motum quendam in labiis eius considerantes, qui aderant, dum tamen toto corpore rigidus ac frigidus more mortuorum iaceret, eum sepelire non audebant, existimantes adhuc in eo animam esse nimio pondere valitudinis sopitam* (ed. Assmann, (B) 1.(1), p. 162, lines 17–20); *Visio Thvrkilli: corpus viri insensibile et immobile* (ed. Schmidt, p. 6, line 22).

This recurrent scenario of the death-like collapse from which the visionary recovers to recount his or her other-world journey has prompted scholars to compare such medieval accounts with latter-day so-called Near-Death Experiences: see Peter Dinzelbacher, 'Mittelalterliche Vision und moderne Sterbeforschung', in *Psychologie in der Mediävistik: Gesamelte Beiträge des Steinheimer Symposions*, ed. J. Kühnel (Göppinger Arbeiten zur Germanistik, 431, Göppingen, 1985), pp. 9–49, and Zaleski; for qualifications, see Marc Van Uytfanghe, 'Les *Visiones* du très haut Moyen Âge et les récentes "expériences de mort temporaire." Sens ou non-sens d'une comparaison. Première partie', *Instrumenta Patristica*, 23 (1991), 447–81, and 'Les *Visiones* du très haut Moyen Âge et les récentes "expériences de mort temporaire." Sens ou non-sens d'une comparaison. Seconde partie', *Sacris Erudiri*, 33 (1992–93), 135–82.

194 *His feete ware ful coolde*: cf. *Visio Sancti Fursei*, 5: *pedes eius frigore ingrauati duruerunt*, Carozzi, p. 681, lines 1–2.

CHAPTER 3

213–15 On the Good Friday *Adoratio Crucis* ceremony, which ends with the kissing of the cross, see Karl Young, *The Drama of the Medieval Church*, 2 vols. (Oxford, 1933, repr. 1962), 1.117–22; the *Regularis Concordia*, ed. Symons, pp. 41–44; and the *Decreta Lanfranci: The Monastic Constitutions of Lanfranc*, ed. David Knowles (London, 1951), pp. 40–41.

218 *they hadd lefte hyt*: I take the translation as warrant for retaining the pluperfect *dimiserant* (S168), as in BdT, albeit S is alone in misreading *diuiserant* against other manuscripts' perfect tense *dimiserunt*.

225 *the .vij. salmys of penanse*: The Seven Penitential Psalms are Vulgate nos. 6, 31, 37, 50, 101, 129, 142.

227–8 *all-mooste tyl the sonne sette*: Edmund revives before compline (243) on Easter Saturday, 20 April 1196, a little before sunset, which in Eynsham that day was about 7.20 p.m.

229 *strengh*: I retain the spelling (see *LALME*, 4.78); elsewhere we find *strenght* 132, 289, 432, and later in the text *strenthe*, 1441, 1803, 2775, 2919, cf. *strenthyd* 2803. The final *-h* in *strengh* has a cross-bar, but this does not signify: the print spells *myth*, e.g., both with and without such a cross-bar.

229 *ius[c]ys*: 'juices', translates *succos* (S178). Neither *OED* nor *MED* records the spelling *iustys* with intrusive *t*, which is probably the result of *c/t* confusion; neither do they record the emended spelling with *-sc-*, but they do record the following: *juce, juic, jouce* (*MED* s.v. *jus*) and *iwisch, wisch* (*OED*) alongside forms with *-s-*.

230 *hit*: The text's *he* is an error for *hit* referring to *what-somme-euer*, cf. *quicquid . . . effluebat*.

234-6 Edmund's insensibility is similar to that reported of other visionaries during their trance, e.g. Boso: *permodicum enim ore et nasibus trahens flatum per tres dies raptus ab humanis rebus quasi mortuus sine ullo sensu permansit* (ed. David Rollason, p. 246); Alberic: *inchoante languore correptus, graviter infirmatus est, quo tempore novem diebus totidemque noctibus immobilis et acsi mortuus sine sensu iacuit* (ed. Schmidt, p. 168); Thurkill (see above, Commentary 190-1).

239 *no-thyng hit botyd*: confirms the accuracy of the S correction *nequicquam* 'in vain'.

CHAPTER 4

249 *They sawe also*: Note that the *Visio* here reads *uidimus*, Adam including himself in the group of witnesses. The *Revelation* here de-personalizes the narrative.

259 Apart from the many other reasons why Edmund should call on the Virgin as he recovers his senses, it is worth noting that the abbey of Eynsham was dedicated to her, see Alison Binns, *Dedications of Monastic Houses in England and Wales 1066-1216* (Woodbridge, 1989), p. 72, and below, Commentary 465-7.

The lament of the other-world visionary on being told to return, or on returning, to this world, *ad saeculum*, is a topos found in other accounts, cf. e.g. Vision of Salvius in Gregory of Tours, *Historia Francorum*, 7.1: *Et ego prostratus super pavimentum cum fletu dicebam: 'Heu, heu, Domine, quur mihi haec ostendisti, si ab his frustrandus eram!'* (MGH, SRM, 1 (1951), 325, lines 20-21); Owein: *lugens eo quod a tanta felicitate ad huius uite miseriam redire cogeretur* (*SPP*, pp. 148-9, lines 1046-7); Visions of Ailsi: *Cumque audisset pater mortem suam, et eius ad seculum reuersionem, ultra quam dici potest indoluit, et stupidus nimis et anxius fuit* (Easting & Sharpe, p. 234, lines 436-7); and also Dryhthelm, Maximus, the monk of Wenlock, Adamnan, and Tnugdal: see further, Zaleski, pp. 75-77.

261 *as I herde theym*: The Middle English shifts to the first person singular the plural *audiuimus*, but note that Adam speaks for himself in the first person plural at S231, for instance.

CHAPTER 5

301-2 Visionaries frequently mistake the duration of their ecstasies in real time: see Dinzelbacher, *Vision und Visionsliteratur*, p. 144. It is now Saturday evening and Edmund thinks it is still early Friday morning after Matins (not Thursday, *pace* Salter, 2.292).

303–5 See above, Commentary 213–15.

CHAPTER 6

335–6 *hit shal be declaryd aftyrward*: i.e. in ch. 58, where, when Edmund hears the bell ring, and not the striking of the Lenten wooden *tabula*, he knows it is the beginning of Easter.

337–8 *a certeyn brother that louyd him famyliarly*: As the recipient of Edmund's story, this brother would appear to be Adam himself, whether or not he and Edmund were blood-brothers.

345 *bare . . . herte*: Dan. 7:28, Luke 2:19, 51.

349–50 *.ii. dayes and .ii. nightys*: i.e. the second half of the night of Thursday/ Friday, Friday, Friday night, and Saturday.

358 *proprite*: 'particulars', translates *proprietatem*, see *MED* s.v. proprete n. Arber, without the benefit of the Latin text, wrongly expands the abbreviation and reads *purprite*.

CHAPTER 7

371 *as he had rose with our Lorde . . .* : On the liturgical parallel of Edmund's vision and the death and resurrection of Christ, see Introduction, p. xcvi.

374–5 *so he did not a .xi. monthis before*: Edmund had been seriously ill for most of the time since he joined the monastery; cf. 124–5.

376–82 On the development of the Easter drama, the *Quem quaeritis* trope and the *Visitatio Sepulchri*, see Young, *The Drama of the Medieval Church*, 1.201 ff; Young does not mention this brief description in Edmund's vision. The Eynsham version presents the three stages identified by Young: stage one: *howe the angel apperid and spake to the wemen at the sepulture of the victoriose resurreccion of ther Kinge*; stage two (Young, 1.307 ff): *and also that they shulde tel to His disciplys His glorious resurreccion*; and stage three (Young, 1.369 ff): *at the laste til our Lord apperyd to his wel-belouyd Mary Mawdelen and named her Maria in the figure of a gardner.*

The *Quem quaeritis* trope had first been incorporated for use in Benedictine monasteries in England in the *Regularis Concordia* of Æthelwold, *c.*973, describing the Winchester performance for the 3rd nocturn at Matins on Easter Sunday: see *Regularis Concordia*, ed. Symons, p. 50. For a detailed study of the *Quem quaeritis* music, a standard melody surviving in the Winchester Troper and in hundreds of manuscripts across Europe, see William L. Smoldon, *The Music of the Medieval Church Dramas*, ed. Cynthia Bourgeault (Oxford, 1980). Ælfric does not mention the Easter drama, but does cover other aspects of liturgical requirements from Maundy Thursday through Easter

Sunday in his abridgement of the *Regularis Concordia*: see Jones, *Ælfric's Letter to the Monks of Eynsham*, pp. 126–36.

On the use of the term *representatio* (S314), see the discussion by G. W. G. Wickham, 'The Romanesque Style in Medieval Drama', in *Tenth-Century Studies: Essays in Commemoration of the Millennium of the Council of Winchester and* Regularis Concordia, ed. David Parsons (London & Chichester, 1975), pp. 115–22 : 'hand in hand with the concepts embraced by the words *officium* and *ordo* [ceremony or rite] went consciousness of the fact that re-enactment of the event by means of dramatic imitation involved the use of artifice for a specific purpose. This came to be expressed in the word *representatio*, or representation. Use of this word implies consciousness of both the symbolic purpose and the emblematic, or figurative, means of commemoration through drama' (p. 117). The term *ludus* 'play' came later.

381 *wel-belouyd*: I gloss 'dearly beloved', though the pp. could be construed with nominal force, 'his wel-belouyd, Mary', translating *dilectricem suam Mariam*. *DMLBS* cites Adam of Eynsham's use of *dilectrix* referring to Mary Magdalene from *MVSH*, 5.14 (not 13 as cited), vol. 2, p. 169: *Christi dilectricis Marie Magdalene*. *OED* does not cite *beloved* as sb. before Tindale, 1526. See John 20:15.

CHAPTER 8

389 *opynily*: LO erroneously read *copynily*, translating *impensius* 'more eagerly'.

S324 *seriatim*: Carozzi (p. 526) gives numerous instances from other texts where the visionary's or redactor's account is claimed to be delivered *seriatim* or in correct order. This is usually indicative of the development of the story as the visionary repeatedly recounts it and as the writer shapes it.

CHAPTER 9

S336–7 The marginal *titulus* in S clearly refers to the section beginning with a coloured capital letter at *Cum inquit . . .* , but Thurston and Salter both begin this chapter one sentence early at *Hoc autem . . . .* The end of the *titulus* has been cropped, though *&* is clear; Thurston and Salter print *facta in somno*, a re-translation of the *Revelation*'s *in his slepe* (405).

429 *perseuerens*: LO have an uncertain single letter between second *r* and *s*; it looks like a two-compartment *s* with *r* over it and a horizontal line beneath.

440–1 *the monastery of nonnys here-by*: As Salter, 2.296, notes, this is most likely the neighbouring nunnery of Godstow, about 4 miles down the Thames towards Oxford.

449–50 *in the night that was nexte afore Shere Thursday*: i.e. early Maundy Thursday morning.

451 *of yow and of youre felowe*: i.e. prior Thomas and sub-prior Adam, if we take it that Adam is here reporting part of what Edmund told the two of them together (cf. 395–402).

458–60 The voice Edmund hears in the next chapter is during sleep before Matins early on Good Friday morning.

CHAPTER 10

465–7 I quote Salter's note, 2.297: 'St. Lawrence was, and is, the patron saint of the parish church of Eynsham, but the chief saints of the abbey were St. Paul, St. Peter, St. Mary, and St. Andrew.'

468 *an ymage of thy Redemer*: *tui Redemptoris ymaginem* (S397–8): Salter's and Thurston's editions both read *cui* for *tui* with no notice taken of S's reading. See Introduction, p. lix.

476 *a senyor, that ʒe knowe wele*: The senior is probably thought by Edmund to be prior Thomas, *ʒe* being addressed to Adam. As we learn in ch. 13 (and in the 'Adigression') he had not actually received any such discipline; it had been another of his hallucinations.

481 *another senyor*: This suggests that the translator's copy of the *Visio* may have had *alius* after *nobis* like A text MS Digby 34, though the presence of two seniors may mean the translator supplied *another* independently.

483–4 *a lityl while*: The translator's copy must have read *parumper* here, but C text manuscripts BdMST and (according to Salter) BN, Réserve des Imprimés MS D.1042, all read *parum*.

487 *Y put of my showys*: Cf. the *Decreta Lanfranci* on rules for Good Friday: *Ad primam pulsata tabula surgentes nudis pedibus uadant ad monasterium, et sic maneant omnes donec impleatur diei officium, nisi iussu abbatis calcientur pro nimia asperitate frigoris. Quod si euenerit, officio tantum intererunt nudis pedibus* (ed. Knowles, p. 39); Knowles notes that the monks go barefoot 'when "creeping to the Cross"'.

488 The *Revelation* omits mention of Edmund's staff here, *baculum manu tenens*.

CHAPTER 11

506–7 *as a mannys flesh is wont to blede whenne hit is cuppid*: Monks were bled regularly, and Adam may have been bled as part of the inefficacious treatments spoken of in ch. 58. Edmund clearly knew what he was talking about.

520 *ʒisterday*: Edmund is here speaking on Easter Day. Edmund's report of his experiences to Adam doubtless took place over days and weeks, if not months; cf. 1661, 1686–8.

CHAPTER 12

533 *old fadyr*: The translator elaborates on S *fratre*, probably prompted by the earlier mention of *senyor* (476).

540–1 *Y desired . . . to take dyscyplynys of hym*: On the discipline or flogging as an instrument of penance, see Dom Louis Gougaud, *Devotional and Ascetic*

Practices in the Middle Ages, English edn. prepared by G. C. Bateman (London, 1927), pp. 179–204.

550 *Y*: Text reads *he*, mistranslating *respondissem*.

550–1 *a certeyne worshipful fadyr, a senyor*: This turns out to be Edmund's other-world guide, St Nicholas.

S468 *angelicum habens vultum*: Judges 13:6.

S471 *Sequere me*: Matt. 8:22, 9:9, Mark 2:14, Luke 5:27, John 1:43.

CHAPTER 13

S473 There is no *titulus* in S at this point. Thurston invented one (*Qualiter se primum raptum sensit*.) by retranslating the *Revelation*'s heading, and this was adopted by Salter, without indication that it was not in the manuscript. The fact that the *Revelation does* have a chapter heading here is another piece of evidence to suggest that the translator was working from a *Visio* manuscript other than S; see Introduction, p. lx.

558 *rapte in spyryte*; *in excessu mentis*: see Dinzelbacher, *Vision und Visions-literatur*, pp. 45–53, for discussion of such expressions used by visionaries to describe their raptures.

559–60 *hys brother . . . thynges aforeseyde*: Again, this seems to be Adam referring to himself in the third person; the *Revelation* adds *that was hys confessor*.

565–8 *Revelation* turns S481–3 into direct speech.

585–6 *matens of the next nyghte. Thanne the next night after, when Y was at matens*: i.e. Matins early on Good Friday morning, *ferie sexte matutinas* (S496).

596 *hit*: inserted for sense, following *ipsum* (S504).

604–17 The *adigression* is the translator's addition, attempting to clarify the reader's probable and understandable confusion at this point by invoking angelic intervention; we would now say that his imagined confessions and flagellations were further examples of his sequence of visionary/hallucinatory experiences, that includes the voice which spoke to him six weeks earlier, and his tasting the blood from the crucifix, and, if Edmund is the visionary of *MVSH*, 5.3, this is all a continuation of a longer-term history of his visions and auditions. Note that the translator here also reveals in advance the name of Edmund's other-world guide.

[CAP. XIII A]

Salter's note is pertinent: 'This chapter is omitted in the English version; that the numbers in the Latin may correspond with those in the printed English version, the number xiii is used twice.'

The *Revelation* omits Adam's account [XIII A] of how seven years before (in 1189) the same crucifix at Eynsham had bled, and how a sick monk had been cured by drinking a potion containing some of the blood (see Introduction,

p. lxiii). As Salter notes (2.301), 'If Adam, the writer, has to trust to the "attestation of the older brethren" [S516], it is evident that in the year 1189 he was not a member of the monastery of Eynsham. If this story is meant to prove how on another occasion the cross gave forth blood, the author has omitted the essential details.'

CHAPTER 14

628 *spiritualle sightis*: not in the *Visio*.

CHAPTER 15

S588 *Ibamus . . .*: cf. the opening of Æneas' other-world journey, *Ibamus obscuri sola sub nocte per umbram . . . (Æneid*, 6.268), alluded to by Bede in the Vision of Dryhthelm (*BEH*, p. 490). Salter, 2.304, also adduces *Æneid* 6.462, *loca senta situ*, cf. *palustri situ & luto* (S590).

632 *zestewarde*: As Dinzelbacher notes, *Vision und Visionsliteratur*, pp. 104–5, it is not clear why purgatory lies in the east in this text, though Owein, following a trajectory first taken by Dryhthelm, travels to purgatory first NE, then SE (see *SPP*, p. 130, lines 361–5 and Commentary), and it is appropriate that purgatory lie eastwards as pilgrimage to Jerusalem was penitential and purgatory a stage en route to Eden. Ernest J. Becker, *A Contribution to the Comparative Study of the Medieval Visions of Heaven and Hell, with Special Reference to the Middle-English Versions*, Diss. Johns Hopkins University (Baltimore, 1899), adduces the *Apocalypse of Peter*, 3, 'there suddenly appeared two men standing before the Lord toward the East' (Becker, p. 32), and *The Book of Enoch*, 27.1, 'From thence I proceeded towards the East' (Becker, p. 24).

639–40 *There were the doers of al synnys ordente to dyuers kyndes of peynes*: Morgan, pp. 123–4, discusses the range of sins and purgatorial punishments in the *Visio*, pointing out, with some justification, 'the confused jumble of individuals and categories, with no apparent order or structure' (p. 124).

646–7 *opynly Y knewe and vndyrstode . . .*: Note that it is with virtually unprecedented specificity that Edmund is granted immediate knowledge of the details of the sins of those he sees punished; cf. the understanding granted to the visionary spoken of by Boniface, *Epistula* 115: *Et omne genus humanum et totum mundum per animas collectum ante conspectum suum; ut discernere, quid quisque vel boni vel mali egisset, nominatim in corpore vivens ea hora, et pene omnium vivorum merita narrare potuiset* (Ciccarese, *Visioni dell'aldilà*, p. 366). Peter Brown aptly comments, 'The basic model for such revelations was no longer a longing to embrace the universe from a high point in the stars. It was a longing to unveil the "hidden things" of the religious life, secret sins, secret virtues . . . in sum, to penetrate the secrets of the individual': 'The Decline of the Empire of God: Amnesty, Penance, and the Afterlife. From Late Antiquity to the Middle Ages', in *Last Things*, ed. Bynum & Freedman, pp. 41–59, at p. 59.

It is stressed hereafter that the satisfaction required of the souls in purgatory is determined by their own efforts of contrition and confession, and by the efforts of others on their behalf, *the remediis and helpinges of othir benefetis done for hem*. These means to salvation, of being *made redy . . . to heuyn-warde*, are fully orthodox, and emphasized throughout the vision.

652 Souls in purgatory have hope of salvation. The degree of that hope varies elsewhere in the vision, cf. the doctor of law, ch. 26.

677 *in this world*: not in the *Visio*.

CHAPTER 16

683–4 *fryed in a panne*: cf. 2 Macc. 7:5; *Apocalypse of Peter*, ed. James, p. 510, §34; *Visio Tnugdali*, ed. Wagner, p. 13, line 7; *SPP*, p. 132, lines 436–7; *Visio Thurkilli*, ed. Schmidt, p. 21, line 4.

The pains briefly listed in this chapter are commonplaces of other-world visions, and it would be redundant to multiply references for them all. More important here is Edmund's point that the clergy suffered more than others (693 ff), especially those of worldly dignity.

695 *spyrytualte* and *temporalte*: For the form, cf. *hospytalte* 1730.

704–5 *afore ther dethe and after ther dethe*, S651–2 *uel antea post obitum*: The discrepancy here suggests that the translator's Latin text at this point read *vel ante vel post obitum* (as in Huber2, p. 663, line 19). The S reading is common to Salter's A and Thurston's B texts, and to C text T. C text M indicates the confusion: *uel antea / post obitum*, but with *vel* added in the right-hand margin after *antea*. Salter (2.306, note to line 32) interprets *antea* as 'before my arrival', and says Huber's reading 'makes nonsense', but the *Revelation* shows that the translator was able to make sense of it.

710 *no man may noumbre*, S656 *nemo . . . dinumerare*: cf. Apoc. 7:9.

711–18, S656–64: The author of the ME *Sawles Warde* adopts these lines from a copy of the *Visio* for his description of the enormity of the pains of hell:

> *Ah þencheð nu herþurh hwuch þe measte pine beo: for the leaste pine is se heard þet hefde a mon islein ba mi feader ant mi moder ant al þe ende of mi cun, ant ido me seoluen al þe scheome ant te hearm þet cwic mon mahte þolien, ant Ich isehe þes mon i þe ilke leaste pine þet Ich iseh in helle, Ich walde, ȝef hit mahte beon, þolien a þusent deaðes to arudden him ut þrof, swa is þe sihðe grislich ant reowðful to bihalden.*

Early Middle English Verse and Prose, ed. J. A. W. Bennett and G. V. Smithers, 2nd edn. (Oxford, 1982), pp. 251–2, lines 130–7. This indebtedness is not signalled in the commentary, but is noted by Bennett in *Middle English Literature*, ed. Douglas Gray (Oxford, 1986), p. 278, and was first noticed by Joseph Hall, *Selections from Early Middle English 1130–1250*, 2 vols. (Oxford, 1920), 2.512, note to line 116, citing the *Visio* B text from Huber2, pp. 663/25–664/4, though Hall oddly omits the clause *quae homini in hac vita constituto possunt irrogari*, the source for *þet cwic mon mahte þolien*. The borrowing helps establish a *terminus a quo* for the composition of *Sawles Warde*: see E. J. Dobson, *The Origins of* Ancrene Wisse (Oxford, 1976), p. 164.

Thurston, p. 257, cites the passages from Dionysius the Carthusian which quote this portion of the *Visio* in *De Quatuor Hominis Novissimis*, art. 47 and *De Particulari Judicio*, art. 23.

717–18 *excede mesure and mode*: Anglicizes *mensuram excedunt & modum* 'exceed moderation and limit' or 'exceed proportion and moderation'. Neither *MED* nor *OED* records this Latinate sense of 'limit' or 'moderation' for *mode* (< *modus*).

734–7 Edmund and his guide St Nicholas witness the torments of purgatory, but Edmund himself is not subjected to any of them, unlike, Tnugdal and Owein.

CHAPTER 17

741 *an hye hylle, vppe al-mooste to the clowdys*: It has been suggested that Dante may have been influenced by Edmund's hill in forming his conception of Mount Purgatory, but this is probably a superfluous supposition. A hill in purgatory is also found in, for example, the visions of Wettin, Charles the Fat, Tnugdal, and Owein: see further, Patch, *The Other World*, pp. 129–30, and Morgan, pp. 157–60.

747 *a full brode ponde*: The *Revelation* ditches the possibility that it might have been a river. Rivers are more frequently encountered by visitors to the other world: see Morgan, pp. 26–29, who notes also that the Styx becomes a lake in Plato, and swamp in Virgil.

758 *hyues . . . of bees*, S699 *aluearia . . . apum*: It may be literary overkill to imagine that Adam's comparison of the multitudes of souls to swarming bees is a reminiscence of Virgil, *Æneid* 6.706–8, but Salter, 2.307, also suggests that a few lines earlier *latice* (S690) 'liquid', *watyr* (747) may recall *Æneid* 6.715, *Securos latices et longa oblivia potant*. Cf. the Vision of Sunniulf, who witnesses crowds of souls swarming about the fiery river, in which some are submerged to varying degrees: *concurrentes populi ceu apes ad alvearia mergebantur*: Gregory of Tours, *Historia Francorum*, 4.33, MGH, SRM, 1 (1951), p. 66, line 25, and *Visio Baronti*, 17: *Vidi ibi innumerabilem milia hominum; a daemonibus ligati et constricti nimium tenebantur graviter, et cum merore gementium et quasi apium similitudinem recurrentium ad vascula sua* (Ciccarese, *Visioni dell'aldilà*, p. 262).

762–4 The alternation of heat and cold is a very widespread form of other-world torment, e.g. Job 24:19, and the visions of Paul, Dryhthelm, Alberic, Godescalc, Thurkill—see Ehlen, 'Vision und Schrift', in *VEME*, p. 254, note 7, for detailed references.

On the souls being borne up in globes of flames like *sparclys*, cf. Vision of Dryhthelm, *BEH*, 5.12, p. 490: *At cum idem globi ignium sine intermissione modo alta peterent, modo ima baratri repeterent, cerno omnia quae ascendebant fastigia flammarum plena esse / spiritibus hominum, qui istar fauillarum cum fumo ascendentium nunc ad sublimiora proicerentur, nunc retractis ignium uaporibus relaberentur in profunda*; *Visio Tnugdali*, ed. Wagner, p. 33, lines 18–22: *Erant enim in ipsa flamma maxima multitudo animarum simul et demonum, que ascendebant more favillarum cum flamma ascendentium et ad nihilum redacto fumo cum demonibus iterum cadebant in fornacem usque ad profundum*; and *SPP*, p. 134, lines 511–14: *quasi homines nudos et igneos utriusque sexus et etatis diuerse sicut scintillas ignis sursum in aere iactari, qui et, flammarum ui deficiente, reciderunt iterum in puteo et igne*.

770–1 *as grapys be compressyd in a pressure*: the English translator substitutes for his audience the more familiar grapes in place of the Latin *oleas* 'olives', which were probably derived from Ps. 80 (see Schmidt, '"Visio diligenti narratione luculenter exarata"', in *VEME*, p. 38, note 19).

797 *thys dyuersiteys*: 'these diversities' translates *ista diuersitas* (sg). The *Revelation* uses *this / thys* for 'these' at 1119, 1632, 2281, though the form *dyuersiteys* may also have been prompted by a too close following of the 'look' of the Latin word.

CHAPTER 18

The prostitute is discussed by Gainer, 'Prolegomenon to Piers Plowman', pp. 181–3, and her inadequate confession is noted by Andrea König, 'Die Zügel der Zunge. Konkrete Mündlichkeit und ihre Reglementierung in mittellateinischen Visionen und Exempla', in *VEME*, pp. 227–50, at pp. 240–1.

821 *tenyse-balle*: the English is more specific than the Latin *pilam*. Devils similarly play with a soul as if it were a ball in the visions of Alpais of Cudot, see Elisabeth Stein, ed. *Leben und Visionen der Alpais von Cudot* (1995), p. 183; in Caesarius of Heisterbach, *Dialogus Miraculorum*, ed. J. Strange, 2 vols. (1851), Dist. 1 cap. 32, where two teams of devils toss the soul of an abbot on an other-world journey back and forth like a ball across a terrible, deep, and sulphurous valley: *et qui* [devils] *stabant ex una parte, animam miseram ad similitudinem ludi pilae proiiciebant; alii ex parte altera per aera volantem manibus suscipiebant* (vol. 1, p. 37); and in Peter of Cornwall's account of St Patrick's Purgatory, where the knight is strung up by a rope around his feet and bashed about the walls like a ball in a squash court: *Sursumque illum paululum trahentes proiecerunt et repulerunt eum quasi pilam de pariete in parietem* (see Easting, 'Peter of Cornwall's Account of St. Patrick's Purgatory', *AB*, 97 (1979), p. 415, lines 137–8).

840, S766 *confusionis operta diploide*: Ps. 108:29.

844–5 *Ducunt . . . descendunt*: Job 21:13.

S769–70 *Merces . . . uermis*: Jud. 16:21.

868–9 *and nothyr God . . . that Y louyd*: The syntax is faulty, possibly because words equivalent to *preter te* (S786) have dropped out.

870 *The only*: i.e. 'Thee only'.

872 *afore thine auter Y offerde vppe candelys*: According to the Sarum Breviary, St Margaret besought God that whoever lit candles for her should be granted whatever was necessary to their salvation: *qui de justo labore suo michi luminaria ministraverit: adipiscatur quicquid utile saluti suæ petierit* (*Breviarium ad usum insignis ecclesiæ Sarum*, 3 vols. (Cambridge, 1882–6), vol. 3, col. 508, Lectio viii). Cf. ME *Seinte Margarete*: 'Hwa se on mi nome makeð chapele oðer chirche, oðer findeð in ham liht oðer lampe, þe leome ʒef him, Lauerd, ant ʒette him, of heouene', ed. Bella Millett and Jocelyn Wogan-Browne, *Medieval English Prose for Women: Selections from the Katherine Group and* Ancrene Wisse (Oxford, 1990), p. 78, lines 23–25.

874 *vtwardly*: 'utterly' not 'outwardly'. The *Revelation* uses this idiosyncratic spelling 14 × plus *vtwardely* 1 ×, mainly to translate *prorsus* 3 × (as here) and *funditus* 6 ×. It is not recorded in *OED* or *MED*; see Appendix 2 §7.

874–9 It is instructive about contemporary lay understanding of penance that the prostitute thinks that confession alone is sufficient, without contrition and satisfaction. Edmund's vision strongly reinforces the need for the other two parts of penance, contrition preceding and satisfaction following confession.

876 *weshe*: LO read *weshte* in error by repeating earlier *weshte* pp.

882 *feytfully*: I retain the spelling without -*h*-: cf. (c1454) Let.Oxf. in OHS 35 324 *We pray yow gefe feytfulle credence yn thys mater*, and a1375 WPal. 337 *Be feiʒtful & fre & euer of faire speche*, cited in *MED* s.v. feithful adj. 2. and 3.(a) respectively, and Cursor 6517 *To þis fait-les lede Manna fel*, cited in *MED* s.v. feithles adj. See also Introduction, p. liii, for other words with *t* for *th*.

889–90 *And thys while sche sorowde*: 'And while she lamented these things' (*dum ista congeminat*), *sorowde* being transitive, and *thys* being pron. pl. (see Glossary for other examples). The English awkwardly follows the Latin OV word order. Alternatively, *thys* might be construed as 'thus', cf. 883.

891 *felows virgyns*: The unusual construction mimics *sodales . . . uirgines* (S804–5); see Introduction, p. lvi.

912 St Margaret flicking away the demons with her sleeve like flies: the comparison, derives, according to Schmidt in *VEME*, p. 38, from Gregory's *Moralia in Job*. For some analogous acts of saints dispelling demons, see Easting, 'Personal Apocalypse'.

925–6 *þat glorius sight of vyrgynys*: translates *uirginalis acies . . . potita* 'powerful battle-line of virgins'. Latin *acies* can also mean 'sharpness of sight', which prompts the translator's use of 'sight' here: see *OED* s.v. sight *sb.*[1] 2.a. 'a great number or quantity; a multitude'. The term is used almost like a collective noun: Ward, 2.499, notes Juliana Berners' phrase *a bomynable syght of monkes*: see Rachel Hands, ed. *English Hawking and Hunting in* The Boke of St. Albans: *A facsimile edition of sigs. A2-f8 of the Boke of St. Albans (1486)* (Oxford, 1975), p. [85] line 131, *a bhomynable sight of mōkis* in the list of 'The Compaynys of beestys and fowlys', following 'a Sculke of freris' (line 130) and 'a Superfluyte of Nunnys' (line 56). As Hands says, when *OED* quotes line 131 (without reference) s.v. abominable B. 'has occasionally been used, like *terrible*, prodigious, a simple intensive', the dictionary translates Berners' expression 'somewhat weakly as "a large company"' (Hands, p. 162), seemingly immune to what I take to be Berners' little linguistic joke of pretending that the initial *a-* is an indefinite article.

CHAPTER 19

Chapters 19–23 concern an alcoholic goldsmith from Osney (just west of Oxford); for discussions, see Gainer, 'Prolegomenon to Piers Plowman', pp. 183–8, and Morgan, pp. 69–70.

938 *Y seyde before*: See 728–32.

943 *ȝe remembre*: Edmund is addressing Adam. The *Revelation* omits the historical detail of S849–50 *qua me . . . descenderatis*: Edmund reminds Adam how Adam visited him while he, Edmund, was lying sick of a quinsy in the vill (presumably Osney) where and when the goldsmith died, which was on 28 December 1194.

949 *Est peccatum . . . quis*: 1 John 5:16.

951–2 *Who so absolute may be seyde that contynewyth hys synne to hys dethe*: translates *Quis uero tam absolute peccatum ad mortem dicetur admittere*. The *Revelation*'s *absolute* could be read as ppl. adj.: 'Who may be said [to be] so completely absorbed [in sin] that . . . ', cf. *OED* s.v. absolute *a*. I.†2.; or as an adverb 'absolutely, positively', like the *Visio*, qualifying either *contynewyth* (translated from *admittere*), or *may be seyde*. Whichever way, this is an example of syntactic awkwardness resulting from the translator sticking so closely to the Latin. Neither *OED* nor *MED* records *absolute* in an equivalent usage.

957 *Dronkinnes excusith no vise*: cited as the sole example in Bartlett Jere Whiting, *Proverbs, Sentences, and Proverbial Phrases from English Writings mainly before 1500* (Cambridge, Mass., 1968), D421. The Latin *Ebrietas nullum uicium excusat* does not appear in Hans Walther, *Lateinische Sprichwörter*, 5 vols. (Göttingen, 1963–7), or the supplement, Nova Series, 3 vols (1982–6).

959 *yn hys wolde days*: in his old days, i.e. former life, *in pristina uita* (S863).

964–5 *my prayur before the ryghtwes Iuge*: Edmund is speaking of prayers offered to assist at the Particular Judgement, on which see Easting, 'Personal Apocalpyse'.

976 *enarrabulle*: glossed 'indescribable', translates *ineffabili*. *OED* first citation, 'Used by mistake for *innarrable* [ad. L. innarrabilis], that cannot be described'. *MED* reads '[L **enarrabilis** describable, confused with **innarrabilis** indescribable.] Indescribable, inexplicable, miraculous', and provides two quotations a1500. Note *inenarrabulle* (637) translates *inenarrabilibus* (S592).

998 Here the goldsmith addresses Edmund familiarly as *thou*, but in the following chapter more formally as *ye*.

CHAPTER 21

1000–1 The *Revelation*'s chapter heading is more explicit, reminding the reader that the goldsmith was in purgatory and had been saved from hell. This is the principal point of his tale, that despite dying drunk and without the sacraments of the church (993–4), he was saved from damnation by his devotion to St Nicholas. It was to teach the benefits of adoration of the saints that the exemplum about him circulated (see Introduction, p. xxviii).

1015 *wylle that no man perysh*: cf. 2 Peter 3:9.

1015–17 *Sent Nycholas, whome now ye folowe . . . and whoys pareshon also Y was*: Salter, 2.264–8, explores the evidence for *Sent Nycholas chapelle* (1023) at Osney, and the likelihood that both the goldsmith and 'also' Edmund were parishioners there; but note that there is no equivalent for *also* in the *Visio*.

1030–1 The drunkard's particular devotion may be signalled by his regular confession twice a year. Christmas and Easter were to become the expected times for confession following the decree of the Fourth Lateran Council *Omnes utriusque sexus* in 1215.

1042 *body and blode*: Salter, 2.316, observes, 'It is worth notice that the laity at this date still communicated in both kinds.' This practice was general until about the 12th century, but the wine was often reserved for the celebrant alone from the 13th century, for according to the doctrine of concomitance the Body and Blood of Christ were both held to be present in both the bread and the wine.

1043 *that holy dayes*: translates *illis sacrosanctis diebus*. For *that* with pl. n. see *OED* s.v. *that* II.1.c.

S967–8 *Uenerunt . . . parturiens*: 4 Reg. 19:3. The appropriateness of this citation—the seemingly hopeless situation of the Israelites under the Assyrians, and the seemingly hopeless situation of the goldsmith facing sudden death—is discussed by Mark Dengler, '"In speculo et enigmate"', in *VEME*, p. 66.

1071 *the thirde daye after Crystynmas daye*: i.e. counting inclusively, viz. 27 December. The 26th is the *morow* (1062); the *derke nyghte* (1074) is the night of the 27th, and the goldsmith dies thinking he has heard the Matins bell on the morning of the 28th, but, as Salter, 2.317, says, 'We are to conclude, it seems, that it was the knell of doom which he heard and mistook for the church bell.'

1090 *owle*: as if translating *bubonis*; S reads *bufonis* 'toad'. (Cf. the frogs emerging from the mouths of false prophets in Apoc. 16:13.) The reading 'owle' may have been quite acceptable for the translator, as 'The owl, creature of night, was regarded in Late Medieval animal symbolism as evil, as unbelief lingering in darkness' (Gertrude Schiller, *The Iconography of Christian Art*, 2 vols., trans. by Janet Seligman (London, 1972), 2.210).

1098–9 *the space of a moment*: The story assures the reader that full intention of reform and appeal to a patron saint whom one has steadfastly revered will save one from damnation even if accomplished only in the last moment of dying, *in extremis* (S1010).

1102–3, S1004 *in ictu oculi*: 1 Cor. 15:52.

1128–9 For the goldsmith condemned to swallow hot coins, cf. the justiciary in *Visio Thvrkilli*, ed. Schmidt, p. 24, lines 14–24, and the figure of the miser or usurer(?) depicted at Chaldon, last quarter of the 12th century: see K. F. N. Flynn, 'The Mural Painting in the Church of Saints Peter and Paul, Chaldon, Surrey', *Surrey Archaeological Collections*, 72 (1980), 127–56, at Fig. 14 and p. 150, where Flynn also instances Thurkill (wrongly dated 1203 instead of 1206, and, like the *Visio*, known to Flynn only from Roger of Wendover). The motif is also found, for example, in Helinand of Froidmont's account of the Vision of the boy William in *Chronicon* (*sub anno* 1146), *PL* 212:1036B; Caesarius of Heisterbach, *Dialogus Miraculorum*, ed. Strange, vol. 2, Dist. 11, cap. 42; and is depicted in the *Hortus Deliciarum* of Herrad of Landsberg, and in Last Judgement portals and murals, e.g. by Taddeo di Bartolo at the Collegiate church in San Gimignano: see further, Morgan, pp. 23–26. The simoniac knight undergoes similar punishment for taking money (see 2401). Cf. also the punishment of the poisoners at 2071 and see Commentary.

CHAPTER 22

1141 *al-moste*: This is a mistake, probably compositorial through homoeoarchy, for 'almost all' < *fere omnes*; I have retained it as it makes its own sense.

1148–50 *Stulte . . . nequissima?*: cf. Luke 12:20.

1174 *Ihesus Nazarenus*: Thurston, 'A Conjectural Chapter', pp. 250–2, compares this with St Edmund's daily practice of tracing these words on his forehead every night before sleeping as instructed by his vision of the Christ child, as part of his argument that the two Edmunds are one and the same—an argument refuted by Salter, 2.260–72: see Matthew Paris, *Vita S. Edmundi*, cap. 3, in C. H. Lawrence, *St. Edmund of Abingdon: A Study in Hagiography and History* (Oxford, 1960), p. 226. The comparison was made by an early reader of L in a note at the foot of f. 230ʳ: *In vita sancti Edmundi archiepiscopi Cantuariensis, qui fuit tempore Henrici regis 3ⁱʲ, habetur quod in prouincia sua apparuit ei Cristus in forma parui, docens eum quod hec verba memoriter semper teneret: Sanctus Ihesus Nazarenus crucifixus rex Iudeorum fili Dei miserere mei et cetera. Et valent contra mortem subitaneam.*

CHAPTER 23

1192 Note that this story of the corroboration of Edmund's vision comes to his notice fifteen days later. We have to remember that Edmund was probably recounting his vision to Adam (and doubtless to others) for many weeks and months after the event and probably discussing it with Adam during its written composition and rewriting for longer.

1202 *fatheris*: text reads *fatherrs*, second *r* is 2-shaped, and had probably been miscast into the *i*'s.

1204–6 On the son's sudden direct speech, see Introduction, p. lxxii.

1211–12 *he was forgoten and putte owte of mynde fro her*: Greenblatt, *Hamlet in Purgatory*, well establishes just how crucial it was to souls in purgatory that they should not be forgotten by their relatives who are charged with offering suffrages on their behalf. He compares this passage with the ghost of Gy appearing to his wife, and notes by contrast how King Hamlet's ghost, though he appears in Gertrude's bedroom, does not communicate with her (p. 305, note 21).

1214–16 *the oncertente of vysyons . . . begylde*: This passing mention of the appearance of the deceased alcoholic goldsmith to his wife, and her reluctance to believe what she had seen, testifies to the readiness with which lay-folk were prepared to countenance the occurrence of visions or ghostly appearances, and also to an instructed caution that the appearances might be demonic and deceptive. The *Visio* and *Revelation* give ample witness to the ubiquity of visions and apparitions in the monastic culture and the secular mentality of the late twelfth century; note, in addition to Edmund's central vision and this mention of the goldsmith's wife, the following: the appearance of St Nicholas to Edmund at the beginning of Lent (425–46); the appearance of the knight guilty of simony to the clerk, detailing masses to be said for him (2416–24); the appearance of Mary to the sexton before his death (2456–75); the vision of the Crucifixion to the souls in paradise (2742–86).

1241 On the omission of the rest of cap. 23, see Introduction, p. lxiv.

S1110–11 *Non est . . . danti*: Eccli. 12:3.

S1112 *vni ex minimis . . . fecisti*: Matt. 25:40.

S1116 *Sicut aqua . . . peccatum*: Eccli. 3:33.

S1122–3 *Non redimuntur . . . deseruntur*: Dan. 4:24, Tob. 4:11.

S1128 *in malis . . . elemosinam*: Eccli. 12:3.

CHAPTER 24

Chapters 24–26 deal with the third place of purgatory, for the sin of sodomy, a term covering a wide range of non-reproductive sexual practices in the Middle Ages, but here meaning homosexual acts, principally male but also, in ch. 25, female. For a richly-documented discussion, see Sven Limbeck, ' "Turpitudo antique passionis"—Sodomie in mittelalterlicher Visionsliteratur' in *VEME*, pp. 165–226, and on the *Visio*, pp. 187–94. As Limbeck shows, earlier attacks on homosexual acts occur in the *Apocalypse of Peter*, *Visio S. Pauli*, Gregory the

Great, *Dialogi*, 4, *Visio Wettini*, *Visio Anselli*, the Vision of the monk of Melrose, and *Visio Tnugdali*.

Adam of Eynsham would have known the representation of homosexuals among those suffering in the carved frieze on the west front of Lincoln Cathedral, *c.*1165–80: there is a clear though small early photograph in Reginald Maxwell Woolley, *St. Hugh of Lincoln* (London, 1927), opp. p. 142, and see F. Saxl, *English Sculptures of the Twelfth Century* (London, 1954), pl. XLVII and Fig. 31, and George Zarnecki, *Romanesque Lincoln: The Sculpture of the Cathedral* (Lincoln, 1988), p. 68, fig. 90, scene 2 of the Torments of the Damned in Hell, and see the schematic drawing opp. p. 108.

1297 *ware ded*: text reads *warded*; emended following *mortui*. The spelling *ware* pa. t. pl. otherwise occurs 24 × in the *Revelation*.

CHAPTER 25

1321 *postre Sent Powelle in hys pystylle*: Rom. 1:26–27. I retain the reading *postre* as a borrowing from French *apostre*, rather than emend it as an error for *postle*, even though this form is not cited in *OED* or *MED*.

1327–9 *I neuyr herde . . . foule synne*: This sentence has been delayed by the translator from S1198–9 *Inauditum . . . deprauatum*.

1337–41 *by experyence . . . in mynde*: The physical or mental or spiritual status of what is witnessed in visions was a recurrent point of discussion at least since the time of Augustine's *De genesi ad litteram* 12. Cf. Hugh of St Victor, *Summa de sacramentis Christianae fidei*, cited by H[enry] of Sawtry in the Prologue to the *Tractatus de Purgatorio Sancti Patricii*: *siue ex responsione conscientie interiori siue per reuelationes exterius factas . . . signa quedam corporalibus similia ad demonstrationem spiritualium nuntiantur* (*SPP*, pp. 121–2, lines 23–24, 67–68), and by Alpais of Cudot, 4.2, ed. Stein, pp. 208 ff and 56–57, and see Ehlen, 'Vision und Schrift' in *VEME*, pp. 277–8 and note 104, for further references. Note that the souls, however, definitely experience the suffering *sencybly* (1342), *sensibiliter*.

1347–8 *voycys . . . was exaltyd and lyfte vppe*: *OED* first cites 1611 Bible for this figurative use of 'exalt' of the voice; it is not recorded in *MED*. For *was* with pl. subject, see Glossary. The *Revelation* provides a duplet with Latinate and English verbs to translate *resultabat* 'resounded'.

CHAPTER 26

Salter, 2.325–6, suggested that the doctor of law in question is Master William of Tunbridge, a prominent legist, connected with Oxford, who worked for the bishop of Worcester. William wrote a charter presenting his body to be buried at Osney, and leaving his books to the abbey after his death. Salter posits that he fell sick at the Domus Dei at Osney in July 1195, and died there in March or April 1196. See Salter for details of the evidence of charters, and of geography which fits Edmund's account. A. B. Emden, *A Biographical Register of the*

University of Oxford, 3 vols. (Oxford, 1957–59), 3.1913, under the entry for William Tunebrigge, says, 'Possibly same as' the anonymous legist who Salter identifies here in the *Visio*. C. R. Cheney, *Hubert Walter* (London, 1967), p. 76, note 1, says 'Master William was still alive in October 1196', i.e. six months after Edmund's vision, but gives no reference.

1354–6 *doctur of lawe . . . Full many lerners of that faculte he ordende yn scolez*: *Visio* has plural faculties (S1225), presumably, as Salter supposes, of civil or Roman and canon law, in Oxford, where Edmund is most likely to have seen and known him (1353). M. B. Hackett, 'The University as a Corporate Body', in *The History of the University of Oxford*, vol. 1, *The Early Oxford Schools*, ed. J. I. Catto (1984), pp. 37–95, at p. 38, points out that in the late twelfth century 'faculty' (first mentioned at Oxford by Gerald of Wales in 1187–8) meant a branch of learning without 'department or structural connotation'. R. W. Southern, 'From Schools to University' in the same volume, pp. 1–36, in an excellent introduction to the development of studies in twelfth-century Oxford, demonstrates that 'by about 1190 a combination of practice in the courts and instruction in the schools was beginning to draw students of canon and Roman law to Oxford' (p. 17). This is precisely the environment in which Edmund's legist operates. Southern also shows the importance of Osney abbey's contribution to legal activity in Oxford, and the presence of the Lincoln canons John of Tynemouth and Simon of Sywell acting as judges delegate in Oxford in the 1180s and 90s. Southern (p. 25, note 3) notes the Cheney discussion of the *Visio* (see previous note). Henry Mayr-Harting discusses evidence for Oxford as a centre of legal learning from the 1170s in 'The Role of the Benedictine Abbeys in the Development of Oxford as a Centre of Legal Learning', in *Benedictines in Oxford*, ed. Henry Wansborough and Anthony Marett-Crosby (London, 1997), pp. 11–19.

1384–7 *after . . . iuggement*: Rom. 2:5.

S1257–80 Thurston, p. 276, cites a brief passage from Dionysius the Carthusian, *De Quatuor Hominis Novissimis*, art. 47, which is derived from this section, and points out that thanks to this and similar passages Dionysius's text was prohibted by the Index from being published in the vernacular, i.e. on account of its mention of sodomy, *representatio sodomitici criminis mei*.

1413–36 König, 'Die Zügel der Zunge' in *VEME*, pp. 240, 242, discusses the jurist's failure to confess privately because of shame and loss of glory, and his public punishment in purgatory. According to Hugh of St Victor, failure to confess when given the opportunity was damnable: *si hac voluntate amissa nollet confiteri et tunc moreretur, nulli est dubium eum damnari pro illo peccato quod confiteri noluit* (*Summa Sententiarum* 6.11, *PL* 176:148D). According to the *De vera et falsa poenitentia* (see above, note S1–2), confession to one who is not a priest is acceptable if a priest is desired but cannot be found: *Tanta itaque vis confessionis est, ut si deest sacerdos, confiteatur proximo. Saepe enim contingit, quod* *poenitens non potest verecundari coram sacerdote, quem desideranti nec locus nec tempus offert. Et si ille cui confitebitur potestatem solvendi non habet, fit tamen dignus venia, ex desiderio sacerdotis, qui socio confitetur turpitudinem criminis* (cap. 10.25, *PL* 40:1122). The jurist could have confessed to the one he sent to find the priest; indeed, *in extremis*, he could have confessed to God without intermediary.

1427–8 *compellyd to doo actually the same foule passyon*: Note that the punishment is the enforced re-enactment of the sin, cf. 1313–14. This concept was developed in the theatrical re-presentations of the sins by the sinners for the enjoyment of the devils in *Visio Thurkilli*.

1445–6, S1291 *nouit corda omnium*: Acts 1:24.

1448 *delyberacyon*: glossed 'deliverance, liberation, salvation', translates *de liberacione*. (It is interesting that S reads *deliberacione* as one word, an error for *de liberacione* or *de deliberacione*.) *MED* deliberacioun n.(2) cites only *St. Anthony* a1425 with the sense 'saving, curing'; *OED* s.v. deliberation² cites only one instance, from 1502.

1450–1 *Non est . . . danti*: Eccli. 12:3.

1455–6 *wise and wyttye in hys owne conceyte*: First citation in *OED* s.v. conceit *sb.* II.4.c. Cf. Is. 5:21.

1462–3 Sap. 6:7. The *Visio* reading is closer to the Vulgate: *exiguo enim conceditur misericordia, potentes autem potenter tormenta patientur.*

1476, S1312–13 *cum hominibus non flagellatur*: Ps. 72:5.

1477 *hangyng*: translates *prominentem*. The text's *hauyng* makes no sense and is unlikely to be a form of 'hoving', which would also be a marginal choice. The compositor seems to have had trouble with the word 'hanging': cf. *hauyng* again at 2077 translating *dependebant*, and *hanuing* 2043 translating *suspendio*.

1480 *takyng . . . persons*: cf. Rom. 2:11.

1484–6 *the ryche man . . . fyre*: cf. Dives in Luke 16:24.

1487 *S[h]ortely*: Text *Sorthely*, but Latin reads *cito*. The compositor has seemingly garbled the word, giving -*th*- instead of *Sh*-, under the influence of the recurrent introductory *Sothely*.

S1313–20 *Quod enim...exuisse*: omitted by *Revelation*: see Introduction, p. lxv.

S1314–15 *superbiam & abundanciam*: Ezech. 16:49; *non conueniunt*: Rom. 1:28.

S1316 *contumeliis . . . semetipsis*: Rom. 1:24.

1487–8 *that worschyppefull pryste to home this clerke was confeste*: This priest, whom Edmund knew well (1418), was probably, as Salter, supposed (2.326), priest of the church of St Nicholas at Osney.

1506–7 *as hyt ys seyde before*: See 728–32.

CHAPTER 27

1511 *a prior, that was father of a relygyous place* . . .: Salter identifies the *rector*/ 'prior' as Godfrey abbot of Eynsham; see also discussions by Gainer, 'Prolego- menon to Piers Plowman', pp. 188–90; Morgan, pp. 65–66; and Wieners, 'König, Bischof und abt im Fegefeuer' in *VEME*, pp. 85–87.

Salter, 1.xv, says that Godfrey was abbot 1152–96 and died between January and Easter 1196. But Godfrey must have died in (about May) 1195, not 1196, despite the expression *anno presenti regimen animarum*, if *MVSH*, 4.8 (vol. 2, p. 41) is correct in stating that there was a two and a half year vacancy before the appointment of his successor, Robert of Dover, who was blessed as abbot of Eynsham at Lincoln, 11 November 1197 (the day before Adam became chaplain to Hugh of Lincoln); see *HRHEW*, p. 49. Godfrey, who had been abbot for 44 years, had therefore served since 1150 x 51, not since 1152. Note that in the *Visio* cap. 29 the bishop there is said to have died 'this year (*anno presenti*) about the feast of St Michael'. As the feast of St Michael is 29 September, *anno presenti* clearly does not mean 'in this year of 1196', the year of the vision, but 'within the past year', viz. Easter 1195 to Easter 1196. This use of *anno presenti* would seem to over-ride the argument of Wieners in *VEME*, p. 86, note 70, that Godfrey died in 1196 because of the use of *mos Anglicanus,* calculating the first day of the year from 25 March; this would mean that Godfrey had died within the 26 days preceding the vision, not merely within the preceding year, and it is likely that his death would have been noted differently if it had been so recent. My argument from the usage in cap. 29 reinforces the statement in *HRHEW*, p. 49, that the two and a half year vacancy 'enforces 1195 not 1196 as the date of d.'

The *Revelation*'s use of *prior* (1511, 1540, 1607) is loose, and properly should be 'abbot', but the *Visio* does not specify the term 'prior' or 'abbot', using instead, respectively, the expressions *rector, regebam, prefuistis*.

1519 *dedful*: may be an error for *dredful*, but I retain it as probably representing 'deathful' translating *exsanguis* 'lifeless'. Although the *Revelation* has no instances of *ded* for 'death', as against *deth* 9× and *dethe* 49×, there are instances of non-initial *d* for *th* in *dedyr* 3×.

1537 *to sum of hem Y gate benefycys of chyrchys*: Salter, 1.xv, and note 5, indicates that of four nephews of Godfrey, Bartholomew had the benefice of Mickleton, Gloucestershire, and Ralph that of Souldern. Wieners (in *VEME*, p. 87) conjectures that these four nephews may be the four (named) persons to whom Edmund is required by Godfrey to convey his warning of hell (lines 1624–36).

1571–2 *to hem and to me . . . succedyth inextynguyble fyre*: I retain *succedyth*, glossed 'ensues'—'inextinguishable fire ensues [hereafter] for them and for me', but it is suspect, translating *alii . . . succendunt ardores* 'others . . . kindle fires'.

Because the *Revelation* substitutes the pr. t. *leuyn* for the *Visio*'s pr. p. *viventes*, *fyre* becomes the subject of *succedyth*, whereas *ardores* is the object of *succendunt*. ME *succendyth* is not recorded intransitively. Note the *Revelation* translates *succensos* (S1423) by *accendyd* (1601).

1575-92 An argument used to justify the length of purgatorial pains was that evil done by others after one's death, but which is attributable to one's influence, also requires satisfaction. Note 1672-81, where purgatorial suffering grows worse for those who have left a bad example to those still living whom they could have corrected, and thereby have contributed to a continuing (potential for the) growth of sin. These features chime with Edmund's thorough-going disapproval of ecclesiastical mis-management. Cf. 1914-21.

1582 *that fowle and abhomynable synne that ought not to be named*: i.e. sodomy, cf. 1305-10.

1600 *sum of the bretheren*: Salter, 2.333, suggests Thomas, the prior, and Adam, the sub-prior (both Edmund's confessors?), are intended. Cf. 1552 ff.

S1435-6 *Confusione . . . adducit peccatum*: Eccli. 4:25.

1624 *foure persons there byn*: possibly Godfrey's four nephews? From the remainder of this chapter it is easy to see why the Eynsham monks were split over the truth of Edmund's vision (see Introduction, p. lxxxi). Such forthrightness, claiming the authority of revelation, would be bound to raise hackles. This chapter is a classic example of a revelation aimed at the recipient's immediate religious community: see Dinzelbacher, *Vision und Visionsliteratur*, pp. 217-22, on *pro-domo* visions.

CHAPTER 28

This *inclusa*, Salter suggests, 'may with much probability' be identified with the *uirgo quedam religiosa ualde* who spent her life in prayers and fasting within the church where Edmund heard the voice bidding him journey to bishop Hugh, *MVSH*, 5.3.

Edmund's visionary experience of encountering the spirit of someone he knows, who he thinks is actually still alive, but who is subsequently discovered to have predeceased the vision, can be matched in other vision texts.

CHAPTER 29

1683 *A certen bisshop*: Thurston, p. 284, suggests that this is Richard Palmer. He was born in England of noble parentage, educated in France, and settled in Sicily under the Norman kings, where he is attested from 1157. In a letter to the bishop of Ostia, Thomas Becket accused Palmer of having supported 'our persecutors with money and advice' and alleged that he been won over by hope of obtaining the bishopric of Lincoln. He was translated from the bishopric of Syracuse to the archbishopric of Messina before 9 February 1183, died 7 August

1195, and was buried in the church of St Nicholas, Messina. (See *DNB,* 43 (1895), 146–7.) Salter points out that Palmer appears not to have visited England during the last thirty years of his life, and as Edmund seems not to have been abroad or far from Oxford, he is unlikely to have seen him.

CHAPTER 30

1723 *scolde and vpbrayde*: Andrea König notes this woman's abusiveness in her discussion of the sins of the tongue: 'Die Zügel der Zunge' in *VEME,* p. 233, note 23.

1730 *hospytalte*: I retain the text's form, rather than emend in accordance with *hospytalyte* 1830, because of the presence also of *spyrytualte* and *temporalte* 695.

1736 *fro*: text reads *for*, Latin *a mera* (1537).

1741–56 This summary of the personal eschatology of Edmund's vision specifies that purgatory is available only to those who die in a state of venial sin. After purgatory, souls pass to places of rest, the Earthly Paradise of ch. 55, where their desire for God fits them for the passage thence to heaven, whither souls are also seen to ascend. Whosoever dies with mortal sins, that have not been converted to venial by confession and penance, will *be presentyd to his iugement in the world þat is to cum* (*in futuro presentetur iudicio*) in the condition he or she is at death. It would appear from the vision's stress on the powers of intercession and suffrage, that this refers to the Particular Judgement following death, where intervention by a patron saint (like Nicholas or Margaret in this vision) or the Virgin, or the suffrages of family or friends, might tip the balance in favour of the soul's good deeds. Edmund's vision does not deal with hell; he does not visit it or hear about it directly, but it is clear that damnation is the destination at the judgement for anyone lacking such help who dies unconfessed of mortal sins (cf. 1816–20, 2012–16). The vision thus conforms to a fourfold view of the other world which was widespread from the time of Bede's account of the Vision of Dryhthelm: see Easting, 'Purgatory and the Earthly Paradise' and 'Personal Apocalypse'.

CHAPTER 31

1762–3 The harsh pains for minor sins committed by religious are in line with the fixed punishments of the early penitentials: see Morgan, p. 120.

1769–81 Here most clearly we see punishments which mirror the sins. For detailed reference to other vision texts which include a similar concept of punishment, e.g. Gregory the Great, *Dialogi* 4.40.1, 4.45.2, *Visio Sancti Fursei*, Visions of Ailsi, Vision of Gunthelm, see Ehlen, 'Vision und Schrift' in *VEME*, p. 254, note 8.

1787 *suerte takyn*: translates the ablative absolute *securitate recepta* (S1581–2), but the sense of the English sentence is incomplete, having no equivalent for *preuaricacionem non uitassent*. The *Visio* means that those were punished who, after making vows in times of peril and having survived the peril (*suerte takyn* 'having achieved safety or freedom from danger') did not avoid failure to fulfil the same vow (i.e. did not fulfil their vow).

CHAPTER 32

The knight who breaks his vow to take the Cross and go to Jerusalem is noted by König, 'Die Zügel der Zunge' in *VEME*, p. 244, as an example of the seriousness of the failure to keep a vow, cf. Deut. 23:21–23 and Prov. 6:2. This knight becomes the subject of a short *exemplum*: see Introduction, p. xxviii. The issue of breaking such a vow had an immediate topicality at the time of Edmund's vision. Roger of Howden reports that Hubert Walter, archbishop of Canterbury, sent to Geoffrey, archbishop of York, a letter containing the text of a letter he (Hubert) had received from Pope Celestine, dated 12 January 1196, complaining about people who had vowed, but failed, to go to the Holy Land. If they did not undertake their vow by 7 April they would, from Easter Sunday 1196, face exclusion from Communion: *in sequenti Pascha Domini proculdubio a perceptione Corporis Christi et communione fidelium exclusandos*: see *Chronica magistri Rogeri de Houedene*, ed. William Stubbs, 4 vols., RS 51.3 (London, 1870), pp. 317–19, cited from p. 319.

S1597 *terrores*: other manuscripts read *tortores*. The *Revelation* does not help to determine the reading of the translator's copy.

CHAPTER 33

S1611–12 *miliciam uite, que super terram est*: Job 7:1.

S1618–19 *ut monet apostolus*: cf. Rom. 12:13, Hebr. 13:2.

1839 *noyeful*: text reads *noysful*, but translates *noxia* (S1628).

1851 i.e.] LO read .*e*., for Latin *est*, for *id est*.

CHAPTER 34

S1646 *ut prefati sumus*: see S724 ff.

CHAPTER 35

1867 *Thre bysshoppys that Y knewe wele sum-tyme*: Note that in the *Visio* Edmund does not make such a claim for familiarity, but says that he had 'often seen' these three bishops whom he encountered in the second place of torment. It is clear that as a clerk in Oxford and a novice at Eynsham he had the opportunity to see or meet many important figures, though it is unlikely that he would have known them all well.

Bishops punished for excessive involvement in secular affairs are found in earlier visions, e.g. *Visio Bernoldi* and *Visio Karoli crassi*.

1874 *he vsyd yn hys lyfe to sytte amonge secler iugys*: Thurston suggested that the first bishop, who used to sit among secular judges, was Hugh du Puiset or Pudsey (1125?–1195), appointed bishop of Durham 1153. In January 1188 he was one of the bishops to whom the monks of Canterbury appealed in their quarrel with archbishop Baldwin (see ch. 36). He was at Woodstock in August 1184, Oxford July 1175, Woodstock 30 September 1186 and the same date in 1189 (see R. W. Eyton, *Court, Household and Itinerary of Henry II* (London, 1878), pp. 192, 273, and G. V. Scammell, *Hugh du Puiset Bishop of Durham* (Cambridge, 1956), pp. 279, 282, 287), and 'doubtless visited Oxford frequently with the king's court' (Salter, 2.341). He bought the office of Justiciar from Richard I, alongside William Longchamp, December 1189 to March 1190, when his jurisdiction was confined north of the Humber. He was summoned to a council in Oxford on 28 February 1193 by William of Coutances, to consider measures rendered necessary by King Richard's captivity, but it is doubtful if the council was held (Roger of Howden, *Chronica*, RS 51.3 (1870), p. xciv). St Godric had prophesied that Hugh du Puiset would have seven years of blindness before his death; after his death this was interpreted as moral blindness 'which immersed him for the last years of his life in political affairs'. His position as a bishop in England was unique being, as earl-palatine of Durham and earl of Northumberland, a secular as well as ecclesiastical potentate. [Sources *DNB*, 47 (1896), 10–16, and Salter.] He died at Howden, 3 March 1195. Scammel (p. 183) says, 'His death so impressed contemporaries (with the unpleasant exception of the visionary monk of Eynsham) that occasional private documents may be found dated "in the year in which Hugh, bishop of Durham, entered the way of all flesh"'.

1874–5 *yn place and tyme of pledyng*: translates *placitatoris loco*, making a pairing by adding *tyme*, and shifting to the action *pledyng* from the actor *placitator* 'litigator, pleader, or judge', see Du Cange, *Glossarium mediæ et infimæ latinitatis*, vol. 6 (1886), p. 348 cols. 2–3.

1883 *The tothyr of hem*: The second bishop, who broke his chastity and became a monk before his death, has been identified by Salter as possibly Joscelin, bishop of Salisbury, and father of Reginald, bishop of Bath and Wells (see ch. 42). Joscelin resigned his bishopric in 1184, entered a Cistercian monastery, and died 18 November 1184. He was at Woodstock in July 1175 (Eyton, *Court, Household and Itinerary of Henry II*, p. 192) and, 'as the bishop whose diocese included Berkshire and part of Grandpont, must often have been in Oxford' (Salter, 2.341).

1897 *The thirde of these byshopys*: is not readily identifiable. Salter says that Bartholomew, bishop of Exeter, who died 15 December 1184, is known to have been often in Oxford. The same is true of Robert Foliot, bishop of Hereford, formerly archdeacon of Oxford, who died 9 May 1186.

   D. H. Farmer, *St. Hugh of Lincoln: An Exhibition to Commemorate the Eighth*

Centenary of his Consecration as Bishop of Lincoln in 1186 (1986), pp. 7–8, has written that the 'bishops whose torments in the next world are graphically described . . . may be plausibly identified with Nigel [*read* William] Longchamp of Ely, once Justiciar of England, and Hugh of Nonant, bishop of Coventry, who tried to expel the monks permanently from Coventry.' These identifications are unlikely, however, if not impossible, for both died after the vision, William Longchamp on 31 January 1197, and Hugh de Nonant on 27 March 1198.

1899 *spyrys*: 'tongues' (of flame or fire), *OED* s.v spire *sb.¹* 5., translates L ablative pl. *spiris*. The LO reading *spyrytys* is an error, there being no appropriate meaning for 'spirit'.

1907–8, S1681 *que sua erant quesisse*: cf. 1 Cor. 13:5.

1911 *dyssymulacyon of her charge*: 'neglect of their office', 'negligence about their responsibility', translates *dissimulacio oneris* (*DMLBS* dissimulatio 2b (1st citation) 'negligence or connivance'). This Latinate meaning of 'dissimulation' is not recorded in *OED* or *MED*.

1915–16 *as Y haue tolde before of a certen prior*: See 1575–92.

CHAPTER 36

For discussions of this chapter on Baldwin, archbishop of Canterbury, see Morgan, pp. 64–65, and Wieners in *VEME*, pp. 81–84.

Baldwin, born of aristocratic or educated stock, studied in Italy, and under Robert Pullen in Paris, was appointed archdeacon of Totnes 1161?, resigned to become a Cistercian monk of Ford Abbey 1169/70–5, was abbot of Ford 1175–80, bishop of Worcester 1180–4, and archbishop of Canterbury 1184–90, and died of a fever in Acre, 19 or 20 November 1190. (For Baldwin's study under Pullen, see A. Morey & C. N. L. Brooke, *Gilbert Foliot and his Letters* (Cambridge, 1965), pp. 54–55, and for his career as teacher, see A. Morey, *Bartholomew of Exeter* (Cambridge, 1937), pp. 105–6.) While at Ford he wrote a number of spiritual works, and was recommended for a cardinal in 1178. He was much 'concerned with the definition and codification of papal jurisdictional authority in England' (D. N. Bell, trans., *Baldwin of Ford: Spiritual Tractates*, 2 vols. (Kalamazoo, 1986), p. 12). He was present with Henry II at the council at Eynsham, 25 May–2 June 1186, which elected Hugh of Avalon as bishop of Lincoln. He was a supporter of Becket, and was embroiled in a protracted and infamous conflict with the monks of Canterbury over his plan to establish at Hackington (half a mile from Canterbury) a collegiate church for secular priests: this seems to be alluded to here: *his promoting of the byshoprye and dignite that he had* (1956). On this controversy, see *Epistolae Cantuarienses*, ed. William Stubbs, RS 38.2 (London, 1865), and for Hugh of Lincoln's advice to Baldwin, see *MVSH*, 3.12, vol. 1, pp. 121–4.

Gerald of Wales, who accompanied Baldwin round Wales as he preached the Third Crusade, wrote a famous comparison of Baldwin and Hugh of Lincoln, in his *Vita sancti Remigii*, cap. 29 (RS 21.7, p. 68): see also *Gerald of Wales (Giraldus Cambrensis), The Life of St. Hugh of Avalon Bishop of Lincoln 1186–1200*, ed. and trans. Richard M. Loomis (New York, 1985), p. xxxi, and see further Richard Loomis, 'Giraldus de Barri's homage to Hugh of Avalon', in *De Cella in Seculum*, ed. Michael G. Sargent (Cambridge, 1989), pp. 29–40. For Baldwin's writings, see also *Baldvini de Forda opera: Sermones de commendatione fidei*, ed. David N. Bell (CCCM 99, Turnhout, 1991).

On the English hospital at Acre founded in 1190 and dedicated to St Thomas Becket, see Wieners in *VEME*, p. 84.

1953 *the King*: Henry II.

1974–80; S1744–8 Salter (2.344) rightly points out that the topic and language of the *Visio* attacking unchaste priests handling the Mass is picked up again by Adam of Eynsham in *MVSH*, 5.3 (vol. 2, p. 87), the chapter detailing the clerk (Edmund's?) audition of the voice directing him to see Hugh of Lincoln (vocabulary items in common in bold): *Sacerdotes enim et aliorum graduum persone omnimodo uitiorum genere, maxime autem luxurie sordibus **fedati sacramentis diuinis** ex indigno accessu iniuriosi existentes, ea irreuerentur sumendo atque tractando, quantum in se est **polluere non uerentur.***

2019–22 *Neuertheles . . . seyde aboue*: On these two final added sentences, see Introduction, p. lxviii.

CHAPTER 37

2041 Thieves are also encountered in the other-world visions of Alberic, cap. 16, ed. Schmidt, p. 182; Tnugdal, ed. Wagner, pp. 19–23; and Gunthelm, ed. Constable, pp. 109–11.

2043–4 *or els opynly*: public confession was an earlier practice: see the discussion by Kreutzer, 'Jenseits und Gesellschaft' in *VEME*, p. 55.

2063 *fyndys al to-bete*: on fiends being party to the purgation of souls in purgatory, as well as tormentors in hell, see Easting, 'Purgatory and the Earthly Paradise'.

CHAPTER 38

2066–7 Women who murder their children are found punished in other-world visions from the time of the Apocalypse of Peter, see J. K. Elliott, *The Apocryphal New Testament* (Oxford, 1993), p. 605; see also *Visio Sancti Pauli*, ed. Theodore Silverstein (1935), Redaction I.7 (p. 154) and Red. III.13 (pp. 176–9).

2071 On the other-world pain of the forced drinking of loathsome matter, see Leopold Kretzenbacher, 'Eschatologisches Erzählgut in Bildkunst und Dichtung: Erscheinungsformen und exemplum-Funktion eines apokryphen Höllenstrafe-Motives', in *Volksüberlieferung: Festschrift für Kurt Ranke zur Vollendung des 60*

Lebensjahres, ed. Fritz Harkort, Karel C. Peeters, & Robert Wildhaber (Göttingen, 1968), pp. 133–50. See also Commentary 1128–9.

2077 *hangyng at her brestys, sokyd her pappys*; S1830–1 *ore uipereo . . . sugentes*: cf. Job 20:16, *Caput aspidum suget, et occidet eum lingua viperae.* Hedwig Röckelein, *Otloh, Gottschalk, Tnugdal. Individuelle und kollektive Visionsmuster des Hochmittelalters* (Frankfurt, 1987), pp. 211–28 (and plates pp. 337–41), discusses occurrences of the image of women whose breasts are sucked by serpents as a negative re-interpretation from the 11th and 12th centuries of the earlier motif of the Earth Mother suckling the Earth in the form of serpents, and instances *Visio Sancti Pauli*, *Visio beati Esdrae*, *Visio Alberici*, and Edmund's vision (pp. 214–15).

CHAPTER 39

S1832 There is no *titulus* in S. Thurston invented *De feneratoribus* (followed by Salter), a retranslation of the *Revelation*'s chapter heading, which itself may have been invented by the translator to accord with the new subject matter of the chapter's one sentence, or may indicate that the translator's copy of the *Visio* had this *titulus*; see Introduction, p. xxxii, and cf. Commentary, Chapter 13, S473.

CHAPTER 41

Attacks on kings and governors have a long history in visions of the other world. Plato's Er witnessed the torment of a tyrant of Pamphylia, Plutarch's Thespesius saw Nero pierced by burning nails, Gregory the Great told of Theodoric in infernal heat, Carolingian visionaries were especially fond of finding kings in torment (see Paul Edward Dutton, *The Politics of Dreaming in the Carolingian Empire* (Lincoln, Nebraska & London, 1994)), and Tnugdal discovered various Irish kings in pain. The monk of Wenlock got in early with his vision, in which he saw king Ceolred of Mercia in torment, even though the king was not dead at the time of the vision (MGH, ES, 1.14). (Adam of Eynsham recounts in *MVSH*, 5.11, how at Fontevrault, Hugh of Lincoln, hammer of kings, warned John Lackland of hell's torments as depicted in the portal sculpture of the Last Judgement.)

Salter identified the king in torment here as Henry II, d. 1189, as indeed did the scribes of the B text of the *Visio* in Chartres, MSS. lat. 84 and 1036 (Huber2, p. 705). See further Wieners in *VEME*, pp. 77–81, especially on Henry's avid delight in hunting.

Henry II was in Oxford January 1180, Woodstock 16 August 1184, Eynsham 25 May-2 June 1186 for the council at which Hugh was elected bishop of Lincoln (*MVSH*, 3.1), Oxford February? 1188, and Woodstock March/April 1188 (see itineraries in L. F. Salzmann, *Henry II* (1917), pp. 240–51, based on Eyton (1878).) His sons, kings Richard I and John, were both born in Oxford, where Beaumont Street preserves the name of his palace.

Edmund's complaint about the harshness of Henry II's forest laws, which were against the *law of kinde* match many such complaints of the reign: see W. L. Warren, *Henry II* (London, 1973), pp. 390–5. For Adam's account of Hugh of Lincoln's dealings with Henry II's foresters, see *MVSH*, 4.5–6, and cf. *Walter Map, De Nugis Curialium, Courtiers' Trifles*, 1.9, ed. and trans. M. R. James, revised by C. N. L. Brooke & R. A. B. Mynors (Oxford, 1983), p. 10, and for Hugh's relationships with Henry II and Richard I, see Karl Leyser, 'The Angevin Kings and the Holy Man', in Karl Leyser, *Communications and Power in Medieval Europe: The Gregorian Revolution and Beyond*, ed. Timothy Reuter (London and Rio Grande, 1994), pp. 157–75 (originally published in Henry Mayr-Harting, ed., *St Hugh of Lincoln* (1987), pp. 49–53). Eynsham's proximity to the royal hunting grounds of Woodstock and Wychwood meant that Edmund's mention of the forest laws had a local impetus. Henry I had 'favoured Eynsham Abbey by releasing its men from the obligation of serving as beaters in the royal hunt while his household was being entertained at the abbey' (Charles R. Young, *The Royal Forests of Medieval England* (Leicester, 1979), p. 16, and see H. W. C. Davis, *et al.*, *Regesta Regum Anglo-Normannorum 1066–1154*, 4 vols. (Oxford, 1913–1969), vol. 2, no. 708). But '[t]here was much dispute over whether Eynsham's woods and heath belonged to the royal forest of Wychwood. . . . Fines paid by the abbot to the Crown in 1185 and 1190 for assarting, waste of timber, and overstocking with pigs may have been incurred at Eynsham' (*A History of the County of Oxford*, VCH, vol. 12 (Oxford, 1990), p. 128, and see Pipe Rolls 31 Henry II (1185), PRS, 34.108, and 2 Richard I (1190), PRS, NS, 1.12–13).

2099–2100 *Quantum . . . luctum*: Apoc. 18:7.

2105–6 *horse . . . pycche*: cf. Apoc. 9:17.

2124 *this cruelly*: See *OED* and *MED* s.v. *this adv.* meaning 'thus' (cf. 883), 'in this manner', or here as an intensifier 'to this extent, so'. *MED* first citation for the use of *this* as an intensifier is a1475 *Wisd.* 932, 978; *MED* says, 'A few exx. could also be construed as ME **thus** adv.'

2125–6 *synne of avowtrye*: Henry II's adultery at Woodstock with Rosamund de Clifford would have been evident to the Eynsham community after it became public in 1174, if not before. See further note to ch. 44.

2138–45 Henry II's failed relationships with his sons were, of course, notorious. Peter of Blois reports a conversation at Le Mans in the first half of 1189, following his eldest son's homage to the king of France on 18 November 1188, in which Henry II opens by saying: *'Filios enutrivi et exaltavi; ipsi autem spreverunt me'*; see Sir Richard Southern, 'Peter of Blois and the Third Crusade', in *Studies in Mediaeval History presented to R. H. C. Davies*, ed. Henry Mayr-Harting & R. I. Moore (London, 1985), pp. 207–18, at p. 210 (the text of the *Dialogus inter regem Henricum II et abbatem Bonævallensem* is in *PL* 207:975–88). Later in the Dialogue (col. 985A), Henry laments: *Novi ego, novi, nec possum aut corde cogitare aut voce* *proferre quantum laboraverim pro populo meo, et hanc retributionem mihi fecit Dominus quod nec in populo meo fidem, nec in filiis meis amorem invenio.*

2147–8 Edmund and Adam may have had in mind Henry II's founding of the first Carthusian house in England at Witham in Somerset, and his appointment of Hugh of Avalon as its third prior.

S1894–1918 On the *Revelation*'s omission of this passage, see Introduction, p. lxiv.

S1899–1900 *testis & conscius*: Cf. Job 16:20.

CHAPTER 42

Reginald, bishop of Bath and Wells, was elected archbishop of Canterbury 27 November 1191 and died the following month, 26 December 1191, before his election was confirmed by the Pope. Reginald would have been known to Adam and Edmund via his connection with Hugh of Lincoln.

Reginald Fitzjocelin de Bohun was born *c.*1140, illegitimate son of Joscelin, bishop of Salisbury, 1141–84 (see ch. 35). He was known as 'the Lombard', probably from his Italian education. A relative, Engelger de Bohun, was one of those who incited Henry II against Thomas Becket. Peter of Blois, archdeacon of Bath, when Reginald was archdeacon of Sarum, speaks of Reginald's love of hawking (*Ep*. 61). Reginald was at one time in the service of Becket, and may have been with him on the embassy in 1158 to arrange the marriage of Henry II's eldest son (then aged 7) to the daughter of Louis VII. He found favour with King Louis, who in 1164 appointed him abbot of St Exuperius in Corbeil, succeeding the king's brother. Reginald withdrew from Becket's party in 1166, in duty to his father who had tried to reconcile Becket with Henry, and whom Becket had consequently excommunicated. Reginald became Henry's representative at the court of Rome in 1167 and 1169 and was a member of the embassy Henry sent to Rome to plead his case after Becket's assassination. In filling sees left vacant during the quarrel with Becket, Henry afterwards nominated Reginald for the bishopric of Bath; his election was confirmed at the Council of Westminster, April 1173. Reginald accompanied Richard, archbishop-elect of Canterbury to Rome to secure papal approval 1173–4. On the return journey, Reginald was consecrated bishop of Bath at St Jean de Maurienne, Savoy, by Richard of Canterbury and St Peter of Tarentaise. As bishop of Bath and Wells, Reginald served as one of Henry's counsellors on a number of important national councils. He was on the commission of inquiry into the Albigensians at Toulouse in 1178 and attended the Third Lateran Council in 1179. It was probably on his return from Rome on this occasion that he was directed by Henry to proceed to the Grande Chartreuse to persuade Hugh of Avalon to become prior of Henry's foundering Carthusian foundation at Witham in Somerset, in the diocese of Bath. Witham was the first Carthusian house in England, established as part of Henry II's penance for the death of Becket.

Reginald's mission was successful, and Witham was to remain Hugh's favourite retreat after he became bishop of Lincoln in 1186. Adam of Eynsham accompanied Hugh to Witham annually during his time at his chaplain.

Reginald supported Baldwin's appointment as archbishop of Canterbury in 1184, though he subsequently took the side of the convent of Christ Church in its famous quarrel with Baldwin over the college at Hackington. Baldwin died at Acre in November 1190 (see Commentary Chapter 36). Reginald was part of the commission ordered by Pope Celestine in May 1191 to destroy Baldwin's new buildings; this was duly performed 21 July 1191. Reginald was nominated to succeed as archbishop of Canterbury the following November, but, as noted above, died a month later. He was buried at Bath on the day of St Thomas the Martyr, 29 December 1191. For fuller details see, C. M. Church, 'Reginald of Bath (1174–1191): His Episcopate, and his Share in the Building of the Church of Wells', *Archaeologia*, 50 (1887), 295–360.

2178, S1946 *corda intuetur*: 1 Reg. 16:7.

2183–5 See Gregory the Great, *Dialogi*, 4.42.

CHAPTER 43

Salter, 2.351, suggested that this chapter might be about Roger, abbot of Abingdon, who died a few days before 11 April 1185.

2217 The *Revelation* omits the horses (S1980) from the list of luxuries.

2267–70 Gal. 4:23, 29. Paul's allegory (Gal. 4:22–5:2) concerns Abraham's two sons, Ismael born by his slave Hagar, and Isaac born by his free-born wife Sarah.

2278 *Trewly, these grete hirtys . . . .*: This is a difficult sentence because of the confusing concatenation of possible subjects and objects. *hirtys* n. pl. 'hurts' translates *dispendia* 'losses', used of those who are lost to (and hence hurt) the religious life by forsaking it for the *corrupcyon . . . of this world* (2276). *the whyche* refers to *relygyous leuyng*. The subject of *beholdyth* v. pl. (in -*th*, see Introduction, p. lv) is *hirtys* (those who lose their religious vocation); the object of *beholdyth* is *prelatys*. *beholdyth* does not fully render *respiciunt*, with its sense that those who have lost their religious way 'look back to', or 'look' to their modern prelates 'for' help. But modern prelates (relative pron. *that*) offer no help to such people; though they know they are being appealed to (*knowen thys*), the prelates so ignore or despise those who have lost their religious life that the prelates do not understand or realize they that themselves have lost their Christian calling also, *that hyt ys so wyth hem*. As the following sentence makes clear, the prelates should be committed to the welfare of those committed to their charge.

2283–4 *knowe* (1): LO read *knewe*, but it translates pr. t. *sciunt*. The combination of eye-skip and compositor's change of folio would account for the loss of *knowe not* to translate *ignorant*.

CHAPTER 44

The abbess, as Salter suggests, is most likely to be of Godstow, the only community of nuns in the vicinity of Eynsham, some 4 miles distant. Salter suggests that Agnes 'seems to have died about 1195' (2.354). *HRHEW*, p. 212, says that Agnes occurs probably 1186 x 1193, and died 1195 x 1196, referring to the *Visio* and Salter's note. (It refers also to Salter page 258 for the date and pages 258–9 for discussion, but these only concern the date of the vision, and contain no reference to Agnes.)

In 1191, during Agnes's term as abbess, Hugh of Lincoln visited Godstow and found the tomb of Henry II's mistress, Fair Rosamund (d. 1176), before the altar in the church, surrounded by candles and lamps. On discovering whose tomb it was, he ordered her body to be removed and buried in the cemetery, because she was a strumpet (*scortum*), and as an example to other women to avoid illicit and adulterous concubinage: see Roger of Howden, *Chronica*, RS 51.3 (1870), 3.167–8. In 1197 Hugh settled a dispute between Godstow and Westminster Abbey concerning the ownership of the church of Bloxham in favour of the nuns: see David M. Smith, ed., *English Episcopal Acta IV*, nos. 67–68.

2319 *vnder the tytyl of virgynyte*: translates *sub uirginitatis titulo*. No equivalent transferred usage of 'title' is recorded in *MED* or *OED*: translate 'in the rank/ order of virginity'.

2341 *that were*: The syntax requires us to understand something like 'to them' before *that were*.

CHAPTER 45

2343–52 Though tender and intimate, the ministrations of the abbess Agnes of Godstow to the two leprous sisters in her charge do not show the extremes of devotional piety to be found in the thirteenth century, such as Angelo of Foligno who drank the scabs from lepers' wounds and found them 'as sweet as communion' (*AASS* Jan. vol. 1, p. 208, and cf. Aldobrandesca, April vol. 3, pp. 473–4, cited by Caroline Walker Bynum, *Fragmentation and Redemption: Essays on Gender and the Human Body in Medieval Religion* (New York, 1991), p. 132). It has been calculated that at the height of its virulence, about the 1180s, 'leprosy affected about one out of every two hundred Europeans' (Edward J. Kealey, *Medieval Medicus: A Social History of Anglo-Norman Medicine* (Baltimore, 1981), p. 94). For a recent discussion of attitudes to leprosy in the twelfth century, which refers to Hugh and the *Revelation*, see Carole Rawcliffe, 'Learning to Love the Leper: Aspects of Institutional Charity in Anglo-Norman England', in *Anglo-Norman Studies XXIII: Proceedings of the Battle Conference 2000*, ed. John Gillingham (Woodbridge, 2001), pp. 231–50.

Salter, 2.275 (cf. Losert in *VEME*, p. 29, note 111) points out the passage in *MVSH*, 4.3, where Adam similarly depicts Hugh of Avalon tending lepers.

2363–7 It seems that Agnes was not so attentive to a certain young cleric who had been entrusted to her care by a bishop *ad educandum, for to be browght vppe* when the boy was *destitute of al hys frendys*. Salter, 2.356, suggests this may well have been Edmund himself, committed to her care by Hugh or some other bishop after the death of his father in the Holy Land. Provided the hypotheses of Edmund's identity with the clerk in *MVSH* and with the boy are sustainable, we can argue as follows. Edmund was born late 1169 (see Introduction, p. xli). We know from cap. 50 that Edmund knew another abbess when he was a child (*quam adhuc puer noueram* (S2255–6)), and she had died fourteen years before the vision, i.e. about 1182, when Edmund was about 13. This is thought to be a second Edith, abbess of Godstow, her predecessor another Edith having been said to reign for 51 years, which is unlikely, though not, as *HRHEW*, p. 212, would have it, impossible. Hugh was elected and consecrated bishop of Lincoln in May and September respectively of 1186, when Edmund was about 17, scarcely *etate paruulum*, so, if the boy in question was Edmund, it is more likely that he was committed to the care of Agnes (Edith II's successor) by bishop Geoffrey (elected 1173, confirmed July 1175, resigned 6 January 1182), or possibly Walter of Coutances (elected 8 May, confirmed 3 July 1183, transferred to Rouen, 17 November 1184). Edmund's father is said to have died *non multos annos* before November 1194. If his father was *Edmundus medicus* (Salter, 2.262, 272) who was mentioned in a deed of 1182–85 but apparently dead by 1190, then 'not many years' suggests he died nearer 1190 than 1182. But Edmund was not *etate paruulum* much beyond the end 1181 when he became twelve. In other words, if the boy neglected by Agnes *was* Edmund, then he was destitute of all his friends before his father died, possibly while his father was overseas. It suggests that Agnes must have succeeded Edith II *c.*1182, and Edmund must have been committed to her charge soon afterwards.

CHAPTER 46

2376–81 *that tyme . . . yourney*: the Third Crusade 1189–92.

2383 Simoniacs are also seen punished by Hildegard of Bingen, *Scivias*, 3.9.20, ed. A. Führkötter and A. Carlevar, CCCM 43a (1978), pp. 531–5, and (without elaboration) in the *Visio Alberici*, cap. 11, ed. Schmidt, p. 178.

2391–5, 2416–24 Here is another mention of the recurrent intercourse between the living and the dead concerning suffrages (cf. ch. 23), effected via dream vision. The simoniac spirit's specificity about which priests should say the masses bespeaks a not uncommon concern; cf. the later text, *A Revelation of Purgatory by an Unknown, Fifteenth-Century Woman Visionary*, ed. Marta Powell Harley (1985), and *VOWME* 5. Note that Edmund's *Revelation* identifies the masses by their most commonly known terms, *Placebo and Dirige*, i.e. Vespers and Matins in the Office for the Dead, replacing the *Visio*'s less specific list of offices (S2118–20). The spirit requires five sets of thirty masses, and names five priests (2418–19) to say them. Edmund gives us to understand that the truth of his conversation in the other world was confirmed for him later by the testimony of the clerk to whom the knight appeared with the instructions, and that this was compounded by the spirit's naming priests unknown to the clerk, his own widowed wife, and indeed himself when he was living. The spirit believes a further seven sets of thirty masses would effect his release from purgatory (2412–15). These requirements are modest in comparison to some provisions for masses, especially in the later Middle Ages.

2401 *compellyd dayly to deuoure tho pensys hoote and brennyng*: cf. the punishment of the frauds of the goldsmith, Commentary 1128–9.

CHAPTER 47

2430 *.iii. or .iiii. ymagys of our blessyd Lady*: Farmer, *St. Hugh of Lincoln* (1986), p. 8, claims that there was a 'famous shrine' of the Virgin at Eynsham, and that this may have prompted the 'majestic and awe-inspiring' figure of the Virgin in an Eynsham manuscript, MS Bodley 269 (see above, Commentary S1–2). I know of no evidence for such a shrine, and if this chapter is it, then the text simply mentions three or four different images of the Virgin and child, and although the story of the sacristan probably *is* set at Eynsham, given 'such knowledge of the customs of the unnamed monastery' (Salter, 2.357), one might expect Adam to have been more specific at least about the number—but his intention was to mask identities.

CHAPTER 48

2495–6 *in connyng of dyuynyte as in other lyberals facultees*: *in diuinis quam in liberalium arcium disciplinis* (S2201): This clerk may well have studied at Oxford, where the liberal arts were established by the 1190s, though study of the law was pre-eminent in Oxford before then (see Commentary 1354–6), and for theology Paris had long been the acknowledged leader. Gerald of Wales in 1195 chose Lincoln as 'the first place in England where sound and healthy theology was most flourishing', where, at this time under Hugh of Lincoln, William de Montibus was chancellor of the cathedral (cited in Southern, 'From Schools to University', p. 21). Like most students of this period, this brilliant clerk had probably studied in more than one centre.

2498 *testymony . . . of a goode consciens*: cf. 2 Cor. 1:12, Rom. 2:15, 9:1.

2518 *ryghte wolde*: justice required.

2527 *Cui . . . exigetur*: Luke 12: 48.

CHAPTER 50

S2237–9 Adam speaks in his own voice, and introduces Edmund, *frater predictus*. In the B text the previous chapter ends with additional lines, finishing the text with a doxology and promising to continue at a future date when the 'storms of opposition' (*contrarietatum procelle*) and other disturbances have subsided. Salter, 2.282, seems to be right in interpreting this as a reference to the continuing struggle between Hugh of Lincoln and Richard I over the patronage of Eynsham (see Introduction, p. xxxvi). Chapters 49–58 seem to have been composed at a later date, therefore, possibly even after Adam became Hugh's chaplain in November 1197.

2560 *a certen abbas*: Edmund meets in paradise another abbess, who died in 1182, most likely Edith II of Godstow. She occurs as *E secunda* in the Godstow Cartulary in 1167 (see *HRHEW*, p. 212, which misdates the *Visio* 1195 instead of 1196). Her predecessor Edith I is said to have reigned for 51 years. This is unlikely (see Commentary, 2363–7). It is more probable that there were indeed two Ediths in succession, as Salter posited (2.361).

CHAPTER 51

2621 *a prior of a monasterye*: In his edition, Salter regards the prior, and his young monk in ch. 52, as belonging to Eynsham, and that the prior was 'probably Bartholomew, who held that post in 1189, whereas in 1196 Thomas was prior' (2.362).

In his unpublished notes, Salter had canvassed the notion that the prior must be Philip, prior of the Augustinian canons' house of St Frideswide's, Oxford, as ch. 52 'shows he was not the prior of an abbey, but of a priory' (Bodleian Library, MS Top Oxon. c.448, f. 159ʳ). According to *HRHEW*, p. 180, Philip last occurs 4 July 1191 and his successor Simon first occurs on 27 November 1195, so Philip could well have died three years before the vision, in 1193. Philip was the author of the 'Miracles of St. Frideswide', *BHL* 3169, *AASS*, October, 8 (1853), 568–89. He recounts that there were many visions and revelations in Oxford about the time of the translation of St Frideswide's relics 12 February 1180, and many miraculous cures were effected at her shrine. Henry Mayr-Harting interestingly explores the 'Miracles' for what they tell of Oxford and its environs (in Edmund's day) in 'Functions of a Twelfth-Century Shrine: The Miracles of St. Frideswide', in *Studies in Mediaeval History*, ed. Mayr-Harting & Moore (1985), pp. 193–206.

Given (a) the level of detail about the prior and his death (ch. 51 tells far more about his behaviour when he was alive than of his state in paradise); (b) how well Edmund says he knew him (*wyth home fro my ryghte yonge aage Y was ful wele acquentyd* (2677–8) < *michique a primeua etate amicissimum*); and (c) the close knowledge the brethren at Eynsham show of the prior's young monk of the same monastery in the next chapter, it seems clear that Salter's published identification of the prior as Bartholomew of Eynsham is to be preferred.

2622 *Y saw hym*: S reads *enim*, which again suggests that the translator was not working from S, where *enim* appears to be a mistake, for MT, and other manuscripts collated by Thurston, read *eum*; Salter prints *eum* without notice of any variants.

S2316 *omnibus omnia*: 1 Cor. 9:22.

S2327 *Salomon*: Prov. 18:14.

CHAPTER 52

2699–2700 *and for othyr diuers fawtys of hys brethirne*: Note again that Edmund reinforces the importance of the responsibilities of those in office. They sin in allowing those in their charge to sin, and their subordinates' misdoings increase their purgatorial pains; cf. ch. 27 in particular.

CHAPTER 53

S2395–7 *Hoc uero . . . inenarrabilis*: omitted by *Revelation*, for no apparent reason.

CHAPTER 54

2744–5 As Morgan (p. 184) says, 'this is the closest any of the popular [otherworld vision] texts comes to foreshadowing Dante's vision of Christ on the Cross in the Heaven of Mars (Par. xiv 94–117)'. Morgan claims that Edmund sees Christ in the two forms that became prominent on French cathedral portals, as discussed by Emile Mâle, 'Christ the King, enthroned as in the tradition of the Apocalypse, and Christ the Son of man, represented with the Cross as in the Last Judgement portals' (pp. 184, 186), but this is not strictly true, because Edmund sees Christ not *with* the Cross but *on* it, in all the agony of the Crucifixion.

In his vision in 1125, the thirteen-year-old Orm sees Christ on a *crux . . . preclarissima* (ed. Farmer, p. 79) beyond the gates of heaven. Although Christ's hands and feet are bloody, Orm does not see the wound in Christ's side, and the vision does not emphasize Christ's suffering.

2756–7 *Marye, not now in heuynes . . . demenyng*: I know of no other account or iconographical representation of Mary joyful at the Crucifixion (joyful in the knowledge of the accomplished Redemption, and, given that this is in Paradise, in the knowledge of the Resurrection). This description within Edmund's vision is itself an account of a *visio* (S2450), a *spectaculum* (S2419, 2421), *ymaginaliter representare* (S2440) *representyd and schewde in a vysyon* (2781–2, cf. *representyd and shewyd* (2738 < *De representacione* (S2406)) or *presented and schewed* (2744–5) to the souls in paradise, *uelut presencialiter* (S2411–12), *as oure Lorde had be present in Hys body* (2746).

Mary is *gaudens* (S2418), and the tradition of *Gaude* sequences most likely lies behind the *Visio*'s image. I am most grateful to Dr Charity Scott Stokes (Clare Hall, Cambridge) for the following references, in which, as she says (private correspondence), 'the Joy is in the present, the focus on the Crucifixion being retrospective, or . . . the Joy is grounded in the prospect of the Resurrection': Commemoration sequence including:

> *Aue, gaude & letare que filium dei de te incarnatum uidisti crucifixum,*
> *mortuum & sepultum in carne pro salute nostra.*
> *Aue, gaude & letare cuius beatissimam animam gladius passionis christi*
> *filii tui domini nostri pertransiuit affectu piissime dilectationis.*

> (BL, MS Cotton Nero C.iv, the Winchester Psalter, f. 134^{va-b})

> Gaude seinte Marie ma ioye e moun socour
> Ke . . . ton fitz suffri peine pur humeine amour
> Mou fut cel dolour graunt mes la ioie greinour
> Quant veites de mort leué ton fiz e ton creatour.

> (BL, MS Royal 16 E.ii, f. 35^v, *Gaude* sequence)

> Gawde, flower of thi lorde and sonne,
> Dieng without gilte for oure redemption:
> To thy grete joye and oure salvation
> *Fulgit resurrectio.*

> (BL, MS Arundel 318, f. 152, from Eleanor Percy's Prayer, 3rd *Gaude*: see Alexandra Barratt, *Women's Writing in Middle English* (London, 1992), pp. 279–81.)

In an unpublished paper ('*Gaudens et hilaris*: A Twelfth-Century Vision of Mary at the Foot of the Cross', read at University College, Oxford, 1996), Robert Penkett calls this depiction of the Virgin in Edmund's vision 'unique', and seeks to explain it by recalling links between the sorrow of the Crucifixion and the joys of the Annunciation and Resurrection; Mary's self-abandonment to God as a pattern of the monastic ideal; and the joy shared by the other souls in the forgiveness accomplished by the Crucifixion, and their achievement thereby of paradise.

S2419 *quem diligebat Ihesus*: John 21:7.

2775, S2433–4 *alligatur fortis . . . diripiuntur*: cf. Mark 3:27.

2791 *my duke and lodisman*: cf. *my duke and leder* 2917; both instances of *duke* in these duplets translate forms of *dux* 'guide, leader', as in *MED* s.v. duke 1.(a), e.g. (a1398) *Trev. Barth. 14a/a.: þey [angels] buþ I-clepid Dukes & leders [L duces] for . . . þey schewiþ & techith [L manifestant] þe way to þe cuntre of blisse. Zaleski, p. 54, notes that 'Edmund addresses Nicholas as "my duke"' as part of her discussion of the way in which Edmund's vision represents the patronage of saints Nicholas and Margaret: their 'advocacy is presented in explicitly feudal terms, as protection in exchange for service'. Her point is true, though in the use of *duke* here the sense of noble, ducal rank is most likely secondary to that of 'leader'.

S2447 *omnia scrutatur*: 1 Cor. 2:10.

CHAPTER 55

2821–2 Elizabeth Willson, writing of the separation of Edmund from St Nicholas by the cross which descends at the entrance gate of Paradise, says it is 'a very peculiar little incident . . . one which I have not seen paralleled anywhere except in romance' (*The Middle English Legends of Visits to the Other World and their Relation to the Metrical Romances* (1917), p. 30), and compares the falling portcullis which bisects the hero's horse in Chrétien's *Yvain*, and a falling barrier in *La Mule sans Frein*.

Morgan (p. 102), under the urge to compare Edmund's being led by the hand of St Nicholas to Dante led by Virgil (*Inferno* 3.19–21), misreads the passage, saying, 'when they reach the entrance to Paradise Nicholas, like Virgil, is forbidden to proceed'. On the contrary, Nicholas goes through unimpeded; it is Edmund who is at first debarred.

2838 *cowpulde*: 'coupled' translates *coaptabat*, and is glossed 'adapted, adjusted' following *DMLBS* coaptare 1d. This sense is not recorded in *OED* or *MED*.

2842 *grycis*: Steps lead souls up to the throne of Christ. On steps or a ladder as the means of passage to a higher realm for the soul, see Morgan, pp. 38–39.

S2510 *exultant . . . Dei*: Response 1st Vespers Feast of All Saints.

S2511–12 *milia . . . ei*: Dan. 7:10.

S2512 *sedentis in trono*: Apoc. 5:7.

S2516 *facie ad faciem*: 1 Cor. 13:12.

S2518–19 *sed nec uidere potest*: 1 Tim. 6:16; *a mundis corde*: cf. Matt. 5:8.

CHAPTER 56

2879 *aftyr they peticion*: Edmund's vision of the other world has been in fulfilment of his prayer made six weeks before (417–32).

2881 *the*: 'thee', cf. *ut tibi*.

2888–9, S2532–3 *si perseueraueris*: cf. Matt. 10:22, Ps. 110:10.

2891–4 It is commonplace for visionaries to regret their return to earth from paradise: see Commentary 259.

S2534–5 *que solus . . . dignus erit*: omitted by the *Revelation*.

S2541 *mandata . . . obserua*: Deut 11:1.

CHAPTER 57

S2561–5 *Eorum nempe . . . sciui*: omitted by the *Revelation*. Possibly the translator's eye skipped from *Eorum* to *Moram* where he picked up.

2932 *at the instauns and commandement of youre holynes: coactus uestre sanctitatis imperio* (S2570) : This expression suggests that Edmund's vision was written down at the instigation of Hugh of Lincoln: as Thurston, p. 317, notes, 'Hugonem Lincolniensem episcopum innuere videtur; haec enim obsequii forma, videlicet *vestra sanctitas*, non ita, credo, minoris dignitatis praesuli conveniret.' It tallies with Adam's statement in *MVSH*, 5.3, that the visions of the clerk, who seems to be Edmund, were written down by order of the bishop: *Cui plurima quoque spiritualium uisionum misteria postmodum fuisse reuelata certissime experti sumus. Ex quibus non pauca, litteris dudum de mandato sancti presulis tradita, longe lateque uulgata noscuntur* (vol. 2, p. 91). Zaleski, pp. 80–81, discusses the reluctance of Edmund and other visionaries to reveal what they have witnessed.

CHAPTER 58

The previous chapter brings to an end Edmund's narration. This final chapter is in Adam's voice. Cf. the claims for veracity at the end of the *Visio Baronti* and in Gregory of Tours, 'Vision of Salvius', *Historia Francorum*, 7.1, MGH, SRM, 1.326; Gervase of Tilbury observes that anyone who writes about the afterlife risks being mocked and dubbed a liar: *Otia Imperialia*, 3.103, ed. G. Leibnitz, *Scriptores rerum Brunsvicensium*, 2 vols. (Hanover, 1701–11), I.994–1002, and see Paolo Cherchi, 'Gervase of Tilbury and the Birth of Purgatory', *Medioevo Romanzo*, 14 (1989), 97–110, p. 101.

S2580–1 *magnorum uirorum compulsus imperio*: cf. S54–57. Salter, 2.370, suggests these great men are Hugh of Lincoln and Thomas, prior of Eynsham. See further, Introduction, above, pp. lxi.

S2582–3 *nunc sensum nunc etiam uerba expressi*: Adam shows that his written account is not throughout a verbatim transcript of Edmund's discussions with him.

2969–70 *yn the space of hys raueshyng, he was so fully helyd*: For healing via a vision, see Dinzelbacher, *Vision und Visionsliteratur*, p. 210: instances include, Alberic, healed a few days after his vision thanks to the intervention of SS Peter and Paul, caps. 49–50, ed. Schmidt, p. 208; Heinrich von Ahorn: *Porro cum inditium quod ad credulitatem eis missum est exposuisset subito de lecto consurgens remotis omnibus ueluti sanus ad focum sedere cepit et, cum sibi stratus esset compositus, reuersus denuo ad grabattum pristina inualitudine uersi cepit. Sequenti autem die ad ianuam domus sue sedentem, ut promissum sibi est, perfecte eum febris deseruit* (ed. Steinmeyer & Sievers, p. 493); Elisabeth of Schönau (F. W. E. Roth, *De Visionen und Briefe der hl. Elisabeth*, 2nd edn. (Brünn, 1886), p. 21 no. 41 (=*PL* 195: 146 no. 50), associated with a vision of Christ crucified (for a useful account of her visions, see also Anne L. Clark, *Elisabeth of Schönau: A Twelfth-Century Life* (Philadelphia, 1992)). Ernst Benz, *Die Vision: Erfahrungsformen und Bilderwelt* (Stuttgart, 1969), pp. 17–34 (chapter 1 'Vision und Krankheit') also instances the later visionaries Julian of Norwich, Caterina Ricci, Maria of Escobar, and Hemme Hayen.

S2624–5 *creauit . . . celum & terram*: Gen. 1:1.

paſſion was ſolemly ſonge wyth grete deuocion .he
wente wyth hys ſtaffe to the chyrche wyth his breꝛ
theren the whiche by cauſe of ſekeneſſe reſtedꝛ hem
alſo with hym in the fermorie were the couent nyght
ly ꝓuice ⁊ laudꝺes offerd ꝺ ꝺype to owꝛ lorꝺ And there
by the reſpecte of heuynly grace ſo grete conpuncci
on anꝺ ſwetenes he reſceuedꝛ that hys holy deuociꝛ
on excedꝓꝛ meſure . wherfore he myght not contey
ne hym fro weppyngꝛ and laudyng goꝺ fro myꝺꝛ
nyght tyl ſex of the belle yn the mornyng . What for
remembryngꝛ wyth worſhippe anꝺ ioye the merceis
of owꝛe lorꝺ .’the whiche haꝺꝛ doon for mankynꝛ
ꝺe . Anꝺ alſo remembryng wyth ſore weppyngꝛ hys
offencys anꝺ ſennys doon by fore tyme . And the
hurte anꝺ the ſtate of hys preſent imꝑfeccion .
And abowte ſex the belle yn the mornyngꝛ he maꝺe
to be calledꝛ to hym ‘ij· of his bretheren one after
a nothꝛ . whiche haꝺꝛ powr to here confeſſeons
anꝺ geue to penitentes abſolucion anꝺ to them
bothe maꝺe purely anꝺ holy as mekylle as he couꝺe
hys confeſſion of al hys ſennys and of the leſt ofꝛ
fence of hys religion or of the comaundementys of
god ⁊ wyth grete contricion ·of herte anꝺ effuſion
of terys deſired hys abſolucion and haꝺ hyt Than
on of hem aſkꝓꝛ hym why he ſorowꝺꝛ ⁊ wepte ſo
imoꝺerately for al they had went yᵗ he ſchulꝺe fele
hym ſelfe ſone to paſſe owte of this worlꝺ Than
he ſerꝺe he felte hym ſelfe no thyng ſo Sothly than
he tolꝺe to his brother yᵗ diligerly enquyꝛꝺ this of
hym ⁊ ſeyꝺ Sir ꝛe ſchal vnꝺerſtonꝺ ⁊ know that

I. British Library, shelfmark IA.55449, folio [a]5ʳ, L208ʳ

Reproduced by permission of the British Library

paſſyon wan ſolenly ſonge wyth grete deuocyon · he
wente with his ſtaffe to the chirche with his brethren
the whiche by cauſe of ſeknelſe reſted them alſo with
hym in the fermorye where the couent nyghly ſeruy-
ce andi laudes offerdi ſype to owre lordi And there
by the reſpecte of heuynly grace ſo grete compunccion andi ſwetenelſe he receyuedi that hys holy deuo
cyon exceodi meſure · wherefore he myght not con
teyne hym fro wepyng andi laudyng godi fro mydi
nyghte tyl ſer of the belle in the mornyng · what for
rememberyng with worſhippe andi ioye the merceis
of owre lordi · the whiche he hath doon for mankin
&e · Andi alſoo rememberyng with ſore wepyng his
offenceps andi ſynnes doon by fore tyme · andi the
harte andi the ſtate of hys preſent imperfeccyon ·
Andi aboue ſer of the belle in the mornyng he made
to be calledi to hym ii of hys brethren one after
anothyr · whyche hadi power to here confeſſyons
andi geue to penytentps abſolucyon andi to them
bothe made purely andi holy as mekyll as he coude
his ſfeſſion of al his tympes andi of the leeſt offece
of his religyon or of the comaundementis of god
andi wyth grete atricion of herte andi effuſion of te-
ris deſired his abſolucion andi hadi hit Than on of
hym aſkid hym why he ſorowd andi wepte ſo imod
rately for al thei hadi wente that he ſhuldi fele hym
ſelfe ſone to paſſe owte of thys worldi Than he ſei-
de he felte hym ſelfe no thyng ſo Sothly tha he took-
de to his brother yt diligently enquyred this of hym
andi ſeid Sir ze ſhal vndirſtondi andi knowd that

APPENDIX 1

VARIANT READINGS IN QUIRE [A] OF L AND O

In addition to the problem of the misimposed sheets in quire [c], an error and correction shared by L and O (see above, p. xlvii), there is a disparity between L and O that has not previously been fully recognized.[1] In quire [a] pages 5, 8, 9, and 12 were reset. This appears to have happened in O (see below), with a resetting of folios [a]3^r, 4^v, 5^r, 6^v, i.e. the second outer forme used to print the second sheet of the first quire. When resetting, the compositor seemingly used the printed text as copy, attempting (not always successfully) to keep to its lineation, but frequently diverging from its spelling. The table below lists the consequent variants in spelling between the two surviving copies. Readings are listed in the order LO, with the line number of each folio, followed in parentheses by the line number in the edition above. I have not attempted to record all the uses of different letter shapes, e.g. occurrences of -d with or without flourish, or -h with or without horizontal line; for instance, O uses 2-shaped r more frequently than L.[2] Changes in lineation are marked by /. I note in the last column, in square brackets, where the change in O is substantive or otherwise significant, either as a correction or an error.

L f. [a]3^r	O	line	Edition line no.	
How	Howe	2	(49)	
yn to	into the	5	(51)	[substantive correction]
dysciplynys	dyscyplynys	6	(52)	
how	howe			
how	Howe	7	(53)	[correction of initial capital]
fyrst	first			
xiij	xiii			
how	Howe	8	(54)	[correction of initial capital]
Nycholas	Nicholas			
xiiij	xiiii	9	(55)	
how	Howe	10	(56)	[correction of initial capital]
broughte	brought			
purgatorie	purgatorye	11		

[1] Sheppard noted that there were changes in f. [a]4^v—see above, pp. xlvi–xlvii.

[2] E.g. in [a]3^r O has roman r for L's two-shaped r 3×, and 2-shaped r for L's roman r 16×; in [a]4^v the figures are 9× and 14×, respectively.

L	O	line	Edition line no.	
diuersyte	diuersite	12	(58)	
þᵗ	that			
saw	sawe			
purgatory	purgatorie	13	(59)	
xvij	xvii			
How	Howe	14	(60)	
xviij	xviii	15	(61)	
goldesmyth	goldsmith	16	(62)	
Nycholas	Nicholas			
How	Howe	18	(63)	
thys	this			
know	knewe			[substantive correction]
fyrst	first			
hys	his	19	(64)	
How	Howe	20	(65)	
goldesmith	goldsmith			
tolde	told			
purgatorye	purgatorie			
How	Howe	22	(67)	
goldesmyth	goldsmith			
tolde	told			
remedye	remedie			
agenst	agenste	23		
xxij	xxii		(68)	
How	Howe	24	(69)	
goldesmyth	goldsmith			
tolde	told			
hys	his	26	(70)	
fadyr	fadir			
apperyd	apperid		(71)	
+iii.	iii			
hys	his			
moder	modyr			
xxiij	xxiii	27		
sodemytis	sodemytys	29	(73)	
xxv	xxvi	30	(74)	[substantive correction]

f. [a]4ᵛ

meruelous	meruailous	1	(118)	
schewyd	shewyd	2		
yn	in	3	(120)	

L	O	line	Edition line no.
Richard	Rychard	4	
owre	our		(121)
callyd	called	6	(122)
yn	in	10	(125)
.xv.	xv	11	
monthys	monthis		
gret	grete		(126)
lytyl	lytyll	15	(128)
euer	euyr	16	(129)
manne	māne		(130)
amendement	amendyment	17	
yn	in	19	(131)
his	hys		
yn	in	22	(134)
dyseasyd	diseasyd	23	(135)
than (*1st*)	thanne	24	
yn	in	26	(137)
hys (*2nd*)	his		
scherethursdaye	sherethursdaye	28	(138)
of/fice	office		(139)
&	and	29	
s~uice	seruyce		
owr	our		
lord	lorde		
cryste	criste		
tradicion	tradycyon		(140)

f. [a]5ʳ (see Plates)

passion	passyon	1	
deuocion	deuocyon		
wyth	with	2	(141)
hys	his		
chyrche	chirche		
wyth	with		
bre-/theren	bretherē		
sekenesse	seknesse	3	(142)
hem/	hem also with/		
in	ni		[introduced error]
fermorie	fermorye	4	
were	where		[regularization]³

³ The predominant spelling in the text is 'where', but there are two other instances of 'were': see Glossary s.v. **wher**.

L	O	line	Edition line no.	
couėt	couent		(143)	
nyght/ly s~uice	nyghly seruy-/ce			[introduced error]
&	and	5		
owῖ	owre			
conpuncci/on	compuncci-/on	6	(144)	
swetenes	swetenesse	7	(145)	
rescyued	resceyued			
deuoci-/on	deuo/cyon			
wherfore	wherefore	8	(146)	
contey/ne	con/teyne			
myd-/nyght	myd/nyghte	9	(147)	
yn	in	10		
had	he hath	12	(149)	[substantive change is a correction]
mankyn-/de	mankin/de			
also	alsoo	13		
hys	his		(150)	
imperfeccion	imperfeccyon	15	(151)	
the	of the	16	(151–2)	[substantive change is a correction]
yn	in			
·ij·	ii	17	(152)	
his	hys			
whiche	whyche	18	(153)	
powr	power			
penitentes	penytentys	19	(154)	
absolucion	absolucyon			
holy	holly	20	(155)	[semantic distinction]
mekylle	mekyll			
hys	his	21		
confession	ɔfession			
hys	his			
lest	leest		(156)	[semantic distinction]
of-/fence	offēce/			
hys	his	22		
religion	religyon			
ɔmawndementys	cōmawndementis			
of/	of god/			
&	and	23	(157)	
contricion	ɔtriciō			
effusion/	effusion of te-/			

L	O	line	Edition line no.
/of terys	of te-/ris	23/24	
hys	his	24	(158)
hyt	hit		
Than/ on of	Than on of/		
askyd	askid	25	
&	and		(159)
so/ īmoderately	so īmode/rately		
they	thei	26	
went	wente		
y^t	that		
schulde	shulde		(160)
fele/hym	fele hym/		
this	thys	27	
Than/he seyde	Than he sei-/de		(160–1)
thyng	thing	28	
than/ he tolde	thā he tool-/de		
diligētly	diligently	29	(162)
enquiryde	enquyryde		
of/ hym	of hym/		
&	and	30	
seyde	seide		
schal	shal		(163)
vndyrstonde &	vndirstonde and		

f. [a]6^v

happyd	happid	1	(207)
yn	in		
wyse	wise		
wythowte	without		
myhht	myght	2	[regularization]
thedyr	thedir		(208)
othyr	othir	3	
thyngys	thynges		(209)
now	nowe		
whyche	whiche	4	
schal	shalle		
wythowte	wyth owte		
thyng	thing	6	(211)
wythowte	wyth owte	7	
fygure	fegure		(212)
affyxed	affixed	8	

L	O	line	Edition line no.
whyche	whiche		(213)
ȝerly	ȝerely	9	
ys	is		
deuowtely	deuowtly		
yn	in	10	(214)
passion	passyon	11	(215)
fresch	fresh		
yn	in	12	(216)
ryhht	right	13	[regularization]
also	alsoo		
ryght	right		
sextense	sextensse	14	(217)
chyrche	chirche		
sche=/wys	she/-wys	17	(219)
brothyr	brother	18	(220)
brethirne	bretheren	19	(221)
ge=/dyr	ge/dyr		
in to	into	20	
thyngys	thynges	21	(222)
wyth	with	22	(223)
contricion	ɔtricion		
discy=/plynys	discyply/nys		(224)
yn	in	23	
.vij.	vii	24	(225)
Trewly	Trewely	25	(226)
thys	this		
all	alle	26	
nyght	night		(227)
fologyng	folowīg	27	[correction]
all	alle		
mooste	moste		
contynewde	ɔtynewde	28	(228)
yn	in		
Also	Alsoo		
wyth	with	29	(229)
yn	in	30	

It is not easy to say which copy was set first, L or O. We do not know why or when the quire was re-set: it may be that the forme came apart during the printing; or was wrongly imposed, as occurred also in quire [c]; or a longer print run was desired after the forme had been undone. Dr Hellinga (in private communication) notes that the only two surviving copies 'may not tell the whole story': 'on present evidence it is not possible to explain with certainty or to reconstruct what had gone on in the printing house, in terms of first causing an error and then correcting it, or probably less likely, second thoughts about the size of the print-run'. The changes are mainly non-substantive: e.g. relative to L, O adds *-e* 23×; O removes *-e* 7×; O has *i* 79× for L's *y*; O has *y* 21× for L's *i*; O has *-yon* 8× for L *-ion*, and *-ion* is shared 5×, but *-ion* occurs elsewhere 142× and *-yon* 164×, so these are not really helpful determiners. L uses *owr* 4× only, all in the first quire; two of these are in O *our* 107 and *owre* 110, and O reads *our* 121 for L *owre*. O could therefore be said to use spellings found frequently throughout the text *our* 17×, *owre* 43× (cf. also *oure* 35×). Whereas L uses the spelling *purgatorie* only twice, at 57 (O *purgatorye*) and 72, O uses *purgatorie* at 59 (L *purgatory*), 65 (L *purgatorye*), and 72; elsewhere in the text *purgatory* occurs 5× and *purgatorye* 18×. Again, the distribution is not sufficient to assist in the question.

Substantive changes are more indicative. Of the variants, O's readings are arguably superior 14× and in error 2× (see the bracketed comments accompanying the table, above). From this it could be argued that O was set first, and that L carelessly introduced seven times as many errors as corrections in the resetting. But it is probably more likely that L represents the earlier setting, and that the opportunity was taken with O to correct a number of features, inadvertently introducing a couple of errors in the process. In support of this supposition, note also that there are three other isolated changes in this quire: [a]2[r] O removes the typographical oddity of a long, undotted *i* followed by a space in L *mocions* to *mocyons* 21; in [a]7[v] O corrects L *thyes* to *yes* 266; and in [a]8[r] L's anomalous inflected relative in the construction *tho thingys whiche es* 283–4 is corrected in O to *thoes thingys whiche*. These instances, I believe, demonstrate that in quire [a] L was printed first and that O is the resetting, for in the course of resetting the four pages of the second outer forme, the opportunity was also taken to correct errors spotted on three other pages in the quire.

APPENDIX 2

THE *REVELATION* AND THE *OED*

The *OED* cites the *Revelation* as *Monk of Evesham* from Arber 255×,[4] dating it 1482 (*c.*1470 s.v. rapt *ppl.* 2). *MED* does not cite the *Revelation*, apart from the single word *colloke*. The following lists present the words cited in *OED*, and others which antedate or do not occur in *OED*, according to various categories, with the line reference for the text printed above, followed by the Latin source word in the *Visio*, where this can be isolated. While not exhaustive, this appendix helps to show the relationship of occurrences in the *Revelation* to what is recorded in *MED*. See also the brief section on Vocabulary in the Introduction, above, p. lvi. I use the following abbreviations in addition to those which are standard in *OED* and *MED*: < 'translated from'; cit(s). 'citation(s)'.

1 The following words, forms, and usages are the sole citation in *OED* and do not occur in *MED*

(I do not list the line references for all the occurrences of a word in the text. Where the *OED* headword is spelt differently, I supply it in parentheses following s.v.)

abrasyng 2070	<	*abrasione* (s.v. abrasing *vbl. sb.*)
adigression 616		perhaps by attraction of indef. art. in phrases like 'to make a digression'
aduocatour 1109	<	*aduocatus* (s.v. advocator)
bocis 745		(s.v. boce²)
fullyor 348	<	*plenius* (s.v. fully *adv.*)
ioyde 976	<	*applaudebat* (s.v. joy *v.* †5.*c. intr.*)
ongoyngable 733	<	*impermeabilis* (s.v. ungoingable *a.*)
plutte 1882	<	*cenoque* [*caenum*](s.v. plud) Sole cit. with -[t]-.
preuent 944		(s.v. †prevent *ppl. a.*) Sole cit. with *of*; no equivalent usage in *MED*.
put (forth to) 636	<	*expositam* (s.v. put *v.* V.43.†d.) Sole cit. with *forth to* = exposed to.
ʒestewarde 632	<	*orientis tramite* (s.v. yestewarde.)
solemly 2769	<	*uenusti decoris pulcritudinem* (s.v. solemnly *a.*)

---

[4] *OED* on CD-ROM calculates 256×, but *chesoun* is cited from another text in Arber's Introduction.

strompetly 839	<	*meretricio operi* (s.v. strumpetly *adv.*)
wepyng 271	<	*plorantes* (s.v. weeping *ppl.* a.1.†b. *absol.*)
wydwardys 1832	<	*uidualem* (s.v. widower 1.a.) Sole cit. with intrusive *-d-*.

2 The following words are the sole citation in *OED* and do occur in
  MED

(Hereafter, where *MED* antedates *OED*, I cite the source for *MED*'s
first usage.)

colloke 387	<	*locutorium* (s.v. colloque *sb.* 1 [from F *colloque* from L *colloquium*]): also sole cit. *MED* (dates *Revelation* 1482)
fugytyuys 2085	<	*fugitiui* (s.v. fugitive *a.* and *sb.* 1.d.) *MED* 1st cit. (a1382) <u>WBible (1)</u>

3 The following words, forms, and usages are the first citation in
  OED and either do not occur in *MED* at all or not in the required
  sense

aftyrward that 285		(s.v. afterward *adv.* and *prep.*, C. *conjunctively*)
alteracyons 1292	<	*uicissitudinum* (s.v. alteration)
(correcte and) amende 1610	<	*probabilius & correccius* (s.v. amend, *ppl. a.*)
attente 317	<	*attencius* (s.v. attent *ppl. a.*)
brackys 745		(s.v. brack *sb.*[4])
ded and gonne 1424	<	*exuisse* (s.v. dead *a.* VI.32.a.)
deprauyd 1328	<	*tantam . . . impudenciam* (s.v. deprave *v.* 2.)
discerpte 1106	<	*discerptus* (s.v. discerp *v.*)
excepte 1474	<	*exceptum* (s.v. except *ppl.* A.1.)
glotyners 2034	<	*commessatores* (s.v. glutton *v.*)
(was) goyng to (be broughte) 849	<	*agitur* (s.v. go *v.* 47.b.)
gratulacyon 2766	<	*congratulatio* (s.v. gratulation 1.)
hedlong 2120	<	*precipicia* (s.v. headlong *adv.* A.1.)
innocentnes 1737	<	*innocencia* (s.v. innocentness)
intercessours 2300	<	*intercessores* (s.v. intercessor 1.)
inuyncyble 1726	<	*inuincibile* (s.v. invincible *a.* 1.b. *transf.* and *fig.*)
lowsing 685	<	*solucionem* (s.v. loosing *vbl. sb.*†2. of joints)
opteyne 2350	<	*confouere* (s.v. obtain *v.* 6.)

ouerfowle 1884   <   *immensum* (s.v. over- II.28.a.)

peruersours 2295   <   *peruersores* (s.v. perverser)

pensys 1128   <   *denarios* (s.v. penny A.2.δ.) Double pl.

pompys 848   <   *pompis* (s.v. pomp *sb.* †2.)

pretendyn 894   (s.v. pretend *v.* 9.)

rectors 2295   <   *rectores* (s.v. rector 2.)

refeccion 368   <   *refeccione* (s.v. refection *sb.* 3.b.)

repletyd 456   <   *infusam* (s.v. replete *v.* †2.)

resperste 2245   <   *respersa* (s.v. resperse *v.* 1. *trans.*)

sex 147   <   *sextam* (s.v. six *a.* and *sb.* A.2.c.)

slowfulnes 1901   <   *torporis* (s.v. slowfulness 1.)

[*rancour and*] *sowernes* 1724   <   *dolorem rancoris* (s.v. sourness 2.)

swarmyn 758   <   *scatere* (s.v. swarm *v.*[1] 4.b. 'swarm full of')

         [*OED* misquotes 'full of *fowlys*' for *sowlys*]

tradicion 140   <   *tradicione* (s.v. tradition *sb.* 2)

tricennarijs 2392   <   *tricennalia* (s.v. tricenary *a.* and *sb.* B.)

voment 1101   <   *uomitum* (s.v. voment: *OED* cites only one other instance, c1510 *Gesta Rom.*); *MED* '[? From L vomens, -entis, ppl. of vomere; ?error for ME vomishment *n.* a1500 Mirk, *IPP*]'

wordly 859   <   *digne* (s.v. worthily *a.* 4.) *MED* does not record this spelling for the *adv.*, but records *wordeliche, wirdliche,* and *wurdlice.* (*MED* records *wordli* and *wordliche* for the adj. *worthli.*)

wrechid (hors) 2119   (s.v. wretched *a.* 5.)

wryte 1171   <   *superscriberentur* (s.v. write *v.* a. *transf.*)

4 The following words are the first or sole citation in *OED* and are antedated in *MED*

(Where *MED* clearly provides an earlier reference or references than *OED*, I give *MED*'s first citation's date.)

adolescente 2682   <   *adolescentulum MED* sense (a) (a1460) Vegetius (2)

alyenacion 170   <   *alienacione* (s.v. alienation 4) *MED* sense 2.?a1425 *Chauliac(1)

ascendyng 2845   <   *ascendencium* (s.v. ascending *vbl. sb.*) *MED* ?a1450 Arderne LW

benyuolente 1832   <   *beneficus* (s.v. benevolent *a.*) *MED* (c1443) Pecock Rule *carke* 1904   <   *cura* (s.v. cark *sb.* 4) *MED* (b) c1440 Lyarde

comyning 383   <   *communionis* (s.v. Commoning *vbl. sb.* 6) Sole cit.
MED s.v. communing ger. 3 Eccl. (b) a1425(c1395) WBible(2)

conceyte 1456   <   *oculis* (s.v. conceit *sb.* II.†4c.) *MED* cf. 3.(a)(1432) Paston

conformyng 2291   <   *conformantes* (s.v. conform *v.* 4.c.) *MED* (c1390) CT.Mel.

cuppid 507   <   *fleubotomo recisa* (s.v. cup *v.* 1.) *MED* sole cit. (a1398) *Trev.Barth.

dedifyed 466   <   *consecratum* (s.v. dedify, dedefy *v.*) *MED* a1475 Godstow Reg.

[confusyon and] despexion 1433   <   *contemptibilitate & ignominia* (s.v. despection) *MED a1500 (a1475)* Ashby Dicta

digestyd 398   <   *digesta* (s.v. digest *v.* 2.) *MED* cf. (1398) *Trev.Barth.

enarrabulle 976   <   *ineffabili* (s.v. enarrable *a.*) ?antedates *MED* a1500 Add.Hymnal

euerlasting 1569   <   *eternaliter* (s.v. everlasting a. and sb. 5. quasi-adv.) *MED* cf. (a) (c1445) Pecock Donet

excedeth 1246   (s.v. exceed v. 5.) *MED* cf. 5.(b) 1543 (1464) Hardyng Chron. B

expyacyon 1631   <   *expiacione* (s.v. expiation) *MED* (a) ?1475 (?a1425) Higd.(2)

fyste 1827   <   *pugno* (s.v. fist sb. 1.d.) *MED* 3(c) c1450 In a noon

generalyte 1855   <   *generalitate* (s.v. generality *sb.* I.1.†b.) *MED* (d) (1450) R.Parl.

inmoderately 159   <   *immoderati* (cited as *imoderately* s.v. immoderately *adv.* 1.) *MED* (a1398) *Trev. Barth.

yncomparable 2625   <   *incomparabiliter* (s.v. incomparable *a.* B. adv.) *MED* c1450 (?c1425) St.Mary.Oign.

incredibulle 543   <   *incredibilis* (s.v. incredible *a.* 1.b.) *MED* cf. (c) a1500 Mirror Salv.

intolerably 1128   <   *intollerabiliter* (s.v. intolerably *adv.*) *MED* ?a1425 *Chauliac (1)

inuoluyd 664   < *inuoluebat* (s.v. involve *v.* 1.) *MED*
                                  (a1382) WBibl(1)Pref.Jer.

iocundnes 2163   < *leticiam* (s.v. jocundness *sb.* 1.) *MED*
                                  (c1426) Audelay *Poems*

perceiuyd 1835   < *percepisset* (s.v. perceive *v.* II.†8.†b.) Cf.
                                  MED 3.(c), 5.(a).

rapte 4   (s.v. rapt pa. pple. 2.) *MED* rapen
                                  v.(2)(c) c1390 11Pains(3)

(blamyng and) resysting 2264 < *increpando* (s.v. resisting *vbl. sb.*) *MED*
                                  1436 Proc.Privy C.

scarpnes 2405   < *asperitate* (s.v. sharpnesss *v.* 4.†d.) *MED*
                                  4.(b). (a1398) *Trev. Barth.

sequestrate 1263   < *sequestratum* (s.v. sequestrate *a. Obs.* 1.)
                                  MED cf. ?a1425 *Chauliac(1)

stupour 339   < *stupore* (s.v. stupor *sb.* 2.b.) *MED* cf.
                                  (a1398) *Trev. Barth.

tedusnes 312   < *tedium* (s.v. tediouness *sb.* †2.) *MED* cf.
                                  ?a1425 Orch.Syon No other instance
                                  with *-dus-* in *OED* and *MED.*

vytalle [veynys] 2957   < *arteriarum* (s.v. vital *a.* 3.) *MED* cf.
                                  1.(b) ?a1425 *Chauliac(1)*

5 The following words antedate *OED* and are not cited in *MED*

affixed 468   < *affixam* (*OED* 1st cit. of affix v. 1533;
                                  with an equivalent use, of an image of
                                  Christ fixed to a crucifix, 1535)

audybille 256   < *audibili* (*OED* 1st cit. 1529)

barenly 1972   < *steriliter* (*OED* 1st cit. 1552)

byshoprye, bysshoppery 1888, 1956, 2169 < *prelationis, inprimis, episcopali officio*
                                  (*OED* 1st cit. 1535)

carnally 2206, 2267, 2577   < *carnaliter, secundum carnem, carnali*
                                  (*OED* 1st cit., 1. corporeally, 1539; 3. in
                                  an unspiritual manner, 1527)

exaltyd 1348   < *resultabat* (of the voice, *OED* 1st cit.
                                  1611)

6 The following words are used in senses not recorded in *OED* or *MED* (See Commentary)

absolute 951   < *absolute* 'unchanging', 'positively'

cowpulde 2838   < *coaptabat* 'adapted, adjusted'

dyssymulacyon 1911   < *dissimulacio* 'negligence, neglect'

mode 718   < *modum* 'limit, moderation'

7 The following spellings are not recorded in *OED* or *MED*

postre 'apostle' 1321   <   *apostolus*. From French *apostre*. Arber reads *postle*.

vtward(e)ly 'utterly' 15×   <   *funditus* 6×, *omnimodis, prorsus* 3×

8 The following words and expressions are uncommon

absent to (my-selfe) 2768   <   *michimet absentem* Not in *OED*. *MED* sole cit. with *to* a1500(1422) Yonge *SSecr.*

briys 243   <   *cilia* (s.v. †bree *sb.*[1] †3) Not in *MED*. 2nd cit. in *OED*, after c1450 *Voc.* in Wr.-Wülcker 631 *Cilium*, [gloss] brye.

(ouer-)carkefulle 1367   <   *solicitus* (s.v. carkful a.) 2nd of 2 cits.; 1st (=sole cit. *MED* s.v. overcarkful) c1449 Pecock, Repr.

lettyngys 2815   <   *demissiones* (s.v. letting *vbl. sb.*[1]) No other pl. usage in *OED* or *MED*.

lyftyngys 2815   <   *eleuaciones* (s.v. lifting *vbl. sb.* 1.a.) 1st pl. usage in *OED*, none in *MED* as ger.

prelacyon 1551, 1558   <   *prelacionis, primatus*; 'pre-eminence, superiority, dignity': *OED* cites only one instance *c.*1420 before 1585; *MED* cites only one instance a1450.

9 The following words, which I have chosen to hyphenate, are not recorded in *MED*

ouer-horabulle 633, *ouer-part* 1265, *ouer-prone* 959, *ouer-teduse* 2030, *ouer-wrechyd* 1519, *ouer-wrechidful* 642.

10 The following words are also cited in *OED*

For most of these words *MED* offers several earlier citations than *OED*, and I therefore offer no further comment. I supply the Latin source word in the *Visio* in selected cases only.

abbas 2314   (s.v. abbess)

abusion 1313

Aduent 1037

agonne 2971   (s.v. ago *v.*)

alye 1694   (s.v. ally *sb.*[1] 5.)

alow 253   (s.v. alow *adv.*[1] 5.)

askynges 2638   (s.v. asking *vbl. sb.*)

a-this-halfe 1407-8   (s.v. a-this-half)

avexid 2454   <   *vexatus* (s.v. avex *v.*)

behauing 976	(s.v. behaving *vbl. sb.*)
be-houable 1029	< *oportunis* (s.v. behovable *a.*)
bore 761	(s.v. bear *v.*[1] str.)
byddyn 577	(s.v. bide *v.*)
chaptur 177	< *[tabula]* (s.v. chapter *sb.* 3) *OED* cites this in the wrong sense: see Commentary.
chastment 409	< *castigare* (s.v. chastement)
cleys 1844	(s.v. clee)
clothyng 2580	< *uestitus* (s.v. clothing *vbl. n.*)
collacyon 332	< *collacionem* (s.v. collation *sb.* 7)
compressyd 250	< *compressis* (s.v. compress *v.* 1) 2nd cit., after c1400 Lanfranc's Cirurg., *MED* adds c1425 Arderne Fistula
consenting 1085	< *consencientibus* (s.v. consenting *vbl. sb.*)
contraryusnes 1803	< *contrarietate* (s.v. contrariousness)
conuersion 124	< *conuersionis* (s.v. conversion 8.c.)
correcte 1549	< *meum opposuissem rigorem* (s.v. correct *pa. pple.* and *a.* A. *pa. pple.*)
cossis 311	(s.v. kiss *sb.*)
Crystynmas 1071	(s.v. christenmas)
dedyr 1815	(s.v. thither *adv.*)
denys 1981	< *decanorum* (s.v. dean *sb.*[1])
deseruynges 675	(s.v. deserving *vbl. n.*)
discyplynys 224	< *disciplinas* (s.v. discipline *sb.* 7.)
discyplyne 478	< *ad dandam . . . disciplinam* ([*OED* spells *discypline*] s.v. discipline *v.* 2.)
disesyd 580	< *inquietatus* (s.v. disease *v.* 1.b.)
dispensacyon 2525	< *dispensacionis* (s.v. dispensation 4.) 2nd cit., after 1382 Wyclif I Cor. ix.17; *MED* adds (a1387 Trev. Higd.)
dyssolucyon 2217	< *luxu* (s.v. dissolution 5.)
doo 1035	(s.v. do *v.* 8.)
erryn 2882	(s.v. err *v.*[1] 4.)
euetyde 627	< *uesperum* (s.v. eve *sb.*[1] 4.) used non-attributively, 2nd cit., after c1460 in Hearne *R.Glouc.* [printed *ene-*]; *MED* a1425 *Medulla 18b/a Crepisculum: an euetyde.
euyn-heyre 2693	< *coheres* (s.v. even *a.* †13.¶c.) Last cit. *MED* one cit. a1425(1395) Wbible(2) Ecclus. 22.29.
euynworthy 878	< *condigne* (s.v. even- 3.†a.) Last cit., after

		c1380 Wyclif *Sermon.* (=*MED* sole cit. s.v. even adv. 17(w) dated. ?c1400)
exempte 2623	<	*exemptum* (s.v. exempt *ppl.* A.1.d.)
facultees 2496	<	*disciplinis* (s.v. faculty II.7.) 2nd cit., after Trevisa <u>Higden</u>, *MED* adds, 2.(b), (1423) <u>Let.Bk.</u> and (c1443) Pecock <u>Rule</u>.
fame 967		(s.v. fame *sb.*¹ 1.a.)
fadyrly 409	<	*paterno* (s.v. fatherly *a.*)
fele 963		(s.v. feel *v.* II.†15.)
fewnes 2262		(s.v. fewness 1)
flayne 1779	<	*excoriabantur* (s.v. flay *v.* 2.)
flockemele 2806	<	*cateruatim* (s.v. flock-meal *adv.*)
gedur 704		(s.v. gather *v.* †5.)
gladsum 2243		(s.v. gladsome *a.* 3.)
growyn 1392		(s.v. grow *v.* 7.)
gyuyd 2061	<	*compediti* (s.v. gyve *v.*)
hangyn 691		(s.v. hang *v.* 3.)
hateful 2035		(s.v. hateful *a.* 1.)
here 16		(s.v. †her *poss. pron. 3rd pl.* A.β) Last cit. (Last cit. under A.γ her 1485 <u>St. Wenefr.</u>)
herns 1662		(s.v. hers *poss. pron.* 1.b. [See Introduction, above, p. lv])
hedir-to 278		(s.v. hitherto *adv.* A. 1.)
holde 339		(s.v. hold *v.* B.I.7.b.)
hoys 2802		(s.v. whose *pron.* I.3.) 'Of inanimate thing.
ȝeffe 1050		(cited as *yeffe* s.v. if *conj.* A.I.3.b.) 2nd cit., after 1382 Wyclif John xi.21.
incorrygyble 1618	<	*incorrigibiles* (s.v. incorrigible *a.* 1.)
indycybylle 748	<	*indicibilis* (s.v. †indicible *a.*) 2nd cit., after 1480 Caxton, <u>Ovid's Met.</u> XII.xix. *MED* one cit. c1475(1459) <u>Pros.Yorkists.</u>
inestymable 752		(s.v. inestimable *a.*)
enfecte 1633	<	*infecerunt* (s.v. infect *v.* 5.)
innumerable 1853	<	*innumeris* (s.v. innumerable *a.*)
intemperans 2513	<	*intemperancia* (s.v. intemperance †1.) Antedated in *OED* and *MED* only by Trevisa, <u>Higden.</u>
intendyng 2656		(s.v. intend *v.* III.†12. trans.β)
hit 11		(s.v. it *pron.* B.I.3.f.) 'In quoting from books, in the phrases *it says, it tells,* etc.'
hordende 1996	<	*instituerat* (s.v. ordain *v.* I.4.)

labouryd 126   (s.v. labour *v.* I.†10.)

lepur 2345   (s.v. †leper *sb.*[1])

a lytyll and a lytill 257   (s.v. little *a.*, *adv.*, and *sb.* B.III.7.†b.)

lodisman 2791   (s.v. †lodesman 1.)

mawncypylle 1026   <   *mancipium* (s.v. manciple 1.)

mawe 823   (cited as *maw* s.v. maw *sb.*[1] 2.†a) Last
                                   cit. *OED*. Last cit. *MED* maue n. 2.(a)
                                   a1500(a1460) TowneleyPl.

medelyng 2911   (s.v. meddling *vbl. sb.* †1.†b.) Last cit.
                                   OED. Last cit. *MED* medling(e ger.
                                   a1500 Mandev.(3)

narracyon 1504   (s.v. narration 1.b.)

naturelly 1326   (s.v. †naturelly *adv.* 1.) Last cit. *OED*.
                                   MED s.v. naturali does not separate
                                   'naturally' and 'naturelly'.

nede 2218   (s.v. need *sb.* I.10.a.)

neglygently 1524   (s.v. negligently *adv.*)

nocturne 587   (s.v. nocturn *sb.* 1.)

none man 14   (s.v. no man 1.a.α.) Last cit. with *non(e*.
                                   Previous cit. c1315 Shoreham; last cit.
                                   MED s.v. non adj. 4.(a) (1340) Ayenb.

nowne 805   (s.v. †nown(e, n'own) 2nd cit., after
                                   c1400 Song Roland

obsecracyons 318   <   *obsecraciones* (s.v. obsecration *sb.* 1.) 2nd
                                   cit., after 1382 Wylif Ps. clii(i) & Prov.
                                   xviii.23 (latter sole cit. *MED* (b))

opynner 348   (s.v. open *a.* B. *adv.*)

ornamentys 1024   (s.v. ornament *sb.* †1.b.Eccl.)

odyr-wise 1955   (s.v. otherwise *sb. phr.*, *adv.*, *a.*
                                   B.adv.1.α)

oncredible 2546   <   *incredibilem* (s.v. †uncredible *a.* 1.) 2nd
                                   cit., after c1440 Wycliffite Bible Judg.
                                   xx.5; *MED* adds only a1500 GLitany
                                   (Lamb) 270

ondyscrete 2490   (s.v. †undiscreet *a.* a.)

onethys 256   (s.v. †uneaths *adv.* 1.α)

onmeserabulle 1013   (s.v. unmeasurable *a.*, *sb.*, and *adv.* 2.b.)

on-mylde 2590   (s.v. †unmild *a.*)

onrightful 2125   (s.v. unrightful *a.*)

onspedeful 430   (s.v. †unspeedful *a.*)

onsufficient 2873   <   *minus* (s.v. †unsufficient *a.*)

ouyr-leyde 192   (s.v. overlay *v.* 2.a.)

ouermekyl 2577   (s.v. over-mickle *a. and adv.*)

pareshon 1017	< *parochianus* (s.v. †parishen 1.β.)
personage 2372	(s.v. parsonage 1.)
passyn 1743	(s.v. pass *v.* I.11.)
pypys 195	< *arteriarum* (s.v. pipe *sb.* II.6.)
playnnes 1270	(s.v. plainness *sb.*†1.)
pledyd 1876	(s.v. plead *v.* II.5.)
posynners 2066	(s.v. poisoner *sb.* a.)
ponissement 1147	(s.v. punishment 1.a.)
purgacyon 1499	(s.v. purgation 3.)
rauyshte 626	(s.v. ravish *v.* 3.b.)
raueshyng 2970	< *dormicione* (s.v. ravishing *vbl. sb.* 2)
reboudye 1783	< *impuritate* (s.v. †ribaldy *sb.*) Last cit. Cf. *MED* ribaudi(e *n.* (b) last cit. c1500(?a1475) <u>Ass. Gods</u>.
refreschyng 2360	(s.v. refreshing *vbl. sb.* 1.)
releuyng 2324	(s.v. relieving *vbl. sb.*)
remaynyn 1244	(s.v. remain *v.* 2.a.)
replecyon 1183	(s.v. repletion 1.)
ryght-wesnes 1479	(s.v. righteousness 1.α)
sacrarye 595	< *sacrarium* (s.v. †sacrary 2.)
sandyr 412	(s.v. †sander *adv.*) 2nd cit., after a1450Myrc <u>Festial</u>, which is sole cit. *MED* s.v. sane adv. dated a1500(a1415)
Sathanas 1047	(s.v. satanas 1.)
scarsnes 2582	(s.v. scarceness †1.)
sey 2013	(s.v. see *v.* A.8. Past Participle β.) Penult. cit. for this form of pp.; last cit. 15.. <u>Adam Bel</u>.
sekyd 1157	(s.v. seek *v.* II.15.)
sende 1186	(s.v. send *v.*¹ I.8.b.)
senyor 476	(s.v. senior *a. and sb.* B.1.a.)
settith 366	(s.v. set *v.*¹ A.1.d. *imperative*) Last cit. in *-th*.
sickelew 2650	(s.v. †sicklew *a.*) Penult. cit.; last cit. ?1503 in *Lett. Rich. III & Hen. VII*. Sole cit. in *-ew* after 1387 Trevisa <u>Higden</u>; last cit. *MED* sikleu(e a1500(a1450) <u>Ashmole SSecr</u>.
sykyng 253	(s.v. sike *v.* 1.intr. β.) Penult. cit.; last cit. 1515 <u>Scottish Field</u>; cf. *MED* siken v.(2)(a).
sykynges 288	(s.v. siking *vbl. sb.*) Last cit. before 1886

	dialectal <u>soikin</u>'; cf. *MED* siking(e ger. 1.(a)
symony 2383	(s.v. simony 1.)
sympylnes 2274	(s.v. simpleness 3.)
sofryn 1589	(s.v. suffer *v.* I.1.a.)
sorowyng 1348	(s.v. sorrowing *vbl. sb.*)
sounned 1783	(s.v. sound *v.*¹ I.†5.†b.(a) 'with simple objective') Last cit.; cf. *MED* sounen v.4.(a) last cit. a1500 Chartier *Treat. Hope*
sownyng 2909	(s.v. sounding *vbl. sb.*¹ 1.a.α.)
sparyd 2810	(s.v. spare *v.*² *north*. †3.) 2nd of 2 cits.; cf. *MED* sparren v.(1)2.(c) last cit. a1500(a1460) <u>Towneley Pl</u>.
sparclys 762	(s.v. sparkle *sb.* 1.)
spedly 1654	(s.v. †speedly *adv.*α.)
succeding 1679	< *successu* (s.v. succeeding *vbl. sb.* †2.) 2nd cit., after c1460 <u>Oseney Reg.</u> (which is sole cit. *MED* succeding ger. (a))
suspycyon 1328	(s.v. suspicion *sb.* 3.) 2nd cit., after c1400 <u>Beryn</u>
sustentacion 374	< *sustentamine* (s.v. sustentation *sb.* 7.a.)
take 622	(s.v. take *v.*)
techyng 806	(s.v. teaching *vbl. sb.* 2.b.)
temporalte 695	< *seculari foro* (s.v. temporalty *sb.* 2.†) 2nd of 2 cits., after c1440 <u>Bone Flor.</u>
thynnyde 796	(s.v. thin *v.*¹ 1.)
thretyng 2467	(s.v. threating *vbl. sb.*)
throwe 1781	(s.v. throw *v.*¹)
to-gedyr 221	(s.v. together *adv.* A.1.a.)
todyr 1697	(s.v. tother *pron. and a.* B.1.a.)
tresur 1385	(s.v. treasure *v.* 2. *fig.*)
trowbulnes 1774	< *inclemenciam* (s.v. †troubleness *a.* 3.) Last cit.
vppe 2809	(s.v. up *adv.* I.2.b.)
vpbrayde 1723	(s.v. upbraid *v.* I.2.)
vpbraydys 2772	(s.v. upbraid *sb.* Obs. 1.)
vtmest 1147	(s.v. utmost *a. and sb.* I.2.)
variant 2911	< *uaria* (s.v. variant *a. and sb.* A.adj.3.a.)
veny 547	< *ueniam* (s.v. †veny¹) Last cit.
white-safe 409	(s.v. vouchsafe *v.* II.6.b.δ².)
wakyngly 1195	< *dum adhuc uigilaret* (s.v. waking *ppl.* 4. <u>transf.</u>) 2nd of 3 cits.

weriful 2030	(s.v. weariful *a.*)
wellid 506	< *emanare* (s.v. well *v.*[1] 6.b. <u>transf.</u>) Construction with *of*, last of 3 cits.
welle 238	(s.v. well *adv.* 12.)
whore 553	(s.v. hoar *a.* and *sb.* A.adj.2.a.)
Wyth Sonday 2450	(cited as *wythssonday* s.v. Whit Sunday 1.)
wulle 1550	(s.v. will *v.* A.4.β)
wytnesse 356	(s.v. witness *sb.* I.†1.)
worschype 2175	< *honorante* (s.v. worship *v.* †2.c.) Last cit.
worschipfulnes 2048	< *uenerabilitate* (s.v. worshipfulness)
wothys 2478	(s.v. oath *sb.* 1.a.)
wrathe 1385	(s.v. wrath *sb.* 4.)
(ouer-)wrechidful 643	< *nimium miserabiles* (s.v. †wretchedful *a.*) Last of 4 cits.

GLOSSARY

The glossary is selective and includes those words, expressions, meanings, spellings, or forms that might give pause to a modern reader, or which are otherwise unusual or interesting; usually only one line reference is given for each instance cited. Variant spellings of a head word are usually listed together but line references are in numerical order, i.e. not necessarily in the order of the cited spellings. I have not necessarily included forms of the pr. 3 sg. *-th(e*, or common spelling variants such as *e/ie*, *i/y*, *u/v*, final *-e*.

Initial and medial *y* used as a vowel are treated as identical with vocalic *i*; *i/y* used as a consonant follow *i/y* used as a vowel; yogh used for initial *y-* is treated as identical with the semi-vowel *y-*; intrusive initial yogh before *e* or *i* is listed separately after *z*. * indicates that the form has been produced by emendation. Superscript n following a line number directs the reader to a note in the Commentary.

a *prep. doctour* ~ *lawe* doctor of law 74.

aage *n.* old age 1848; *oolde* ~2628; *yong(e* ~ youth 1382, 1399; *ryghte yonge* ~ childhood 2677.

abashyd *pa. t. 1 pl. intrans.* were confused 992; **abasshid** *pp.* discomfited 2468.

abbas, abasse, abbasse *n.* abbess 96, 2313, 2314.

abboth *n.* abbot 103; **abbot is** *poss.* 187.

abhomynable *adj.* hateful, execrable 1430.

abhortyd *pa. 3 sg.* abhorred 127.

abyde *v.* await 2895; *pr. p.* **abydyng** 2813.

abiecte *adj.* menial 2341.

aboue *prep.* beyond, after 2973.

aboute, abowte *adv. as adj. and prep.* be ~ be diligent 1965, be attending to 2633; in the vicinity of 595.

aboutys *adv. al* ~ everywhere 2829.

abrasyng *vbl. n.* 'The act of scraping or rubbing off; abrading' (*OED*) 2070.

abrode *adv.* about, around 1102, 1270.

absolute *adj.* completely absorbed, unchanging, *or adv.* absolutely, positively 951.

abusion *n.* shameful practice 1313; *pl.* **abusyons** 1567.

accendyd *pp.* kindled, inflamed (fig.) 1601, 2783.

accept *pp. or ppl. adj.* ~ *of* pleasing to 471.

acomtys *n. pl.* accounts 2220, 2525.

acquentanse, aquentans *n.* acquaintance 792, 1862.

acquentyd *pp.* acquainted 2678.

actually *adv.* in reality 1427.

adigression *n.* digression 604, 616.

aduocatour *n.* intercessor, patron (saint) 1109, 1230, 1470.

aferd(e *adj.* frightened, terrified 2468, 2823.

a-ferre *adv.* afar, at a distance 811.

affeccyon *n. carnal* ~ feeling through ties of kinship or worldly association 1535, 2603.

affectualy *adv.* earnestly 869.

affyxed, affixed *ppl. adj.* fixed 212, 468.

afore *adv.* before 274.

afore *conj.* ~ *þat* before 341.

afore *prep.* before 217, in front of 185.

after, aftyr *adv.* afterwards 211, 422.

after, aftyr *conj.* ~ *that* after 308, 1056.

after, aftyr *prep.* in accordance with 846, 1937, 2879, 2899; according to 2673.

afterward, aftirward, aftyrward(e *adv.* afterwards 269, 346, 764, 920.

aftyrward *conj.* ~ *that* after 285.

agaste *ppl. adj.* aghast, horrified 1571.

agayne *adv.* back again 111.

agenst(e, agaynest, ageynst *prep.* against 67, 1007, 1151, 1724; **ageynste** *prep.* next to 735.

ageyn(e *adv.* in return 980, 2465, 2679.

agoe *pp.* ago 2203; **agoo** 2188; **agon(e** 1234, 1823; **agonne** 2622; gone away 2971.

al(le *adj.* ~ *thing* everything 348, 1245; ~ *maner* every kind of 1286, 2046; ~ *maner of* every kind of 2340; *adv.* entirely, utterly 684; ~ *only* especially, in particular 2639, merely 2927, 2973, solely, exclusively 2863.

albys *n. pl.* albs (ecclesiastical vestments) 545, 562; **aubys** 169.

algate *adv.* at any rate 1408.

alyenacion *n.* 'withdrawal, loss, or derangement of mental faculties' (*OED*) 170.

alyenate *ppl. adj.* estranged 1865; ~ *fro my-selfe* deranged 2768.

allonly *adv.* solely 554.

almys *n. pl.* alms 1373; charity 1371; charitable action 1375; ~ *-dede*, ~ *-dedys*, *almis-dede* deeds of mercy 1454, 1457, 1917.

alow *adv.* in a low voice, quietly 253.

also *adv.* as, just as 32.

alteracyons *n.pl.* changes 1292.

alwey *adv.* always 2163.

alye *n.* relative, kinsman 1694.

amende *v.* recover, get well 137; make amends for (faults) 1155; improve (behaviour) 720; **amendyng** *pr. p.* getting better 202; ~ *pp.* amended, reformed 1610.

amend(e)ment *n.* atonement, penance 1619, 2470; (moral) improvement 1088; (physical) recovery 130; benefit 1809.

amonge *adv.* from time to time 350; *prep.* ~ *this* meanwhile 659, 1014.

ancres(se *n.* anchoress 77, 1647.

ancrys *n. pl.* anchorites 2197.

and *conj.* if 18, 167; ~ *yf* if 1339.

andswerde *pa. 3 sg.* answered 2463.

anguys(she *n.* anguish, distress 717, 834.

anoyntid *pa. 1 sg.* smeared 514.

anoyntyng *vbl. n. laste* ~ sacrament of extreme unction 2655.

anon(e, anoon *adv.* at once, right away 199, 211, 492; ~ *as* as soon as 351.

answarde, an(d)swerde *pa. 3 sg.* answered 550, 1217, 2463; **answard** *pp.* 2011.

any-thing *adv.* in any way 201-2.

aperyd *pp.* appeared 1190.

apon(e *prep.* upon 488, 1080; about 222.

apostasye *n.* abandonment of holy orders 2092.

appetite, appetyte *n.* craving or passion for food 1014, 1772.

approfe *n.* proof, endorsement 114.

approuyd *pa. 1 sg.* approved, endorsed 1565; *pp.* proved 19.

arayed *ppl. adj.* adorned 2433.

archedekons *n. pl.* archdeacons 1981.

armyr *n.* armour 2109.

as *conj.* as if 183, 244; in so far as 1003; *lyke* ~ just as 15, in the same way as 269; (introducing an oath) 824.

asaye *v.* attempt 2532; **asayde** *pa.3 sg.* 289.

ascendyng *vbl. n.* ascent, ascension 2845.

ascendyt *pa. 3 sg.* ascended 926.

aside *adv. put* ~ abandoned 410.

asking *vbl. n.* question 563; **askynges** *pl.* prayers, supplication 2638.

assoyled, assoylyd *pa. t.* absolved 548, 607; ~ *pp.* 538.

astonyd *ppl. adj.* ~ *apon* amazed by, astonished at 222.

a-this-halfe *prep. phr.* on this side (of) 1407-8.

atte *prep.* at the 245, 290.

attendans *n.* diligent service 203.

attente *ppl. adj.* full of attention 317.

aubys *see* **albys**.

auctorite *n.* authority, power to influence people 1959.

auctors *n. pl. her* ~ those who promoted them 1989.

audybille *adj.* audible 256.

auisement, auysement *n.* consideration, deliberation 402; *were put in . . .* ~ *for-to* with forethought undertook to 1143; ~ *takyn* having considered 222-3.

auowtres *n. pl.* adulterers 2033.

auowtrye *n.* adultery 2126.

auter, awter *n.* altar 219, 467.

a-vexid *pp.* distressed 2454.

axces *n.* attack (of illness) 2454.

bade *pa. t.* asked . . . (to) 534; urged 1419; commanded 2322; implored 2477.

bare *see* **bere**.

baren *adj.* worthless, unproductive 1794.

barenly *adv.* unproductively 1972.

bashyd *pa. t. sg.* was ashamed, embarrassed 1615.

be *pr. sg. subj.* be 936, 1285; ~ *pr. pl.* are 354, 920, 1453, **ben** 210, 716, **byn** 298; ~ *cum to* have come to 2283; ~ *pr. pl. subj.* 1395; **ware** *pa. t. 3 sg. subj.* were 266, 1296; **ware** *pa. t. pl.* 7, where 682, was 1348, 1908, **wes** 669, 2795; ~ *pp.* 183, 301; **ben** 33; **bene** 1215.

be *prep.* by, thanks to 1117.

be(-)cause, by(-)cause, by(-)cawse *conj.* ~ *that* because 281, 1211, 1845.

becke *n.* gesture 2640.

beckid *pa. t. sg.* signalled, beckoned 483.

be-fyll(e *pa. t. sg.* hyt so ~ hym it happened to him like this 946; *pa. t. pl.* happened (to) 222, 341.

begunne *pa. t. sg.* began 1422; *pa. t. pl.* 1679; *pp.* 475, **begonne** 351.

begylde *pa. t. sg.* beguiled 1123; *pp.* 1216.

behauing, behauyng *vbl. n.* conduct, behaviour 976, 1776.

behauyd *pa. t. sg.* ~ hym/her(selfe behaved 180, 2338, 2587.

beholdyth *pr. t. pl.* observe 2280; **behilde, behylde** *pa. t. sg.* 505, 519; *pa. t. pl.* 1245, 2762; *pp.* **beholde** 2541.

beholdyng *vbl. n.* sight 804; visual appearance, 'looks' 857, 1650.

be-houable *adj.* helpful, beneficial 1029*.

beyng *vbl. n.* condition 206.

beleue *v.* ~ to give credence to, trust 1621.

belouyd *pp.* ~ of loved/cherished by 1720; wel- ~ dearly loved 381 (*see Commentary*).

benefetis, benefet(t)ys, benefitys, benefytys *n. pl.* favours, good deeds, acts of piety 314, 676, 2175, 2525, 2657.

beneficys, benefycys *n. pl.* ecclesiastical livings, offices or positions in the Church 1358, 1537, 1951.

beneson *n.* blessing 538.

bere *v.* endure 1531; ~ my-selfe move, walk 166; **bare** *pa. t. sg.* carried 1826; held (office) 2605; kept (sth. in heart/mind) 345; raised 2832; wore 2626; *pl.* endured 658; **bore** *pp.* born 1684; carried 761; given birth to 2068.

besy(e *adj.* diligent 1534; constantly occupied 1451; **besyur** *comp.* 2637.

besyde *adv.* to one side 2237.

besyly *adv.* constantly 1478, **bysyly** 748; rapidly 1134; scrupulously, zealously 2256; diligently, attentively 2651; **besily, besely** devoutly, sedulously 416, 497.

besynes *n.* effort 2139; solicitude 2609; attention 2610; **besynesses** *pl.* affairs, activities 1045.

be-toke *pa. t. sg.* consigned 2586; **betakyn** *pp.* assigned to 2201; allotted 2528; (*refl.*) surrended 2720-1.

betwene *adv.* put ~ interspersed 328.

betwhene *prep.* between 2674.

betwyxe *prep.* between 218.

betyd *pa. t. pl.* happened (to) 346.

be-yonde *prep.* ~ see overseas 1685.

bydyng *vbl. n.* certen ~ that he boode secure hope with which he waited 2625.

bylle *n.* bill, beak 1844.

byshoprye, bysshoppery *n.* office of a bishop, bishopric 1888, 1956, 2169.

byttyrste *adj. superl.* mooste ~ most bitter 836.

blamyng *vbl. n.* accusation 2264.

blessyd *pp. adj.* ~ of blessed by 2862.

bleynys *n. pl.* (leprous) sores 2347.

blowyn *pp.* blown 239.

blyster *pp.* ~ owte of swollen up with, blistered with 2347.

bocis *n. pl.* bushes 745.

bode *pa. t. sg.* remained 337; **boode** waited 2626; **byddyn** *pp.* remained 577.

bonde *pa. t. pl.* bound, tied on 233; **bownde** *pp.* ~ 2966, bound 1012, **bounden** 643; ~ to destined for 1929; committed 2086, **bownde** 2604.

boocke *n.* buck, male deer 2129.

borowe *n.* protector 1098.

borthyn* *n.* burden 2114.

bothe *conj.* ~ of both 807, 1322.

botyd *pa. t. sg.* no-thyng hit ~ it was of no use 239.

boundys *n. pl.* bonds 1777.

bowde *pa. t.* bowed 904, 977; **bowyd** *pp.* submitted 1635.

brackys *n. pl.* bracken 745.

brake, breke *pr. t. pl.* break (vow) 1819; *pa. t. sg.* 82; ~ vppe escaped 664; *pa. t. pl.* broke (vow) 1790.

brekerys *n. pl.* violators (of holy vows) 1556.

breking, brekyng *vbl. n.* breaking of rules/vows 1765, 1817,/chastity 2010.

brenne *v.* (*trans. and intrans.*) burn 2451; **brenning, brennyng** *pr. p.* (and *adj.*) 510, 1478, 2081; **brende** *pa. t.* 1703, **brent(e** 1128, 1296; **brent(e** *pp.* 668, 1653.

brennyng *vbl. n.* burning 1132.

breste *n.* chest 198; *pl.* **brestys** breasts 2077.

bretheren, brethirne, brethyrne *n. pl.* brethren, fellow monks 41, 221, 2648.

brighte, bryght *adv.* brightly 2110, 2804.

briys *n. pl.* eye-lashes 243.

brochys *n. pl.* spits, skewers 2121.

brode *adv.* fer(re and ~ far and wide 1605, 2714.

broder *n.* brother 724.

bronde *n.* ~ *of fyre* firebrand, torch 1478.
brought(e *pp.* ~ *of* brought by 387; ~ *to nought* destroyed 1290, 1293; **browghte forthe** brought up, educated 2599.
broysyd *pp.* bruised 1779.
brydyl *n.* bridle 1547.
by *prep.* ~ *the space of* for the duration of 125; ~ *the relygion* according to the rules of the (religious) order 167, ~ *the ordyr* 188.
bye *v.* buy, purchase 2195.
by-fore-tyme *adv.* previously 150.
byn *see* be.

can *pr. sg.* ~ *and may* know how and am able 2539; *nethir . . . we may or* ~ *pr. pl.* nor are we able . . . or know how to 357; **cowde** *pa. t.* could 155, 411, **kowd(e** 292, 1006.
canker *n.* ulcer 2963.
carke, karke *n.* care, heed, concern 1904, 2286.
carnal(le *adj.* worldly, sinful 1535, 2210.
carnaly *adv.* in an unspiritual manner 2206, 2267, 2577.
caste *v.* ~ *awey* give up, renounce 1008; ~ *pa. t. pl.* poured 229; **castyd** threw 820; ~ *vndyr pp.* subjected (to) 709, 2770.
causis *n. pl.* cases 1876.
causyn *pr. t. pl.* cause 326.
cellys *n. pl.* (subordinate) houses of religion, or monastic cells 1768.
certenly *adv.* definitely 2983.
certifide *pp.* informed, assured 967.
cesse *v.* (+ *of*) become silent, cease speaking (about) 2557; **cese** *pr. t. sg.* ~ *of* 2215; **cessyd** *pp. was* ~ had ceased 2916.
chafer *n.* a commodity 2445.
chambyr *n.* bedroom 1196.
chapitres *n. pl.* chapters 28.
chaptur *n.* ~ *was ronge* monks were all summoned by ringing 177 (*see Commentary*).
chaptur-hous, -hows(e *n.* monks' meeting-place 32, 182, 186.
charge *n.* burden (of office), responsibility 1911; (to have) ~ *and cure of* (to have) responsibility for and care of 1530.
charyte *n.* love, charity, act of kindness 2240.
chaste *v.* correct, discipline 409.
chast(e)ment *n.* chastisement 409, 2353; **chastmentys** *pl.* 2168.

chaystyng *vbl. n.* chastising 719.
chere *n.* expression, demeanour 551; manner, bearing 2464.
cherysshe *v.* favour, promote the well-being of 1556.
chesyng *pr. p.* choosing 2262; **chose** *pp.* chosen 2155.
childe *n. of a* ~ since childhood 2672.
chirch(e, chyrche, chirce *n.* church 141, 179, 292, 533; *Holy* ~ the Church of Rome 315.
chose *see* **chesyng.**
clarke, *n.* clerk, cleric 1398; **clarkys** *pl.* 1975.
clathyr *v.* babble 1559.
clene *adj.* clean, pure 1841; *adv.* fully (confess) 1031; completely 2971.
clennes *n.* purity 2249.
clensyd, *pp.* expiated 1382; purified 920; *vbl. n.* **clensyng** 1159.
clepynges *vbl. n. pl.* sexual encounters 1317.
cleppyd *see* **clippid.**
clere *adj.* unadulterated 1737; clear 2728.
clerely *adv.* with purity 1178.
cleuyth *pr. 3 sg.* sticks 1743; **cleuyn** *pr. pl.* 879.
cley *n.* clay 634.
cleys *n. pl.* claws 1844.
clippid, clyppyd *pa. 3 sg.* held 311, 556; **clypte** squeezed 1100; **cleppyd** *pa. t. pl.* embraced 2075.
clothyng *vbl. n.* 'The action of covering or providing with clothes; dressing' (*OED*), being clothed 2580.
clothles *adj.* without clothes 2407.
collacion *n.* monastic evening assembly for devotion or reading from homilies, etc. 243; *hit range to the collacyon* the bell was sounded for this gathering 332.
colloke *n.* place for conversation in a monastery 387.
colur *n.* ruse: *by a* ~ *of* by the deceptive means of 1954.
colys *n. pl.* coals 1770.
comfort *see* **confort(e.**
commandement, commawndement *n.* command, bidding 621; *of the* ~ according to the instruction 1036; **commandmentis, commaundmentys** *pl.* (our Lord's) ~ 1864, 2715; **commaundementys, commawndementys** *of God* Ten Commandments 156, 2898.

commaundyd *pp.* ~ *of* commanded by 1034.

comme, cum(me *v.* come 185, 208, 511; **comythe, cummyth** *pr. 3 sg.* 1810, 1891; **cummyng** *pr. p.* 2660, **commyng** *on the feste of Estur* as the feast of Easter approached 136; *pp.* ~ . . . *to [oneself]* regained consciousness 36, 392, 1189; **commyn** come 2811; **cum** 2283.

commendacyon *n. of grete* ~ highly praiseworthy 2307; applause 2573.

commytid, committed *pp.* given 2528; **comyttyd** . . . *of* entrusted . . . by 2365; delegated as superior 2564; *ppl. adj.* entrusted 2287.

comonne *n. in* ~ together 305.

companyse *n. pl.* multitudes 1275.

comparyson *n. in* ~ *of* in comparison with 1574; *wythowte any* **comparsone** incomparably 210.

compassyon *n.* ~ *of* compassion on 2519; ~ *to* 2636.

compendeusly *adv.* concisely and comprehensively 2930.

complen(ne *n.* compline, the last of the seven daily monastic services or 'hours' 241, 243.

compressyd *pp.* pressed or squeezed together 250.

compunccion, compunccyon, conpunccion, cumpunctyon *n.* remorse 144, 326, 1849; ~ *of teeris* tearful repentance 30; ~ *of herte* contrition 2674.

comyn(ne *adj.* common, shared 759, 1902, 2647.

comyning *n.* Communion, the Eucharist 383.

comyning *vbl. n.* conversing 678.

comyrd *pp.* burdened 2737.

conceue *v.* ~ (in mind) comprehend 708; *imp. pl.* **conceyue*** understand 1459; **conceuyd** *pa. 1 sg.* experienced 2871; **conseyued** comprehended 678; **conceuyd** *pp.* formed 1067; **conceyued** ~ *of* comprehended by 1246.

conceyte *n.* private opinion, estimation, or judgement 1456; conception 2945.

concurs *n.* a gathering 2762.

condempnyth *v. pr. 3 sg.* condemns 1322.

condicion *n.* status in society 638; **condicions, condycyons** *pl.* 316, 2027; **condycyons** behaviour, character 720, 1513.

condicionde, condicyonde, condy-

cyonde *ppl. adj. wele* ~ well disposed, of good character 1718, 1834, 2194.

condigne *adj.* appropriate 2055.

confermethe *v. pr. 3 sg.* confirms 1461.

confesse *v.* (*refl.*) + *of* confess 1031; **confeste** *me pa. 1 sg.* 1417; **confest(e** *pp.* 396, 1411.

confessour *n.* adherent of the faith 1222.

Confiteor *n.* prayer '*Confiteor Domino meo*' said as part of confession 537.

conforme *v.* (*refl.*) ~ *hym* adapt, accommodate himself 1841; *conformyd* . . . *after pa. 3 sg.* modelled . . . according to 2160.

conformyng *vbl. n.* showing obedience 2291.

confort(e *n.* encouragement, help 13, 130; comfort 391.

confortyd *pa. t. 3 sg.* encouraged 835; *pp.* ~, **conforted, confortid** encouraged, strengthened 652, 1121, 2511.

confowndyd *pp.* destroyed 2298; disgraced 1434; **confounded** *of* overcome with 1429.

confusyon *n.* humiliation 1433.

conning, connyng *n.* learning, knowledge, understanding 1466, 1970.

conplaynyd *pa. 3 sg.* ~ *of* bemoaned, attacked 2305.

consciens, conscyens *n. of ther* ~ according to their conscience 655; consciousness, remorse 841.

conselle *n. by* ~ after due consideration 202; **consels** *pl.* advice 1621; **councelys** 2277.

conseyued *see* conceue.

consentyng *vbl. n.* giving consent 1085.

contenans, contynauns, contynawnse *n.* demeanour 909, 1650, 2163.

conteyne *v.* ~ *hym* restrain himself 146; **conteynyth** *pr. 3 pl.* contains 1173; **conteynyd** *pp.* 1979.

contynally *adv.* permanently 2481; **contynwaly** 1022.

continew, contynew *v.* continue 2667, 2716; **contynewyth** *pr. 3 sg.* 951; **contynwyde** *pa. 1 sg.* 1004; **conteynuyd** *pa. 3 sg.* 1882, **continewyde** 961, **contynewde** 228, **contynewid** 376; **contynued** *pa. pl.* 1568; **contynewde** *pp.* 950.

contradiccion *n.* opposition 1083.

contrary(e *adj.* adverse 131; *adv.* on the contrary 1044.

contrary(e)-wyse *adv.* on the contrary

1366; *euyn* ~ in just the opposite manner 1472.

contraryusnes *n.* opposition, antagonism 1803.

contyd *see* **cownte.**

contynauns, contynawnse *see* **contenans.**

conuenient *adj.* fitting, appropriate 2717.

conuersacion, conuersacyon *n.* manner of living, conduct, behaviour 443, 1648.

conuersion *n.* entry into monastic life 124.

coostys *n. pl.* regions 735, 2378.

corect, correcte *v.* correct, amend, punish 1155, 1364; **correcte** *pp.* 1549, set right 1610, reproved 1613.

correccyon *n.* correction (of faults in conduct) 1547; rebuke 1615; **correccions** *pl.* 1613.

corrupcion, corrupcyon *n.* moral contamination 2276*, 2870.

cossis *n. pl.* kisses 311.

coste *n. of myne owne* ~ at my own expense 1023.

cosyn *n.* kinsman, blood relation 1694; **cosynis** *pl.* kinsfolk 2583, 2589.

couent *n.* (monastic company of) monks 143.

couetyse *adj.* covetous, greedy 1544, 2034.

couetyse *n.* covetousness 2083.

coueytyd *pa. 3 sg.* coveted, strongly desired 1359; **koueyten** *pr. pl.* 1394; **coueytyng** *pr. p.* 1155.

councelys *see* **conselle.**

cowde *see* **can.**

cownte *pr. 1 sg.* ~ *hit lightly* hold it of little account 1114; **counted** *pa. 3 sg. ful lytyl* ~ *hyt* thought very little of it 1653; **countyd** considered 1467; **countid** *pl.* ~ *lyghtly* reckoned as not burdensome 657; **contyd** *pp.* counted 1751.

cowpuld(e *pa. t. 3 sg.* joined 2630; united (in marriage) 2586; adapted, adjusted 2838.

crafte *n.* craft, profession 1122*; skill 2068.

creye *n.* cry 813.

Cristen, Cristyn, Crysten, Crystin, Crystyn *adj.* Christian 13, 23, 316, 383, 2377.

Cristynmas, Crystenmas, Crystynmas *n.* Christmas 1030, 1040, 1056.

Crystendame, Crystyndome *n.* Christendom 1324, 1984.

cruelnes *n.* cruelty 1116.

cumbrid *pp.* ruined 1634.

cuppid *pp.* bled by means of a cupping glass 507.

curacion, curacyon *n.* healing 2961, 2973.

cure *n.* ecclesiastical position, spiritual responsibility 1950; those for whom one has spiritual responsibility 2287; (have) ~ of (souls) have (spiritual) responsibility for 1530, 1904; **curys** *pl.* cares 2166.

cursydnes *n.* sinfulness 1632.

custome *n. of an euyl* ~ by/because of a bad habit 1005.

cytson *n.* citizen 944; **cytsonnys** *pl.* 2734.

dammage *n.* harm 1169.

dampde *pp.* damned 986.

dampnably *adv.* damnably 1589.

dampnacion, dampnacyon *n.* damnation 833*, 1678.

dat *conj. whyle* ~ while [that] 1429.

dayly *adv.* daily 615.

de *def. art.* the 2319.

deceuabul *adj.* deceitful 2141.

declare *v.* make knowing, describe 942, 2090.

ded(e, dedde *adj.* dead 33, 194, 1318; ~ *and gonne* dead and gone 1424.

dede *n.* deed, action 803; **dedis, dedys** *pl.* 726, 2713.

dede-doyng *n.* performance 1144.

dedful *adj.* lifeless 1519 (*see Commentary*).

dedifyed *pp.* dedicated 466.

dedly *adj.* mortal 1752; ~ *synne(s* mortal sin(s 953, 1785; *adv.* heinously 1366; in a manner destructive to the soul 1920.

dedyr *adv.* thither 1264; *see* **hethur.**

defende *pp.* defended 1168.

defoule *v.* pollute, defile 1980.

defoyled *pp.* polluted, defiled 1329.

degreys *n. pl.* social positions, ranks 316.

dele *n. neuer a* ~ not at all 672.

dele *v.* distribute 2189.

delectable *adj.* delightful 2976.

delectacion *n.* ~ *of* pleasure in 1069; delight in 1910.

delyberacyon *n.[1] were putte in* ~ *. . . forto* with deliberation undertook to 1143.

delyberacyon *n.[2]* deliverance, liberation, salvation 1448.

delycately *adv.* in luxury 1838.

delyng *n.* apportioning 2241.

delyte *n.* delight 1876; **delytys** *pl.* pleasures 2102.

delyte *v.* delight, take pleasure 473; **delytyd** *pa. t. 3 sg.* delighted 2838; **delyted** took pleasure 1897; **delytyd . . . of** *pl.* delighted in 2038; **delytyd** (*refl.*) 2354.

delyuer(e)d *pa. t.* freed, rescued 60, 80; passed on 2242; **delyuerd** *pp.* freed 726; ~ *of* freed from 723; **delyueryd** 1053.

demenyd *pp.* disposed 2230.

demening, demenyng *vbl. n.* behaviour 430, 2299; demeanour 2757.

denys *n. pl.* deans 1981.

departyd *pa. t. 3 sg.* separated 2822; ~ *fro(m)* *pp.* separated from 268, 816, 1263, 2916.

departyng *vbl. n.* death 1157; ~ *of* departure from 1184.

deprauyd *pp.* perverted, corrupted 1328.

dere *adj.* dear 724.

derisions *n. pl.* mockery, ridicule 2128.

desceyued *pp.* deceived 1216.

deseruingys, deseruynges *vbl. n. pl. merytys and* ~ merits and deserts 675, 779.

desesid *ppl. adj.* diseased, tormented 1362.

desyre *pr. 2. sg. subj.* desire 998; **desyren** *pr. pl.* desire 1394; **desiring** *pr. p.* requesting 389; **desired** *pa. t. 1 sg.* asked, begged 540; **desired** (*of*) *pp.* earnestly requested (by) 41, 365.

desperacion, desperacyon *n.* despair, lack of faith or hope in God's mercy 865, 1923, 1931; ~ *of* despair concerning 837.

despexion *n.* contempt, scorn 1433; ~ *of* contempt for 1905.

despysen *pr. pl.* despise 2281.

destitute, destytute *adj.* forlorn 1066; ~ *of* deprived of 132, 623, 835, 2364.

destruccyon *n.* destruction 1392.

detracte *v.* disparage, slander 1555.

deuyl(le *n.* devil 820, 852; *pl.* **deuelys, deuyllys, deuyl(y)s** 61, 665, 842, 1066.

deuowter *adj. comp. (more)* ~ more devout 1199, *(more)* **deuowtur** 1044, 2637.

dew(e *adj.* due, fitting, proper 1532, 2717.

dewty *n. of* ~ as a matter of right 1638.

deye *v.* die 1422; **deyon** *pr. 3 pl.* 1670; **deyed** *pa. t. 1, 3 sg.* 1082, 1685; **deydyst, didest, dydest** *pa. t. 2 sg.* 991, 996, 1412; **deyde, deyed, dide, dyde,**

dyed *pa. t. 3 sg.* 66, 945, 1512, 1830, 1685; **dyde** *pa. t. pl.* 1141; **dyed** *pp.* 962.

differens *n.* difference 2973.

difficulte *n.* difficulty 2845.

digestyd *pp.* reduced and condensed into a systematic form *pa. t. pl.* 398.

dignite, dignyte, dygnyte *n.* high position or rank, honour 699, 1888, 1954; **dignitees** *pl.* 694.

Dirige n. Matins in the Office for the Dead 2393, 2414.

discerpte *pa. t. pl.* tore . . . to pieces 1106.

disceste, dysceste *pa. t. 3 sg.* died, deceased 1512, 2156; ~ *pp.* 1400, 1665.

disceyte *n.* deceit 1414, 2052.

dysceyued *pa. t. 1 sg.* deceived 1124; **dysceyuyd** *pp.* 2274.

dyscipil *n.* disciple 2758; **disciplys** *pl.* 380.

disciplyne *n.* penitential flogging 483; **disciplinis, disciplynys, discyplynis, dysciplynys, dyscyplynys** 52, 168, 477, 539, 561; *discyplynys of roddys* 224.

discyplyne *v.* beat, flog by way of penance 478; **discyplyned** *pp.* 534.

disese, dyssese *n.* discomfort, pain, suffering 308, 1809, 2353; **dissese** illness, disease 2643; **dyssesis** *pl.* 2645.

disesyth *pr. t. 3 sg.* vexes, distresses 1933; **disesyd** *pp.* disturbed 580; tormented 1120; **dyseasyd, dyssesyd, dissesid** troubled, afflicted 135, 2512, 2922; **dissesyd** *ppl. adj.* suffering from an illness 2569; **dyssesyd** suffering hardship 2639.

disfigurde *pp.* disfigured 2751.

dispensacion, *n. of a . . .* ~ *by a . . .* arrangement of events 1363; **dispensacyon** stewardship 2525.

dispose, dyspose *v.* arrange, ordain 1364; (*refl.*) be willing 1369; ~ *me* prepared myself 2894; ~ *imper. sg.* regulate 2899; **disposed, dysposed** *me* *pa. t. 1 sg.* behaved 1002; resolved, made up my mind 411; **disposyd, dysposyd** *pp., ppl. adj.* designed, arranged 2843; inclined 2187; *wele* ~ morally or kindly inclined 1719, 1730, 2157; *euyl* ~ ill willed, wickedly inclined 1556; *euyl(l)-* ~ 2265, 2278.

dissenteria *n.* dysentery 2653.

dyssymulacyon *n.* negligence, neglect 1911 (*see Commentary*).

dyssymylle *v.* disregard 2263; **dissymylyd** *pa. t. 3 sg.* concealed 395.

dissolucyon, dyssolucyon n. extravagance 2217; laxity, dissipation 1775,
1986.

distinccyon n. differentiation 775.

distrey, distroye, dystroye v. destroy
1963, 2255, 2289.

diuers, dyuers adj. various 80, 2023; many
~ tymys many different times 253.

diuersite, diuersyte, dyuersyte n. variety
58, 640, 708; diuersitees, diuersytees,
dyuersiteys, dyuersytees pl. 681, 682,
797, 1286.

dyuynyte n. theology 2495.

do n. doe 2129.

do(o v. perform 1427; ~ awey remove 876;
~ to his worschippe do in his honour
1018; doyth pr. t. 3 sg. does 2145; doth
pl. 271; pa. t. dede did 1237, 1675;
dydde 2101, 2596; ~ pp. done 1035,
2006; done of done by 566, 676, 712,
done according to 654; doon(e 149, 383.

doyng vbl. n. performance 1454.

doctour n. ~ a lawe authority on Canon
Law 74.

document n. precept 806.

dolour n. pain 832.

dome n. day of ~ Judgement Day 1444;
domys-daye 1408.

don(e adv. down 49, 217; doon(e 319, 488;
doun 191.

doute, dowte n. doubt 571, 1754.

dout(e)les, doutheles, dowtheles adv.
without doubt 434, 569, 609, 1183, 2825.

dowbulle adj. double 696.

dowte v. doubt 18; ~ (of) be uncertain
(about) 14; douted, dowtyd pa. t. pl. ~
(of) were uncertain (about) 200, 1922.

dowtefulle adj. uncertain 424.

drawe v. bring 283; drag 1083; ~ . . . to-
gedyr heal 2969; drewe pa. t. pl. tore . . .
apart 1106; drawyn pp. drawn 1012.

drede n.[1] fear 424.

drede n.[2] thread 2957.

drede v. fear 24; be feared 2524; ~ pr. 1
sg. 1583; ~ pa. t. 3 sg. 1086; dredde
1952; dred(de dreaded 210, 959.

dreme n. dream 1656.

dronken(n)es, dronkinnes, dronkyn-
nes(se n. drunkenness 954, 957, 960,
1059, 1096.

dronkyn ppl. adj. drunk 1183.

dround, drownd(e pp. drowned 760,
1885, 2080.

duke n. leader, guide 2791, 2917.

dullyd pp. stunned 852; dimmed 2836.

dyffamyd pp. slandered 1616.

dyfferde pa. t. 3 sg. deferred 1214.

dysceyued pa. t. sg. deceived 1124; dysceyuyd by pp. deceived on account of
[their] 2274.

dyspensours n. pl. those in charge of the
administration or distribution of goods
and services 2213.

ede pa. t. pl. went 185.

edifie v. edify, spiritually strengthen 1966.

edifiyng vbl. n. edification, spiritual
improvement 390.

elacyon n. arrogance, vainglory 1795.

ellys adv. else 713; els 675; adj. as n. 174.

emplastur n. medical salvelike preparation, plaster 2967; emplasters pl. 232.

enarrabulle adj. indescribable 976.

encrese v. increase 2481; encresythe pr. 3
sg. 838; encresyn pr. pl. 1391; encresyng pr. p. 1591; vbl. n. 1584; encresyd
pp. 1579.

enfecte see infecte.

enformid pa. t. 3 sg. informed 2713;
enfourmed pp. 678.

enmy, ennemy n. enemy 714, 812;
enmyes pl. 317.

enquyre v. investigate 2590; enquyryng
pr. p. questioning 1204; pa. t. sg.
enquered therof asked about it 1999.

ensonge n. evensong 2438.

entent n. purpose, intention 2255.

entryd pa. t. sg. ~ into relygyon entered
the religious life 2683.

entysyd pp. enticed 2277.

enuyus adj. envious 2034.

equite, equyte n. justice, equity 1738,
1742.

ere conj. before 938; зere 2228; yere 1185.

erryn pr. pl. err, sin, go astray morally
2882.

erthe n. yn ~ in the world 2465.

erthely adj. earthly, material 1375; worldly
2299.

eschewe v. avoid 1164; eschue shun 2161.

especyalle adv. phr. in ~ especially 1505.

estymacyon n. apprehension, comprehension 707, 1272.

esy adj. moderate 2049; зesy 2041; зesyor
comp. more bearable 784; more esyur
660; more esuer 1575.

esyd *pa. t. sg.* relieved 2389; ~ *pp.* eased, soothed 2146.

ete *v.* eat 41.

eting, etyng *vbl. n.* eating 1771, 2490.

euangeliste, euangelyste *n.* evangelist 2099, 2759; euangelystys *pl.* 2673.

euer *adv.* always 1252.

euerichon, euerych(e-on *pron.* every one 1344, 1853, 1907, 2790.

euerlasting *adv.* for ever, throughout eternity 1569.

euermore *adv.* always, at all times 407; forever 2988.

euetyde *n.* evening 627.

euydentely *adv.* conclusively 2944.

euyl(l *n.* ill 1555; suffering 1902; evil, wrong-doing 956, 1452, 2250; euyllys *pl.* sufferings 723.

euyll(e, euyl *adj.* evil, wicked 278, 829, 1381; harmful 2083. *See also* custome, dispose.

euylle *adv.* wickedly 1090.

euyn *adv. see* contrarye-wyse.

euyn *n.* evening 365. *See also* Estur.

euyn-heyre *n.* joint heir 2693.

euynworthy* *adj.* suitable, comparable 878.

exaltyd *pp.* raised 1348.

example *n.* punishment (as a deterrent or warning to others) 692, 1476; by ~ by (following his) example 1227; exampulle model (of vice) 1674; examples *pl.* signs, indications 2943.

examynde *pp.* examined 2607.

excedeth *pr. 3 sg.* ~ *of* exceeds in 1246.

excepte *ppl. adj.* exempted 1474.

excludyd *pp.* eliminated 23; removed 2923.

exempte *ppl. adj.* removed from liability to 2623.

exercyse *v.* ~ *vs* devote ourselves 721.

extende *v.* exalt 2101.

faculte *n.* (university) faculty, branch of learning 1356; *pl.* facultees 2496.

fader, fadyr *n.* father 70, 621; faders *pl.* 2223; the Church Fathers 2279.

fadyrly *adj.* fatherly 409.

faites *n. pl.* acts 1381.

falle *pr. t. pl.* ~ *done fro* abandon 2275; fyl, fylle *pa. t.* fell 29, 124, 1318; fille *fro* departed from 1899; fal, falle, *fro*

fallyn *pp.* fallen 171, 251, 1943; sunken 191, 2954.

fallyng *vbl. n.* occurrence 1170.

fame *n.* report 967.

famylyar *adj.* household 1026.

famyliarly, famylyarly *adv.* intimately, closely 331, 338.

farthir, farthyr *adj.* ~ *syde* far side 744, 913.

farthir *adv.* further 659.

fauer *n.* charm, attractiveness 2162; fauyr esteem 1541.

fauerth *pr. 3 sg.* favours 443; faueryd, fauyrde *pa. t. 1 sg.* 1553, 1621; fauerd *pa. t. pl.* 1920.

fauyr *see* fauer.

fawte *n.* fault 2609; fautes, fautys, fawtes, fawtys *pl.* 81, 1155, 1757, 2166.

fawtye *adj.* faulty, guilty 2591.

fayling *vbl. n.* hardship 673.

fayne *adv.* gladly 995.

fayre, feire, feyre *adj.* morally good 803; splendid 1416; beautiful 1650, 2544; *more* feyrer *comp.* 1705; *mooste* feyryste *superl.* 860.

feblyd *pp.* weakened 135.

febul(l *adj.* feeble, weak 2174, 2651.

febulnes(se *n.* feebleness, weakness 126, 170; deficiency 1803.

fede *pr. t. pl.* feed 2289; fedde *pp.* 2648.

fegure *see* figure.

feyerness *n.* beauty 1712.

feyghtyng *n. worldys* ~ struggles against evil in the world 2886.

feire, feyre *adj. see* fayre.

feyre *adv.* beautifully 2433.

feytfully *adv.* faithfully 882.

feyth(e)ful(e *adj.* faithful 123, 1926, 2391; feythfullir *comp.* 1198.

feithe, feythe *n.* faith 2723, 2825.

felawe, felow(e *n.* companion 451, 622, 2822; felawys *pl.* colleagues 2496.

feleschippe, feleshyppe, felishyppe, felysschippe, felysshyppe *n.* fellowship, company 1010, 1255, 1258, 1839, 2901.

felows *adj. pl.* ~ *virgyns* fellow virgins 891.

fenne *n.* filth 1881.

fer, ferre *adv.* far 1605, 2717.

fere *n.* fear 737.

feriis *n. pl. sexte* ~ Fridays 453.

fermorie, fermorye *n.* (monastic) infirmary 138, 142, 294.

ferre *adj.* far, remote 1865.
ferther *adv. the* ~ ... *the* ... the farther
... the ... 669.
feruent *adj.* hot 1183; ardent 2251.
feryd *pp.* feared 210.
feste *n.* feast-day 136.
fesyke *n.* medical treatment 129.
feturs *n. pl.* fetters 2061.
fewnes *n.* small number 2262.
fier(e *n.* fire 664, 761.
figure, fygure, fegure *n.* image 34, 204,
212; likeness 382.
filde, fylde *n.* field 641, 1262.
fille *see* **falle**.
fynde *v.* find 414; **fonde** *pa. t. 1 sg.* 1866;
fownde provided, paid for 1022; **fonde,
fondyn** *pp.* found 35, 220.
fyndis, fyndys *n. pl.* fiends 2063, 2127.
fyry(e *adj.* fiery 684, 690.
flayne *pp.* flayed 713.
flat(e)ring, flatryng *vbl. n.* flattering,
flattery 1905, 2141, 2573.
fleyn *pr. pl.* flee 2291; **flyd** *pp.* fled 1581.
fleyn *pr. pl.* fly 1806; **fleyd** *pa. t. pl.* flew
912; **flowe** 1847.
flockemel(e *adv.* in groups 643, 2806.
floure *n.* flower 2629.
flowryd *pa. t. pl.* flourished 694, 2279.
flowrys *n. pl.* floors 1271.
fole *n.* fool 1150.
folow(e *v.* follow 1548, 2661; **foloweth(e,
folowth, folowyth** 2, 11, 403, 928;
folo(w)yn *pr. pl.* 209, 2357; **folo(w)ing,
folo(w)yng** *pr. p.* 176, 181, 1071, 1681;
foloude, folowd(e, folowyde *pa. t. sg.*
54, 618, 814, 2791.
folowing *n.* imitation 2286.
folusnesse *n.* foolishness 1393.
fonde, fondyn *see* **fynde**.
for *prep.* because of 115; on account of 658;
what ~ ... *and* both because of ... and
because of 147, 832; **fore** for 1618; ~
conj. ~ *by-cause* because 2150; ~ *as
moche that* adv. phrase to such a degree
that 2345.
fornece, fornes *n.* furnace 762, 1733.
forsake *pp.* abandoned 2067.
forswerers *n. pl.* perjurers 2034.
forto *inf. particle* to 774.
foughtyn *pp.* fought 2774.
fraudys *n. pl.* dishonest acts 2267.
frawardnes *n.* contrariness 2271.
frayter *n.* refectory 2647.

frende, frynde *n.* friend 985, 1665; **frendys** *pl.* 318.
fresch *adv.* freshly 215; **fresche** recently
2749.
fro *prep.* from 61.
froryn *pp.* frozen 1880.
froward *adj.* disobedient 1617.
frowardly *adv.* pervertedly 1481.
frute *n.* benefit 1611; **frutys** *pl.* 1771.
frynde *see* **frende**.
fugytyuys, fygytyuys *n. pl.* those who
abandon the monastic life 91, 2084.
fulfille, fulfylle *v.* carry out, complete,
accomplish 774, 1033; *subj.* 1739, 2231;
fulfilde *pa. t. sg.* 1068; **fulfylled** 2191;
fulfylled, fulfyllede *pp.* 843, 1445;
fulfeldyn 1735; **fulfylde** filled 1271.
ful(l *adv.* very 194, 744.
fullyor *adv. comp. more* ~ more fully 348;
fullyur 2183.

gast(e)ful, gastfull(e *adj.* terrifying 634,
909, 2075, 2122.
gastfulnesse *n.* dread 1257.
gat(t)e *pa. t. sg.* procured 1537; *(refl.)*
acquired, obtained 1122, 1357; **gotyn**
pp. 2329, earned 1994.
gedur *v.* bring together, compile 704;
gedirde *pp.* amassed 2142; **gedyrd(e**
gathered 1298, 2378.
generalyte *n. vnder a certen* ~ in general
terms 1855.
gestur *n.* bearing, manner, gesture 976,
1767, 1775.
geue *v.* give 168; **gaue** *pa. t. 1 sg. (refl.)*
yielded 1019; **geuyn** *pp.* 2117. *See also*
3eue.
gladlyur *adv. more* ~ more gladly 933.
gladsum *adj.* joyful, happy 2243.
glotyners *n. pl.* gluttons 2034.
gnawyn *pp.* gnawed 688.
go *v.* ~ *ageyne* return 2886.
God-ward *prep. phrase to* ~ towards God
1200.
godys *see* **goodys**.
goyng *vbl. n.* progress 672.
goyth *pr. 3 sg.* leads 1654; **gone oute of
kynde** *pr. pl.* deviate from what is natural, decline 1736; **gon** *pa. t. 3 sg.* (+ *inf.*)
began 402.
gon(e *see* **goyth**.
goodys *n. pl.* wealth 846; **godys** goods
1375.

Go(o)ste *n. Holy* ~ Holy Spirit 314, 2495.

goostly, gostely *adj.* spiritual 390, 1034.

gotyn *see* gat(t)e.

gratulacyon *n.* (shared) rejoicing, exaltation 2766.

grefe *n.* suffering 658.

grete *pa. t. sg.* greeted 1521, 2679.

gret(e)ly *adv.* greatly 23, 127.

greter *adj. comp. more* ~ greater 2704; **grettur** 781; *adv. comp. more* **grettur, grettyr** more abundantly (of weeping) 279, 303.

greuossor *adv. comp. more* ~ more grievous 1681.

greuys *adj.* grievous, severe 29.

greuysly *adv.* gravely, seriously 1677; violently 1780; severely 2059; bitterly 2150.

greuyth *pr. t. 3 sg.* causes sorrow 1535; **greuyd** *pp.* pained, injured 700.

grice *n.* step (of a stairway) 2457; **gricis, grycis** *pl.* 598, 2842.

growyn *pr. pl.* grow, increase 1392.

gruggyng *n.* resentment, grumbling 2608.

gyde *n.* guide 1200.

gyuyd* *pp.* shackled 2061.

habet(te *n.* robe of a monk 1889, 2255.

haburgyn *n.* coat of mail 2114.

halowed *pa. t. pl.* honoured 2747; **halowd** *pp.* consecrated 466.

hangyn *see* hynge.

haply *adv.* perhaps 1549.

happe *n.* unforeseen experience 206; occurrence 967.

happonde *pa. t. 3 sg.* happened 2441.

happyd *pa. t. 3 sg.* happened 207.

hard(e *pa. t. sg.* heard 811, 2918; ~ *pp.* 1209.

harde *adj.* difficult, troublesome 2166; *more* **harder** *comp.* more severe 787; more callous, more strict 2517.

harder *adv. more* ~ more intensely 1126.

hardenes(se *n.* obduracy 1384, 1734; niggardliness 2408; difficulty 2861.

harm(e)les *adj.* unharmed 1176; not liable to punishment 2052.

harmys *n. pl.* arms 2075, 2350.

harnes *n.* armour 2115.

harte *n.* hart 2129. *See also* herte.

hast(e)ly *adv.* suddenly 944, 2155.

hastid, hastyd *pa. t. 3 sg.* (*refl.*) hastened, went speedily 1654, 2235; ~ *pa. pl.* 662.

hastynes *n.* anger 2265.

hatfull *adj.* repugnant 1303; **hateful** malignant 2035.

haue *v.* ~ . . . *out of* displace . . . from 1550; **haue** *pr. pl.* regard 985; **hadyste** *pa. t. 2 sg.* had 992; **had(de** *pa. t. sg. subj.* would have 713 (1), 1048; **had** *pa. pl.* took, brought 202; **had** *pp.* held to be 1355; **hade** *pp.* taken 1104.

hauke *n.* hawk 1843; **haukys** *pl.* 1847.

haukyng *n.* hawking 1845.

hed(d, hed(d)e, heed, heedde *n.* head 170, 192, 198, 270, 319, 553; **hedys** *pl.* leaders 1970.

hede *n.* heed, (+ take) pay attention to 1949.

hedir-to *see* hetherto.

hedlong(e *adv.* head foremost 765, 2120.

hedyr *adv.* hither 299.

heere *n.* hair 553.

heiers *n. pl.* heirs 2140.

helme *n.* helmet 2114.

helpe *pp.* helped 1443; **holpe(n, holpyn** 675, 782, 1992.

helping, helpyng *vbl. n.* spiritual aid 727; assistance, relief 1637; **helpinges** *pl.* 650.

helpys *n. pl.* alms 780.

helthe *n.* spiritual well-being 1173.

hem *pron.* them 10; themselves 142; her, here *poss.* their 16, 88.

hemself(e *pron. pl.* themselves 662, 2086.

hens *adv.* hence 1743.

hens-forth *adv.* henceforth 431.

hepe *n.* heap 1127; **hepys** *pl.* 1299.

here *v.* hear 153; **herith** *pr. pl.* 24; **heryng** *pr. p.* 819; **herd(e, hard(e** *pa. t.* 112, 211, 811, 2918; **harde, herd(e** *pp.* 1148, 1209, 1349.

herns *see* herre *pron.*

herre *n.* (garment of) hair cloth 2159.

herre *pron.* her 2758; *of* **herns** *poss.* of hers 1662.

herte, harte *n.* heart 157, 1092; **hertys** *pl.* 1178.

hertely *adv.* heartily, devoutly 871.

hete *n.* heat 1132.

hetherto, hethir-to *adv.* hitherto, until now 569, 1130; **hedir-to** 278.

hethur *adv.* ~ *and thedur* hither and thither 912; **hethyr** *and dedyr* 2855.

hethyn *adj.* heathen 1310.

heuely *adv.* severely 843; intensely 1912.

heuene, heuin, heuyn *n.* heaven 751, 871, 2180; heuyns *pl.* 2857.

heuenly, heuynly *adj.* heavenly 144, 2357.

heuy *adj.* sorrowful, sad 731.

heuynes(se *n.* sorrow 802, 830.

heuyn-ward(e *adv. to* ~ towards heaven 646, 2884.

hey *see* hy(e.

hyenesse *n.* excellence 323.

heyth(e *n.* height 553, 2802.

hye, hey *adj.* high 741, 2862; *an* hy(e *adv. phr.* aloft 761, 2809; above 850.

hier *adv. comp.* higher 2846.

hild, hylde *see* holde.

hille, hylle *n.* hill 741, 1741; hyllys *pl.* 1269.

hym *pron.* (*refl.*) himself 30.

hynge *pa. t. sg.* hung 2435; hangyn *pp.* hanged 691.

hirte *n.* hurt 1338; hirtys *pl.* hurts, losses 2278 (*see Commentary*).

hit, hyt *pron.* it 11, 158; hym (2) *obj.* it 2113.

ho(o *pron.* who 822, 2037, how 2104; hois, hoys *poss.* whose 187, 1519, (of inanimate thing) 2802; home *obj.* whom 1488, 1650; see also whois.

ho-sum-euer *pron.* whoever 1961.

hokys *n. pl.* hooks 691.

holde *v.* hold 2350; hild, hylde *pa. t.* 518, 555; holde *pp.* kept in a certain state 339; holdyn 782.

hole, hoolle *adj.* whole 2962; healthy, sound 573, 873.

holpe(n, holpyn *see* helpe.

holsum *adj.* spiritually beneficial 472; holsummur *comp. more* ~ 1393.

holy *adv.* wholly 155, 1095.

home *see* ho(o.

hooly *adj.* holy 168; holyur *comp. more* ~ more holy 1043.

hondred *n.* hundred 2851.

hondyrdfolde *n.* hundred 1287.

honest *adj.* decent, virtuous 1405; beautiful 1703.

honeste *n.* virtue 1604; purity, decorum 1784; decency, moral integrity 1967.

honorabulle *adj.* honourable 1436.

hoote *adj.* hot 1770.

hopynne *adj.* open 512.

hordende *see* orden.

hor(r)able, horabul(l)e, horrabul, horrabull(e) *adj.* horrible 657, 686, 747, 757, 981, 1101, 2075.

horrabulnes *n.* dreadfulness 1249.

hospitalle *n.* hospice 1996.

hospytalte *n.* hospitality 1730.

hosylde *pp. be* ~ receive Communion 1041.

how *see* ho(o.

how(e)-be-(h)yt, (-hit, -it) *adv.* nevertheless 736, 785; ~ *that* albeit, although 172, 1113, 1528, 1972, 2053, 2448.

howr(e *n.* hour, time 369, 2669; howris *pl.* 2956.

humour *n.* liquid 246.

hungery *adj.* hungry 2193.

ydelnes *n.* vain pursuits 1561.

idyle, ydyl *adj.* foolish 1481, 1763.

ydylly *adv.* uselessly 2140.

ye *n.* eye 846; yes *n. pl.* 191, 246, 266; *my* nyes mine eyes 502.

ye-lyddys *n. pl.* eyelids 244.

ymage *n.* image 468; ymages, ymagys *pl.* 2430, 2439.

ymagynacyon *n.* imagination, power of forming mental images 1659.

inclyned, inclynde *pa. t. sg.* bowed 319, 488; inclynyd *pp.* inclined 1635.

yncomparable *adv.* incomparably 2625.

incredibulle *adj.* incredible, supreme 543.

indycyble, indycybylle *adj.* unspeakable 748, 1628.

inenarrabulle *adj.* inexpressible 637.

inestymable, ynestymable *adj.* inestimable, too profound or intense to be estimated 543, 858, 2796.

ynestymably *adv.* inestimably 2837.

inextynguyble *adj.* inextinguishable 1572.

infecte, enfecte *pp.* infected 1633, 2344.

infenyte *adj.* infinite 635.

infirmyte, infyrmyte *n.* sickness 171; weakness 2947.

infydelite, infydelyte *n.* lack of faith 21, 2947.

iniurye *n.* detriment 1060; dishonour 1976; iniuriis *pl.* injustices 712; harm, injuries 2770.

inmoderate *adj.* excessive 172, 1763.

inmoderately *adv.* excessively 159.

inmortalite *n.* immortality 2866.

inmortalle, ynmortalle *adj.* immortal 905, 2779.

innocentnes *n.* innocency 1737.

innumerabulle, inumerable *adj.* innumerable 314, 1990.

inordenatly *adv.* excessively 1554.

ynow *adv.* enough 361.

inpacyently *adv.* impatiently 1723.

inpenytente *adj.* impenitent 1385.

inperfeccyon *n.* imperfection 1727.

inportable *adj.* unbearable 1116.

ynportune *adj.* grievous 894.

inportunyte *n.* importunity, insistence 1010.

inpossible *adj.* impossible 281.

insensybulle *adj.* devoid of sensation 200.

insta(u)ns *n.* request 339, 2932; *with grete* ~, **instaunce** very vehemently, persistently 394, 1224.

instruccyons *n. pl.* instructive examples 2943.

instrumentys *n. pl.* implements 821.

intemperans *n.* severity 2513.

intendyng *pr. p.* turning his thoughts to, fixing (his) mind on 2656.

intercessours *n. pl.* mediators 2300.

intollerabul *adj.* unbearable 2109.

intytylde *pa. t. sg.* named 1996.

inuyncyble *adj.* insuperable 1726.

inuoluyd *pa. t. sg.* enveloped 664; ~ *pp.* 1652.

inward(e *adj.* earnest 326; ~ *bowel(l)ys* guts 823, 1133.

ynward *adv. more* ~ farther in 2727.

ynward(e)ly *adv.* inwardly 829, 2603.

yrne *n.* iron 2966 (cf. **3irne**).

is, ys *poss. pron. following (proper) n.* his 139, 187.

iangelyng *vbl. n.* chattering 1485.

iangyl *v.* chatter 1481.

iapyng *vbl. n.* joking 2492.

iapys *n. pl.* jokes 1560.

iocunde, yocunde *adj.* cheerful 2534, 2548.

iocundnes *n.* jocundity, cheerfulness 1501, 2163.

ioyde *pa. t. 3 sg.* offered honour or salutation 976.

ioy(e *n.* joy 109, 856; **ioyes, ioys, iowys** *pl.* 6, 1501, 1722.

ioyful(l *adj.* joyful 373, 543.

ioifully, ioyfully, yoyfully *adv.* joyfully 922, 980, 2534.

yoynde see **ioynyng**.

ioyin *pr. t. pl.* rejoice 2858; **ioyng** *pr. p.* 2757; **ioyde** *pa. t. sg.* expressed joy 976.

ioyntys *n. pl.* joints 685.

ioynyng *pr. p.* joining 271; **yoynde** *pa. 3 sg.* 2379; **ioynyd** *pp.* 2710.

iourney, iornay, iorney, yourney *n.* journey 1654, 1805, 2040, 2381.

iuge *n.* judge 897; **iugys** *pl.* 701.

iugement(e, iuggement *n.* judgement 1387, 1754, 2297.

iugit *pp.* judged, condemned 2042.

iuscys* *n. pl.* juices, medicinal potions 229.

karyd *pa. t. sg.* took care 1375.

kendler *n.* kindler, instigator 1048.

kepe *v.* ~ *forthe* maintain 2481; **kepyth** *pr. 3 sg.* keeps, preserves 1738; **keped** *pa. t. sg.* 2629*.

kepers *n. pl.* those with personal responsibility for the care of another 203.

kepyng *vbl. n.* ~ *of ... relygyon* adherence to prescribed religious practice 2488; taking care 2287.

keuerd, keueryde *pp.* covered 840, 1266.

kinde *n. the law of* ~ natural moral law 2130; **kynde** natural desires 1328; *see* **goyth**.

kynnefolke, kynnys-folke *n.* kinsfolk 1906, 2207.

kynred *n.* family, kindred 2210.

kyssyngys *n. pl.* acts of kissing 2675.

kneys *n. pl.* knees 273.

knyhht *n.* knight 1821.

knockyng *vbl. n.* being beaten 1779.

knowe *pr. 2 sg. subj.* know 974; **knowyst** *pr. 2 sg.* 441; **knowyth** *pr. 3 sg.* 898; **know** *pa. t. 3 sg.* 63; **know(e** *pp.* 576, 962; **knowen, knowyn** 195, 1153.

knowlege, knoulege, knoweleg, knowleche *n.* knowledge 798, 1259, 1353, 2019.

knowlege, knouleche *pr. 1 sg.* declare 1247; **knowleged** *pa. t. 3 sg.* acknowledged 1209.

koueyten see **coueytyd**.

laborus *adj.* painful 1650.

labur, labore *n.* hand work 1475, 1947; *dyd grete* ~ took great pains 1602; hardship 2002.

labur(e *v.* strive 721, 1389; ~ *pr. 1 sg.* journey painfully 1802; **laborde** *pa. t. sg.* suffered 1991; **laborid, labouryd** *pp.* afflicted, overwhelmed 126, 406.

ladde *pp.* led 4.

ladyd *pa. t. sg.* weighed down 2113.

layde *pa. t. 1 sg. refl.* ~ *my* lay 1078; **leide** *ouer with pp.* surmounted by 2805.

lappe *n.* lap 2350; **lappys** *pl.* 2431.

largely *adv.* fully 19; abundantly, copiously 1358, 2754; generously 2222; greatly 1584; widely 1747.

last(e *adj.* ~ *ende* death 1004, 1046; *quasi-n. at the* ~, *atte* ~ in the end 202, 245.

laste *adv.* finally 2956.

late *adv.* lately 816, 873, 931.

laudable *adj.* praiseworthy 442.

laude, lawde *n.* praise 2307, 2482; **laudes, laudys** *pl.* 143, 2795.

laudyng *vbl. n.* praising 146.

leche *n.* healer, *heuynly* ~ Christ 1376; *of lechis pl.* by doctors 2968.

leche-crafte *n.* medical care 129.

led(d)e *n.* lead (metal) 687, 1441.

lede *pr. pl.* spend 845; **ledyng** *pr. p.* leading 815.

leder *n.* leader, guide 54.

leding *vbl. n.* ~ *of hande* leading by the hand 621.

lefte *pa. t. 1 sg.* omitted 1018.

lefte *ppl. adj.* remaining 796.

leful *adj.* permitted, allowed 1561.

lefully *adv.* properly, rightfully 2448.

leide *see* **layde.**

lenger, lengur *adv. comp.* longer 360, 767.

lenthe *n.* length 746.

lepur *n.* leprosy 2345.

lepurs *n. pl.* lepers 97.

lese *pr. 1 sg.* lose 263; **lesyth** *pr. 3 sg.* 953; **lesyn** *pr. pl.* cause to be lost (spiritually), damn 2291.

lessid, lessyd *pp.* lessened, alleviated 660, 1918; diminished 795.

lessur *adj. comp.* less intense 669, 1809.

lest(e *adj. superl.* least 156, 1762.

lest(e *conj.* lest 581; ~ *that* 1215.

lette, lettyn *pp.* let 763, 2810.

lettyd *pa. t.* hindered, prevented (from happening) 1614, 2251; *pa. t. pl.* prevented, impeded 798; *pp.* hindered 675, 1804.

lettynges *n.¹ pl.* hindrances 598.

lettyngys *n.² pl.* ~ *done* (actions of) letting (the cross) down 2815.

leue *v.¹* leave off, desist from (vices, sin) 1007, 2714; leave 1546; ~ *out* omit 2786;

~ *pr. 1 sg.* 1514; ~ *pr. pl.* leave aside 283; **leuyng** *pr. p.* leaving 913.

leue *v.²* live 360; **leuyn** *pr. pl.* 1238; **leuyd, lyued, lyuyd** *pa. t. sg. and pl.* 10, 100, 799, 1088; **leuid** *pp.* 1939.

leuefulle *adj.* permissible 2297.

leuing, leuyng(e), lyuyng *vbl. n.* manner of living, behaviour 16, 720, 1002, 1380.

lewde *adj.* idle, worthless 1559, 1778.

lewdnesse *n.* silliness 1560.

leyde *pa. t. pl.* inflicted 817; ~ *pp.* placed, laid 1299, 2968.

leyser *n. bi* ~ without haste 346.

lyberale *adj.* generous 2522; **lyberals** *facultees pl.* faculties of the (seven) liberal arts 2495.

lyberally *adv.* generously 1711, 1829.

lyers *n. pl.* liars 2033.

lift *pa. t. sg.* lifted 502; **lyfte** 270, 911; **lyftyd** *pa. t. pl.* 904; **lyfte** *pp.* 2808; raised (of voices) 1348.

lyfte *adj.* left 2963.

lyftyng *vbl. n.* lifting 2813; **lyftyngys** *pl.* 2815.

light, lyght(e *adj.* light-hearted 387; frivolous, foolish 1485, 1766, 2489; venial 1749; trivial 2570; easy to bear 1574; **lyghtys** *superl.* easiest to bear 707.

lyght *adv.* readily 1765; **lyghter** *comp.* more easily 412.

lyghted *pp.* lit 2436.

light(e)ly, lyght(e)ly *adv.* quickly 479, 2760; easily 743, 971, 2736; *see* **cownte.**

lightnes(se, lyghtnes *n.* gladness 585; fickleness 1558; frivolousness 1551; leniency 1562.

lyghtnyd *pa. t. pl.* illuminated 2440.

lyghtynde *pp.* lit 2479.

like *adj.* similar 928.

like, lyke *adv. forming compound conj.* ~ *as* just as 15, 2029; just as if 269, 5889.

likenesse *n.* similarity 644; **liknes** likeness 573, 608; **lykenesse** appearance 1311; **lykenes** the bodily form 2850.

lykyth *pr. 3 sg. impers.* hit ~ *me* it pleases me 803; pleases 2297.

lymmys *n. pl.* limbs 1781.

lyste *pr. pl.* wish, choose 942.

lyth(e *pr. 3 sg.* lies, is situated 597, 1886.

litil(l, lityl(l, lytil(l, lytyl(l *adj., adv.* little 128, 177, 196, 199, 235, 244; *a lytyll and a lytill adv. phrase* gradually 257.

lyuys *adj.* living 235.

lodisman *n.* leader, guide 2791.

loke *pr. pl.* ~ *ther-aftur* seek them out 2294.

lo(o, loe *interj.* lo! 298, 1150, 1458.

long(e *adj. in adv. phr.* ~ *tyme* for a long time 196, 782.

longeth *pr. 3 sg. yt* ~ *to* it is fitting for/ required by 1921; **longyth** *to pr. pl.* are appropriate for 1908; **longyng** *to pr. p.* pertaining to 2413; belonging to 2594; **longed** *to pa. t. pl.* were necessary for 2580.

lothyd *pa. t. pl.* loathed 2348.

louers *n. pl.* those who love 725.

lowsyd *pa. t. 1 sg.* loosened 1546; ~ *pp.* freed 1052.

lowsing *vbl. n.* rendering loose in the socket 685.

luste *n.* pleasure 1009; enjoyment 2285; **lustys** *pl.* passions, desires 850, 1548.

madeness *n.* madness 1394.

mageste *n.* majesty 1623.

magnifyde, magnyfyde *pa. t. sg.* exalted, promoted 1622; ~ glorified 2101.

makyn *pr. pl.* make 2767; **made** *pa. t.* (causal) ~ *to be called* had summoned 152; ~ . . . *to be blowyn* had . . . blown 238.

maner(e *n.* kind 910; *no* ~ . . . no kind of . . . whatever 1206, 1264; *in* ~ *of* in the likeness of 246; **maners** *pl.* behaviour, conduct 1513, 1842. *al(l)e* ~ *(of) see* al(l)e; ~ *of wise see* wise.

mannis, mannys *n. gen. sg.* man's 22, 79; **mennys** *gen. pl.* 1480.

marke *n.*[1] boundary 1294.

marke *n.*[2] *pl.* marks 2372 (1 mark = 13s 4d, or 2/3 of a pound sterling, hence 27 marks = £18).

markid *pp.* assigned 1893.

matens *n. pl.* matins, morning prayers 178.

maw(e *n.* belly, abdominal cavity 823, 2122.

mawncypylle *n.* manciple, one who purchases provisions for an institution 1026.

may(e *see* **can.**

mayme *v.* maim 2132.

me *pron. refl.* myself 411, 455; **my** 1078; **my** *obj.* me 1205, 2337, **my** *thoughte* it seemed to me 1339; **myn(e** *poss.* (followed by (semi-)vowel or *h*-) 516, 872,

2920; (followed by consonant) 865, 1046, 1184.

mede *n.* reward 1611; *in* ~ as a blessing 655.

medelyng *n.* mixture, blend 2911.

medeson, medicyn, medsyn *n.* medicine 1379, 1772, 2967.

medy *adj.* medium 553.

medylle *v.* ~ *with* have sexual relations with 1314; **medylde, medild** *pp.* mixed 1267, 1518.

meke *adj.* gentle, humble, meek 339, 402.

mekely *adv.* humbly 469.

mekenes *n.* humility 2630, 2771.

mekil, mekyl(l)(e *adv.* much, greatly 282, 698, 1250, 1583.

mekyl(l *adj.* much 193, 919, 1609.

mekyl(l)(e *n. as* ~ *as* as much as 155, 1351, 1802.

membre *n.* member, limb 191, 1279.

mencion, mencyon, mension *n. (make)* ~ (*to*) mention, report 351, 728, 857.

mene *adj.* moderate 2382, 2497.

mene *n.* means 1443, 1469.

mene while, mene whyle *n. the* ~ in the mean while 205, 332, 502, 979.

men-sleers* *n. pl.* murderers, homicides 2033.

merceis, mercijs *n. pl.* mercies 148, 1093.

merite *n.* excellence, worthiness 935; **meritys, merytys** merits, deserts 674, 1892, 2573.

meruail(o)us, meruaylous, merueles, meruel(o)us *adj.* wonderful, marvelous, miraculous 118, 173, 318, 393, 1619, 2915.

meruaylously, meruelusly *adv.* astonishingly, wonderfully 237, 2837.

meruel(le *n.* ~ *of* astonishment at 2767; *no* ~ no wonder 1483, 2468.

meruel *v.* marvel, wonder (at); ~ *on* be filled with wonder at 2778; **meruelyng** *pr. p.* 809; **meruelde, merueled, meruelyd(e, merueylde, merueyled** (*of*) *pa. t.* 189, 205, 970, 1404, 1833, 2246, 2581; **merueld, merueylyde** *pp.* 1836, 2962.

merueling *vbl. n.* marveling 373.

merytorye *adj.* deserving of spiritual reward, meritorious 1658.

messis, messys *n. pl.* masses (Eucharistic services) 382, 2396.

mesure *n.* quantity 648, 1011; size 793; (*exceed*) ~ exceed the bounds of propriety

or moderation 145, (are) excessive 717;
oute/owt of ~ excessive 1544, (*adv.*) 1142.

mete *n.* food 127; *at* ~ at table 1485;
metys *pl.* foods 2217; *fles(s)che* ~ meat
2650.

mette *pa. t.* ~ *with* met 476, 665.

meuyng *vbl. n.* movement 2957.

meyny *n.* household 1180.

my *see* me.

myddys *n.* midst, middle 770, 2743, 2808.

might, myght *n.* might, power, strength
929, 1619; **myghtys** *pl.* 137.

might, myght(e, myhht *pa. t.* might 165,
195, 207, 1674.

mighty, myghty *adj.* powerful, great 814,
2140; keen, strong 1067.

mightily, myghtyly *adv.* powerfully
1111; severely 1464.

minystrys, mynystrys *n. pl.* servants,
agents 852, 1597.

myry *adj.* muddy 634.

mysdedys *n. pl.* misdeeds 1391, 2050.

myserable, myserabul(le *adj.* miserable,
wretched 673, 1331, 2276.

myserably, myserabully *adv.* miserably,
wretchedly 863, 1769.

mysgouernaunce *n.* misconduct, wrong-
doing 1529.

mystruste *v.* ~ *of* lack faith in 14.

mo *adj.* more 1343; *as n.* more 791.

moche *adv.* greatly 1210.

moche *n.* much 1213; *for as* ~ *that* to such
an extent that 2345.

mocyon *n.* motion, movement 190; impulse,
prompting 2572; **mocions** *of pl.* inclina-
tions to 21.

mockyng *vbl. n.* mockery 842.

mockys *n. pl.* jeering, derision 813, 2064.

mode *n. excede . . .* ~ exceed all limits 718
(*see Commentary*).

moder(e, modyr, moeder *n.* mother 71,
1195, 2326, 2503; **moders** *pl.* 2223.

moment *n. a* ~ *whyle* for a moment's
time 1336.

monasterie, monastery(e *n.* monastery
122, 440, 2698; **monasteriis** *pl.* 2258.

mon(e)thys, monthis *n. pl.* months 125,
134, 375.

monstrus, monsturs *n. pl.* monsters
1310, 2075.

mony *adj.* many 344; *as n.* 315.

monyfold *adj.* manifold 775.

more *adj.* greater 219.

mornyng *n.* mourning 2756.

most(e *pr. sg.* must 2940; *pr. pl.* 15.

moth, mowth(e *n.* mouth 11, 229, 621.

moue *v.* encourage, stir 1027, 1225, 2264;
mouyd *pa. t. sg.* roused 338; **mouyd
wyth** *pp.* oppressed by 842; **mouid**
afflicted 2771.

multe, multyn *pp.* melted, molten 1442,
2071.

musyd *pa. t. pl.* pondered 200.

nakyd *adj.* ill-clad 1711.

named *pp.* praised 1960.

narracion, narracyon *n.* story, account
617, 1504.

naturale *adj.* by blood 2319.

naturelly *adv.* by nature 1326.

ne *conj.* nor 26, 2741; or 993, 1611.

necessarijs *n. pl.* necessities 2585.

necys *n. pl.* nieces 2585.

nede *n.* need 1239; *to her* ~ to cover their
needs 2218.

nedeful(le *adj.* necessary 1028; needy 2406.

nedy *adj.* needy 2192.

nedys *adv.* necessarily 114, 2940.

neglygens *n.* neglect 1903.

neybur *n.* neighbour 1662.

neldys, nyldys *n. pl.* needles 234, 2952.

nere *adv.*[1] not (at all) 512, 517.

nere *adv.*[2] near 910; *more* ~ *comp.* nearer
783.

neris *n. pl. my* ~ my ears 514.

nether, nethir, nethyr *conj.* ~ . . . ~
neither . . . nor 354–7, 358, ~ . . . *ne*
2741; (after negative) nor 536, 566,
1372–3–4.

neuertelesse *conj.* nevertheless 1402.

neueys *n. pl.* nephews 2585.

newe *adv.* newly 2566.

nyce, nyse *adj.* foolish 1766; extravagant
1795.

nyes *n. pl. my* ~ my eyes 497, 502, 514.

nygh *prep.* near 487.

nyldys *see* neldys.

nyse *see* nyce.

no *adj.* not any 565; (*following neg.*) any
457, 2636. *See* meruel(le, nother,
nothir, wise.

no(o *adv. or* ~ or not 517; no 1339.

nobulnes *n.* worthiness 1966.

nobylle *adj.* valuable 806.

nocturne *n.* one of the divisions of the
office of matins 587.

noyeful *adj.* harmful 1839*.

noysyd *pp.* reported, rumoured 945, 1605.

noythe *pr. 3 sg.* torments 1542.

nombre *n.* number 635.

nombre *v.* count 636.

non(e *adj.* (*before a vowel or h-*) no 1294, 1309; (*before a consonant*) none *man* no man 14.

nonnys, noonys *n. pl.* nuns 97, 697, 2368.

noo *see* no-thing.

nor *conj.* Y *vndyrstode* ∼ Y *knewe not* I neither understode nor knew 1399.

norishte, noryshte *pp.* nurtured 1054, 1838.

nose-thrillys *n. pl.* nostrils 514.

not *pr. sg.* see wytte.

nother, nothyr, nowther *conj.* nor 826; *no* . . . ∼ *no* . . . *nor* 17; *not* . . . ∼ *not* . . . *nor* 201; ∼ . . . *ne* neither . . . nor 868.

no-thing, no-thyng, noo-thing *adv.* not, in no respect 161, 965, 1553; not at all 256.

no-thing, no-thyng, noo thing *n.* nothing 128; none 521; *yn* ∼ in no way, not at all 797.

nothir *adj.* no ∼ no other 608, 1338.

nothir *adv.* neither, not 352.

nothir, nothyr *pron. ne in no* ∼ nor in any other 26; *no* ∼ no other, no-one else 2323.

not(h)withstondyng *adv.* nevertheless 1092, 1340.

notwithstonding *prep.* despite 2645.

notyd *pp.* mentioned 486.

nought *n.* nothing 1288. *See* brought(e.

noumbre, nowmbre *n.* number 870, 1040; *aboue* ∼ innumerably 2261.

noumbre, nowmbre *v.* count 710; enumerate 2731.

nowne *adj. myn* ∼ my own 865.

obite *n.* death 2644.

obsecracyons *n. pl.* supplications, entreaties 318.

obseruyd *pp.* maintained 2593.

occasion, occasyon *n.* ∼ (*of*) opportunity (for) 1018, 1228; temptation 1065.

odyr *pron. pl.* others 691.

odyrwise, odyr-wyse *adv.* differently 2228, 2230; ∼ *then* differently than 1955.

of *adv.* off 487.

of *prep.* from 22; off 177; at 1036 (2); with 1731.

offende *v.* displease 1622; sin 1837; offendythe *pr. 3 sg.* sins, does wrong 2575; offendyn *pr. pl.* 2882; offendyd *pa. t.* 98, 1678; offendyd *pp.* 1957.

office, offyce *n.* office, duty 1910; ecclesiastical service or mass 139; offices, officys, offycys *pl.* 437, 2393, 2413.

ofte *adj.* frequent, repeated 1533, 2069, 2168.

ofte *adv.* repeatedly 977; often 1836, 2340; *as* ∼ *as* as often as, whenever 1589, 2977.

often-tyme *adv.* frequently 1126.

often-times, often-tymes, often-tymys, oftyn-times, oftyn-tymes *adv.* many a time, frequently, often 22, 236, 262, 1130, 2119.

oft(e)-tymes, ofte-tymys *adv.* many a time, frequently, often 488, 496, 1652.

on *adj.* one 1353, 1805.

on *pron.* one 158, 477, 821.

on *conj.* and (*unstressed*) 2432.

onauysyd *pp. as adv.* without warning, unexpectedly 2821.

onberyde *pp.* not buried 1180.

oncertente *n.* unreliability 1214; state of not being definitely known 1924.

onchaste *adj.* unchaste 1974.

onchastyte *n.* unchastity, fornication 2005.

onclene *see* vnclene.

onclenesse, onclennes *n.* wantoness 1783; sinfulness 2553.

oncredyble *adj.* incredible 2546.

ondue *adj.* excessive 2151.

ondyscrete *adj.* immoderate 2490.

ondyscretely *adv.* imprudently, recklessly 1539.

onely *adv.* only 256; alone, solely 1445.

on(n)ethe *adv.* scarcely, barely, hardly at all 1098, 1236, 2955; rarely 2013.

onethis, onethys, onnethis *adv.* barely, hardly 165, 256, 1422; with difficulty 196; scarcely 1634.

ongoyngable *adj.* impossible to traverse 733.

onhappy *adj.* wretched, miserable 848.

onknowen *pp.* unknown 2424.

onleful *adj.* seductive, sinful 850, 2102.

only *see* al(le *adv.*

onmeserabulle *adj.* immoderate, immeasurable 1013.

onmyghty *adj.* powerless 853.

on-mylde *adj.* harsh 2590.

onnaturally *adv.* unnaturally 1311.

onponyshte *pp.* unpunished 2452.

onprofetable *adj.* useless, worthless 988.

onprofetably, onprofetabully *adv.* uselessly, for no good purpose 1768, 1959.

onrightful *adj.* unrightful, unjust, wrong 2125.

onspedeful *adj.* of no avail, inefficacious 430.

onspekable, onspekehabule *adj.* unspeakable 1274, 1573.

onstable, onstabule *adj.* irresolute, morally weak 1468; vagrant 1780.

onstabulnes *n.* irresoluteness, moral weakness 2274.

onsufficient *adj.* insufficient 2873.

onto *prep.* (un)to 751.

onworthy *adj.* unworthy 409, 1538.

onwyse *adj.* unwise 1459.

onwysyly *adv.* unwisely 1951.

onys *adv.* once 289.

oppressure *n.* tyrant 1877.

opteyne *v.* obtain 434; hold 2350.

opyn *adj.* clear, intelligible 25, 705; public 1974.

opynd *pa. t. 1 sg.* opened 1091; opinde, opynde *pa. t. pl.* 229, 2920; opynd *pp.* 1747.

opynly, opinly, opynily *adv.* certainly 346; plainly, openly 358; clearly 420, 941, 2695; publicly, generally 945; freely 389*.

opynner, opynnor *adv. comp.* more ~ more clearly 348, 616.

orden *v.* arrange, organize 1025, 2392; ordende *pa. t. 3 sg.* appointed 1356; hordende established, founded 1996; ordend(e, ordente *pp.* assigned 295, 1670, 2226; sentenced (to punishment) 639, 698, 1962; founded 2101; arranged 2228, 2842; decreed 2393.

ordenans *n.* decree 2231.

ordyr *n. by the* ~ in accordance with the monastic rule 188.

ornamentys *n. pl.* accessories, furnishings 1024.

other, othir, othyr *pron. pl.* others 265, 401, 662, 724, 886, 1027, 1264.

otherwhile *adv.* occasionally 2091.

othyr-whyles *adv.* sometimes 1883; ~ amonge from time to time 2515.

othyr-wyse *adv.* ~ than different from what 995. *See also* odyr-wise.

ouer-all *adv.* everywhere 1616.

ouer-carkefulle *adj.* ~ *of* full of care about, anxious about 1367.

ouercome *pa. t. 3 sg.* overcame 2632.

ouerfowle *adj.* excessively disgraceful 1884.

ouer-grete *adj.* exceedingly intense 1132.

ouer-horabulle *adj.* exceedingly horrible 633.

ouerkeuryde *pp.* covered over 1881.

ouer-large *adj.* over-generous 2207.

ouer-longe *adj.* too long 281, 702.

ouermekyl *adj.* excessive 1069, 2608.

ouermekyl, ouer-mekyl(le, ouyr-mekyl *adv.* excessively, too much 946, 1367, 1764, 2206, 2577.

ouer-moche *adj.* excessive 1058.

ouer-part *n.* upper part 1265.

ouer-prone *adj.* too inclined 959.

ouer-sore *adv.* too severely 1119.

ouer-teduse *adj.* too wearisome 2030.

ouer-wrechyd *adj.* exceedingly miserable 1519.

ouer-wrechidful *adj.* exceedingly miserable 642.

ouyr-leyde *pp.* smeared . . . all over 192.

ouyr-mekyl *see* ouermekyl.

owre *n.* hour 242, 590.

owther, owthir *conj.* ~ . . . *or* either . . . or 649, 675, 2273.

palys *n. pl.* poles 690.

pament *n.* paved floor 488, 589.

pappys *n. pl.* nipples, breasts 2077.

pareshon *n.*[1] parishioner 1017.

parishons(e), paryshons *n.*[2] *pl.* parishes 2222, 2712, 2714.

parfet *adj.* perfect 2723.

part(e *n.* side 528; *a* ~ (*of*) *adv. phrase* partly (because of) 1557, 1558.

particularly *adv.* separately, specifically 343.

party *n.* some, a certain amount 2879.

passage *n.* passing from one place to another 671.

passe *v.* ~ *owte of this worlde,* ~ *fro this worlde,* ~ *hens* die 160, 422, 2663; passyth *pr. 3 sg.* 1755; passyn *pr. pl.*

1743; **paste** *pa. t.* went 528, 596; **passyd** surpassed 2496; **paste** *pp.* 1594, 2735.

passing, passyng *vbl. n.* death 1687, 1693.

passyon *n.* sin 1428.

pecys *n. pl.* pieces; *armyd at al* ~ completely armed 2108.

peynde, peynyd *pp.* tormented, afflicted 772, 2098.

peyne *n.* pain, torment 542; **peinys, peynes, peynis, peynys** *pl.* 6, 631, 659, 1301.

peyse *n.* weight 2115.

pele *n.* peal 2903.

penans(e, penaunce, penauns *n.* penance 225, 879, 1156, 1629.

penanse-doyng *n.* the performance of penance 2723.

pensys *n. pl.* pence 1128, 2401.

peple, pepul(e, pepull(e *n.* people 13, 88, 1372, 1670, 2174.

perauenture *adv.* perhaps, perchance 171, 2591.

perceue *v.* obtain, experience 1671, 2887; **perceyued** *pa. t. 1 sg.* heard 463; saw 504; **perceyuyd, perseuyd, perseyuyd** *pp.* observed 196, 235, 2956; **perceiuyd** obtained 1835.

perelle *n.* danger, peril 892; **perels** *pl.* 2308.

perfet *v.* become perfect 2716.

perfetly *adv.* completely 2411.

perfette *adj.* perfect 1748.

person *n.* parson 2402; **persons** *pl.* 2226.

personage *n.* benefice of a parson, parsonage 2372.

persyd *pp.* pierced 2752.

peruersours *n. pl.* perverters, corrupters 2295.

pete, pety *n.* pity 727, 804.

pilgrymage *n. went . . . a* ~ went on (a) pilgrimage 1995.

pypys *n. pl.* respiratory passages 195.

pystylle *n.* epistle 948, 1321.

Placebo *n.* ~ *and Dirige* vespers and matins of the Office for the Dead 2393, 2413–14.

plage *n.* disease 2344.

playnnes *n.* level ground, flatness 1270.

pledyd *pa. t. pl.* maintained their cause by argument in a court of law 1876.

pledyng *vbl. n.* legal dispute, litigation 1875.

pleyn *adj.* level, flat 632.

pleys *n. pl.* amusements 1778.

plutte *n.* muddy puddle 1882.

pompys *n. pl.* parades, processions 848; ~ of the world worldly glory 2217.

ponyshe, ponyssh *v.* punish 2165, 2592; **ponyshte** *pa. pl.* 1278; **ponisht, ponyscht(e, ponysht(e, ponyssht(e** *pp.* 647, 696, 1054, 1141, 1265, 1307, 1439.

ponissement, ponyshment *n.* punishment 777, 1147.

pore *see* **poure** *adj.*

posseste *pp. was* ~ *with* (was) possessed of, owned 1358.

possybylle *adj.* possible 715.

postre *n.* apostle 1321.

posynners, poysynners *n. pl.* poisoners 89, 2065.

posynyd* *pa. pl.* poisoned 2066.

pouerte *n.* poverty 1124; *Crystes* ~ voluntary poverty undertaken for religious reasons 2286.

poure, powre, pore *adj.* poor 79, 1372, 1717; **powrer** *comp.* 2522.

power, powr(e, poure *n.* power 1153, 929, 1913; *after . . .* ~ to the best of (one's) ability 416, 2196.

prayng *pr. p. and vbl. n.* praying 321, 905.

prayor, prayur, preyer *n.* prayer 30, 369, 907.

precius *adj.* precious 856.

prelacyon *n.* pre-eminence, superiority, dignity 1551, 1558.

presens *n.* presence 430.

pressure *n.* wine-press 771.

pressyd *pp.* tormented 2097.

presydent *n.* one in a position of authority in a religious house 188.

presyng *vbl. n.* praising 176.

pretendyn *pr. pl.* lay claim, aspire, try 894.

preuent(e *pp.* spiritually led or encouraged 2385; ~ *of dethe* prematurely overtaken by death 944, 2155, 2686.

Prime *n.* canonical service of Prime 185.

prinspaly *adv.* principally 1542.

priour, *n.* prior 104; **priowrs** *pl.* 167.

priste, pryste *n.* priest 106, 1022; **pristys, prystys** *pl.* 1974, 2004.

procedyd *pa. t. 3 sg. trans.* ~ *forthe* carried on 1473.

proces *n. sesid the* ~ stopped telling the story 352.

procuron *pr. pl.* bring about 2294.

profeste *pp.* professed 2212.

profet *pa. t. 3 sg.* benefited 2001; **profeting** *pr. p.* gaining spiritual benefit 1654; **profet** *pp.* been spiritually helpful 1961.

profetyng *vbl. n.* spiritual progress 13, 673.

proffe *n.* proof 2940.

propre, propyr *adj.* individual, personal 865, 1395; particular 1761.

proprite *n.* particulars 358.

prouyn *pr. pl.* prove 2944; **prouid, prouyd** *pp.* tested 1732, 2202.

purpos *n.* intention 1067.

put(te) *pp.* ~ *aside* abandoned 410, 1603; ~ *forth to* exposed to 636; ~ *oute* excluded 628; ~ *(vn)to* consigned to 698, 1319; ~ *thens* expelled 2377; ~ *vppe* kept 655.

quenchid *pp.* eliminated 23.
quere, quire *n.* choir 374, 2647.

rapte *pp. & adj.* carried away in spirit, in an ecstatic trance 52, 341, 557; ~ *in spirite* 4, 558*.

rasyd *pa. t. pl.* tore 1280.

raueshte *pa. t. 3 sg.* enraptured 2832; **rauesht, rauyshte** *(in spirite) pp.* transported (into an ecstasy) 525, 626.

raueshyng *vbl. n.* being transported, ecstasy 2970.

reboudye *n.* scurrility 1783.

recompensacyon *n. into the* ~ ... *of* in compensation for 1630.

record(e *n. take God to* ~ call God to witness (that something is so) 888, 1493, 1655.

recouere *v.* regain 264; **rekeuerythe** *pr. 3 sg.* 1738; **recoueryd** *(of sekness) pp.* recovered from sickness 362.

rectors *n. pl.* leaders, directors 2295.

red(d)er *n.* reader 1140, 2030.

redy *adj.* well chosen 322; clear 799.

refeccion, refeccyon *n.* portion of food or drink 368, 2648.

refraynde *pp. trans.* restrained 1549.

refreschyng, refresshyng *n.* mitigation (of pain), comfort, consolation 2360, 2510.

reherse *v.* repeat 540; recount 2025.

releue *v.* relieve 1711; assist, comfort 2196, 2224; **releuyth** *pr. 3 sg.* 837; **releuyd** *pp.* 675, 1121, 2146.

releuyng *vbl. n. for hys* ~ for his relief, to

cure him 230; mitigation 919; assistance 2360.

religion, religyon, relygion, relygyon *n.* the religious life, (rule of a) religious order 91, 167, 2084, 2254, 2255, 2587, 2897.

religi(o)us, religyous, relygy(o)us *adj.* ~ *man* monk 2000; ~ *men pl.* 80, 294, 2037, 2147.

religyously, religyusly, relygyously *adv.* devoutly, piously 2157, 2428; in accordance with a monastic rule 2187*.

remayneth *pr. 3 sg.* remains 1302; **remaynyn, remeynyth** *pr. pl.* are left over and above 1244, 2220; **remanyng to hym** *pr. p.* there being reserved for him 2179; **remaynyd to hym of** *pa. t. sg.* was reserved for him by 2507.

remediis *n. pl.* remedies 650.

remembre *v. refl.* ~ *me after* recall to mind 1932.

remnand(e *n.* rest 194*, 518; remaining part 2336.

remys *n. pl.* realms 2298.

renne *v.* run 2119; **rennyng** *pr. p.* flowing 271.

rentys *n. pl.* revenues, incomes 1358, 2143.

repente *v. refl.* repent 1817, 2373.

replecyon *n.* surfeit 1183.

repletyd *pa. t. pl.* (spiritually) filled 456; ~ *pp. and adj.* filled 322, 1270; spiritually satisfied 2792.

reproues *n. pl.* reproaches, insults 2253.

reprouyd *pp.* ~ *of* reproved on account of 581.

requyryth *pr. 3 sg.* demands, requires 1988, 2211; **requyred, requyryd** *pa. t.* 178, 332.

resceyue, reseyue *v.* be able to take in 128; take (the sacrament) 1041; attain, receive 2411; **resceyued, rescyued, resceyuyd** *pa. t.* 145, 164, 571; **resceuyd, resceyued, resceyuid, resceyuyd** *pp.* 250, 383, 1056, 2324.

resceyuyng *vbl. n.* receiving 456.

resoluyd *pp. was* ~ *al into terys* wept copiously 492.

respecte *n. by the* ~ *of* by means of 144.

resperste *pp.* bespattered, stained 2245.

resyn *see* **risith.**

reuoluyd *pa. t. 3 sg.* repeated 254.

rewle *n.* rule 2226.

reynynge *vbl. n.* reigning 2885.

right, ryght *adv.* very 440, 1719.
ryghtfull *adj.* righteous 1387.
ryghtfully *adv.* justly 866, 1446.
rightwes, ryghtwes, ryghtwys *adj.* righteous 965, 2297, 2858.
ryghtwesly *adv.* justly 1053.
rightwysnes, ryghtewesenes, ryghtwesnes, ryghtwysnes, ryhhtwysnes *n.* righteousness 1479, 1602, 1743, 1877, 2290.
ryhht *adj.* right 216.
risith *pr. 3 sg.* ~ . . . *of* arises from 22; resyn *pp.* risen 1077; rose 371.
ronge *n.* harm 1060.
ronge, rongyn *pp.* rung 1077; summoned by ringing 178, 2909.
roryd *pa. t. pl.* roared 1317.
rotyd *ppl. adj.* rooted, ingrained 1964.

sacrarye *n.* sanctuary, area immediately around an altar 595.
sakyrment *n.* sacrament 2654.
salmys *n. pl.* psalms 225, 2635, 2674.
salute *pa. t. sg.* greeted 980.
sander, sandyr *adv. comp.* sooner 412, 662, 1944.
satisfaccion, satysfaccion, satysfaccyon *n.* satisfaction, penance 648, 1890, 2486.
saue *prep. & conj.* except 235, 2323, 2805; ~ *onely* 255.
sauer, sauyr *n.* smell, fragrance 2545, 2728, 2795.
Sauyur *n.* saviour 470, 906, 1363*.
saye, sey(e *v.* say 185, 343, 828; seyst(e *pr. 2 sg.* 562, 990; seith, seyth(e *pr. 3 sg.* 956, 1449, 2099; seying, seyng *pr. p.* 427, 844; seide, seyd(e *pa. t. sg.* 161, 292, 361; sayde, seyde(n *pa. t. pl.* 193, 224, 1563; seide, seyd(e *pp.* 170, 296, 903.
seying, seyyng, seyng *vbl. n.* saying, talking 324, 1320, 2489.
scape *v.* escape 360; scapydyste *pa. t. 2 sg.* 997; scapyd *pa. t. pl.* 661; scapyd *pp.* 2334; ~ 2387.
scarpe *see* scharpe.
scarpnes *see* scharpenesse.
scarsly *adv.* frugally 2218.
scarnes(se) *n.* dearth 2442; niggardliness 2582.
scepulcur *n.* sepulchre 2375.
schal(l, schalle, shal(le *pr. 1 sg.* shall 209,

260, 361, 883, 1408; schal, schalt(e *pr. 2 sg.* 434, 919, 2901; schal(l, schalle, shal(le *pr. 3 sg.* 19, 335, 1445, 1712, 2183; schal(l, schalle, scalle, shal *pr. pl.* 163, 881, 1503, 1665, 1748; schuld(e, sculd, shuld(e *pa. t. 1, 3 sg.* 14, 160, 360, 414, 417, 963, 1215, 1371, 2414; schuldyst *pa. t. 2 sg.* 918; schuld(e, sculde, shold, shuld(e *pa. t. pl.* 167, 380, 721, 1160, 1432, 1918.
schame *n.* shame, disgrace, embarrassment 840, 1429.
schameful, schamfull *adj.* causing shame 841, 1304; modest 1327.
schamfully *adv.* ignominiously 1616.
schapyne *ppl. adj.* shaped 1311.
scharpe, scarpe, sharpe *adj.* sharp 689, 1394, 2751; violent 1869; prickly 2159; acute 2454; intense, severe 2205, 2335; scharper *comp.* 787.
scharpe, scharply *adv.* keenly 1854; sharply 2463.
scharpenesse, scharpnes, scarpnes, sharpenesse *n.* sharpness 2124; sharp pain, painfulness 1154; intensity 2405; hardship 1804; fierceness 764.
scharpyd *pa. t. 3 sg.* made more acute 2836.
schast *v.* chasten 1533.
sche, she *pron.* she 832, 838.
scheding *n.* shedding 2125.
Schere *see* Shere.
schew(e, shewe *v.* show, reveal 357, 822, 2028; schewyng, shewyng *pr. p.* 2291, 2472; schewyd, schoyd, shewed, shewid, shewyd *pa. t.* 94, 115, 572, 1311, 1378, 2153; schewde, schewed, schewyd, shewde, shewed, shewid, shewyd *pp.* 12, 20, 26, 118, 394, 1659, 1985, 2173.
schewyng *vbl. n.* showing, revealing 1386.
schewys *see* showis.
schod *pp.* shod 1076.
schone *pa. t.* shone 2279.
schonne *v.* ensure safety from 1163.
schorge *n.* scourge 910, 1364.
schorte, shorte *adj.* short 329, 1286.
schort(e)ly, shortly *adv.* shortly, briefly 283, 730, 1854.
schortenes *n. by-cause of* ~ for the sake of brevity 1514.
schortyd *pp.* shortened 1390.
schoyd *see* schew(e).

schoys *see* showis.

schrewdenes *n.* wickedness 1631.

schynyd *pa. t. 3 sg.* shone 2837; schyning, schynyng *pr. p. and adj.* 855, 2552, 2831.

sciens *n.* branch of knowledge 1355.

sclaunder *n.* stumbling-block, offence 1962.

sclaunderers *n. pl.* slanderers 2035.

scoler *n.* scholar 2364; scolers *n. pl.* 2198.

scolez, scolys *n. pl.* schools 1356, 2500.

scorgis, scorgys, scurgys *n. pl.* scourges, whips 665, 692, 2063. *See* schorge.

scornes, scornys *n. pl.* insults 813, 1590.

scurfe *n.* dross 1734*.

se(e *v.* see 5, 1748; seyst *pr. 2 sg.* 2248; seithe, seyth *pr. 3 sg.* 827, 2868; seyng *pr. p.* 189; sene, sey, seyen, seyn(e) *pp.* 40, 252, 1323, 2013, 2453.

seying *vbl. n.* seeing 2921.

seche, suche *adj.* such 25, 331.

seche *v.* (*after*) seek, look for 291, 432; sechyth *of pr. 3 sg.* requires of 1969; sechith *imper. pl.* 292; sekyd *after pa. t. pl.* tried to obtain 1157.

secler *adj.* secular 1561, 1874, 2161.

see *n.* sea 1685.

seyghte *n.* sight 2859.

seint *see* sent(e.

seith, seith(e *see* say(e, se(e.

seke *adj.* sick 131.

sekelew *adj.* ill, ailing 485.

sekenes(se, seknes *n.* sickness 29, 134, 360.

sekyd *see* seche *v.*

seldyn(ne *adv.* seldom 782, 2013.

seluyr *n.* silver 310.

sembly *adj.* handsome 2244; *more* semlyor *comp.* more beautiful 1705.

semyth *pr. 3 sg. impers. me* ~ it seems to me 1574; semyd *pa. t.* seemed 244, 254; *me* semyd 2349, 2583.

semyng *vbl. n. to owre* ~ in our judgement 733.

sen *prep.* since 1118.

sencybly *adv.* in a manner perceptible to the senses 1342.

sende *pa. t. 3 sg.* sent (*followed by inf. indicating the purpose*) 1186.

sene *see* se(e.

sent(e, seint, seynt(e *adj.* saint 5, 54, 466, 614, 908.

sentence *n.* maxim 1461.

sentis, sentys, seyntys *n. pl.* saints 807, 869, 871, 1373.

senyor *n.* one superior by reason of age or appointment 476, 561.

sepulture *n.* sepulchre 379.

sequestrate *ppl. adj.* separated, cut off from 1263.

seruant(e, seruaunt(e *n.* servant 893, 988, 1026, 1658; seruantis, seruantys, seruauntes, seruawntys *pl.* 133, 1052, 2326, 2594.

serues, seruys *n.* service 1230, 1469.

sesid, sesyd *pa. t.* ~ (*of*) ceased, stopped 199, 321, 351; sesyd *pp.* 1116.

sesyn(e *n.* time, season 1038, 2444.

set *pr. 3 sg.* ~ *ful lytel* scarcely undertook 1456; settith *imper. pl.* set, place 366; sette *abowte pp.* adorned 855.

seth(e *conj.* since 1192, 1409; setthe *adv.* since then 1576.

seurer *adv. comp.* more safely 1250.

sewer, sewre *adj.* secure, safe 2266; ~ *and safe* 1169.

sewerly, sewurly *adv.* firmly 555, 1007.

sex *num.* six 147.

sexte *see* feriis.

sexten(ne *n.* sexton 99, 2426; sextenys *poss.* 2441; sextense *pl.* 217.

sh- *see also* sch-.

shappys *n. pl.* shapes 797.

Shere, Schere *adj.* ~ *Thursday(e* Maundy Thursday 138, 396*, 450, 624.

showis, showys, schewys, shewys, schoys *n. pl.* shoes 37, 219, 286, 293, 2197.

shylde *n.* shield 2114.

sickelew *adj.* ill, sickly 2650.

syde *n. in prep. phr. on euery* ~ *me* on every side of me 2309.

sygne *n.* gesture 2660; sygnys *pl.* 1767.

sykyng *pr. p.* sighing 253.

syking *vbl. n.* sighing 399; sykynges *pl.* 288, 459.

sympylnes *n.* ignorance, foolishness 2274.

simulacyon, symulacyon *n.* dissimulation, deceit 1954, 1983.

synfyl *adj.* sinful 1299.

synglerly, singlerly *adv.* one by one, individually 343, 702; especially 315.

synguler, syngler *adj.* individual, single 329, 1761, 2029.

synnarys *n. pl.* sinners 2542.

synne, sinne, sine *n.* sin 73, 958, 1013;

synnes, synnis, synnys, synys *pl.* 150, 640, 781, 1369.

synne *v.* sin 1143; **sinnyd** *pa. t.* 2370.

synning *vbl. n.* sinning 1676.

slayne *pp.* ~ *of* killed by 2040; ~ *to* killed for 2130.

sloufulnes, slowfulnes *n.* sloth 1901, 1986.

slowthyd *pa. t. sg.* neglected through slothfulness 880.

smothe *adj.* smooth 2831.

smytyth *pr. 3 sg.* strikes (fire) 2111; **smytte, smyt(e, smitte** *pp.* smitten, struck 588, 689, 911, 2454.

so(o *adv.* such 263, 264, 522; ~ . . . *as* as . . . as 555.

sobirnes, soburnes *n.* self-restraint 2188; sobriety in regard to drink 1067.

socoure, socur, sokyr *n.* spiritual comfort 836, 2654; help 1997.

sode(n *pp.* boiled 245, 685.

soden *adj.* sudden 68.

sodenly *adv.* suddenly 66.

sof(f)ragys *see* **suffragys**.

sof(f)yr, sofyrre, sofre *v.* suffer 644, 653, 715, 1291; **sofre, sofyr** *pr. 1 sg.* 1114, 1425; **sofryth** *pr. 3 sg.* 828; **sofryn** *pr. pl.* 1589; tolerate 2262; **sofryng** *pr. p.* 971; **soffryd, sofred, sofreyd, sofrid, sofryd, sofyrd** *pa. t.* 80, 703, 1517, 1522, 1922, 2038; permitted 1547; **sofrid, sofryd** *pp.* 982, 2514; permitted 987.

softe *adj.* mild 2049; **softyr** *comp.* 784.

softly *adv.* gently 556.

sogettys *n. pl.* subjects 1547.

sokyd *pa. t. pl.* sucked 2077.

sokyr *see* **socoure**.

sokyrde *pp.* helped 2511.

solemly *adj.* of a solemn or sacred character 2769.

solenly *adv.* with due religious reverence 140, 2982.

solenne *adj.* awe-inspiring, reverent 2907, 2977.

solennyte *n.* solemn feast 2985.

som(m)e-tyme *see* **sum-tyme**.

sone *adv.* soon 160; **soner** *comp.* 726.

songe *pp.* sung 140.

sonne *n.* son 69; **sonnys** *pl.* 2134.

soo *see* **so(o**.

sore *adj.* painful 29; bitter 150.

sore *adv.* greatly, bitterly, painfully 126, 276, 665; (*more*) **sorer** *comp.* 134, 789.

soroful *adj.* sad, sorrowful 967, 2924.

sorofully *adv.* sorrowfully 271.

sorow(e *n.* sorrow 542, 2765; *alas, for* ~ exclamatory *phr.* alas 876, 1942; **sorow(y)s** *pl.* 413, 1926.

sorow(e *v.* (feel) sorrow, be sad 274, 2769; be lamented 2272; **sorowyng** *pr. p.* being sorry for, lamenting 1863; **sorowd(e, sorowyd(e** *pa. t.* 159, 279, 1006, 1912, *trans.* 890.

sorowyng *vbl. n.* lamenting 1348.

sortyd *pp.* assigned, allotted 947.

sothe *adj.* true 2602.

soth(e)ly *adv.* truly 355, 2529.

soule, sowle *n.* soul 60, 815; **soulys, sowlis, sowl(l)ys** *pl.* 7, 108, 419, 831.

sounned *pa. t. pl.* concerned, had a tendency towards 1783.

sowernes *n.* a sour disposition 1724.

sownde *adj.* sound, healthy 2453.

sowne *n.* sound 532.

sownnyng *vbl. n.* sounding 2913; *of* sownyng that makes a loud noise 2909.

sownyd *pa. t. 3 sg.* uttered 258; sounded 2911.

sowthe *adj.* south 528.

sowyn *pp.* sown 1964.

space *n.* length or span (of time) 5; ~ *of* (*penance*) opportunity or time for 1156. *See* **while**.

sparclys *n.pl.* sparks 762, 2111.

sparhauke *n.* sparrowhawk 1827.

sparyd *pa. t. 3 sg.* ~ . . . *oute* shut out 2810.

speche *n.* gossip 1773.

spectacul *n.* spectacle, sight 2755.

spede *pp.* assisted (to pass) 1235.

spedly *adv.* speedily, promptly 1654, 2200.

speke *v.* speak 255; ~ *pr. pl.* 958; **spekyth** *pr. 3 sg.* 948; **spekyng** *pr. p.* 1203; **spake** *pa. t.* 10; **spokyn** *pp.* 1233.

speking, spekyng *vbl. n.* speaking 679, 1485.

spende *pa. t. 1 sg.* spent 1030; **spendyd** *pa. t. 3 sg.* 175; **spende** *pp.* 2219.

spredyd *pa. t.* spread 1270.

spyrys* *n. pl.* tongues (of fire) 1899.

spyrytualte *n.* clergy 695.

stabulle, stabylle *adj.* stable, firm, constant 908, 1094.

stabulnes *n.* steadfastness 1066.

stabylle *v. refl.* make oneself morally steadfast 423.

stekyd *pa. t. pl.* pierced 1106; **stykyd** *pa. t. pl.* stuck 2076; ~ *pp.* stuck 2120.

stere *v.* persuade, exhort 1224; urge on 2119; incite 2264; **steryng** *pr. p.* 1066; **steryd** *pa. t. 3 sg.* prompted, moved 324.

sterne *adv.* sternly 2587.

steyer *n. wyndyng* ~ spiral staircase 2459.

stydde *n. in the* ~ *of* instead of 542.

stidfastly *adv.* fixedly 972.

styed *pp.* ~ *vppe* ascended 2852.

styftely *adv.* stiffly 1880.

stykyd *see* stekyd.

stode *ppl. adj.* ~ *opyn* ([gate] which was) stood open 2805.

stole *n.* long robe 1713.

stomake *n.* stomach 127.

stondyng *pr. p.* standing 312; **stode** *pa. t.* stood 2308.

stopped *pp.* blocked 232.

strangulde *pa. t. 3 sg.* strangled, choked 1089.

strawyn *pp.* strewn, covered 1271.

straytely, streytely *adv.* tightly 1868; exactly 2219, 2524.

strengh, strenght, strenthe *n.* strength 132, 229, 1441.

strenthyd *pa. t. pl.* supported, strengthened 2308.

streyte *adj.* strict 2606.

stroke *n.* blow 541; **strokys** *pl.* 574.

strompetly *adv.* like a strumpet 839.

studeyng *vbl. n.* studying 2500.

studyd *pa. t. sg.* made an effort 1375; took pains (to do sth.) 1954; *pp.* devoted (myself) 884.

stupour *n.* a state of amazement 339.

succeding *vbl. n.* succession 1679.

succedyth *pr. 3 sg.* ensues 1572.

suerly *adv.* surely, truly 2630.

suerte *n.* ~ *takyn* having achieved safety 1787.

sufficient *adj.* able 354.

suffragys, suffragiis, sof(f)ragys *n. pl.* intercessions 780, 1470, 1638, 2328, 2403.

suffyse *v.* be able 1248.

sum-tyme, summe-tyme, som(m)e-tyme *adv.* sometimes 127, 1203; once 371; at some time 653, 2427; at one time 725, 791, 2732.

sum-tymes *adv.* sometimes 2579.

superfluyte *n.* excess use or number 1777; **superfluyteis** *pl.* extravagances 2612.

suspendyd *pp. my mynde was* ~ my rational faculty was in abeyance, i.e. was in an ecstasy 2914.

suspycyon *n.* inkling 1328.

sustentacion *n.* being supported 374.

svm *adj.* some 1139.

swagyth *pr. 3 sg.* alleviates, assuages 1925.

swarmyn *pr. pl.* swarm 758.

swelowd(e *pa. t. 1 sg.* swallowed 516; ~ *pp.* 250.

swerde *n.* sword 1394.

swete *adj.* spiritually pleasing 324; **swhete** 2674; blessed 2748; **swetur** *comp.* more delightful 2728.

take *pr. t. 1 sg.* in asseverations: ~ *God to wytnesse*, ~ *God to record(e* call God to/ as witness, swear by God 710, 888, 1655; **takyth** *pr. 3 sg.* receives 953; **take** *pr. 3 sg. subj.* ~ *mercy* have mercy 1543; **toke** *pa. t.* received (flogging) 51; ~ *the crosse* joined a crusade 1799; ~ *pp.* taken 2464; adopted (custom) 1578; ~ *of* received from 1713; ~ *me vp* befriended 622; **takyn** understood 941, 1749.

taking *vbl. n.* consumption (of drink) 1013.

talkyng *vbl. n.* conversation 810.

tamyd *pa. t. 3 sg.* subdued (flesh) 2159.

tankyde *pa. pl.* thanked 2353.

tapers *n. pl.* candles 510.

tare *pa. t. 3 sg.* tore 1844.

tary(e *v.* wait, delay (*trans. and intrans.*) 483, 534; **taryde** *pa. t.* 1207, 2812; **taryde, teryde** *pp.* 768, 2929.

tar(y)yng *vbl. n.* delay 903, 1217.

tawarde *prep.* toward 2315, 2388.

tawghte *pa. t. 3 sg.* taught 2713.

te *unstressed infin. particle* to 2175. *See also* too.

techyng *vbl. n.* doctrine, precept 806.

ted(e)usnes *n.* ennui, boredom, distaste 312; discomfort 1335, 1844.

teeris, terys *n. pl.* tears 31, 157.

tel(le *v.* ~ *(of)* recount, tell (about) 209, 354, 380, 1343; ~ count 1131.

temporal *adj.* temporary 715; worldly 2136.

temporalte *n.* condition or estate of a layman 695.

tenyse-balle *n.* tennis-ball 821.

terme *n.* limit 1294; period 2900.

teryde *see* tary(e.

terys *see* teeris.

teth(e *n. pl.* teeth 688, 901.

Tewsday, The-wysday *n.* Tuesday 2455, 2485.

than(ne, þan *adv.* then 136, 257, 298, 913*.

thankynges, thankyngys *vbl. n. pl.* thanks 496, 1051.

thaugh, thaught, thawgh(e, thawght *adv., conj.* though 32, 966, 1148, 1810, 2266.

thay *pron. 3 pl.* they 1922; ther *poss.* 379; ther *obj. gen.* of them 798; theym *obj.* 261, 1145. *See also* hem.

that *demon. adj. pl.* ~ holy dayes on those holy days 1043.

the *pron. see* thou.

theder, thedir, thedur, thedyr *adv.* thither, to that place 189, 208, 2566, 2806. *See also* hethur.

thees *see* thes.

then(ne *conj.* than 767, 778, 1044, 1327.

thens(e *adv.* thence, from that place 180, 334; *in prep. phr. fro* ~ 726.

ther *pron. see* thay.

ther-as *adv.* where 1401.

therby *adv.* because of that 1942, 2148.

therf(f)or(e *adv.* for this reason 895, 1126, 2592; for the purpose 1025.

therof *adv.* about it 353; of it 368; by it 2454; as a result 1891.

therto *adv.* for it 2056.

thes *adj.* this 138; the(e)s, this, thys *pl.* 8, 397, 797, 1119, 1632, 1735, 1903, 2281.

theuys *n. pl.* thieves 811.

The-wysday *see* Tewsday.

they *see* thou.

theym *see* thay.

theyselfe *n.* thyself 2886.

thylke *demons. adj.* those 2440.

thyne *see* thou.

thing(e, thyng(e *n.* thing 129, 251, 1701, 1742; thing(h)es, thinghys*, thingis, thingys, thynges, thynghes, thynghys, thyngis, thyngys 40, 43, 209, 283, 329, 1352, 1643, 2305, 2532, 2574.

thynkyn *pr. pl.* think 2296.

thynnyde *pp.* made thin 796.

this *adj. see* thes.

this, thys *adv.* thus, in this manner 883; thus, to this extent, so 2124[n].

this, thys *pron. to* ~ to this end, for this purpose 1097; *pl.* these (things) 659[n], 1014.

thoes *demons. adj.* those 43.

tho(o *demons. adj.* those 192, 809.

tho(o *demons. pron.* those persons 651, 1307.

thoon *n. the* ~ the one 400.

thorow(e *adv., prep.* through 823, 1091, 1349, 2120.

thou, thow *pron. nom.* thou 562, 613, þou, þow(e 433, 434, 467; they *poss.* 917, 994, 2900; thyne *as n.* thy people 2886; the *obj.* 472, 1150, 2881*.

thought(e, thowghte *pa. t. 3 sg. impers. me/my* ~ it seemed to me 754, 1339, 2834.

thowsand *n.* thousand 1424; thousandys, thowsondis *pl.* 2548, 2860.

thrall *adj.* captive, conquered 862.

thretyng *pr. p.* threatening 909; ~ *vbl. n.* 2467, 2471.

thries *adv.* thrice 289, 1190.

throte, throwte *n.* throat 232, 1133.

throw(e *adv., prep.* through 111, 689, 774, 2841.

throwe *pp.* thrown 1781.

til, tyl(e *conj., prep.* until 147, 369, 632, 1207, 1739.

tyrandys *n. pl.* ruffians, fiends 820.

tyrse *n.* tierce (about 9 a.m.) 2670.

tytyl *n.* title, rank 2319. *See Commentary.*

tytyngys *n. pl.* tidings, report 1049.

to-bete *pa. t. pl.* severely beat 1106.

to-brend *pa. t. pl.* burned up 1106; to-brende *pp.* 2112.

toche *v.* touch 2348; tochyd *pp.* 1653.

tochyng, touchyng, touching *adv. phr. as* ~ concerning, in regard to 605, 610, 1501, 2114.

towchyng *vbl. n.* touching 1131.

to-drawyn *pp.* pulled apart 691.

todyr *adj.* the other 2974; *the* ~ 1125, 1697, 1902.

togeder, togedir, togedyr, togedur *adv.* together 164, 272, 283, 388.

to-gnew *pa. t. pl.* gnawed away at 2078.

tokyn *n.* sign, gesture 2661; sign, mark 1179; indication 2960; tokyn(y)s *pl.* 1220, 2321.

tonge *n.* tongue 706.

too *infin. particle* to 880. *See also* te.

too *num., adj., n.* two 2126, 2632.

toon *adj. the* ~ (the) one 749.

to-rasyd *pp.* slashed to pieces 684.

torment *pp.* tormented, tortured 661, 714.

to-teryd *pa. t. pl.* mutilated, ripped 1280, **to-tore** 1275; **to-toryn** *pp.* 692.

tother, tothir, tothyr *adj.* the other 751; *the* ~ 367, 530; *pron.* 401, 1883.

tradicion *n.* betrayal 140.

trayturs *n. pl.* traitors 2034.

tremyl *v.* tremble 199.

tresowre, tresur *n.* treasure 523, 2143.

trespas *n.* sin, transgression 2470, 2487; **trespassys** *pl.* 2047.

trespast *pa. t. 3 sg.* ~ ... *to* sinned against 1366.

tresur *pr. 3 pl.* ~ *to hem* keep in store/lay up for themselves 1385.

tretyth *pr. 3 sg.* concerns 2.

treuly, trew(e)ly(e, tru(e)ly *adv.* properly 1029; indeed, certainly, truly 191, 658, 809, 1234, 1541, 2887.

trew(e *adj.* true 115, 1052.

tricennariis, tricennarijs *n. pl.* series of masses said on thirty consecutive days 2392, 2413.

tryfullys *n. pl.* foolish or vulgar nonsense 1559.

troble *v.* trouble, harrass 1955; **troubulde** *pp.* disturbed 579; **trowbuld** disordered 2298.

trone *n.* throne 2849.

tro(u)the, trowth(e *n.* (the) truth 17, 564, 1482*.

trowbullus *adj.* troublesome 2265.

trowbulnes *n.* turbidity, turbulence 1774*.

trowe *v.* believe 2411; ~ *pr. 1 sg.* 25; **trowiste** *pr. 2 sg.* 560.

twies, twyes *adv.* twice 289, 1030.

twynkeling, twynkelyng *n. in the (space of a)* ~ *of an ye* in a moment, suddenly 846, 1102*.

vnclene, onclene *adj.* unchaste, morally impure 868, 1305.

vnclenes(se *n.* impurity 1315, 1742.

vnderstonde, vndirstonde, vndyrstande, vndyrstonde *v.* understand 163, 421, 1665, 2720; **vndyrstonde** *pr. sg.* 2928; **vndirstonde** *pr. 3 sg. subj.* 18; **vndirstonde** *pr. pl.* 2282; **vnderstode, vndirstode, vndyrstode** *pa. t sg.* 574, 1185, 2148; **vndyrstode** *pa. t. pl.* 391; **vndyrstond(e** *pp.* 259, 2416.

vnderstanding, vnderstonding, vnder-

stondyng, vndyrstondyng *vbl. n.* understanding 1968, 1971, 2176, 2796.

vnshappely *adj.* ugly 1273.

vnther *prep.* under 1299.

vnto *prep.* to 20.

vnyuersally *adv.* collectively 315.

vpbrayde *v.* reproach, reprove 1723; **vpbraydyn** *pr. pl.* 1598; **vpbrayde, vpbraydyd** *pa. pl.* 2064, 2128.

vpbraydys *n. pl.* reproaches 1591, 2772.

vp(p)e *adv.* up 143, 544.

vppur *adj. comp.* upper 2855.

vse *n.* customary practice 537; **vsus, vsys** *n. pl.* uses, purposes 1029, 2446.

vtmest *adj.* extreme 1147.

vtturmaste *adj.* last, final 2607.

vtwarde *adj.* outward 828.

vtward(e)ly *adv.* utterly, completely, absolutely 22, 874, 2015, 2945.

vanyshte *pa. 3 sg.* vanished 2475.

vanyte *n.* frivolity 123.

variant, varyante *adj.* diverse, varied 2911; changeable 1774.

vayne *adj.* of no avail 233; empty, useless, foolish 1065, 1566, 1765.

vayne-glorye *n.* vainglory 1800.

vaynely *adv.* vainly, foolishly 1368.

vellonye *n.* disgrace 840.

venery *n. pl.* game animals 2129.

vengans *n.* punishment 2227*.

venummys *adj.* venomous 688.

veny *n.* pardon, forgiveness 547.

venyne *n.* venom 1101.

verely *adv.* truly 278.

verey *adv.* very 2567; *adj.* very true 1737.

vertuus *adj.* vertuous 2256, 2716.

vexid, vexyd *pp.* afflicted 1362, 2772.

victoriose, vyctoryose *adj.* victorious 379, 848*, 925.

vycy(o)us *adj.* depraved, sinful 1699, 1795, 2004.

vycyusly *adv.* dissolutely 839.

virgyn(ne, vyrgyn(e *n.* virgin 861, 890, 2482, 2503; **virgenis, virgenys, virgyns, vyrgyn(y)s** *pl.* 855, 891, 926, 2320, 2344.

vise, vyce, vyse *n.* vice 73, 957, 1007; **vysys** *pl.* 2214.

vyset, vysyte *v.* visit 2348, 2374.

visitacyon *n.* presence, visit, act of visiting 1121.

vytalle *adj.* essential to life 2957.

voluptuous *adj.* sensually gratifying 2217.

vome(n)t *n.* vomit 1101, 2088.

wachyd *pa. t. 3 sg.* kept vigil 2505.

wacchyng *vbl. n.* keeping vigil 2631.

wakyd *pa. t. 1 sg.* woke 446, 474.

waking *pr. p.* keeping vigil 369, 585.

wakyngly *adv.* while awake 573, 1195.

walowyng *pr. p.* tossing from side to side 1869.

wandyr *v.* wander 1560, 1765; **wandryng** *pr. p.* 1768, 1780.

war(r)e *adj.* cautious, prudent 1200, 2408, 2563, 2611; ~ *of* careful about 1036; careful to avoid 1064.

warly *adv.* watchfully, prudently 2591.

wars *adj., adv., n.* worse 1568, 1570, 1679.

wastyn *pr. pl.* waste, squander 2215; **wasted, wastyd** *pp.* enfeebled 1276, 1288, 1297.

watrid, watryd *pa. t. sg.* watered 311, 497.

watsumeuer *see* w(h)atsumeuer.

waxen *pr. pl.* grow, become 1133; **waxed** *pa. t. pl.* 784; **waxin** *pp.* 2521.

wedowys *n. pl.* widows 2197.

wedyr *n.* weather 1804.

weke *n.* week 2452, 2456; **wekis** *pl.* 449.

wekednesse, wekydnes, wy(c)kydnes *n.* wickedness 1474, 1529, 1633, 2044.

wekenes *n.* weakness 126.

wekid, wekyd, wy(c)kyd *adj.* wicked 720, 814, 852, 1381.

wel-belouyd *ppl. adj.* dearly loved 381*.

wellid *pa. t. 3 sg.* hit ~ *oute of blode* it poured out blood 506.

wemen *n. pl.* women 378.

wende *pa. t.* thought 601, 995; **wend(e, went(e** *pp.* 159, 1077, 1349, 1431.

weping, wepyng *vbl. n.* weeping 146, 172; **wepyngs** *pl.* 2168.

wepyng *pr. p. adj.* (*used absolutely as n. pl. translating* plorantes) weeping persons 271.

wepyngly *adv.* in a weeping manner 225.

wepynys *n. pl.* weapons 1396.

were *conj.* see **wher**.

were *pa. t. 3 sg.* wore 2109.

weriful *adj.* tiresome 2030.

werke *n.* work, act 803, 930; **werkys** *pl.* 654; creations 25.

wers *adj. comp.* worse 674.

wery *adj.* weary 2520.

weryde *pp.* made weary 1651.

weryng *vbl. n.* wearing 2159.

wes *see* **be**.

weshe*, wesse *v.* wash 876, 2351; **weshid** *pa. pl.* 197; **weshte** *pp.* 875.

wey(e *n.* way 175, 622; **wey(e)s** *pl.* 895, 1534.

weyfaring *pr. p. adj.* wayfaring 2040.

whan(ne, when, when(n)e *adv.* when 299; *conj.* when 10, 163, 180, 292, 1365.

what *conj.* ~ *for* on account of, what with 147, 832, 1641, 1838.

w(h)atsumeuer *adj., pron.* 129, 2833, 2871, 2909.

whe *pron.* we 2529.

wheder *adv.* whither 1107.

whedir *conj.* whether 2765.

whens *adv.* whence 464, 511.

whent *pa. pl.* went 1814.

wher *conj.* where 1026; **were** 142, 2251, 2856.

wherby *adv.* whereby, by which 1011.

where *conj.* whereas 2355.

where *v.* see **be**.

where-as *conj.* where 588.

wherefore, wherfor(e *conj.* for which reason 193, 2445, 2891.

whersumeuer *conj.* wherever 2358.

wherto *conj.* why, to what end 1151, 2730.

whethir, whethyr *conj.* if, whether 1406, 1408.

which(e, whyche, wiche, wyche, wyiche *rel. pron. the* ~ which, who, whom 3, 9, 209, 388, 898, 1146, 1927.

whyle *conj.* ~ *dat* while 1429.

while, whyle *n. thys* ~ during this time that 889; *space of on matens* ~ the length of one matins 2928; *a moment* ~ for a moment 1336.

whilys, whylys *conj.* while 1338, 1832.

whyrlewynde *n.* whirlwind 912; **whyrle-wyndys** *pl.* 1870.

whyt *prep.* with 1878, 2106, 2111.

white-safe, whytesaue, whytsafe, with-saue, wythsaue *v.* vouchsafe, deign 409, 417, 898, 1664, 2780, 2934.

whitnes, whythnes, wythnes *n.* white-ness 2703, 2794, 2972.

whytowte *prep.* without 1083.

whyt-owte-forthe *adv.* on the outside 2112.

whytowtyn *see* **withouten**.

whittir *adj. comp.* whiter 552, 612; *more* **whyttur** 2729.

who-sum-euer *pron.* whoever 645, 1785.

whois, whoys *pron. poss.* whose 356, 958; (of inanimate thing) 641, 690; *see also* ho(o.

wholde *pp.* held 1009.

whore *adj.* hoar, white 553.

wyche *see* **which(e).**

wyckyd *see* **wekid.**

wyckydlye *adv.* wickedly 841.

wyckydnes *see* **wekednesse.**

wydwardys *n. poss.* widower's 1832.

wyf(e) *n.* wife 79, 1078.

wykyd *see* **wekid.**

wykydnes *see* **wekednesse.**

wil, wyl, wille, wylle *pr. 1 sg.* will 679, 704, 730, 933; *pr. 3 sg.* 302, 438, 1620; **wole** 1446; **wyl** *pr. 1 pl.* 2532; **will** *pr. 2 pl.* wish 2934; **wulle** *pr. 3 pl.* 1550; **wold(e, wuld(e** *pa. t.* 350, 939, 1039, 2128.

wille, wylle *n.* will, wish 4, 1005; **willes, willys** *pl.* wills, desires 443, 1547.

wyndyng *see* **steyer.**

wyntyr *n. pl.* winters 1831.

wisdam, wysdom *n.* wisdom 173, 1959.

wyse *n.*[1] vice 1096.

wise, wyse *n.*[2] manner, way 18, 207; *in lyke* ~ in the same way 479; *thys* ~ in this way 2906; *in this* ~ thus 464; *maner of* ~ way 418; **wysys** *pl.* ways 1439; ways of behaving 1964.

wist, wyste *see* **wytte.**

wysyly *adv.* wisely 2190.

wyte *v.* blame, impute 1675.

withal, wyth-alle *adv.* as well, in addition 2544, 2911.

withdrew *pa. t. sg.* took away 2447.

wythyn *adv.* inwardly 840.

within(-)forth(e, wythinforth(e, wyth-ynforthe *adv.* within, inside 110, 2804, 2840; inwardly 830, 2112, 2164.

wythnes *see* **whitnes.**

without(e, withowte, wythowt(e *prep.* without 190, 207, 373, 737, 818.

withoute *adv.* outside 2816.

withouten, withoutyn, withowtyn, whytowtyn, wyhtowtyn, wythoutyn, wythowten, wythowtyn *prep.* without 571, 903, 1175, 1217, 1754, 2333, 2357, 2861.

wythoutforth *adv.* from outside, 'physically' 842.

withsaue, wythsaue *see* **white-safe.**

wythstonde *pp.* withstood 1051.

witnes, wytnes(s)e *n.* witness, testimony 2498, 2950; understanding, wisdom 356. *See also* **take.**

wytnesyd *pa. t. 3 sg.* testified 1201.

witte *n.* intelligence 323; **wittis, wyttys** *pl. bodily* ~ senses 623; wits 1073.

wytte *v. that ys to* ~ *and to saye* namely 1174; **wote** *pr. 1 sg.* know 267, not know not 535; **wist** *pa. t. 1 sg.* 463; **wyste** *pa. t. 3 sg.* 2446.

wyttye *adj.* clever 1456.

wodde *adj.* mad 1277; *more* **wodder** *comp.* 818.

wodenes(se *n.* madness 667, 1105.

wold(e *see* **wil.**

wolde *adj.* old 2198; *yn hys* ~ *days* i.e. during his (former) life 959.

woluys *n. pl.* wolves 2292.

wondyr *n.* wonder 219; astonishment 340, 2767.

wondyrful(l, wundyrfull *adj.* admirable 2755; remarkable 688; astonishing 1272.

wondirfully *adv.* wonderfully 2838.

wondrede *pa. t. 3 sg.* was amazed, wondered 563; **wondred, wondrid** *pa. pl.* 205, 206; **wondride** *pa. p.* marvelled at 2913.

wont(e *pp.* accustomed 213, 377; *with impers v.* = customary 1610.

worde *n. in* ~, *by* ~ in words 2743, 2830.

word(e)ly *adj.* worldly 2088, 2613, 2737.

wordly *see* **worthely.**

worschip(p)e, worschuppe, worschyppe, worshippe, worshyp(p)e *n.* worship, honour 148, 466, 807, 1019, 1179, 1254, 2464.

worschippe, worschype, worship(p)e *v.* worship, honour 47, 309, 2175, 2789; **worshippyng** *pr. p.* 978; **worshipt(e** *pa. t. sg.* 34, 287; **worschipte, worschypte** *pa. t. pl.* 2747, 2853*; **worschipped, worschipte, worshipte, worshypte** *pp.* 210, 304, 1111, 1253.

worschipping *vbl. n.* worshipping 2763.

worshippeful, worschip(p)ful, worschyfful, worschypful, worschyppefull, worshipful(l *adj.* honourable 106, 611, 1357, 1487, 1489, 2615, 2677, 2684.

worschipfulness *n.* reverence 2048.

worthely, worthily, wordly *adv.* worthily, fittingly 859; rightly 2742; fittingly 2743.

worthy *adj. were* ~ deserved 2398; *more*
worthior *comp.* more fitting 964.
wote *see* wytte.
wothys *n. pl.* oaths 2478.
wownde *n.* wound 2969; wowndys *pl.*
1395.
wrathe *n.* wrath (of God/Christ) 1385,
1386.
wrecche *n.* wretch, miserable person 2935;
wrechys *pl.* 1278.
wrechid, wrechyd *adj.* miserable 642,
899; of poor abilities 2119.
wrechidnes, wrechydnes *n.* miserable
condition 1094, 1438; great misery 717.
wreten, wretyn *pp.* written 398, 1178.
wrought *pp.* brought about, created 1458.
wuld(e, wulle *see* wil.
wundyrfull *see* wondyrful(l.

ye, ȝe *pron.* you 163, 406; you, yow *obj.*
297, 576; youre, yowre *poss.* 298, 451.
yef(fe, ȝef(fe, ȝefe *conj.* if 317, 433, 1050,
2025, 2946.
ȝeftys, ȝyftys *n. pl.* gifts 1028*, 1480.
ȝellyd *pa. t. pl.* yelled 1317.

yere *n.* year 121; *a .xiiii.* ~ *pl.* fourteen
years 2562; ȝere 1823; ȝerys 2642.
yere *conj. see* ere.
ȝesterday, ȝisterday, ȝysterdaye *adv.*
yesterday 520, 1069, 1999.
yet, ȝet(te *conj., adv.* yet, still 93, 266, 339,
560, 1404, 1581.
ȝeue v. give 1502, 2524.
yldyn *pp.* rendered 1705.
yong(e *adj.* young 105, 1193. *See* aage.
youthe, yowthe *n.* youth, young age 1523,
1837.
ȝys *adv.* yes 2412.
ȝystys *n. pl.* works, deeds 882.

zele *n.* zeal 1552, 1602.
zwifte *adj.* swift 1184.

ȝere *conj. see* ere.
ȝere *adv.* ever 728.
ȝese *v.* ease 2968.
ȝesely *adv.* acting in a kindly manner 2589.
ȝestewarde *adv.* eastward 632.
ȝesy, ȝesyor *see* esy.
ȝirne *n.* iron 2110 (cf. yrne).

INDEX OF PROPER NAMES

SELECT BIBLIOGRAPHY

See also Abbreviations and Short Titles; works cited there are not listed again here.

Anciaux, P., *La Théologie du Sacrement de Pénitence au XIIe Siècle* (Louvain, 1949).

Apocalypse of Peter. See *The Apocryphal New Testament*, trans. M. R. James (Oxford, 1924), pp. 504–24.

Beadle, Richard, 'Middle English Texts and their Transmission, 1350–1500: Some Geographical Criteria', in *Speaking in our tongues: Proceedings of a Colloquium on Medieval Dialectology and Related Disciplines*, ed. Margaret Laing and Keith Williamson (Cambridge, 1994), pp. 69–91.

Becker, Ernest J., *A Contribution to the Comparative Study of the Medieval Visions of Heaven and Hell, with Special Reference to the Middle-English Versions*, Diss. Johns Hopkins University (Baltimore, 1899).

Benz, Ernst, *Die Vision: Erfahrungsformen und Bilderwelt* (Stuttgart, 1969).

Bihrer, Andreas, 'Die Bearbeitungspraxis mittelalterlicher Visionsliteratur. Eine spätmittelalterliche Redaktion der "Visio Edmundi monachi de Eynsham"', in *VEME*, pp. 91–112.

Braswell, Mary Flowers, *The Medieval Sinner: Characterization and Confession in the Literature of the Middle Ages* (Rutherford, New Jersey, 1983).

Browe, Peter, *Die eucharistischen Wunder des Mittelalters* (Breslauer Studien zur historischen Theologie, Neue Folge 4, Breslau, 1938).

Bynum, Caroline Walker, *Jesus as Mother: Studies in the Spirituality of the High Middle Ages* (Berkeley and Los Angeles, 1982).

—— *The Resurrection of the Body in Western Christianity, 200–1336* (New York, 1995).

Caesarii Heisterbacensis monachi ordinis Cisterciensis Dialogus miraculorum, ed. Joseph Strange, 2 vols. (Cologne, Bonn, Brussels, 1851).

Chambers, Edmund, *Eynsham under the Monks* (Oxfordshire Record Society Series 18, 1936).

Cheney, C. R., *From Becket to Langton: English Church Government 1170–1213* (Manchester, 1956).

Church, C. M., 'Reginald of Bath (1174–1191): His Episcopate, and his Share in the Building of the Church of Wells', *Archaeologia*, 50 (1887), 295–360.

Ciccarese, Maria Pia, ed., *Visioni dell'aldilà in occidente: Fonti, modelli, testi* (Bibliotheca Patristica, Florence, 1987).

Clark, Anne L., *Elisabeth of Schönau: A Twelfth-Century Life* (Philadelphia, 1992).

Clayton, Joseph, *St Hugh of Lincoln: A Biography* (London, 1931).

Constable, Giles, 'The Vision of Gunthelm and other Visiones attributed to Peter the Venerable', *Revue bénédictine*, 66 (1956), 92–114. Repr. with addenda in Giles Constable, *Cluniac Studies* (London, 1980).

—— *Cluniac Studies* (London, 1980).

Cosmo, Umberto, 'Una nuova fonte dantesca?', *Studi medievali*, 1 (1904–5), 77–93.

Coulton, G. G., *Life in the Middle Ages*, vol. 1 (Cambridge, 1928).

The Customary of the Benedictine Abbey of Eynsham in Oxfordshire, ed. Antonia Gransden (Corpus consuetudinum monasticarum 2, Siegburg, 1963).

De Cella in Seculum: Religious and Secular Life and Devotion in Late Medieval England, ed. Michael G. Sargent (Cambridge, 1989).

Decreta Lanfranci: The Monastic Constitutions of Lanfranc, ed. David Knowles (London, 1951).

Dengler, Mark., '"In speculo et enigmate". Zur Auswahl und Funktion biblischer Zitate in der "Visio Edmundi monachi de Eynsham"', in *VEME*, pp. 59–71.

Dionysius the Carthusian, 'De Particulari Judicio in Obitu Singulorum Dialogus', in *Doctoris Ecstatici D. Dionysii Cartusiani Opera Omnia*, vol. 41, *Opera Minora*, vol. 9 (Tournai, 1912), pp. 421–88.

—— 'De Quatuor Hominis Novissimis', in *Doctoris Ecstatici D. Dionysii Cartusiani Opera Omnia*, vol. 41, *Opera Minora*, vol. 9 (Tournai, 1912), pp. 491–594.

Dinzelbacher, Peter, *Vision und Visionsliteratur im Mittelalter* (Monographien zur Geschichte des Mittelalters 23, Stuttgart, 1981).

—— 'Das Christusbild der heiligen Lutgard von Tongeren im Rahmen der Passionsmystik und Bildkunst des 12. und 13. Jahrhunderts', *Ons geestelijk Erf*, 56 (1982), 217–77.

—— 'Körperliche und seelische Vorbedingungen religiöser Träume und Visionen', in *I sogni nel medioevo*, ed. Tullio Gregory (Lessico Intellettuale Europeo 35, Rome, 1985), 57–86.

—— 'Mittelalterliche Vision und moderne Sterbeforschung', in *Psychologie in der Mediävistik: Gesamelte Beiträge des Steinheimer Symposions*, ed. J. Kühnel (Göppinger Arbeiten zur Germanistik 431, Göppingen, 1985), pp. 9–49.

—— 'The Beginnings of Mysticism Experienced in Twelfth-Century England', *The Medieval Mystical Tradition in England. Exeter Symposium IV: Papers read at Dartington Hall, July 1987*, ed. Marion Glasscoe (Cambridge, 1987), pp. 111–31.

—— *Mittelalterliche Visionsliteratur: Eine Anthologie* (Darmstadt, 1989).

—— *Revelationes* (Typologie des sources du Moyen Âge occidental 57, Turnhout, 1991).

—— *Christliche Mystik im Abendland. Ihre Geschichte von den Anfängen bis zum Ende des Mittelalters* (Paderborn, 1994).

—— 'Das Fegefeuer in der schriftlichen und bildlichen Katechese des Mittelalters', *Studi Medievali*, 3rd series, 38 (1997), 1–66.

—— 'Edmund von Eynsham', in *Lexikon des Mittelalters*, ed. R. Auty *et al*, 9 vols. and Index (Munich and Zurich, 1977–99), 3 (1986), 1581–2.

Dobson, E. J., *English Pronunciation 1500–1700*, 2 vols., 2nd edn. (Oxford, 1968).

Doyle, A. Ian, 'A Survey of the Origins and Circulation of Theological Writings in English in the 14th, 15th and Early 16th Centuries with Special Consideration of the Part of the Clergy Therein', Dissertation, Cambridge University, 1953.

Duff, E. Gordon, *Fifteenth Century English Books: A Bibliography of Books and Documents Printed in England and of Books for the English Market Printed Abroad* (The Bibliographical Society, Illustrated Monographs 18, Oxford, 1917).

—— *The Printers, Stationers and Bookbinders of Westminster and London from 1476 to 1535* (Cambridge, 1906).

Duffy, Eamon, *The Stripping of the Altars: Traditional Religion in England c.1400–c.1580* (New Haven & London, 1992).

Easting, Robert, 'The Date and Dedication of the "Tractatus de Purgatorio Sancti Patricii"', *Speculum*, 53 (1978), 778–83.

—— 'Peter of Cornwall's Account of St Patrick's Purgatory', *AB*, 97 (1979), 397–416.

—— 'Owein at St Patrick's Purgatory', *Medium Ævum*, 55 (1986), 159–75.

—— 'Purgatory and the Earthly Paradise in the *Tractatus de Purgatorio Sancti Patricii*', *Cîteaux*, 37 (1986), 23–48.

—— 'Peter of Bramham's Account of a Chaplain's Vision of Purgatory (*c.*1343?)', *Medium Ævum*, 65 (1996), 211–29.

—— '"Send thine heart into purgatory": Visionaries of the Other World', in *The Long Fifteenth Century: Essays for Douglas Gray*, ed. Helen Cooper and Sally Mapstone (Oxford, 1997), pp. 185–203.

—— 'Personal Apocalypse: Judgement in some Other-world Visions', [forthcoming] in *The Millennium, Social Disorder and the Day of Doom: Proceedings of the 2000 Harlaxton Symposium*, ed. Nigel Morgan (2003).

—— and Richard Sharpe, 'The Visions of Ailsi and his Sons', *Mediaevistik*, 1 (1988), 207–62.

Ehlen, Thomas, 'Vision und Schrift—Interessen, Prozeß und Typik der Verschriftlichung hochmittelalterlicher Jenseitsreisen in lateinischer Sprache am Beispiel der "Visio Edmundi monachi de Eynsham"', in *VEME*, pp. 251–300.

English Episcopal Acta IV: Lincoln 1186–1200, ed. David M. Smith (London, 1986).

Exordium Magnum, ed. B. Griesser, CCCM 138 (Turnhout, 1994).

Eyton, R. W., *Court, Household and Itinerary of Henry II* (London, 1878).

Farmer, [David] Hugh, 'The Canonization of St Hugh of Lincoln', *Lincolnshire Architectural and Archaeological Society Papers*, 6 (1956), 86–117.

Farmer, [David] Hugh, *Saint Hugh of Lincoln* (Kalamazoo, 1985).

—— *St. Hugh of Lincoln: An Exhibition to Commemorate the Eighth Centenary of his Consecration as Bishop of Lincoln in 1186* (Oxford, 1986).

—— [See also Vision of Orm, and Vision of the monk of Melrose.]

Gainer, Kim Dian, 'Prolegomenon to Piers Plowman: Latin Visions of the Otherworld from the Beginnings to the Thirteenth Century', Dissertation, Ohio State University, 1987. [*DAI* 48 (1987), 131A.]

Gardiner, Eileen, ed., *Visions of Heaven and Hell before Dante* (New York, 1989).

—— *Medieval Visions of Heaven and Hell: A Sourcebook* (Garland Medieval Bibliographies 11, New York, 1993).

Gerald of Wales (Giraldus Cambrensis), The Life of St. Hugh of Avalon Bishop of Lincoln 1186–1200, ed. and trans. Richard M. Loomis (Garland Library of Medieval Literature 31, Series A, New York, 1985).

Gordon, Eric, 'Eynsham Charters. 2. Provision for Retired Abbots', *The Eynsham Record*, 3 (1986), 6–11.

—— *Eynsham Abbey 1005–1228: A Small Window into a Large Room* (Chichester, 1990).

Greenblatt, Stephen, *Hamlet in Purgatory* (Princeton & Oxford, 2001).

Greenway, Diana E., *John Le Neve. Fasti Ecclesiae Anglicanae 1066–1300. III Lincoln* (London, 1977).

Hauréau, B., *Notices et extraits de quelques manuscrits latins de la Bibliothèque Nationale*, 6 vols., 1890–1893, vol. 1 (Paris, 1890), 126–36.

Haren, Michael and Yolande de Pontfarcy, eds., *The Medieval Pilgrimage to St Patrick's Purgatory: Lough Derg and the European Tradition* (Enniskillen, 1988).

Jones, Charles W., *Saint Nicholas of Myra, Bari, and Manhattan* (Chicago & London, 1978).

Jones, Christopher A., *Ælfric's Letter to the Monks of Eynsham* (Cambridge Studies in Anglo-Saxon England 24, Cambridge, 1998).

Keiser, George R., 'The Progress of Purgatory: Visions of the Afterlife in Later Middle English Literature', in *Zeit, Tod und Ewigkeit in der Renaissance Literatur*, ed. James Hogg, *Analecta Cartusiana*, 117.3 (Salzburg, 1987), 72–100.

König, Andrea., 'Die Zügel der Zunge: Konkrete Mündlichkeit und ihre Reglementierung in mittellateinischen Visionen und Exempla', in *VEME*, pp. 227–50.

Kreutzer, Thomas, 'Jenseits und Gesellschaft. Zur Soziologie der "Visio Edmundi monachi de Eynsham"', in *VEME*, pp. 39–58.

Last Things: Death and the Apocalypse in the Middle Ages, ed. Caroline Walker Bynum & Paul Freedman (Philadelphia, 2000).

Le Coulteux, Carolo, *Annales Ordinis Cartusiensis ab anno 1084 ad annum 1429* (Monstrolii, 1888).

Le Goff, Jacques, *La Naissance du Purgatoire* (Paris, 1981); trans. Arthur Goldhammer, *The Birth of Purgatory* (Chicago & Aldershot, 1984).

Limbeck, Sven, '"Turpitudo antique passionis." Sodomie in mittelalterlicher Visionsliteratur', in *VEME*, pp. 165–226.

Losert, Kerstin, 'Adam von Eynsham—Erstredaktor der "Visio Edmundi monachi de Eynsham"?', in *VEME*, pp. 3–30.

Magna Vita S. Hugonis episcopi Lincolniensis, ed. James F. Dimock, RS 37 (London, 1864).

Mangei, Johannes, 'Die Bedeutung der Kartäuser für die Überlieferung der "Visio Edmundi monachi de Eynsham"', in *VEME*, pp. 135–61.

Matsuda, Takami, *Death and Purgatory in Middle English Didactic Poetry* (Cambridge, 1997).

Matthæi Parisiensis, monachi Sancti Albani, Historia Anglorum, ed. Frederic Madden, 3 vols., RS 44 (London, 1866–9).

Matthæi Parisiensis, monachi Sancti Albani, Chronica Major, ed. Henry Richards Luard, 7 vols., RS 57 (London, 1872–3, repr. Wiesbaden, 1964).

Mayr-Harting, Henry, ed., *St Hugh of Lincoln: Lectures Delivered at Oxford and Lincoln to Celebrate the Eighth Centenary of St Hugh's Consecration as Bishop of Lincoln* (Oxford, 1987).

McGuire, Brian Patrick, 'The Cistercians and the Rise of the Exemplum in Early Thirteenth Century France: A Reevaluation of *Paris BN lat. 15912*', *Classica et Mediaevalia*, 34 (1983), 211–67.

—— 'Purgatory, the Communion of the Saints, and Medieval Change', *Viator*, 20 (1989), 61–84.

Oliphant, T. L. Kington, *The New English*, 2 vols. (London, 1886).

Os, Arnold Barel van, *Religious Visions: The Development of the Eschatological Elements in Medieval English Religious Literature* (Amsterdam, 1932).

Palmer, Nigel F., '*Visio Tnugdali': The German and Dutch Translations and their Circulation in the Later Middle Ages* (Münchener Texte und Untersuchungen zur deutschen Literatur des Mittelalters 76, Munich, 1982).

Patch, Howard Rollins, *The Other World according to Descriptions in Medieval Literature* (Cambridge, Mass., 1950, repr. New York, 1970).

Penkett, Robert, 'Sinners and the Community of Saints: Aspects of Repentance in a Late Twelfth-Century Visio', Lambeth MA thesis (1996).

Radulphi de Coggeshall Chronicon Anglicanum, ed. Joseph Stevenson, RS 66 (London, 1875, repr. Wiesbaden, 1965).

The Registrum Antiquissimum of the Cathedral Church of Lincoln, vol. 1, ed. C. W. Foster (The Lincoln Record Society 27, Lincoln, 1931).

Regularis Concordia, ed. and trans. Dom T. Symons (London, 1953).

A Revelation of Purgatory by an Unknown, Fifteenth-Century Woman Visionary: Introduction, Critical Text, and Translation, ed. Marta Powell Harley (Studies in Women and Religion 18, Lewiston, NY, 1985).

The Revelation to the Monk of Evesham Abbey in the Year of Our Lord Eleven Hundred and Ninety Six, concerning the Places of Purgatory and Paradise, Rendered into Modern English by Valerian Paget (London, 1909).

Röckelein, Hedwig, *Otloh, Gottschalk, Tnugdal. Individuelle und kollektive Visionsmuster des Hochmittelalters* (Europäische Hochschulschriften, III, 319, Frankfurt, Bern, New York, 1987).

[Roger of Howden] *Chronica magistri Rogeri de Houedene*, ed. William Stubbs, 4 vols., RS 51 (London, 1868–71).

Roger of Wendover, *Flores Historiarum*, ed. H.O. Coxe, 4 vols. (Publications of the English Historical Society 12, London, 1841–4).

Rogeri de Wendover Liber qui dicitur Flores Historiarum, ed. Henry G. Hewlett, 3 vols., RS 84 (London, 1886–9, repr. Wiesbaden, 1965).

Royster, James Finch, and John Marcellus Steadman, jun., 'The *"Going-to"* future.' *The Manly Anniversary Studies in Language and Literature* (Chicago, 1923), pp. 394–403.

Russell, Jeffrey Burton, *A History of Heaven: The Singing Silence* (Princeton, 1997).

Russell, Josiah Cox, *Dictionary of Writers of Thirteenth Century England* (London, 1936).

Samuels, M. L., 'Spelling and Dialect in the late and post-Middle English Periods', in *So meny people longages and tonges: Philological Essays in Scots and Mediæval English presented to Angus McIntosh* (Edinburgh, 1981), pp. 43–54; repr. in *The English of Chaucer and his Contemporaries: Essays by M L Samuels and J J Smith*, ed. J. J. Smith (Aberdeen, 1988), pp. 86–95.

Scammell, G. V., *Hugh du Puiset Bishop of Durham* (Cambridge, 1956).

Schmidt, Paul Gerhard, 'Luzifer in Kaisheim. Die Sakramentsvision des Zisterziensers Rudolf (ca. 1207) und Abt Eberhard von Salem', in *Litterae Medii Aevi: Festschrift für Johanne Autenrieth zu ihrem 65. Geburtstag*, ed. Michael Borgholte and Herrad Spilling (Sigmaringen, 1988).

——'"Visio diligenti narratione luculenter exarata." Zu Sprache und Stil der "Visio Edmundi monachi de Eynsham"', in *VEME*, pp. 31–38.

——[See also *Visio Alberici* and *Visio Thvrkilli*.]

Schmitt, Jean-Claude, *Les revenants: les vivants et les morts dans la société médiévale* (Paris, 1994); trans. Teresa Lavender Fagan, *Ghosts in the Middle Ages: The Living and the Dead in Medieval Society* (Chicago & London, 1998).

Smith, David M., 'Hugh's Administration of the Diocese of Lincoln', in *St Hugh of Lincoln: Lectures Delivered at Oxford and Lincoln to Celebrate the Eighth Centenary of St Hugh's Consecration as Bishop of Lincoln*, ed. Henry Mayr-Harting (Oxford, 1987), pp. 18–47.

Smith, George, *William de Machlinia: The Primer on Vellum Printed by him in London about 1484* (London, 1929).

Soliño, José Secundino Gómez, 'Variación y estandardización en el Ingés moderno temprano:1470–1540', Dissertation, University of Oviedo, 1984.

Southern, R. W., 'From Schools to University', in *The History of the University of Oxford*, vol. 1, *The Early Oxford Schools*, ed. J. I. Catto (Oxford, 1984), pp. 1–36.

Spilling, Herrad, *Die Visio Tnugdali: Eigenart und Stellung in der mittelalterlichen Visionsliteratur bis zum Ende des 12. Jahrhunderts* (Münchener Beiträge zur Mediävistik und Renaissance-Forschung 21, Munich, 1975).

Stein, Elisabeth, ed., *Leben und Visionen der Alpais von Cudot (1150–1211): Neuedition des lateinischen Textes mit begleitenden Untersuchungen zu Autor, Werk, Quellen und Nachwirkung* (ScriptOralia 77, Tübingen, 1995).

—— '". . . de Gallica edicione rithmice composita in Latinam transtuli . . ." Eine Rückübersetzung der "Visio Edmundi monachi de Eynsham"', in *VEME*, pp. 113–33.

Studies in Mediaeval History presented to R. H. C. Davies, ed. Henry Mayr-Harting & R. I. Moore (London, 1985).

Symeon of Durham, *Libellvs de Exordio atque Procvrsv istivs, hoc est Dvnhelmensis, Ecclesie: Tract on the Origins and Progress of this the Church of Durham*, ed. and trans. David Rollason, Oxford Medieval Texts (Oxford, 2000).

Thomson, John, *The Revelation to the Monk of Evesham: A Remarkable Psychological Production of the Middle Ages, now for the first time sufficiently rendered into present-day English* (Glasgow, 1904).

Thurston, Herbert, *The Life of Saint Hugh of Lincoln Translated from the French Carthusian Life and Edited with Large Additions* (London, 1898).

—— 'The Vision of the Monk of Eynsham', *The Month*, 91 (1898), 49–63.

—— 'A Conjectural Chapter in the Life of St. Edmund of Canterbury', *The Dublin Review*, 135, 4th ser. 52 (1904), 229–57.

—— *The Physical Phenomena of Mysticism* (London, 1952).

Tractatus de Purgatorio Sancti Patricii. See *SPP*.

Tubach, Frederic C., *Index Exemplorum: A Handbook of Medieval Religious Tales* (FF Communications 204, Helsinki, 1969).

Van Uytfanghe, Marc, 'Les *Visiones* du très haut Moyen Âge et les récentes "expériences de mort temporaire." Sens ou non-sens d'une comparaison. Première partie', *Instrumenta Patristica*, 23 (1991), 447–81.

—— 'Les *Visiones* du très haut Moyen Âge et les récentes "expériences de mort temporaire." Sens ou non-sens d'une comparaison. Seconde partie', *Sacris Erudiri*, 33 (1992–93), 135–82.

Visio Alberici: Die Jenseitswanderung des neunjährigen Alberich in der vom Visionär um 1127 in Monte Cassino revidierten Fassung, ed. Paul Gerhard Schmidt (Sitzungsberichte der wissenschaftlichen Gesellschaft an der Johann Wolfgang Goethe-Universität Frankfurt an Main, 35:4, Stuttgart, 1997).

Visio Anselli. See Jean Leclercq, 'Une redaction en prose de la "Visio Anselli" dans un manuscrit de Subiaco', *Benedictina*, 16 (1969), 188–95.

Visio Baronti. Ed. W. Levison, MGH, SRM, 5.377–94; and see Ciccarese, pp. 236–68.

Visio Bernoldi. See Maaike Van Der Lugt, 'The Textual Tradition of Hincmar of Rheims *Visio Bernoldi* with a New Critical Edition', *Bulletin du Cange*, 52 (1994), 109–149.

Visio Sancti Fursei. See Carozzi, pp. 679–92.

Visio Sancti Pauli. The History of the Apocalypse in Latin together with Nine Texts, ed. Theodore Silverstein (Studies and Documents 4, London, 1935).

Visio Thvrkilli. Relatore vt videtur Radvlpho de Coggeshall, ed. Paul Gerhard Schmidt (Leipzig, 1978).

Visio Tnugdali. Lateinisch und altdeutsch, ed. Albrecht Wagner (Erlangen, 1882, repr. Hildesheim, 1989).

Visio Wettini. Ed. E. Dümmler, MGH, PLAC, 2.267–75; and see Ciccarese (1987), pp. 406–38.

[Vision of Boso] See Symeon of Durham (2000), pp. 246–51.

[Vision of Dryhthelm] See *BEH*, 5.12.

The Vision of Edmund Leversedge: A 15th-century Account of a Visit to the Otherworld Edited from BL MS Additional 34,193 with an Introduction, Commentary and Glossary, ed. W. F. Nijenhuis (Middeleeuwse Studies 8, Nijmegen, 1991).

[Vision of Godescalc] See *Godeschalcus und Visio Godeschalci*, ed. Erwin Assmann (Quellen und Forschungen zur Geschichte Schleswig-Holstein 74, Neumünster, 1979).

[Vision of Gunthelm] See Constable (1956).

[Vision of Heinrich von Ahorn] See E. Steinmeyer and E. Sievers, *Die althochdeutschen Glossen*, 5 vols. (Berlin, 1879–1922), vol. 4 (1898), 491–3.

[Vision of Orm] See Hugh Farmer, 'The Vision of Orm', *AB*, 75 (1957), 72–82.

[Vision of Salvius] See *Gregorii Episcopi Tvronensis Libri Historiarum X*, ed. B. Krusch & W. Levison, 7.1, MGH, SRM, 1.1 (1951), 323–7.

[Vision of Sunniulf] See *Gregorii Episcopi Tvronensis Libri Historiarum X*, ed. B. Krusch & W. Levison, 4.33, MGH, SRM, 1.1 (1951), 166.

[Vision of the boy William] See Helinand of Froidmont, *Chronicon*, *PL*, 212:1036–7.

[Vision of the monk of Melrose] See Hugh Farmer, 'A Letter of St. Waldef of Melrose Concerning a Recent Vision', *Analecta Monastica. Textes et études sur la vie des moines au Moyen Âge* 5 (Studia Anselmiana 43, Rome, 1958), 91–101.

[Vision of the monk of Wenlock]. See Boniface, *Epistola* 10, ed. Michael Tangl, *Die Briefe des heiligen Bonifatius und Lullius*, MGH, ES, 1 (Berlin, 1916), 7–15.

Visiones Georgii: Visiones quas in Purgatorio Sancti Patricii vidit Georgius miles de Ungaria A. D. MCCCLIII, ed. L. L. Hammerich (Det. Kgl. Danske Videnskabernes Selskab. historisk-filologiske Meddelelser, 18.2, Copenhagen, 1930).

[Visions of Ailsi] See Easting & Sharpe (1988).

[Visions of Alpais of Cudot] See Stein (1995).

[Visions of Elisabeth of Schönau] See F. W. E. Roth, *De Visionen und Briefe der hl. Elisabeth*, 1884, 2nd edn. (Brünn, 1886).

Warren, W. L., *Henry II* (London, 1973).

Whiting, Bartlett Jere, and Whiting H. W., *Proverbs, Sentences and Proverbial Phrases from English Writings mainly before 1500* (Harvard, 1968).

Wieners, Thomas H. T., 'König, Bischof und Abt im Fegefeuer. Historische Personen, Fürsten- und Prälatenkritik in der "Visio Edmundi monachi de Eynsham"', in *VEME*, pp. 73–87.

Willson, Elizabeth, *The Middle English Legends of Visits to the Other World and their Relation to the Metrical Romances* (Chicago, 1917).

Woolley, Reginald Maxwell, *St. Hugh of Lincoln* (London, 1927).

Wyld, Henry Cecil, *A Short History of English*, 3rd edn. (London, 1927).

Young, Karl, *The Drama of the Medieval Church*, 2 vols. (Oxford, 1933, repr. with corrections 1962).